Regular Expressions Cookbook

Regular Expressions Cookbook

Jan Goyvaerts and Steven Levithan

O'REILLY®

Beijing · Cambridge · Farnham · Köln · Sebastopol · Taipei · Tokyo

Regular Expressions Cookbook

by Jan Goyvaerts and Steven Levithan

Copyright © 2009 Jan Goyvaerts and Steven Levithan. All rights reserved.
Printed in the United States of America.

Published by O'Reilly Media, Inc., 1005 Gravenstein Highway North, Sebastopol, CA 95472.

O'Reilly books may be purchased for educational, business, or sales promotional use. Online editions
are also available for most titles (*http://my.safaribooksonline.com*). For more information, contact our
corporate/institutional sales department: (800) 998-9938 or *corporate@oreilly.com*.

Editor: Andy Oram	**Indexer:** Seth Maislin
Production Editor: Sumita Mukherji	**Cover Designer:** Karen Montgomery
Copyeditor: Genevieve d'Entremont	**Interior Designer:** David Futato
Proofreader: Kiel Van Horn	**Illustrator:** Robert Romano

Printing History:

May 2009: First Edition.

RepKover™

This book uses RepKover™, a durable and flexible lay-flat binding.

ISBN: 978-0-596-52068-7

[M]

1242309024

Table of Contents

Preface

Over the past decade, regular expressions have experienced a remarkable rise in popularity. Today, all the popular programming languages include a powerful regular expression library, or even have regular expression support built right into the language. Many developers have taken advantage of these regular expression features to provide the users of their applications the ability to search or filter through their data using a regular expression. Regular expressions are everywhere.

Many books have been published to ride the wave of regular expression adoption. Most do a good job of explaining the regular expression syntax along with some examples and a reference. But there aren't any books that present solutions based on regular expressions to a wide range of real-world practical problems dealing with text on a computer and in a range of Internet applications. We, Steve and Jan, decided to fill that need with this book.

We particularly wanted to show how you can use regular expressions in situations where people with limited with regular expression experience would say it can't be done, or where software purists would say a regular expression isn't the right tool for the job. Because regular expressions are everywhere these days, they are often a readily available tool that can be used by end users, without the need to involve a team of programmers. Even programmers can often save time by using a few regular expressions for information retrieval and alteration tasks that would take hours or days to code in procedural code, or that would otherwise require a third-party library that needs prior review and management approval.

Caught in the Snarls of Different Versions

As with anything that becomes popular in the IT industry, regular expressions come in many different implementations, with varying degrees of compatibility. This has resulted in many different regular expression *flavors* that don't always act the same way, or work at all, on a particular regular expression.

Many books do mention that there are different flavors and point out some of the differences. But they often leave out certain flavors here and there—particularly when a flavor lacks certain features—instead of providing alternative solutions or workarounds. This is frustrating when you have to work with different regular expression flavors in different applications or programming languages.

Casual statements in the literature, such as "everybody uses Perl-style regular expressions now," unfortunately trivialize a wide range of incompatibilities. Even "Perl-style" packages have important differences, and meanwhile Perl continues to evolve. Oversimplified impressions can lead programmers to spend half an hour or so fruitlessly running the debugger instead of checking the details of their regular expression implementation. Even when they discover that some feature they were depending on is not present, they don't always know how to work around it.

This book is the first book on the market that discusses the most popular and feature-rich regular expression flavors side by side, and does so consistently throughout the book.

Intended Audience

You should read this book if you regularly work with text on a computer, whether that's searching through a pile of documents, manipulating text in a text editor, or developing software that needs to search through or manipulate text. Regular expressions are an excellent tool for the job. *Regular Expressions Cookbook* teaches you everything you need to know about regular expressions. You don't need any prior experience whatsoever, because we explain even the most basic aspects of regular expressions.

If you do have experience with regular expressions, you'll find a wealth of detail that other books and online articles often gloss over. If you've ever been stumped by a regex that works in one application but not another, you'll find this book's detailed and equal coverage of seven of the world's most popular regular expression flavors very valuable. We organized the whole book as a cookbook, so you can jump right to the topics you want to read up on. If you read the book cover to cover, you'll become a world-class chef of regular expressions.

This book teaches you everything you need to know about regular expressions and then some, regardless of whether you are a programmer. If you want to use regular expressions with a text editor, search tool, or any application with an input box labeled "regex," you can read this book with no programming experience at all. Most of the recipes in this book have solutions purely based on one or more regular expressions.

If you are a programmer, Chapter 3 provides all the information you need to implement regular expressions in your source code. This chapter assumes you're familiar with the basic language features of the programming language of your choice, but it does not assume you have ever used a regular expression in your source code.

Technology Covered

.NET, Java, JavaScript, PCRE, Perl, Python, and Ruby aren't just back-cover buzzwords. These are the seven regular expression flavors covered by this book. We cover all seven flavors equally. We've particularly taken care to point out all the inconsistencies that we could find between those regular expression flavors.

The programming chapter (Chapter 3) has code listings in C#, Java, JavaScript, PHP, Perl, Python, Ruby, and VB.NET. Again, every recipe has solutions and explanations for all eight languages. While this makes the chapter somewhat repetitive, you can easily skip discussions on languages you aren't interested in without missing anything you should know about your language of choice.

Organization of This Book

The first three chapters of this book cover useful tools and basic information that give you a basis for using regular expressions; each of the subsequent chapters presents a variety of regular expressions while investigating one area of text processing in depth.

Chapter 1, *Introduction to Regular Expressions*, explains the role of regular expressions and introduces a number of tools that will make it easier to learn, create, and debug them.

Chapter 2, *Basic Regular Expression Skills*, covers each element and feature of regular expressions, along with important guidelines for effective use.

Chapter 3, *Programming with Regular Expressions*, specifies coding techniques and includes code listings for using regular expressions in each of the programming languages covered by this book.

Chapter 4, *Validation and Formatting*, contains recipes for handling typical user input, such as dates, phone numbers, and postal codes in various countries.

Chapter 5, *Words, Lines, and Special Characters*, explores common text processing tasks, such as checking for lines that contain or fail to contain certain words.

Chapter 6, *Numbers*, shows how to detect integers, floating-point numbers, and several other formats for this kind of input.

Chapter 7, *URLs, Paths, and Internet Addresses*, shows you how to take apart and manipulate the strings commonly used on the Internet and Windows systems to find things.

Chapter 8, *Markup and Data Interchange*, covers the manipulation of HTML, XML, comma-separated values (CSV), and INI-style configuration files.

Conventions Used in This Book

The following typographical conventions are used in this book:

Italic
> Indicates new terms, URLs, email addresses, filenames, and file extensions.

`Constant width`
> Used for program listings, program elements such as variable or function names, values returned as the result of a regular expression replacement, and subject or input text that is applied to a regular expression. This could be the contents of a text box in an application, a file on disk, or the contents of a string variable.

`Constant width italic`
> Shows text that should be replaced with user-supplied values or by values determined by context.

‹Regular●expression›
> Represents a regular expression, standing alone or as you would type it into the search box of an application. Spaces in regular expressions are indicated with gray circles, except when spaces are used in free-spacing mode.

«Replacement●text»
> Represents the text that regular expression matches will be replaced with in a search-and-replace operation. Spaces in replacement text are indicated with gray circles.

Matched text
> Represents the part of the subject text that matches a regular expression.

…
> A gray ellipsis in a regular expression indicates that you have to "fill in the blank" before you can use the regular expression. The accompanying text explains what you can fill in.

CR, LF, *and* CRLF
> CR, LF, and CRLF in boxes represent actual line break characters in strings, rather than character escapes such as \r, \n, and \r\n. Such strings can be created by pressing Enter in a multiline edit control in an application, or by using multiline string constants in source code such as verbatim strings in C# or triple-quoted strings in Python.

↵
> The return arrow, as you may see on the Return or Enter key on your keyboard, indicates that we had to break up a line to make it fit the width of the printed page. When typing the text into your source code, you should not press Enter, but instead type everything on a single line.

This icon signifies a tip, suggestion, or general note.

 This icon indicates a warning or caution.

Using Code Examples

This book is here to help you get your job done. In general, you may use the code in this book in your programs and documentation. You do not need to contact us for permission unless you're reproducing a significant portion of the code. For example, writing a program that uses several chunks of code from this book does not require permission. Selling or distributing a CD-ROM of examples from O'Reilly books does require permission. Answering a question by citing this book and quoting example code does not require permission. Incorporating a significant amount of example code from this book into your product's documentation does require permission.

We appreciate, but do not require, attribution. An attribution usually includes the title, author, publisher, and ISBN. For example: "*Regular Expressions Cookbook* by Jan Goyvaerts and Steven Levithan. Copyright 2009 Jan Goyvaerts and Steven Levithan, 978-0-596-2068-7."

If you feel your use of code examples falls outside fair use or the permission given here, feel free to contact us at *permissions@oreilly.com*.

Safari® Books Online

 When you see a Safari® Books Online icon on the cover of your favorite technology book, that means the book is available online through the O'Reilly Network Safari Bookshelf.

Safari offers a solution that's better than e-books. It's a virtual library that lets you easily search thousands of top tech books, cut and paste code samples, download chapters, and find quick answers when you need the most accurate, current information. Try it for free at *http://my.safaribooksonline.com*.

How to Contact Us

Please address comments and questions concerning this book to the publisher:

O'Reilly Media, Inc.
1005 Gravenstein Highway North

Sebastopol, CA 95472
800-998-9938 (in the United States or Canada)
707-829-0515 (international or local)
707-829-0104 (fax)

We have a web page for this book where we list errata, examples, and any additional information. You can access this page at:

http://www.regexcookbook.com

or at:

http://oreilly.com/catalog/9780596520687

To comment or ask technical questions about this book, send email to:

bookquestions@oreilly.com

For more information about our books, conferences, Resource Centers, and the O'Reilly Network, see our website at:

http://www.oreilly.com

Acknowledgments

We thank Andy Oram, our editor at O'Reilly Media, Inc., for helping us see this project from start to finish. We also thank Jeffrey Friedl, Zak Greant, Nikolaj Lindberg, and Ian Morse for their careful technical reviews, which made this a more comprehensive and accurate book.

## CHAPTER 1

Introduction to Regular Expressions

Having opened this cookbook, you are probably eager to inject some of the ungainly strings of parentheses and question marks you find in its chapters right into your code. If you are ready to plug and play, be our guest: the practical regular expressions are listed and described in Chapters 4 through 8.

But the initial chapters of this book may save you a lot of time in the long run. For instance, this chapter introduces you to a number of utilities—some of them created by one of the authors, Jan—that let you test and debug a regular expression before you bury it in code where errors are harder to find. And these initial chapters also show you how to use various features and options of regular expressions to make your life easier, help you understand regular expressions in order to improve their performance, and learn the subtle differences between how regular expressions are handled by different programming languages—and even different versions of your favorite programming language.

So we've put a lot of effort into these background matters, confident that you'll read it before you start or when you get frustrated by your use of regular expressions and want to bolster your understanding.

Regular Expressions Defined

In the context of this book, a *regular expression* is a specific kind of text pattern that you can use with many modern applications and programming languages. You can use them to verify whether input fits into the text pattern, to find text that matches the pattern within a larger body of text, to replace text matching the pattern with other text or rearranged bits of the matched text, to split a block of text into a list of subtexts, and to shoot yourself in the foot. This book helps you understand exactly what you're doing and avoid disaster.

History of the Term 'Regular Expression'

The term *regular expression* comes from mathematics and computer science theory, where it reflects a trait of mathematical expressions called *regularity*. Such an expression can be implemented in software using a deterministic finite automaton (DFA). A DFA is a finite state machine that doesn't use backtracking.

The text patterns used by the earliest *grep* tools were regular expressions in the mathematical sense. Though the name has stuck, modern-day Perl-style regular expressions are not regular expressions at all in the mathematical sense. They're implemented with a nondeterministic finite automaton (NFA). You will learn all about backtracking shortly. All a practical programmer needs to remember from this note is that some ivory tower computer scientists get upset about their well-defined terminology being overloaded with technology that's far more useful in the real world.

If you use regular expressions with skill, they simplify many programming and text processing tasks, and allow many that wouldn't be at all feasible without the regular expressions. You would need dozens if not hundreds of lines of procedural code to extract all email addresses from a document—code that is tedious to write and hard to maintain. But with the proper regular expression, as shown in Recipe 4.1, it takes just a few lines of code, or maybe even one line.

But if you try to do too much with just one regular expression, or use regexes where they're not really appropriate, you'll find out why some people say:[*]

> Some people, when confronted with a problem, think "I know, I'll use regular expressions." Now they have two problems.

The second problem those people have is that they didn't read the owner's manual, which you are holding now. Read on. Regular expressions are a powerful tool. If your job involves manipulating or extracting text on a computer, a firm grasp of regular expressions will save you plenty of overtime.

Many Flavors of Regular Expressions

All right, the title of the previous section was a lie. We didn't define what regular expressions are. We can't. There is no official standard that defines exactly which text patterns are regular expressions and which aren't. As you can imagine, every designer of programming languages and every developer of text processing applications has a different idea of exactly what a regular expression should be. So now we're stuck with a whole palate of regular expression *flavors*.

Fortunately, most designers and developers are lazy. Why create something totally new when you can copy what has already been done? As a result, all modern regular expression flavors, including those discussed in this book, can trace their history back to

---

[*] Jeffrey Friedl traces the history of this quote in his blog at *http://regex.info/blog/2006-09-15/247*.

the Perl programming language. We call these flavors *Perl-style regular expressions*. Their regular expression syntax is very similar, and mostly compatible, but not completely so.

Writers are lazy, too. We'll usually type *regex* or *regexp* to denote a single regular expression, and *regexes* to denote the plural.

Regex flavors do not correspond one-to-one with programming languages. Scripting languages tend to have their own, built-in regular expression flavor. Other programming languages rely on libraries for regex support. Some libraries are available for multiple languages, while certain languages can draw on a choice of different libraries.

This introductory chapter deals with regular expression flavors only and completely ignores any programming considerations. Chapter 3 begins the code listings, so you can peek ahead to "Programming Languages and Regex Flavors" in Chapter 3 to find out which flavors you'll be working with. But ignore all the programming stuff for now. The tools listed in the next section are an easier way to explore the regex syntax through "learning by doing."

Regex Flavors Covered by This Book

For this book, we selected the most popular regex flavors in use today. These are all *Perl-style* regex flavors. Some flavors have more features than others. But if two flavors have the same feature, they tend to use the same syntax. We'll point out the few annoying inconsistencies as we encounter them.

All these regex flavors are part of programming languages and libraries that are in active development. The list of flavors tells you which versions this book covers. Further along in the book, we mention the flavor without any versions if the presented regex works the same way with all flavors. This is almost always the case. Aside from bug fixes that affect corner cases, regex flavors tend not to change, except to add features by giving new meaning to syntax that was previously treated as an error:

Perl
> Perl's built-in support for regular expressions is the main reason why regexes are popular today. This book covers Perl 5.6, 5.8, and 5.10.
>
> Many applications and regex libraries that claim to use Perl or Perl-compatible regular expressions in reality merely use Perl-style regular expressions. They use a regex syntax similar to Perl's, but don't support the same set of regex features. Quite likely, they're using one of the regex flavors further down this list. Those flavors are all Perl-style.

PCRE
> PCRE is the "Perl-Compatible Regular Expressions" C library developed by Philip Hazel. You can download this open source library at *http://www.pcre.org*. This book covers versions 4 through 7 of PCRE.

Though PCRE claims to be Perl-compatible, and probably is more than any other flavor in this book, it really is just Perl-style. Some features, such as Unicode support, are slightly different, and you can't mix Perl code into your regex, as Perl itself allows.

Because of its open source license and solid programming, PCRE has found its way into many programming languages and applications. It is built into PHP and wrapped into numerous Delphi components. If an application claims to support "Perl-compatible" regular expressions without specifically listing the actual regex flavor being used, it's likely PCRE.

.NET

The Microsoft .NET Framework provides a full-featured Perl-style regex flavor through the `System.Text.RegularExpressions` package. This book covers .NET versions 1.0 through 3.5. Strictly speaking, there are only two versions of `System.Text.RegularExpressions`: 1.0 and 2.0. No changes were made to the Regex classes in .NET 1.1, 3.0, and 3.5.

Any .NET programming language, including C#, VB.NET, Delphi for .NET, and even COBOL.NET, has full access to the .NET regex flavor. If an application developed with .NET offers you regex support, you can be quite certain it uses the .NET flavor, even if it claims to use "Perl regular expressions." A glaring exception is Visual Studio (VS) itself. The VS integrated development environment (IDE) still uses the same old regex flavor it has had from the beginning, which is not Perl-style at all.

Java

Java 4 is the first Java release to provide built-in regular expression support through the `java.util.regex` package. It has quickly eclipsed the various third-party regex libraries for Java. Besides being standard and built in, it offers a full-featured Perl-style regex flavor and excellent performance, even when compared with applications written in C. This book covers the `java.util.regex` package in Java 4, 5, and 6.

If you're using software developed with Java during the past few years, any regular expression support it offers likely uses the Java flavor.

JavaScript

In this book, we use the term *JavaScript* to indicate the regular expression flavor defined in version 3 of the ECMA-262 standard. This standard defines the ECMAScript programming language, which is better known through its JavaScript and JScript implementations in various web browsers. Internet Explorer 5.5 through 8.0, Firefox, Opera, and Safari all implement Edition 3 of ECMA-262. However, all browsers have various corner case bugs causing them to deviate from the standard. We point out such issues in situations where they matter.

If a website allows you to search or filter using a regular expression without waiting for a response from the web server, it uses the JavaScript regex flavor, which is the only cross-browser client-side regex flavor. Even Microsoft's VBScript and Adobe's ActionScript 3 use it.

Python

Python supports regular expressions through its **re** module. This book covers Python 2.4 and 2.5. Python's regex support has remained unchanged for many years.

Ruby

Ruby's regular expression support is part of the Ruby language itself, similar to Perl. This book covers Ruby 1.8 and 1.9. A default compilation of Ruby 1.8 uses the regular expression flavor provided directly by the Ruby source code. A default compilation of Ruby 1.9 uses the Oniguruma regular expression library. Ruby 1.8 can be compiled to use Oniguruma, and Ruby 1.9 can be compiled to use the older Ruby regex flavor. In this book, we denote the native Ruby flavor as Ruby 1.8, and the Oniguruma flavor as Ruby 1.9.

To test which Ruby regex flavor your site uses, try to use the regular expression ‹a++›. Ruby 1.8 will say the regular expression is invalid, because it does not support possessive quantifiers, whereas Ruby 1.9 will match a string of one or more **a** characters.

The Oniguruma library is designed to be backward-compatible with Ruby 1.8, simply adding new features that will not break existing regexes. The implementors even left in features that arguably should have been changed, such as using (?m) to mean "the dot matches line breaks," where other regex flavors use (?s).

Searching and Replacing with Regular Expressions

Search-and-replace is a common job for regular expressions. A search-and-replace function takes a subject string, a regular expression, and a replacement string as input. The output is the subject string with all matches of the regular expression replaced with the replacement text.

Although the replacement text is not a regular expression at all, you can use certain special syntax to build dynamic replacement texts. All flavors let you reinsert the text matched by the regular expression or a capturing group into the replacement. Recipes 2.20 and 2.21 explain this. Some flavors also support inserting matched context into the replacement text, as Recipe 2.22 shows. In Chapter 3, Recipe 3.16 teaches you how to generate a different replacement text for each match in code.

Many Flavors of Replacement Text

Different ideas by different regular expression software developers have led to a wide range of regular expression flavors, each with different syntax and feature sets. The story for the replacement text is no different. In fact, there are even more replacement text flavors than regular expression flavors. Building a regular expression engine is difficult. Most programmers prefer to reuse an existing one, and bolting a search-and-replace function onto an existing regular expression engine is quite easy. The result is that there are many replacement text flavors for regular expression libraries that do not have built-in search-and-replace features.

Fortunately, all the regular expression flavors in this book have corresponding replacement text flavors, except PCRE. This gap in PCRE complicates life for programmers who use flavors based on it. The open source PCRE library does not include any functions to make replacements. Thus, all applications and programming languages that are based on PCRE need to provide their own search-and-replace function. Most programmers try to copy existing syntax, but never do so in exactly the same way.

This book covers the following replacement text flavors. Refer to "Many Flavors of Regular Expressions" on page 2 for more details on the regular expression flavors that correspond with the replacement text flavors:

Perl

> Perl has built-in support for regular expression substitution via the `s/regex/replace/` operator. The Perl replacement text flavor corresponds with the Perl regular expression flavor. This book covers Perl 5.6 to Perl 5.10. The latter version adds support for named backreferences in the replacement text, as it adds named capture to the regular expression syntax.

PHP

> In this book, the PHP replacement text flavor refers to the `preg_replace` function in PHP. This function uses the PCRE regular expression flavor and the PHP replacement text flavor.
>
> Other programming languages that use PCRE do not use the same replacement text flavor as PHP. Depending on where the designers of your programming language got their inspiration, the replacement text syntax may be similar to PHP or any of the other replacement text flavors in this book.
>
> PHP also has an `ereg_replace` function. This function uses a different regular expression flavor (POSIX ERE), and a different replacement text flavor, too. PHP's `ereg` functions are not discussed in this book.

.NET

> The `System.Text.RegularExpressions` package provides various search-and-replace functions. The .NET replacement text flavor corresponds with the .NET regular expression flavor. All versions of .NET use the same replacement text flavor. The new regular expression features in .NET 2.0 do not affect the replacement text syntax.

Java

> The `java.util.regex` package has built-in search-and-replace functions. This book covers Java 4, 5, and 6. All use the same replacement text syntax.

JavaScript

> In this book, we use the term *JavaScript* to indicate both the replacement text flavor and the regular expression flavor defined in Edition 3 of the ECMA-262 standard.

Python

> Python's re module provides a sub function to search-and-replace. The Python replacement text flavor corresponds with the Python regular expression flavor. This book covers Python 2.4 and 2.5. Python's regex support has been stable for many years.

Ruby

> Ruby's regular expression support is part of the Ruby language itself, including the search-and-replace function. This book covers Ruby 1.8 and 1.9. A default compilation of Ruby 1.8 uses the regular expression flavor provided directly by the Ruby source code, whereas a default compilation of Ruby 1.9 uses the Oniguruma regular expression library. Ruby 1.8 can be compiled to use Oniguruma, and Ruby 1.9 can be compiled to use the older Ruby regex flavor. In this book, we denote the native Ruby flavor as Ruby 1.8, and the Oniguruma flavor as Ruby 1.9.
>
> The replacement text syntax for Ruby 1.8 and 1.9 is the same, except that Ruby 1.9 adds support for named backreferences in the replacement text. Named capture is a new feature in Ruby 1.9 regular expressions.

Tools for Working with Regular Expressions

Unless you have been programming with regular expressions for some time, we recommend that you first experiment with regular expressions in a tool rather than in source code. The sample regexes in this chapter and Chapter 2 are plain regular expressions that don't contain the extra escaping that a programming language (even a Unix shell) requires. You can type these regular expressions directly into an application's search box.

Chapter 3 explains how to mix regular expressions into your source code. Quoting a literal regular expression as a string makes it even harder to read, because string escaping rules compound regex escaping rules. We leave that until Recipe 3.1. Once you understand the basics of regular expressions, you'll be able to see the forest through the backslashes.

The tools described in this section also provide debugging, syntax checking, and other feedback that you won't get from most programming environments. Therefore, as you develop regular expressions in your applications, you may find it useful to build a complicated regular expression in one of these tools before you plug it in to your program.

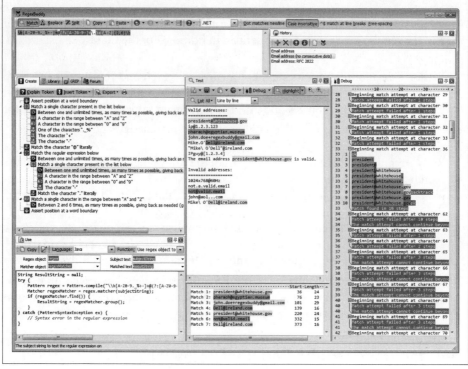

Figure 1-1. RegexBuddy

RegexBuddy

RegexBuddy (Figure 1-1) is the most full-featured tool available at the time of this writing for creating, testing, and implementing regular expressions. It has the unique ability to emulate all the regular expression flavors discussed in this book, and even convert among the different flavors.

RegexBuddy was designed and developed by Jan Goyvaerts, one of this book's authors. Designing and developing RegexBuddy made Jan an expert on regular expressions, and using RegexBuddy helped get coauthor Steven hooked on regular expressions to the point where he pitched this book to O'Reilly.

If the screenshot (Figure 1-1) looks a little busy, that's because we've arranged most of the panels side by side to show off RegexBuddy's extensive functionality. The default view tucks all the panels neatly into a row of tabs. You also can drag panels off to a secondary monitor.

To try one of the regular expressions shown in this book, simply type it into the edit box at the top of RegexBuddy's window. RegexBuddy automatically applies syntax highlighting to your regular expression, making errors and mismatched brackets obvious.

The Create panel automatically builds a detailed English-language analysis while you type in the regex. Double-click on any description in the regular expression tree to edit that part of your regular expression. You can insert new parts to your regular expression by hand, or by clicking the Insert Token button and selecting what you want from a menu. For instance, if you don't remember the complicated syntax for positive look-ahead, you can ask RegexBuddy to insert the proper characters for you.

Type or paste in some sample text on the Test panel. When the Highlight button is active, RegexBuddy automatically highlights the text matched by the regex.

Some of the buttons you're most likely to use are:

List All
> Displays a list of all matches.

Replace
> The Replace button at the top displays a new window that lets you enter replacement text. The Replace button in the Test box then lets you view the subject text after the replacements are made.

Split (The button on the Test panel, not the one at the top)
> Treats the regular expression as a separator, and splits the subject into tokens based on where matches are found in your subject text using your regular expression.

Click any of these buttons and select Update Automatically to make RegexBuddy keep the results dynamically in sync as you edit your regex or subject text.

To see exactly how your regex works (or doesn't), click on a highlighted match or at the spot where the regex fails to match on the Test panel, and click the Debug button. RegexBuddy will switch to the Debug panel, showing the entire matching processes step by step. Click anywhere on the debugger's output to see which regex token matched the text you clicked on. Click on your regular expression to highlight that part of the regex in the debugger.

On the Use panel, select your favorite programming language. Then, select a function to instantly generate source code to implement your regex. RegexBuddy's source code templates are fully editable with the built-in template editor. You can add new functions and even new languages, or change the provided ones.

To test your regex on a larger set of data, switch to the GREP panel to search (and replace) through any number of files and folders.

When you find a regex in source code you're maintaining, copy it to the clipboard, including the delimiting quotes or slashes. In RegexBuddy, click the Paste button at the top and select the string style of your programming language. Your regex will then appear in RegexBuddy as a plain regex, without the extra quotes and escapes needed for string literals. Use the Copy button at the top to create a string in the desired syntax, so you can paste it back into your source code.

As your experience grows, you can build up a handy library of regular expressions on the Library panel. Make sure to add a detailed description and a test subject when you store a regex. Regular expressions can be cryptic, even for experts.

If you really can't figure out a regex, click on the Forum panel and then the Login button. If you've purchased RegexBuddy, the login screen appears. Click OK and you are instantly connected to the RegexBuddy user forum. Steven and Jan often hang out there.

RegexBuddy runs on Windows 98, ME, 2000, XP, and Vista. For Linux and Apple fans, RegexBuddy also runs well on VMware, Parallels, CrossOver Office, and with a few issues on WINE. You can download a free evaluation copy of RegexBuddy at *http://www.regexbuddy.com/RegexBuddyCookbook.exe*. Except for the user forum, the trial is fully functional for seven days of actual use.

RegexPal

RegexPal (Figure 1-2) is an online regular expression tester created by Steven Levithan, one of this book's authors. All you need to use it is a modern web browser. RegexPal is written entirely in JavaScript. Therefore, it supports only the JavaScript regex flavor, as implemented in the web browser you're using to access it.

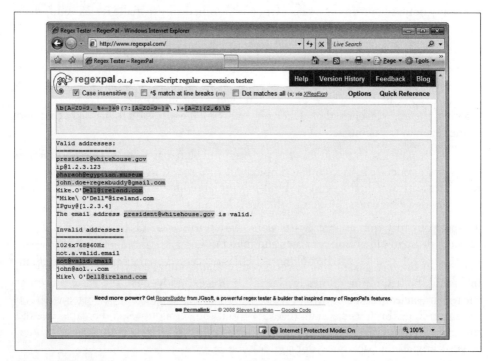

Figure 1-2. RegexPal

To try one of the regular expressions shown in this book, browse to *http://www.regexpal* *.com*. Type the regex into the box that says "Enter regex here." RegexPal automatically applies syntax highlighting to your regular expression, which immediately reveals any syntax errors in the regex. RegexPal is aware of the cross-browser issues that can ruin your day when dealing with JavaScript regular expressions. If certain syntax doesn't work correctly in some browsers, RegexPal will highlight it as an error.

Now type or paste some sample text into the box that says "Enter test data here." RegexPal automatically highlights the text matched by your regex.

There are no buttons to click, making RegexPal one of the most convenient online regular expression testers.

More Online Regex Testers

Creating a simple online regular expression tester is easy. If you have some basic web development skills, the information in Chapter 3 is all you need to roll your own. Hundreds of people have already done this; a few have added some extra features that make them worth mentioning.

regex.larsolavtorvik.com

Lars Olav Torvik has put a great little regular expression tester online at *http://regex* *.larsolavtorvik.com* (see Figure 1-3).

To start, select the regular expression flavor you're working with by clicking on the flavor's name at the top of the page. Lars offers PHP PCRE, PHP POSIX, and JavaScript. PHP PCRE, the PCRE regex flavor discussed in this book, is used by PHP's **preg** functions. POSIX is an old and limited regex flavor used by PHP's **ereg** functions, which are not discussed in this book. If you select JavaScript, you'll be working with your browser's JavaScript implementation.

Type your regular expression into the Pattern field and your subject text into the Subject field. A moment later, the Matches field displays your subject text with highlighted regex matches. The Code field displays a single line of source code that applies your regex to your subject text. Copying and pasting this into your code editor saves you the tedious job of manually converting your regex into a string literal. Any string or array returned by the code is displayed in the Result field. Because Lars used Ajax technology to build his site, results are updated in just a few moments for all flavors. To use the tool, you have to be online, as PHP is processed on the server rather than in your browser.

The second column displays a list of regex commands and regex options. These depend on the regex flavor. The regex commands typically include match, replace, and split operations. The regex options consist of common options such as case insensitivity, as well as implementation-specific options. These commands and options are described in Chapter 3.

Figure 1-3. regex.larsolavtorvik.com

Nregex

http://www.nregex.com (Figure 1-4) is a straightforward online regex tester built on .NET technology by David Seruyange. Although the site doesn't say which flavor it implements, it's .NET 1.x at the time of this writing.

The layout of the page is somewhat confusing. Enter your regular expression into the field under the Regular Expression label, and set the regex options using the checkboxes below that. Enter your subject text in the large box at the bottom, replacing the default `If I just had $5.00 then "she" wouldn't be so @#$! mad.`. If your subject is a web page, type the URL in the Load Target From URL field, and click the Load button under that input field. If your subject is a file on your hard disk, click the Browse button, find the file you want, and then click the Load button under that input field.

Your subject text will appear duplicated in the "Matches & Replacements" field at the center of the web page, with the regex matches highlighted. If you type something into

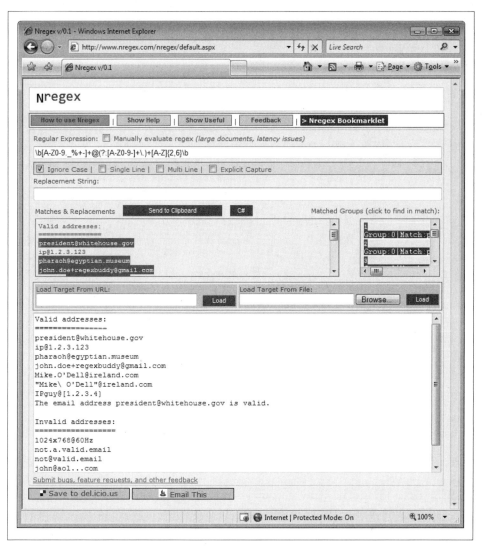

Figure 1-4. Nregex

the Replacement String field, the result of the search-and-replace is shown instead. If your regular expression is invalid, … appears.

The regex matching is done in .NET code running on the server, so you need to be online for the site to work. If the automatic updates are slow, perhaps because your subject text is very long, tick the Manually Evaluate Regex checkbox above the field for your regular expression to show the Evaluate button. Click that button to update the "Matches & Replacements" display.

Rubular

Michael Lovitt put a minimalistic regex tester online at *http://www.rubular.com* (Figure 1-5), using the Ruby 1.8 regex flavor.

Figure 1-5. Rubular

Enter your regular expression in the box between the two forward slashes under "Your regular expression." You can turn on case insensitivity by typing an **i** in the small box after the second slash. Similarly, if you like, turn on the option "a dot matches a line break" by typing an **m** in the same box. **im** turns on both options. Though these conventions may seem a bit user-unfriendly if you're new to Ruby, they conform to the */regex/*im syntax used to specify a regex in Ruby source code.

Type or paste your subject text into the "Your test string" box, and wait a moment. A new "Match result" box appears to the right, showing your subject text with all regex matches highlighted.

myregexp.com

Sergey Evdokimov created several regular expression testers for Java developers. The home page at *http://www.myregexp.com* (Figure 1-6) offers an online regex tester. It's a Java applet that runs in your browser. The Java 4 (or later) runtime needs to be installed on your computer. The applet uses the **java.util.regex** package to evaluate

Figure 1-6. myregexp.com

your regular expressions, which is new in Java 4. In this book, the "Java" regex flavor refers to this package.

Type your regular expression into the Regular Expression box. Use the Flags menu to set the regex options you want. Three of the options also have direct checkboxes.

If you want to test a regex that already exists as a string in Java code, copy the whole string to the clipboard. In the myregexp.com tester, click on the Edit menu, and then "Paste Regex from Java String". In the same menu, pick "Copy Regex for Java Source" when you're done editing the regular expression. The Edit menu has similar commands for JavaScript and XML as well.

Below the regular expression, there are four tabs that run four different tests:

Find

Highlights all regular expression matches in the sample text. These are the matches found by the `Matcher.find()` method in Java.

Match

Tests whether the regular expression matches the sample text entirely. If it does, the whole text is highlighted. This is what the `String.matches()` and `Matcher.matches()` methods do.

Split

The second box at the right shows the array of strings returned by `String.split()` or `Pattern.split()` when used with your regular expression and sample text.

Replace

Type in a replacement text, and the box at the right shows the text returned by `String.replaceAll()` or `Matcher.replaceAll()`.

You can find Sergey's other regex testers via the links at the top of the page at *http://www.myregexp.com*. One is a plug-in for Eclipse, and the other is a plug-in for IntelliJ IDEA.

reAnimator

Oliver Steele's reAnimator at *http://osteele.com/tools/reanimator* (Figure 1-7) won't bring a dead regex back to life. Rather, it's a fun little tool that shows a graphic representation of the finite state machines that a regular expression engine uses to perform a regular expression search.

reAnimator's regex syntax is very limited. It is compatible with all the flavors discussed in this book. Any regex you can animate with reAnimator will work with any of this book's flavors, but the reverse is definitely not true. This is because reAnimator's regular expressions are regular in the mathematical sense. The sidebar "History of the Term 'Regular Expression'" on page 2 explains this briefly.

Start by going up to the Pattern box at the top of the page and pressing the Edit button. Type your regular expression into the Pattern field and click Set. Slowly type the subject text into the Input field.

As you type in each character, colored balls will move through the state machine to indicate the end point reached in the state machine by your input so far. Blue balls indicate that the state machine accepts the input, but needs more input for a full match. Green balls indicate that the input matches the whole pattern. No balls means the state machine can't match the input.

reAnimator will show a match only if the regular expression matches the whole input string, as if you had put it between ‹^› and ‹$› anchors. This is another property of expressions that are regular in the mathematical sense.

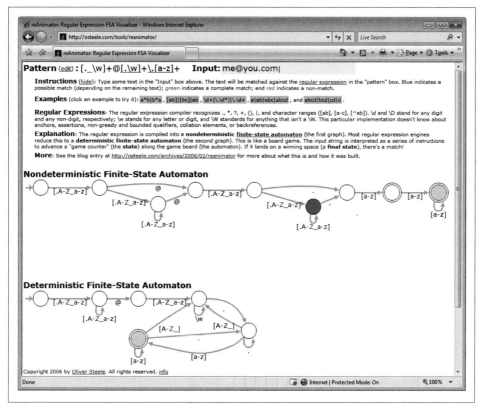

Figure 1-7. reAnimator

More Desktop Regular Expression Testers

Expresso

Expresso (not to be confused with caffeine-laden espresso) is a .NET application for creating and testing regular expressions. You can download it at *http://www.ultrapico .com/Expresso.htm*. The .NET framework 2.0 or later must be installed on your computer.

The download is a free 60-day trial. After the trial, you have to register or Expresso will (mostly) stop working. Registration is free, but requires you to give the Ultrapico folks your email address. The registration key is sent by email.

Expresso displays a screen like the one shown in Figure 1-8. The Regular Expression box where you type in your regular expression is permanently visible. No syntax highlighting is available. The Regex Analyzer box automatically builds a brief English-language analysis of your regular expression. It too is permanently visible.

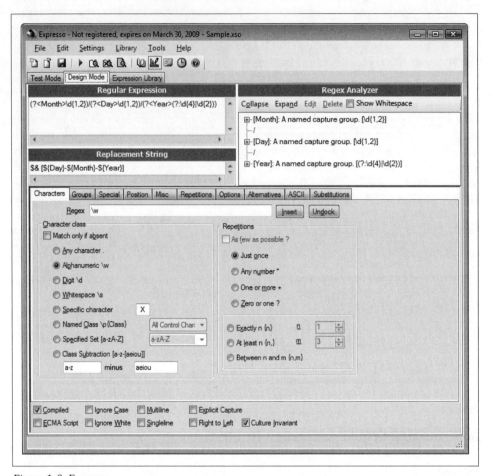

Figure 1-8. Expresso

In Design Mode, you can set matching options such as "Ignore Case" at the bottom of the screen. Most of the screen space is taken up by a row of tabs where you can select the regular expression token you want to insert. If you have two monitors or one large monitor, click the Undock button to float the row of tabs. Then you can build up your regular expression in the other mode (Test Mode) as well.

In Test Mode, type or paste your sample text in the lower-left corner. Then, click the Run Match button to get a list of all matches in the Search Results box. No highlighting is applied to the sample text. Click on a match in the results to select that match in the sample text.

The Expression Library shows a list of sample regular expressions and a list of recent regular expressions. Your regex is added to that list each time you press Run Match. You can edit the library through the Library menu in the main menu bar.

The Regulator

The Regulator, which you can download from *http://sourceforge.net/projects/regulator*, is not safe for SCUBA diving or cooking-gas canisters; it is another .NET application for creating and testing regular expressions. The latest version requires .NET 2.0 or later. Older versions for .NET 1.x can still be downloaded. The Regulator is open source, and no payment or registration required.

The Regulator does everything in one screen (Figure 1-9). The New Document tab is where you enter your regular expression. Syntax highlighting is automatically applied, but syntax errors in your regex are not made obvious. Right-click to select the regex token you want to insert from a menu. You can set regular expression options via the buttons on the main toolbar. The icons are a bit cryptic. Wait for the tooltip to see which option you're setting with each button.

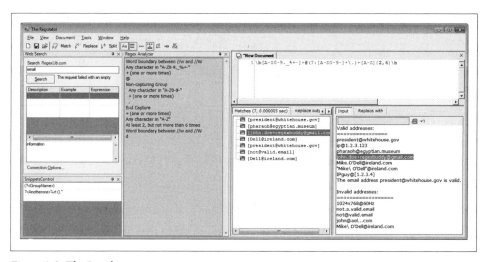

Figure 1-9. The Regulator

Below the area for your regex and to the right, click on the Input button to display the area for pasting in your sample text. Click the "Replace with" button to type in the replacement text, if you want to do a search-and-replace. Below the regex and to the left, you can see the results of your regex operation. Results are not updated automatically; you must click the Match, Replace, or Split button in the toolbar to update the results. No highlighting is applied to the input. Click on a match in the results to select it in the subject text.

The Regex Analyzer panel shows a simple English-language analysis of your regular expression, but it is not automatic or interactive. To update the analysis, select Regex Analyzer in the View menu, even if it is already visible. Clicking on the analysis only moves the text cursor.

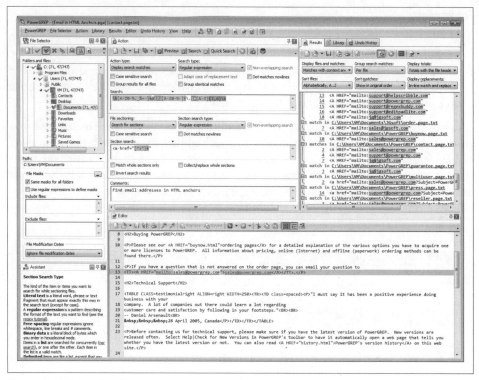

Figure 1-10. PowerGREP

grep

The name *grep* is derived from the g/re/p command that performed a regular expression search in the Unix text editor *ed*, one of the first applications to support regular expressions. This command was so popular that all Unix systems now have a dedicated grep utility for searching through files using a regular expression. If you're using Unix, Linux, or OS X, type man grep into a terminal window to learn all about it.

The following three tools are Windows applications that do what grep does, and more.

PowerGREP

PowerGREP, developed by Jan Goyvaerts, one of this book's authors, is probably the most feature-rich *grep* tool available for the Microsoft Windows platform (Figure 1-10). PowerGREP uses a custom regex flavor that combines the best of the flavors discussed in this book. This flavor is labeled "JGsoft" in RegexBuddy.

To run a quick regular expression search, simply select Clear in the Action menu and type your regular expression into the Search box on the Action panel. Click on a folder in the File Selector panel, and select "Include File or Folder" or "Include Folder and

Subfolders" in the File Selector menu. Then, select Execute in the Action menu to run your search.

To run a search-and-replace, select "search-and-replace" in the "action type" drop-down list at the top-left corner of the Action panel after clearing the action. A Replace box will appear below the Search box. Enter your replacement text there. All the other steps are the same as for searching.

PowerGREP has the unique ability to use up to three lists of regular expressions at the same time, with any number of regular expressions in each list. While the previous two paragraphs provide all you need to run simple searches like you can in any grep tool, unleashing PowerGREP's full potential will take a bit of reading through the tool's comprehensive documentation.

PowerGREP runs on Windows 98, ME, 2000, XP, and Vista. You can download a free evaluation copy at *http://www.powergrep.com/PowerGREPCookbook.exe*. Except for saving results and libraries, the trial is fully functional for 15 days of actual use. Though the trial won't save the results shown on the Results panel, it will modify all your files for search-and-replace actions, just like the full version does.

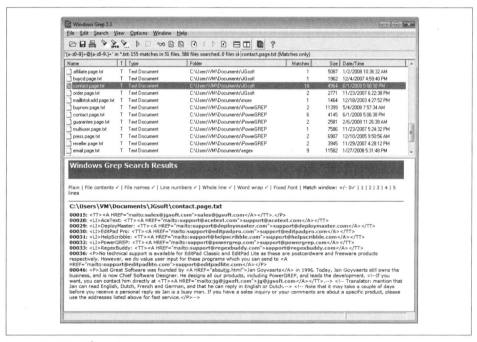

Figure 1-11. Windows Grep

Windows Grep

Windows Grep (*http://www.wingrep.com*) is one of the oldest grep tools for Windows. Its age shows a bit in its user interface (Figure 1-11), but it does what it says on the tin just fine. It supports a limited regular expression flavor called POSIX ERE. For the features that it supports, it uses the same syntax as the flavors in this book. Windows Grep is shareware, which means you can download it for free, but payment is expected if you want to keep it.

To prepare a search, select Search in the Search menu. The screen that appears differs depending on whether you've selected Beginner Mode or Expert Mode in the Options menu. Beginners get a step-by-step wizard, whereas experts get a tabbed dialog.

When you've set up the search, Windows Grep immediately executes it, presenting you with a list of files in which matches were found. Click once on a file to see its matches in the bottom panel, and double-click to open the file. Select "All Matches" in the View menu to make the bottom panel show everything.

To run a search-and-replace, select Replace in the Search menu.

RegexRenamer

RegexRenamer (Figure 1-12) is not really a grep tool. Instead of searching through the contents of files, it searches and replaces through the names of files. You can download it at *http://regexrenamer.sourceforge.net*. RegexRenamer requires version 2.0 or later of the Microsoft .NET framework.

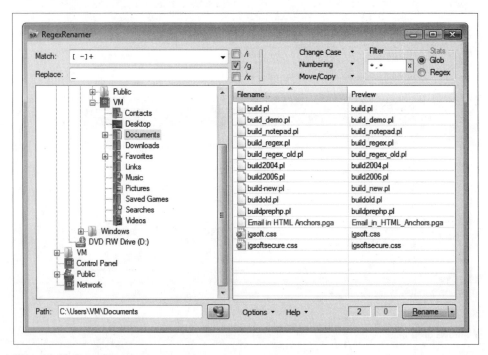

Figure 1-12. RegexRenamer

Type your regular expression into the Match box and the replacement text into the Replace box. Click /i to turn on case insensitivity, and /g to replace all matches in each filename rather than just the first. /x turns on free-spacing syntax, which isn't very useful, since you have only one line to type in your regular expression.

Use the tree at the left to select the folder that holds the files you want to rename. You can set a file mask or a regex filter in the top-right corner. This restricts the list of files to which your search-and-replace regex will be applied. Using one regex to filter and another to replace is much handier than trying to do both tasks with just one regex.

Popular Text Editors

Most modern text editors have at least basic support for regular expressions. In the search or search-and-replace panel, you'll typically find a checkbox to turn on regular expression mode. Some editors, such as EditPad Pro, also use regular expressions for various features that process text, such as syntax highlighting or class and function lists. The documentation with each editor explains all these features. Some popular text editors with regular expression support include:

- Boxer Text Editor (PCRE)
- Dreamweaver (JavaScript)
- EditPad Pro (custom flavor that combines the best of the flavors discussed in this book; labeled "JGsoft" in RegexBuddy)
- Multi-Edit (PCRE, if you select the "Perl" option)
- NoteTab (PCRE)
- UltraEdit (PCRE)
- TextMate (Ruby 1.9 [Oniguruma])

## CHAPTER 2

Basic Regular Expression Skills

The problems presented in this chapter aren't the kind of real-world problems that your boss or your customers ask you to solve. Rather, they're technical problems you'll encounter while creating and editing regular expressions to solve real-world problems. The first recipe, for example, explains how to match literal text with a regular expression. This isn't a goal on its own, because you don't need a regex when all you want to do is to search for literal text. But when creating a regular expression, you'll likely need it to match certain text literally, and you'll need to know which characters to escape. Recipe 2.1 tells you how.

The recipes start out with very basic regular expression techniques. If you've used regular expressions before, you can probably skim or even skip them. The recipes further down in this chapter will surely teach you something new, unless you have already read *Mastering Regular Expressions* by Jeffrey E. F. Friedl (O'Reilly) cover to cover.

We devised the recipes in this chapter in such a way that each explains one aspect of the regular expression syntax. Together, they form a comprehensive tutorial to regular expressions. Read it from start to finish to get a firm grasp of regular expressions. Or dive right in to the real-world regular expressions in Chapters 4 through 8, and follow the references back to this chapter whenever those chapters use some syntax you're not familiar with.

This tutorial chapter deals with regular expressions only and completely ignores any programming considerations. The next chapter is the one with all the code listings. You can peek ahead to "Programming Languages and Regex Flavors" in Chapter 3 to find out which regular expression flavor your programming language uses. The flavors themselves, which this chapter talks about, were introduced in "Regex Flavors Covered by This Book" on page 3.

2.1 Match Literal Text

Problem

Create a regular expression to exactly match this gloriously contrived sentence: `The punctuation characters in the ASCII table are: !"#$%&'()*+,-./:;<=>?@[\]^_`{|}~.`

Solution

```
The•punctuation•characters•in•the•ASCII•table•are:•↵
!"#\$%&'\(\)\*\+,-\./:;<=>\?@\[\\]\^_`\{\|}~
```
Regex options: None
Regex flavors: .NET, Java, JavaScript, PCRE, Perl, Python, Ruby

Discussion

Any regular expression that does not include any of the dozen characters `$()*+.?[\^{|` simply matches itself. To find whether `Mary had a little lamb` in the text you're editing, simply search for ‹`Mary•had•a•little•lamb`›. It doesn't matter whether the "regular expression" checkbox is turned on in your text editor.

The 12 punctuation characters that make regular expressions work their magic are called *metacharacters*. If you want your regex to match them literally, you need to *escape* them by placing a backslash in front of them. Thus, the regex:

```
\$\(\)\*\+\.\?\[\\\^\{\|
```

matches the text:

```
$()*+.?[\^{|
```

Notably absent from the list are the closing square bracket], the hyphen -, and the closing curly bracket }. The first two become metacharacters only after an unescaped [, and the } only after an unescaped {. There's no need to ever escape }. Metacharacter rules for the blocks that appear between [and] are explained in Recipe 2.3.

Escaping any other nonalphanumeric character does not change how your regular expression works—at least not when working with any of the flavors discussed in this book. Escaping an alphanumeric character either gives it a special meaning or throws a syntax error.

People new to regular expressions often escape every punctuation character in sight. Don't let anyone know you're a newbie. Escape judiciously. A jungle of needless backslashes makes regular expressions hard to read, particularly when all those backslashes have to be doubled up to quote the regex as a literal string in source code.

Variations

Block escape

```
The•punctuation•characters•in•the•ASCII•table•are:•↵
\Q!"#$%&'()*+,-./:;<=>?@[\]^_`{|}~\E
```
Regex options: None
Regex flavors: Java 6, PCRE, Perl

Perl, PCRE and Java support the regex tokens ‹\Q› and ‹\E›. ‹\Q› suppresses the meaning of all metacharacters, including the backslash, until ‹\E›. If you omit ‹\E›, all characters after the ‹\Q› until the end of the regex are treated as literals.

The only benefit of ‹\Q...\E› is that it is easier to read than ‹\.\.\.›.

 Though Java 4 and 5 support this feature, you should not use it. Bugs in the implementation cause regular expressions with ‹\Q···\E› to match different things from what you intended, and from what PCRE, Perl, or Java 6 would match. These bugs were fixed in Java 6, making it behave the same way as PCRE and Perl.

Case-insensitive matching

```
ascii
```
Regex options: Case insensitive
Regex flavors: .NET, Java, JavaScript, PCRE, Perl, Python, Ruby

```
(?i)ascii
```
Regex options: None
Regex flavors: .NET, Java, PCRE, Perl, Python, Ruby

By default, regular expressions are case sensitive. ‹regex› matches <u>regex</u> but not Regex, REGEX, or ReGeX. To make ‹regex› match all of those, you need to turn on case insensitivity.

In most applications, that's a simple matter of marking or clearing a checkbox. All programming languages discussed in the next chapter have a flag or property that you can set to make your regex case insensitive. Recipe 3.4 in the next chapter explains how to apply the regex options listed with each regular expression solution in this book in your source code.

If you cannot turn on case insensitivity outside the regex, you can do so within by using the ‹(?i)› mode modifier, such as ‹(?i)regex›. This works with the .NET, Java, PCRE, Perl, Python, and Ruby flavors.

.NET, Java, PCRE, Perl, and Ruby support local mode modifiers, which affect only part of the regular expression. ‹sensitive(?i)caseless(?-i)sensitive› matches <u>sensitive</u> <u>CASELESSsensitive</u> but not SENSITIVEcaselessSENSITIVE. ‹(?i)› turns on case insensitivity for the remainder of the regex, and ‹(?-i)› turns it off for the remainder of the regex. They act as toggle switches.

Recipe 2.10 shows how to use local mode modifiers with groups instead of toggles.

See Also

Recipes 2.3 and 5.14

2.2 Match Nonprintable Characters

Problem

Match a string of the following ASCII control characters: bell, escape, form feed, line feed, carriage return, horizontal tab, vertical tab. These characters have the hexadecimal ASCII codes 07, 1B, 0C, 0A, 0D, 09, 0B.

Solution

```
\a\e\f\n\r\t\v
```
Regex options: None
Regex flavors: .NET, Java, PCRE, Perl, Python, Ruby

```
\x07\x1B\f\n\r\t\v
```
Regex options: None
Regex flavors: .NET, Java, JavaScript, PCRE, Perl, Python, Ruby

Discussion

Seven of the most commonly used ASCII control characters have dedicated escape sequences. These all consist of a backslash followed by a letter. This is the same syntax that is used for string literals in many programming languages. Table 2-1 shows the common nonprinting characters and how they are represented.

Table 2-1. Nonprinting characters

Representation	Meaning	Hexadecimal representation
‹\a›	bell	0x07
‹\e›	escape	0x1B
‹\f›	form feed	0x0C
‹\n›	line feed (newline)	0x0A
‹\r›	carriage return	0x0D
‹\t›	horizontal tab	0x09
‹\v›	vertical tab	0x0B

The ECMA-262 standard does not support ‹\a› and ‹\e›. Therefore, we use a different syntax for the JavaScript examples in this book, even though many browsers do support ‹\a› and ‹\e›.

These control characters, as well as the alternative syntax shown in the following section, can be used equally inside and outside character classes in your regular expression.

Variations on Representations of Nonprinting Characters

The 26 control characters

\cG\x1B\cL\cJ\cM\cI\cK
Regex options: None
Regex flavors: .NET, Java, JavaScript, PCRE, Perl, Ruby 1.9

Using ‹\cA› through ‹\cZ›, you can match one of the 26 control characters that occupy positions 1 through 26 in the ASCII table. The c must be lowercase. The letter that follows the c is case insensitive in most flavors. We recommend that you always use an uppercase letter. Java requires this.

This syntax can be handy if you're used to entering control characters on console systems by pressing the Control key along with a letter. On a terminal, Ctrl-H sends a backspace. In a regex, ‹\cH› matches a backspace.

Python and the classic Ruby engine in Ruby 1.8 do not support this syntax. The Oniguruma engine in Ruby 1.9 does.

The escape control character, at position 27 in the ASCII table, is beyond the reach of the English alphabet, so we leave it as ‹\x1B› in our regular expression.

The 7-bit character set

\x07\x1B\x0C\x0A\x0D\x09\x0B
Regex options: None
Regex flavors: .NET, Java, JavaScript, PCRE, Perl, Python, Ruby

A lowercase \x followed by two uppercase hexadecimal digits matches a single character in the ASCII set. Figure 2-1 shows which hexadecimal combinations from ‹\x00› through ‹\x7F› match each character in the entire ASCII character set. The table is arranged with the first hexadecimal digit going down the left side and the second digit going across the top.

Which characters ‹\x80› through ‹\xFF› match depends on how your regex engine interprets them, and which code page your subject text is encoded in. We recommend that you not use ‹\x80› through ‹\xFF›. Instead, use the Unicode code point token described in Recipe 2.7.

If you're using Ruby 1.8 or you compiled PCRE without UTF-8 support, you cannot use Unicode code points. Ruby 1.8 and PCRE without UTF-8 are 8-bit regex engines.

	0	1	2	3	4	5	6	7	8	9	A	B	C	D	E	F
0	NUL	SOH	STX	ETX	EOT	ENQ	ACK	BEL	BS	HT	LF	VT	FF	CR	SO	SI
1	DLE	DC1	DC2	DC3	DC4	NAK	SYN	ETB	CAN	EM		SUB	ESC	FS	GS	RS	US
2	SP	!	"	#	$	%	&	'	(	)	*	+	,	-	.	/
3	0	1	2	3	4	5	6	7	8	9	:	;	<	=	>	?
4	@	A	B	C	D	E	F	G	H	I	J	K	L	M	N	O
5	P	Q	R	S	T	U	V	W	X	Y	Z	[	\	]	^	_
6	`	a	b	c	d	e	f	g	h	i	j	k	l	m	n	o
7	p	q	r	s	t	u	v	w	x	y	z	{	|	}	~	DEL

Figure 2-1. ASCII Table

They are completely ignorant about text encodings and multibyte characters. ‹\xAA› in these engines simply matches the byte 0xAA, regardless of which character 0xAA happens to represent or whether 0xAA is part of a multibyte character.

See Also

Recipe 2.7

2.3 Match One of Many Characters

Problem

Create one regular expression to match all common misspellings of calendar, so you can find this word in a document without having to trust the author's spelling ability. Allow an a or e to be used in each of the vowel positions. Create another regular expression to match a single hexadecimal character. Create a third regex to match a single character that is not a hexadecimal character.

Solution

Calendar with misspellings

c[ae]l[ae]nd[ae]r
Regex options: None
Regex flavors: .NET, Java, JavaScript, PCRE, Perl, Python, Ruby

Hexadecimal character

[a-fA-F0-9]
Regex options: None
Regex flavors: .NET, Java, JavaScript, PCRE, Perl, Python, Ruby

Nonhexadecimal character

    [^a-fA-F0-9]
        Regex options: None
        Regex flavors: .NET, Java, JavaScript, PCRE, Perl, Python, Ruby

Discussion

The notation using square brackets is called a *character class*. A character class matches a single character out of a list of possible characters. The three classes in the first regex match either an a̲ or an e̲. They do so independently. When you test `calendar` against this regex, the first character class matches a̲, the second e̲, and the third a̲.

Outside character classes, a dozen punctuation characters are metacharacters. Inside a character class, only four characters have a special function: \, ^, -, and]. If you're using Java or .NET, the opening bracket [is also a metacharacter inside character classes. All other characters are literals and simply add themselves to the character class. The regular expression ‹[$()*+.?{|]› matches any one of the nine characters between the square brackets.

The backslash always escapes the character that follows it, just as it does outside character classes. The escaped character can be a single character, or the start or end of a range. The other four metacharacters get their special meanings only when they're placed in a certain position. It is possible to include them as literal characters in a character class without escaping them, by positioning them in a way that they don't get their special meaning. ‹[][^-]› pulls off this trick, at least if you're not using a JavaScript implementation that strictly adheres to the standard. But we recommend that you always escape these metacharacters, so the previous regex should be ‹[\]\[\^\-]›. Escaping the metacharacters makes your regular expression easier to understand.

Alphanumeric characters cannot be escaped with a backslash. Doing so is either an error or creates a regular expression token (something with a special meaning in a regular expression). In our discussions of certain other regex tokens, such as in Recipe 2.2, we mention that they can be used inside character classes. All these tokens consist of a backslash and a letter, sometimes followed by a bunch of other characters. Thus, ‹[\r\n]› matches a carriage return (\r) or line break (\n).

The *caret* (^) negates the character class if you place it immediately after the opening bracket. It makes the character class match any character that is *not* in the list. A negated character class matches line break characters, unless you add them to the negated character class.

The *hyphen* (-) creates a *range* when it is placed between two characters. The range consists of the character class with the character before the hyphen, the character after the hyphen, and all characters that lie between them in numerical order. To know which characters those are, you have to look at the ASCII or Unicode character table. ‹[A-z]› includes all characters in the ASCII table between the uppercase A and the lowercase z. The range includes some punctuation, so ‹[A-Z\[\\\]\^_`a-z]› matches the same characters more explicitly. We recommend that you create ranges only between two digits or between two letters that are both upper- or lowercase.

Reversed ranges, such as ‹[z-a]›, are not permitted.

Variations

Shorthands

```
[a-fA-F\d]
```
   Regex options: None
   Regex flavors: .NET, Java, PCRE, Perl, Python, Ruby

Six regex tokens that consist of a backslash and a letter form *shorthand* character classes. You can use these both inside and outside character classes. ‹\d› and ‹[\d]› both match a single digit. Each lowercase shorthand character has an associated uppercase shorthand character with the opposite meaning. Thus ‹\D› matches any character that is *not* a digit, and is equivalent to ‹[^\d]›.

‹\w› matches a single *word character*. A word character is a character that can occur as part of a word. That includes letters, digits, and the underscore. The particular choice of characters here may seem odd, but it was chosen because these are the characters that are typically allowed in identifiers in programming languages. ‹\W› matches any character that is not part of such a propellerhead word.

In Java, JavaScript, PCRE, and Ruby, ‹\w› is always identical to ‹[a-zA-Z0-9_]›. In .NET and Perl, it includes letters and digits from all other scripts (Cyrillic, Thai, etc.). In Python, the other scripts are included only if you pass the UNICODE or U flag when creating the regex. ‹\d› follows the same rule in all these flavors. In .NET and Perl, digits from other scripts are always included, whereas Python includes them only if you pass the UNICODE or U flag.

‹\s› matches any *whitespace character*. This includes spaces, tabs, and line breaks. In .NET, Perl, and JavaScript, ‹\s› also matches any character defined as whitespace by the Unicode standard. Notice that JavaScript uses Unicode for ‹\s› but ASCII for ‹\d› and ‹\w›. ‹\S› matches any character not matched by ‹\s›.

Further inconsistency arises when we add ‹\b› to the mix. ‹\b› is not a shorthand character class, but a word boundary. Though you'd expect ‹\b› to support Unicode when ‹\w› does and to be ASCII-only when ‹\w› is ASCII-only, this isn't always the case. The subsection "Word Characters" on page 42 in Recipe 2.6 has the details.

Case insensitivity

```
(?i)[A-F0-9]
```
   Regex options: None
   Regex flavors: .NET, Java, PCRE, Perl, Python, Ruby

```
(?i)[^A-F0-9]
```
   Regex options: None
   Regex flavors: .NET, Java, PCRE, Perl, Python, Ruby

Case insensitivity, whether set with an external flag (see Recipe 3.4) or a mode modifier inside the regex (see Recipe 2.1), also affects character classes. The two regexes just shown are equivalent to the ones in the original solution.

JavaScript follows the same rule, but it doesn't support ‹(?i)›. To make a regular expression case-insensitive in JavaScript, set the /i flag when creating it.

Flavor-Specific Features

.NET character class subtraction

```
[a-zA-Z0-9-[g-zG-Z]]
```

This regular expression matches a single hexadecimal character, but in a roundabout way. The base character class matches any alphanumeric character, and a nested class then subtracts the letters g through z. This nested class must appear at the end of the base class, preceded by a hyphen: ‹[class-[subtract]]›.

Character class *subtraction* is particularly useful when working with Unicode properties, blocks, and scripts. As an example, ‹\p{IsThai}› matches any character in the Thai block. ‹\P{N}› matches any character that doesn't have the Number property. Combining them with subtraction, ‹[\p{IsThai}-[\P{N}]]› matches any of the 10 Thai digits.

Java character class union, subtraction, and intersection

```
[a-f[A-F][0-9]]
```

```
[a-f[A-F[0-9]]]
```

Java allows one character class to be nested inside another. If the nested class is included directly, the resulting class is the *union* of the two. You can nest as many classes as you like. Both of the two regexes just shown have the same effect as the original without the extra square brackets:

```
[\w&&[a-fA-F0-9\s]]
```

This one could win a prize in a regex obfuscation contest. The base character class matches any word character. The nested class matches any hexadecimal digit and any whitespace character. The resulting class is the *intersection* of the two, matching hexadecimal digits and nothing else. Because the base class does not match whitespace and the nested class does not match ‹[g-zG-Z_]›, those are dropped from the final character class, leaving only the hexadecimal digits:

```
[a-zA-Z0-9&&[^g-zG-Z]]
```

This regular expression matches a single hexadecimal character, also in a roundabout way. The base character class matches any alphanumeric character, and a nested class then subtracts the letters g through z. This nested class must be a negated character class, preceded by two ampersands: ‹[class&&[^subtract]]›.

Character class intersection and subtraction are particularly useful when working with Unicode properties, blocks, and scripts. Thus, ‹\p{InThai}› matches any character in the Thai block, whereas ‹\p{N}› matches any character that has the Number property. In consequence, ‹[\p{InThai}&&[\p{N}]]› matches any of the 10 Thai digits.

If you're wondering about the subtle differences in the ‹\p› regex tokens, you'll find those all explained in Recipe 2.7.

See Also

Recipes 2.1, 2.2, and 2.7

2.4 Match Any Character

Problem

Match a quoted character. Provide one solution that allows any single character, except a line break, between the quotes. Provide another that truly allows any character, including line breaks.

Solution

Any character except line breaks

```
'.'
```

Regex options: None (the "dot matches line breaks" option must not be set)
Regex flavors: .NET, Java, JavaScript, PCRE, Perl, Python, Ruby

Any character including line breaks

```
'.'
```

Regex options: Dot matches line breaks
Regex flavors: .NET, Java, PCRE, Perl, Python, Ruby

```
'[\s\S]'
```

Regex options: None
Regex flavor: JavaScript

Discussion

Any character except line breaks

The dot is one of the oldest and simplest regular expression features. Its meaning has always been to match any single character.

There is, however, some confusion as to what *any character* truly means. The oldest tools for working with regular expressions processed files line by line, so there was never an opportunity for the subject text to include a line break. The programming languages discussed in this book process the subject text as a whole, no matter how many line breaks you put into it. If you want true line-by-line processing, you have to write a bit of code that splits the subject into an array of lines and applies the regex to each line in the array. Recipe 3.21 in the next chapter shows how to do this.

Larry Wall, the developer of Perl, wanted Perl to retain the traditional behavior of line-based tools, in which the dot never matched a line break (\n). All the other flavors discussed in this book followed suit. ‹'.'› thus matches any single character *except* a newline character.

Any character including line breaks

If you do want to allow your regular expression to span multiple lines, turn on the "dot matches line breaks" option. This option masquerades under different names. Perl and many others confusingly call it "single line" mode, whereas Java calls it "dot all" mode. Recipe 3.4 in the next chapter has all the details. Whatever the name of this option in your favorite programming language is, think of it as "dot matches line breaks" mode. That's all the option does.

An alternative solution is needed for JavaScript, which doesn't have a "dot matches line breaks" option. As Recipe 2.3 explains, ‹\s› matches any whitespace character, whereas ‹\S› matches any character that is not matched by ‹\s›. Combining these into ‹[\s\S]› results in a character class that includes all characters, including line breaks. ‹[\d\D]› and ‹[\w\W]› have the same effect.

Dot abuse

The dot is the most abused regular expression feature. ‹\d\d.\d\d.\d\d› is not a good way to match a date. It does match <u>05/16/08</u> just fine, but it also matches <u>99/99/99</u>. Worse, it matches <u>12345678</u>.

A proper regex for matching only valid dates is a subject for a later chapter. But replacing the dot with a more appropriate character class is very easy. ‹\d\d[/.\-]\d\d[/.\-]\d\d› allows a forward slash, dot, or hyphen to be used as the date separator. This regex still matches <u>99/99/99</u>, but not 12345678.

It's just a coincidence that the previous example includes a dot inside the character classes. Inside a character class, the dot is just a literal character. It's worth including in this particular regular expression because in some countries, such as Germany, the dot is used as a date separator.

Use the dot only when you really want to allow any character. Use a character class or negated character class in any other situation.

Variations

(?s)'.'
  Regex options: None
  Regex flavors: .NET, Java, PCRE, Perl, Python

(?m)'.'
  Regex options: None
  Regex flavors: Ruby

If you cannot turn on "dot matches line breaks" mode outside the regular expression, you can place a mode modifier at the start of the regular expression. We explain the concept of mode modifiers, and JavaScript's lack of support for them, in the subsection "Case-insensitive matching" on page 27 under Recipe 2.1.

‹(?s)› is the mode modifier for "dot matches line breaks" mode in .NET, Java, PCRE, Perl, and Python. The s stands for "single line" mode, which is Perl's confusing name for "dot matches line breaks."

The terminology is so confusing that the developer of Ruby's regex engine copied it wrongly. Ruby uses ‹(?m)› to turn on "dot matches line breaks" mode. Other than the different letter, the functionality is exactly the same. The new engine in Ruby 1.9 continues to use ‹(?m)› for "dot matches line breaks." Perl's meaning for ‹(?m)› is explained in Recipe 2.5.

See Also

Recipes 2.3, 3.4, and 3.21

2.5 Match Something at the Start and/or the End of a Line

Problem

Create four regular expressions. Match the word <u>alpha</u>, but only if it occurs at the very beginning of the subject text. Match the word <u>omega</u>, but only if it occurs at the very end of the subject text. Match the word <u>begin</u>, but only if it occurs at the beginning of a line. Match the word <u>end</u>, but only if it occurs at the end of a line.

Solution

Start of the subject

^alpha
Regex options: None ("^ and $ match at line breaks" must not be set)
Regex flavors: .NET, Java, JavaScript, PCRE, Perl, Python

\Aalpha
Regex options: None
Regex flavors: .NET, Java, PCRE, Perl, Python, Ruby

End of the subject

omega$
Regex options: None ("^ and $ match at line breaks" must not be set)
Regex flavors: .NET, Java, JavaScript, PCRE, Perl, Python

omega\Z
Regex options: None
Regex flavors: .NET, Java, PCRE, Perl, Python, Ruby

Start of a line

^begin
Regex options: ^ and $ match at line breaks
Regex flavors: .NET, Java, JavaScript, PCRE, Perl, Python, Ruby

End of a line

end$
Regex options: ^ and $ match at line breaks
Regex flavors: .NET, Java, JavaScript, PCRE, Perl, Python, Ruby

Discussion

Anchors and lines

The regular expression tokens ‹^›, ‹$›, ‹\A›, ‹\Z›, and ‹\z› are called *anchors*. They do not match any characters. Instead, they match at certain positions, effectively anchoring the regular expression match at those positions.

A *line* is the part of the subject text that lies between the start of the subject and a line break, between two line breaks, or between a line break and the end of the subject. If there are no line breaks in the subject, then the whole subject is considered to be one line. Thus, the following text consists of four lines, one each for one, two, an empty string, and four:

```
one
two

four
```

The text could be represented in a program as one⟨LF⟩two⟨LF⟩⟨LF⟩four.

Start of the subject

The anchor ‹\A› always matches at the very start of the subject text, before the first character. That is the only place where it matches. Place ‹\A› at the start of your regular expression to test whether the subject text begins with the text you want to match. The "A" must be uppercase.

JavaScript does not support ‹\A›.

The anchor ‹^› is equivalent to ‹\A›, as long as you do not turn on the "^ and $ match at line breaks" option. This option is off by default for all regex flavors except Ruby. Ruby does not offer a way to turn this option off.

Unless you're using JavaScript, we recommend that you always use ‹\A› instead of ‹^›. The meaning of ‹\A› never changes, avoiding any confusion or mistakes in setting regex options.

End of the subject

The anchors ‹\Z› and ‹\z› always match at the very end of the subject text, after the last character. Place ‹\Z› or ‹\z› at the end of your regular expression to test whether the subject text ends with the text you want to match.

.NET, Java, PCRE, Perl, and Ruby support both ‹\Z› and ‹\z›. Python supports only ‹\Z›. JavaScript does not support ‹\Z› or ‹\z› at all.

The difference between ‹\Z› and ‹\z› comes into play when the last character in your subject text is a line break. In that case, ‹\Z› can match at the very end of the subject text, after the final line break, as well as immediately before that line break. The benefit is that you can search for ‹omega\Z› without having to worry about stripping off a trailing line break at the end of your subject text. When reading a file line by line, some tools include the line break at the end of the line, whereas others don't; ‹\Z› masks this difference. ‹\z› matches only at the very end of the subject text, so it will not match text if a trailing line break follows.

The anchor ‹$› is equivalent to ‹\Z›, as long as you do not turn on the "^ and $ match at line breaks" option. This option is off by default for all regex flavors except Ruby. Ruby does not offer a way to turn this option off. Just like ‹\Z›, ‹$› matches at the very end of the subject text, as well as before the final line break, if any.

To help clarify this subtle and somewhat confusing situation, lets look at an example in Perl. Assuming that $/ (the current record separator) is set to its default \n, the following Perl statement reads a single line from the terminal (standard input):

```
$line = <>;
```

Perl leaves the newline on the content of the variable $line. Therefore, an expression such as ‹end•of•input.\z› will not match the variable. But ‹end•of•input.\Z› and ‹end•of•input.$› will both match, because they ignore the trailing newline.

To make processing easier, Perl programmers often strip newlines with:

```
chomp $line;
```

After that operation is performed, all three anchors will match. (Technically, chomp strips a string of the current record separator.)

Unless you're using JavaScript, we recommend that you always use ‹\Z› instead of ‹$›. The meaning of ‹\Z› never changes, avoiding any confusion or mistakes in setting regex options.

Start of a line

By default, ‹^› matches only at the start of the subject text, just like ‹\A›. Only in Ruby does ‹^› always match at the start of a line. All the other flavors require you to turn on the option to make the caret and dollar sign match at line breaks. This option is typically referred to as "multiline" mode.

Do not confuse this mode with "single line" mode, which would be better known as "dot matches line breaks" mode. "Multiline" mode affects only the caret and dollar sign; "single line" mode affects only the dot, as Recipe 2.4 explains. It is perfectly possible to turn on both "single line" and "multiline" mode at the same time. By default, both options are off.

With the correct option set, ‹^› will match at the start of each line in the subject text. Strictly speaking, it matches before the very first character in the file, as it always does, and also after each line break character in the subject text. The caret in ‹\n^› is redundant because ‹^› always matches after ‹\n›.

End of a line

By default, ‹$› matches only at the end of the subject text or before the final line break, just like ‹\Z›. Only in Ruby does ‹$› always match at the end of each line. All the other flavors require you to turn on the "multiline" option to make the caret and dollar match at line breaks.

With the correct option set, ‹$› will match at the end of each line in the subject text. (Of course, it also matches after the very last character in the text because that is always the end of a line as well.) The dollar in ‹$\n› is redundant because ‹$› always matches before ‹\n›.

Zero-length matches

It is perfectly valid for a regular expression to consist of nothing but one or more anchors. Such a regular expression will find a zero-length match at each position where the anchor can match. If you place several anchors together, all of them need to match at the same position for the regex to match.

You could use such a regular expression in a search-and-replace. Replace ‹\A› or ‹\Z› to prepend or append something to the whole subject. Replace ‹^› or ‹$›, in "^ and $ match at line breaks" mode, to prepend or append something in each line in the subject text.

Combine two anchors to test for blank lines or missing input. ‹\A\Z› matches the empty string, as well as the string that consists of a single newline. ‹\A\z› matches only the empty string. ‹^$›, in "^ and $ match at line breaks" mode, matches each empty line in the subject text.

Variations

> (?m)^begin
> **Regex options:** None
> **Regex flavors:** .NET, Java, PCRE, Perl, Python

> (?m)end$
> **Regex options:** None
> **Regex flavors:** .NET, Java, PCRE, Perl, Python

If you cannot turn on "^ and $ match at line breaks" mode outside the regular expression, you can place a mode modifier at the start of the regular expression. The concept of mode modifiers and JavaScript's lack of support for them are both explained in the subsection "Case-insensitive matching" on page 27 under Recipe 2.1.

‹(?m)› is the mode modifier for "^ and $ match at line breaks" mode in .NET, Java, PCRE, Perl, and Python. The m stands for "multiline" mode, which is Perl's confusing name for "^ and $ match at line breaks."

As explained earlier, the terminology was so confusing that the developer of Ruby's regex engine copied it incorrectly. Ruby uses ‹(?m)› to turn on "dot matches line breaks" mode. Ruby's ‹(?m)› has nothing to do with the caret and dollar anchors. In Ruby, ‹^› and ‹$› always match at the start and end of each line.

Except for the unfortunate mix-up in letters, Ruby's choice to use ‹^› and ‹$› exclusively for lines is a good one. Unless you're using JavaScript, we recommend that you copy this choice in your own regular expressions.

Jan followed the same idea in his designs of EditPad Pro and PowerGREP. You won't find a checkbox labeled "^ and $ match at line breaks," even though there is one labeled "dot matches newlines." Unless you prefix your regular expression with ‹(?-m)›, you'll have to use ‹\A› and ‹\Z› to anchor your regex to the beginning or end of your file.

See Also

Recipes 3.4 and 3.21

2.6 Match Whole Words

Problem

Create a regex that matches <u>cat</u> in `My cat is brown`, but not in `category` or `bobcat`. Create another regex that matches <u>cat</u> in `staccato`, but not in any of the three previous subject strings.

Solution

Word boundaries

`\bcat\b`
> **Regex options:** None
> **Regex flavors:** .NET, Java, JavaScript, PCRE, Perl, Python, Ruby

Nonboundaries

`\Bcat\B`
> **Regex options:** None
> **Regex flavors:** .NET, Java, JavaScript, PCRE, Perl, Python, Ruby

Discussion

Word boundaries

The regular expression token ‹\b› is called a *word boundary*. It matches at the start or the end of a word. By itself, it results in a zero-length match. ‹\b› is an *anchor*, just like the tokens introduced in the previous section.

Strictly speaking, ‹\b› matches in these three positions:

- Before the first character in the subject, if the first character is a word character
- After the last character in the subject, if the last character is a word character
- Between two characters in the subject, where one is a word character and the other is not a word character

None of the flavors discussed in this book have separate tokens for matching only before or only after a word. Unless you wanted to create a regex that consists of nothing but a word boundary, these aren't needed. The tokens before or after the ‹\b› in your regular expression will determine where ‹\b› can match. The ‹\b› in ‹\bx› and ‹!\b› could match only at the start of a word. The ‹\b› in ‹x\b› and ‹\b!› could match only at the end of a word. ‹x\bx› and ‹!\b!› can never match anywhere.

To run a "whole words only" search using a regular expression, simply place the word between two word boundaries, as we did with ‹\bcat\b›. The first ‹\b› requires the ‹c› to occur at the very start of the string, or after a nonword character. The second ‹\b› requires the ‹t› to occur at the very end of the string, or before a nonword character.

Line break characters are nonword characters. ‹\b› will match after a line break if the line break is immediately followed by a word character. It will also match before a line break immediately preceded by a word character. So a word that occupies a whole line by itself will be found by a "whole words only" search. ‹\b› is unaffected by "multiline" mode or ‹(?m)›, which is one of the reasons why this book refers to "multiline" mode as "^ and $ match at line breaks" mode.

Nonboundaries

‹\B› matches at every position in the subject text where ‹\b› does not match. ‹\B› matches at every position that is not at the start or end of a word.

Strictly speaking, ‹\B› matches in these five positions:

- Before the first character in the subject, if the first character is not a word character
- After the last character in the subject, if the last character is not a word character
- Between two word characters
- Between two nonword characters
- The empty string

‹\Bcat\B› matches <u>cat</u> in staccato, but not in My cat is brown, category, or bobcat.

To do the opposite of a "whole words only" search (i.e., excluding My cat is brown and including staccato, category, and bobcat), you need to use alternation to combine ‹\Bcat› and ‹cat\B› into ‹\Bcat|cat\B›. ‹\Bcat› matches <u>cat</u> in staccato and bobcat. ‹cat\B› matches <u>cat</u> in category (and staccato if ‹\Bcat› hadn't already taken care of that). Recipe 2.8 explains alternation.

Word Characters

All this talk about word boundaries, but no talk about what a *word character* is. A word character is a character that can occur as part of a word. The subsection "Short-hands" on page 32 in Recipe 2.3 discussed which characters are included in ‹\w›, which matches a single word character. Unfortunately, the story is not the same for ‹\b›.

Although all the flavors in this book support ‹\b› and ‹\B›, they differ in which characters are word characters.

.NET, JavaScript, PCRE, Perl, Python, and Ruby have ‹\b› match between two characters where one is matched by ‹\w› and the other by ‹\W›. ‹\B› always matches between two characters where both are matched by ‹\w› or ‹\W›.

JavaScript, PCRE, and Ruby view only ASCII characters as word characters. ‹\w› is identical to ‹[a-zA-Z0-9_]›. With these flavors, you can do a "whole words only" search on words in languages that use only the letters A to Z without diacritics, such as English. But these flavors cannot do "whole words only" searches on words in other languages, such as Spanish or Russian.

.NET and Perl treat letters and digits from all scripts as word characters. With these flavors, you can do a "whole words only" search on words in any language, including those that don't use the Latin alphabet.

Python gives you an option. Non-ASCII characters are included only if you pass the **UNICODE** or **U** flag when creating the regex. This flag affects both ‹\b› and ‹\w› equally.

Java behaves inconsistently. ‹\w› matches only ASCII characters. But ‹\b› is Unicode-enabled, supporting any script. In Java, ‹\b\w\b› matches a single English letter, digit, or underscore that does not occur as part of a word in any language. ‹\bкошка\b› will correctly match the Russian word for cat, because ‹\b› supports Unicode. But ‹\w+› will not match any Russian word, because ‹\w› is ASCII-only.

See Also

Recipe 2.3

2.7 Unicode Code Points, Properties, Blocks, and Scripts

Problem

Use a regular expression to find the trademark sign (™) by specifying its Unicode code point rather than copying and pasting an actual trademark sign. If you like copy and paste, the trademark sign is just another literal character, even though you cannot type it directly on your keyboard. Literal characters are discussed in Recipe 2.1.

Create a regular expression that matches any character that has the "Currency Symbol" Unicode property. Unicode properties are also called Unicode categories.

Create a regular expression that matches any character in the "Greek Extended" Unicode block.

Create a regular expression that matches any character that, according to the Unicode standard, is part of the Greek script.

Create a regular expression that matches a grapheme, or what is commonly thought of as a character: a base character with all its combining marks.

Solution

Unicode code point

`\u2122`
Regex options: None
Regex flavors: .NET, Java, JavaScript, Python

This regex works in Python only when quoted as a Unicode string: `u"\u2122"`.

`\x{2122}`
Regex options: None
Regex flavors: PCRE, Perl, Ruby 1.9

PCRE must be compiled with UTF-8 support; in PHP, turn on UTF-8 support with the /u pattern modifier. Ruby 1.8 does not support Unicode regular expressions.

Unicode property or category

`\p{Sc}`
Regex options: None
Regex flavors: .NET, Java, PCRE, Perl, Ruby 1.9

PCRE must be compiled with UTF-8 support; in PHP, turn on UTF-8 support with the /u pattern modifier. JavaScript and Python do not support Unicode properties. Ruby 1.8 does not support Unicode regular expressions.

Unicode block

`\p{IsGreekExtended}`
Regex options: None
Regex flavors: .NET, Perl

`\p{InGreekExtended}`
Regex options: None
Regex flavors: Java, Perl

JavaScript, PCRE, Python, and Ruby do not support Unicode blocks.

Unicode script

`\p{Greek}`
Regex options: None
Regex flavors: PCRE, Perl, Ruby 1.9

Unicode script support requires PCRE 6.5 or later, and PCRE must be compiled with UTF-8 support. In PHP, turn on UTF-8 support with the /u pattern modifier. .NET, JavaScript, and Python do not support Unicode properties. Ruby 1.8 does not support Unicode regular expressions.

Unicode grapheme

\X
> **Regex options:** None
> **Regex flavors:** PCRE, Perl

PCRE and Perl have a dedicated token for matching graphemes, but also support the workaround syntax using Unicode properties.

\P{M}\p{M}*
> **Regex options:** None
> **Regex flavors:** .NET, Java, PCRE, Perl, Ruby 1.9

PCRE must be compiled with UTF-8 support; in PHP, turn on UTF-8 support with the /u pattern modifier. JavaScript and Python do not support Unicode properties. Ruby 1.8 does not support Unicode regular expressions.

Discussion

Unicode code point

A *code point* is one entry in the Unicode character database. A code point is not the same as a *character*, depending on the meaning you give to "character." What appears as a character on screen is called a *grapheme* in Unicode.

The Unicode code point U+2122 represents the "trademark sign" character. You can match this with ‹\u2122› or ‹\x{2122}›, depending on the regex flavor you're working with.

The ‹\u› syntax requires exactly four hexadecimal digits. This means you can only use it for Unicode code points U+0000 through U+FFFF. The ‹\x› syntax allows any number of hexadecimal digits, supporting all code points U+000000 through U+10FFFF. You can match U+00E0 with ‹\x{E0}› or ‹\x{00E0}›. Code points U+100000 are used very infrequently, and are poorly supported by fonts and operating systems.

Code points can be used inside and outside character classes.

Unicode property or category

Each Unicode code point has exactly one *Unicode property*, or fits into a single *Unicode category*. These terms mean the same thing. There are 30 Unicode categories, grouped into 7 super-categories:

‹\p{L}›
> Any kind of letter from any language

> ‹\p{Ll}›
>> A lowercase letter that has an uppercase variant

⟨\p{Lt}⟩
> A letter that appears at the start of a word when only the first letter of the word is capitalized

⟨\p{Lo}⟩
> A letter or ideograph that does not have lowercase and uppercase variants

⟨\p{M}⟩
> A character intended to be combined with another character (accents, umlauts, enclosing boxes, etc.)

⟨\p{Mn}⟩
> > A character intended to be combined with another character that does not take up extra space (e.g., accents, umlauts, etc.)

⟨\p{Me}⟩
> > A character that encloses another character (circle, square, keycap, etc.)

⟨\p{Z}⟩
> Any kind of whitespace or invisible separator

⟨\p{Zs}⟩
> > A whitespace character that is invisible, but does take up space

⟨\p{Zl}⟩
> > The line separator character U+2028

⟨\p{Zp}⟩
> > The paragraph separator character U+2029

⟨\p{S}⟩
> Math symbols, currency signs, dingbats, box-drawing characters, etc.

⟨\p{Sm}⟩
> > Any mathematical symbol

⟨\p{Sc}⟩
> > Any currency sign

⟨\p{Sk}⟩
> > A combining character (mark) as a full character on its own

⟨\p{So}⟩
> > Various symbols that are not math symbols, currency signs, or combining characters

⟨\p{N}⟩
> Any kind of numeric character in any script

⟨\p{Nd}⟩
> > A digit 0 through 9 in any script except ideographic scripts

⟨\p{Nl}⟩
> > A number that looks like a letter, such as a Roman numeral

⟨\p{No}⟩
> A superscript or subscript digit, or a number that is not a digit 0...9 (excluding numbers from ideographic scripts)

⟨\p{P}⟩
> Any kind of punctuation character

⟨\p{Pd}⟩
> Any kind of hyphen or dash

⟨\p{Ps}⟩
> Any kind of opening bracket

⟨\p{Pe}⟩
> Any kind of closing bracket

⟨\p{Pi}⟩
> Any kind of opening quote

⟨\p{Pf}⟩
> Any kind of closing quote

⟨\p{Pc}⟩
> A punctuation character such as an underscore that connects words

⟨\p{Po}⟩
> Any kind of punctuation character that is not a dash, bracket, quote or connector

⟨\p{C}⟩
> Invisible control characters and unused code points

⟨\p{Cc}⟩
> An ASCII 0x00...0x1F or Latin-1 0x80...0x9F control character

⟨\p{Cf}⟩
> An invisible formatting indicator

⟨\p{Co}⟩
> Any code point reserved for private use

⟨\p{Cs}⟩
> One half of a surrogate pair in UTF-16 encoding

⟨\p{Cn}⟩
> Any code point to which no character has been assigned

⟨\p{Ll}⟩ matches a single code point that has the Ll, or "lowercase letter," property. ⟨\p{L}⟩ is a quick way of writing ⟨[\p{Ll}\p{Lu}\p{Lt}\p{Lm}\p{Lo}]⟩ that matches a single code point in any of the "letter" categories.

⟨\P⟩ is the negated version of ⟨\p⟩. ⟨\P{Ll}⟩ matches a single code point that does not have the Ll property. ⟨\P{L}⟩ matches a single code point that does not have any of the "letter" properties. This is not the same as ⟨[\P{Ll}\P{Lu}\P{Lt}\P{Lm}\P{Lo}]⟩, which matches all code points. ⟨\P{Ll}⟩ matches the code points with the Lu property (and every other property except `Ll`), whereas ‹`\P{Lu}`› includes the `Ll` code points. Combining just these two in a code point class already matches all possible code points.

Unicode block

The Unicode character database divides all the code points into blocks. Each block consists of a single range of code points. The code points U+0000 through U+FFFF are divided into 105 blocks:

U+0000...U+007F	‹\p{InBasic_Latin}›
U+0080...U+00FF	‹\p{InLatin-1_Supplement}›
U+0100...U+017F	‹\p{InLatin_Extended-A}›
U+0180...U+024F	‹\p{InLatin_Extended-B}›
U+0250...U+02AF	‹\p{InIPA_Extensions}›
U+02B0...U+02FF	‹\p{InSpacing_Modifier_Letters}›
U+0300...U+036F	‹\p{InCombining_Diacritical_Marks}›
U+0370...U+03FF	‹\p{InGreek_and_Coptic}›
U+0400...U+04FF	‹\p{InCyrillic}›
U+0500...U+052F	‹\p{InCyrillic_Supplementary}›
U+0530...U+058F	‹\p{InArmenian}›
U+0590...U+05FF	‹\p{InHebrew}›
U+0600...U+06FF	‹\p{InArabic}›
U+0700...U+074F	‹\p{InSyriac}›
U+0780...U+07BF	‹\p{InThaana}›
U+0900...U+097F	‹\p{InDevanagari}›
U+0980...U+09FF	‹\p{InBengali}›
U+0A00...U+0A7F	‹\p{InGurmukhi}›
U+0A80...U+0AFF	‹\p{InGujarati}›
U+0B00...U+0B7F	‹\p{InOriya}›
U+0B80...U+0BFF	‹\p{InTamil}›
U+0C00...U+0C7F	‹\p{InTelugu}›
U+0C80...U+0CFF	‹\p{InKannada}›
U+0D00...U+0D7F	‹\p{InMalayalam}›
U+0D80...U+0DFF	‹\p{InSinhala}›
U+0E00...U+0E7F	‹\p{InThai}›
U+0E80...U+0EFF	‹\p{InLao}›
U+0F00...U+0FFF	‹\p{InTibetan}›
U+1000...U+109F	‹\p{InMyanmar}›

U+10A0...U+10FF	⟨\p{InGeorgian}⟩
U+1100...U+11FF	⟨\p{InHangul_Jamo}⟩
U+1200...U+137F	⟨\p{InEthiopic}⟩
U+13A0...U+13FF	⟨\p{InCherokee}⟩
U+1400...U+167F	⟨\p{InUnified_Canadian_Aboriginal_Syllabics}⟩
U+1680...U+169F	⟨\p{InOgham}⟩
U+16A0...U+16FF	⟨\p{InRunic}⟩
U+1700...U+171F	⟨\p{InTagalog}⟩
U+1720...U+173F	⟨\p{InHanunoo}⟩
U+1740...U+175F	⟨\p{InBuhid}⟩
U+1760...U+177F	⟨\p{InTagbanwa}⟩
U+1780...U+17FF	⟨\p{InKhmer}⟩
U+1800...U+18AF	⟨\p{InMongolian}⟩
U+1900...U+194F	⟨\p{InLimbu}⟩
U+1950...U+197F	⟨\p{InTai_Le}⟩
U+19E0...U+19FF	⟨\p{InKhmer_Symbols}⟩
U+1D00...U+1D7F	⟨\p{InPhonetic_Extensions}⟩
U+1E00...U+1EFF	⟨\p{InLatin_Extended_Additional}⟩
U+1F00...U+1FFF	⟨\p{InGreek_Extended}⟩
U+2000...U+206F	⟨\p{InGeneral_Punctuation}⟩
U+2070...U+209F	⟨\p{InSuperscripts_and_Subscripts}⟩
U+20A0...U+20CF	⟨\p{InCurrency_Symbols}⟩
U+20D0...U+20FF	⟨\p{InCombining_Diacritical_Marks_for_Symbols}⟩
U+2100...U+214F	⟨\p{InLetterlike_Symbols}⟩
U+2150...U+218F	⟨\p{InNumber_Forms}⟩
U+2190...U+21FF	⟨\p{InArrows}⟩
U+2200...U+22FF	⟨\p{InMathematical_Operators}⟩
U+2300...U+23FF	⟨\p{InMiscellaneous_Technical}⟩
U+2400...U+243F	⟨\p{InControl_Pictures}⟩
U+2440...U+245F	⟨\p{InOptical_Character_Recognition}⟩
U+2460...U+24FF	⟨\p{InEnclosed_Alphanumerics}⟩
U+2500...U+257F	⟨\p{InBox_Drawing}⟩
U+2580...U+259F	⟨\p{InBlock_Elements}⟩
U+25A0...U+25FF	⟨\p{InGeometric_Shapes}⟩
U+2600...U+26FF	⟨\p{InMiscellaneous_Symbols}⟩
U+2700...U+27BF	⟨\p{InDingbats}⟩

```
U+27C0...U+27EF    ‹\p{InMiscellaneous_Mathematical_Symbols-A}›

U+27F0...U+27FF    ‹\p{InSupplemental_Arrows-A}›

U+2800...U+28FF    ‹\p{InBraille_Patterns}›

U+2900...U+297F    ‹\p{InSupplemental_Arrows-B}›

U+2980...U+29FF    ‹\p{InMiscellaneous_Mathematical_Symbols-B}›

U+2A00...U+2AFF    ‹\p{InSupplemental_Mathematical_Operators}›

U+2B00...U+2BFF    ‹\p{InMiscellaneous_Symbols_and_Arrows}›

U+2E80...U+2EFF    ‹\p{InCJK_Radicals_Supplement}›

U+2F00...U+2FDF    ‹\p{InKangxi_Radicals}›

U+2FF0...U+2FFF    ‹\p{InIdeographic_Description_Characters}›

U+3000...U+303F    ‹\p{InCJK_Symbols_and_Punctuation}›

U+3040...U+309F    ‹\p{InHiragana}›

U+30A0...U+30FF    ‹\p{InKatakana}›

U+3100...U+312F    ‹\p{InBopomofo}›

U+3130...U+318F    ‹\p{InHangul_Compatibility_Jamo}›

U+3190...U+319F    ‹\p{InKanbun}›

U+31A0...U+31BF    ‹\p{InBopomofo_Extended}›

U+31F0...U+31FF    ‹\p{InKatakana_Phonetic_Extensions}›

U+3200...U+32FF    ‹\p{InEnclosed_CJK_Letters_and_Months}›

U+3300...U+33FF    ‹\p{InCJK_Compatibility}›

U+3400...U+4DBF    ‹\p{InCJK_Unified_Ideographs_Extension_A}›

U+4DC0...U+4DFF    ‹\p{InYijing_Hexagram_Symbols}›

U+4E00...U+9FFF    ‹\p{InCJK_Unified_Ideographs}›

U+A000...U+A48F    ‹\p{InYi_Syllables}›

U+A490...U+A4CF    ‹\p{InYi_Radicals}›

U+AC00...U+D7AF    ‹\p{InHangul_Syllables}›

U+D800...U+DB7F    ‹\p{InHigh_Surrogates}›

U+DB80...U+DBFF    ‹\p{InHigh_Private_Use_Surrogates}›

U+DC00...U+DFFF    ‹\p{InLow_Surrogates}›

U+E000...U+F8FF    ‹\p{InPrivate_Use_Area}›

U+F900...U+FAFF    ‹\p{InCJK_Compatibility_Ideographs}›

U+FB00...U+FB4F    ‹\p{InAlphabetic_Presentation_Forms}›

U+FB50...U+FDFF    ‹\p{InArabic_Presentation_Forms-A}›

U+FE00...U+FE0F    ‹\p{InVariation_Selectors}›

U+FE20...U+FE2F    ‹\p{InCombining_Half_Marks}›

U+FE30...U+FE4F    ‹\p{InCJK_Compatibility_Forms}›
```

U+FE50...U+FE6F	⟨\p{InSmall_Form_Variants}⟩
U+FE70...U+FEFF	⟨\p{InArabic_Presentation_Forms-B}⟩
U+FF00...U+FFEF	⟨\p{InHalfwidth_and_Fullwidth_Forms}⟩
U+FFF0...U+FFFF	⟨\p{InSpecials}⟩

A Unicode block is a single, contiguous range of code points. Although many blocks have the names of Unicode scripts and Unicode categories, they do not correspond 100% with them. The name of a block only indicates its primary use.

The Currency block does not include the dollar and yen symbols. Those are found in the Basic_Latin and Latin-1_Supplement blocks, for historical reasons. Both do have the Currency Symbol property. To match any currency symbol, use \p{Sc} instead of \p{InCurrency}.

Most blocks include unassigned code points, which are covered by the property ⟨\p{Cn}⟩. No other Unicode property, and none of the Unicode scripts, include unassigned code points.

The ⟨\p{InBlockName}⟩ syntax works with .NET and Perl. Java uses the ⟨\p{IsBlockName}⟩ syntax.

Perl also supports the Is variant, but we recommend you stick with the In syntax, to avoid confusion with Unicode scripts. For scripts, Perl supports ⟨\p{Script}⟩ and ⟨\p{IsScript}⟩, but not ⟨\p{InScript}⟩.

Unicode script

Each Unicode code point, except unassigned ones, is part of exactly one Unicode script. Unassigned code points are not part of any script. The assigned code points up to U+FFFF are assigned to these scripts:

⟨\p{Common}⟩	⟨\p{Katakana}⟩
⟨\p{Arabic}⟩	⟨\p{Khmer}⟩
⟨\p{Armenian}⟩	⟨\p{Lao}⟩
⟨\p{Bengali}⟩	⟨\p{Latin}⟩
⟨\p{Bopomofo}⟩	⟨\p{Limbu}⟩
⟨\p{Braille}⟩	⟨\p{Malayalam}⟩
⟨\p{Buhid}⟩	⟨\p{Mongolian}⟩
⟨\p{CanadianAboriginal}⟩	⟨\p{Myanmar}⟩
⟨\p{Cherokee}⟩	⟨\p{Ogham}⟩
⟨\p{Cyrillic}⟩	⟨\p{Oriya}⟩
⟨\p{Devanagari}⟩	⟨\p{Runic}⟩
⟨\p{Ethiopic}⟩	⟨\p{Sinhala}⟩
⟨\p{Georgian}⟩	⟨\p{Syriac}⟩
⟨\p{Greek}⟩	⟨\p{Tagalog}⟩
⟨\p{Gujarati}⟩	⟨\p{Tagbanwa}⟩

```
‹\p{Gurmukhi}›            ‹\p{TaiLe}›
‹\p{Han}›                 ‹\p{Tamil}›
‹\p{Hangul}›              ‹\p{Telugu}›
‹\p{Hanunoo}›             ‹\p{Thaana}›
‹\p{Hebrew}›              ‹\p{Thai}›
‹\p{Hiragana}›            ‹\p{Tibetan}›
‹\p{Inherited}›           ‹\p{Yi}›
‹\p{Kannada}›
```

A script is a group of code points used by a particular human writing system. Some scripts, such as Thai, correspond with a single human language. Other scripts, such as Latin, span multiple languages. Some languages are composed of multiple scripts. For instance, there is no Japanese Unicode script; instead, Unicode offers the Hiragana, Katakana, Han, and Latin scripts that Japanese documents are usually composed of.

We listed the Common script first, out of alphabetical order. This script contains all sorts of characters that are common to a wide range of scripts, such as punctuation, white-space, and miscellaneous symbols.

Unicode grapheme

The difference between code points and characters comes into play when there are *combining marks*. The Unicode code point U+0061 is "Latin small letter a," whereas U+00E0 is "Latin small letter a with grave accent." Both represent what most people would describe as a character.

U+0300 is the "combining grave accent" combining mark. It can be used sensibly only after a letter. A string consisting of the Unicode code points U+0061 U+0300 will be displayed as à, just like U+00E0. The combining mark U+0300 is displayed on top of the character U+0061.

The reason for these two different ways of displaying an accented letter is that many historical character sets encode "a with grave accent" as a single character. Unicode's designers thought it would be useful to have a one-on-one mapping with popular legacy character sets, in addition to the Unicode way of separating marks and base letters, which makes arbitrary combinations not supported by legacy character sets possible.

What matters to you as a regex user is that all regex flavors discussed in this book operate on code points rather than graphical characters. When we say that the regular expression ‹.› matches a single character, it really matches just a single code point. If your subject text consists of the two code points U+0061 U+0300, which can be represented as the string literal "\u0061\u0300" in a programming language such as Java, the dot will match only the code point U+0061, or a, without the accent U+0300. The regex ‹..› will match both.

Perl and PCRE offer a special regex token ‹\X›, which matches any single Unicode grapheme. Essentially, it is the Unicode version of the venerable dot. It matches any Unicode code point that is not a combining mark, along with all the combining marks that follow it, if any. ‹\P{M}\p{M}*› does the same thing using the Unicode property syntax. ‹\X› will find two matches in the text àà, regardless of how it is encoded. If it is encoded as "\u00E0\u0061\u0300" the first match is "\u00E0", and the second "\u0061\u0300".

Variations

Negated variant

The uppercase ‹\P› is the negated variant of the lowercase ‹\p›. For instance, ‹\P{Sc}› matches any character that does not have the "Currency Symbol" Unicode property. ‹\P› is supported by all flavors that support ‹\p›, and for all the properties, block, and scripts that they support.

Character classes

All flavors allow all the ‹\u›, ‹\x›, ‹\p›, and ‹\P› tokens they support to be used inside character classes. The character represented by the code point, or the characters in the category, block, or script, are then added to the character class. For instance, you could match a character that is either an opening quote (initial punctuation property), a closing quote (final punctuation property), or the trademark symbol (U+2122) with:

[\p{Pi}\p{Pf}\x{2122}]
Regex options: None
Regex flavors: .NET, Java, PCRE, Perl, Ruby 1.9

Listing all characters

If your regular expression flavor does not support Unicode categories, blocks, or scripts, you can list the characters that are in the category, block, or script in a character class. For blocks this is very easy: each block is simply a range between two code points. The Greek Extended block comprises the characters U+1F00 to U+1FFF:

[\u1F00-\u1FFF]
Regex options: None
Regex flavors: .NET, Java, JavaScript, Python

[\x{1F00}-\x{1FFF}]
Regex options: None
Regex flavors: PCRE, Perl, Ruby 1.9

For most categories and many scripts, the equivalent character class is a long list of individual code points and short ranges. The characters that comprise each category and many of the scripts are scattered throughout the Unicode table. This is the Greek script:

```
[\u0370-\u0373\u0375\u0376-\u0377\u037A\u037B-\u037D\u0384\u0386↵
\u0388-\u038A\u038C\u038E-\u03A1\u03A3-\u03E1\u03F0-\u03F5\u03F6↵
\u03F7-\u03FF\u1D26-\u1D2A\u1D5D-\u1D61\u1D66-\u1D6A\u1DBF\u1F00-\u1F15↵
\u1F18-\u1F1D\u1F20-\u1F45\u1F48-\u1F4D\u1F50-\u1F57\u1F59\u1F5B\u1F5D↵
\u1F5F-\u1F7D\u1F80-\u1FB4\u1FB6-\u1FBC\u1FBD\u1FBE\u1FBF-\u1FC1↵
\u1FC2-\u1FC4\u1FC6-\u1FCC\u1FCD-\u1FCF\u1FD0-\u1FD3\u1FD6-\u1FDB↵
\u1FDD-\u1FDF\u1FE0-\u1FEC\u1FED-\u1FEF\u1FF2-\u1FF4\u1FF6-\u1FFC↵
\u1FFD-\u1FFE\u2126]
```
Regex options: None
Regex flavors: .NET, Java, JavaScript, Python

We built this regular expression by copying the listing for the Greek script from *http://www.unicode.org/Public/UNIDATA/Scripts.txt*, searching and replacing with three regular expressions:

1. Searching for the regular expression ‹;.*› and replacing its matches with nothing deletes the comments. If it deletes everything, undo and turn off "dot matches line breaks."

2. Searching for ‹^› with "^ and $ match at line breaks" turned on, and replacing with «\u», prefixes the code points with \u. Replacing ‹\.\.› with «-\u» corrects the ranges.

3. Finally, replacing ‹\s+› with nothing removes the line breaks. Adding the brackets around the character class finishes the regex. You may have to add \u at the start of the character class and/or remove it at the end, depending on whether you included any leading or trailing blank lines when copying the listing from Scripts.txt.

This may seem like a lot of work, but it actually took Jan less than a minute. Writing the description took much longer. Doing this for the \x{} syntax is just as easy:

1. Searching for the regular expression ‹;.*› and replacing its matches with nothing deletes the comments. If it deletes everything, undo and turn off "dot matches line breaks."

2. Searching for ‹^› with "^ and $ match at line breaks" turned on and replacing with «\x{» prefixes the code points with \x{. Replacing ‹\.\.› with «}-\x{» corrects the ranges.

3. Finally, replacing ‹\s+› with «}» adds the closing braces and removes the line breaks. Adding the brackets around the character class finishes the regex. You may have to add \x{ at the start of the character class and/or remove it at the end, depending on whether you included any leading or trailing blank lines when copying the listing from Scripts.txt.

The results are:

```
[\x{0370}-\x{0373}\x{0375}\x{0376}-\x{0377}\x{037A}\x{037B}-\x{037D}↵
\x{0384}\x{0386}\x{0388}-\x{038A}\x{038C}\x{038E}-\x{03A1}↵
\x{03A3}-\x{03E1}\x{03F0}-\x{03F5}\x{03F6}\x{03F7}-\x{03FF}↵
\x{1D26}-\x{1D2A}\x{1D5D}-\x{1D61}\x{1D66}-\x{1D6A}\x{1DBF}↵
\x{1F00}-\x{1F15}\x{1F18}-\x{1F1D}\x{1F20}-\x{1F45}\x{1F48}-\x{1F4D}↵
\x{1F50}-\x{1F57}\x{1F59}\x{1F5B}\x{1F5D}\x{1F5F}-\x{1F7D}↵
\x{1F80}-\x{1FB4}\x{1FB6}-\x{1FBC}\x{1FBD}\x{1FBE}\x{1FBF}-\x{1FC1}↵
\x{1FC2}-\x{1FC4}\x{1FC6}-\x{1FCC}\x{1FCD}-\x{1FCF}\x{1FD0}-\x{1FD3}↵
\x{1FD6}-\x{1FDB}\x{1FDD}-\x{1FDF}\x{1FE0}-\x{1FEC}\x{1FED}-\x{1FEF}↵
\x{1FF2}-\x{1FF4}\x{1FF6}-\x{1FFC}\x{1FFD}-\x{1FFE}\x{2126}↵
\x{10140}-\x{10174}\x{10175}-\x{10178}\x{10179}-\x{10189}↵
\x{1018A}\x{1D200}-\x{1D241}\x{1D242}-\x{1D244}\x{1D245}]
```

Regex options: None
Regex flavors: PCRE, Perl, Ruby 1.9

See Also

http://www.unicode.org is the official website of the Unicode Consortium, where you can download all the official Unicode documents, character tables, etc.

Unicode is a vast topic, on which entire books have been written. One such book is *Unicode Explained* by Jukka K. Korpela (O'Reilly).

We can't explain everything you should know about Unicode code points, properties, blocks, and scripts in just one section. We haven't even tried to explain why you should care—you should. The comfortable simplicity of the extended ASCII table is a lonely place in today's globalized world.

2.8 Match One of Several Alternatives

Problem

Create a regular expression that when applied repeatedly to the text `Mary, Jane, and Sue went to Mary's house` will match <u>Mary</u>, <u>Jane</u>, <u>Sue</u>, and then <u>Mary</u> again. Further match attempts should fail.

Solution

```
Mary|Jane|Sue
```

Regex options: None
Regex flavors: .NET, Java, JavaScript, PCRE, Perl, Python, Ruby

Discussion

The *vertical bar*, or *pipe symbol*, splits the regular expression into multiple *alternatives*. ‹Mary|Jane|Sue› matches <u>Mary</u>, or <u>Jane</u>, or <u>Sue</u> with each match attempt. Only one name matches each time, but a different name can match each time.

All regular expression flavors discussed in this book use a regex-directed engine. The *engine* is simply the software that makes the regular expression work. *Regex-directed* means that all possible permutations of the regular expression are attempted at each character position in the subject text, before the regex is attempted at the next character position.

When you apply ‹Mary|Jane|Sue› to Mary, Jane, and Sue went to Mary's house, the match <u>Mary</u> is immediately found at the start of the string.

When you apply the same regex to the remainder of the string—e.g., by clicking "Find Next" in your text editor—the regex engine attempts to match ‹Mary› at the first comma in the string. That fails. Then, it attempts to match ‹Jane› at the same position, which also fails. Attempting to match ‹Sue› at the comma fails, too. Only then does the regex engine advance to the next character in the string. Starting at the first space, all three alternatives fail in the same way.

Starting at the J, the first alternative, ‹Mary›, fails to match. The second alternative, ‹Jane›, is then attempted starting at the J. It matches <u>Jane</u>. The regex engine declares victory.

Notice that <u>Jane</u> was found even though there is another occurrence of <u>Mary</u> in the subject text, and that ‹Mary› appears before ‹Jane› in the regex. At least in this case, the order of the alternatives in the regular expression does not matter. The regular expression finds the *leftmost* match. It scans the text from left to right, tries all alternatives in the regular expression at each step, and stops at the first position in the text where any of the alternatives produces a valid match.

If we do another search through the remainder of the string, <u>Sue</u> will be found. The fourth search will find <u>Mary</u> once more. If you tell the regular engine to do a fifth search, that will fail, because none of the three alternatives match the remaining , house string.

The order of the alternatives in the regex matters only when two of them can match at the same position in the string. The regex ‹Jane|Janet› has two alternatives that match at the same position in the text Her name is Janet. There are no word boundaries in the regular expression. The fact that ‹Jane› matches the word Janet in Her name is Janet only partially does not matter.

---

* The other kind of engine is a *text-directed* engine. The key difference is that a text-directed engine visits each character in the subject text only once, whereas a regex-directed engine may visit each character many times. Text-directed engines are much faster, but support regular expressions only in the mathematical sense described at the beginning of Chapter 1. The fancy Perl-style regular expressions that make this book so interesting can be implemented only with a regex-directed engine.

‹Jane|Janet› matches <u>Jane</u> in `Her name is Janet` because a regex-directed regular expression engine is *eager*. In addition to scanning the subject text from left to right, finding the leftmost match, it also scans the alternatives in the regex from left to right. The engine stops as soon as it finds an alternative that matches.

When ‹Jane|Janet› reaches the `J` in `Her name is Janet`, the first alternative, ‹Jane›, matches. The second alternative is not attempted. If we tell the engine to look for a second match, the `t` is all that is left of the subject text. Neither alternative matches there.

There are two ways to stop Jane from stealing Janet's limelight. One way is to put the longer alternative first: ‹Janet|Jane›. A more solid solution is to be explicit about what we're trying to do: we're looking for names, and names are complete words. Regular expressions don't deal with words, but they can deal with word boundaries.

So ‹\bJane\b|\bJanet\b› and ‹\bJanet\b|\bJane\b› will both match <u>Janet</u> in `Her name is Janet`. Because of the word boundaries, only one alternative can match. The order of the alternatives is again irrelevant.

Recipe 2.12 explains the best solution: ‹\bJanet?\b›.

See Also

Recipe 2.9

2.9 Group and Capture Parts of the Match

Problem

Improve the regular expression for matching <u>Mary</u>, <u>Jane</u>, or <u>Sue</u> by forcing the match to be a whole word. Use grouping to achieve this with one pair of word boundaries for the whole regex, instead of one pair for each alternative.

Create a regular expression that matches any date in yyyy-mm-dd format, and separately captures the year, month, and day. The goal is to make it easy to work with these separate values in the code that processes the match. You can assume all dates in the subject text to be valid. The regular expression does not have to exclude things like 9999-99-99, as these won't occur in the subject text at all.

Solution

> \b(Mary|Jane|Sue)\b
> **Regex options:** None
> **Regex flavors:** .NET, Java, JavaScript, PCRE, Perl, Python, Ruby

> \b(\d\d\d\d)-(\d\d)-(\d\d)\b
> **Regex options:** None
> **Regex flavors:** .NET, Java, JavaScript, PCRE, Perl, Python, Ruby

Discussion

The alternation operator, explained in the previous section, has the lowest precedence of all regex operators. If you try ‹\bMary|Jane|Sue\b›, the three alternatives are ‹\bMary›, ‹Jane›, and ‹Sue\b›. This regex matches <u>Jane</u> in `Her name is Janet`.

If you want something in your regex to be excluded from the alternation, you have to *group* the alternatives. Grouping is done with parentheses. They have the highest precedence of all regex operators, just as in most programming languages. ‹\b(Mary|Jane|Sue)\b› has three alternatives—‹Mary›, ‹Jane›, and ‹Sue›—between two word boundaries. This regex does not match anything in `Her name is Janet`.

When the regex engine reaches the `J` in `Janet` in the subject text, the first word boundary matches. The engine then enters the group. The first alternative in the group, ‹Mary›, fails. The second alternative, ‹Jane›, succeeds. The engine exits the group. All that is left is ‹\b›. The word boundary fails to match between the `e` and `t` at the end of the subject. The overall match attempt starting at `J` fails.

A pair of parentheses isn't just a group; it's a *capturing group*. For the Mary-Jane-Sue regex, the capture isn't very useful, because it's simply the overall regex match. Captures become useful when they cover only part of the regular expression, as in ‹\b(\d\d\d\d)-(\d\d)-(\d\d)\b›.

This regular expression matches a date in yyyy-mm-dd format. The regex ‹\b\d\d\d\d-\d\d-\d\d\b› does exactly the same. Because this regular expression does not use any alternation or repetition, the grouping function of the parentheses is not needed. But the capture function is very handy.

The regex ‹\b(\d\d\d\d)-(\d\d)-(\d\d)\b› has three capturing groups. Groups are numbered by counting opening parentheses from left to right. ‹(\d\d\d\d)› is group number 1. ‹(\d\d)› is number 2. The second ‹(\d\d)› is group number 3.

During the matching process, when the regular expression engine exits the group upon reaching the closing parenthesis, it stores the part of the text matched by the capturing group. When our regex matches <u>2008-05-24</u>, <u>2008</u> is stored in the first capture, <u>05</u> in the second capture, and <u>24</u> in the third capture.

There are three ways you can use the captured text. Recipe 2.10 in this chapter explains how you can match the captured text again within the same regex match. Recipe 2.21 shows how to insert the captured text into the replacement text when doing a search-and-replace. Recipe 3.9 in the next chapter describes how your application can use the parts of the regex match.

Variations

Noncapturing groups

In the regex ‹\b(Mary|Jane|Sue)\b›, we need the parentheses for grouping only. Instead of using a capturing group, we could use a noncapturing group:

> \b(?:Mary|Jane|Sue)\b
> **Regex options:** None
> **Regex flavors:** .NET, Java, JavaScript, PCRE, Perl, Python, Ruby

The three characters ‹(?:› open the noncapturing group. The parenthesis ‹)› closes it. The noncapturing group provides the same grouping functionality, but does not capture anything.

When counting opening parentheses of capturing groups to determine their numbers, do not count the parenthesis of the noncapturing group. This is the main benefit of noncapturing groups: you can add them to an existing regex without upsetting the references to numbered capturing groups.

Another benefit of noncapturing groups is performance. If you're not going to use a backreference to a particular group (Recipe 2.10), reinsert it into the replacement text (Recipe 2.21), or retrieve its match in source code (Recipe 3.9), a capturing group adds unnecessary overhead that you can eliminate by using a noncapturing group. In practice, you'll hardly notice the performance difference, unless you're using the regex in a tight loop and/or on lots of data.

Group with mode modifiers

In the "Case-insensitive matching" variation of Recipe 2.1, we explain that .NET, Java, PCRE, Perl, and Ruby support local mode modifiers, using the mode toggles: ‹sensitive(?i)caseless(?-i)sensitive›. Although this syntax also involves parentheses, a toggle such as ‹(?i)› does not involve any grouping.

Instead of using toggles, you can specify mode modifiers in a noncapturing group:

> \b(?i:Mary|Jane|Sue)\b
> **Regex options:** None
> **Regex flavors:** .NET, Java, PCRE, Perl, Ruby

> sensitive(?i:caseless)sensitive
> **Regex options:** None
> **Regex flavors:** .NET, Java, PCRE, Perl, Ruby

Adding mode modifiers to a noncapturing group sets that mode for the part of the regular expression inside the group. The previous settings are restored at the closing parenthesis. Since case sensitivity is the default, only the part of the regex inside:

> (?i:⋯)

is case insensitive.

You can combine multiple modifiers. ⟨(?ism:group)⟩. Use a hyphen to turn off modifiers: ⟨(?-ism:group)⟩ turns off the three options. ⟨(?i-sm)⟩ turns on case insensitivity (i), and turns off both "dot matches line breaks" (s) and "caret and dollar match at line breaks" (m). These options are explained in Recipes 2.4 and 2.5.

See Also

Recipes 2.10, 2.11, 2.21, and 3.9

2.10 Match Previously Matched Text Again

Problem

Create a regular expression that matches "magical" dates in yyyy-mm-dd format. A date is magical if the year minus the century, the month, and the day of the month are all the same numbers. For example, 2008-08-08 is a magical date. You can assume all dates in the subject text to be valid. The regular expression does not have to exclude things like 9999-99-99, as these won't occur in the subject text. You only need to find the magical dates.

Solution

```
\b\d\d(\d\d)-\1-\1\b
```
Regex options: None
Regex flavors: .NET, Java, JavaScript, PCRE, Perl, Python, Ruby

Discussion

To match previously matched text later in a regex, we first have to capture the previous text. We do that with a capturing group, as shown in Recipe 2.9. After that, we can match the same text anywhere in the regex using a *backreference*. You can reference the first nine capturing groups with a backslash followed by a single digit one through nine. For groups 10 through 99, use ⟨\10⟩ to ⟨\99⟩.

 Do not use ⟨\01⟩. That is either an octal escape or an error. We don't use octal escapes in this book at all, because the ⟨\xFF⟩ hexadecimal escapes are much easier to understand.

When the regular expression ⟨\b\d\d(\d\d)-\1-\1\b⟩ encounters 2008-08-08, the first ⟨\d\d⟩ matches **20**. The regex engine then enters the capturing group, noting the position reached in the subject text.

The ⟨\d\d⟩ inside the capturing group matches **08**, and the engine reaches the group's closing parenthesis. At this point, the partial match **08** is stored in capturing group 1.

The next token is the hyphen, which matches literally. Then comes the backreference. The regex engine checks the contents of the first capturing group: <u>08</u>. The engine tries to match this text literally. If the regular expression is case-insensitive, the captured text is matched in this way. Here, the backreference succeeds. The next hyphen and backreference also succeed. Finally, the word boundary matches at the end of the subject text, and an overall match is found: <u>2008-08-08</u>. The capturing group still holds <u>08</u>.

If a capturing group is repeated, either by a quantifier (Recipe 2.12) or by backtracking (Recipe 2.13), the stored match is overwritten each time the capturing group matches something. A backreference to the group matches only the text that was last captured by the group.

If the same regex encounters 2008-05-24 2007-07-07, the first time the group captures something is when ‹\b\d\d(\d\d)› matches <u>2008</u>, storing <u>08</u> for the first (and only) capturing group. Next, the hyphen matches itself. The backreference, which tries to match ‹08›, fails against 05.

Since there are no other alternatives in the regular expression, the engine gives up the match attempt. This involves clearing all the capturing groups. When the engine tries again, starting at the first 0 in the subject, ‹\1› holds no text at all.

Still processing 2008-05-24 2007-07-07, the next time the group captures something is when ‹\b\d\d(\d\d)› matches <u>2007</u>, storing <u>07</u>. Next, the hyphen matches itself. Now the backreference tries to match ‹07›. This succeeds, as do the next hyphen, backreference, and word boundary. <u>2007-07-07</u> has been found.

Because the regex engine proceeds from start to end, you should put the capturing parentheses before the backreference. The regular expressions ‹\b\d\d\1-(\d\d)-\1› and ‹\b\d\d\1-\1-(\d\d)\b› could never match anything. Since the backreference is encountered before the capturing group, it has not captured anything yet. Unless you're using JavaScript, a backreference always fails if it points to a group that hasn't already participated in the match attempt.

A group that hasn't participated is not the same as a group that has captured a zero-length match. A backreference to a group with a zero-length capture always succeeds. When ‹(^)\1› matches at the start of the string, the first capturing group captures the caret's zero-length match, causing ‹1› to succeed. In practice, this can happen when the contents of the capturing group are all optional.

> JavaScript is the only flavor we know that goes against decades of back-reference tradition in regular expressions. In JavaScript, or at least in implementations that follow the JavaScript standard, a backreference to a group that hasn't participated always succeeds, just like a backreference to a group that captured a zero-length match. So, in JavaScript, ‹\b\d\d\1-\1-(\d\d)\b› can match <u>12--34</u>.

See Also

Recipes 2.9, 2.11, 2.21, and 3.9

2.11 Capture and Name Parts of the Match

Problem

Create a regular expression that matches any date in yyyy-mm-dd format and separately captures the year, month, and day. The goal is to make it easy to work with these separate values in the code that processes the match. Contribute to this goal by assigning the descriptive names "year", "month", and "day" to the captured text.

Create another regular expression that matches "magical" dates in yyyy-mm-dd format. A date is magical if the year minus the century, the month, and the day of the month are all the same numbers. For example, 2008-08-08 is a magical date. Capture the magical number (08 in the example), and label it "magic."

You can assume all dates in the subject text to be valid. The regular expressions don't have to exclude things like 9999-99-99, because these won't occur in the subject text.

Solution

Named capture

```
\b(?<year>\d\d\d\d)-(?<month>\d\d)-(?<day>\d\d)\b
```
Regex options: None
Regex flavors: .NET, PCRE 7, Perl 5.10, Ruby 1.9

```
\b(?'year'\d\d\d\d)-(?'month'\d\d)-(?'day'\d\d)\b
```
Regex options: None
Regex flavors: .NET, PCRE 7, Perl 5.10, Ruby 1.9

```
\b(?P<year>\d\d\d\d)-(?P<month>\d\d)-(?P<day>\d\d)\b
```
Regex options: None
Regex flavors: PCRE 4 and later, Perl 5.10, Python

Named backreferences

```
\b\d\d(?<magic>\d\d)-\k<magic>-\k<magic>\b
```
Regex options: None
Regex flavors: .NET, PCRE 7, Perl 5.10, Ruby 1.9

```
\b\d\d(?'magic'\d\d)-\k'magic'-\k'magic'\b
```
Regex options: None
Regex flavors: .NET, PCRE 7, Perl 5.10, Ruby 1.9

```
\b\d\d(?P<magic>\d\d)-(?P=magic)-(?P=magic)\b
```
Regex options: None
Regex flavors: PCRE 4 and later, Perl 5.10, Python

Discussion

Named capture

Recipes 2.9 and 2.10 illustrate *capturing groups* and *backreferences*. To be more precise: these recipes use *numbered* capturing groups and numbered backreferences. Each group automatically gets a number, which you use for the backreference.

Modern regex flavors support *named* capturing groups in addition to numbered groups. The only difference between named and numbered groups is your ability to assign a descriptive name, instead of being stuck with automatic numbers. Named groups make your regular expression more readable and easier to maintain. Inserting a capturing group into an existing regex can change the numbers assigned to all the capturing groups. Names that you assign remain the same.

Python was the first regular expression flavor to support named capture. It uses the syntax ‹(?P<name>regex)›. The name must consist of word characters matched by ‹\w›. ‹(?P<name>)› is the group's opening bracket, and ‹)› is the closing bracket.

The designers of the .NET Regex class came up with their own syntax for named capture, using two interchangeable variants. ‹(?<name>regex)› mimics Python's syntax, minus the P. The name must consist of word characters matched by ‹\w›. ‹(?<name>)› is the group's opening bracket, and ‹)› is the closing bracket.

The angle brackets in the named capture syntax are annoying when you're coding in XML, or writing this book in DocBook XML. That's the reason for .NET's alternate named capture syntax: ‹(?'name'regex)›. The angle brackets are replaced with single quotes. Choose whichever syntax is easier for you to type. Their functionality is identical.

Perhaps due to .NET's popularity over Python, the .NET syntax seems to be the one that other regex library developers prefer to copy. Perl 5.10 has it, and so does the Oniguruma engine in Ruby 1.9.

PCRE copied Python's syntax long ago, at a time when Perl did not support named capture at all. PCRE 7, the version that adds the new features in Perl 5.10, supports both the .NET syntax and the Python syntax. Perhaps as a testament to the success of PCRE, in a reverse compatibility move, Perl 5.10 also supports the Python syntax. In PCRE and Perl 5.10, the functionality of the .NET syntax and the Python syntax for named capture is identical.

Choose the syntax that is most useful to you. If you're coding in PHP and you want your code to work with older versions of PHP that incorporate older versions of PCRE, use the Python syntax. If you don't need compatibility with older versions and you also work with .NET or Ruby, the .NET syntax makes it easier to copy and paste between all these languages. If you're unsure, use the Python syntax for PHP/PCRE. People recompiling your code with an older version of PCRE are going to be unhappy if the regexes in your code suddenly stop working. When copying a regex to .NET or Ruby, deleting a few Ps is easy enough.

Documentation for PCRE 7 and Perl 5.10 barely mention the Python syntax, but it is by no means deprecated. For PCRE and PHP, we actually recommend it.

Named backreferences

With named capture comes named backreferences. Just as named capturing groups are functionally identical to numbered capturing groups, named backreferences are functionally identical to numbered backreferences. They're just easier to read and maintain.

Python uses the syntax ‹(?P=name)› to create a backreference to the group name. Although this syntax uses parentheses, the backreference is not a group. You cannot put anything between the name and the closing parenthesis. A backreference ‹(?P=name)› is a singular regex token, just like ‹\1›.

.NET uses the syntax ‹\k<name>› and ‹\k'name'›. The two variants are identical in functionality, and you can freely mix them. A named group created with the bracket syntax can be referenced with the quote syntax, and vice versa.

We strongly recommend you don't mix named and numbered groups in the same regex. Different flavors follow different rules for numbering unnamed groups that appear between named groups. Perl 5.10 and Ruby 1.9 copied .NET's syntax, but they do not follow .NET's way of numbering named capturing groups or of mixing numbered capturing groups with named groups. Instead of trying to explain the differences, I simply recommend not mixing named and numbered groups. Avoid the confusion and either give all unnamed groups a name or make them noncapturing.

See Also

Recipes 2.9, 2.10, 2.21, and 3.9

2.12 Repeat Part of the Regex a Certain Number of Times

Problem

Create regular expressions that match the following kinds of numbers:

- A googol (a decimal number with 100 digits).
- A 32-bit hexadecimal number.
- A 32-bit hexadecimal number with an optional h suffix.

- A floating-point number with an optional integer part, a mandatory fractional part, and an optional exponent. Each part allows any number of digits.

Solution

Googol

`\b\d{100}\b`
> **Regex options:** None
> **Regex flavors:** .NET, Java, JavaScript, PCRE, Perl, Python, Ruby

Hexadecimal number

`\b[a-z0-9]{1,8}\b`
> **Regex options:** Case insensitive
> **Regex flavors:** .NET, Java, JavaScript, PCRE, Perl, Python, Ruby

Hexadecimal number

`\b[a-z0-9]{1,8}h?\b`
> **Regex options:** Case insensitive
> **Regex flavors:** .NET, Java, JavaScript, PCRE, Perl, Python, Ruby

Floating-point number

`\b\d*\.\d+(e\d+)?`
> **Regex options:** Case insensitive
> **Regex flavors:** .NET, Java, JavaScript, PCRE, Perl, Python, Ruby

Discussion

Fixed repetition

The *quantifier* ‹{n}›, where *n* is a positive number, repeats the preceding regex token *n* number of times. The ‹\d{100}› in ‹\b\d{100}\b› matches a string of 100 digits. You could achieve the same by typing ‹\d› 100 times.

‹{1}› repeats the preceding token once, as it would without any quantifier. ‹ab{1}c› is the same regex as ‹abc›.

‹{0}› repeats the preceding token zero times, essentially deleting it from the regular expression. ‹ab{0}c› is the same regex as ‹ac›.

Variable repetition

For *variable repetition*, we use the quantifier ‹{n,m}›, where *n* is a positive number and *m* is greater than *n*. ‹\b[a-f0-9]{1,8}\b› matches a hexadecimal number with one to eight digits. With variable repetition, the order in which the alternatives are attempted comes into play. Recipe 2.13 explains that in detail.

If *n* and *m* are equal, we have fixed repetition. ‹\b\d{100,100}\b› is the same regex as ‹\b\d{100}\b›.

Infinite repetition

The quantifier ‹{n,}›, where *n* is a positive number, allows for *infinite repetition*. Essentially, infinite repetition is variable repetition without an upper limit.

‹\d{1,}› matches one or more digits, and ‹\d+› does the same. A plus after a regex token that's not a quantifier means "one or more." Recipe 2.13 shows the meaning of a plus after a quantifier.

‹\d{0,}› matches zero or more digits, and ‹\d*› does the same. The asterisk always means "zero or more." In addition to allowing infinite repetition, ‹{0,}› and the asterisk also make the preceding token optional.

Making something optional

If we use variable repetition with *n* set to zero, we're effectively making the token that precedes the quantifier optional. ‹h{0,1}› matches the ‹h› once or not at all. If there is no h, ‹h{0,1}› results in a zero-length match. If you use ‹h{0,1}› as a regular expression all by itself, it will find a zero-length match before each character in the subject text that is not an h. Each h will result in a match of one character (the h).

‹h?› does the same as ‹h{0,1}›. A question mark after a valid and complete regex token that is not a quantifier means "zero or once." The next recipe shows the meaning of a question mark after a quantifier.

 A question mark, or any other quantifier, after an opening parenthesis is a syntax error. Perl and the flavors that copy it use this to add "Perl extensions" to the regex syntax. Preceding recipes show noncapturing groups and named capturing groups, which all use a question mark after an opening parenthesis as part of their syntax. These question marks are not quantifiers at all; they're simply part of the syntax for noncapturing groups and named capturing groups. Following recipes will show more styles of groups using the ‹(?› syntax.

Repeating groups

If you place a quantifier after the closing parenthesis of a group, the whole group is repeated. ‹(?:abc){3}› is the same as ‹abcabcabc›.

Quantifiers can be nested. ‹(e\d+)?› matches an <u>e</u> followed by one or more digits, or a zero-length match. In our floating-point regular expression, this is the optional exponent.

Capturing groups can be repeated. As explained in Recipe 2.9, the group's match is captured each time the engine exits the group, overwriting any text previously matched by the group. ‹(\d\d){3}› matches a string of two, four, or six digits. The engine exits the group three times. When this regex matches <u>123456</u>, the capturing group will hold <u>56</u>, because <u>56</u> was stored by the last iteration of the group. The other two matches by the group, <u>12</u> and <u>34</u>, cannot be retrieved.

‹(\d\d){3}› captures the same text as ‹\d\d\d\d(\d\d)›. If you want the capturing group to capture all two, four, or six digits rather than just the last two, you have to place the capturing group around the quantifier instead of repeating the capturing group: ‹((?: \d\d){3})›. Here we used a noncapturing group to take over the grouping function from the capturing group. We also could have used two capturing groups: ‹((\d\d) {3})›. When this last regex matches <u>123456</u>, ‹\1› holds <u>123456</u> and ‹\2› holds <u>56</u>.

.NET's regular expression engine is the only one that allows you to retrieve all the iterations of a repeated capturing group. If you directly query the group's `Value` property, which returns a string, you'll get <u>56</u>, as with every other regular expression engine. Backreferences in the regular expression and replacement text also substitute <u>56</u>, but if you use the group's `CaptureCollection`, you'll get a stack with <u>56</u>, <u>34</u>, and <u>12</u>.

See Also

Recipes 2.9, 2.13, 2.14

2.13 Choose Minimal or Maximal Repetition

Problem

Match a pair of ‹p› and ‹/p› XHTML tags and the text between them. The text between the tags can include other XHTML tags.

Solution

```
<p>.*?</p>
```
Regex options: Dot matches line breaks
Regex flavors: .NET, Java, JavaScript, PCRE, Perl, Python, Ruby

Discussion

All the quantifiers discussed in Recipe 2.12 are *greedy*, meaning they try to repeat as many times as possible, giving back only when required to allow the remainder of the regular expression to match.

This can make it hard to pair tags in XHTML (which is a version of XML and therefore requires every opening tag to be matched by a closing tag). Consider the following simple excerpt of XHTML:

```
<p>
The very <em>first</em> task is to find the beginning of a paragraph.
</p>
<p>
Then you have to find the end of the paragraph
</p>
```

There are two opening `<p>` tags and two closing `</p>` tags in the excerpt. You want to match the first `<p>` with the first `</p>`, because they mark a single paragraph. Note that this paragraph contains a nested `<em>` tag, so the regex can't simply stop when it encounters a `<` character.

Take a look at one incorrect solution for the problem in this recipe:

`<p>.*</p>`
   Regex options: Dot matches line breaks
   Regex flavors: .NET, Java, JavaScript, PCRE, Perl, Python, Ruby

The only difference is that this incorrect solution lacks the extra question mark after the asterisk. The incorrect solution uses the same greedy asterisk explained in Recipe 2.12.

After matching the first ‹p› tag in the subject, the engine reaches ‹.*›. The dot matches any character, including line breaks. The asterisk repeats it zero or more times. The asterisk is greedy, and so ‹.*› matches everything all the way to the end of the subject text. Let me say that again: ‹.*› eats up your whole XHTML file, starting with the first paragraph.

When the ‹.*› has its belly full, the engine attempts to match the ‹<› at the end of the subject text. That fails. But it's not the end of the story: the regex engine *backtracks*.

The asterisk prefers to grab as much text as possible, but it's also perfectly satisfied to match nothing at all (zero repetitions). With each repetition of a quantifier beyond the quantifier's minimum, the regular expression stores a backtracking position. Those are positions the engine can go back to, in case the part of the regex following the quantifier fails.

When ‹<› fails, the engine backtracks by making the ‹.*› give up one character of its match. Then ‹<› is attempted again, at the last character in the file. If it fails again, the engine backtracks once more, attempting ‹<› at the second-to-last character in the file. This process continues until ‹<› succeeds. If ‹<› never succeeds, the ‹.*› eventually runs out of backtracking positions and the overall match attempt fails.

If ‹<› does match at some point during all that backtracking, ‹/› is attempted. If ‹/› fails, the engine backtracks again. This repeats until ‹</p>› can be matched entirely.

So what's the problem? Because the asterisk is greedy, the incorrect regular expression matches everything from the first `<p>` in the XHTML file to the last `</p>`. But to correctly match an XHTML paragraph, we need to match the first `<p>` with the first `</p>` that follows it.

That's where *lazy* quantifiers come in. You can make any quantifier lazy by placing a question mark after it: ⟨*?⟩, ⟨+?⟩, ⟨??⟩, and ⟨{7,42}?⟩ are all lazy quantifiers.

Lazy quantifiers backtrack too, but the other way around. A lazy quantifier repeats as few times as it has to, stores one backtracking position, and allows the regex to continue. If the remainder of the regex fails and the engine backtracks, the lazy quantifier repeats once more. If the regex keeps backtracking, the quantifier will expand until its maximum number of repetitions, or until the regex token it repeats fails to match.

⟨<p>.*?</p>⟩ uses a lazy quantifier to correctly match an XHTML paragraph. When ⟨<p>⟩ matches, the ⟨.*?⟩, lazy as it is, initially does nothing but procrastinate. If ⟨</p>⟩ immediately occurs after <u>p></u>, an empty paragraph is matched. If not, the engine backtracks to ⟨.*?⟩, which matches one character. If ⟨</p>⟩ still fails, ⟨.*?⟩ matches the next character. This continues until either ⟨</p>⟩ succeeds or ⟨.*?⟩ fails to expand. Since the dot matches everything, failure won't occur until the ⟨.*?⟩ has matched everything up to the end of the XHTML file.

The quantifiers ⟨*⟩ and ⟨*?⟩ allow all the same regular expression matches. The only difference is the order in which the possible matches are tried. The greedy quantifier will find the longest possible match. The lazy quantifier will find the shortest possible match.

If possible, the best solution is to make sure there is only one possible match. The regular expressions for matching numbers in Recipe 2.12 will still match the same numbers if you make all their quantifiers lazy. The reason is that the parts of those regular expressions that have quantifiers and the parts that follow them are mutually exclusive. ⟨\d⟩ matches a digit, and ⟨\b⟩ matches after ⟨\d⟩ only if the next character is not a digit (or letter).

It may help to understand the operation of greedy and lazy repetition by comparing how ⟨\d+\b⟩ and ⟨\d+?\b⟩ act on a couple of different subject texts. The greedy and lazy versions produce the same results, but test the subject text in a different order.

If we use ⟨\d+\b⟩ on 1234, ⟨\d+⟩ will match all the digits. ⟨\b⟩ then matches, and an overall match is found. If we use ⟨\d+?\b⟩, ⟨\d+?⟩ first matches only <u>1</u>. ⟨\b⟩ fails between 1 and 2. ⟨\d+?⟩ expands to <u>12</u>, and ⟨\b⟩ still fails. This continues until ⟨\d+?⟩ matches <u>1234</u>, and ⟨\b⟩ succeeds.

If our subject text is 1234X, the first regex, ⟨\d+\b⟩, still has ⟨\d+⟩ match <u>1234</u>. But then ⟨\b⟩ fails. ⟨\d+⟩ backtracks to <u>123</u>. ⟨\b⟩ still fails. This continues until ⟨\d+⟩ has backtracked to its minimum <u>1</u>, and ⟨\b⟩ still fails. Then the whole match attempt fails.

If we use ⟨\d+?\b⟩ on 1234X, ⟨\d+?⟩ first matches only <u>1</u>. ⟨\b⟩ fails between 1 and 2. ⟨\d+?⟩ expands to <u>12</u>. ⟨\b⟩ still fails. This continues until ⟨\d+?⟩ matches <u>1234</u>, and ⟨\b⟩ still fails. The regex engine attempts to expand ⟨\d+?⟩ once more, but ⟨\d⟩ does not match X. The overall match attempt fails.

If we put ⟨\d+⟩ between word boundaries, it must match all the digits in the subject text, or it fails. Making the quantifier lazy won't affect the final regex match or its eventual failure. In fact, ‹\b\d+\b› would be better off without any backtracking at all. The next recipe explains how you can use a possessive quantifier ‹\b\d++\b› to achieve that, at least with some flavors.

See Also

Recipes 2.8, 2.9, 2.12, 2.14, and 2.15

2.14 Eliminate Needless Backtracking

Problem

The previous recipe explains the difference between greedy and lazy quantifiers, and how they backtrack. In some situations, this backtracking is unnecessary.

‹\b\d+\b› uses a greedy quantifier, and ‹\b\d+?\b› uses a lazy quantifier. They both match the same thing: an integer. Given the same subject text, both will find the exact same matches. Any backtracking that is done is unnecessary. Rewrite this regular expression to explicitly eliminate all backtracking, making the regular expression more efficient.

Solution

> \b\d++\b
> **Regex options:** None
> **Regex flavors:** Java, PCRE, Perl 5.10, Ruby 1.9

The easiest solution is to use a possessive quantifier. But it is supported only in a few recent regex flavors.

> \b(?>\d+)\b
> **Regex options:** None
> **Regex flavors:** .NET, Java, PCRE, Perl, Ruby

An atomic group provides exactly the same functionality, using a slightly less readable syntax. Support for atomic grouping is more widespread than support for possessive quantifiers.

JavaScript and Python do not support possessive quantifiers or atomic grouping. There is no way to eliminate needless backtracking with these two regex flavors.

Discussion

A *possessive quantifier* is similar to a greedy quantifier: it tries to repeat as many times as possible. The difference is that a possessive quantifier will never give back, not even when giving back is the only way that the remainder of the regular expression could match. Possessive quantifiers do not keep backtracking positions.

You can make any quantifier possessive by placing a plus sign after it. For example, ⟨*+⟩, ⟨++⟩, ⟨?+⟩, and ⟨{7,42}+⟩ are all possessive quantifiers.

Possessive quantifiers are supported by Java 4 and later, the first Java release to include the `java.util.regex` package. All versions of PCRE discussed in this book (version 4 to 7) support possessive quantifiers. Perl supports them starting with Perl 5.10. Classic Ruby regular expressions do not support possessive quantifiers, but the Oniguruma engine, which is the default in Ruby 1.9, does support them.

Wrapping a greedy quantifier inside an *atomic group* has the exact same effect as using a possessive quantifier. When the regex engine exits the atomic group, all backtracking positions remembered by quantifiers and alternation inside the group are thrown away. The syntax is ⟨(?>*regex*)⟩, where ⟨*regex*⟩ is any regular expression. An atomic group is essentially a noncapturing group, with the extra job of refusing to backtrack. The question mark is not a quantifier; the opening bracket simply consists of the three characters ⟨(?>⟩.

When you apply the regex ⟨\b\d++\b⟩ (possessive) to 123abc 456, ⟨\b⟩ matches at the start of the subject, and ⟨\d++⟩ matches 123. So far, this is no different from what ⟨\b\d+\b⟩ (greedy) would do. But then the second ⟨\b⟩ fails to match between 3 and a.

The possessive quantifier did not store any backtracking positions. Since there are no other quantifiers or alternation in this regular expression, there are no further options to try when the second word boundary fails. The regex engine immediately declares failure for the match attempt starting at 1.

The regex engine does attempt the regex starting at the next character positions in the string, and using a possessive quantifier does not change that. If the regex must match the whole subject, use anchors, as discussed in Recipe 2.5. Eventually, the regex engine will attempt the regex starting at the 4 and find the match 456.

The difference with the greedy quantifier is that when the second ⟨\b⟩ fails during the first match attempt, the greedy quantifier will backtrack. The regex engine will then (needlessly) test ⟨\b⟩ between 2 and 3, and between 1 and 2.

The matching process using atomic grouping is essentially the same. When you apply the regex ⟨\b(?>\d+)\b⟩ (possessive) to 123abc 456, the word boundary matches at the start of the subject. The regex engine enters the atomic group, and ⟨\d+⟩ matches 123. Now the engine exits the atomic group. At this point, the backtracking positions remembered by ⟨\d+⟩ are thrown away. When the second ⟨\b⟩ fails, the regex engine is left without any further options, causing the match attempt to fail immediately. As with the possessive quantifier, eventually 456 will be found.

We describe the possessive quantifier as failing to remember backtracking positions, and the atomic group as throwing them away. This makes it easier to understand the matching process, but don't get hung up on the difference, as it may not even exist in the regex flavor you're working with. In many flavors, ⟨x++⟩ is merely syntactic sugar for ⟨(?>x+)⟩, and both are implemented in exactly the same way. Whether the engine never remembers backtracking positions or throws them away later is irrelevant for the final outcome of the match attempt.

Where possessive quantifiers and atomic grouping differ is that a possessive quantifier applies only to a single regular expression token, whereas an atomic group can wrap a whole regular expression.

‹\w++\d++› and ‹(?>\w+\d+)› are not the same at all. ‹\w++\d++›, which is the same as ‹(?>\w+)(?>\d+)›, will not match abc123. ‹\w++› matches <u>abc123</u> entirely. Then, the regex engine attempts ‹\d++› at the end of the subject text. Since there are no further characters that can be matched, ‹\d++› fails. Without any remembered backtracking positions, the match attempt fails.

‹(?>\w+\d+)› has two greedy quantifiers inside the same atomic group. Within the atomic group, backtracking occurs normally. Backtracking positions are thrown away only when the engine exits the whole group. When the subject is abc123, ‹\w+› matches <u>abc123</u>. The greedy quantifier does remember backtracking positions. When ‹\d+› fails to match, ‹\w+› gives up one character. ‹\d+› then matches <u>3</u>. Now, the engine exits the atomic group, throwing away all backtracking positions remembered for ‹\w+› and ‹\d+›. Since the end of the regex has been reached, this doesn't really make any difference. An overall match is found.

If the end had not been reached, as in ‹(?>\w+\d+)\d+›, we would be in the same situation as with ‹\w++\d++›. The second ‹\d+› has nothing left to match at the end of the subject. Since the backtracking positions were thrown away, the regex engine can only declare failure.

Possessive quantifiers and atomic grouping don't just optimize regular expressions. They can alter the matches found by a regular expression by eliminating those that would be reached through backtracking.

This recipe shows how to use possessive quantifiers and atomic grouping to make minor optimizations, which may not even show any difference in benchmarks. The next recipe will showcase how atomic grouping can make a dramatic difference.

See Also

Recipes 2.12 and 2.15

2.15 Prevent Runaway Repetition

Problem

Use a single regular expression to match a complete HTML file, checking for properly nested html, head, title, and body tags. The regular expression must fail efficiently on HTML files that do not have the proper tags.

Solution

```
<html>(?>.*?<head>)(?>.*?<title>)(?>.*?</title>)↵
(?>.*?</head>)(?>.*?<body[^>]*>)(?>.*?</body>).*?</html>
```
Regex options: Case insensitive, dot matches line breaks
Regex flavors: .NET, Java, PCRE, Perl, Ruby

JavaScript and Python do not support atomic grouping. There is no way to eliminate needless backtracking with these two regex flavors. When programming in JavaScript or Python, you can solve this problem by doing a literal text search for each of the tags one by one, searching for the next tag through the remainder of the subject text after the one last found.

Discussion

The proper solution to this problem is more easily understood if we start from this naïve solution:

```
<html>.*?<head>.*?<title>.*?</title>↵
.*?</head>.*?<body[^>]*>.*?</body>.*?</html>
```
Regex options: Case insensitive, dot matches line breaks
Regex flavors: .NET, Java, JavaScript, PCRE, Perl, Python, Ruby

When you test this regex on a proper HTML file, it works perfectly well. ‹.*?› skips over anything, because we turn on "dot matches line breaks." The lazy asterisk makes sure the regex goes ahead only one character at a time, each time checking whether the next tag can be matched. Recipes 2.4 and 2.13 explain all this.

But this regex gets you into trouble when it needs to deal with a subject text that does not have all the HTML tags. The worst case occurs when </html> is missing.

Imagine the regex engine has matched all the preceding tags and is now busy expanding the last ‹.*?›. Since ‹</html>› can never match, the ‹.*?› expands all the way to the end of the file. When it can no longer expand, it fails.

But that is not the end of the story. The other six ‹.*?› have all remembered a backtracking position that allows them to expand further. When the last ‹.*?› fails, the one before expands, gradually matching </body>. That same text was previously matched by the literal ‹</body>› in the regex. This ‹.*?› too will expand all the way to the end of the file, as will all preceding lazy dots. Only when the first one reaches the end of the file will the regex engine declare failure.

This regular expression has a worst-case complexity of $O(n^7)$, the length of the subject text to the seventh power. There are seven lazy dots that can potentially expand all the way to the end of the file. If the file is twice the size, the regex can need up to 128 times as many steps to figure out it doesn't match.

We call this *catastrophic backtracking*. So much backtracking occurs that the regex either takes forever or crashes your application. Some regex implementations are clever and will abort runaway match attempts early, but even then the regex will still kill your application's performance.

 Catastrophic backtracking is an instance of a phenomenon known as a *combinatorial explosion,* in which several orthogonal conditions intersect and all combinations have to be tried. You could also say that the regex is a *Cartesian product* of the various repetition operators.

The solution is to use atomic grouping to prevent needless backtracking. There is no need for the sixth ‹.*?› to expand after ‹</body>› has matched. If ‹</html>› fails, expanding the sixth lazy dot will not magically produce a closing html tag.

To make a quantified regular expression token stop when the following delimiter matches, place both the quantified part of the regex and the delimiter together in an atomic group: ‹(?>.*?</body>)›. Now the regex engine throws away all the matching positions for ‹.*?</body>› when ‹</body>› is found. If ‹</html>› later fails, the regex engine has forgotten about ‹.*?</body>›, and no further expansion will occur.

If we do the same for all the other ‹.*?› in the regex, none of them will expand further. Although there are still seven lazy dots in the regex, they will never overlap. This reduces the complexity of the regular expression to O(*n*), which is linear with respect to the length of the subject text. A regular expression can never be more efficient than this.

Variations

If you really want to see catastrophic backtracking at work, try ‹(x+x+)+y› on xxxxxxxxxx. If it fails quickly, add one x to the subject. Repeat this until the regex starts to take very long to match or your application crashes. It won't take many more x characters, unless you're using Perl.

Of the regex flavors discussed in this book, only Perl is able to detect that the regular expression is too complex and then abort the match attempt without crashing.

The complexity of this regex is $O(2^n)$. When ‹y› fails to match, the regex engine will try all possible permutations of repeating each ‹x+› and the group containing them. For instance, one such permutation, far down the match attempt, is ‹x+› matching xxx, the second ‹x+› matching x, and then the group being repeated three more times with each ‹x+› matching x. With 10 x characters, there are 1,024 such permutations. If we increase the number to 32, we're at over 4 billion permutations, which will surely cause any regex engine to run out of memory, unless it has a safety switch that allows it to give up and say that your regular expression is too complicated.

In this case, this nonsensical regular expression is easily rewritten as ‹xx+y›, which finds exactly the same matches in linear time. In practice, the solution may not be so obvious with more complicated regexes.

Essentially, you have to watch out when two or more parts of the regular expression can match the same text. In these cases, you may need atomic grouping to make sure the regex engine doesn't try all possible ways of dividing the subject text between those two parts of the regex. Always test your regex on (long) test subjects that contain text that can be partially but not entirely matched by the regex.

See Also

Recipes 2.13 and 2.14

2.16 Test for a Match Without Adding It to the Overall Match

Problem

Find any word that occurs between a pair of HTML bold tags, without including the tags in the regex match. For instance, if the subject is My cat is furry, the only valid match should be <u>cat</u>.

Solution

```
(?<=<b>)\w+(?=</b>)
```
Regex options: Case insensitive
Regex flavors: .NET, Java, PCRE, Perl, Python, Ruby 1.9

JavaScript and Ruby 1.8 support the lookahead ‹(?=</b>)›, but not the lookbehind ‹(?<=<b>)›.

Discussion

Lookaround

The four kinds of *lookaround* groups supported by modern regex flavors have the special property of giving up the text matched by the part of the regex inside the lookaround. Essentially, lookaround checks whether certain text can be matched without actually matching it.

Lookaround that looks backward is called *lookbehind*. This is the only regular expression construct that will traverse the text from right to left instead of from left to right. The syntax for *positive lookbehind* is ‹(?<=*text*)›. The four characters ‹(?<=› form the opening bracket. What you can put inside the lookbehind, here represented by ‹*text*›, varies among regular expression flavors. But simple literal text, such as ‹(?<=<b>)›, always works.

Lookbehind checks to see whether the text inside the lookbehind occurs immediately to the left of the position that the regular expression engine has reached. If you match ‹(?<=<b>)› against My <b>cat</b> is furry, the lookbehind will fail to match until the regular expression starts the match attempt at the letter c in the subject. The regex engine then enters the lookbehind group, telling it to look to the left. ‹b› matches to the left of c. The engine exits the lookbehind at this point, and discards any text matched by the lookbehind from the match attempt. In other words, the match-in-progress is back at where it was when the engine entered the lookbehind. In this case, the match-in-progress is the zero-length match before the c in the subject string. The lookbehind only tests or asserts that ‹b› can be matched; it does not actually match it. Lookaround constructs are therefore called *zero-length assertions*.

After the lookbehind has matched, the shorthand character class ‹\w+› attempts to match one or more word characters. It matches <u>cat</u>. The ‹\w+› is not inside any kind of lookaround or group, and so it matches the text <u>cat</u> normally. We say that ‹\w+› matches and *consumes* <u>cat</u>, whereas lookaround can match something but can never consume anything.

Lookaround that looks forward, in the same direction that the regular expression normally traverses the text, is called *lookahead*. Lookahead is equally supported by all regex flavors in this book. The syntax for *positive lookahead* is ‹(?=*regex*)›. The three characters ‹(?=› form the opening bracket of the group. Everything you can use in a regular expression can be used inside lookahead, here represented by ‹*regex*›.

When the ‹\w+› in ‹(?<=<b>)\w+(?=</b>)› has matched <u>cat</u> in My <b>cat</b> is furry, the regex engine enters the lookahead. The only special behavior for the lookahead at this point is that the regex engine remembers which part of the text it has matched so far, associating it with the lookahead. ‹</b>› is then matched normally. Now the regex engine exits the lookahead. The regex inside the lookahead matches, so the lookahead itself matches. The regex engine discards the text matched by the lookahead, by restoring the match-in-progress it remembered when entering the lookahead. Our overall match-in-progress is back at <u>cat</u>. Since this is also the end of our regular expression, <u>cat</u> becomes the final match result.

Negative lookaround

‹(?!*regex*)›, with an explanation point instead of an equals sign, is *negative lookahead*. Negative lookahead works just like positive lookahead, except that whereas positive lookahead matches when the regex inside the lookahead matches, negative lookahead matches when the regex inside the lookahead fails to match.

The matching process is exactly the same. The engine saves the match-in-progress when entering the negative lookahead, and attempts to match the regex inside the lookahead normally. If the sub-regex matches, the lookahead fails, and the regex engine backtracks. If the sub-regex fails to match, the engine restores the match-in-process and proceeds with the remainder of the regex.

Similarly, (?<!*text*) is *negative lookbehind*. Negative lookbehind matches when none of the alternatives inside the lookbehind can be found looking backward from the position the regex has reached in the subject text.

Different levels of lookbehind

Lookahead is easy. All regex flavors discussed in this book allow you to put a complete regular expression inside the lookahead. Everything you can use in a regular expression can be used inside lookahead. You can even nest other lookahead and lookbehind groups inside lookahead. Your brain might get into a twist, but the regex engine will handle everything nicely.

Lookbehind is a different story. Regular expression software has always been designed to search the text from left to right only. Searching backward is often implemented as a bit of a hack: the regex engine determines how many characters you put inside the lookbehind, jumps back that many characters, and then compares the text in the lookbehind with the text in the subject from left to right.

For this reason, the earliest implementations allowed only fixed-length literal text inside lookbehind. Perl, Python, and Ruby 1.9 take this one step further, allowing you to use alternation and character classes to put multiple fixed-length literal strings inside the lookbehind. Something like ‹(?<=one|two|three|forty-two|gr[ae]y)› is all they can handle.

Internally, Perl, Python, and Ruby 1.9 expand this into six lookbehind tests. First, they jump back three characters to test ‹one|two›, then four characters to test ‹gray|grey›, then five to test ‹three›, and finally nine to test ‹forty-two›.

PCRE and Java take lookbehind one step further. They allow any finite-length regular expression inside lookbehind. This means you can use anything except the infinite quantifiers ‹*›, ‹+›, and ‹{42,}› inside lookbehind. Internally, PCRE and Java calculate the minimum and maximum length of the text that could possibly be matched by the part of the regex in the lookbehind. They then jump back the minimum number of characters, and apply the regex in the lookbehind from left to right. If it fails, they jump back one more character and try again, until either the lookbehind matches or the maximum number of characters has been tried.

If all this sounds rather inefficient, it is. Lookbehind is very convenient, but it won't break any speed records. Later, we present a solution for JavaScript and Ruby 1.8, which don't support lookbehind at all. This solution is actually far more efficient than using lookbehind.

The regular expression engine in the .NET framework is the only one in the world[†] that can actually apply a full regular expression from right to left. .NET allows you to use anything inside lookbehind, and it will actually apply the regular expression from right to left. Both the regular expression inside the lookbehind and the subject text are scanned from right to left.

[†] RegexBuddy's regex engine also allows a full regex inside lookbehind, but does not (yet) have a feature similar to .NET's RegexOptions.RightToLeft to reverse the whole regular expression.

Matching the same text twice

If you use lookbehind at the start of the regex or lookahead at the end of the regex, the net effect is that you're requiring something to appear before or after the regex match, without including it in the match. If you use lookaround in the middle of your regular expression, you can apply multiple tests to the same text.

In "Flavor-Specific Features" on page 33 (a subsection of Recipe 2.3), we showed how to use character class subtraction to match a Thai digit. Only .NET and Java support character class subtraction.

A character is a Thai digit if it is both a Thai character (any sort) and a digit (any script). With lookahead, you can test both requirements on the same character:

```
(?=\p{Thai})\p{N}
```
Regex options: None
Regex flavors: PCRE, Perl, Ruby 1.9

This regex works only with the three flavors that support Unicode scripts, as we explain in Recipe 2.7. But the principle of using lookahead to match the same character more than once works with all flavors discussed in this book.

When the regular expression engine searches for ‹(?=\p{Thai})\p{N}›, it starts by entering the lookahead at each position in the string where it begins a match attempt. If the character at that position is not in the Thai script (i.e., ‹\p{Thai}› fails to match), the lookahead fails. This causes the whole match attempt to fail, forcing the regex engine to start over at the next character.

When the regex reaches a Thai character, ‹\p{Thai}› matches. Thus, the ‹(?=\p{Thai})› lookaround matches, too. As the engine exits the lookaround, it restores the match-in-progress. In this case, that's the zero-length match before the character just found to be Thai. Next up is ‹\p{N}›. Because the lookahead discarded its match, ‹\p{N}› is compared with the same character that ‹\p{Thai}› already matched. If this character has the Unicode property Number, ‹\p{N}› matches. Since ‹\p{N}› is not inside a lookaround, it consumes the character, and we have found our Thai digit.

Lookaround is atomic

When the regular expression engine exits a lookaround group, it discards the text matched by the lookaround. Because the text is discarded, any backtracking positions remembered by alternation or quantifiers inside the lookaround are also discarded. This effectively makes lookahead and lookbehind atomic. Recipe 2.15 explains atomic groups in detail.

In most situations, the atomic nature of lookaround is irrelevant. A lookaround is merely an assertion to check whether the regex inside the lookaround matches or fails. How many different ways it can match is irrelevant, as it does not consume any part of the subject text.

The atomic nature comes into play only when you use capturing groups inside look-ahead (and lookbehind, if your regex flavor allows you to). While the lookahead does not consume any text, the regex engine will remember which part of the text was matched by any capturing groups inside the lookahead. If the lookahead is at the end of the regex, you will indeed end up with capturing groups that match text not matched by the regular expression itself. If the lookahead is in the middle of the regex, you can end up with capturing groups that match overlapping parts of the subject text.

The only situation in which the atomic nature of lookaround can alter the overall regex match is when you use a backreference outside the lookaround to a capturing group created inside the lookaround. Consider this regular expression:

(?=(\d+))\w+\1
Regex options: None
Regex flavors: .NET, Java, JavaScript, PCRE, Perl, Python, Ruby

At first glance, you may think that this regex would match **123x12**. ‹\d+› would capture **12** into the first capturing group, then ‹\w+› would match **3x**, and finally ‹\1› would match **12** again.

But that never happens. The regular expression enters the lookaround and the capturing group. The greedy ‹\d+› matches **123**. This match is stored into the first capturing group. The engine then exits the lookahead, resetting the match-in-progress to the start of the string, discarding the backtracking positions remembered by the greedy plus but keeping the **123** stored in the first capturing group.

Now, the greedy ‹\w+› is attempted at the start of the string. It eats up **123x12**. ‹\1›, which references **123**, fails at the end of the string. ‹\w+› backtracks one character. ‹\1› fails again. ‹\w+› keeps backtracking until it has given up everything except the first **1** in the subject. ‹\1› also fails to match after the first **1**.

The final **12** would match ‹\1› if the regex engine could return to the lookahead and give up **123** in favor of **12**, but the regex engine doesn't do that.

The regex engine has no further backtracking positions to go to. ‹\w+› backtracked all the way, and the lookaround forced ‹\d+› to give up its backtracking positions. The match attempt fails.

Solution Without Lookbehind

All the preceding arcania is of no use if you're using Python or JavaScript, because you cannot use lookbehind at all. There's no way to solve the problem as stated with these regex flavors, but you can work around the need for lookbehind by using capturing groups. This alternative solution also works with all the other regex flavors:

()(\w+)(?=)
Regex options: Case insensitive
Regex flavors: .NET, Java, JavaScript, PCRE, Perl, Python, Ruby

Instead of using lookbehind, we used a capturing group for the opening tag `<b>`. We also placed the part of the match we're interested in, the `\w+`, into a capturing group.

When you apply this regular expression to `My <b>cat</b> is furry`, the overall regex match will be <u>`<b>cat`</u>. The first capturing group will hold <u>`<b>`</u>, and the second, <u>`cat`</u>.

If the requirement is to match only <u>`cat`</u> (the word between the `<b>` tags) because you want to extract only that from the text, you can reach that goal by simply storing the text matched by the second capturing group instead of the overall regex.

If the requirement is that you want to do a search-and-replace, replacing only the word between the tags, simply use a backreference to the first capturing group to reinsert the opening tag into the replacement text. In this case, you don't really need the capturing group, as the opening tag is always the same. But when it's variable, the capturing group reinserts exactly what was matched. Recipe 2.21 explains this in detail.

Finally, if you really want to simulate lookbehind, you can do so with two regular expressions. First, search for your regex without the lookbehind. When it matches, copy the part of the subject text before the match into a new string variable. Do the test you did inside the lookbehind with a second regex, appending an end-of-string anchor (`\z` or `$`). The anchor makes sure the match of the second regex ends at the end of the string. Since you cut the string at the point where the first regex matched, that effectively puts the second match immediately to the left of the first match.

In JavaScript, you could code this along these lines:

```javascript
var mainregexp = /\w+(?=<\/b>)/;
var lookbehind = /<b>$/;
if (match = mainregexp.exec("My <b>cat</b> is furry")) {
    // Found a word before a closing tag </b>
    var potentialmatch = match[0];
    var leftContext = match.input.substring(0, match.index);
    if (lookbehind.exec(leftContext)) {
        // Lookbehind matched:
        // potentialmatch occurs between a pair of <b> tags
    } else {
        // Lookbehind failed: potentialmatch is no good
    }
} else {
    // Unable to find a word before a closing tag </b>
}
```

See Also

Recipes 5.5 and 5.6

2.17 Match One of Two Alternatives Based on a Condition

Problem

Create a regular expression that matches a comma-delimited list of the words one, two, and three. Each word can occur any number of times in the list, but each word must appear at least once.

Solution

```
\b(?:(?:(one)|(two)|(three))(?:,|\b)){3,}(?(1)|(?!))(?(2)|(?!))(?(3)|(?!))
```

Regex options: None
Regex flavors: .NET, JavaScript, PCRE, Perl, Python

Java and Ruby do not support conditionals. When programming in Java or Ruby (or any other language), you can use the regular expression without the conditionals, and write some extra code to check if each of the three capturing groups matched something.

```
\b(?:(?:(one)|(two)|(three))(?:,|\b)){3,}
```

Regex options: None
Regex flavors: .NET, Java, JavaScript, PCRE, Perl, Python, Ruby

Discussion

.NET, JavaScript, PCRE, Perl, and Python support *conditionals* using numbered capturing groups. ‹(?(1)*then*|*else*)› is a conditional that checks whether the first capturing group has already matched something. If it has, the regex engine attempts to match ‹*then*›. If the capturing group has not participated in the match attempt thus far, the ‹*else*› part is attempted.

The parentheses, question mark, and vertical bar are all part of the syntax for the conditional. They don't have their usual meaning. You can use any kind of regular expression for the ‹*then*› and ‹*else*› parts. The only restriction is that if you want to use alternation for one of the parts, you have to use a group to keep it together. Only one vertical bar is permitted directly in the conditional.

If you want, you can omit either the ‹*then*› or ‹*else*› part. The empty regex always finds a zero-length match. The solution for this recipe uses three conditionals that have an empty ‹*then*› part. If the capturing group participated, the conditional simply matches.

An empty negative lookahead, ‹(?!)›, fills the ‹*else*› part. Since the empty regex always matches, a negative lookahead containing the empty regex always fails. Thus, the conditional ‹(?(1)|(?!))› always fails when the first capturing group did not match anything.

By placing each of the three required alternatives in their own capturing group, we can use three conditionals at the end of the regex to test if all the capturing groups captured something.

.NET also supports named conditionals. ‹(?(*name*)*then*|*else*)› checks whether the named capturing group name participated in the match attempt thus far.

To better understand how conditionals work, let's examine the regular expression ‹(a)?b(?(1)c|d)›. This is essentially a complicated way of writing ‹abc|bd›.

If the subject text starts with an a, this is captured in the first capturing group. If not, the first capturing group does not participate in the match attempt at all. It is important that the question mark is outside the capturing group because this makes the whole group optional. If there is no a, the group is repeated zero times, and never gets the chance to capture anything at all. It can't capture a zero-length string.

If you use ‹(a?)›, the group always participates in the match attempt. There's no quantifier after the group, so it is repeated exactly once. The group will either capture a̲ or capture nothing.

Regardless of whether ‹a› was matched, the next token is ‹b›. The conditional is next. If the capturing group participated in the match attempt, even if it captured the zero-length string (not possible here), ‹c› will be attempted. If not, ‹d› will be attempted.

In English, ‹(a)?b(?(1)c|d)› either matches a̲b̲ followed by c̲, or matches b̲ followed by d̲.

With .NET, PCRE, and Perl, but not with Python, conditionals can also use lookaround. ‹(?(?=*if*)*then*|*else*)› first tests ‹(?=*if*)› as a normal lookahead. Recipe 2.16 explains how this works. If the lookaround succeeds, the ‹*then*› part is attempted. If not, the ‹*else*› part is attempted. Since lookaround is zero-width, the ‹*then*› and ‹*else*› regexes are attempted at the same position in the subject text where ‹*if*› either matched or failed.

You can use lookbehind instead of lookahead in the conditional. You can also use negative lookaround, though we recommend against it, as it only confuses things by reversing the meaning of "then" and "else."

> A conditional using lookaround can be written without the conditional as ‹(?=*if*)*then*|(?!*if*)*else*›. If the positive lookahead succeeds, the ‹*then*› part is attempted. If the positive lookahead fails, the alternation kicks in. The negative lookahead then does the same test. The negative lookahead succeeds when ‹*if*› fails, which is already guaranteed because ‹(?=*if*)› failed. Thus, ‹*else*› is attempted. Placing the lookahead in a conditional saves time, as the conditional attempts ‹*if*› only once.

Recipes 2.9 and 2.16

2.18 Add Comments to a Regular Expression

Problem

⟨\d{4}-\d{2}-\d{2}⟩ matches a date in yyyy-mm-dd format, without doing any validation of the numbers. Such a simple regular expression is appropriate when you know your data does not contain any invalid dates. Add comments to this regular expression to indicate what each part of the regular expression does.

Solution

```
\d{4}      # Year
-          # Separator
\d{2}      # Month
-          # Separator
\d{2}      # Day
```
Regex options: Free-spacing
Regex flavors: .NET, Java, PCRE, Perl, Python, Ruby

Discussion

Free-spacing mode

Regular expressions can quickly become complicated and difficult to understand. Just as you should comment source code, you should comment all but the most trivial regular expressions.

All regular expression flavors in this book, except JavaScript, offer an alternative regular expression syntax that makes it very easy to clearly comment your regular expressions. You can enable this syntax by turning on the *free-spacing* option. It has different names in various programming languages.

In .NET, set the `RegexOptions.IgnorePatternWhitespace` option. In Java, pass the `Pattern.COMMENTS` flag. Python expects `re.VERBOSE`. PHP, Perl, and Ruby use the `/x` flag.

Turning on free-spacing mode has two effects. It turns the hash symbol (#) into a metacharacter, outside character classes. The hash starts a comment that runs until the end of the line or the end of the regex (whichever comes first). The hash and everything after it is simply ignored by the regular expression engine. To match a literal hash sign, either place it inside a character class ⟨[#]⟩ or escape it ⟨\#⟩.

The other effect is that whitespace, which includes spaces, tabs, and line breaks, is also ignored outside character classes. To match a literal space, either place it inside a character class ⟨[●]⟩ or escape it ⟨\●⟩. If you're concerned about readability, you could use the hexadecimal escape ⟨\x20⟩ or the Unicode escape ⟨\u0020⟩ or ⟨\x{0020}⟩ instead. To match a tab, use ⟨\t⟩. For line breaks, use ⟨\r\n⟩ (Windows) or ⟨\n⟩ (Unix/Linux/OS X).

Free-spacing mode does not change anything inside character classes. A character class is a single token. Any whitespace characters or hashes inside character classes are literal characters that are added to the character class. You cannot break up character classes to comment their parts.

Java has free-spacing character classes

Regular expressions wouldn't live up to their reputation unless at least one flavor was incompatible with the others. In this case, Java is the odd one out.

In Java, character classes are not parsed as single tokens. If you turn on free-spacing mode, Java ignores whitespace in character classes, and hashes inside character classes do start comments. This means you cannot use ⟨[●]⟩ and ⟨[#]⟩ to match these characters literally. Use ⟨\u0020⟩ and ⟨\#⟩ instead.

Variations

```
(?#Year)\d{4}(?#Separator)-(?#Month)\d{2}-(?#Day)\d{2}
```
Regex options: None
Regex flavors: .NET, PCRE, Perl, Python, Ruby

If, for some reason, you can't or don't want to use free-spacing syntax, you can still add comments by way of ⟨(?#comment)⟩. All characters between ⟨(?#⟩ and ⟨)⟩ are ignored.

Unfortunately, JavaScript, the only flavor in this book that doesn't support free-spacing, also doesn't support this comment syntax. Java does not support it either.

```
(?x)\d{4}       # Year
-               # Separator
\d{2}           # Month
-               # Separator
\d{2}           # Day
```
Regex options: None
Regex flavors: .NET, Java, PCRE, Perl, Python, Ruby

If you cannot turn on free-spacing mode outside the regular expression, you can place the mode modifier ⟨(?x)⟩ at the very start of the regular expression. Make sure there's no whitespace before the ⟨(?x)⟩. Free-spacing mode begins only at this mode modifier; any whitespace before it is significant.

Mode modifiers are explained in detail in "Case-insensitive matching" on page 27, a subsection of Recipe 2.1.

2.19 Insert Literal Text into the Replacement Text

Problem

Search and replace any regular expression match literally with the eight characters $%*$1\1.

Solution

$%*$$1\1
> **Replacement text flavors:** .NET, JavaScript

\$%*\$1\\1
> **Replacement text flavor:** Java

$%*\$1\\1
> **Replacement text flavor:** PHP

\$%*\$1\\1
> **Replacement text flavor:** Perl

$%*$1\\1
> **Replacement text flavors:** Python, Ruby

Discussion

When and how to escape characters in replacement text

This recipe shows you the different escape rules used by the various replacement text flavors. The only two characters you may ever need to escape in the replacement text are the dollar sign and the backslash. The escape characters are also the dollar sign and the backslash.

The percentage sign and asterisk in this example are always literal characters, though a preceding backslash may be treated as an escape instead of a literal backslash. «$1» and/or «\1» are a backreference to a capturing group. Recipe 2.21 tells you which flavors use which syntax for backreferences.

The fact that this problem has five different solutions for seven replacement text flavors demonstrates that there really is no standard for replacement text syntax.

.NET and JavaScript

.NET and JavaScript always treat a backslash as a literal character. Do not escape it with another backslash, or you'll end up with two backslashes in the replacement.

A lone dollar sign is a literal character. Dollar signs need to be escaped only when they are followed by a digit, ampersand, backtick, straight quote, underscore, plus sign, or another dollar sign. To escape a dollar sign, precede it with another dollar sign.

You can double up all dollar signs if you feel that makes your replacement text more readable. This solution is equally valid:

```
$$%\*$$1\1
```

Replacement text flavors: .NET, JavaScript

.NET also requires dollar signs followed by an opening curly brace to be escaped. «${group}» is a named backreference in .NET. JavaScript does not support named backreferences.

Java

In Java, the backslash is used to escape backslashes and dollar signs in the replacement text. All literal backslashes and all literal dollar signs must be escaped. If you do not escape them, Java will throw an exception.

PHP

PHP requires backslashes followed by a digit, and dollar signs followed by a digit or opening curly brace, to be escaped with a backslash.

A backslash also escapes another backslash. Thus, you need to write «\\\\» to replace with two literal backslashes. All other backslashes are treated as literal backslashes.

Perl

Perl is a bit different from the other replacement text flavors: it does not really have a replacement text flavor. Whereas the other programming languages have special logic in their search-and-replace routines to substitute things such as «$1», in Perl that's just normal variable interpolation. In the replacement text, you need to escape all literal dollar signs with a backslash, just as you would in any double-quoted string.

One exception is that Perl does support the «\1» syntax for backreferences. Thus, you need to escape a backslash followed by a digit if you want the backslash to be a literal. A backslash followed by a dollar sign also needs to be escaped, to prevent the backslash from escaping the dollar sign.

A backslash also escapes another backslash. Thus, you need to write «\\\\» to replace with two literal backslashes. All other backslashes are treated as literal backslashes.

Python and Ruby

The dollar sign has no special meaning in the replacement text in Python and Ruby. Backslashes need to be escaped with another backslash when followed by a character that gives the backslash a special meaning.

With Python, «\1» through «\9» and «\g<» create backreferences. These backslashes need to be escaped.

For Ruby, you need to escape a backslash followed by a digit, ampersand, backtick, straight quote, or plus sign.

In both languages, a backslash also escapes another backslash. Thus, you need to write «\\\\» to include two literal backslashes in replacement text. All other backslashes are treated as literal backslashes.

More escape rules for string literals

Remember that in this chapter, we deal only with the regular expressions and replacement text themselves. The next chapter covers programming languages and string literals.

The replacement texts shown earlier will work when the actual string variable you're passing to the `replace()` function holds this text. In other words, if your application provides a text box for the user to type in the replacement text, these solutions show what the user would have to type in order for the search-and-replace to work as intended. If you test your search-and-replace commands with RegexBuddy or another regex tester, the replacement texts included in this recipe will show the expected results.

But these same replacement texts will not work if you paste them directly into your source code and put quote characters around them. String literals in programming languages have their own escape rules, and you need to follow those rules on top of the replacement text escape rules. You may indeed end up with a mess of backslashes.

See Also

Recipe 3.14

2.20 Insert the Regex Match into the Replacement Text

Problem

Perform a search-and-replace that converts URLs into HTML links that point to the URL, and use the URL as the text for the link. For this exercise, define a URL as "http:" and all nonwhitespace characters that follow it. For instance, `Please visit http://www.regexcookbook.com` becomes `Please visit <a href="http://www.regexcook book.com">http://www.regexcookbook.com</a>`.

Solution

Regular expression

```
http:\S+
```
Regex options: None
Regex flavors: .NET, Java, JavaScript, PCRE, Perl, Python, Ruby

Replacement

> `<a•href="$&">$&</a>`
> **Replacement text flavors:** .NET, JavaScript, Perl

> `<a•href="$0">$0</a>`
> **Replacement text flavors:** .NET, Java, PHP

> `<a•href="\0">\0</a>`
> **Replacement text flavors:** PHP, Ruby

> `<a•href="\&">\&</a>`
> **Replacement text flavor:** Ruby

> `<a•href="\g<0>">\g<0></a>`
> **Replacement text flavor:** Python

Discussion

Inserting the whole regex match back into the replacement text is an easy way to insert new text before, after, or around the matched text, or even between multiple copies of the matched text. Unless you're using Python, you don't have to add any capturing groups to your regular expression to be able to reuse the overall match.

In Perl, «$&» is actually a variable. Perl stores the overall regex match in this variable after each successful regex match.

.NET and JavaScript have adopted the «$&» syntax to insert the regex match into the replacement text. Ruby uses backslashes instead of dollar signs for replacement text tokens, so use «\&» for the overall match.

Java, PHP, and Python do not have a special token to reinsert the overall regex match, but they do allow text matched by capturing groups to be inserted into the replacement text, as the next section explains. The overall match is an implicit capturing group number 0. For Python, we need to use the syntax for named capture to reference group zero. Python does not support «\0».

.NET and Ruby also support the zeroth capturing group syntax, but it doesn't matter which syntax you use. The result is the same.

See Also

"Searching and Replacing with Regular Expressions" in Chapter 1, and Recipe 3.15

2.21 Insert Part of the Regex Match into the Replacement Text

Problem

Match any contiguous sequence of 10 digits, such as 1234567890. Convert the sequence into a nicely formatted phone number, for example, (123) 456-7890.

Solution

Regular expression

`\b(\d{3})(\d{3})(\d{4})\b`

Regex options: None
Regex flavors: .NET, Java, JavaScript, PCRE, Perl, Python, Ruby

Replacement

`($1)•$2-$3`

Replacement text flavors: .NET, Java, JavaScript, PHP, Perl

`(${1})•${2}-${3}`

Replacement text flavors: .NET, PHP, Perl

`(\1)•\2-\3`

Replacement text flavors: PHP, Python, Ruby

Discussion

Replacements using capturing groups

Recipe 2.10 explains how you can use capturing groups in your regular expression to match the same text more than once. The text matched by each capturing group in your regex is also available after each successful match. You can insert the text of some or all capturing groups—in any order, or even more than once—into the replacement text.

Some flavors, such as Python and Ruby, use the same «\1» syntax for backreferences in both the regular expression and the replacement text. Other flavors use Perl's «$1» syntax, using a dollar sign instead of a backslash. PHP supports both.

In Perl, «$1» and above are actually variables that are set after each successful regex match. You can use them anywhere in your code until the next regex match. .NET, Java, JavaScript, and PHP support «$1» only in the replacement syntax. These programming languages do offer other ways to access capturing groups in code. Chapter 3 explains that in detail.

$10 and higher

All regex flavors in this book support up to 99 capturing groups in a regular expression. In the replacement text, ambiguity can occur with «$10» or «\10» and above. These can be interpreted as either the 10th capturing group, or the first capturing group followed by a literal zero.

.NET, PHP, and Perl allow you to put curly braces around the number to make your intention clear. «${10}» is always the 10th capturing group, and «${1}0» is always the first followed by a literal zero.

Java and JavaScript try to be clever with «$10». If a capturing group with the specified two-digit number exists in your regular expression, both digits are used for the capturing group. If fewer capturing groups exist, only the first digit is used to reference the group, leaving the second as a literal. Thus «$23» is the 23rd capturing group, if it exists. Otherwise, it is the second capturing group followed by a literal «3».

.NET, PHP, Perl, Python, and Ruby always treat «$10» and «\10» as the 10th capturing group, regardless of whether it exists. If it doesn't, the behavior for nonexistent groups comes into play.

References to nonexistent groups

The regular expression in the solution for this recipe has three capturing groups. If you type «$4» or «\4» into the replacement text, you're adding a reference to a capturing group that does not exist. This triggers one of three different behaviors.

Java and Python will cry foul by raising an exception or returning an error message. Do not use invalid backreferences with these flavors. (Actually, you shouldn't use invalid backreferences with any flavor.) If you want to insert «$4» or «\4» literally, escape the dollar sign or backslash. Recipe 2.19 explains this in detail.

PHP, Perl, and Ruby substitute all backreferences in the replacement text, including those that point to groups that don't exist. Groups that don't exist did not capture any text and therefore references to these groups are simply replaced with nothing.

Finally, .NET and JavaScript leave backreferences to groups that don't exist as literal text in the replacement.

All flavors do replace groups that do exist in the regular expression but did not capture anything. Those are replaced with nothing.

Solution Using Named Capture

Regular expression

```
\b(?<area>\d{3})(?<exchange>\d{3})(?<number>\d{4})\b
```
   Regex options: None
   Regex flavors: .NET, PCRE 7, Perl 5.10, Ruby 1.9

```
\b(?'area'\d{3})(?'exchange'\d{3})(?'number'\d{4})\b
```
   Regex options: None
   Regex flavors: .NET, PCRE 7, Perl 5.10, Ruby 1.9

```
\b(?P<area>\d{3})(?P<exchange>\d{3})(?P<number>\d{4})\b
```
    Regex options: None
    Regex flavors: PCRE 4 and later, Perl 5.10, Python

Replacement

```
(${area})•${exchange}-${number}
```
    Replacement text flavor: .NET

```
(\g<area>)•\g<exchange>-\g<number>
```
    Replacement text flavor: Python

```
(\k<area>)•\k<exchange>-\k<number>
```
    Replacement text flavor: Ruby 1.9

```
(\k'area')•\k'exchange'-\k'number'
```
    Replacement text flavor: Ruby 1.9

```
($1)•$2-$3
```
    Replacement text flavors: .NET, PHP, Perl 5.10

```
(${1})•${2}-${3}
```
    Replacement text flavors: .NET, PHP, Perl 5.10

```
(\1)•\2-\3
```
    Replacement text flavors: PHP, Python, Ruby 1.9

Flavors that support named capture

.NET, Python, and Ruby 1.9 allow you to use named backreferences in the replacement text if you used named capturing groups in your regular expression.

With .NET and Python, the syntax for named backreferences works equally with named and numbered capturing groups. Simply specify the name or number of the group between the curly braces or angle brackets.

Ruby uses the same syntax for backreferences in the replacement text as it does in the regular expression. For named capturing groups in Ruby 1.9, this syntax is «\k<group>» or «\k'group'». The choice between angle brackets and single quotes is merely a notational convenience.

Perl 5.10 and PHP (using PCRE) support named capturing groups in regular expressions, but not in the replacement text. You can use numbered backreferences in the replacement text to named capturing groups in the regular expression. Perl 5.10 and PCRE assign numbers to both named and unnamed groups, from left to right.

.NET, Python, and Ruby 1.9 also allow numbered references to named groups. However, .NET uses a different numbering scheme for named groups, as Recipe 2.11 explains. Mixing names and numbers with .NET, Python, or Ruby is not recommended. Either give all your groups names or don't name any groups at all. Always use named backreferences for named groups.

See Also

"Searching and Replacing with Regular Expressions" in Chapter 1, and Recipes 2.9, 2.10, 2.11, and 3.15

2.22 Insert Match Context into the Replacement Text

Problem

Create replacement text that replaces the regex match with the text before the regex match, followed by the whole subject text, followed by the text after the regex match. For example, if `Match` is found in `BeforeMatchAfter`, replace the match with `BeforeBefore MatchAfterAfter`, yielding the new text `BeforeBeforeBeforeMatchAfterAfterAfter`.

Solution

```
$`$_$'
```
Replacement text flavors: .NET, Perl

```
\`\'\&\'\'
```
Replacement text flavor: Ruby

```
$`$`$&$'$'
```
Replacement text flavor: JavaScript

Discussion

The term *context* refers to the subject text that the regular expression was applied to. There are three pieces of context: the subject text before the regex match, the subject text after the regex match, and the whole subject text. The text before the match is sometimes called the *left context*, and the text after the match is correspondingly the *right context*. The whole subject text is the left context, the match, and the right context.

.NET and Perl support «$`», «$'», and «$_» to insert all three forms of context into the replacement text. Actually, in Perl these are variables set after a successful regex match and are available in any code until the next match attempt. Dollar backtick is the left context. You can type the backtick on a U.S. keyboard by pressing the key to the left of the 1 key in the top-left corner of your keyboard. Dollar straight quote is the right context. The straight quote is the usual single quote. On a U.S. keyboard, it sits between the semicolon and Enter keys. Dollar underscore is the whole subject text. Like .NET and Perl, JavaScript uses «$`» and «$'» for left and right context. However, JavaScript does not have a token for inserting the entire subject text. You can recompose the subject text by inserting the whole regex match with «$&» between the left and right context.

Ruby supports left and right context via «\`» and «\'», and uses «\&» to insert the whole regex match. Like JavaScript, there is no token for the whole subject text.

See Also

"Searching and Replacing with Regular Expressions" in Chapter 1, and Recipe 3.15

CHAPTER 3

Programming with Regular Expressions

Programming Languages and Regex Flavors

This chapter explains how to implement regular expressions with your programming language of choice. The recipes in this chapter assume you already have a working regular expression at your disposal; the previous chapters can help in that regard. Now you face the job of putting a regular expression into your source code and actually making it do something.

We've done our best in this chapter to explain exactly how and why each piece of code works the way it does. Because of the level of detail in this chapter, reading it from start to finish may get a bit tedious. If you're reading *Regular Expression Cookbook* for the first time, we recommend you skim this chapter to get an idea of what can or needs to be done. Later, when you want to implement one of the regular expressions from the following chapters, come back here to learn exactly how to integrate the regexes with your programming language of choice.

Chapters 4 through 8 use regular expressions to solve real-world problems. Those chapters focus on the regular expressions themselves, and many recipes in those chapters don't show any source code at all. To make the regular expressions you find in those chapters work, simply plug them into one of the code snippets in this chapter.

Because the other chapters focus on regular expressions, they present their solutions for specific regular expression flavors, rather than for specific programming languages. Regex flavors do not correspond one-on-one with programming languages. Scripting languages tend to have their own regular expression flavor built-in, and other programming languages rely on libraries for regex support. Some libraries are available for multiple languages, while certain languages have multiple libraries available for them.

"Many Flavors of Regular Expressions" on page 2 describes all the regular expression flavors covered in this book. "Many Flavors of Replacement Text" on page 5 lists the replacement text flavors, used for searching and replacing with a regular expression. All of the programming languages covered in this chapter use one of these flavors.

Languages Covered in This Chapter

This chapter covers seven programming languages. Each recipe has separate solutions for all seven programming languages, and many recipes also have separate discussions for all seven languages. If a technique applies to more than one language, we repeat it in the discussion for each of those languages. We've done this so you can safely skip the discussions of programming languages that you're not interested in:

C#
> C# uses the Microsoft .NET framework. The `System.Text.RegularExpressions` classes use the ".NET" regular expression and replacement text flavor. This book covers C# 1.0 through 3.5, or Visual Studio 2002 until 2008.

VB.NET
> This book uses VB.NET and Visual Basic.NET to refer to Visual Basic 2002 and later, to distinguish these versions from Visual Basic 6 and earlier. Visual Basic now uses the Microsoft .NET framework. The `System.Text.RegularExpressions` classes use the ".NET" regular expression and replacement text flavor. This book covers Visual Basic 2002 until 2008.

Java
> Java 4 is the first Java release to provide built-in regular expression support through the `java.util.regex` package. The `java.util.regex` package uses the "Java" regular expression and replacement text flavor. This book covers Java 4, 5, and 6.

JavaScript
> This is the regex flavor used in the programming language commonly known as JavaScript. All modern web browsers implement it: Internet Explorer (as of version 5.5), Firefox, Opera, Safari, and Chrome. Many other applications also use JavaScript as a scripting language.
>
> Strictly speaking, in this book we use the term *JavaScript* to indicate the programming language defined in version 3 of the ECMA-262 standard. This standard defines the ECMAScript programming language, which is better known through its implementations JavaScript and JScript in various web browsers.
>
> ECMA-262v3 also defines the regular expression and replacement text flavors used by JavaScript. Those flavors are labeled as "JavaScript" in this book.

PHP
> PHP has three sets of regular expression functions. We strongly recommend using the `preg` functions. Therefore, this book only covers the `preg` functions, which are built into PHP as of version 4.2.0. This book covers PHP 4 and 5. The `preg` functions are PHP wrappers around the PCRE library. The PCRE regex flavor is indicated as

"PCRE" in this book. Since PCRE does not include search-and-replace functionality, the PHP developers devised their own replacement text syntax for preg_replace. This replacement text flavor is labeled "PHP" in this book.

The mb_ereg functions are part of PHP's "multibyte" functions, which are designed to work well with languages that are traditionally encoded with multibyte character sets, such as Japanese and Chinese. In PHP 5, the mb_ereg functions use the Oniguruma regex library, which was originally developed for Ruby. The Oniguruma regex flavor is indicated as "Ruby 1.9" in this book. Using the mb_ereg functions is recommended only if you have a specific requirement to deal with multibyte code pages and you're already familiar with the mb_ functions in PHP.

The ereg group of functions is the oldest set of PHP regex functions, and are officially deprecated as of PHP 5.3.0. They don't depend on external libraries, and implement the POSIX ERE flavor. This flavor offers only a limited feature set, and is not discussed in this book. POSIX ERE is a strict subset of the Ruby 1.9 and PCRE flavors. You can take the regex from any ereg function call and use it with mb_ereg or preg. For preg, you have to add Perl-style delimiters (Recipe 3.1).

Perl

Perl's built-in support for regular expressions is the main reason why regexes are popular today. The regular expression and replacement text flavors used by Perl's m// and s/// operators are labeled as "Perl" in this book. This book covers Perl 5.6, 5.8, and 5.10.

Python

Python supports regular expressions through its re module. The regular expression and replacement text flavor used by this module are labeled "Python" in this book. This book covers Python 2.4 and 2.5.

Ruby

Ruby has built-in support for regular expressions. This book covers Ruby 1.8 and Ruby 1.9. These two versions of Ruby have different default regular expression engines. Ruby 1.9 uses the Oniguruma engine, which has more regex features than the classic engine in Ruby 1.8. "Regex Flavors Covered by This Book" on page 3 has more details on this.

In this chapter, we don't talk much about the differences between Ruby 1.8 and 1.9. The regular expressions in this chapter are very basic, and they don't use the new features in Ruby 1.9. Because the regular expression support is compiled into the Ruby language itself, the Ruby code you use to implement your regular expressions is the same, regardless of whether you've compiled Ruby using the classic regex engine or the Oniguruma engine. You could recompile Ruby 1.8 to use the Oniguruma engine if you need its features.

More Programming Languages

The programming languages in the following list aren't covered by this book, but they do use one of the regular expression flavors in this book. If you use one of these languages, you can skip this chapter, but all the other chapters are still useful:

ActionScript

ActionScript is Adobe's implementation of the ECMA-262 standard. As of version 3.0, ActionScript has full support for ECMA-262v3 regular expressions. This regex flavor is labeled "JavaScript" in this book. The ActionScript language is also very close to JavaScript. You should be able to adapt the JavaScript examples in this chapter for ActionScript.

C

C can use a wide variety of regular expression libraries. The open source PCRE library is likely the best choice out of the flavors covered by this book. You can download the full C source code at *http://www.pcre.org*. The code is written to compile with a wide range of compilers on a wide range of platforms.

C++

C++ can use a wide variety of regular expression libraries. The open source PCRE library is likely the best choice out of the flavors covered by this book. You can either use the C API directly or use the C++ class wrappers included with the PCRE download itself (see *http://www.pcre.org*).

On Windows, you could import the VBScript 5.5 RegExp COM object, as explained later for Visual Basic 6. That could be useful for regex consistency between a C++ backend and a JavaScript frontend.

Delphi for Win32

At the time of this writing, the Win32 version of Delphi does not have any built-in support for regular expressions. There are many VCL components available that provide regular expression support. I recommend that you choose one based on PCRE. Delphi has the ability to link C object files into your applications, and many VCL wrappers for PCRE use such object files. This allows you to keep your application as a single *.exe* file.

You can download my own TPerlRegEx component at *http://www.regexp.info/del phi.html*. This is a VCL component that installs itself onto the component palette, so you can easily drop it into a form. Another popular PCRE wrapper for Delphi is the `TJclRegEx` class part of the `JCL` library at *http://www.delphi-jedi.org*. `TJclRegEx` descends from `TObject`, so you can't drop it into a form.

Both libraries are open source under the Mozilla Public License.

Delphi Prism

In Delphi Prism, you can use the regular expression support provided by the .NET framework. Simply add `System.Text.RegularExpressions` to the `uses` clause of any Delphi Prism unit in which you want to use regular expressions.

Once you've done that, you can use the same techniques shown in the C# and VB.NET code snippets in this chapter.

Groovy

You can use regular expressions in Groovy with the `java.util.regex` package, just as you can in Java. In fact, all of the Java solutions in this chapter should work with Groovy as well. Groovy's own regular expression syntax merely provides notational shortcuts. A literal regex delimited with forward slashes is an instance of `java.lang.String` and the `=~` operator instantiates `java.util.regex.Matcher`. You can freely mix the Groovy syntax with the standard Java syntax—the classes and objects are all the same.

PowerShell

PowerShell is Microsoft's shell-scripting language, based on the .NET framework. PowerShell's built-in `-match` and `-replace` operators use the .NET regex flavor and replacement text as described in this book.

R

The R Project supports regular expressions via the `grep`, `sub`, and `regexpr` functions in the `base` package. All these functions take an argument labeled `perl`, which is `FALSE` if you omit it. Set it to `TRUE` to use the PCRE regex flavor as described in this book. The regular expressions shown for PCRE 7 work with R 2.5.0 and later. For earlier versions of R, use the regular expressions marked as "PCRE 4 and later" in this book. The "basic" and "extended" flavors supported by R are older and limited regex flavors not discussed in this book.

REALbasic

REALbasic has a built-in `RegEx` class. Internally, this class uses the UTF-8 version of the PCRE library. This means that you can use PCRE's Unicode support, but you have to use REALbasic's `TextConverter` class to convert non-ASCII text into UTF-8 before passing it to the `RegEx` class.

All regular expressions shown in this book for PCRE 6 will work with REALbasic. One caveat is that in REALbasic, the "case insensitive" and "caret and dollar match at line breaks" ("multi line") options are on by default in REALbasic. If you want to use a regular expression from this book that does not tell you to turn on these matching modes, you have to turn them off explicitly in REALbasic.

Scala

Scala provides built-in regex support through the `scala.util.matching` package. This support is built on the regular expression engine in Java's `java.util.regex` package. The regular expression and replacement text flavors used by Java and Scala are labeled "Java" in this book.

Visual Basic 6

Visual Basic 6 is the last version of Visual Basic that does not require the .NET framework. That also means Visual Basic 6 cannot use the excellent regular expression support of the .NET framework. The VB.NET code samples in this chapter won't work with VB 6 at all.

Visual Basic 6 does make it very easy to use the functionality provided by ActiveX and COM libraries. One such library is Microsoft's VBScript scripting library, which has decent regular expression capabilities starting with version 5.5. The scripting library implements the same regular expression flavor used in JavaScript, as standardized in ECMA-262v3. This library is part of Internet Explorer 5.5 and later. It is available on all computers running Windows XP or Vista, and previous versions of Windows if the user has upgraded to IE 5.5 or later. That includes almost every Windows PC that is used to connect to the Internet.

To use this library in your Visual Basic application, select Project|References in the VB IDE's menu. Scroll down the list to find the item "Microsoft VBScript Regular Expressions 5.5", which is immediately below the "Microsoft VBScript Regular Expressions 1.0" item. Make sure to tick the 5.5 version, not the 1.0 version. The 1.0 version is only provided for backward compatibility, and its capabilities are less than satisfactory.

After adding the reference, you can see which classes and class members the library provides. Select View|Object Browser in the menu. In the Object Browser, select the "VBScript_RegExp_55" library in the drop-down list in the upper-left corner.

3.1 Literal Regular Expressions in Source Code

Problem

You have been given the regular expression ‹[$"'\n\d/\\]› as the solution to a problem. This regular expression consists of a single character class that matches a dollar sign, a double quote, a single quote, a line feed, any digit between 0 and 9, a forward slash, or a backslash. You want to hardcode this regular expression into your source code as a string constant or regular expression operator.

Solution

C#

As a normal string:

```
"[$\"'\n\\d/\\\\]"
```

As a verbatim string:

```
@"[$""'\n\d/\\]"
```

VB.NET

```
"[$""'\n\d/\\]"
```

Java

```
"[$\"'\n\\d/\\\\]"
```

JavaScript

```
/[$"'\n\d\/\\]/
```

PHP

```
'%[$"\'\n\d/\\\\]%'
```

Perl

Pattern-matching operator:

```
/[\$"'\n\d\/\\]/
m![\$"'\n\d/\\]!
```

Substitution operator:

```
s![\$"'\n\d/\\]!!
```

Python

Raw triple-quoted string:

```
r"""[$"'\n\d/\\]"""
```

Normal string:

```
"[$\"'\n\\d/\\\\]"
```

Ruby

Literal regex delimited with forward slashes:

```
/[$"'\n\d\/\\]/
```

Literal regex delimited with punctuation of your choice:

```
%r![$"'\n\d/\\]!
```

Discussion

When this book shows you a regular expression by itself (as opposed to as part of a larger source code snippet), it always shows regular expressions unadorned. This recipe is the only exception. If you're using a regular expression tester such as RegexBuddy or RegexPal, you would type in the regex this way. If your application accepts a regular expression as user input, the user would type it in this way.

But if you want to hardcode the regular expression into your source code, you have extra work. Carelessly copying and pasting regular expressions from a regular expression tester into your source code—or vice versa—will often leave you scratching your head as to why the regular expression works in your tool but not in your source code, or why the tester fails on a regex you've copied from somebody else's code. All programming languages discussed in this book require literal regular expressions to be delimited in a certain way, with some languages requiring strings and some requiring a special regex constant. If your regex includes the language's delimiters or certain other characters with special meanings in the language, you have to escape them.

The backslash is the most commonly used escape character. That's why most of the solutions to this problem have far more backslashes in them than the four in the original regular expression.

C#

In C#, you can pass literal regular expressions to the `Regex()` constructor, and to various member functions in the `Regex` class. The parameter that takes the regular expression is always declared as a string.

C# supports two kinds of string literals. The most common kind is the double-quoted string, well-known from languages such as C++ and Java. Within double-quoted strings, double quotes and backslashes must be escaped with a backslash. Escapes for nonprintable characters, such as ‹\n›, are also supported in strings. There is a difference between "\n" and "\\n" when using `RegexOptions.IgnorePatternWhitespace` (see Recipe 3.4) to turn on free-spacing mode, as explained in Recipe 2.18. "\n" is a string with a literal line break, which is ignored as whitespace. "\\n" is a string with the regex token ‹\n›, which matches a newline.

Verbatim strings start with an at sign and a double quote, and end with a double quote on its own. To include a double quote in a verbatim string, double it up. Backslashes do not need to be escaped, resulting in a significantly more readable regular expression. @"\n" is always the regex token ‹\n›, which matches a newline, even in free-spacing mode. Verbatim strings do not support ‹\n› at the string level, but can span multiple lines instead. That makes verbatim strings ideal for free-spacing regular expressions.

The choice is clear: use verbatim strings to put regular expressions into your C# source code.

VB.NET

In VB.NET, you can pass literal regular expressions to the `Regex()` constructor, and to various member functions in the `Regex` class. The parameter that takes the regular expression is always declared as a string.

Visual Basic uses double-quoted strings. Double quotes within the string must be doubled. No other characters need to be escaped.

Java

In Java, you can pass literal regular expressions to the `Pattern.compile()` class factory, and to various functions of the `String` class. The parameter that takes the regular expression is always declared as a string.

Java uses double-quoted strings. Within double-quoted strings, double quotes and backslashes must be escaped with a backslash. Escapes for nonprintable characters, such as ‹\n›, and Unicode escapes such as ‹\uFFFF› are also supported in strings.

There is a difference between "\n" and "\\n" when using `Pattern.COMMENTS` (see Recipe 3.4) to turn on free-spacing mode, as explained in Recipe 2.18. "\n" is a string with a literal line break, which is ignored as whitespace. "\\n" is a string with the regex token ‹\n›, which matches a newline.

JavaScript

In JavaScript, regular expressions are best created by using the special syntax for declaring literal regular expressions. Simply place your regular expression between two forward slashes. If any forward slashes occur within the regular expression itself, escape those with a backslash.

Although it is possible to create a `RegExp` object from a string, it makes little sense to use the string notation for literal regular expressions in your code. You would have to escape quotes and backslashes, which generally leads to a forest of backslashes.

PHP

Literal regular expressions for use with PHP's `preg` functions are a curious contraption. Unlike JavaScript or Perl, PHP does not have a native regular expression type. Regular expressions must always be quoted as strings. This is true for the `ereg` and `mb_ereg` functions as well. But in their quest to mimic Perl, the developers of PHP's wrapper functions for PCRE added an additional requirement.

Within the string, the regular expression must be quoted as a Perl-style literal regular expression. That means that where you would write `/regex/` in Perl, the string for PHP's `preg` functions becomes `'/regex/'`. As in Perl, you can use any pair of punctuation characters as the delimiters. If the regex delimiter occurs within the regex, it must be escaped with a backslash. To avoid this, choose a delimiter that does not occur in the regex. For this recipe, I used the percentage sign, because the forward slash occurs in the regex but the percentage sign does not. If the forward slash does not occur in the regex, use that, as it's the most commonly used delimiter in Perl and the required delimiter in JavaScript and Ruby.

PHP supports both single-quoted and double-quoted strings. Both require the quote (single or double) and the backslash within a regex to be escaped with a backslash. In double-quoted strings, the dollar sign also needs to be escaped. For regular expressions, you should use single-quoted strings, unless you really want to interpolate variables in your regex.

Perl

In Perl, literal regular expressions are used with the pattern-matching operator and the substitution operator. The pattern-matching operator consists of two forward slashes, with the regex between it. Forward slashes within the regular expression must be escaped with a backslash. There's no need to escape any other characters, except perhaps $ and @, as explained at the end of this subsection.

An alternative notation for the pattern-matching operator puts the regular expression between any pair of punctuation characters, preceded by the letter m. If you use any kind of opening and closing punctuation (parentheses, braces, or brackets) as the delimiter, they need to match up: for example, m{*regex*}. If you use other punctuation, simply use the same character twice. The solution for this recipe uses the exclamation point. That saves us having to escape the literal forward slash in the regular expression. Only the closing delimiter needs to be escaped with a backslash.

The substitution operator is similar to the pattern-matching operator. It starts with s instead of m, and tacks on the replacement text. When using brackets or similar punctuation as the delimiters, you need two pairs: s[*regex*][*replace*]. For all other punctuation, use it three times: s/*regex*/*replace*/.

Perl parses the pattern-matching and substitution operators as double-quoted strings. If you write m/I am $name/ and $name holds "Jan", you end up with the regular expression ‹I•am•Jan›. $" is also a variable in Perl, so we have to escape the literal dollar sign in the character class in our regular expression in this recipe.

Never escape a dollar sign that you want to use as an anchor (see Recipe 2.5). An escaped dollar sign is always a literal. Perl is smart enough to differentiate between dollars used as anchors, and dollars used for variable interpolation, due to the fact that anchors can be used sensibly only at the end of a group or the whole regex, or before a newline. You shouldn't escape the dollar in ‹m/^*regex*$/› if you want to check whether "regex" matches the subject string entirely.

The at sign does not have a special meaning in regular expressions, but it is used for variable interpolation in Perl. You need to escape it in literal regular expressions in Perl code, as you do for double-quoted strings.

Python

The functions in Python's re module expect literal regular expressions to be passed as strings. You can use any of the various ways that Python provides to quote strings. Depending on the characters that occur in your regular expression, different ways of quoting it may reduce the number of characters you need to escape with backslashes.

Generally, raw strings are the best option. Python raw strings don't require any characters to be escaped. If you use a raw string, you don't need to double up the backslashes in your regular expression. r"\d+" is easier to read than "\\d+", particularly as your regex gets long.

The only situation where raw strings aren't ideal is when your regular expression includes both the single quote and double quote characters. Then you can't use a raw string delimited with one pair of single or double quotes, because there's no way to escape the quotes inside the regular expression. In that case, you can triple-quote the raw string, as we did in the Python solution for this recipe. The normal string is shown for comparison.

If you want to use the Unicode features explained in Recipe 2.7 in your regular expression, you need to use Unicode strings. You can turn a string into a Unicode string by preceding it with a u.

Raw strings don't support nonprintable character escapes such as \n. Raw strings treat escape sequences as literal text. This is not a problem for the re module. It supports these escapes as part of the regular expression syntax, and as part of the replacement text syntax. A literal \n in a raw string will still be interpreted as a newline in your regular expressions and replacement texts.

There is a difference between the string "\n" on one side, and the string "\\n" and the raw string r"\n" on the other side when using re.VERBOSE (see Recipe 3.4) to turn on free-spacing mode, as explained in Recipe 2.18. "\n" is a string with a literal line break, which is ignored as whitespace. "\\n" and r"\n" are both strings with the regex token ‹\n›, which matches a newline.

When using free-spacing mode, triple-quoted raw strings such as r"""\n""" are the best solution, because they can span multiple lines. Also, ‹\n› is not interpreted at the string level, so it can be interpreted at the regex level to match a line break.

Ruby

In Ruby, regular expressions are best created by using the special syntax for declaring literal regular expressions. Simply place your regular expression between two forward slashes. If any forward slashes occur within the regular expression itself, escape those with a backslash.

If you don't want to escape forward slashes in your regex, you can prefix your regular expression with %r and then use any punctuation character of your choice as the delimiter.

Although it is possible to create a Regexp object from a string, it makes little sense to use the string notation for literal regular expressions in your code. You then would have to escape quotes and backslashes, which generally leads to a forest of backslashes.

Ruby is very similar to JavaScript in this respect, except that the name of the class is `Regexp` as one word in Ruby, whereas it is `RegExp` with camel caps in JavaScript.

See Also

Recipe 2.3 explains how character classes work, and why two backslashes are needed in the regular expression to include just one in the character class.

Recipe 3.4 explains how to set regular expression options, which is done as part of literal regular expressions in some programming languages.

3.2 Import the Regular Expression Library

Problem

To be able to use regular expressions in your application, you want to import the regular expression library or namespace into your source code.

 The remainder of the source code snippets in this book assume that you have already done this, if needed.

Solution

C#

```
using System.Text.RegularExpressions;
```

VB.NET

```
Imports System.Text.RegularExpressions
```

Java

```
import java.util.regex.*;
```

Python

```
import re
```

Discussion

Some programming languages have regular expressions built-in. For these languages, you don't need to do anything to enable regular expression support. Other languages provide regular expression functionality through a library that needs to be imported with an import statement in your source code. Some languages don't have regex support at all. For those, you'll have to compile and link in the regular expression support yourself.

C#

If you place the `using` statement at the top of your C# source file, you can reference the classes that provide regular expression functionality directly, without having to fully qualify them. For instance, you can write `Regex()` instead of `System.Text.RegularExpressions.Regex()`.

VB.NET

If you place the `Imports` statement at the top of your VB.NET source file, you can reference the classes that provide regular expression functionality directly, without having to fully qualify them. For instance, you can write `Regex()` instead of `System.Text.RegularExpressions.Regex()`.

Java

You have to import the `java.util.regex` package into your application to be able to use Java's built-in regular expression library.

JavaScript

JavaScript's regular expression support is built-in and always available.

PHP

The `preg` functions are built-in and always available in PHP 4.2.0 and later.

Perl

Perl's regular expression support is built-in and always available.

Python

You have to import the `re` module into your script to be able to use Python's regular expression functions.

Ruby

Ruby's regular expression support is built-in and always available.

3.3 Creating Regular Expression Objects

Problem

You want to instantiate a regular expression object or otherwise compile a regular expression so you can use it efficiently throughout your application.

Solution

C#

If you know the regex to be correct:

```
Regex regexObj = new Regex("regex pattern");
```

If the regex is provided by the end user (UserInput being a string variable):

```
try {
    Regex regexObj = new Regex(UserInput);
} catch (ArgumentException ex) {
    // Syntax error in the regular expression
}
```

VB.NET

If you know the regex to be correct:

```
Dim RegexObj As New Regex("regex pattern")
```

If the regex is provided by the end user (UserInput being a string variable):

```
Try
    Dim RegexObj As New Regex(UserInput)
Catch ex As ArgumentException
    'Syntax error in the regular expression
End Try
```

Java

If you know the regex to be correct:

```
Pattern regex = Pattern.compile("regex pattern");
```

If the regex is provided by the end user (userInput being a string variable):

```
try {
    Pattern regex = Pattern.compile(userInput);
} catch (PatternSyntaxException ex) {
    // Syntax error in the regular expression
}
```

To be able to use the regex on a string, create a `Matcher`:

```
Matcher regexMatcher = regex.matcher(subjectString);
```

To use the regex on another string, you can create a new `Matcher`, as just shown, or reuse an existing one:

```
regexMatcher.reset(anotherSubjectString);
```

JavaScript

Literal regular expression in your code:

```
var myregexp = /regex pattern/;
```

Regular expression retrieved from user input, as a string stored in the variable `userinput`:

```
var myregexp = new RegExp(userinput);
```

Perl

```
$myregex = qr/regex pattern/
```

Regular expression retrieved from user input, as a string stored in the variable `$userinput`:

```
$myregex = qr/$userinput/
```

Python

```
reobj = re.compile("regex pattern")
```

Regular expression retrieved from user input, as a string stored in the variable `userinput`:

```
reobj = re.compile(userinput)
```

Ruby

Literal regular expression in your code:

```
myregexp = /regex pattern/;
```

Regular expression retrieved from user input, as a string stored in the variable `userinput`:

```
myregexp = Regexp.new(userinput);
```

Discussion

Before the regular expression engine can match a regular expression to a string, the regular expression has to be compiled. This compilation happens while your application is running. The regular expression constructor or compile function parses the string that holds your regular expression and converts it into a tree structure or state machine. The function that does the actual pattern matching will traverse this tree or state machine as it scans the string. Programming languages that support literal regular expressions do the compilation when execution reaches the regular expression operator.

.NET

In C# and VB.NET, the .NET class `System.Text.RegularExpressions.Regex` holds one compiled regular expression. The simplest constructor takes just one parameter: a string that holds your regular expression.

If there's a syntax error in the regular expression, the `Regex()` constructor will throw an `ArgumentException`. The exception message will indicate exactly which error was encountered. It is important to catch this exception if the regular expression is provided by the user of your application. Display the exception message and ask the user to correct the regular expression. If your regular expression is a hardcoded string literal, you can omit catching the exception if you use a code coverage tool to make sure the line is executed without throwing an exception. There are no possible changes to state or mode that could cause the same literal regex to compile in one situation and fail to compile in another. Note that if there is a syntax error in your literal regex, the exception will occur when your application is run, not when your application is compiled.

You should construct a `Regex` object if you will be using the regular expression inside a loop or repeatedly throughout your application. Constructing the regex object involves no extra overhead. The static members of the `Regex` class that take the regex as a string parameter construct a `Regex` object internally anyway, so you might just as well do it in your own code and keep a reference to the object.

If you plan to use the regex only once or a few times, you can use the static members of the Regex class instead, to save a line of code. The static `Regex` members do not throw away the internally constructed regular expression object immediately; instead, they keep a cache of the 15 most recently used regular expressions. You can change the cache size by setting the `Regex.CacheSize` property. The cache lookup is done by looking up your regular expression string in the cache. But don't go overboard with the cache. If you need lots of regex objects frequently, keep a cache of your own that you can look up more efficiently than with a string search.

Java

In Java, the `Pattern` class holds one compiled regular expression. You can create objects of this class with the `Pattern.compile()` class factory, which requires just one parameter: a string with your regular expression.

If there's a syntax error in the regular expression, the `Pattern.compile()` factory will throw a `PatternSyntaxException`. The exception message will indicate exactly which error was encountered. It is important to catch this exception if the regular expression is provided by the user of your application. Display the exception message and ask the user to correct the regular expression. If your regular expression is a hardcoded string literal, you can omit catching the exception if you use a code coverage tool to make sure the line is executed without throwing an exception. There are no possible changes to state or mode that could cause the same literal regex to compile in one situation and fail to compile in another. Note that if there is a syntax error in your literal regex, the exception will occur when your application is run, not when your application is compiled.

Unless you plan to use a regex only once, you should create a `Pattern` object instead of using the static members of the `String` class. Though it takes a few lines of extra code, that code will run more efficiently. The static calls recompile your regex each and every time. In fact, Java provides static calls for only a few very basic regex tasks.

A `Pattern` object only stores a compiled regular expression; it does not do any actual work. The actual regex matching is done by the `Matcher` class. To create a `Matcher`, call the `matcher()` method on your compiled regular expression. Pass the subject string as the only argument to `matcher()`.

You can call `matcher()` as many times as you like to use the same regular expression on multiple strings. You can work with multiple matchers using the same regex at the same time, as long as you keep everything in a single thread. The `Pattern` and `Matcher` classes are not thread-safe. If you want to use the same regex in multiple threads, call `Pattern.compile()` in each thread.

If you're done applying a regex to one string and want to apply the same regex to another string, you can reuse the `Matcher` object by calling `reset()`. Pass the next subject string as the only argument. This is more efficient than creating a new `Matcher` object. `reset()` returns the same `Matcher` you called it on, allowing you to easily reset and use a matcher in one line of code, e.g., `regexMatcher.reset(nextString).find()`.

JavaScript

The notation for literal regular expressions shown in Recipe 3.2 already creates a new regular expression object. To use the same object repeatedly, simply assign it to a variable.

If you have a regular expression stored in a string variable (e.g., because you asked the user to type in a regular expression), use the `RegExp()` constructor to compile the regular expression. Notice that the regular expression inside the string is not delimited by forward slashes. Those slashes are part of JavaScript's notation for literal `RegExp` objects, rather than part of the regular expression itself.

Since assigning a literal regex to a variable is trivial, most of the JavaScript solutions in this chapter omit this line of code and use the literal regular expression directly. In your own code, when using the same regex more than once, you should assign the regex to a variable and use that variable instead of pasting the same literal regex multiple times into your code. This increases performance and makes your code easier to maintain.

PHP

PHP does not provide a way to store a compiled regular expression in a variable. Whenever you want to do something with a regular expression, you have to pass it as a string to one of the preg functions.

The preg functions keep a cache of up to 4,096 compiled regular expressions. Although the hash-based cache lookup is not as fast as referencing a variable, the performance hit is not as dramatic as having to recompile the same regular expression over and over. When the cache is full, the regex that was compiled the longest ago is removed.

Perl

You can use the "quote regex" operator to compile a regular expression and assign it to a variable. It uses the same syntax as the match operator described in Recipe 3.1, except that it starts with the letters qr instead of the letter m.

Perl is generally quite efficient at reusing previously compiled regular expressions. Therefore, we don't use qr// in the code samples in this chapter. Only Recipe 3.5 demonstrates its use.

qr// is useful when you're interpolating variables in the regular expression or when you've retrieved the whole regular expression as a string (e.g., from user input). With qr/$regexstring/, you can control when the regex is recompiled to reflect the new contents of $regexstring. m/$regexstring/ would recompile the regex every time, whereas m/$regexstring/o never recompiles it. Recipe 3.4 explains /o.

Python

The compile() function in Python's re module takes a string with your regular expression, and returns an object with your compiled regular expression.

You should call compile() explicitly if you plan to use the same regular expression repeatedly. All the functions in the re module first call compile(), and then call the function you wanted on the compiled regular expression object.

The compile() function keeps a reference to the last 100 regular expressions that it compiled. This reduces the recompilation of any of the last 100 used regular expressions to a dictionary lookup. When the cache is full, it is cleared out entirely.

If performance is not an issue, the cache works well enough that you can use the functions in the `re` module directly. But when performance matters, calling `compile()` is a good idea.

Ruby

The notation for literal regular expressions shown in Recipe 3.2 already creates a new regular expression object. To use the same object repeatedly, simply assign it to a variable.

If you have a regular expression stored in a string variable (e.g., because you asked the user to type in a regular expression), use the `Regexp.new()` factory or its synonym `Regexp.compile()` to compile the regular expression. Notice that the regular expression inside the string is not delimited by forward slashes. Those slashes are part of Ruby's notation for literal `Regexp` objects and are not part of the regular expression itself.

 Since assigning a literal regex to a variable is trivial, most of the Ruby solutions in this chapter omit this line of code and use the literal regular expression directly. In your own code, when using the same regex more than once, you should assign the regex to a variable and use the variable instead of pasting the same literal regex multiple times into your code. This increases performance and makes your code easier to maintain.

Compiling a Regular Expression Down to CIL

C#

```
Regex regexObj = new Regex("regex pattern", RegexOptions.Compiled);
```

VB.NET

```
Dim RegexObj As New Regex("regex pattern", RegexOptions.Compiled)
```

Discussion

When you construct a `Regex` object in .NET without passing any options, the regular expression is compiled in the way we described in "Discussion" on page 109. If you pass `RegexOptions.Compiled` as a second parameter to the `Regex()` constructor, the `Regex` class does something rather different: it compiles your regular expression down to CIL, also known as MSIL. CIL stands for Common Intermediate Language, a low-level programming language that is closer to assembly than to C# or Visual Basic. All .NET compilers produce CIL. The first time your application runs, the .NET framework compiles the CIL further down to machine code suitable for the user's computer.

The benefit of compiling a regular expression with `RegexOptions.Compiled` is that it can run up to 10 times faster than a regular expression compiled without this option.

The drawback is that this compilation can be up to two orders of magnitude slower than simply parsing the regex string into a tree. The CIL code also becomes a permanent part of your application until it is terminated. CIL code is not garbage collected.

Use `RegexOptions.Compiled` only if a regular expression is either so complex or needs to process so much text that the user experiences a noticeable wait during operations using the regular expression. The compilation and assembly overhead is not worth it for regexes that do their job in a split second.

See Also

Recipes 3.1, 3.2, and 3.4

3.4 Setting Regular Expression Options

Problem

You want to compile a regular expression with all of the available matching modes: free-spacing, case insensitive, dot matches line breaks, and caret and dollar match at line breaks.

Solution

C#

```
Regex regexObj = new Regex("regex pattern",
    RegexOptions.IgnorePatternWhitespace | RegexOptions.IgnoreCase |
    RegexOptions.Singleline | RegexOptions.Multiline);
```

VB.NET

```
Dim RegexObj As New Regex("regex pattern",
    RegexOptions.IgnorePatternWhitespace Or RegexOptions.IgnoreCase Or
    RegexOptions.Singleline Or RegexOptions.Multiline)
```

Java

```
Pattern regex = Pattern.compile("regex pattern",
    Pattern.COMMENTS | Pattern.CASE_INSENSITIVE | Pattern.UNICODE_CASE |
    Pattern.DOTALL | Pattern.MULTILINE);
```

JavaScript

Literal regular expression in your code:

```
var myregexp = /regex pattern/im;
```

Regular expression retrieved from user input, as a string:

```
var myregexp = new RegExp(userinput, "im");
```

PHP

```
regexstring = '/regex pattern/simx';
```

Perl

```
m/regex pattern/simx;
```

Python

```
reobj = re.compile("regex pattern",
    re.VERBOSE | re.IGNORECASE |
    re.DOTALL | re.MULTILINE)
```

Ruby

Literal regular expression in your code:

```
myregexp = /regex pattern/mix;
```

Regular expression retrieved from user input, as a string:

```
myregexp = Regexp.new(userinput,
    Regexp::EXTENDED or Regexp::IGNORECASE or
    Regexp::MULTILINE);
```

Discussion

Many of the regular expressions in this book, and those that you find elsewhere, are written to be used with certain regex matching modes. There are four basic modes that nearly all modern regex flavors support. Unfortunately, some flavors use inconsistent and confusing names for the options that implement the modes. Using the wrong modes usually breaks the regular expression.

All the solutions in this recipe use flags or options provided by the programming language or regular expression class to set the modes. Another way to set modes is to use mode modifiers within the regular expression. Mode modifiers within the regex always override options or flags set outside the regular expression.

.NET

The Regex() constructor takes an optional second parameter with regular expressions options. You can find the available options in the RegexOptions enumeration.

Free-spacing: RegexOptions.IgnorePatternWhitespace
Case insensitive: RegexOptions.IgnoreCase
Dot matches line breaks: RegexOptions.Singleline
Caret and dollar match at line breaks: RegexOptions.Multiline

Java

The `Pattern.compile()` class factory takes an optional second parameter with regular expressions options. The `Pattern` class defines several constants that set the various options. You can set multiple options by combining them with the bitwise inclusive or operator |.

Free-spacing: `Pattern.COMMENTS`
Case insensitive: `Pattern.CASE_INSENSITIVE | Pattern.UNICODE_CASE`
Dot matches line breaks: `Pattern.DOTALL`
Caret and dollar match at line breaks: `Pattern.MULTILINE`

There are indeed two options for case insensitivity, and you have to set both for full case insensitivity. If you set only `Pattern.CASE_INSENSITIVE`, only the English letters A to Z are matched case insensitively. If you set both options, all characters from all scripts are matched case insensitively. The only reason not to use `Pattern.UNICODE_CASE` is performance, in case you know in advance you'll be dealing with ASCII text only. When using mode modifiers inside your regular expression, use ‹(?i)› for ASCII-only case insensitivity and ‹(?iu)› for full case insensitivity.

JavaScript

In JavaScript, you can specify options by appending one or more single-letter flags to the `RegExp` literal, after the forward slash that terminates the regular expression. When talking about these flags in documentation, they are usually written as /i and /m, even though the flag itself is only one letter. No additional slashes are added to specify regex mode flags.

When using the `RegExp()` constructor to compile a string into a regular expression, you can pass an optional second parameter with flags to the constructor. The second parameter should be a string with the letters of the options you want to set. Do not put any slashes into the string.

Free-spacing: Not supported by JavaScript.
Case insensitive: /i
Dot matches line breaks: Not supported by JavaScript.
Caret and dollar match at line breaks: /m

PHP

Recipe 3.1 explains that the PHP `preg` functions require literal regular expressions to be delimited with two punctuation characters, usually forward slashes, and the whole lot formatted as a string literal. You can specify regular expression options by appending one or more single-letter modifiers to the end of the string. That is, the modifier letters come after the closing regex delimiter, but still inside the string's single or double quotes. When talking about these modifiers in documentation, they are usually written as /x, even though the flag itself is only one letter, and even though the delimiter between the regex and the modifiers doesn't have to be a forward slash.

Free-spacing: /x
Case insensitive: /i
Dot matches line breaks: /s
Caret and dollar match at line breaks: /m

Perl

You can specify regular expression options by appending one or more single-letter modifiers to the end of the pattern-matching or substitution operator. When talking about these modifiers in documentation, they are usually written as /x, even though the flag itself is only one letter, and even though the delimiter between the regex and the modifiers doesn't have to be a forward slash.

Free-spacing: /x
Case insensitive: /i
Dot matches line breaks: /s
Caret and dollar match at line breaks: /m

Python

The `compile()` function (explained in the previous recipe) takes an optional second parameter with regular expression options. You can build up this parameter by using the | operator to combine the constants defined in the `re` module. Many of the other functions in the `re` module that take a literal regular expression as a parameter also accept regular expression options as a final and optional parameter.

The constants for the regular expression options come in pairs. Each option can be represented either as a constant with a full name or as just a single letter. Their functionality is equivalent. The only difference is that the full name makes your code easier to read by developers who aren't familiar with the alphabet soup of regular expression options. The basic single-letter options listed in this section are the same as in Perl.

Free-spacing: `re.VERBOSE` or `re.X`
Case insensitive: `re.IGNORECASE` or `re.I`
Dot matches line breaks: `re.DOTALL` or `re.S`
Caret and dollar match at line breaks: `re.MULTILINE` or `re.M`

Ruby

In Ruby, you can specify options by appending one or more single-letter flags to the `Regexp` literal, after the forward slash that terminates the regular expression. When talking about these flags in documentation, they are usually written as /i and /m, even though the flag itself is only one letter. No additional slashes are added to specify regex mode flags.

When using the `Regexp.new()` factory to compile a string into a regular expression, you can pass an optional second parameter with flags to the constructor. The second parameter should be either `nil` to turn off all options, or a combination of constants from the `Regexp` class combined with the **or** operator.

Free-spacing: /r or Regexp::EXTENDED

Case insensitive: /i or Regexp::IGNORECASE

Dot matches line breaks: /m or Regexp::MULTILINE. Ruby indeed uses "m" and "multi line" here, whereas all the other flavors use "s" or "single line" for "dot matches line breaks".

Caret and dollar match at line breaks: The caret and dollar always match at line breaks in Ruby. You cannot turn this off. Use ‹\A› and ‹\Z› to match at the start or end of the subject string.

Additional Language-Specific Options

.NET

`RegexOptions.ExplicitCapture` makes all groups, except named groups, noncapturing. With this option, ‹(group)› is the same as ‹(?:group)›. If you always name your capturing groups, turn on this option to make your regular expression more efficient without the need to use the ‹(?:group)› syntax. Instead of using `RegexOptions.Explicit Capture`, you can turn on this option by putting ‹(?n)› at the start of your regular expression. See Recipe 2.9 to learn about grouping. Recipe 2.11 explains named groups.

Specify `RegexOptions.ECMAScript` if you're using the same regular expression in your .NET code and in JavaScript code, and you want to make sure it behaves in the same way. This is particularly useful when you're developing the client side of a web application in JavaScript and the server side in ASP.NET. The most important effect is that with this option, \w and \d are restricted to ASCII characters, as they are in JavaScript.

Java

An option unique to Java is `Pattern.CANON_EQ`, which enables "canonical equivalence." As explained in the discussion in "Unicode grapheme" on page 52, Unicode provides different ways to represent characters with diacritics. When you turn on this option, your regex will match a character, even if it is encoded differently in the subject string. For instance, the regex ‹\u00E0› will match both "\u00E0" and "\u0061\u0300", because they are canonically equivalent. They both appear as "à" when displayed on screen, indistinguishable to the end user. Without canonical equivalence, the regex ‹\u00E0› does not match the string "\u0061\u0300". This is how all other regex flavors discussed in this book behave.

Finally, `Pattern.UNIX_LINES` tells Java to treat only ‹\n› as a line break character for the dot, caret, and dollar. By default, all Unicode line breaks are treated as line break characters.

JavaScript

If you want to apply a regular expression repeatedly to the same string—e.g., to iterate over all matches or to search and replace all matches instead of just the first—specify the /g or "global" flag.

PHP

/u tells PCRE to interpret both the regular expression and the subject string as UTF-8 strings. This modifier also enables Unicode regex tokens such as ‹\p{FFFF}› and ‹\p{L}›. These are explained in Recipe 2.7. Without this modifier, PCRE treats each byte as a separate character, and Unicode regex tokens cause an error.

/U flips the "greedy" and "lazy" behavior of adding an extra question mark to a quantifier. Normally, ‹.*› is greedy and ‹.*?› is lazy. With /U, ‹.*› is lazy and ‹.*?› is greedy. I strongly recommend that you never use this flag, as it will confuse programmers who read your code later and miss the extra /U modifier, which is unique to PHP. Also, don't confuse /U with /u if you encounter it in somebody else's code. Regex modifiers are case sensitive.

Perl

If you want to apply a regular expression repeatedly to the same string (e.g., to iterate over all matches or to search-and-replace all matches instead of just the first one), specify the /g ("global") flag.

If you interpolate a variable in a regex—e.g., m/I am $name/—Perl will recompile the regular expression each time it needs to be used, because the contents of $name may have changed. You can suppress this with the /o modifier. m/I am $name/o is compiled the first time Perl needs to use it, and then reused the way it is after that. If the contents of $name change, the regex will not reflect the change. See Recipe 3.3 if you want to control when the regex is recompiled.

Python

Python has two extra options that change the meaning of word boundaries (see Recipe 2.6) and the shorthand character classes ‹\w›, ‹\d›, and ‹\s›, as well as their negated counterparts (see Recipe 2.3). By default, these tokens deal only with ASCII letters, digits, and whitespace.

The `re.LOCALE` or `re.L` option makes these tokens dependent on the current locale. The locale then determines which characters are treated as letters, digits, and whitespace by these regex tokens. You should specify this option when the subject string is not a

Unicode string and you want characters such as letters with diacritics to be treated as such.

The re.UNICODE or re.U makes these tokens dependent on the Unicode standard. All characters defined by Unicode as letters, digits, and whitespace are then treated as such by these regex tokens. You should specify this option when the subject string you're applying the regular expression to is a Unicode string.

Ruby

The Regexp.new() factory takes an optional third parameter to select the string encoding your regular expression supports. If you do not specify an encoding for your regular expression, it will use the same encoding as your source file. Most of the time, using the source file's encoding is the right thing to do.

To select a coding explicitly, pass a single character for this parameter. The parameter is case-insensitive. Possible values are:

n

This stands for "None." Each byte in your string is treated as one character. Use this for ASCII text.

e

Enables the "EUC" encoding for Far East languages.

s

Enables the Japanese "Shift-JIS" encoding.

u

Enables UTF-8, which uses one to four bytes per character and supports all languages in the Unicode standard (which includes all living languages of any significance).

When using a literal regular expression, you can set the encoding with the modifiers /n, /e, /s, and /u. Only one of these modifiers can be used for a single regular expression. They can be used in combination with any or all of the /x, /i, and /m modifiers.

 Do not mistake Ruby's /s for that of Perl, Java, or .NET. In Ruby, /s forces the Shift-JIS encoding. In Perl and most other regex flavors, it turns on "dot matches line breaks" mode. In Ruby, you can do that with /m.

See Also

The effects of the matching modes are explained in detail in Chapter 2. Those sections also explain the use of mode modifiers within the regular expression.

Free-spacing: Recipe 2.18
Case insensitive: "Case-insensitive matching" on page 27 in Recipe 2.1
Dot matches line breaks: Recipe 2.4
Caret and dollar match at line breaks: Recipe 2.5

Recipes 3.1 and 3.3 explain how to use literal regular expressions in your source code and how to create regular expression objects. You set the regular expression options while creating a regular expression.

3.5 Test Whether a Match Can Be Found Within a Subject String

Problem

You want to check whether a match can be found for a particular regular expression in a particular string. A partial match is sufficient. For instance, the regex ‹regex•pattern› partially matches `The regex pattern can be found`. You don't care about any of the details of the match. You just want to know whether the regex matches the string.

Solution

C#

For quick one-off tests, you can use the static call:

```
bool foundMatch = Regex.IsMatch(subjectString, "regex pattern");
```

If the regex is provided by the end user, you should use the static call with full exception handling:

```
bool foundMatch = false;
try {
    foundMatch = Regex.IsMatch(subjectString, UserInput);
} catch (ArgumentNullException ex) {
    // Cannot pass null as the regular expression or subject string
} catch (ArgumentException ex) {
    // Syntax error in the regular expression
}
```

To use the same regex repeatedly, construct a **Regex** object:

```
Regex regexObj = new Regex("regex pattern");
bool foundMatch = regexObj.IsMatch(subjectString);
```

If the regex is provided by the end user, you should use the **Regex** object with full exception handling:

```
bool foundMatch = false;
try {
```

```
        Regex regexObj = new Regex(UserInput);
        try {
            foundMatch = regexObj.IsMatch(subjectString);
        } catch (ArgumentNullException ex) {
            // Cannot pass null as the regular expression or subject string
        }
    } catch (ArgumentException ex) {
        // Syntax error in the regular expression
    }
```

VB.NET

For quick one-off tests, you can use the static call:

```
Dim FoundMatch = Regex.IsMatch(SubjectString, "regex pattern")
```

If the regex is provided by the end user, you should use the static call with full exception handling:

```
Dim FoundMatch As Boolean
Try
    FoundMatch = Regex.IsMatch(SubjectString, UserInput)
Catch ex As ArgumentNullException
    'Cannot pass Nothing as the regular expression or subject string
Catch ex As ArgumentException
    'Syntax error in the regular expression
End Try
```

To use the same regex repeatedly, construct a **Regex** object:

```
Dim RegexObj As New Regex("regex pattern")
Dim FoundMatch = RegexObj.IsMatch(SubjectString)
```

The IsMatch() call should have SubjectString as the only parameter, and the call should be made on the RegexObj instance rather than the Regex class:

```
Dim FoundMatch = RegexObj.IsMatch(SubjectString)
```

If the regex is provided by the end user, you should use the **Regex** object with full exception handling:

```
Dim FoundMatch As Boolean
Try
    Dim RegexObj As New Regex(UserInput)
    Try
        FoundMatch = Regex.IsMatch(SubjectString)
    Catch ex As ArgumentNullException
        'Cannot pass Nothing as the regular expression or subject string
    End Try
Catch ex As ArgumentException
    'Syntax error in the regular expression
End Try
```

Java

The only way to test for a partial match is to create a `Matcher`:

```
Pattern regex = Pattern.compile("regex pattern");
Matcher regexMatcher = regex.matcher(subjectString);
boolean foundMatch = regexMatcher.find();
```

If the regex is provided by the end user, you should use exception handling:

```
boolean foundMatch = false;
try {
    Pattern regex = Pattern.compile(UserInput);
    Matcher regexMatcher = regex.matcher(subjectString);
    foundMatch = regexMatcher.find();
} catch (PatternSyntaxException ex) {
    // Syntax error in the regular expression
}
```

JavaScript

```
if (/regex pattern/.test(subject)) {
    // Successful match
} else {
    // Match attempt failed
}
```

PHP

```
if (preg_match('/regex pattern/', $subject)) {
    # Successful match
} else {
    # Match attempt failed
}
```

Perl

With the subject string held in the special variable $_:

```
if (m/regex pattern/) {
    # Successful match
} else {
    # Match attempt failed
}
```

With the subject string held in the variable $subject:

```
if ($subject =~ m/regex pattern/) {
    # Successful match
} else {
    # Match attempt failed
}
```

Using a precompiled regular expression:

```
$regex = qr/regex pattern/;
if ($subject =~ $regex) {
    # Successful match
} else {
    # Match attempt failed
}
```

Python

For quick one-off tests, you can use the global function:

```
if re.search("regex pattern", subject):
    # Successful match
else:
    # Match attempt failed
```

To use the same regex repeatedly, use a compiled object:

```
reobj = re.compile("regex pattern")
if reobj.search(subject):
    # Successful match
else:
    # Match attempt failed
```

Ruby

```
if subject =~ /regex pattern/
    # Successful match
else
    # Match attempt failed
end
```

This code does exactly the same thing:

```
if /regex pattern/ =~ subject
    # Successful match
else
    # Match attempt failed
end
```

Discussion

The most basic task for a regular expression is to check whether a string matches the regex. In most programming languages, a partial match is sufficient for the match function to return true. The match function will scan through the entire subject string to see whether the regular expression matches any part of it. The function returns true as soon as a match is found. It returns false only when it reaches the end of the string without finding any matches.

The code examples in this recipe are useful for checking whether a string contains certain data. If you want to check whether a string fits a certain pattern in its entirety (e.g., for input validation), use the next recipe instead.

C# and VB.NET

The `Regex` class provides four overloaded versions of the `IsMatch()` method, two of which are static. This makes it possible to call `IsMatch()` with different parameters. The subject string is always the first parameter. This is the string in which the regular expression will try to find a match. The first parameter must not be `null`. Otherwise, `IsMatch()` will throw an `ArgumentNullException`.

You can perform the test in a single line of code by calling `Regex.IsMatch()` without constructing a `Regex` object. Simply pass the regular expression as the second parameter and pass regex options as an optional third parameter. If your regular expression has a syntax error, an `ArgumentException` will be thrown by `IsMatch()`. If your regex is valid, the call will return `true` if a partial match was found, or `false` if no match could be found at all.

If you want to use the same regular expression on many strings, you can make your code more efficient by constructing a `Regex` object first, and calling `IsMatch()` on that object. The first parameter, which holds the subject string, is then the only required parameter. You can specify an optional second parameter to indicate the character index at which the regular expression should begin the check. Essentially, the number you pass as the second parameter is the number of characters at the start of your subject string that the regular expression should ignore. This can be useful when you've already processed the string up to a point, and you want to check whether the remainder should be processed further. If you specify a number, it must be greater than or equal to zero and less than or equal to the length of the subject string. Otherwise, `IsMatch()` throws an `ArgumentOutOfRangeException`.

The static overloads do not allow for the parameter that specifies where the regex attempt should start in the string. There is no overload that allows you to tell `IsMatch()` to stop before the end of the string. If you want to do that, you could call `Regex.Match("subject", start, stop)` and check the `Success` property of the returned `Match` object. See Recipe 3.8 for details.

Java

To test whether a regex matches a string partially or entirely, instantiate a `Matcher` object as explained in Recipe 3.3. Then call the `find()` method on your newly created or newly reset matcher.

Do not call `String.matches()`, `Pattern.matches()`, or `Matcher.matches()`. Those all require the regex to match the whole string.

JavaScript

To test whether a regular expression can match part of a string, call the `test()` method on your regular expression. Pass the subject string as the only parameter.

`regexp.test()` returns `true` if the regular expression matches part or all of the subject string, and `false` if it does not.

PHP

The `preg_match()` function can be used for a variety of purposes. The most basic way to call it is with only the two required parameters: the string with your regular expression, and the string with the subject text you want the regex to search through. `preg_match()` returns `1` if a match can be found and `0` when the regex cannot match the subject at all.

Later recipes in this chapter explain the optional parameters you can pass to `preg_match()`.

Perl

In Perl, `m//` is in fact a regular expression operator, not a mere regular expression container. If you use `m//` by itself, it uses the `$_` variable as the subject string.

If you want to use the matching operator on the contents of another variable, use the `=~` binding operator to associate the regex operator with your variable. Binding the regex to a string immediately executes the regex. The pattern-matching operator returns true if the regex matches part of the subject string, and false if it doesn't match at all.

If you want to check whether a regular expression does not match a string, you can use `!~`, which is the negated version of `=~`.

Python

The `search()` function in the `re` module searches through a string to find whether the regular expression matches part of it. Pass your regular expression as the first parameter and the subject string as the second parameter. You can pass the regular expression options in the optional third parameter.

The `re.search()` function calls `re.compile()`, and then calls the `search()` method on the compiled regular expression object. This method takes just one parameter: the subject string.

If the regular expression finds a match, `search()` returns a `MatchObject` instance. If the regex fails to match, `search()` returns `None`. When you evaluate the returned value in an `if` statement, the `MatchObject` evaluates to `True`, whereas `None` evaluates to `False`. Later recipes in this chapter show how to use the information stored by `MatchObject`.

Don't confuse search() with match(). You cannot use match() to find a match in the middle of a string. The next recipe uses match().

Ruby

The =~ operator is the pattern-matching operator. Place it between a regular expression and a string to find the first regular expression match. The operator returns an integer with the position at which the regex match begins in the string. It returns nil if no match can be found.

This operator is implemented in both the Regexp and String classes. In Ruby 1.8, it doesn't matter which class you place to the left and which to the right of the operator. In Ruby 1.9, doing so has a special side effect involving named capturing groups. Recipe 3.9 explains this.

In all the other Ruby code snippets in this book, we place the subject string to the left of the =~ operator and the regular expression to the right. This maintains consistency with Perl, from which Ruby borrowed the =~ syntax, and avoids the Ruby 1.9 magic with named capturing groups that people might not expect.

See Also

Recipes 3.6 and 3.7

3.6 Test Whether a Regex Matches the Subject String Entirely

Problem

You want to check whether a string fits a certain pattern in its entirety. That is, you want to check that the regular expression holding the pattern can match the string from start to end. For instance, if your regex is ‹regex•pattern›, it will match input text consisting of regex pattern but not the longer string The regex pattern can be found.

Solution

C#

For quick one-off tests, you can use the static call:

```
bool foundMatch = Regex.IsMatch(subjectString, @"\Aregex pattern\Z");
```

To use the same regex repeatedly, construct a **Regex** object:

```
Regex regexObj = new Regex(@"\Aregex pattern\Z");
bool foundMatch = regexObj.IsMatch(subjectString);
```

VB.NET

For quick one-off tests, you can use the static call:

```
Dim FoundMatch = Regex.IsMatch(SubjectString, "\Aregex pattern\Z")
```

To use the same regex repeatedly, construct a **Regex** object:

```
Dim RegexObj As New Regex("\Aregex pattern\Z")
Dim FoundMatch = RegexObj.IsMatch(SubjectString)
```

The `IsMatch()` call should have `SubjectString` as the only parameter, and the call should be made on the `RegexObj` instance rather than the `Regex` class:

```
Dim FoundMatch = RegexObj.IsMatch(SubjectString)
```

Java

If you want to test just one string, you can use the static call:

```
boolean foundMatch = subjectString.matches("regex pattern");
```

If you want to use the same regex on multiple strings, compile your regex and create a matcher:

```
Pattern regex = Pattern.compile("regex pattern");
Matcher regexMatcher = regex.matcher(subjectString);
boolean foundMatch = regexMatcher.matches(subjectString);
```

JavaScript

```
if (/^regex pattern$/.test(subject)) {
    // Successful match
} else {
    // Match attempt failed
}
```

PHP

```
if (preg_match('/\Aregex pattern\Z/', $subject)) {
    # Successful match
} else {
    # Match attempt failed
}
```

Perl

```
if ($subject =~ m/\Aregex pattern\Z/) {
    # Successful match
} else {
    # Match attempt failed
}
```

Python

For quick one-off tests, you can use the global function:

```
if re.match(r"regex pattern\Z", subject):
    # Successful match
else:
    # Match attempt failed
```

To use the same regex repeatedly, use a compiled object:

```
reobj = re.compile(r"regex pattern\Z")
if reobj.match(subject):
    # Successful match
else:
    # Match attempt failed
```

Ruby

```
if subject =~ /\Aregex pattern\Z/
    # Successful match
else
    # Match attempt failed
end
```

Discussion

Normally, a successful regular expression match tells you that the pattern you want is *somewhere* within the subject text. In many situations you also want to make sure it *completely* matches, with nothing else in the subject text. Probably the most common situation calling for a complete match is validating input. If a user enters a phone number or IP address but includes extraneous characters, you want to reject the input.

The solutions that use the anchors ‹$› and ‹\Z› also work when you're processing a file line by line (Recipe 3.21), and the mechanism you're using to retrieve the lines leaves the line breaks at the end of the line. As Recipe 2.5 explains, these anchors also match before a final line break, essentially allowing the final line break to be ignored.

In the following subsections, we explain the solutions for various languages in detail.

C# and VB.NET

The `Regex()` class in the .NET framework does not have a function for testing whether a regex matches a string entirely. The solution is to add the start-of-string anchor ‹\A› to the start of your regular expression, and the end-of-string anchor ‹\Z› to the end of your regular expression. This way, the regular expression can only match a string either in its entirety or not at all. If your regular expression uses alternation, as in ‹one|two| three›, make sure to group the alternation before adding the anchors: ‹\A(?:one|two| three)\Z›.

With your regular expression amended to match whole strings, you can use the same `IsMatch()` method as described in the previous recipe.

Java

Java has three methods called `matches()`. They all check whether a regex can match a string entirely. These methods are a quick way to do input validation, without having to enclose your regex with start-of-string and end-of-string anchors.

The `String` class has a `matches()` method that takes a regular expression as the only parameter. It returns `true` or `false` to indicate whether the regex can match the whole string. The `Pattern` class has a static `matches()` method, which takes two strings: the first is the regular expression, and the second is the subject string. Actually, you can pass any `CharSequence` as the subject string to `Pattern.matches()`. That's the only reason for using `Pattern.matches()` instead of `String.matches()`.

Both `String.matches()` and `Pattern.matches()` recompile the regular expression each time by calling `Pattern.compile("regex").matcher(subjectString).matches()`. Because the regex is recompiled each time, you should use these calls only when you want to use the regex only once (e.g., to validate one field on an input form) or when efficiency is not an issue. These methods don't provide a way to specify matching options outside of the regular expression. A `PatternSyntaxException` is thrown if your regular expression has a syntax error.

If you want to use the same regex to test many strings efficiently, you should compile your regex and create and reuse a `Matcher`, as explained in Recipe 3.3. Then call `matches()` on your `Matcher` instance. This function does not take any parameters, because you've already specified the subject string when creating or resetting the matcher.

JavaScript

JavaScript does not have a function for testing whether a regex matches a string entirely. The solution is to add ‹^› to the start of your regular expression, and ‹$› to the end of your regular expression. Make sure that you do not set the /m flag for your regular expression. Only without /m do the caret and dollar match only at the start and end of the subject string. When you set /m, they also match at line breaks in the middle of the string.

With the anchors added to your regular expression, you can use the same `regexp.test()` method described in the previous recipe.

PHP

PHP does not have a function for testing whether a regex matches a string entirely. The solution is to add the start-of-string anchor ‹\A› to the start of your regular expression, and the end-of-string anchor ‹\Z› to the end of your regular expression. This way, the regular expression can only match a string either in its entirety or not at all. If your regular expression uses alternation, as in ‹one|two|three›, make sure to group the alternation before adding the anchors: ‹\A(?:one|two|three)\Z›.

With your regular expression amended to match whole strings, you can use the same `preg_match()` function as described in the previous recipe.

Perl

Perl has only one pattern-matching operator, which is satisfied with partial matches. If you want to check whether your regex matches the whole subject string, add the start-of-string anchor ‹\A› to the start of your regular expression, and the end-of-string anchor ‹\Z› to the end of your regular expression. This way, the regular expression can only match a string either in its entirety or not at all. If your regular expression uses alternation, as in ‹one|two|three›, make sure to group the alternation before adding the anchors: ‹\A(?:one|two|three)\Z›.

With your regular expression amended to match whole strings, use it as described in the previous recipe.

Python

The `match()` function is very similar to the `search()` function described in the previous recipe. The key difference is that `match()` evaluates the regular expression only at the very beginning of the subject string. If the regex does not match at the start of the string, `match()` returns None right away. The `search()` function, however, will keep trying the regex at each successive position in the string until it either finds a match or reaches the end of the subject string.

The `match()` function does not require the regular expression to match the whole string. A partial match is accepted, as long as it begins at the start of the string. If you want to check whether your regex can match the whole string, append the end-of-string anchor ‹\Z› to your regular expression.

Ruby

Ruby's `Regexp` class does not have a function for testing whether a regex matches a string entirely. The solution is to add the start-of-string anchor ‹\A› to the start of your regular expression, and the end-of-string anchor ‹\Z› to the end of your regular expression. This way, the regular expression can only match a string either in its entirety or not at all. If your regular expression uses alternation, as in ‹one|two|three›, make sure to group the alternation before adding the anchors: ‹\A(?:one|two|three)\Z›.

With your regular expression amended to match whole strings, you can use the same =~ operator as described in the previous recipe.

See Also

Recipe 2.5 explains in detail how anchors work.

Recipes 2.8 and 2.9 explain alternation and grouping. If your regex uses alternation outside of any groups, you need to group your regex before adding the anchors. If your regex does not use alternation, or if it uses alternation only within groups, then no extra grouping is needed to make the anchors work as intended.

Follow Recipe 3.7 when partial matches are acceptable.

3.7 Retrieve the Matched Text

Problem

You have a regular expression that matches a part of the subject text, and you want to extract the text that was matched. If the regular expression can match the string more than once, you want only the first match. For example, when applying the regex ‹\d+› to the string Do you like 13 or 42?, 13 should be returned.

Solution

C#

For quick one-off matches, you can use the static call:

```
string resultString = Regex.Match(subjectString, @"\d+").Value;
```

If the regex is provided by the end user, you should use the static call with full exception handling:

```
string resultString = null;
try {
    resultString = Regex.Match(subjectString, @"\d+").Value;
} catch (ArgumentNullException ex) {
    // Cannot pass null as the regular expression or subject string
} catch (ArgumentException ex) {
    // Syntax error in the regular expression
}
```

To use the same regex repeatedly, construct a Regex object:

```
Regex regexObj = new Regex(@"\d+");
string resultString = regexObj.Match(subjectString).Value;
```

If the regex is provided by the end user, you should use the Regex object with full exception handling:

```
string resultString = null;
try {
    Regex regexObj = new Regex(@"\d+");
    try {
        resultString = regexObj.Match(subjectString).Value;
    } catch (ArgumentNullException ex) {
        // Cannot pass null as the subject string
    }
} catch (ArgumentException ex) {
    // Syntax error in the regular expression
}
```

VB.NET

For quick one-off matches, you can use the static call:

```
Dim ResultString  = Regex.Match(SubjectString, "\d+").Value
```

If the regex is provided by the end user, you should use the static call with full exception handling:

```
Dim ResultString As String = Nothing
Try
    ResultString = Regex.Match(SubjectString, "\d+").Value
Catch ex As ArgumentNullException
    'Cannot pass Nothing as the regular expression or subject string
Catch ex As ArgumentException
    'Syntax error in the regular expression
End Try
```

To use the same regex repeatedly, construct a Regex object:

```
Dim RegexObj As New Regex("\d+")
Dim ResultString = RegexObj.Match(SubjectString).Value
```

If the regex is provided by the end user, you should use the Regex object with full exception handling:

```
Dim ResultString As String = Nothing
Try
    Dim RegexObj As New Regex("\d+")
    Try
        ResultString = RegexObj.Match(SubjectString).Value
    Catch ex As ArgumentNullException
        'Cannot pass Nothing as the subject string
    End Try
```

```
Catch ex As ArgumentException
    'Syntax error in the regular expression
End Try
```

Java

Create a `Matcher` to run the search and store the result:

```java
String resultString = null;
Pattern regex = Pattern.compile("\\d+");
Matcher regexMatcher = regex.matcher(subjectString);
if (regexMatcher.find()) {
    resultString = regexMatcher.group();
}
```

If the regex is provided by the end user, you should use full exception handling:

```java
String resultString = null;
try {
    Pattern regex = Pattern.compile("\\d+");
    Matcher regexMatcher = regex.matcher(subjectString);
    if (regexMatcher.find()) {
        resultString = regexMatcher.group();
    }
} catch (PatternSyntaxException ex) {
    // Syntax error in the regular expression
}
```

JavaScript

```javascript
var result = subject.match(/\d+/);
if (result) {
    result = result[0];
} else {
    result = '';
}
```

PHP

```php
if (preg_match('/\d+/', $subject, $groups)) {
    $result = $groups[0];
} else {
    $result = '';
}
```

Perl

```perl
if ($subject =~ m/\d+/) {
    $result = $&;
} else {
```

```
    $result = '';
}
```

Python

For quick one-off matches, you can use the global function:

```
matchobj = re.search("regex pattern", subject)
if matchobj:
    result = matchobj.group()
else:
    result = ""
```

To use the same regex repeatedly, use a compiled object:

```
reobj = re.compile("regex pattern")
matchobj = reobj.search(subject)
if match:
    result = matchobj.group()
else:
    result = ""
```

Ruby

You can use the =~ operator and its magic $& variable:

```
if subject =~ /regex pattern/
    result = $&
else
    result = ""
end
```

Alternatively, you can call the match method on a Regexp object:

```
matchobj = /regex pattern/.match(subject)
if matchobj
    result = matchobj[0]
else
    result = ""
end
```

Discussion

Extracting the part of a longer string that fits the pattern is another prime job for regular expressions. All programming languages discussed in this book provide an easy way to get the first regular expression match from a string. The function will attempt the regular expression at the start of the string and continue scanning through the string until the regular expression matches.

.NET

The .NET Regex class does not have a member that returns the string matched by the regular expression. But it does have a Match() method that returns an instance of the Match class. This Match object has a property called Value, which holds the text matched by the regular expression. If the regular expression fails to match, it still returns a Match object, but the Value property holds an empty string.

A total of five overloads allows you to call the Match() method in various ways. The first parameter is always the string that holds the subject text in which you want the regular expression to find a match. This parameter should not be null. Otherwise, Match() will throw an ArgumentNullException.

If you want to use the regular expression only a few times, you can use a static call. The second parameter is then the regular expression you want to use. You can pass regex options as an optional third parameter. If your regular expression has a syntax error, an ArgumentException will be thrown.

If you want to use the same regular expression on many strings, you can make your code more efficient by constructing a Regex object first and then calling Match() on that object. The first parameter with the subject string is then the only required parameter. You can specify an optional second parameter to indicate the character index at which the regular expression should begin to search. Essentially, the number you pass as the second parameter is the number of characters at the start of your subject string that the regular expression should ignore. This can be useful when you've already processed the string up to a point and want to search the remainder of the string. If you specify this number, it must be in the range from zero to the length of the subject string. Otherwise, IsMatch() throws an ArgumentOutOfRangeException.

If you specify the second parameter with the starting position, you can specify a third parameter that indicates the length of the substring the regular expression is allowed to search through. This number must be greater than or equal to zero and must not exceed the length of the subject string (first parameter) minus the starting offset (second parameter). For instance, regexObj.Match("123456", 3, 2) tries to find a match in "45". If the third parameter is greater than the length of the subject string, Match() throws an ArgumentOutOfRangeException. If the third parameter is not greater than the length of the subject string, but the sum of the second and third parameters is greater than the length of the string, then another IndexOutOfRangeException is thrown. If you allow the user to specify starting and ending positions, either check them before calling Match() or make sure to catch both out-of-range exceptions.

The static overloads do not allow for the parameters that specify which part of the string the regular expression can search through.

Java

To get the part of a string matched by a regular expression, you need to create a `Matcher`, as explained in Recipe 3.3. Then call the `find()` method on your matcher, without any parameters. If `find()` returns `true`, call `group()` without any parameters to retrieve the text matched by your regular expression. If `find()` returns `false`, you should not call `group()`, as all you'll get is an `IllegalStateException`.

`Matcher.find()` takes one optional parameter with the starting position in the subject string. You can use this to begin the search at a certain position in the string. Specify zero to begin the match attempt at the start of the string. An `IndexOutOf BoundsException` is thrown if you set the starting position to a negative number, or to a number greater than the length of the subject string.

If you omit the parameter, `find()` starts at the character after the previous match found by `find()`. If you're calling `find()` for the first time after `Pattern.matcher()` or `Matcher.reset()`, then `find()` begins searching at the start of the string.

JavaScript

The `string.match()` method takes a regular expression as its only parameter. You can pass the regular expression as a literal regex, a regular expression object, or as a string. If you pass a string, `string.match()` creates a temporary `regexp` object.

When the match attempt fails, `string.match()` returns `null`. This allows you to differentiate between a regex that finds no matches, and a regex that finds a zero-length match. It does mean that you cannot directly display the result, as "null" or an error about a null object may appear.

When the match attempt succeeds, `string.match()` returns an array with the details of the match. Element zero in the array is a string that holds the text matched by the regular expression.

Make sure that you do not add the /g flag to your regular expression. If you do, `string.match()` behaves differently, as Recipe 3.10 explains.

PHP

The `preg_match()` function discussed in the previous two recipes takes an optional third parameter to store the text matched by the regular expression and its capturing groups. When `preg_match()` returns `1`, the variable holds an array of strings. Element zero in the array holds the overall regular expression match. The other elements are explained in Recipe 3.9.

Perl

When the pattern-matching operator `m//` finds a match, it sets several special variables. One of those is the `$&` variable, which holds the part of the string matched by the regular expression. The other special variables are explained in later recipes.

Python

Recipe 3.5 explains the `search()` function. This time, we store the `MatchObject` instance returned by `search()` into a variable. To get the part of the string matched by the regular expression, we call the `group()` method on the match object without any parameters.

Ruby

Recipe 3.8 explains the `$~` variable and the `MatchData` object. In a string context, this object evaluates to the text matched by the regular expression. In an array context, this object evaluates to an array with element number zero holding the overall regular expression match.

`$&` is a special read-only variable. It is an alias for `$~[0]`, which holds a string with the text matched by the regular expression.

See Also

Recipes 3.5, 3.8, 3.9, 3.10, and 3.11

3.8 Determine the Position and Length of the Match

Problem

Instead of extracting the substring matched by the regular expression, as shown in the previous recipe, you want to determine the starting position and length of the match. With this information, you can extract the match in your own code or apply whatever processing you fancy on the part of the original string matched by the regex.

Solution

C#

For quick one-off matches, you can use the static call:

```
int matchstart, matchlength = -1;
Match matchResult = Regex.Match(subjectString, @"\d+");
if (matchResult.Success) {
    matchstart = matchResult.Index;
    matchlength = matchResult.Length;
}
```

To use the same regex repeatedly, construct a **Regex** object:

```
int matchstart, matchlength = -1;
Regex regexObj = new Regex(@"\d+");
Match matchResult = regexObj.Match(subjectString).Value;
if (matchResult.Success) {
    matchstart = matchResult.Index;
    matchlength = matchResult.Length;
}
```

VB.NET

For quick one-off matches, you can use the static call:

```
Dim MatchStart = -1
Dim MatchLength = -1
Dim MatchResult = Regex.Match(SubjectString, "\d+")
If MatchResult.Success Then
    MatchStart = MatchResult.Index
    MatchLength = MatchResult.Length
End If
```

To use the same regex repeatedly, construct a **Regex** object:

```
Dim MatchStart = -1
Dim MatchLength = -1
Dim RegexObj As New Regex("\d+")
Dim MatchResult = Regex.Match(SubjectString, "\d+")
If MatchResult.Success Then
    MatchStart = MatchResult.Index
    MatchLength = MatchResult.Length
End If
```

Java

```
int matchStart, matchLength = -1;
Pattern regex = Pattern.compile("\\d+");
Matcher regexMatcher = regex.matcher(subjectString);
if (regexMatcher.find()) {
    matchStart = regexMatcher.start();
    matchLength = regexMatcher.end() - matchStart;
}
```

JavaScript

```
var matchstart = -1;
var matchlength = -1;
var match = /\d+/.exec(subject);
if (match) {
    matchstart = match.index;
```

```
        matchlength = match[0].length;
    }
```

PHP

```php
if (preg_match('/\d+/', $subject, $groups, PREG_OFFSET_CAPTURE)) {
    $matchstart = $groups[0][1];
    $matchlength = strlen($groups[0][0]);
}
```

Perl

```perl
if ($subject =~ m/\d+/g) {
    $matchlength = length($&);
    $matchstart = length($`);
}
```

Python

For quick one-off matches, you can use the global function:

```python
matchobj = re.search(r"\d+", subject)
if matchobj:
    matchstart = matchobj.start()
    matchlength = matchobj.end() - matchstart
```

To use the same regex repeatedly, use a compiled object:

```python
reobj = re.compile(r"\d+")
matchobj = reobj.search(subject)
if matchobj:
    matchstart = matchobj.start()
    matchlength = matchobj.end() - matchstart
```

Ruby

You can use the =~ operator and its magic $~ variable:

```ruby
if subject =~ /regex pattern/
    matchstart = $~.begin()
    matchlength = $~.end() - matchstart
end
```

Alternatively, you can call the match method on a Regexp object:

```ruby
matchobj = /regex pattern/.match(subject)
if matchobj
    matchstart = matchobj.begin()
    matchlength = matchobj.end() - matchstart
end
```

Discussion

.NET

To get the match index and length, we use the same `Regex.Match()` method described in the previous recipe. This time, we use the `Index` and `Length` properties of the `Match` object returned by `Regex.Match()`.

`Index` is the index in the subject string at which the regex match begins. If the regex match begins at the start of the string, `Index` will be zero. If the match starts at the second character in the string, `Index` will be one. The maximum value for `Index` is the length of the string. That can happen when the regex finds a zero-length match at the end of the string. For example, the regex consisting solely of the end-of-string anchor ‹\Z› always matches at the end of the string.

`Length` indicates the number of characters that were matched. It is possible for a valid match to be zero characters long. For example, the regex consisting only of the word boundary ‹\b› will find a zero-length match at the start of the first word in the string.

If the match attempt fails, `Regex.Match()` still returns a `Match` object. Its `Index` and `Length` properties will both be zero. These values can also happen with a successful match. The regex consisting of the start-of-string anchor ‹\A› will find a zero-length match at the start of the string. Thus, you cannot rely on `Match.Index` or `Match.Length` to indicate whether the match attempt was successful. Use `Match.Success` instead.

Java

To get the position and length of the match, call `Matcher.find()` as described in the previous recipe. When `find()` returns true, call `Matcher.start()` without any parameters to obtain the index of the first character that is part of the regex match. Call `end()` without any parameters to get the index of the first character after the match. Subtract the start from the end to get the length of the match, which can be zero. If you call `start()` or `end()` without a prior call to `find()`, you'll get an `IllegalStateException`.

JavaScript

Call the `exec()` method on a `regexp` object to get an array with details about the match. This array has a few additional properties. The `index` property stores the position in the subject string at which the regex match begins. If the match begins at the start of the string, `index` will be zero. Element zero in the array holds a string with the overall regex match. Get the `length` property of that string to determine the length of the match.

If the regular expression cannot match the string at all, `regexp.exec()` returns `null`.

Do not use the `lastIndex` property of the array returned by `exec()` to determine the ending position of the match. In a strict JavaScript implementation, the `lastIndex` does not exist in the returned array at all, but only in the `regexp` object itself. You shouldn't use `regexp.lastIndex` either. It is unreliable, due to cross-browser differences (see Recipe 3.11 for more details). Instead, simply add up `match.index` and `match[0].length` to determine where the regex match ended.

PHP

The previous recipe explains how you can get the text matched by the regular expression by passing a third parameter to `preg_match()`. You can get the position of the match by passing the constant `PREG_OFFSET_CAPTURE` as a fourth parameter. This parameter changes what `preg_match()` stores in the third parameter when it returns `1`.

When you either omit the fourth parameter or set it to zero, the variable passed as the third parameter receives an array of strings. When you pass `PREG_OFFSET_CAPTURE` as the fourth parameter, the variable receives an array of arrays. Element zero in the overall array is still the overall match (see the preceding recipe), and elements one and beyond are still capturing groups one and beyond (see the next recipe). But instead of holding a string with the text matched by the regex or a capturing group, the element holds an array with two values: the text that was matched and the position in the string at which it was matched.

To get the details of the overall match, subelement zero of element zero gives us the text matched by the regex. We pass this to the `strlen()` function to calculate its length. Subelement one of element zero holds an integer with the position in the subject string at which the match starts.

Perl

To get the length of the match, we simply calculate the length of the `$&` variable, which holds the overall regular expression match. To get the start of the match, we calculate the length of the `` $` `` variable, which holds the text in the string before the regex match.

Python

The `start()` method of `MatchObject` returns the position in the string at which the regular expression match begins. The `end()` method returns the position of the first character after the match. Both methods return the same value when a zero-length regular expression match is found.

You can pass a parameter to `start()` and `end()` to retrieve the range of text matched by one of the capturing groups in the regular expressions. Call `start(1)` for the first capturing group, `end(2)` for the second group, and so on. Python supports up to 99 capturing groups. Group number 0 is the overall regular expression match. Any number other than zero up to the number of capturing groups in the regular expression (with 99 being the ceiling) causes `start()` and `end()` to raise an `IndexError` exception. If the group number is valid but the group did not participate in the regex match, `start()` and `end()` both return `-1` for that group.

If you want to store both the starting and ending positions in a tuple, call the `span()` method on the match object.

Ruby

Recipe 3.5 uses the `=~` operator to find the first regex match in a string. A side effect of this operator is that it fills the special `$~` variable with an instance of the `MatchData` class. This variable is thread-local and method-local. That means you can use the contents of this variable until your method exits or until the next time you use the `=~` operator in your method, without worrying that another thread or another method in your thread will overwrite it.

If you want to keep the details of multiple regex matches, call the `match()` method on a `Regexp` object. This method takes a subject string as its only parameter. It returns a `MatchData` instance when a match can be found, or `nil` otherwise. It also sets the `=~` variable to the same `MatchObject` instance, but does not overwrite other `MatchObject` instances stored in other variables.

The `MatchData` object stores all the details about a regular expression match. Recipes 3.7 and 3.9 explain how to get the text matched by the regular expression and by capturing groups.

The `begin()` method returns the position in the subject string at which the regex match begins. `end()` returns the position of the first character after the regex match. `offset()` returns an array with the beginning and ending positions. These three methods take one parameter. Pass `0` to get the positions of the overall regex match, or pass a positive number to get the positions of the specified capturing group. For example, `begin(1)` returns the start of the first capturing group.

Do not use `length()` or `size()` to get the length of the match. Both these methods return the number of elements in the array that `MatchData` evaluates to in array context, as explained in Recipe 3.9.

See Also

Recipes 3.5 and 3.9

3.9 Retrieve Part of the Matched Text

Problem

As in Recipe 3.7, you have a regular expression that matches a substring of the subject text, but this time you want to match just one part of that substring. To isolate the part you want, you added a capturing group to your regular expression, as described in Recipe 2.9.

For example, the regular expression ‹http://([a-z0-9.-]+)› matches http://www.regexcookbook.com in the string Please visit http://www.regexcookbook.com for more information. The part of the regex inside the first capturing group matches www.regexcookbook.com, and you want to retrieve the domain name captured by the first capturing group into a string variable.

We're using this simple regex to illustrate the concept of capturing groups. See Chapter 7 for more accurate regular expressions for matching URLs.

Solution

C#

For quick one-off matches, you can use the static call:

```
string resultString = Regex.Match(subjectString,
                    "http://([a-z0-9.-]+)").Groups[1].Value;
```

To use the same regex repeatedly, construct a Regex object:

```
Regex regexObj = new Regex("http://([a-z0-9.-]+)");
string resultString = regexObj.Match(subjectString).Groups[1].Value;
```

VB.NET

For quick one-off matches, you can use the static call:

```
Dim ResultString = Regex.Match(SubjectString,
                    "http://([a-z0-9.-]+)").Groups(1).Value
```

To use the same regex repeatedly, construct a Regex object:

```
Dim RegexObj As New Regex("http://([a-z0-9.-]+)")
Dim ResultString = RegexObj.Match(SubjectString).Groups(1).Value
```

Java

```
String resultString = null;
Pattern regex = Pattern.compile("http://([a-z0-9.-]+)");
Matcher regexMatcher = regex.matcher(subjectString);
if (regexMatcher.find()) {
    resultString = regexMatcher.group(1);
}
```

JavaScript

```
var result = "";
var match = /http:\/\/([a-z0-9.-]+)/.exec(subject);
if (match) {
    result = match[1];
} else {
```

```
    result = '';
}
```

PHP

```php
if (preg_match('%http://([a-z0-9.-]+)%', $subject, $groups)) {
    $result = $groups[1];
} else {
    $result = '';
}
```

Perl

```perl
if ($subject =~ m!http://([a-z0-9.-]+)!) {
    $result = $1;
} else {
    $result = '';
}
```

Python

For quick one-off matches, you can use the global function:

```python
matchobj = re.search("http://([a-z0-9.-]+)", subject)
if matchobj:
    result = matchobj.group(1)
else:
    result = ""
```

To use the same regex repeatedly, use a compiled object:

```python
reobj = re.compile("http://([a-z0-9.-]+)")
matchobj = reobj.search(subject)
if match:
    result = matchobj.group(1)
else:
    result = ""
```

Ruby

You can use the =~ operator and its magic numbered variables, such as $1:

```ruby
if subject =~ %r!http://([a-z0-9.-]+)!
    result = $1
else
    result = ""
end
```

Alternatively, you can call the match method on a Regexp object:

```ruby
matchobj = %r!http://([a-z0-9.-]+)!.match(subject)
if matchobj
```

```
        result = matchobj[1]
    else
        result = ""
    end
```

Discussion

Recipe 2.10 and Recipe 2.21 explain how you can use numbered backreferences in the regular expression and the replacement text to match the same text again, or to insert part of the regex match into the replacement text. You can use the same reference numbers to retrieve the text matched by one or more capturing groups in your code.

In regular expressions, capturing groups are numbered starting at one. Programming languages typically start numbering arrays and lists at zero. All programming languages discussed in this book that store capturing groups in an array or list use the same numbering for capturing groups as the regular expression, starting at one. The zeroth element in the array or list is used to store the overall regular expression match. This means that if your regular expression has three capturing groups, the array storing their matches will have four elements. Element zero holds the overall match, and elements one, two, and three store the text matched by the three capturing groups.

.NET

To retrieve details about capturing groups, we again resort to the `Regex.Match()` member function, first explained in Recipe 3.7. The returned `Match` object has a property called `Groups`. This is a collection property of type `GroupCollection`. The collection holds the details for all the capturing groups in your regular expression. `Groups[1]` holds the details for the first capturing group, `Groups[2]` the second group, and so on.

The `Groups` collection holds one `Group` object for each capturing group. The `Group` class has the same properties as the `Match` class, except for the `Groups` property. `Match.Groups[1].Value` returns the text matched by the first capturing group, in the same way that `Match.Value` returns the overall regex match. `Match.Groups[1].Index` and `Match.Groups[1].Length` return the starting position and length of the text matched by the group. See Recipe 3.8 for more details on `Index` and `Length`.

`Groups[0]` holds the details for the overall regex match, which are also held by the match object directly. `Match.Value` and `Match.Groups[0].Value` are equivalent.

The `Groups` collection does not throw an exception if you pass an invalid group number. For example, `Groups[-1]` still returns a `Group` object, but the properties of that `Group` object will indicate that the fictional capturing group -1 failed to match. The best way to test this is to use the `Success` property. `Groups[-1].Success` will return `false`.

To determine how many capturing groups there are, check `Match.Groups.Count`. The `Count` property follows the same convention as the `Count` property for all collection objects in .NET: it returns the number of elements in the collection, which is the highest allowed index plus one. In our example, the Groups collection holds Groups[0] and Groups[1]. Groups.Count thus returns 2.

Java

The code for getting either the text matched by a capturing group or the match details of a capturing group is practically the same as that for the whole regex match, as shown in the preceding two recipes. The group(), start() and end(), methods of the Matcher class all take one optional parameter. Without this parameter, or with this parameter set to zero, you get the match or positions of the whole regex match.

If you pass a positive number, you get the details of that capturing group. Groups are numbered starting at one, just like backreferences in the regular expression itself. If you specify a number higher than the number of capturing groups in your regular expression, these three functions throw an IndexOutOfBoundsException. If the capturing group exists but did not participate in the match, group(n) returns null, whereas start() and end() both return -1.

JavaScript

As explained in the previous recipe, the exec() method of a regular expression object returns an array with details about the match. Element zero in the array holds the overall regex match. Element one holds the text matched by the first capturing group, element two stores the second group's match, etc.

If the regular expression cannot match the string at all, regexp.exec() returns null.

PHP

Recipe 3.7 explains how you can get the text matched by the regular expression by passing a third parameter to preg_match(). When preg_match() returns 1, the parameter is filled with an array. Element zero holds a string with the overall regex match.

Element one holds the text matched by the first capturing group, element two the text from the second group, and so on. The length of the array is the number of capturing groups plus one. Array indexes correspond to backreference numbers in the regular expression.

If you specify the PREG_OFFSET_CAPTURE constant as the fourth parameter, as explained in the previous recipe, then the length of the array is still the number of capturing groups plus one. But instead of holding a string at each index, the array will hold subarrays with two elements. Subelement zero is the string with the text matched by the overall regex or the capturing group. Subelement one is an integer that indicates the position in the subject string at which the matched text starts.

Perl

When the pattern-matching operator `m//` finds a match, it sets several special variables. Those include the numbered variables `$1`, `$2`, `$3`, etc., which hold the part of the string matched by the capturing groups in the regular expression.

Python

The solution to this problem is almost identical to the one in Recipe 3.7. Instead of calling `group()` without any parameters, we specify the number of the capturing group we're interested in. Call `group(1)` to get the text matched by the first capturing group, `group(2)` for the second group, and so on. Python supports up to 99 capturing groups. Group number 0 is the overall regular expression match. If you pass a number greater than the number of capturing groups in your regular expression, then `group()` raises an `IndexError` exception. If the group number is valid but the group did not participate in the regex match, `group()` returns `None`.

You can pass multiple group numbers to `group()` to get the text matched by several capturing groups in one call. The result will be a list of strings.

If you want to retrieve a tuple with the text matched by all the capturing groups, you can call the `groups()` method of `MatchObject`. The tuple will hold `None` for groups that did not participate in the match. If you pass a parameter to `groups()`, that value is used instead of `None` for groups that did not participate in the match.

If you want a dictionary instead of a tuple with the text matched by the capturing groups, call `groupdict()` instead of `groups()`. You can pass a parameter to `groupdict()` to put something other than `None` in the dictionary for groups that did not participate in the match.

Ruby

Recipe 3.8 explains the `$~` variable and the `MatchData` object. In an array context, this object evaluates to an array with the text matched by all the capturing groups in your regular expression. Capturing groups are numbered starting at `1`, just like backreferences in the regular expression. Element `0` in the array holds the overall regular expression match.

`$1`, `$2`, and beyond are special read-only variables. `$1` is a shortcut to `$~[1]`, which holds the text matched by the first capturing group. `$2` retrieves the second group, and so on.

Named Capture

If your regular expression uses named capturing groups, you can use the group's name to retrieve its match in your code.

C#

For quick one-off matches, you can use the static call:

```
string resultString = Regex.Match(subjectString,
            "http://(?<domain>[a-z0-9.-]+)").Groups["domain"].Value;
```

To use the same regex repeatedly, construct a `Regex` object:

```
Regex regexObj = new Regex("http://(?<domain>[a-z0-9.-]+)");
string resultString = regexObj.Match(subjectString).Groups["domain"].Value;
```

In C#, there's no real difference in the code for getting the `Group` object for a named group compared with a numbered group. Instead of indexing the `Groups` collection with an integer, index it with a string. Also in this case, .NET will not throw an exception if the group does not exist. `Match.Groups["nosuchgroup"].Success` merely returns `false`.

VB.NET

For quick one-off matches, you can use the static call:

```
Dim ResultString = Regex.Match(SubjectString,
            "http://(?<domain>[a-z0-9.-]+)").Groups("domain").Value
```

To use the same regex repeatedly, construct a `Regex` object:

```
Dim RegexObj As New Regex("http://(?<domain>[a-z0-9.-]+)")
Dim ResultString = RegexObj.Match(SubjectString).Groups("domain").Value
```

In VB.NET, there's no real difference in the code for getting the `Group` object for a named group compared with a numbered group. Instead of indexing the `Groups` collection with an integer, index it with a string. Also in this case, .NET will not throw an exception if the group does not exist. `Match.Groups("nosuchgroup").Success` merely returns `False`.

PHP

```
if (preg_match('%http://(?P<domain>[a-z0-9.-]+)%', $subject, $groups)) {
    $result = $groups['domain'];
} else {
    $result = '';
}
```

If your regular expression has named capturing groups, then the array assigned to `$groups` is an associative array. The text matched by each named capturing group is added to the array twice. You can retrieve the matched text by indexing the array with either the group's number or the group's name. In the code sample, `$groups[0]` stores the overall regex match, whereas both `$groups[1]` and `$groups['domain']` store the text matched by the regular expression's only capturing group.

Perl

```
if ($subject =~ '!http://(?<domain>[a-z0-9.-]+)%!) {
    $result = $+{'domain'};
} else {
    $result = '';
}
```

Perl supports named capturing groups starting with version 5.10. The **$+** hash stores the text matched by all named capturing groups. Perl numbers named groups along with numbered groups. In this example, both **$1** and **$+{name}** store the text matched by the regular expression's only capturing group.

Python

```
matchobj = re.search("http://(?P<domain>[a-z0-9.-]+)", subject)
if matchobj:
    result = matchobj.group("domain")
else:
    result = ""
```

If your regular expression has named capturing groups, you can pass the group's name instead of its number to the **group()** method.

See Also

Recipe 2.9 explains numbered capturing groups.

Recipe 2.11 explains named capturing groups.

3.10 Retrieve a List of All Matches

Problem

All the preceding recipes in this chapter deal only with the first match that a regular expression can find in the subject string. But in many cases, a regular expression that partially matches a string can find another match in the remainder of the string. And there may be a third match after the second, and so on. For example, the regex ‹\d+› can find six matches in the subject string The lucky numbers are 7, 13, 16, 42, 65, and 99: 7, 13, 16, 42, 65, and 99.

You want to retrieve the list of all substrings that the regular expression finds when it is applied repeatedly to the remainder of the string, after each match.

Solution

C#

You can use the static call when you process only a small number of strings with the same regular expression:

```
MatchCollection matchlist = Regex.Matches(subjectString, @"\d+");
```

Construct a `Regex` object if you want to use the same regular expression with a large number of strings:

```
Regex regexObj = new Regex(@"\d+");
MatchCollection matchlist = regexObj.Matches(subjectString);
```

VB.NET

You can use the static call when you process only a small number of strings with the same regular expression:

```
Dim matchlist = Regex.Matches(SubjectString, "\d+")
```

Construct a `Regex` object if you want to use the same regular expression with a large number of strings:

```
Dim RegexObj As New Regex("\d+")
Dim MatchList = RegexObj.Matches(SubjectString)
```

Java

```
List<String> resultList = new ArrayList<String>();
Pattern regex = Pattern.compile("\\d+");
Matcher regexMatcher = regex.matcher(subjectString);
while (regexMatcher.find()) {
    resultList.add(regexMatcher.group());
}
```

JavaScript

```
var list = subject.match(/\d+/g);
```

PHP

```
preg_match_all('/\d+/', $subject, $result, PREG_PATTERN_ORDER);
$result = $result[0];
```

Perl

```
@result = $subject =~ m/\d+/g;
```

This only works for regular expressions that don't have capturing groups, so use noncapturing groups instead. See Recipe 2.9 for details.

Python

If you process only a small number of strings with the same regular expression, you can use the global function:

```
result = re.findall(r"\d+", subject)
```

To use the same regex repeatedly, use a compiled object:

```
reobj = re.compile(r"\d+")
result = reobj.findall(subject)
```

Ruby

```
result = subject.scan(/\d+/)
```

Discussion

.NET

The `Matches()` method of the `Regex` class applies the regular expression repeatedly to the string, until all matches have been found. It returns a `MatchCollection` object that holds all the matches. The subject string is always the first parameter. This is the string in which the regular expression will try to find a match. The first parameter must not be `null`. Otherwise, `Matches()` will throw an `ArgumentNullException`.

If you want to get the regex matches in only a small number of strings, you can use the static overload of `Matches()`. Pass your subject string as the first parameter and your regular expression as the second paramater. You can pass regular expression options as an optional third parameter.

If you'll be processing many strings, construct a `Regex` object first, and use that to call `Matches()`. The subject string is then the only required parameter. You can specify an optional second parameter to indicate the character index at which the regular expression should begin the check. Essentially, the number you pass as the second parameter is the number of characters at the start of your subject string that the regular expression should ignore. This can be useful when you've already processed the string up to a point and want to check whether the remainder should be processed further. If you specify the number, it must be between zero and the length of the subject string. Otherwise, `IsMatch()` throws an `ArgumentOutOfRangeException`.

The static overloads do not allow for the parameter that specifies where the regex attempt should start in the string. There is no overload that allows you to tell `Matches()` to stop before the end of the string. If you want to do that, you could call `Regex.Match("subject", start, stop)` in a loop, as shown in the next recipe, and add all the matches it finds to a list of your own.

Java

Java does not provide a function that retrieves the list of matches for you. You can easily do this in your own code by adapting Recipe 3.7. Instead of calling `find()` in an `if` statement, do it in a `while` loop.

To use the `List` and `ArrayList` classes, as in the example, put `import java.util.*;` at the start of your code.

JavaScript

This code calls `string.match()`, just like the JavaScript solution to Recipe 3.7. There is one small but very important difference: the `/g` flag. Regex flags are explained in Recipe 3.4.

The `/g` flag tells the `match()` function to iterate over all matches in the string and put them into an array. In the code sample, `list[0]` will hold the first regex match, `list[1]` the second, and so on. Check `list.length` to determine the number of matches. If no matches can be found at all, `string.match` returns `null` as usual.

The elements in the array are strings. When you use a regex with the `/g` flag, `string.match()` does not provide any further details about the regular expression match. If you want to get match details for all regex matches, iterate over the matches as explained in Recipe 3.11.

PHP

All the previous PHP recipes used `preg_match()`, which finds the first regex match in a string. `preg_match_all()` is very similar. The key difference is that it will find all matches in the string. It returns an integer indicating the number of times the regex could match.

The first three parameters for `preg_match_all()` are the same as the first three for `preg_match()`: a string with your regular expression, the string you want to search through, and a variable that will receive an array with the results. The only differences are that the third parameter is required and the array is always multidimensional.

For the fourth parameter, specify either the constant `PREG_PATTERN_ORDER` or `PREG_SET_ORDER`. If you omit the fourth parameter, `PREG_PATTERN_ORDER` is the default.

If you use `PREG_PATTERN_ORDER`, you will get an array that stores the details of the overall match at element zero, and the details of capturing groups one and beyond at elements one and beyond. The length of the array is the number of capturing groups plus one. This is the same order used by `preg_match()`. The difference is that instead of each element holding a string with the only regex match found by `preg_match()`, each element holds a subarray with all the matches found by `preg_matches()`. The length of each subarray is the same as the value returned by `preg_matches()`.

To get a list of all the regex matches in the string, discarding text matched by capturing groups, specify `PREG_PATTERN_ORDER` and retrieve element zero in the array. If you're only interested in the text matched by a particular capturing group, use PREG_PATTERN_ORDER and the capturing group's number. For example, specifying $result[1] after calling preg_match('%http://([a-z0-9.-]+)%', $subject, $result) gives you the list of domain names of all the URLs in your subject string.

PREG_SET_ORDER fills the array with the same strings, but in a different way. The length of the array is the value returned by preg_matches(). Each element in the array is a subarray, with the overall regex match in subelement zero and the capturing groups in elements one and beyond. If you specify PREG_SET_ORDER, then $result[0] holds the same array as if you had called preg_match().

You can combine PREG_OFFSET_CAPTURE with PREG_PATTERN_ORDER or PREG_SET_ORDER. Doing so has the same effect as passing PREG_OFFSET_CAPTURE as the fourth parameter to preg_match(). Instead of each element in the array holding a string, it will hold a two-element array with the string and the offset at which that string occurs in the original subject string.

Perl

Recipe 3.4 explains that you need to add the /g modifier to enable your regex to find more than one match in the subject string. If you use a global regex in a list context, it will find all the matches and return them. In this recipe, the list variable to the left of the assignment operator provides the list context.

If the regular expression does not have any capturing groups, the list will contain the overall regex matches. If the regular expression does have capturing groups, the list will contain the text matched by all the capturing groups for each regex match. The overall regex match is not included, unless you put a capturing group around the whole regex. If you only want to get a list of overall regex matches, replace all capturing groups with noncapturing groups. Recipe 2.9 explains both kinds of grouping.

Python

The findall() function in the re module searches repeatedly through a string to find all matches of the regular expression. Pass your regular expression as the first parameter and the subject string as the second parameter. You can pass the regular expression options in the optional third parameter.

The re.findall() function calls re.compile(), and then calls the findall() method on the compiled regular expression object. This method has only one required parameter: the subject string.

The findall() method takes two optional parameters that the global re.findall() function does not support. After the subject string, you can pass the character position in the string at which findall() should begin its search. If you omit this parameter, findall() processes the whole subject string. If you specify a starting position, you can also specify an ending position. If you don't specify an ending position, the search runs until the end of the string.

No matter how you call `findall()`, the result is always a list with all the matches that could be found. If the regex has no capturing groups, you get a list of strings. If it does have capturing groups, you get a list of tuples with the text matched by all the capturing groups for each regex match.

Ruby

The `scan()` method of the `String` class takes a regular expression as its only parameter. It iterates over all the regular expression matches in the string. When called without a block, `scan()` returns an array of all regex matches.

If your regular expression does not contain any capturing groups, `scan()` returns an array of strings. The array has one element for each regex match, holding the text that was matched.

When there are capturing groups, `scan()` returns an array of arrays. The array has one element for each regex match. Each element is an array with the text matched by each of the capturing groups. Subelement zero holds the text matched by the first capturing group, subelement one holds the second capturing group, etc. The overall regex match is not included in the array. If you want the overall match to be included, enclose your entire regular expression with an extra capturing group:

Ruby does not provide an option to make `scan()` return an array of strings when the regex has capturing groups. Your only solution is to replace all named and numbered capturing groups with noncapturing groups.

See Also

Recipes 3.7, 3.11, and 3.12

3.11 Iterate over All Matches

Problem

The previous recipe shows how a regex could be applied repeatedly to a string to get a list of matches. Now you want to iterate over all the matches in your own code.

Solution

C#

You can use the static call when you process only a small number of strings with the same regular expression:

```
Match matchResult = Regex.Match(subjectString, @"\d+");
while (matchResult.Success) {
    // Here you can process the match stored in matchResult
    matchResult = matchResult.NextMatch();
}
```

Construct a **Regex** object if you want to use the same regular expression with a large number of strings:

```
Regex regexObj = new Regex(@"\d+");
matchResult = regexObj.Match(subjectString);
while (matchResult.Success) {
    // Here you can process the match stored in matchResult
    matchResult = matchResult.NextMatch();
}
```

VB.NET

You can use the static call when you process only a small number of strings with the same regular expression:

```
Dim MatchResult = Regex.Match(SubjectString, "\d+")
While MatchResult.Success
    'Here you can process the match stored in MatchResult
    MatchResult = MatchResult.NextMatch
End While
```

Construct a **Regex** object if you want to use the same regular expression with a large number of strings:

```
Dim RegexObj As New Regex("\d+")
Dim MatchResult = RegexObj.Match(SubjectString)
While MatchResult.Success
    'Here you can process the match stored in MatchResult
    MatchResult = MatchResult.NextMatch
End While
```

Java

```
Pattern regex = Pattern.compile("\\d+");
Matcher regexMatcher = regex.matcher(subjectString);
while (regexMatcher.find()) {
    // Here you can process the match stored in regexMacher
}
```

JavaScript

If your regular expression may yield a zero-length match, or if you're simply not sure about that, make sure to work around cross-browser issues dealing with zero-length matches and exec():

```
var regex = /\d+/g;
var match = null;
while (match = regex.exec(subject)) {
  // Don't let browsers such as Firefox get stuck in an infinite loop
  if (match.index == regex.lastIndex) regex.lastIndex++;
  // Here you can process the match stored in the match variable
}
```

If you know for sure your regex can never find a zero-length match, you can iterate over the regex directly:

```
var regex = /\d+/g;
var match = null;
while (match = regex.exec(subject)) {
  // Here you can process the match stored in the match variable
}
```

PHP

```
preg_match_all('/\d+/', $subject, $result, PREG_PATTERN_ORDER);
for ($i = 0; $i < count($result[0]); $i++) {
    # Matched text = $result[0][$i];
}
```

Perl

```
while ($subject =~ m/\d+/g) {
    # matched text = $&
}
```

Python

If you process only a small number of strings with the same regular expression, you can use the global function:

```
for matchobj in re.finditer(r"\d+", subject):
    # Here you can process the match stored in the matchobj variable
```

To use the same regex repeatedly, use a compiled object:

```
reobj = re.compile(r"\d+")
for matchobj in reobj.finditer(subject):
    # Here you can process the match stored in the matchobj variable
```

Ruby

```
subject.scan(/\d+/) {|match|
    # Here you can process the match stored in the match variable
}
```

Discussion

.NET

Recipe 3.7 explains how to use the `Match()` member function of the `Regex` class to retrieve the first regular expression match in the string. To iterate over all matches in the string, we again call the `Match()` function to retrieve the details of the first match. The `Match()` function returns an instance of the `Match` class, which we store in the variable `matchResult`. If the `Success` property of the `matchResult` object holds `true`, we can begin our loop.

At the start of the loop, you can use the properties of the `Match` class to process the details of the first match. Recipe 3.7 explains the `Value` property, Recipe 3.8 explains the `Index` and `Length` properties, and Recipe 3.9 explains the `Groups` collection.

When you're done with the first match, call the `NextMatch()` member function on the `matchResult` variable. `Match.NextMatch()` returns an instance of the `Match` class, just like `Regex.Match()` does. The newly returned instance holds the details of the second match.

Assigning the result from `matchResult.NextMatch()` to the same `matchResult` variable makes it easy to iterate over all matches. We have to check `matchResult.Success` again to see whether `NextMatch()` did in fact find another match. When `NextMatch()` fails, it still returns a `Match` object, but its `Success` property will be set to `false`. By using a single `matchResult` variable, we can combine the initial test for success and the test after the call to `NextMatch()` into a single `while` statement.

Calling `NextMatch()` does not invalidate the `Match` object you called it on. If you want, you could keep the full `Match` object for each regular expression match.

The `NextMatch()` method does not accept any parameters. It uses the same regular expression and subject string as you passed to the `Regex.Match()` method. The `Match` object keeps references to your regular expression and subject string.

You can use the static `Regex.Match()` call, even when your subject string contains a very large number of regex matches. `Regex.Match()` will compile your regular expression once, and the returned `Match` object will hold a reference to the compiled regular expression. `Match.MatchAgain()` uses the previously compiled regular expression referenced by the `Match` object, even when you used the static `Regex.Match()` call. You need to instantiate the `Regex` class only if you want to call `Regex.Match()` repeatedly, i.e., use the same regex on many strings.

Java

Iterating over all the matches in a string is very easy in Java. Simply call the `find()` method introduced in Recipe 3.7 in a `while` loop. Each call to `find()` updates the `Matcher` object with the details about the match and the starting position for the next match attempt.

JavaScript

Before you begin, make sure to specify the /g flag if you want to use your regex in a loop. This flag is explained in Recipe 3.4. `while (regexp.exec())` finds all numbers in the subject string when `regexp = /\d+/g`. If `regexp = /\d+/`, then `while (regexp.exec())` finds the first number in the string again and again, until your script crashes or is forcibly terminated by the browser.

Note that `while (/\d+/g.exec())` (looping over a literal regex with /g) also will get stuck in the same infinite loop, at least with certain JavaScript implementations, because the regular expression is recompiled during each iteration of the `while` loop. When the regex is recompiled, the starting position for the match attempt is reset to the start of the string. Assign the regular expression to a variable outside the loop, to make sure it is compiled only once.

Recipes 3.8 and 3.9 explain the object returned by `regexp.exec()`. This object is the same, regardless of whether you use `exec()` in a loop. You can do whatever you want with this object.

The only effect of the /g is that it updates the `lastIndex` property of the `regexp` object on which you're calling `exec()`. This works even when you're using a literal regular expression, as shown in the second JavaScript solution for this recipe. Next time you call `exec()`, the match attempt will begin at `lastIndex`. If you assign a new value to `lastIndex`, the match attempt will begin at the position you specified.

There is, unfortunately, one major problem with `lastIndex`. If you read the ECMA-262v3 standard for JavaScript literally, then `exec()` should set `lastIndex` to the first character after the match. This means that if the match is zero characters long, the next match attempt will begin at the position of the match just found, resulting in an infinite loop.

All regular expression engines discussed in this book (except JavaScript) deal with this by automatically starting the next match attempt one character further in the string, if the previous match was zero-length. Internet Explorer does this by incrementing `lastIndex` by one if the match is zero-length. This is why Recipe 3.7 claims that you cannot use `lastIndex` to determine the end of the match, as you'll get incorrect values in Internet Explorer.

The Firefox developers, however, are adamant about implementing the ECMA-262v3 standard literally, even if it means `regexp.exec()` may get stuck in an infinite loop. This outcome is not unlikely. For example, you can use `re = /^.*$/gm; while (re.exec())` to iterate over all lines in a multiline string, and if the string has a blank line, Firefox will get stuck on it.

The workaround is to increment `lastIndex` in your own code if the `exec()` function hasn't already done this. The first JavaScript solution to this recipe shows you how. If you're unsure, simply paste in this one line of code and be done with it.

This problem does not exist with `string.match()` (Recipe 3.10) or `string.replace()` (Recipe 3.14). For these methods, which use `lastIndex` internally, the ECMA-262v3 standard does state that `lastIndex` must be incremented for each zero-length match.

PHP

The `preg_match()` function takes an optional fifth parameter to indicate the position in the string at which the match attempt should start. You could adapt Recipe 3.8 to pass `$matchstart + $matchlength` as the fifth parameter upon the second call to `preg_match()` to find the second match in the string, and repeat that for the third and following matches until `preg_match()` returns 0. Recipe 3.18 uses this method.

In addition to requiring extra code to calculate the starting offset for each match attempt, repeatedly calling `preg_match()` is inefficient, because there's no way to store a compiled regular expression in a variable. `preg_match()` has to look up the compiled regular expression in its cache each time you call it.

An easier and more efficient solution is to call `preg_match_all()`, as explained in the previous recipe, and iterate over the array with the match results.

Perl

Recipe 3.4 explains that you need to add the `/g` modifier to enable your regex to find more than one match in the subject string. If you use a global regex in a scalar context, it will try to find the next match, continuing at the end of the previous match. In this recipe, the `while` statement provides the scalar context. All the special variables, such as `$&` (explained in Recipe 3.7), are available inside the `while` loop.

Python

The `finditer()` function in `re` returns an iterator that you can use to find all the matches of the regular expression. Pass your regular expression as the first parameter and the subject string as the second parameter. You can pass the regular expression options in the optional third parameter.

The `re.finditer()` function calls `re.compile()`, and then calls the `finditer()` method on the compiled regular expression object. This method has only one required parameter: the subject string.

The `finditer()` method takes two optional parameters that the global `re.finditer()` function does not support. After the subject string, you can pass the character position in the string at which `finditer()` should begin its search. If you omit this parameter, the iterator will process the whole subject string. If you specify a starting position, you can also specify an ending position. If you don't specify an ending position, the search runs until the end of the string.

Ruby

The `scan()` method of the `String` class takes a regular expression as its only parameter and iterates over all the regular expression matches in the string. When called with a block, you can process each match as it is found.

If your regular expression does not contain any capturing groups, specify one iterator variable in the block. This variable will receive a string with the text matched by the regular expression.

If your regex does contain one or more capturing groups, list one variable for each group. The first variable will receive a string with the text matched by the first capturing group, the second variable receives the second capturing group, and so on. No variable will be filled with the overall regex match. If you want the overall match to be included, enclose your entire regular expression with an extra capturing group.

```ruby
subject.scan(/(a)(b)(c)/) {|a, b, c|
    # a, b, and c hold the text matched by the three capturing groups
}
```

If you list fewer variables than there are capturing groups in your regex, you will be able to access only those capturing groups for which you provided variables. If you list more variables than there are capturing groups, the extra variables will be set to `nil`.

If you list only one iterator variable and your regex has one or more capturing groups, the variable will be filled with an array of strings. The array will have one string for each capturing group. If there is only one capturing group, the array will have a single element:

```ruby
subject.scan(/(a)(b)(c)/) {|abc|
    # abc[0], abc[1], and abc[2] hold the text
    # matched by the three capturing groups
}
```

See Also

Recipes 3.7, 3.8, 3.10, and 3.12

3.12 Validate Matches in Procedural Code

Problem

Recipe 3.10 shows how you can retrieve a list of all matches a regular expression can find in a string when it is applied repeatedly to the remainder of the string after each match. Now you want to get a list of matches that meet certain extra criteria that you cannot (easily) express in a regular expression. For example, when retrieving a list of lucky numbers, you only want to retain those that are an integer multiple of 13.

Solution

C#

You can use the static call when you process only a small number of strings with the same regular expression:

```
StringCollection resultList = new StringCollection();
Match matchResult = Regex.Match(subjectString, @"\d+");
while (matchResult.Success) {
    if (int.Parse(matchResult.Value) % 13 == 0) {
        resultList.Add(matchResult.Value);
    }
    matchResult = matchResult.NextMatch();
}
```

Construct a Regex object if you want to use the same regular expression with a large number of strings:

```
StringCollection resultList = new StringCollection();
Regex regexObj = new Regex(@"\d+");
matchResult = regexObj.Match(subjectString);
while (matchResult.Success) {
    if (int.Parse(matchResult.Value) % 13 == 0) {
        resultList.Add(matchResult.Value);
    }
    matchResult = matchResult.NextMatch();
}
```

VB.NET

You can use the static call when you process only a small number of strings with the same regular expression:

```
Dim ResultList = New StringCollection
Dim MatchResult = Regex.Match(SubjectString, "\d+")
While MatchResult.Success
    If Integer.Parse(MatchResult.Value) Mod 13 = 0 Then
        ResultList.Add(MatchResult.Value)
    End If
    MatchResult = MatchResult.NextMatch
End While
```

Construct a Regex object if you want to use the same regular expression with a large number of strings:

```
Dim ResultList = New StringCollection
Dim RegexObj As New Regex("\d+")
Dim MatchResult = RegexObj.Match(SubjectString)
While MatchResult.Success
```

```
        If Integer.Parse(MatchResult.Value) Mod 13 = 0 Then
            ResultList.Add(MatchResult.Value)
        End If
        MatchResult = MatchResult.NextMatch
    End While
```

Java

```java
List<String> resultList = new ArrayList<String>();
Pattern regex = Pattern.compile("\\d+");
Matcher regexMatcher = regex.matcher(subjectString);
while (regexMatcher.find()) {
    if (Integer.parseInt(regexMatcher.group()) % 13 == 0) {
        resultList.add(regexMatcher.group());
    }
}
```

JavaScript

```javascript
var list = [];
var regex = /\d+/g;
var match = null;
while (match = regex.exec(subject)) {
    // Don't let browsers such as Firefox get stuck in an infinite loop
    if (match.index == regex.lastIndex) regex.lastIndex++;
    // Here you can process the match stored in the match variable
    if (match[0] % 13 == 0) {
        list.push(match[0]);
    }
}
```

PHP

```php
preg_match_all('/\d+/', $subject, $matchdata, PREG_PATTERN_ORDER);
for ($i = 0; $i < count($matchdata[0]); $i++) {
    if ($matchdata[0][$i] % 13 == 0) {
      $list[] = $matchdata[0][$i];
    }
}
```

Perl

```perl
while ($subject =~ m/\d+/g) {
    if ($& % 13 == 0) {
        push(@list, $&);
    }
}
```

Python

If you process only a small number of strings with the same regular expression, you can use the global function:

```
list = []
for matchobj in re.finditer(r"\d+", subject):
    if int(matchobj.group()) % 13 == 0:
        list.append(matchobj.group())
```

To use the same regex repeatedly, use a compiled object:

```
list = []
reobj = re.compile(r"\d+")
for matchobj in reobj.finditer(subject):
    if int(matchobj.group()) % 13 == 0:
        list.append(matchobj.group())
```

Ruby

```
list = []
subject.scan(/\d+/) {|match|
    list << match if (Integer(match) % 13 == 0)
}
```

Discussion

Regular expressions deal with text. Though the regular expression ‹\d+› matches what we call a number, to the regular expression engine it's just a string of one or more digits.

If you want to find specific numbers, such as those divisible by 13, it is much easier to write a general regex that matches all numbers, and then use a bit of procedural code to skip the regex matches you're not interested in.

The solutions for this recipe all are based on the solutions for the previous recipe, which shows how to iterate over all matches. Inside the loop, we convert the regular expression match into a number.

Some languages do this automatically; other languages require an explicit function call to convert the string into an integer. We then check whether the integer is divisible by 13. If it is, the regex match is added to the list. If it is not, the regex match is skipped.

See Also

Recipes 3.7, 3.10, and 3.11

3.13 Find a Match Within Another Match

Problem

You want to find all the matches of a particular regular expression, but only within certain sections of the subject string. Another regular expression matches each of the sections in the string.

Suppose you have an HTML file in which various passages are marked as bold with `<b>` tags. You want to find all numbers marked as bold. If some bold text contains multiple numbers, you want to match all of them separately. For example, when processing the string 1 `<b>2</b>` 3 4 `<b>5 6 7</b>`, you want to find four matches: 2, 5, 6, and 7.

Solution

C#

```
StringCollection resultList = new StringCollection();
Regex outerRegex = new Regex("<b>(.*?)</b>", RegexOptions.Singleline);
Regex innerRegex = new Regex(@"\d+");
// Find the first section
Match outerMatch = outerRegex.Match(subjectString);
while (outerMatch.Success) {
    // Get the matches within the section
    Match innerMatch = innerRegex.Match(outerMatch.Groups[1].Value);
    while (innerMatch.Success) {
        resultList.Add(innerMatch.Value);
        innerMatch = innerMatch.NextMatch();
    }
    // Find the next section
    outerMatch = outerMatch.NextMatch();
}
```

VB.NET

```
Dim ResultList = New StringCollection
Dim OuterRegex As New Regex("<b>(.*?)</b>", RegexOptions.Singleline)
Dim InnerRegex As New Regex("\d+")
'Find the first section
Dim OuterMatch = OuterRegex.Match(SubjectString)
While OuterMatch.Success
    'Get the matches within the section
    Dim InnerMatch = InnerRegex.Match(OuterMatch.Groups(1).Value)
    While InnerMatch.Success
        ResultList.Add(InnerMatch.Value)
        InnerMatch = InnerMatch.NextMatch
    End While
```

```
    OuterMatch = OuterMatch.NextMatch
End While
```

Java

Iterating using two matchers is easy, and works with Java 4 and later:

```java
List<String> resultList = new ArrayList<String>();
Pattern outerRegex = Pattern.compile("<b>(.*?)</b>", Pattern.DOTALL);
Pattern innerRegex = Pattern.compile("\\d+");
Matcher outerMatcher = outerRegex.matcher(subjectString);
while (outerMatcher.find()) {
    Matcher innerMatcher = innerRegex.matcher(outerMatcher.group());
    while (innerMatcher.find()) {
        resultList.add(innerMatcher.group());
    }
}
```

The following code is more efficient (because `innerMatcher` is created only once), but requires Java 5 or later:

```java
List<String> resultList = new ArrayList<String>();
Pattern outerRegex = Pattern.compile("<b>(.*?)</b>", Pattern.DOTALL);
Pattern innerRegex = Pattern.compile("\\d+");
Matcher outerMatcher = outerRegex.matcher(subjectString);
Matcher innerMatcher = innerRegex.matcher(subjectString);
while (outerMatcher.find()) {
    innerMatcher.region(outerMatcher.start(), outerMatcher.end());
    while (innerMatcher.find()) {
        resultList.add(innerMatcher.group());
    }
}
```

JavaScript

```javascript
var result = [];
var outerRegex = /<b>([\s\S]*?)<\/b>/g;
var innerRegex = /\d+/g;
var outerMatch = null;
while (outerMatch = outerRegex.exec(subject)) {
    if (outerMatch.index == outerRegex.lastIndex)
        outerRegex.lastIndex++;
    var innerSubject = subject.substr(outerMatch.index,
                                      outerMatch[0].length);
    var innerMatch = null;
    while (innerMatch = innerRegex.exec(innerSubject)) {
        if (innerMatch.index == innerRegex.lastIndex)
            innerRegex.lastIndex++;
        result.push(innerMatch[0]);
```

```
        }
    }
```

PHP

```php
$list = array();
preg_match_all('%<b>(.*?)</b>%s', $subject, $outermatches,
               PREG_PATTERN_ORDER);
for ($i = 0; $i < count($outermatches[0]); $i++) {
    if (preg_match_all('/\d+/', $outermatches[0][$i], $innermatches,
                       PREG_PATTERN_ORDER)) {
        $list = array_merge($list, $innermatches[0]);
    }
}
```

Perl

```perl
while ($subject =~ m!<b>(.*?)</b>!gs) {
    push(@list, ($& =~ m/\d+/g));
}
```

This only works if the inner regular expression (‹\d+›, in this example) doesn't have any capturing groups, so use noncapturing groups instead. See Recipe 2.9 for details.

Python

```python
list = []
innerre = re.compile(r"\d+")
for outermatch in re.finditer("(?s)<b>(.*?)</b>", subject):
    list.extend(innerre.findall(outermatch.group(1)))
```

Ruby

```ruby
list = []
subject.scan(/<b>(.*?)<\/b>/m) {|outergroups|
    list += outergroups[0].scan(/\d+/)
}
```

Discussion

Regular expressions are well-suited for tokenizing input, but they are not well-suited for parsing input. Tokenizing means to identify different parts of a string, such as numbers, words, symbols, tags, comments, etc. It involves scanning the text from left to right, trying different alternatives and quantities of characters to be matched. Regular expressions handle this very well.

Parsing means to process the relationship between those tokens. For example, in a programming language, combinations of such tokens form statements, functions, classes, namespaces, etc. Keeping track of the meaning of the tokens within the larger context of the input is best left to procedural code. In particular, regular expressions cannot keep track of nonlinear context, such as nested constructs.[*]

Trying to find one kind of token within another kind of token is a task that people commonly try to tackle with regular expressions. A pair of HTML bold tags is easily matched with the regular expression ‹(.*?)›.[†] A number is even more easily matched with the regex ‹\d+›. But if you try to combine these into a single regex, you'll end up with something rather different:

\d+(?=(?:.(?!))*)
Regex options: None
Regex flavors: .NET, Java, JavaScript, PCRE, Perl, Python, Ruby

Though the regular expression just shown is a solution to the problem posed by this recipe, it is hardly intuitive. Even a regular expression expert will have to carefully scrutinize the regex to determine what it does, or perhaps resort to a tool to highlight the matches. And this is the combination of just two simple regexes.

A better solution is to keep the two regular expressions as they are and use procedural code to combine them. The resulting code, while a bit longer, is much easier to understand and maintain, and creating simple code is the reason for using regular expressions in the first place. A regex such as ‹(.*?)› is easy to understand by anyone with a modicum of regex experience, and quickly does what would otherwise take many more lines of code that are harder to maintain.

Though the solutions for this recipe are some of the most complex ones in this chapter, they're very straightforward. Two regular expressions are used. The "outer" regular expression matches the HTML bold tags and the text between them, and the text in between is captured by the first capturing group. This regular expression is implemented with the same code shown in Recipe 3.11. The only difference is that the placeholder comment saying where to use the match has been replaced with code that lets the "inner" regular expression do its job.

The second regular expression matches a digit. This regex is implemented with the same code as shown in Recipe 3.10. The only difference is that instead of processing the subject string entirely, the second regex is applied only to the part of the subject string matched by the first capturing group of the outer regular expression.

There are two ways to restrict the inner regular expressions to the text matched by (a capturing group of) the outer regular expressions. Some languages provide a function that allows the regular expression to be applied to part of a string. That can save an extra string copy if the match function doesn't automatically fill a structure with the

---

[*] A few modern regex flavors have tried to introduce features for balanced or recursive matching. These features result in such complex regular expessions, however, that they only end up proving my point that parsing is best left to procedural code.

[†] To allow the tag to span multiple lines, turn on "dot matches line breaks" mode. For JavaScript, use ‹([\s \S]*?)›.

text matched by the capturing groups. We can always simply retrieve the substring matched by the capturing group and apply the inner regex to that.

Either way, using two regular expressions together in a loop will be faster than using the one regular expression with its nested lookahead groups. The latter requires the regex engine to do a whole lot of backtracking. On large files, using just one regex will be much slower, as it needs to determine the section boundaries (HTML bold tags) for each number in the subject string, including numbers that are not between <b> tags. The solution that uses two regular expressions doesn't even begin to look for numbers until it has found the section boundaries, which it does in linear time.

See Also

Recipes 3.8, 3.10, and 3.11

3.14 Replace All Matches

Problem

You want to replace all matches of the regular expression ‹before› with the replacement text «after».

Solution

C#

You can use the static call when you process only a small number of strings with the same regular expression:

```
string resultString = Regex.Replace(subjectString, "before", "after");
```

If the regex is provided by the end user, you should use the static call with full exception handling:

```
string resultString = null;
try {
    resultString = Regex.Replace(subjectString, "before", "after");
} catch (ArgumentNullException ex) {
    // Cannot pass null as the regular expression, subject string,
    // or replacement text
} catch (ArgumentException ex) {
    // Syntax error in the regular expression
}
```

Construct a Regex object if you want to use the same regular expression with a large number of strings:

```
Regex regexObj = new Regex("before");
string resultString = regexObj.Replace(subjectString, "after");
```

If the regex is provided by the end user, you should use the Regex object with full exception handling:

```csharp
string resultString = null;
try {
    Regex regexObj = new Regex("before");
    try {
        resultString = regexObj.Replace(subjectString, "after");
    } catch (ArgumentNullException ex) {
        // Cannot pass null as the subject string or replacement text
    }
} catch (ArgumentException ex) {
    // Syntax error in the regular expression
}
```

VB.NET

You can use the static call when you process only a small number of strings with the same regular expression:

```vbnet
Dim ResultString = Regex.Replace(SubjectString, "before", "after")
```

If the regex is provided by the end user, you should use the static call with full exception handling:

```vbnet
Dim ResultString As String = Nothing
Try
    ResultString = Regex.Replace(SubjectString, "before", "after")
Catch ex As ArgumentNullException
    'Cannot pass null as the regular expression, subject string,
    'or replacement text
Catch ex As ArgumentException
    'Syntax error in the regular expression
End Try
```

Construct a Regex object if you want to use the same regular expression with a large number of strings:

```vbnet
Dim RegexObj As New Regex("before")
Dim ResultString = RegexObj.Replace(SubjectString, "after")
```

If the regex is provided by the end user, you should use the Regex object with full exception handling:

```vbnet
Dim ResultString As String = Nothing
Try
    Dim RegexObj As New Regex("before")
    Try
        ResultString = RegexObj.Replace(SubjectString, "after")
    Catch ex As ArgumentNullException
        'Cannot pass null as the subject string or replacement text
```

```
        End Try
Catch ex As ArgumentException
    'Syntax error in the regular expression
End Try
```

Java

You can use the static call when you process only one string with the same regular expression:

```
String resultString = subjectString.replaceAll("before", "after");
```

If the regex or replacement text is provided by the end user, you should use the static call with full exception handling:

```
try {
    String resultString = subjectString.replaceAll("before", "after");
} catch (PatternSyntaxException ex) {
    // Syntax error in the regular expression
} catch (IllegalArgumentException ex) {
    // Syntax error in the replacement text (unescaped $ signs?)
} catch (IndexOutOfBoundsException ex) {
    // Non-existent backreference used the replacement text
}
```

Construct a Matcher object if you want to use the same regular expression with a large number of strings:

```
Pattern regex = Pattern.compile("before");
Matcher regexMatcher = regex.matcher(subjectString);
String resultString = regexMatcher.replaceAll("after");
```

If the regex or replacement text is provided by the end user, you should use the Regex object with full exception handling:

```
String resultString = null;
try {
    Pattern regex = Pattern.compile("before");
    Matcher regexMatcher = regex.matcher(subjectString);
    try {
        resultString = regexMatcher.replaceAll("after");
    } catch (IllegalArgumentException ex) {
        // Syntax error in the replacement text (unescaped $ signs?)
    } catch (IndexOutOfBoundsException ex) {
        // Non-existent backreference used the replacement text
    }
} catch (PatternSyntaxException ex) {
    // Syntax error in the regular expression
}
```

JavaScript

```
result = subject.replace(/before/g, "after");
```

PHP

```
$result = preg_replace('/before/', 'after', $subject);
```

Perl

With the subject string held in the special variable $_, storing the result back into $_:

```
s/before/after/g;
```

With the subject string held in the variable $subject, storing the result back into $subject:

```
$subject =~ s/before/after/g;
```

With the subject string held in the variable $subject, storing the result into $result:

```
($result = $subject) =~ s/before/after/g;
```

Python

If you have only a few strings to process, you can use the global function:

```
result = re.sub("before", "after", subject)
```

To use the same regex repeatedly, use a compiled object:

```
reobj = re.compile("before")
result = reobj.sub("after", subject)
```

Ruby

```
result = subject.gsub(/before/, 'after')
```

Discussion

.NET

In .NET, you will always use the `Regex.Replace()` method to search and replace with a regular expression. The `Replace()` method has 10 overloads. Half of those take a string as the replacement text; those are discussed here. The other half take a `MatchEvaluator` delegate as the replacement, and those are discussed in Recipe 3.16.

The first parameter expected by `Replace()`, is always the string that holds the original subject text you want to search and replace through. This parameter should not be `null`. Otherwise, `Replace()` will throw an `ArgumentNullException`. The return value of `Replace()` is always the string with the replacements applied.

If you want to use the regular expression only a few times, you can use a static call. The second parameter is then the regular expression you want to use. Specify the replacement text as the third parameter. You can pass regex options as an optional fourth parameter. If your regular expression has a syntax error, an `ArgumentException` will be thrown.

If you want to use the same regular expression on many strings, you can make your code more efficient by constructing a `Regex` object first, and then calling `Replace()` on that object. Pass the subject string as the first parameter and the replacement text as the second parameter. Those are the only required parameters.

When calling `Replace()` on an instance of the `Regex` class, you can pass additional parameters to limit the search-and-replace. If you omit these parameters, all matches of the regular expression in the subject string will be replaced. The static overloads of `Replace()` do not allow these additional parameters; they always replace all matches.

As the optional third parameter, after the subject and replacement, you can pass the number of replacements to be made. If you pass a number greater than one, that is the maximum number of replacements that will be made. For example, `Replace(subject, replacement, 3)` replaces only the first three regular expression matches, and further matches are ignored. If there are fewer than three possible matches in the string, all matches will be replaced. You will not receive any indication that fewer replacements were made than you requested. If you pass zero as the third parameter, no replacements will be made at all and the subject string will be returned unchanged. If you pass `-1`, all regex matches are replaced. Specifying a number less than `-1` will cause `Replace()` to throw an `ArgumentOutOfRangeException`.

If you specify the third parameter with the number of replacements to be made, then you can specify an optional fourth parameter to indicate the character index at which the regular expression should begin to search. Essentially, the number you pass as the fourth parameter is the number of characters at the start of your subject string that the regular expression should ignore. This can be useful when you've already processed the string up to a point, and you want to search and replace only through the remainder of the string. If you specify the number, it must be between zero and the length of the subject string. Otherwise, `Replace()` throws an `ArgumentOutOfRangeException`. Unlike `Match()`, `Replace()` does not allow you to provide a parameter that specifies the length of the substring the regular expression is allowed to search through.

Java

If you only want to search and replace through one string with the same regex, you can call either the `replaceFirst()` or `replaceAll()` method directly on your string. Both methods take two parameters: a string with your regular expression and a string with your replacement text. These are convenience functions that call `Pattern.compile("before").matcher(subjectString).replaceFirst("after")` and `Pattern.compile("before").matcher(subjectString).replaceAll("after")`.

If you want to use the same regex on multiple strings, you should create the `Matcher` object as explained in Recipe 3.3. Then, call `replaceFirst()` or `replaceAll()` on your matcher, passing the replacement text as the only parameter.

There are three different exception classes you have to contend with if the regex and replacement text are provided by the end user. The exception class `PatternSyntaxException` is thrown by `Pattern.compile()`, `String.replaceFirst()`, and `String.replaceAll()` if the regular expression has a syntax error. `Illegal ArgumentException` is thrown by `replaceFirst()` and `replaceAll()` if there's a syntax error in the replacement text. If the replacement text is syntactically valid but references a capturing group that does not exist, then `IndexOutOfBoundsException` is thrown instead.

JavaScript

To search and replace through a string using a regular expression, call the `replace()` function on the string. Pass your regular expression as the first parameter and the string with your replacement text as the second parameter. The `replace()` function returns a new string with the replacements applied.

If you want to replace all regex matches in the string, set the /g flag when creating your regular expression object. Recipe 3.4 explains how this works. If you don't use the /g flag, only the first match will be replaced.

PHP

You can easily search and replace through a string with `preg_replace()`. Pass your regular expression as the first parameter, the replacement text as the second parameter, and the subject string as the third parameter. The return value is a string with the replacements applied.

The optional fourth parameter allows you to limit the number of replacements made. If you omit the parameter or specify `-1`, all regex matches are replaced. If you specify `0`, no replacements are made. If you specify a positive number, `preg_replace()` will replace up to as many regex matches as you specified. If there are fewer matches, all of them are replaced without error.

If you want to know how many replacements were made, you can add a fifth parameter to the call. This parameter will receive an integer with the number of replacements that were actually made.

A special feature of `preg_replace()` is that you can pass arrays instead of strings for the first three parameters. If you pass an array of strings instead of a single string as the third parameter, `preg_replace()` will return an array with the search-and-replace done on all the strings.

If you pass an array of regular expression strings as the first parameter, preg_replace() will use the regular expressions one by one to search and replace through the subject string. If you pass an array of subject strings, all the regular expressions are used on all the subject strings. When searching for an array or regular expressions, you can specify either a single string as the replacement (to be used by all the regexes) or an array of replacements. When using two arrays, preg_replace() walks through both the regex and replacement arrays, using a different replacement text for each regex. preg_replace() walks through the array as it is stored in memory, which is not necessarily the numerical order of the indexes in the array. If you didn't build the array in numerical order, call ksort() on the arrays with the regular expressions and replacement texts before passing them to preg_replace().

This example builds the $replace array in reverse order:

```
$regex[0] = '/a/';
$regex[1] = '/b/';
$regex[2] = '/c/';
$replace[2] = '3';
$replace[1] = '2';
$replace[0] = '1';

echo preg_replace($regex, $replace, "abc");
ksort($replace);
echo preg_replace($regex, $replace, "abc");
```

The first call to preg_replace() displays 321, which is not what you might expect. After using ksort(), the replacement returns 123 as we intended. ksort() modifies the variable you pass to it. Don't pass its return value (true or false) to preg_replace.

Perl

In Perl, s/// is in fact a substitution operator. If you use s/// by itself, it will search and replace through the $_ variable, storing the result back into $_.

If you want to use the substitution operator on another variable, use the =~ binding operator to associate the substitution operator with your variable. Binding the substitution operator to a string immediately executes the search-and-replace. The result is stored back into the variable that holds the subject string.

The s/// operator always modifies the variable you bind it to. If you want to store the result of the search-and-replace in a new variable without modifying the original, first assign the original string to the result variable, and then bind the substitution operator to that variable. The Perl solution to this recipe shows how you can take those two steps in one line of code.

Use the /g modifier explained in Recipe 3.4 to replace all regex matches. Without it, Perl replaces only the first match.

Python

The `sub()` function in the `re` module performs a search-and-replace using a regular expression. Pass your regular expression as the first parameter, your replacement text as the second parameter, and the subject string as the third parameter. The global `sub()` function does not accept a parameter with regular expression options.

The `re.sub()` function calls `re.compile()`, and then calls the `sub()` method on the compiled regular expression object. This method has two required parameters: the replacement text and the subject string.

Both forms of `sub()` return a string with all the regular expressions replaced. Both take one optional parameter that you can use to limit the number of replacements to be made. If you omit it or set it to zero, all regex matches are replaced. If you pass a positive number, that is the maximum number of matches to be replaced. If fewer matches can be found than the count you specified, all matches are replaced without error.

Ruby

The `gsub()` method of the `String` class does a search-and-replace using a regular expression. Pass the regular expression as the first parameter and a string with the replacement text as the second parameter. The return value is a new string with the replacements applied. If no regex matches can be found, then `gsub()` returns the original string.

`gsub()` does not modify the string on which you call the method. If you want the original string to be modified, call `gsub!()` instead. If no regex matches can be found, `gsub!()` returns `nil`. Otherwise, it returns the string you called it on, with the replacements applied.

See Also

"Searching and Replacing with Regular Expressions" in Chapter 1, and Recipes 3.15 and 3.16

3.15 Replace Matches Reusing Parts of the Match

Problem

You want to run a search-and-replace that reinserts parts of the regex match back into the replacement. The parts you want to reinsert have been isolated in your regular expression using capturing groups, as described in Recipe 2.9.

For example, you want to match pairs of words delimited by an equals sign, and swap those words in the replacement.

Solution

C#

You can use the static call when you process only a small number of strings with the same regular expression:

```
string resultString = Regex.Replace(subjectString, @"(\w+)=(\w+)",
                                     "$2=$1");
```

Construct a Regex object if you want to use the same regular expression with a large number of strings:

```
Regex regexObj = new Regex(@"(\w+)=(\w+)");
string resultString = regexObj.Replace(subjectString, "$2=$1");
```

VB.NET

You can use the static call when you process only a small number of strings with the same regular expression:

```
Dim ResultString = Regex.Replace(SubjectString, "(\w+)=(\w+)", "$2=$1")
```

Construct a Regex object if you want to use the same regular expression with a large number of strings:

```
Dim RegexObj As New Regex("(\w+)=(\w+)")
Dim ResultString = RegexObj.Replace(SubjectString, "$2=$1")
```

Java

You can call String.replaceAll() when you process only one string with the same regular expression:

```
String resultString = subjectString.replaceAll("(\\w+)=(\\w+)", "$2=$1");
```

Construct a Matcher object if you want to use the same regular expression with a large number of strings:

```
Pattern regex = Pattern.compile("(\\w+)=(\\w+)");
Matcher regexMatcher = regex.matcher(subjectString);
String resultString = regexMatcher.replaceAll("$2=$1");
```

JavaScript

```
result = subject.replace(/(\w+)=(\w+)/g, "$2=$1");
```

PHP

```
$result = preg_replace('/(\w+)=(\w+)/', '$2=$1', $subject);
```

Perl

```
$subject =~ s/(\w+)=(\w+)/$2=$1/g;
```

Python

If you have only a few strings to process, you can use the global function:

```
result = re.sub(r"(\w+)=(\w+)", r"\2=\1", subject)
```

To use the same regex repeatedly, use a compiled object:

```
reobj = re.compile(r"(\w+)=(\w+)")
result = reobj.sub(r"\2=\1", subject)
```

Ruby

```
result = subject.gsub(/(\w+)=(\w+)/, '\2=\1')
```

Discussion

The regular expression ‹(\w+)=(\w+)› matches the pair of words and captures each word into its own capturing group. The word before the equals sign is captured by the first group, and the word after the sign by the second group.

For the replacement, you need to specify that you want to use the text matched by the second capturing group, followed by an equals sign, followed by the text matched by the first capturing group. You can do this with special placeholders in the replacement text. The replacement text syntax varies widely between different programming languages. "Searching and Replacing with Regular Expressions" in Chapter 1 describes the replacement text flavors, and Recipe 2.21 explains how to reference capturing groups in the replacement text.

.NET

In .NET, you can use the same `Regex.Replace()` method described in the previous recipe, using a string as the replacement. The syntax for adding backreferences to the replacement text follows the .NET replacement text flavor Recipe 2.21.

Java

In Java, you can use the same `replaceFirst()` and `replaceAll()` methods described in the previous recipe. The syntax for adding backreferences to the replacement text follows the Java replacement text flavor described in this book.

JavaScript

In JavaScript, you can use the same `string.replace()` method described in the previous recipe. The syntax for adding backreferences to the replacement text follows the JavaScript replacement text flavor described in this book.

PHP

In PHP, you can use the same `preg_replace()` function described in the previous recipe. The syntax for adding backreferences to the replacement text follows the PHP replacement text flavor described in this book.

Perl

In Perl, the `replace` part in `s/regex/replace/` is simply interpreted as a double-quoted string. You can use the special variables `$&`, `$1`, `$2`, etc. explained in Recipe 3.7 and Recipe 3.9 in the replacement string. The variables are set right after the regex match is found, before it is replaced. You can also use these variables in all other Perl code. Their values persist until you tell Perl to find another regex match.

All the other programming languages in this book provide a function call that takes the replacement text as a string. The function call parses the string to process backreferences such as `$1` or `\1`. But outside the replacement text string, `$1` has no meaning with these languages.

Python

In Python, you can use the same `sub()` function described in the previous recipe. The syntax for adding backreferences to the replacement text follows the Python replacement text flavor described in this book.

Ruby

In Ruby, you can use the same `String.gsub()` method described in the previous recipe. The syntax for adding backreferences to the replacement text follows the Ruby replacement text flavor described in this book.

You cannot interpolate variables such as `$1` in the replacement text. That's because Ruby does variable interpolation before the `gsub()` call is executed. Before the call, `gsub()` hasn't found any matches yet, so backreferences can't be substituted. If you try to interpolate `$1`, you'll get the text matched by the first capturing group in the last regex match before the call to `gsub()`.

Instead, use replacement text tokens such as «\1». The `gsub()` function substitutes those tokens in the replacement text for each regex match. I recommend that you use single-quoted strings for the replacement text. In double-quoted strings, the backslash is used as an escape, and escaped digits are octal escapes. '\1' and "\\1" use the text matched by the first capturing group as the replacement, whereas "\1" substitutes the single literal character 0x01.

Named Capture

If you use named capturing groups in your regular expression, you can reference the groups by their names in your replacement string.

C#

You can use the static call when you process only a small number of strings with the same regular expression:

```csharp
string resultString = Regex.Replace(subjectString,
                          @"(?<left>\w+)=(?<right>\w+)", "${right}=${left}");
```

Construct a `Regex` object if you want to use the same regular expression with a large number of strings:

```csharp
Regex regexObj = new Regex(@"(?<left>\w+)=(?<right>\w+)");
string resultString = regexObj.Replace(subjectString, "${right}=${left}");
```

VB.NET

You can use the static call when you process only a small number of strings with the same regular expression:

```vbnet
Dim ResultString = Regex.Replace(SubjectString,
                      "(?<left>\w+)=(?<right>\w+)", "${right}=${left}")
```

Construct a `Regex` object if you want to use the same regular expression with a large number of strings:

```vbnet
Dim RegexObj As New Regex("(?<left>\w+)=(?<right>\w+)")
Dim ResultString = RegexObj.Replace(SubjectString, "${right}=${left}")
```

PHP

```php
$result = preg_replace('/(?P<left>\w+)=(?P<right>\w+)/',
                      '$2=$1', $subject);
```

PHP's `preg` functions use the PCRE library, which supports named capture. The `preg_match()` and `preg_match_all()` functions add named capturing groups to the array with match results. Unfortunately, `preg_replace()` does not provide a way to use named backreferences in the replacement text. If your regex has named capturing groups, count both the named and numbered capturing groups from left to right to determine the backreference number of each group. Use those numbers in the replacement text.

Perl

```perl
$subject =~ s/(?<left>\w+)=(?<right>\w+)/$+{right}=$+{left}/g;
```

Perl supports named capturing groups starting with version 5.10. The `$+` hash stores the text matched by all named capturing groups in the regular expression last used. You can use this hash in the replacement text string, as well as anywhere else.

Python

If you have only a few strings to process, you can use the global function:

```
result = re.sub(r"(?P<left>\w+)=(?P<right>\w+)", r"\g<right>=\g<left>",
              subject)
```

To use the same regex repeatedly, use a compiled object:

```
reobj = re.compile(r"(?P<left>\w+)=(?P<right>\w+)")
result = reobj.sub(r"\g<right>=\g<left>", subject)
```

Ruby

```
result = subject.gsub(/(?<left>\w+)=(?<right>\w+)/, '\k<left>=\k<right>')
```

See Also

"Searching and Replacing with Regular Expressions" in Chapter 1 describes the replacement text flavors.

Recipe 2.21 explains how to reference capturing groups in the replacement text.

3.16 Replace Matches with Replacements Generated in Code

Problem

You want to replace all matches of a regular expression with a new string that you build up in procedural code. You want to be able to replace each match with a different string, based on the text that was actually matched.

For example, suppose you want to replace all numbers in a string with the number multiplied by two.

Solution

C#

You can use the static call when you process only a small number of strings with the same regular expression:

```
string resultString = Regex.Replace(subjectString, @"\d+",
                    new MatchEvaluator(ComputeReplacement));
```

Construct a Regex object if you want to use the same regular expression with a large number of strings:

```
Regex regexObj = new Regex(@"\d+");
string resultString = regexObj.Replace(subjectString,
                    new MatchEvaluator(ComputeReplacement));
```

Both code snippets call the function ComputeReplacement. You should add this method to the class in which you're implementing this solution:

```
public String ComputeReplacement(Match matchResult) {
    int twiceasmuch = int.Parse(matchResult.Value) * 2;
    return twiceasmuch.ToString();
}
```

VB.NET

You can use the static call when you process only a small number of strings with the same regular expression:

```
Dim MyMatchEvaluator As New MatchEvaluator(AddressOf ComputeReplacement)
Dim ResultString = Regex.Replace(SubjectString, "\d+", MyMatchEvaluator)
```

Construct a Regex object if you want to use the same regular expression with a large number of strings:

```
Dim RegexObj As New Regex("\d+")
Dim MyMatchEvaluator As New MatchEvaluator(AddressOf ComputeReplacement)
Dim ResultString = RegexObj.Replace(SubjectString, MyMatchEvaluator)
```

Both code snippets call the function ComputeReplacement. You should add this method to the class in which you're implementing this solution:

```
Public Function ComputeReplacement(ByVal MatchResult As Match) As String
    Dim TwiceAsMuch = Int.Parse(MatchResult.Value) * 2;
    Return TwiceAsMuch.ToString();
End Function
```

Java

```
StringBuffer resultString = new StringBuffer();
Pattern regex = Pattern.compile("\\d+");
Matcher regexMatcher = regex.matcher(subjectString);
while (regexMatcher.find()) {
    Integer twiceasmuch = Integer.parseInt(regexMatcher.group()) * 2;
    regexMatcher.appendReplacement(resultString, twiceasmuch.toString());
}
regexMatcher.appendTail(resultString);
```

JavaScript

```
var result = subject.replace(/\d+/g,
                             function(match) { return match * 2; }
                             );
```

PHP

Using a declared callback function:

```
$result = preg_replace_callback('/\d+/', compute_replacement, $subject);

function compute_replacement($groups) {
```

```
        return $groups[0] * 2;
    }
```

Using an anonymous callback function:

```
$result = preg_replace_callback(
    '/\d+/',
    create_function(
        '$groups',
        'return $groups[0] * 2;'
    ),
    $subject
);
```

Perl

```
$subject =~ s/\d+/$& * 2/eg;
```

Python

If you have only a few strings to process, you can use the global function:

```
result = re.sub(r"\d+", computereplacement, subject)
```

To use the same regex repeatedly, use a compiled object:

```
reobj = re.compile(r"\d+")
result = reobj.sub(computereplacement, subject)
```

Both code snippets call the function computereplacement. This function needs to be declared before you can pass it to sub().

```
def computereplacement(matchobj):
    return str(int(matchobj.group()) * 2)
```

Ruby

```
result = subject.gsub(/\d+/) {|match|
    Integer(match) * 2
}
```

Discussion

When using a string as the replacement text, you can do only basic text substitution. To replace each match with something totally different that varies along with the match being replaced, you need to create the replacement text in your own code.

C#

Recipe 3.14 discusses the various ways in which you can call the Regex.Replace() method, passing a string as the replacement text. When using a static call, the replacement is the third parameter, after the subject and the regular expression. If you passed the regular expression to the `Regex()` constructor, you can call `Replace()` on that object with the replacement as the second parameter.

Instead of passing a string as the second or third parameter, you can pass a `Match Evaluator` delegate. This delegate is a reference to a member function that you add to the class where you're doing the search-and-replace. To create the delegate, use the `new` keyword to call the `MatchEvaluator()` constructor. Pass your member function as the only parameter to `MatchEvaluator()`.

The function you want to use for the delegate should return a string and take one parameter of class `System.Text.RegularExpressions.Match`. This is the same `Match` class returned by the `Regex.Match()` member used in nearly all the previous recipes in this chapter.

When you call `Replace()` with a `MatchEvaluator` as the replacement, your function will be called for each regular expression match that needs to be replaced. Your function needs to return the replacement text. You can use any of the properties of the `Match` object to build your replacement text. The example shown earlier uses `matchResult.Value` to retrieve the string with the whole regex match. Often, you'll use `matchResult.Groups[]` to build up your replacement text from the capturing groups in your regular expression.

If you do not want to replace certain regex matches, your function should return `matchResult.Value`. If you return `null` or an empty string, the regex match is replaced with nothing (i.e., deleted).

VB.NET

Recipe 3.14 discusses the various ways in which you can call the `Regex.Replace()` method, passing a string as the replacement text. When using a static call, the replacement text is the third parameter, after the subject and the regular expression. If you used the `Dim` keyword to create a variable with your regular expression, you can call `Replace()` on that object with the replacement as the second parameter.

Instead of passing a string as the second or third parameter, you can pass a `Match Evaluator` object. This object holds a reference to a function that you add to the class where you're doing the search-and-replace. Use the `Dim` keyword to create a new variable of type `MatchEvaluator`. Pass one parameter with the `AddressOf` keyword followed by the name of your member function. The `AddressOf` operator returns a reference to your function, without actually calling the function at that point.

The function you want to use for `MatchEvaluator` should return a string and should take one parameter of class `System.Text.RegularExpressions.Match`. This is the same `Match` class returned by the `Regex.Match()` member used in nearly all the previous recipes in this chapter. The parameter will be passed by value, so you have to declare it with `ByVal`.

When you call `Replace()` with a `MatchEvaluator` as the replacement, your function will be called for each regular expression match that needs to be replaced. Your function needs to return the replacement text. You can use any of the properties of the `Match` object to build your replacement text. The example uses `MatchResult.Value` to retrieve the string with the whole regex match. Often, you'll use `MatchResult.Groups()` to build up your replacement text from the capturing groups in your regular expression.

If you do not want to replace certain regex matches, your function should return `MatchResult.Value`. If you return `Nothing` or an empty string, the regex match is replaced with nothing (i.e., deleted).

Java

The Java solution is very straightforward. We iterate over all the regex matches as explained in Recipe 3.11. Inside the loop, we call `appendReplacement()` on our `Matcher` object. When `find()` fails to find any further matches, we call `appendTail()`. The two methods `appendReplacement()` and `appendTail()` make it very easy to use a different replacement text for each regex match.

`appendReplacement()` takes two parameters. The first is the `StringBuffer` where you're (temporarily) storing the result of the search-and-replace in progress. The second is the replacement text to be used for the last match found by `find()`. This replacement text can include references to capturing groups, such as `"$1"`. If there is a syntax error in your replacement text, an `IllegalArgumentException` is thrown. If the replacement text references a capturing group that does not exist, an `IndexOutOfBoundsException` is thrown instead. If you call `appendReplacement()` without a prior successful call to `find()`, it throws an `IllegalStateException`.

If you call `appendReplacement()` correctly, it does two things. First, it copies the text located between the previous and current regex match to the string buffer, without making any modifications to the text. If the current match is the first one, it copies all the text before that match. After that, it appends your replacement text, substituting any backreferences in it with the text matched by the referenced capturing groups.

If you want to delete a particular match, simply replace it with an empty string. If you want to leave a match in the string unchanged, you can omit the call to `appendReplacement()` for that match. When I say "previous regex match," I mean the previous match for which you called `appendReplacement()`. If you don't call `appendReplacement()` for certain matches, those become part of the text between the matches that you do replace, which is copied unchanged into the target string buffer.

When you're done replacing matches, call `appendTail()`. That copies the text at the end of the string after the last regex match for which you called `appendReplacement()`.

JavaScript

In JavaScript, a function is really just another object that can be assigned to a variable. Instead of passing a literal string or a variable that holds a string to the `string.replace()` function, we can pass a function that returns a string. This function is then called each time a replacement needs to be made.

You can make your replacement function accept one or more parameters. If you do, the first parameter will be set to the text matched by the regular expression. If your regular expression has capturing groups, the second parameter will hold the text matched by the first capturing group, the third parameter gives you the text of the second capturing group, and so on. You can set these parameters to use bits of the regular expression match to compose the replacement.

The replacement function in the JavaScript solution for this recipe simply takes the text matched by the regular expression, and returns it multiplied by two. JavaScript handles the string-to-number and number-to-string conversions implicitly.

PHP

The `preg_replace_callback()` function works just like the `preg_replace()` function described in Recipe 3.14. It takes a regular expression, replacement, subject string, optional replacement limit, and optional replacement count. The regular expression and subject string can be single strings or arrays.

The difference is that `preg_replace_callback()` doesn't accept a string or array of strings for the replacement; it accepts a function. You can declare this function in your code or use `create_function()` to create an anonymous function. The function should take one parameter and return a string (or something that can be coerced into a string).

Each time `preg_replace_callback()` finds a regex match, it will call your callback function. The parameter will be filled with an array of strings. Element zero holds the overall regex match, and elements one and beyond hold the text matched by capturing groups one and beyond. You can use this array to build up your replacement text using the text matched by the regular expression or one or more capturing groups.

Perl

The `s///` operator supports one extra modifier that is ignored by the `m//` operator: `/e`. The `/e`, or "execute," modifier tells the substitution operator to execute the replacement part as Perl code, instead of interpreting it as the contents of a double-quoted string. Using this modifier, we can easily retrieve the matched text with the `$&` variable, and then multiply it by two. The result of the code is used as the replacement string.

Python

Python's `sub()` function allows you to pass the name of a function instead of a string as the replacement text. This function is then called for each regex match to be replaced.

You need to declare this function before you can reference it. It should take one parameter to receive a `MatchObject` instance, which is the same object returned by the `search()` function. You can use it to retrieve (part of) the regex match to build your replacement. See Recipe 3.7 and Recipe 3.9 for details.

Your function should return a string with the replacement text.

Ruby

The previous two recipes called the `gsub()` method of the `String` class with two parameters: the regex and the replacement text. This method also exists in block form.

In block form, `gsub()` takes your regular expression as its only parameter. It fills one iterator variable with a string that holds the text matched by the regular expression. If you supply additional iterator variables, they are set to `nil`, even if your regular expression has capturing groups.

Inside the block, place an expression that evaluates to the string that you want to use as the replacement text. You can use the special regex match variables, such as `$~`, `$&`, and `$1`, inside the block. Their values change each time the block is evaluated to make another replacement. See Recipes 3.7, 3.8, and 3.9 for details.

You cannot use replacement text tokens such as «\1». Those remain as literal text.

See Also

Recipes 3.9 and 3.15

3.17 Replace All Matches Within the Matches of Another Regex

Problem

You want to replace all the matches of a particular regular expression, but only within certain sections of the subject string. Another regular expression matches each of the sections in the string.

Say you have an HTML file in which various passages are marked as bold with `<b>` tags. Between each pair of bold tags, you want to replace all matches of the regular expression ‹before› with the replacement text ‹after›. For example, when processing the string `before <b>first before</b> before <b>before before</b>`, you want to end up with: `before <b>first after</b> before <b>after after</b>`.

Solution

C#

```
Regex outerRegex = new Regex("<b>.*?</b>", RegexOptions.Singleline);
Regex innerRegex = new Regex("before");
```

```
string resultString = outerRegex.Replace(subjectString,
                        new MatchEvaluator(ComputeReplacement));

public String ComputeReplacement(Match matchResult) {
    // Run the inner search-and-replace on each match of the outer regex
    return innerRegex.Replace(matchResult.Value, "after");
}
```

VB.NET

```
Dim OuterRegex As New Regex("<b>.*?</b>", RegexOptions.Singleline)
Dim InnerRegex As New Regex("before")
Dim MyMatchEvaluator As New MatchEvaluator(AddressOf ComputeReplacement)
Dim ResultString = OuterRegex.Replace(SubjectString, MyMatchEvaluator)

Public Function ComputeReplacement(ByVal MatchResult As Match) As String
    'Run the inner search-and-replace on each match of the outer regex
    Return InnerRegex.Replace(MatchResult.Value, "after");
End Function
```

Java

```
StringBuffer resultString = new StringBuffer();
Pattern outerRegex = Pattern.compile("<b>.*?</b>");
Pattern innerRegex = Pattern.compile("before");
Matcher outerMatcher = outerRegex.matcher(subjectString);
while (outerMatcher.find()) {
    outerMatcher.appendReplacement(resultString,
        innerRegex.matcher(outerMatcher.group()).replaceAll("after"));
}
outerMatcher.appendTail(resultString);
```

JavaScript

```
var result = subject.replace(/<b>.*?<\/b>/g,
                        function(match) {
                            return match.replace(/before/g, "after");
                        }
                    );
```

PHP

```
$result = preg_replace_callback('%<b>.*?</b>%',
                        replace_within_tag, $subject);

function replace_within_tag($groups) {
    return preg_replace('/before/', 'after', $groups[0]);
}
```

Perl

```
$subject =~ s%<b>.*?</b>%($match = $&) =~ s/before/after/g; $match;%eg;
```

Python

```
innerre = re.compile("before")
def replacewithin(matchobj):
    return innerre.sub("after", matchobj.group())

result = re.sub("<b>.*?</b>", replacewithin, subject)
```

Ruby

```
innerre = /before/
result = subject.gsub(/<b>.*?<\/b>/) {|match|
    match.gsub(innerre, 'after')
}
```

Discussion

This solution is again the combination of two previous solutions, using two regular expressions. The "outer" regular expression, ‹<b>.*?</b>›, matches the HTML bold tags and the text between them. The "inner" regular expression matches the "before," which we'll replace with "after."

Recipe 3.16 explains how you can run a search-and-replace and build the replacement text for each regex match in your own code. Here, we do this with the outer regular expression. Each time it finds a pair of opening and closing <b> tags, we run a search-and-replace using the inner regex, just as we do in Recipe 3.14. The subject string for the search-and-replace with the inner regex is the text matched by the outer regex.

See Also

Recipes 3.11, 3.13, and 3.16

3.18 Replace All Matches Between the Matches of Another Regex

Problem

You want to replace all the matches of a particular regular expression, but only within certain sections of the subject string. Another regular expression matches the text between the sections. In other words, you want to search and replace through all parts of the subject string not matched by the other regular expression.

Say you have an HTML file in which you want to replace straight double quotes with smart (curly) double quotes, but you only want to replace the quotes outside of HTML tags. Quotes within HTML tags must remain plain ASCII straight quotes, or your web browser won't be able to parse the HTML anymore. For example, you want to turn "text" <span class="middle">"text"</span> "text" into "text" <span class="middle">"text"</span> "text".

Solution

C#

```
string resultString = null;
Regex outerRegex = new Regex("<[^<>]*>");
Regex innerRegex = new Regex("\"([^\"]*)\"");
// Find the first section
int lastIndex = 0;
Match outerMatch = outerRegex.Match(subjectString);
while (outerMatch.Success) {
    // Search-and-replace through the text between this match,
    // and the previous one
    string textBetween =
        subjectString.Substring(lastIndex, outerMatch.Index - lastIndex);
    resultString = resultString +
        innerRegex.Replace(textBetween, "\u201C$1\u201D");
    lastIndex = outerMatch.Index + outerMatch.Length;
    // Copy the text in the section unchanged
    resultString = resultString + outerMatch.Value;
    // Find the next section
    outerMatch = outerMatch.NextMatch();
}
// Search-and-replace through the remainder after the last regex match
string textAfter = subjectString.Substring(lastIndex,
                    subjectString.Length - lastIndex);
resultString = resultString + innerRegex.Replace(textAfter,
                                            "\u201C$1\u201D");
```

VB.NET

```
Dim ResultString As String = Nothing
Dim OuterRegex As New Regex("<[^<>]*>")
Dim InnerRegex As New Regex("""([^""]*)""")
'Find the first section
Dim LastIndex = 0
Dim OuterMatch = OuterRegex.Match(SubjectString)
While OuterMatch.Success
    'Search-and-replace through the text between this match,
    'and the previous one
    Dim TextBetween = SubjectString.Substring(LastIndex,
```

```
                        OuterMatch.Index - LastIndex);
        ResultString = ResultString + InnerRegex.Replace(TextBetween,
                    ChrW(&H201C) + "$1" + ChrW(&H201D))
        LastIndex = OuterMatch.Index + OuterMatch.Length
        'Copy the text in the section unchanged
        ResultString = ResultString + OuterMatch.Value
        'Find the next section
        OuterMatch = OuterMatch.NextMatch
End While
'Search-and-replace through the remainder after the last regex match
Dim TextAfter = SubjectString.Substring(LastIndex,
                                SubjectString.Length - LastIndex);
ResultString = ResultString +
    InnerRegex.Replace(TextAfter, ChrW(&H201C) + "$1" + ChrW(&H201D))
```

Java

```
StringBuffer resultString = new StringBuffer();
Pattern outerRegex = Pattern.compile("<[^<>]*>");
Pattern innerRegex = Pattern.compile("\"([^\"]*)\"");
Matcher outerMatcher = outerRegex.matcher(subjectString);
int lastIndex = 0;
while (outerMatcher.find()) {
    // Search-and-replace through the text between this match,
    // and the previous one
    String textBetween = subjectString.substring(lastIndex,
                                    outerMatcher.start());
    Matcher innerMatcher = innerRegex.matcher(textBetween);
    resultString.append(innerMatcher.replaceAll("\u201C$1\u201D"));
    lastIndex = outerMatcher.end();
    // Append the regex match itself unchanged
    resultString.append(outerMatcher.group());
}
// Search-and-replace through the remainder after the last regex match
String textAfter = subjectString.substring(lastIndex);
Matcher innerMatcher = innerRegex.matcher(textAfter);
resultString.append(innerMatcher.replaceAll("\u201C$1\u201D"));
```

JavaScript

```
var result = "";
var outerRegex = /<[^<>]*>/g;
var innerRegex = /"([^"]*)"/g;
var outerMatch = null;
var lastIndex = 0;
while (outerMatch = outerRegex.exec(subject)) {
    if (outerMatch.index == outerRegex.lastIndex) outerRegex.lastIndex++;
    // Search-and-replace through the text between this match,
    // and the previous one
```

```
        var textBetween = subject.substring(lastIndex, outerMatch.index);
        result = result + textBetween.replace(innerRegex, "\u201C$1\u201D");
        lastIndex = outerMatch.index + outerMatch[0].length;
        // Append the regex match itself unchanged
        result = result + outerMatch[0];
    }
    // Search-and-replace through the remainder after the last regex match
    var textAfter = subject.substr(lastIndex);
    result = result + textAfter.replace(innerRegex, "\u201C$1\u201D");
```

PHP

```
    $result = '';
    $lastindex = 0;
    while (preg_match('/<[^<>]*>/', $subject, $groups, PREG_OFFSET_CAPTURE,
                      $lastindex)) {
        $matchstart = $groups[0][1];
        $matchlength = strlen($groups[0][0]);
        // Search-and-replace through the text between this match,
        // and the previous one
        $textbetween = substr($subject, $lastindex, $matchstart-$lastindex);
        $result .= preg_replace('/"([^"]*)"/', '"“$1”"', $textbetween);
        // Append the regex match itself unchanged
        $result .= $groups[0][0];
        // Move the starting position for the next match
        $lastindex = $matchstart + $matchlength;
        if ($matchlength == 0) {
            // Don't get stuck in an infinite loop
            // if the regex allows zero-length matches
            $lastindex++;
        }
    }
    // Search-and-replace through the remainder after the last regex match
    $textafter = substr($subject, $lastindex);
    $result .= preg_replace('/"([^"]*)"/', '"“$1”"', $textafter);
```

Perl

```
    use encoding "utf-8";
    $result = '';
    while ($subject =~ m/<[^<>]*>/g) {
        $match = $&;
        $textafter = $';
        ($textbetween = $`) =~ s/"([^"]*)"/\x{201C}$1\x{201D}/g;
        $result .= $textbetween . $match;
    }
    $textafter =~ s/"([^"]*)"/\x{201C}$1\x{201D}/g;
    $result .= $textafter;
```

Python

```
innerre = re.compile('"([^"]*)"')
result = "";
lastindex = 0;
for outermatch in re.finditer("<[^<>]*>", subject):
    # Search-and-replace through the text between this match,
    # and the previous one
    textbetween = subject[lastindex:outermatch.start()]
    result += innerre.sub(u"\u201C\\1\u201D", textbetween)
    lastindex = outermatch.end()
    # Append the regex match itself unchanged
    result += outermatch.group()
# Search-and-replace through the remainder after the last regex match
textafter = subject[lastindex:]
result += innerre.sub(u"\u201C\\1\u201D", textafter)
```

Ruby

```
result = '';
textafter = ''
subject.scan(/<[^<>]*>/) {|match|
    textafter = $'
    textbetween = $`.gsub(/"([^"]*)"/, '"\1"')
    result += textbetween + match
}
result += textafter.gsub(/"([^"]*)"/, '"\1"')
```

Discussion

Recipe 3.13 explains how to use two regular expressions to find matches (of the second regex) only within certain sections of the file (matches of the first regex). The solution for this recipe uses the same technique to search and replace through only certain parts of the subject string.

It is important that the regular expression you use to find the sections continues to work on the original subject string. If you modify the original subject string, you have to shift the starting position for the regex that finds the section as the inner regex adds or deletes characters. More importantly, the modifications can have unintended side effects. For example, if your outer regex uses the anchor ‹^› to match something at the start of a line, and your inner regex inserts a line break at the end of the section found by the outer regex, then ‹^› will match right after the previous section because of the newly inserted line break.

Though the solutions for this recipe are quite long, they're very straightforward. Two regular expressions are used. The "outer" regular expression, ‹<[^<>]*>›, matches a pair of angle brackets and anything between them, except angle brackets. This is a crude way of matching any HTML tag. This regex works fine as long as the HTML file does not contain any literal angle brackets that were (incorrectly) not encoded as entities. We implement this regular expression with the same code shown in Recipe 3.11. The only difference is that the placeholder comment in that code that said where to use the match was replaced by the code that does the actual search-and-replace.

The search-and-replace within the loop follows the code shown in Recipe 3.14. The subject string for the search-and-replace is the text between the previous match of the outer regex and the current match. We append the result of the inner search-and-replace to the overall result string. We also append the current match of the outer regular expression unchanged.

When the outer regex fails to find further matches, we run the inner search-and-replace once more, on the text after the last match of the outer regex.

The regex ‹"([^"]*)"›, used for the search-and-replace inside the loop, matches a pair of double-quote characters and anything between them, except double quotes. The text between the quotes is captured into the first capturing group.

For the replacement text, we use a reference to the first capturing group, which is placed between two smart quotes. The smart quotes occupy Unicode code points U+201C and U+201D. Normally, you can simply paste the smart quotes directly into your source code. Visual Studio 2008, however, insists on being clever and automatically replaces literal smart quotes with straight quotes.

In a regular expression, you can match a Unicode code point with ‹\u201C› or ‹\x{201C}›, but none of the programming languages discussed in this book support such tokens as part of the replacement text. If an end user wants to insert smart quotes into the replacement text he types into an edit control, he'll have to paste them in literally from a character map. In your source code, you can use Unicode escapes in the replacement text, if your language supports such escapes as part of literal strings. For example, C# and Java support \u201C at the string level, but VB.NET does not offer a way to escape Unicode characters in strings. In VB.NET, you can use the ChrW function to convert a Unicode code point into a character.

Perl and Ruby

The Perl and Ruby solutions use two special variables available in these languages that we haven't explained yet. $` (dollar backtick) holds the part of the text to the left of the subject match, and $' (dollar single quote) holds the part of the text to the right of the subject match. Instead of iterating over the matches in the original subject string, we start a new search on the part of the string after the previous match. This way, we can easily retrieve the text between the match and the previous one with $`.

Python

The result of this code is a Unicode string because the replacement text is specified as a Unicode string. You may need to call encode() to be able to display it, e.g.:

```
print result.encode('1252')
```

See Also

Recipes 3.11, 3.13, and 3.16

3.19 Split a String

Problem

You want to split a string using a regular expression. After the split, you will have an array or list of strings with the text between the regular expression matches.

For example, you want to split a string with HTML tags in it along the HTML tags. Splitting I•like•bold•and•<i>italic</i>•fonts should result in an array of five strings: I•like•, bold, •and•, italic, and •fonts.

Solution

C#

You can use the static call when you process only a small number of strings with the same regular expression:

```
string[] splitArray = Regex.Split(subjectString, "<[^<>]*>");
```

If the regex is provided by the end user, you should use the static call with full exception handling:

```
string[] splitArray = null;
try {
    splitArray = Regex.Split(subjectString, "<[^<>]*>");
} catch (ArgumentNullException ex) {
    // Cannot pass null as the regular expression or subject string
} catch (ArgumentException ex) {
    // Syntax error in the regular expression
}
```

Construct a Regex object if you want to use the same regular expression with a large number of strings:

```
Regex regexObj = new Regex("<[^<>]*>");
string[] splitArray = regexObj.Split(subjectString);
```

If the regex is provided by the end user, you should use the Regex object with full exception handling:

```
string[] splitArray = null;
try {
    Regex regexObj = new Regex("<[^<>]*>");
```

```
    try {
        splitArray = regexObj.Split(subjectString);
    } catch (ArgumentNullException ex) {
        // Cannot pass null as the subject string
    }
} catch (ArgumentException ex) {
    // Syntax error in the regular expression
}
```

VB.NET

You can use the static call when you process only a small number of strings with the same regular expression:

```
Dim SplitArray = Regex.Split(SubjectString, "<[^<>]*>")
```

If the regex is provided by the end user, you should use the static call with full exception handling:

```
Dim SplitArray As String()
Try
    SplitArray = Regex.Split(SubjectString, "<[^<>]*>")
Catch ex As ArgumentNullException
    'Cannot pass null as the regular expression or subject string
Catch ex As ArgumentException
    'Syntax error in the regular expression
End Try
```

Construct a **Regex** object if you want to use the same regular expression with a large number of strings:

```
Dim RegexObj As New Regex("<[^<>]*>")
Dim SplitArray = RegexObj.Split(SubjectString)
```

If the regex is provided by the end user, you should use the **Regex** object with full exception handling:

```
Dim SplitArray As String()
Try
    Dim RegexObj As New Regex("<[^<>]*>")
    Try
        SplitArray = RegexObj.Split(SubjectString)
    Catch ex As ArgumentNullException
        'Cannot pass null as the subject string
    End Try
Catch ex As ArgumentException
    'Syntax error in the regular expression
End Try
```

Java

You can call `String.Split()` directly when you want to split only one string with the same regular expression:

```java
String[] splitArray = subjectString.split("<[^<>]*>");
```

If the regex is provided by the end user, you should use full exception handling:

```java
try {
    String[] splitArray = subjectString.split("<[^<>]*>");
} catch (PatternSyntaxException ex) {
    // Syntax error in the regular expression
}
```

Construct a `Pattern` object if you want to use the same regular expression with a large number of strings:

```java
Pattern regex = Pattern.compile("<[^<>]*>");
String[] splitArray = regex.split(subjectString);
```

If the regex is provided by the end user, you should use the `Pattern` object with full exception handling:

```java
String[] splitArray = null;
try {
    Pattern regex = Pattern.compile("<[^<>]*>");
    splitArray = regex.split(subjectString);
} catch (ArgumentException ex) {
    // Syntax error in the regular expression
}
```

JavaScript

The `string.split()` function can split a string using a regular expression:

```javascript
result = subject.split(/<[^<>]*>/);
```

Unfortunately, there are a lot of cross-browser issues when using `string.split()` with a regular expression. Building the list in your own code is more reliable:

```javascript
var list = [];
var regex = /<[^<>]*>/g;
var match = null;
var lastIndex = 0;
while (match = regex.exec(subject)) {
    // Don't let browsers such as Firefox get stuck in an infinite loop
    if (match.index == regex.lastIndex) regex.lastIndex++;
    // Add the text before the match
    list.push(subject.substring(lastIndex, match.index));
    lastIndex = match.index + match[0].length;
}
```

```
// Add the remainder after the last match
list.push(subject.substr(lastIndex));
```

PHP

```
$result = preg_split('/<[^<>]*>/', $subject);
```

Perl

```
@result = split(m/<[^<>]*>/, $subject);
```

Python

If you have only a few strings to split, you can use the global function:

```
result = re.split("<[^<>]*>", subject))
```

To use the same regex repeatedly, use a compiled object:

```
reobj = re.compile("<[^<>]*>")
result = reobj.split(subject)
```

Ruby

```
result = subject.split(/<[^<>]*>/)
```

Discussion

Splitting a string using a regular expression essentially produces the opposite result of Recipe 3.10. Instead of retrieving a list with all the regex matches, you get a list of the text between the matches, including the text before the first and after the last match. The regex matches themselves are omitted from the output of the split function.

C# and VB.NET

In .NET, you will always use the Regex.Split() method to split a string with a regular expression. The first parameter expected by Split() is always the string that holds the original subject text you want to split. This parameter should not be null. If it is, Split() will throw an ArgumentNullException. The return value of Split() is always an array of strings.

If you want to use the regular expression only a few times, you can use a static call. The second parameter is then the regular expression you want to use. You can pass regex options as an optional third parameter. If your regular expression has a syntax error, an ArgumentException will be thrown.

If you want to use the same regular expression on many strings, you can make your code more efficient by constructing a Regex object first, and then calling Split() on that object. The subject string is then the only required parameter.

When calling `Split()` on an instance of the `Regex` class, you can pass additional parameters to limit the split operation. If you omit these parameters, the string will be split at all matches of the regular expression in the subject string. The static overloads of `Split()` do not allow these additional parameters. They always split the whole string at all matches.

As the optional second parameter, after the subject string, you can pass the maximum number of split strings you want to end up with. For example, if you call `regexObj.Split(subject, 3)`, you will receive an array with at most three strings in it. The `Split()` function will try to find two regex matches, and return an array with the text before the first match, the text between the two matches, and the text after the second match. Any further possible regex matches within the remainder of the subject string are ignored, and left in the last string in the array.

If there are not enough regex matches to reach your limit, `Split()` will split along all the available regex matches and return an array with fewer strings than you specified. `regexObj.Split(subject, 1)` does not split the string at all, returning an array with the original string as the only element. `regexObj.Split(subject, 0)` splits at all regex matches, just like `Split()` does when you omit the second parameter. Specifying a negative number will cause `Split()` to throw an `ArgumentOutOfRangeException`.

If you specify the second parameter with the maximum number of strings in the returned array, you also can specify an optional third parameter to indicate the character index at which the regular expression should begin to find matches. Essentially, the number you pass as the third parameter is the number of characters at the start of your subject string that the regular expression should ignore. This can be useful when you've already processed the string up to a point, and you only want to split the remainder of the string.

The characters skipped by the regular expression will still be added to the returned array. The first string in the array is the whole substring before the first regex match found after the starting position you specified, including the characters before that starting position. If you specify the third parameter, it must be between zero and the length of the subject string. Otherwise, `Split()` throws an `ArgumentOutOfRangeException`. Unlike `Match()`, `Split()` does not allow you to specify a parameter that sets the length of the substring the regular expression is allowed to search through.

If a match occurs at the start of the subject string, the first string in the resulting array will be an empty string. When two regex matches can be found right next to each other in the subject string, with no text between them, an empty string will be added to the array. If a match occurs at the end of the subject string, the last element in the array will be an empty string.

Java

If you have only one string to split, you can call the `split()` method directly on your subject string. Pass the regular expression as the only parameter. This method simply calls `Pattern.compile("regex").split(subjectString)`.

If you want to split multiple strings, use the `Pattern.compile()` factory to create a `Pattern` object. This way, your regular expression needs to be compiled only once. Then, call the `split()` method on your `Pattern` instance, and pass your subject string as the parameter. There's no need to create a `Matcher` object. The `Matcher` class does not have a `split()` method at all.

`Pattern.split()` takes an optional second parameter, but `String.split()` does not. You can use the second parameter to pass the maximum number of split strings you want to end up with. For example, if you call `Pattern.split(subject, 3)`, you will receive an array with at most three strings in it. The `split()` function will try to find two regex matches, and return an array with the text before the first match, the text between the two matches, and the text after the second match. Any further possible regex matches within the remainder of the subject string are ignored, and left in the last string in the array. If there are not enough regex matches to reach your limit, `split()` will split along all the available regex matches, and return an array with fewer strings than you specified. `Pattern.split(subject, 1)` does not split the string at all, returning an array with the original string as the only element.

If a match occurs at the start of the subject string, the first string in the resulting array will be an empty string. When two regex matches can be found right next to each other in the subject string, with no text between them, an empty string will be added to the array. If a match occurs at the end of the subject string, the last element in the array will be an empty string.

Java, however, will eliminate empty strings at the end of the array. If you want the empty strings to be included, pass a negative number as the second parameter to `Pattern.split()`. This tells Java to split the string as many times as possible, and leave any empty strings at the end of the array. The actual value of the second parameter makes no difference when it is negative. You cannot tell Java to split a string a certain number of times and also leave empty strings at the end of the array at the same time.

JavaScript

In JavaScript, call the `split()` method on the string you want to split. Pass the regular expression as the only parameter to get an array with the string split as many times as possible. You can pass an optional second parameter to specify the maximum number of strings you want to have in the returned array. This should be a positive number. If you pass zero, you get an empty array. If you omit the second parameter or pass a negative number, the string is split as many times as possible. Setting the /g flag for the regex (Recipe 3.4) makes no difference.

Unfortunately, none of the popular web browsers implement each aspect of the `split()` method as specified in the JavaScript standard. In particular, some browsers include the text matched by capturing groups in the array, and others don't. Those that include capturing groups don't handle nonparticipating groups consistently. To avoid such issues, use only noncapturing groups (Recipe 2.9) in regular expressions you pass to `split()`.

Some JavaScript implementations omit zero-length strings from the returned array. Zero-length strings should be in the array when two regex matches occur right next to each other, or when the regex matches at the start or the end of the string that is being split. Since you can't work around this with a simple change to your regular expression, it is probably safer to use the longer JavaScript solution to this recipe. That solution includes all zero-length strings, but you can easily edit it to exclude zero-length strings.

The long solution is an adaptation of Recipe 3.12. It adds the text between the regex matches and the regex matches themselves to an array. To get the text between the matches, we use the match details explained in Recipe 3.8.

If you want an implementation of `String.prototype.split` that follows the standard and also works with all browsers, Steven Levithan has a solution for you at *http://blog .stevenlevithan.com/archives/cross-browser-split*.

PHP

Call `preg_split()` to split a string into an array of strings along the regex matches. Pass the regular expression as the first parameter and the subject string as the second parameter. If you omit the second parameter, `$_` is used as the subject string.

You can pass an optional third parameter to specify the maximum number of split strings you want to end up with. For example, if you call `preg_split($regex, $subject, 3)`, you will receive an array with at most three strings in it. The `preg_split()` function will try to find two regex matches, and return an array with the text before the first match, the text between the two matches, and the text after the second match. Any further possible regex matches within the remainder of the subject string are ignored, and left in the last string in the array. If there are not enough regex matches to reach your limit, `preg_split()` will split along all the available regex matches and return an array with fewer strings than you specified. If you omit the third parameter or set it to `-1`, the string is split as many times as possible.

If a match occurs at the start of the subject string, the first string in the resulting array will be an empty string. When two regex matches can be found right next to each other in the subject string, with no text between them, an empty string will be added to the array. If a match occurs at the end of the subject string, the last element in the array will be an empty string. By default, `preg_split()` includes those empty strings in the array it returns. If you don't want empty strings in the array, pass the constant `PREG_SPLIT_NO_EMPTY` as the fourth parameter.

Perl

Call the `split()` function to split a string into an array of strings along the regex matches. Pass a regular expression operator as the first parameter and the subject string as the second parameter.

You can pass an optional third parameter to specify the maximum number of split strings you want to end up with. For example, if you call `split(/regex/, subject, 3)`, you will receive an array with at most three strings in it. The `split()` function will try to find two regex matches, and return an array with the text before the first match, the text between the two matches, and the text after the second match. Any further possible regex matches within the remainder of the subject string are ignored, and left in the last string in the array. If there are not enough regex matches to reach your limit, `split()` will split along all the available regex matches and return an array with fewer strings than you specified.

If you omit the third parameter, Perl will determine the appropriate limit. If you assign the result to an array variable, as the solution for this recipe does, the string is split as many times as possible. If you assign the result to a list of scalar variables, Perl sets the limit to the number of variables plus one. In other words, Perl will attempt to fill all the variables, and will discard the unsplit remainder. For example, `($one, $two, $three) = split(/,/)` splits `$_` with a limit of 4.

If a match occurs at the start of the subject string, the first string in the resulting array will be an empty string. When two regex matches can be found right next to each other in the subject string, with no text between them, an empty string will be added to the array. If a match occurs at the end of the subject string, the last element in the array will be an empty string.

Python

The `split()` function in the `re` module splits a string using a regular expression. Pass your regular expression as the first parameter and the subject string as the second parameter. The global `split()` function does not accept a parameter with regular expression options.

The `re.split()` function calls `re.compile()`, and then calls the `split()` method on the compiled regular expression object. This method has only one required parameter: the subject string.

Both forms of `split()` return a list with the text between all the regex matches. Both take one optional parameter that you can use to limit the number of times the string should be split. If you omit it or set it to zero, the string is split as many times as possible. If you pass a positive number, that is the maximum number of regex matches at which the string will be split. The resulting list will contain one more string than the count you specified. The last string is the unsplit remainder of the subject string after the last regex match. If fewer matches can be found than the count you specified, the string is split at all regex matches without error.

Ruby

Call the `split()` method on the subject string and pass your regular expression as the first parameter to divide the string into an array of strings along the regex matches.

The `split()` method takes an optional second parameter, which you can use to indicate the maximum number of split strings you want to end up with. For example, if you call `subject.split(re, 3)`, you will receive an array with at most three strings in it. The `split()` function will try to find two regex matches, and return an array with the text before the first match, the text between the two matches, and the text after the second match. Any further possible regex matches within the remainder of the subject string are ignored, and left in the last string in the array. If there are not enough regex matches to reach your limit, `split()` will split along all the available regex matches, and return an array with fewer strings than you specified. `split(re, 1)` does not split the string at all, returning an array with the original string as the only element.

If a match occurs at the start of the subject string, the first string in the resulting array will be an empty string. When two regex matches can be found right next to each other in the subject string, with no text between them, an empty string will be added to the array. If a match occurs at the end of the subject string, the last element in the array will be an empty string.

Ruby, however, will eliminate empty strings at the end of the array. If you want the empty strings to be included, pass a negative number as the second parameter to `split()`. This tells Ruby to split the string as many times as possible and leave any empty strings at the end of the array. The actual value of the second parameter makes no difference when it is negative. You cannot tell Ruby to split a string a certain number of times and also leave empty strings at the end of the array at the same time.

See Also

Recipe 3.20

3.20 Split a String, Keeping the Regex Matches

Problem

You want to split a string using a regular expression. After the split, you will have an array or list of strings with the text between the regular expression matches, as well as the regex matches themselves.

Suppose you want to split a string with HTML tags in it along the HTML tags, and also keep the HTML tags. Splitting I•like•bold•and•<i>italic</i>•fonts should result in an array of nine strings: I•like•, , bold, , •and•, <i>, italic, </i>, and •fonts.

Solution

C#

You can use the static call when you process only a small number of strings with the same regular expression:

```
string[] splitArray = Regex.Split(subjectString, "(<[^<>]*>)");
```

Construct a Regex object if you want to use the same regular expression with a large number of strings:

```
Regex regexObj = new Regex("(<[^<>]*>)");
string[] splitArray = regexObj.Split(subjectString);
```

VB.NET

You can use the static call when you process only a small number of strings with the same regular expression:

```
Dim SplitArray = Regex.Split(SubjectString, "(<[^<>]*>)")
```

Construct a Regex object if you want to use the same regular expression with a large number of strings:

```
Dim RegexObj As New Regex("(<[^<>]*>)")
Dim SplitArray = RegexObj.Split(SubjectString)
```

Java

```
List<String> resultList = new ArrayList<String>();
Pattern regex = Pattern.compile("<[^<>]*>");
Matcher regexMatcher = regex.matcher(subjectString);
int lastIndex = 0;
while (regexMatcher.find()) {
    resultList.add(subjectString.substring(lastIndex,
                                           regexMatcher.start()));
    resultList.add(regexMatcher.group());
    lastIndex = regexMatcher.end();
}
resultList.add(subjectString.substring(lastIndex));
```

JavaScript

```
var list = [];
var regex = /<[^<>]*>/g;
var match = null;
var lastIndex = 0;
```

```
while (match = regex.exec(subject)) {
    // Don't let browsers such as Firefox get stuck in an infinite loop
    if (match.index == regex.lastIndex) regex.lastIndex++;
    // Add the text before the match, as well as the match itself
    list.push(subject.substring(lastIndex, match.index), match[0]);
    lastIndex = match.index + match[0].length;
}
// Add the remainder after the last match
list.push(subject.substr(lastIndex));
```

PHP

```
$result = preg_split('/(<[^<>]*>)/', $subject, -1,
                     PREG_SPLIT_DELIM_CAPTURE);
```

Perl

```
@result = split(m/(<[^<>]*>)/, $subject);
```

Python

If you have only a few strings to split, you can use the global function:

```
result = re.split("(<[^<>]*>)", subject))
```

To use the same regex repeatedly, use a compiled object:

```
reobj = re.compile("(<[^<>]*>)")
result = reobj.split(subject)
```

Ruby

```
list = []
lastindex = 0;
subject.scan(/<[^<>]*>/) {|match|
    list << subject[lastindex..$~.begin(0)-1];
    list << $&
    lastindex = $~.end(0)
}
list << subject[lastindex..subject.length()]
```

Discussion

.NET

In .NET, the Regex.Split() method includes the text matched by capturing groups into the array. .NET 1.0 and 1.1 include only the first capturing group. .NET 2.0 and later include all capturing groups as separate strings into the array. If you want to include the overall regex match into the array, place the whole regular expression inside a capturing group. For .NET 2.0 and later, all other groups should be noncapturing, or they will be included in the array.

The capturing groups are not included in the string count that you can pass to the `Split()` function. If you call `regexObj.Split(subject, 4)` with the example string and regex of this recipe, you'll get an array with seven strings. Those will be the four strings with the text before, between, and after the first three regex matches, plus three strings between them with the regex matches, as captured by the only capturing group in the regular expression. Simply put, you'll get an array with: `I•like•`, `<b>`, `bold`, `</b>`, `•and•`, `<italic>`, and `italic</italic>•fonts`. If your regex has 10 capturing groups and you're using .NET 2.0 or later, `regexObj.Split(subject, 4)` returns an array with 34 strings.

.NET does not provide an option to exclude the capturing groups from the array. Your only solution is to replace all named and numbered capturing groups with noncapturing groups. An easy way to do this in .NET is to use `RegexOptions.ExplicitCapture`, and replace all named groups with normal groups (i.e., just a pair of parentheses) in your regular expression.

Java

Java's `Pattern.split()` method does not provide the option to add the regex matches to the resulting array. Instead, we can adapt Recipe 3.12 to add the text between the regex matches along with the regex matches themselves to a list. To get the text between the matches, we use the match details explained in Recipe 3.8.

JavaScript

JavaScript's `string.split()` function does not provide an option to control whether regex matches should be added to the array. According to the JavaScript standard, all capturing groups should have their matches added to the array. Unfortunately, the popular web browsers either don't do this at all or do so inconsistently.

For a solution that works with all browsers, we can adapt Recipe 3.12 to add the text between the regex matches along with the regex matches themselves to a list. To get the text between the matches, we use the match details explained in Recipe 3.8.

PHP

Pass `PREG_SPLIT_DELIM_CAPTURE` as the fourth parameter to `preg_split()` to include the text matched by capturing groups in the returned array. You can use the | operator to combine `PREG_SPLIT_DELIM_CAPTURE` with `PREG_SPLIT_NO_EMPTY`.

The capturing groups are not included in the string count that you specify as the third argument to the `preg_split()` function. If you set the limit to four with the example string and regex of this recipe, you'll get an array with seven strings. Those will be the four strings with the text before, between, and after the first three regex matches, plus three strings between them with the regex matches, as captured by the only capturing group in the regular expression. Simply put, you'll get an array with: I●like●, , bold, , ●and●, <italic>, and italic</italic>●fonts.

Perl

Perl's `split()` function includes the text matched by all capturing groups into the array. If you want to include the overall regex match into the array, place the whole regular expression inside a capturing group.

The capturing groups are not included in the string count that you can pass to the `split()` function. If you call `split(/(<[^<>]*>)/, $subject, 4)` with the example string and regex of this recipe, you'll get an array with seven strings. Those will be the four strings with the text before, between, and after the first three regex matches, plus three strings between them with the regex matches, as captured by the only capturing group in the regular expression. Simply put, you'll get an array with: I●like●, , bold, , ●and●, <italic>, and italic</italic>●fonts. If your regex has 10 capturing groups, `split($regex, $subject, 4)` returns an array with 34 strings.

Perl does not provide an option to exclude the capturing groups from the array. Your only solution is to replace all named and numbered capturing groups with noncapturing groups.

Python

Python's `split()` function includes the text matched by all capturing groups into the array. If you want to include the overall regex match into the array, place the whole regular expression inside a capturing group.

The capturing groups do not affect the number of times the string is split. If you call `split(/(<[^<>]*>)/, $subject, 3)` with the example string and regex of this recipe, you'll get an array with seven strings. The string is split three times, which results in four pieces of text between the matches, plus three pieces of text matched by the capturing group. Simply put, you'll get an array with: "I like", "", "bold", "", " and ", "<i>", and "italic</i> fonts". If your regex has 10 capturing groups, `split($regex, $subject, 3)` returns an array with 34 strings.

Python does not provide an option to exclude the capturing groups from the array. Your only solution is to replace all named and numbered capturing groups with non-capturing groups.

Ruby

Ruby's `String.split()` method does not provide the option to add the regex matches to the resulting array. Instead, we can adapt Recipe 3.11 to add the text between the regex matches along with the regex matches themselves to a list. To get the text between the matches, we use the match details explained in Recipe 3.8.

See Also

Recipe 2.9 explains capturing and noncapturing groups.

Recipe 2.11 explains named groups.

3.21 Search Line by Line

Problem

Traditional grep tools apply your regular expression to one line of text at a time, and display the lines matched (or not matched) by the regular expression. You have an array of strings, or a multiline string, that you want to process in this way.

Solution

C#

If you have a multiline string, split it into an array of strings first, with each string in the array holding one line of text:

```
string[] lines = Regex.Split(subjectString, "\r?\n");
```

Then, iterate over the lines array:

```
Regex regexObj = new Regex("regex pattern");
for (int i = 0; i < lines.Length; i++) {
    if (regexObj.IsMatch(lines[i])) {
        // The regex matches lines[i]
    } else {
        // The regex does not match lines[i]
    }
}
```

VB.NET

If you have a multiline string, split it into an array of strings first, with each string in the array holding one line of text:

```
Dim Lines = Regex.Split(SubjectString, "\r?\n")
```

Then, iterate over the lines array:

```
Dim RegexObj As New Regex("regex pattern")
For i As Integer = 0 To Lines.Length - 1
    If RegexObj.IsMatch(Lines(i)) Then
        'The regex matches Lines(i)
    Else
        'The regex does not match Lines(i)
```

```
        End If
    Next
```

Java

If you have a multiline string, split it into an array of strings first, with each string in the array holding one line of text:

```
String[] lines = subjectString.split("\r?\n");
```

Then, iterate over the `lines` array:

```
Pattern regex = Pattern.compile("regex pattern");
Matcher regexMatcher = regex.matcher("");
for (int i = 0; i < lines.length; i++) {
    regexMatcher.reset(lines[i]);
    if (regexMatcher.find()) {
        // The regex matches lines[i]
    } else {
        // The regex does not match lines[i]
    }
}
```

JavaScript

If you have a multiline string, split it into an array of strings first, with each string in the array holding one line of text. As mentioned in Recipe 3.19, some browsers exclude empty lines from the array.

```
var lines = subject.split(/\r?\n/);
```

Then, iterate over the `lines` array:

```
var regexp = /regex pattern/;
for (var i = 0; i < lines.length; i++) {
    if (lines[i].match(regexp)) {
        // The regex matches lines[i]
    } else {
        // The regex does not match lines[i]
    }
}
```

PHP

If you have a multiline string, split it into an array of strings first, with each string in the array holding one line of text:

```
$lines = preg_split('/\r?\n/', $subject)
```

Then, iterate over the `$lines` array:

```
foreach ($lines as $line) {
    if (preg_match('/regex pattern/', $line)) {
```

```
        // The regex matches $line
    } else {
        // The regex does not match $line
    }
}
```

Perl

If you have a multiline string, split it into an array of strings first, with each string in the array holding one line of text:

```
$lines = split(m/\r?\n/, $subject)
```

Then, iterate over the $lines array:

```
foreach $line ($lines) {
    if ($line =~ m/regex pattern/) {
        # The regex matches $line
    } else {
        # The regex does not match $line
    }
}
```

Python

If you have a multiline string, split it into an array of strings first, with each string in the array holding one line of text:

```
lines = re.split("\r?\n", subject);
```

Then, iterate over the lines array:

```
reobj = re.compile("regex pattern")
for line in lines[:]:
    if re.search(line):
        # The regex matches line
    else:
        # The regex does not match line
```

Ruby

If you have a multiline string, split it into an array of strings first, with each string in the array holding one line of text:

```
lines = subject.split(/\r?\n/)
```

Then, iterate over the lines array:

```
re = /regex pattern/
lines.each { |line|
    if line =~ re
        # The regex matches line
    else
```

```
    # The regex does not match line
}
```

Discussion

When working with line-based data, you can save yourself a lot of trouble if you split the data into an array of lines, instead of trying to work with one long string with embedded line breaks. Then, you can apply your actual regex to each string in the array, without worrying about matching more than one line. This approach also makes it easy to keep track of the relationship between lines. For example, you could easily iterate over the array using one regex to find a header line and then another to find the footer line. With the delimiting lines found, you can then use a third regex to find the data lines you're interested in. Though this may seem like a lot of work, it's all very straight-forward, and will yield code that performs well. Trying to craft a single regex to find the header, data, and footer all at once will be a lot more complicated, and will result in a much slower regex.

Processing a string line by line also makes it easy to negate a regular expression. Regular expressions don't provide an easy way of saying "match a line that does not contain this or that word." Only character classes can be easily negated. But if you've already split your string into lines, finding the lines that don't contain a word becomes as easy as doing a literal text search in all the lines, and removing the ones in which the word can be found.

Recipe 3.19 shows how you can easily split a string into an array. The regular expression ‹\r\n› matches a pair of CR and LF characters, which delimit lines on the Microsoft Windows platforms. ‹\n› matches an LF character, which delimits lines on Unix and its derivatives, such as Linux and even OS X. Since these two regular expressions are essentially plain text, you don't even need to use a regular expression. If your programming language can split strings using literal text, by all means split the string that way.

If you're not sure which line break style your data uses, you could split it using the regular expression ‹\r?\n›. By making the CR optional, this regex matches either a CRLF Windows line break or an LF Unix line break.

Once you have your strings into the array, you can easily loop over it. Inside the loop, follow the recipe shown in Recipe 3.5 to check which lines match, and which don't.

See Also

Recipes 3.11 and 3.19

Validation and Formatting

This chapter contains recipes for validating and formatting common types of user input. Some of the solutions show how to allow variations of valid input, such as U.S. postal codes that can contain either five or nine digits. Others are designed to harmonize or fix commonly understood formats for things such as phone numbers, dates, and credit card numbers.

Beyond helping you get the job done by eliminating invalid input, these recipes can also improve the user experience of your applications. Messages such as "no spaces or hyphens" next to phone or credit card number fields often frustrate users or are simply ignored. Fortunately, in many cases regular expressions allow you to let users enter data in formats that they find familiar and comfortable with very little extra work on your part.

Certain programming languages provide functionality similar to some recipes in this chapter through their native classes or libraries. Depending on your needs, it might make more sense to use these built-in options, so we'll point them out along the way.

4.1 Validate Email Addresses

Problem

You have a form on your website or a dialog box in your application that asks the user for an email address. You want to use a regular expression to validate this email address before trying to send email to it. This reduces the number of emails returned to you as undeliverable.

Solution

Simple

The first solution does a very simple check. It only verifies that the email address has a single at (@) sign and no whitespace:

```
^\S+@\S+$
```
Regex options: None
Regex flavors: .NET, Java, JavaScript, PCRE, Perl, Python

```
\A\S+@\S+\Z
```
Regex options: None
Regex flavors: .NET, Java, PCRE, Perl, Python, Ruby

Simple, with restrictions on characters

The *domain name*, the part after the @ sign, is restricted to characters allowed in domain names. The *username*, the part before the @ sign, is restricted to characters commonly used in email usernames, which is more restrictive than what most email clients and servers will accept:

```
^[A-Z0-9+_.-]+@[A-Z0-9.-]+$
```
Regex options: Case insensitive
Regex flavors: .NET, Java, JavaScript, PCRE, Perl, Python

```
\A[A-Z0-9+_.-]+@[A-Z0-9.-]+\Z
```
Regex options: Case insensitive
Regex flavors: .NET, Java, PCRE, Perl, Python, Ruby

Simple, with all characters

This regular expression expands the previous one by allowing a larger set of rarely used characters in the username. Not all email software can handle all these characters, but we've included all the characters permitted by RFC 2822, which governs the email message format. Among the permitted characters are some that present a security risk if passed directly from user input to an SQL statement, such as the single quote (') and the pipe character (|). Be sure to escape sensitive characters when inserting the email address into a string passed to another program, in order to prevent security holes such as SQL injection attacks:

```
^[\w!#$%&'*+/=?`{|}~^.-]+@[A-Z0-9.-]+$
```
Regex options: Case insensitive
Regex flavors: .NET, Java, JavaScript, PCRE, Perl, Python

```
\A[\w!#$%&'*+/=?`{|}~^.-]+@[A-Z0-9.-]+\Z
```
Regex options: Case insensitive
Regex flavors: .NET, Java, PCRE, Perl, Python, Ruby

No leading, trailing, or consecutive dots

Both the username and the domain name can contain one or more dots, but no two dots can appear right next to each other. Furthermore, the first and last characters in the username and in the domain name must not be dots:

```
^[\w!#$%&'*+/=?`{|}~^-]+(?:\.[!#$%&'*+/=?`{|}~^-]+)*@↵
[A-Z0-9-]+(?:\.[A-Z0-9-]+)*$
```
Regex options: Case insensitive
Regex flavors: .NET, Java, JavaScript, PCRE, Perl, Python

```
\A[\w!#$%&'*+/=?`{|}~^-]+(?:\.[!#$%&'*+/=?`{|}~^-]+)*@↵
[A-Z0-9-]+(?:\.[A-Z0-9-]+)*\Z
```
Regex options: Case insensitive
Regex flavors: .NET, Java, PCRE, Perl, Python, Ruby

Top-level domain has two to six letters

This regular expression adds to the previous versions by specifying that the domain name must include at least one dot, and that the part of the domain name after the dot can only consist of letters. That is, the domain must contain at least two levels, such as secondlevel.com or thirdlevel.secondlevel.com. The top-level domain, .com, must consist of two to six letters. All country-code top-level domains have two letters. The generic top-level domains have between three (.com) and six letters (.museum):

```
^[\w!#$%&'*+/=?`{|}~^-]+(?:\.[!#$%&'*+/=?`{|}~^-]+)*@↵
(?:[A-Z0-9-]+\.)+[A-Z]{2,6}$
```
Regex options: Case insensitive
Regex flavors: .NET, Java, JavaScript, PCRE, Perl, Python

```
\A[\w!#$%&'*+/=?`{|}~^-]+(?:\.[!#$%&'*+/=?`{|}~^-]+)*@↵
(?:[A-Z0-9-]+\.)+[A-Z]{2,6}\Z
```
Regex options: Case insensitive
Regex flavors: .NET, Java, PCRE, Perl, Python, Ruby

Discussion

About email addresses

If you thought something as conceptually simple as validating an email address would have a simple one-size-fits-all regex solution, you're quite wrong. This recipe is a prime example that before you can start writing a regular expression, you have to decide *exactly* what you want to match. There is no universally agreed upon rule as to which email addresses are valid and which not. It depends on your definition of *valid*.

asdf@asdf.asdf is valid according to RFC 2822, which defines the syntax for email addresses. But it is not valid if your definition specifies that a valid email address is one that accepts mail. There is no top-level asdf domain.

The short answer to the validity problem is that you can't know whether john.doe@somewhere.com is an email address that can actually receive email until you try to send email to it. And even then, you can't be sure if the lack of response signals that the somewhere.com domain is silently discarding mail sent to nonexistent mailboxes, or if John Doe hit the Delete button on his keyboard, or if his spam filter beat him to it.

Because you ultimately have to check whether the address exists by actually sending email to it, you can decide to use a simpler or more relaxed regular expression. Allowing invalid addresses to slip through may be preferable to annoying people by blocking valid addresses. For this reason, you may want to select the "simple, with all characters" regular expression. Though it obviously allows many things that aren't email addresses, such as `#$%@.-`, the regex is quick and simple, and will never block a valid email address.

If you want to avoid sending too many undeliverable emails, while still not blocking any real email addresses, the regex in "Top-level domain has two to six letters" on page 215 is a good choice.

You have to consider how complex you want your regular expression to be. If you're validating user input, you'll likely want a more complex regex, because the user could type in anything. But if you're scanning database files that you know contain only valid email addresses, you can use a very simple regex that merely separates the email addresses from the other data. Even the solution in the earlier subsection "Simple" may be enough in this case.

Finally, you have to consider how future-proof you want your regular expression to be. In the past, it made sense to restrict the top-level domain to only two-letter combinations for the country codes, and exhaustively list the generic top-level domains, i.e., ‹com|net|org|mil|edu›. With new top-level domains being added all the time, such regular expressions now quickly go out of date.

Regular expression syntax

The regular expressions presented in this recipe show all the basic parts of the regular expression syntax in action. If you read up on these parts in Chapter 2, you can already do 90% of the jobs that are best solved with regular expressions.

All the regular expressions require the case-insensitive matching option to be turned on. Otherwise, only uppercase characters will be allowed. Turning on this option allows you to type ‹[A-Z]› instead of ‹[A-Za-z]›, saving a few keystrokes. If you use one of the last two regular expressions, the case-insensitivity option is very handy. Otherwise, you'd have to replace every letter ‹X› with ‹[Xx]›.

‹\S› and ‹\w› are shorthand character classes, as the recipe in Recipe 2.3 explains. ‹\S› matches any nonwhitespace character, whereas ‹\w› matches a word character.

‹@› and ‹\.› match a literal @ sign and a dot, respectively. Since the dot is a metacharacter when used outside character classes, it needs to be escaped with a backslash. The @ sign never has a special meaning with any of the regular expression flavors in this book. Recipe 2.1 gives you a list of all the metacharacters that need to be escaped.

‹[A-Z0-9.-]› and the other sequences between square brackets are character classes. This one allows all letters between A and Z, all digits between 0 and 9, as well as a literal dot and hyphen. Though the hyphen normally creates a range in a character class, the hyphen is treated as a literal when it occurs as the last character in a character class.

The recipe in Recipe 2.3 tells you all about character classes, including combining them with shorthands, as in ‹[\w!#$%&'*+/=?`{|}~^.-]›. This class matches a word character, as well as any of the 19 listed punctuation characters.

‹+› and ‹*›, when used outside character classes, are quantifiers. The plus sign repeats the preceding regex token one or more times, whereas the asterisk repeats it zero or more times. In these regular expressions, the quantified token is usually a character class, and sometimes a group. Therefore, ‹[A-Z0-9.-]+› matches one or more letters, digits, dots, and/or hyphens.

As an example of the use of a group, ‹(?:[A-Z0-9-]+\.)+› matches one or more letters, digits, and/or hyphens, followed by one literal dot. The plus sign repeats this group one or more times. The group must match at least once, but can match as many times as possible. Recipe 2.12 explains the mechanics of constructs such as these in detail.

‹(?:group)› is a noncapturing group. Use it to create a group from part of the regular expression so you can apply a quantifier to the group as a whole. The capturing group ‹(group)› does the same thing with a cleaner syntax, so you could replace ‹(?:› with ‹(› in all of the regular expressions we've used so far without changing the overall match results.

But since we're not interested in separately capturing parts of the email address, the noncapturing group is somewhat more efficient, although it makes the regular expression somewhat harder to read. Recipe 2.9 tells you all about capturing and noncapturing groups.

The anchors ‹^› and ‹$› force the regular expression to find its match at the start and end of the subject text, respectively. Placing the whole regular expression between these characters effectively requires the regular expression to match the entire subject.

This is important when validating user input. You do not want to accept `drop database; -- joe@server.com haha!` as a valid email address. Without the anchors, all the previous regular expressions will match because they find joe@server.com in the middle of the given text. See Recipe 2.5 for details. That recipe also explains why the "caret and dollar match at line breaks" matching option must be off.

In Ruby, the caret and dollar always match at line breaks. The regular expressions using the caret and dollar work correctly in Ruby, but only if the string you're trying to validate contains no line breaks. If the string may contain line breaks, all the regexes using ‹^› and ‹$› will match the email address in `drop database; --` LF joe@server.com LF haha!, where LF represents a line break.

To avoid this, use the anchors ‹\A› and ‹\Z› instead. These match at the start and end of the string only, regardless of any options, in all flavors discussed in this book, except JavaScript. JavaScript does not support ‹\A› and ‹\Z› at all. Recipe 2.5 explains these anchors.

The issue with ‹^› and ‹$› versus ‹\A› and ‹\Z› applies to all regular expressions that validate input. There are a lot of these in this book. Although we will offer the occasional reminder, we will not constantly repeat this advice or show separate solutions for JavaScript and Ruby for each and every recipe. In many cases, we'll show only one solution using the caret and dollar, and list Ruby as a compatible flavor. If you're using Ruby, remember to use ‹\A› and ‹\Z› if you want to avoid matching one line in a multiline string.

Building a regex step-by-step

This recipe illustrates how you can build a regular expression step-by-step. This technique is particularly handy with an interactive regular expression tester, such as RegexBuddy.

First, load a bunch of valid and invalid sample data into the tool. In this case, that would be a list of valid email addresses and a list of invalid email addresses.

Then, write a simple regular expression that matches all the valid email addresses. Ignore the invalid addresses for now. ‹^\S+@\S+$› already defines the basic structure of an email address: a username, an at sign, and a domain name.

With the basic structure of your text pattern defined, you can refine each part until your regular expression no longer matches any of the invalid data. If your regular expression only has to work with previously existing data, that can be a quick job. If your regex has to work with any user input, editing the regular expression until it is restrictive enough will be a much harder job than just getting it to match the valid data.

Variations

If you want to search for email addresses in larger bodies of text instead of checking whether the input as a whole is an email address, you cannot use the anchors ‹^› and ‹$›. Merely removing the anchors from the regular expression is not the right solution. If you do that with the final regex, which restricts the top-level domain to letters, it will match asdf@asdf.as in asdf@asdf.as99, for example. Instead of anchoring the regex match to the start and end of the subject, you have to specify that the start of the username and the top-level domain cannot be part of longer words.

This is easily done with a pair of word boundaries. Replace both ‹^› and ‹$› with ‹\b›. For instance, ‹^[A-Z0-9+_.-]+@(?:[A-Z0-9-]+\.)+[A-Z]{2,6}$› becomes ‹\b[A-Z0-9+_.-]+@(?:[A-Z0-9-]+\.)+[A-Z]{2,6}\b›.

This regex indeed combines the username portion from "Simple, with restrictions on characters" on page 214 and the domain name portion from "Top-level domain has two to six letters" on page 215. We find that this regular expression works quite well in practice.

See Also

RFC 2822 defines the structure and syntax of email messages, including the email addresses used in email messages. You can download RFC 2822 at *http://www.ietf.org/rfc/rfc2822.txt*.

4.2 Validate and Format North American Phone Numbers

Problem

You want to determine whether a user entered a North American phone number in a common format, including the local area code. These formats include 1234567890, 123-456-7890, 123.456.7890, 123 456 7890, (123) 456 7890, and all related combinations. If the phone number is valid, you want to convert it to your standard format, (123) 456-7890, so that your phone number records are consistent.

Solution

A regular expression can easily check whether a user entered something that looks like a valid phone number. By using capturing groups to remember each set of digits, the same regular expression can be used to replace the subject text with precisely the format you want.

Regular expression

```
^\(?([0-9]{3})\)?[-.•]?([0-9]{3})[-.•]?([0-9]{4})$
```
Regex options: None
Regex flavors: .NET, Java, JavaScript, PCRE, Perl, Python, Ruby

Replacement

```
($1)•$2-$3
```
Replacement text flavors: .NET, Java, JavaScript, Perl, PHP

```
(\1)•\2-\3
```
Replacement text flavors: Python, Ruby

C#

```csharp
Regex regexObj =
    new Regex(@"^\(?([0-9]{3})\)?[-. ]?([0-9]{3})[-. ]?([0-9]{4})$");

if (regexObj.IsMatch(subjectString)) {
    string formattedPhoneNumber =
        regexObj.Replace(subjectString, "($1) $2-$3");
} else {
```

```
        // Invalid phone number
    }
```

JavaScript

```javascript
var regexObj = /^\(?([0-9]{3})\)?[-. ]?([0-9]{3})[-. ]?([0-9]{4})$/;
if (regexObj.test(subjectString)) {
    var formattedPhoneNumber =
        subjectString.replace(regexObj, "($1) $2-$3");
} else {
    // Invalid phone number
}
```

Other programming languages

See Recipes 3.5 and 3.15 for help implementing this regular expression with other programming languages.

Discussion

This regular expression matches three groups of digits. The first group can optionally be enclosed with parentheses, and the first two groups can optionally be followed with a choice of three separators (a hyphen, dot, or space). The following layout breaks the regular expression into its individual parts, omitting the redundant groups of digits:

```
^           # Assert position at the beginning of the string.
\(          # Match a literal "("...
    ?       #   between zero and one time.
(           # Capture the enclosed match to backreference 1...
  [0-9]     #   Match a digit...
    {3}     #     exactly three times.
)           # End capturing group 1.
\)          # Match a literal ")"...
    ?       #   between zero and one time.
[-. ]       # Match one character from the set "-. "...
    ?       #   between zero and one time.
...         # [Match the remaining digits and separator.]
$           # Assert position at the end of the string.
```

Let's look at each of these parts more closely.

The ‹^› and ‹$› at the beginning and end of the regular expression are a special kind of metacharacter called an *anchor* or *assertion*. Instead of matching text, assertions match a position within the text. Specifically, ‹^› matches at the beginning of the text, and ‹$› at the end. This ensures that the phone number regex does not match within longer text, such as 123-456-78901.

As we've repeatedly seen, parentheses are special characters in regular expressions, but in this case we want to allow a user to enter parentheses and have our regex recognize

---

them. This is a textbook example of where we need a backslash to escape a special character so the regular expression treats it as literal input. Thus, the ‹\(› and ‹\)› sequences that enclose the first group of digits match literal parenthesis characters. Both are followed by a question mark, which makes them optional. We'll explain more about the question mark after discussing the other types of tokens in this regular expression.

The parentheses that appear without backslashes are capturing groups and are used to remember the values matched within them so that the matched text can be recalled later. In this case, backreferences to the captured values are used in the replacement text so we can easily reformat the phone number as needed.

Two other types of tokens used in this regular expression are character classes and quantifiers. Character classes allow you to match any one out of a set of characters. ‹[0-9]› is a character class that matches any digit. The regular expression flavors covered by this book all include the shorthand character class ‹\d› that also matches a digit, but in some flavors ‹\d› matches a digit from any language's character set or script, which is not what we want here. See Recipe 2.3 for more information about ‹\d›.

‹[-.•]› is another character class, one that allows any one of three separators. It's important that the hyphen appears first in this character class, because if it appeared between other characters, it would create a range, as with ‹[0-9]›. Another way to ensure that a hyphen inside a character class matches a literal version of itself is to escape it with a backslash. ‹[.\-•]› is therefore equivalent.

Finally, quantifiers allow you to repeat a token or group. ‹{3}› is a quantifier that causes its preceding element to be repeated exactly three times. The regular expression ‹[0-9]{3}› is therefore equivalent to ‹[0-9][0-9][0-9]›, but is shorter and hopefully easier to read. A question mark (mentioned earlier) is a special quantifier that causes its preceding element to repeat zero or one time. It could also be written as ‹{0,1}›. Any quantifier that allows something to be repeated zero times effectively makes that element optional. Since a question mark is used after each separator, the phone number digits are allowed to run together.

Note that although this recipe claims to handle North American phone numbers, it's actually designed to work with *North American Numbering Plan* (NANP) numbers. The NANP is the telephone numbering plan for the countries that share the country code "1". This includes the United States and its territories, Canada, Bermuda, and 16 Caribbean nations. It excludes Mexico and the Central American nations.

Variations

Eliminate invalid phone numbers

So far, the regular expression matches any 10-digit number. If you want to limit matches to valid phone numbers according to the North American Numbering Plan, here are the basic rules:

- *Area codes* start with a number from 2–9, followed by 0–8, and then any third digit.
- The second group of three digits, known as the *central office* or *exchange code*, starts with a number from 2–9, followed by any two digits.
- The final four digits, known as the *station code*, have no restrictions.

These rules can easily be implemented with a few character classes.

```
^\(?([2-9][0-8][0-9])\)?[-.•]?([2-9][0-9]{2})[-.•]?([0-9]{4})$
```
Regex options: None
Regex flavors: .NET, Java, JavaScript, PCRE, Perl, Python, Ruby

Beyond the basic rules just listed, there are a variety of reserved, unassigned, and restricted phone numbers. Unless you have very specific needs that require you to filter out as many phone numbers as possible, don't go overboard trying to eliminate unused numbers. New area codes that fit the rules listed earlier are made available regularly, and even if a phone number is valid, that doesn't necessarily mean it was issued or is in active use.

Find phone numbers in documents

Two simple changes allow the previous regular expression to match phone numbers within longer text:

```
\(?\b([0-9]{3})\)?[-.•]?([0-9]{3})[-.•]?([0-9]{4})\b
```
Regex options: None
Regex flavors: .NET, Java, JavaScript, PCRE, Perl, Python, Ruby

Here, the ‹^› and ‹$› assertions that bound the regular expression to the beginning and end of the text have been removed. In their place, word boundary tokens (‹\b›) have been added to ensure that the matched text stands on its own and is not part of a longer number or word.

Similar to ‹^› and ‹$›, ‹\b› is an assertion that matches a position rather than any actual text. Specifically, ‹\b› matches the position between a word character and either a nonword character or the beginning or end of the text. Letters, numbers, and underscore are all considered word characters (see Recipe 2.6).

Note that the first word boundary token appears after the optional, opening parenthesis. This is important because there is no word boundary to be matched between two nonword characters, such as the opening parenthesis and a preceding space character. The first word boundary is relevant only when matching a number without parentheses, since the word boundary always matches between the opening parenthesis and the first digit of a phone number.

Allow a leading "1"

You can allow an optional, leading "1" for the country code (which covers the North American Numbering Plan region) via the addition shown in the following regex:

```
^(?:\+?1[-.•]?)?\(?(?:([0-9]{3})\)?[-.•]?([0-9]{3})[-.•]?([0-9]{4})$
```
Regex options: None
Regex flavors: .NET, Java, JavaScript, PCRE, Perl, Python, Ruby

In addition to the phone number formats shown previously, this regular expression will also match strings such as +1 (123) 456-7890 and 1-123-456-7890. It uses a non-capturing group, written as ‹(?:⋯)›. When a question mark follows an unescaped left parenthesis like this, it's not a quantifier, but instead helps to identify the type of grouping. Standard capturing groups require the regular expression engine to keep track of backreferences, so it's more efficient to use noncapturing groups whenever the text matched by a group does not need to be referenced later. Another reason to use a noncapturing group here is to allow you to keep using the same replacement string as in the previous examples. If we added a capturing group, we'd have to change $1 to $2 (and so on) in the replacement text shown earlier in this recipe.

The full addition to this version of the regex is ‹(?:\+?1[-.•]?)?›. The "1" in this pattern is preceded by an optional plus sign, and optionally followed by one of three separators (hyphen, dot, or space). The entire, added noncapturing group is also optional, but since the "1" is required within the group, the preceding plus sign and separator are not allowed if there is no leading "1".

Allow seven-digit phone numbers

To allow matching phone numbers that omit the local area code, enclose the first group of digits together with its surrounding parentheses and following separator in an optional, noncapturing group:

```
^(?:\(?([0-9]{3})\)?[-.•]?)?([0-9]{3})[-.•]?([0-9]{4})$
```
Regex options: None
Regex flavors: .NET, Java, JavaScript, PCRE, Perl, Python, Ruby

Since the area code is no longer required as part of the match, simply replacing any match with «($1)•$2-$3» might now result in something like () 123-4567, with an empty set of parentheses. To work around this, add code outside the regex that checks whether group 1 matched any text, and adjust the replacement text accordingly.

See Also

Recipe 4.3 shows how to validate international phone numbers.

The North American Numbering Plan (NANP) is the telephone numbering plan for the United States and its territories, Canada, Bermuda, and 16 Caribbean nations. More information is available at *http://www.nanpa.com*.

4.3 Validate International Phone Numbers

Problem

You want to validate international phone numbers. The numbers should start with a plus sign, followed by the country code and national number.

Solution

Regular expression

```
^\+(?:[0-9]●?){6,14}[0-9]$
```
Regex options: None
Regex flavors: .NET, Java, JavaScript, PCRE, Perl, Python, Ruby

JavaScript

```javascript
function validate (phone) {
    var regex = /^\+(?:[0-9] ?){6,14}[0-9]$/;

    if (regex.test(phone)) {
        // Valid international phone number
    } else {
        // Invalid international phone number
    }
}
```

Other programming languages

See Recipe 3.5 for help implementing this regular expression with other programming languages.

Discussion

The rules and conventions used to print international phone numbers vary significantly around the world, so it's hard to provide meaningful validation for an international phone number unless you adopt a strict format. Fortunately, there is a simple, industry-standard notation specified by ITU-T E.123. This notation requires that international phone numbers include a leading plus sign (known as the *international prefix symbol*), and allows only spaces to separate groups of digits. Although the tilde character (~) can appear within a phone number to indicate the existence of an additional dial tone, it has been excluded from this regular expression since it is merely a procedural element (in other words, it is not actually dialed) and is infrequently used. Thanks to the international phone numbering plan (ITU-T E.164), phone numbers cannot contain more than 15 digits. The shortest international phone numbers in use contain seven digits.

With all of this in mind, let's look at the regular expression again after breaking it into its pieces. Because this version is written using free-spacing style, the literal space character has been replaced with ‹\x20›:

```
^           # Assert position at the beginning of the string.
\+          # Match a literal "+" character.
(?:         # Group but don't capture...
  [0-9]     #   Match a digit.
  \x20      #   Match a space character...
      ?     #       Between zero and one time.
)           # End the noncapturing group.
  {6,14}  #   Repeat the preceding group between 6 and 14 times.
[0-9]       # Match a digit.
$           # Assert position at the end of the string.
```
Regex options: Free-spacing
Regex flavors: .NET, Java, PCRE, Perl, Python, Ruby

The ‹^› and ‹$› anchors at the edges of the regular expression ensure that it matches the whole subject text. The noncapturing group—enclosed with ‹(?:···)›—matches a single digit, followed by an optional space character. Repeating this grouping with the interval quantifier ‹{6,14}› enforces the rules for the minimum and maximum number of digits, while allowing space separators to appear anywhere within the number. The second instance of the character class ‹[0-9]› completes the rule for the number of digits (bumping it up from between 6 and 14 digits to between 7 and 15), and ensures that the phone number does not end with a space.

Variations

Validate international phone numbers in EPP format

```
^\+[0-9]{1,3}\.[0-9]{4,14}(?:x.+)?$
```
Regex options: None
Regex flavors: .NET, Java, JavaScript, PCRE, Perl, Python, Ruby

This regular expression follows the international phone number notation specified by the Extensible Provisioning Protocol (EPP). EPP is a relatively recent protocol (finalized in 2004), designed for communication between domain name registries and registrars. It is used by a growing number of domain name registries, including *.com*, *.info*, *.net*, *.org*, and *.us*. The significance of this is that EPP-style international phone numbers are increasingly used and recognized, and therefore provide a good alternative format for storing (and validating) international phone numbers.

EPP-style phone numbers use the format *+CCC.NNNNNNNNNNxEEEE*, where *C* is the 1–3 digit country code, *N* is up to 14 digits, and *E* is the (optional) extension. The leading plus sign and the dot following the country code are required. The literal "x" character is required only if an extension is provided.

See Also

Recipe 4.2 provides more options for validating North American phone numbers.

ITU-T Recommendation E.123 ("Notation for national and international telephone numbers, e-mail addresses and Web addresses") can be downloaded here: *http://www .itu.int/rec/T-REC-E.123*.

ITU-T Recommendation E.164 ("The international public telecommunication numbering plan") can be downloaded at *http://www.itu.int/rec/T-REC-E.164*.

National numbering plans can be downloaded at *http://www.itu.int/ITU-T/inr/nnp*.

RFC 4933 defines the syntax and semantics of EPP contact identifiers, including international phone numbers. You can download RFC 4933 at *http://tools.ietf.org/html/ rfc4933*.

4.4 Validate Traditional Date Formats

Problem

You want to validate dates in the traditional formats mm/dd/yy, mm/dd/yyyy, dd/mm/yy, and dd/mm/yyyy. You want to use a simple regex that simply checks whether the input looks like a date, without trying to weed out things such as February 31st.

Solution

Match any of these date formats, allowing leading zeros to be omitted:

```
^[0-3]?[0-9]/[0-3]?[0-9]/(?:[0-9]{2})?[0-9]{2}$
```
Regex options: None
Regex flavors: .NET, Java, JavaScript, PCRE, Perl, Python, Ruby

Match any of these date formats, requiring leading zeros:

```
^[0-3][0-9]/[0-3][0-9]/(?:[0-9][0-9])?[0-9][0-9]$
```
Regex options: None
Regex flavors: .NET, Java, JavaScript, PCRE, Perl, Python, Ruby

Match m/d/yy and mm/dd/yyyy, allowing any combination of one or two digits for the day and month, and two or four digits for the year:

```
^(1[0-2]|0?[1-9])/(3[01]|[12][0-9]|0?[1-9])/(?:[0-9]{2})?[0-9]{2}$
```
Regex options: None
Regex flavors: .NET, Java, JavaScript, PCRE, Perl, Python, Ruby

Match mm/dd/yyyy, requiring leading zeros:

```
^(1[0-2]|0[1-9])/(3[01]|[12][0-9]|0[1-9])/[0-9]{4}$
```
Regex options: None
Regex flavors: .NET, Java, JavaScript, PCRE, Perl, Python, Ruby

Match d/m/yy and dd/mm/yyyy, allowing any combination of one or two digits for the day and month, and two or four digits for the year:

```
^(3[01]|[12][0-9]|0?[1-9])/(1[0-2]|0?[1-9])/(?:[0-9]{2})?[0-9]{2}$
```
Regex options: None
Regex flavors: .NET, Java, JavaScript, PCRE, Perl, Python, Ruby

Match dd/mm/yyyy, requiring leading zeros:

```
^(3[01]|[12][0-9]|0[1-9])/(1[0-2]|0[1-9])/[0-9]{4}$
```
Regex options: None
Regex flavors: .NET, Java, JavaScript, PCRE, Perl, Python, Ruby

Match any of these date formats with greater accuracy, allowing leading zeros to be omitted:

```
^(?:(1[0-2]|0?[1-9])/(3[01]|[12][0-9]|0?[1-9])|↵
(3[01]|[12][0-9]|0?[1-9])/(1[0-2]|0?[1-9]))/(?:[0-9]{2})?[0-9]{2}$
```
Regex options: None
Regex flavors: .NET, Java, JavaScript, PCRE, Perl, Python, Ruby

Match any of these date formats with greater accuracy, requiring leading zeros:

```
^(?:(1[0-2]|0[1-9])/(3[01]|[12][0-9]|0[1-9])|↵
(3[01]|[12][0-9]|0[1-9])/(1[0-2]|0[1-9]))/[0-9]{4}$
```
Regex options: None
Regex flavors: .NET, Java, JavaScript, PCRE, Perl, Python, Ruby

The free-spacing option makes these last two a bit more readable:

```
^(?:
  # m/d or mm/dd
  (1[0-2]|0?[1-9])/(3[01]|[12][0-9]|0?[1-9])
|
  # d/m or dd/mm
  (3[01]|[12][0-9]|0?[1-9])/(1[0-2]|0?[1-9])
)
# /yy or /yyyy
/(?:[0-9]{2})?[0-9]{2}$
```
Regex options: Free-spacing
Regex flavors: .NET, Java, PCRE, Perl, Python, Ruby

```
^(?:
  # mm/dd
  (1[0-2]|0[1-9])/(3[01]|[12][0-9]|0[1-9])
|
  # dd/mm
  (3[01]|[12][0-9]|0[1-9])/(1[0-2]|0[1-9])
)
# /yyyy
/[0-9]{4}$
```
Regex options: Free-spacing
Regex flavors: .NET, Java, PCRE, Perl, Python, Ruby

Discussion

You might think that something as conceptually trivial as a date should be an easy job for a regular expression. But it isn't, for two reasons. Because dates are such an everyday thing, humans are very sloppy with them. 4/1 may be April Fools' Day to you. To somebody else, it may be the first working day of the year, if New Year's Day is on a Friday. The solutions shown match some of the most common date formats.

The other issue is that regular expressions don't deal directly with numbers. You can't tell a regular expression to "match a number between 1 and 31", for instance. Regular expressions work character by character. We use ‹3[01]|[12][0-9]|0?[1-9]› to match 3 followed by 0 or 1, or to match 1 or 2 followed by any digit, or to match an optional 0 followed by 1 to 9. In character classes, we can use ranges for single digits, such as ‹[1-9]›. That's because the characters for the digits 0 through 9 occupy consecutive positions in the ASCII and Unicode character tables. See Chapter 6 for more details on matching all kinds of numbers with regular expressions.

Because of this, you have to choose how simple or how accurate you want your regular expression to be. If you already know your subject text doesn't contain any invalid dates, you could use a trivial regex such as ‹\d{2}/\d{2}/\d{4}›. The fact that this matches things like 99/99/9999 is irrelevant if those don't occur in the subject text. You can quickly type in this simple regex, and it will be quickly executed.

The first two solutions for this recipe are quick and simple, too, and they also match invalid dates, such as 0/0/00 and 31/31/2008. They only use literal characters for the date delimiters, and character classes (see Recipe 2.3) for the digits and the question mark (see Recipe 2.12) to make certain digits optional. ‹(?:[0-9]{2})?[0-9]{2}› allows the year to consist of two or four digits. ‹[0-9]{2}› matches exactly two digits. ‹(?:[0-9]{2})?› matches zero or two digits. The noncapturing group (see Recipe 2.9) is required, because the question mark needs to apply to the character class and the quantifier ‹{2}› combined. ‹[0-9]{2}?› matches exactly two digits, just like ‹[0-9]{2}›. Without the group, the question mark makes the quantifier lazy, which has no effect because ‹{2}› cannot repeat more than two times or fewer than two times.

Solutions 3 through 6 restrict the month to numbers between 1 and 12, and the day to numbers between 1 and 31. We use alternation (see Recipe 2.8) inside a group to match various pairs of digits to form a range of two-digit numbers. We use capturing groups here because you'll probably want to capture the day and month numbers anyway.

The final two solutions are a little more complex, so we're presenting these in both condensed and free-spacing form. The only difference between the two forms is readability. JavaScript does not support free-spacing. The final solutions allow all of the date formats, just like the first two examples. The difference is that the last two use an extra level of alternation to restrict the dates to 12/31 and 31/12, disallowing invalid months, such as 31/31.

Variations

If you want to search for dates in larger bodies of text instead of checking whether the input as a whole is a date, you cannot use the anchors ‹^› and ‹$›. Merely removing the anchors from the regular expression is not the right solution. That would allow any of these regexes to match **12/12/2001** within 9912/12/200199, for example. Instead of anchoring the regex match to the start and end of the subject, you have to specify that the date cannot be part of longer sequences of digits.

This is easily done with a pair of word boundaries. In regular expressions, digits are treated as characters that can be part of words. Replace both ‹^› and ‹$› with ‹\b›. As an example:

```
\b(1[0-2]|0[1-9])/(3[01]|[12][0-9]|0[1-9])/[0-9]{4}\b
```
Regex options: None
Regex flavors: .NET, Java, JavaScript, PCRE, Perl, Python, Ruby

See Also

Recipes 4.5, 4.6, and 4.7

4.5 Accurately Validate Traditional Date Formats

Problem

You want to validate dates in the traditional formats mm/dd/yy, mm/dd/yyyy, dd/mm/yy, and dd/mm/yyyy. You want to weed out invalid dates, such as February 31st.

Solution

C#

Month before day:

```
    DateTime foundDate;
    Match matchResult = Regex.Match(SubjectString,
        "^(?<month>[0-3]?[0-9])/(?<day>[0-3]?[0-9])/" +
        "(?<year>(?:[0-9]{2})?[0-9]{2})$");
    if (matchResult.Success) {
        int year = int.Parse(matchResult.Groups["year"].Value);
        if (year < 50) year += 2000;
        else if (year < 100) year += 1900;
        try {
            foundDate = new DateTime(year,
                int.Parse(matchResult.Groups["month"].Value),
                int.Parse(matchResult.Groups["day"].Value));
        } catch {
            // Invalid date
        }
    }
```

Day before month:

```
    DateTime foundDate;
    Match matchResult = Regex.Match(SubjectString,
        "^(?<day>[0-3]?[0-9])/(?<month>[0-3]?[0-9])/" +
        "(?<year>(?:[0-9]{2})?[0-9]{2})$");
    if (matchResult.Success) {
        int year = int.Parse(matchResult.Groups["year"].Value);
        if (year < 50) year += 2000;
        else if (year < 100) year += 1900;
        try {
            foundDate = new DateTime(year,
                int.Parse(matchResult.Groups["month"].Value),
                int.Parse(matchResult.Groups["day"].Value));
        } catch {
            // Invalid date
        }
    }
```

Perl

Month before day:

```
    @daysinmonth = (31, 28, 31, 30, 31, 30, 31, 31, 30, 31, 30, 31);
    $validdate = 0;
    if ($subject =~ m!^([0-3]?[0-9])/([0-3]?[0-9])/((?:[0-9]{2})?[0-9]{2})$!) {
        $month = $1;
        $day = $2;
        $year = $3;
        $year += 2000 if $year < 50;
        $year += 1900 if $year < 100;
        if ($month == 2 && $year % 4 == 0 && ($year % 100 != 0 ||
                                              $year % 400 == 0)) {
```

```
            $validdate = 1 if $day >= 1 && $day <= 29;
        } elsif ($month >= 1 && $month <= 12) {
            $validdate = 1 if $day >= 1 && $day <= $daysinmonth[$month-1];
        }
    }
```

Day before month:

```
@daysinmonth = (31, 28, 31, 30, 31, 30, 31, 31, 30, 31, 30, 31);
$validdate = 0;
if ($subject =~ m!^([0-3]?[0-9])/([0-3]?[0-9])/((?:[0-9]{2})?[0-9]{2})$!) {
    $day = $1;
    $month = $2;
    $year = $3;
    $year += 2000 if $year < 50;
    $year += 1900 if $year < 100;
    if ($month == 2 && $year % 4 == 0 && ($year % 100 != 0 ||
                                         $year % 400 == 0)) {
        $validdate = 1 if $day >= 1 && $day <= 29;
    } elsif ($month >= 1 && $month <= 12) {
        $validdate = 1 if $day >= 1 && $day <= $daysinmonth[$month-1];
    }
}
```

Pure regular expression

Month before day:

```
^(?:
  # February (29 days every year)
  (?<month>0?2)/(?<day>[12][0-9]|0?[1-9])
|
  # 30-day months
  (?<month>0?[469]|11)/(?<day>30|[12][0-9]|0?[1-9])
|
  # 31-day months
  (?<month>0?[13578]|1[02])/(?<day>3[01]|[12][0-9]|0?[1-9])
)
# Year
/(?<year>(?:[0-9]{2})?[0-9]{2})$
```
Regex options: Free-spacing
Regex flavors: .NET

```
^(?:
  # February (29 days every year)
  (0?2)/([12][0-9]|0?[1-9])
|
  # 30-day months
  (0?[469]|11)/(30|[12][0-9]|0?[1-9])
|
```

```
  # 31-day months
  (0?[13578]|1[02])/(3[01]|[12][0-9]|0?[1-9])
)
# Year
/((?:[0-9]{2})?[0-9]{2})$
```
Regex options: Free-spacing
Regex flavors: .NET, Java, PCRE, Perl, Python, Ruby

```
^(?:(0?2)/([12][0-9]|0?[1-9])|(0?[469]|11)/(30|[12][0-9]|0?[1-9])|↵
(0?[13578]|1[02])/(3[01]|[12][0-9]|0?[1-9]))/((?:[0-9]{2})?[0-9]{2})$
```
Regex options: None
Regex flavors: .NET, Java, JavaScript, PCRE, Perl, Python, Ruby

Day before month:

```
^(?:
  # February (29 days every year)
  (?<day>[12][0-9]|0?[1-9])/(?<month>0?2)
|
  # 30-day months
  (?<day>30|[12][0-9]|0?[1-9])/(?<month>0?[469]|11)
|
  # 31-day months
  (?<day>3[01]|[12][0-9]|0?[1-9])/(?<month>0?[13578]|1[02])
)
# Year
/(?<year>(?:[0-9]{2})?[0-9]{2})$
```
Regex options: Free-spacing
Regex flavors: .NET

```
^(?:
  # February (29 days every year)
  ([12][0-9]|0?[1-9])/(0?2)
|
  # 30-day months
  (30|[12][0-9]|0?[1-9])/([469]|11)
|
  # 31-day months
  (3[01]|[12][0-9]|0?[1-9])/(0?[13578]|1[02])
)
# Year
/((?:[0-9]{2})?[0-9]{2})$
```
Regex options: Free-spacing
Regex flavors: .NET, Java, PCRE, Perl, Python, Ruby

```
^(?:([12][0-9]|0?[1-9])/(0?2)|(30|[12][0-9]|0?[1-9])/([469]|11)|↵
(3[01]|[12][0-9]|0?[1-9])/(0?[13578]|1[02]))/((?:[0-9]{2})?[0-9]{2})$
```
Regex options: None
Regex flavors: .NET, Java, JavaScript, PCRE, Perl, Python, Ruby

Discussion

There are essentially two ways to accurately validate dates with a regular expression. One method is to use a simple regex that merely captures groups of numbers that look like a month/day/year combination, and then use procedural code to check whether the date is correct. I used the first regex from the previous recipe that allows any number between 0 and 39 for the day and month. That makes it easy to change the format from mm/dd/yy to dd/mm/yy by changing which capturing group is treated as the month.

The main benefit of this method is that you can easily add additional restrictions, such as limiting dates to certain periods. Many programming languages provide specific support for dealing with dates. The C# solution uses .NET's `DateTime` structure to check whether the date is valid and return the date in a useful format, all in one step.

The other method is to do everything with a regular expression. The solution is manageable, if we take the liberty of treating every year as a leap year. We can use the same technique of spelling out the alternatives as we did for the more final solutions presented with the preceding recipe.

The problem with using a single regular expression is that it no longer neatly captures the day and month in a single capturing group. We now have three capturing groups for the month, and three for the day. When the regex matches a date, only three of the seven groups in the regex will actually capture something. If the month is February, groups 1 and 2 capture the month and day. If the month has 30 days, groups 3 and 4 return the month and day. If the month has 31 days, groups 5 and 6 take action. Group 7 always captures the year.

Only the .NET regex flavor helps us in this situation. .NET allows multiple named capturing groups (see Recipe 2.11) to have the same name, and uses the same storage space for groups with the same name. If you use the .NET-only solution with named capture, you can simply retrieve the text matched by the groups "month" and "day" without worrying about how many days the month has. All the other flavors discussed in this book either don't support named capture, don't allow two groups to have the same name, or return only the text captured by the last group with any given name. For those flavors, numbered capture is the only way to go.

The pure regex solution is interesting only in situations where one regex is all you can use, such as when you're using an application that offers one box to type in a regex. When programming, make things easier with a bit of extra code. This will be particularly helpful if you want to add extra checks on the date later. Here's a pure regex solution that matches any date between 2 May 2007 and 29 August 2008 in d/m/yy or dd/mm/yyyy format:

```
# 2 May 2007 till 29 August 2008
^(?:
  # 2 May 2007 till 31 December 2007
  (?:
    # 2 May till 31 May
```

```
  (?<day>3[01]|[12][0-9]|0?[2-9])/(?<month>0?5)/(?<year>2007)
|
  # 1 June till 31 December
  (?:
    # 30-day months
    (?<day>30|[12][0-9]|0?[1-9])/(?<month>0?[69]|11)
  |
    # 31-day months
    (?<day>3[01]|[12][0-9]|0?[1-9])/(?<month>0?[78]|1[02])
  )
  /(?<year>2007)
)
|
  # 1 January 2008 till 29 August 2008
  (?:
    # 1 August till 29 August
    (?<day>[12][0-9]|0?[1-9])/(?<month>0?8)/(?<year>2008)
  |
    # 1 Janary till 30 June
    (?:
      # February
      (?<day>[12][0-9]|0?[1-9])/(?<month>0?2)
    |
      # 30-day months
      (?<day>30|[12][0-9]|0?[1-9])/(?<month>0?[46])
    |
      # 31-day months
      (?<day>3[01]|[12][0-9]|0?[1-9])/(?<month>0?[1357])
    )
    /(?<year>2008)
  )
)$
```
Regex options: Free-spacing
Regex flavors: .NET, Java, PCRE, Perl, Python, Ruby

See Also

Recipes 4.4, 4.6, and 4.7

4.6 Validate Traditional Time Formats

Problem

You want to validate times in various traditional time formats, such as hh:mm and hh:mm:ss in both 12-hour and 24-hour formats.

Solution

Hours and minutes, 12-hour clock:

```
^(1[0-2]|0?[1-9]):([0-5]?[0-9])$
```
Regex options: None
Regex flavors: .NET, Java, JavaScript, PCRE, Perl, Python, Ruby

Hours and minutes, 24-hour clock:

```
^(2[0-3]|[01]?[0-9]):([0-5]?[0-9])$
```
Regex options: None
Regex flavors: .NET, Java, JavaScript, PCRE, Perl, Python, Ruby

Hours, minutes and seconds, 12-hour clock:

```
^(1[0-2]|0?[1-9]):([0-5]?[0-9]):([0-5]?[0-9])$
```
Regex options: None
Regex flavors: .NET, Java, JavaScript, PCRE, Perl, Python, Ruby

Hours, minutes and seconds, 24-hour clock:

```
^(2[0-3]|[01]?[0-9]):([0-5]?[0-9]):([0-5]?[0-9])$
```
Regex options: None
Regex flavors: .NET, Java, JavaScript, PCRE, Perl, Python, Ruby

The question marks in all of the preceding regular expressions make leading zeros optional. Remove the question marks to make leading zeros mandatory.

Discussion

Validating times is considerably easier than validating dates. Every hour has 60 minutes, and every minute has 60 seconds. This means we don't need any complicated alternations in the regex. For the minutes and seconds, we don't use alternation at all. ‹[0-5]?[0-9]› matches a digit between 0 and 5, followed by a digit between 0 and 9. This correctly matches any number between 0 and 59. The question mark after the first character class makes it optional. This way, a single digit between 0 and 9 is also accepted as a valid minute or second. Remove the question mark if the first 10 minutes and seconds should be written as 00 to 09. See Recipe 2.3 and Recipe 2.12 for details on character classes and quantifiers such as the question mark.

For the hours, we do use alternation (see Recipe 2.8). The second digit allows different ranges, depending on the first digit. On a 12-hour clock, if the first digit is 0, the second digit allows all 10 digits, but if the first digit is 1, the second digit must be 0, 1, or 2. In a regular expression, we write this as ‹1[0-2]|0?[1-9]›. On a 24-hour clock, if the first digit is 0 or 1, the second digit allows all 10 digits, but if the first digit is 2, the second digit must be between 0 and 3. In regex syntax, this can be expressed as 2[0-3]|[01]?[0-9]. Again, the question mark allows the first 10 hours to be written with a single digit. Remove the question mark to require two digits.

We put parentheses around the parts of the regex that match the hours, minutes, and seconds. That makes it easy to retrieve the digits for the hours, minutes, and seconds without the colons. Recipe 2.9 explains how parentheses create capturing groups. Recipe 3.9 explains how you can retrieve the text matched by those capturing groups in procedural code.

The parentheses around the hour part keeps two alternatives for the hour together. If you remove those parentheses, the regex won't work correctly. Removing the parentheses around the minutes and seconds has no effect, other than making it impossible to retrieve their digits separately.

Variations

If you want to search for times in larger bodies of text instead of checking whether the input as a whole is a time, you cannot use the anchors ‹^› and ‹$›. Merely removing the anchors from the regular expression is not the right solution. That would allow the hour and minute regexes to match **12:12** within **9912:1299**, for instance. Instead of anchoring the regex match to the start and end of the subject, you have to specify that the date cannot be part of longer sequences of digits.

This is easily done with a pair of word boundaries. In regular expressions, digits are treated as characters that can be part of words. Replace both ‹^› and ‹$› with ‹\b›. As an example:

> \b(2[0-3]|[01]?[0-9]):([0-5]?[0-9])\b
> **Regex options:** None
> **Regex flavors:** .NET, Java, JavaScript, PCRE, Perl, Python, Ruby

Word boundaries don't disallow everything; they only disallow letters, digits and underscores. The regex just shown, which matches hours and minutes on a 24-hour clock, matches **16:08** within the subject text The time is 16:08:42 sharp. The space is not a word character, whereas the 1 is, so the word boundary matches between them. The 8 is a word character, whereas the colon isn't, so ‹\b› also matches between those two.

If you want to disallow colons as well as word characters, you need to use lookaround (see Recipe 2.16). The following regex will not match any part of The time is 16:08:42 sharp. It only works with flavors that support lookbehind:

> (?<![:\w])(2[0-3]|[01]?[0-9]):([0-5]?[0-9])(?![:\w])
> **Regex options:** None
> **Regex flavors:** .NET, Java, PCRE, Perl, Python, Ruby 1.9

See Also

Recipes 4.4, 4.5, and 4.7

4.7 Validate ISO 8601 Dates and Times

Problem

You want to match dates and/or times in the official ISO 8601 format, which is the basis for many standardized date and time formats. For example, in XML Schema, the built-in `date`, `time`, and `dateTime` types are all based on ISO 8601.

Solution

The following matches a calendar month, e.g., 2008-08. The hyphen is required:

```
^([0-9]{4})-(1[0-2]|0[1-9])$
```
Regex options: None
Regex flavors: .NET, Java, JavaScript, PCRE, Perl, Python, Ruby

```
^(?<year>[0-9]{4})-(?<month>1[0-2]|0[1-9])$
```
Regex options: None
Regex flavors: .NET, PCRE 7, Perl 5.10, Ruby 1.9

```
^(?P<year>[0-9]{4})-(?P<month>1[0-2]|0[1-9])$
```
Regex options: None
Regex flavors: PCRE, Python

Calendar date, e.g., 2008-08-30. The hyphens are optional. This regex allows YYYY-MMDD and YYYYMM-DD, which do not follow ISO 8601:

```
^([0-9]{4})-?(1[0-2]|0[1-9])-?(3[0-1]|0[1-9]|[1-2][0-9])$
```
Regex options: None
Regex flavors: .NET, Java, JavaScript, PCRE, Perl, Python, Ruby

```
^(?<year>[0-9]{4})-?(?<month>1[0-2]|0[1-9])-?↵
(?<day>3[0-1]|0[1-9]|[1-2][0-9])$
```
Regex options: None
Regex flavors: .NET, PCRE 7, Perl 5.10, Ruby 1.9

Calendar date, e.g., 2008-08-30. The hyphens are optional. This regex uses a conditional to exclude YYYY-MMDD and YYYYMM-DD. There is an extra capturing group for the first hyphen:

```
^([0-9]{4})(-)?(1[0-2]|0[1-9])(?(2)-)(3[0-1]|0[1-9]|[1-2][0-9])$
```
Regex options: None
Regex flavors: .NET, PCRE, Perl, Python

Calendar date, e.g., 2008-08-30. The hyphens are optional. This regex uses alternation to exclude YYYY-MMDD and YYYYMM-DD. There are two capturing groups for the month:

```
^([0-9]{4})(?:(1[0-2]|0[1-9])|-?(1[0-2]|0[1-9])-?)↵
(3[0-1]|0[1-9]|[1-2][0-9])$
```
Regex options: None
Regex flavors: .NET, Java, JavaScript, PCRE, Perl, Python, Ruby

Week of the year, e.g., 2008-W35. The hyphen is optional:

```
^([0-9]{4})-?W(5[0-3]|[1-4][0-9]|0[1-9])$
```
Regex options: None
Regex flavors: .NET, Java, JavaScript, PCRE, Perl, Python, Ruby

```
^(?<year>[0-9]{4})-?W(?<week>5[0-3]|[1-4][0-9]|0[1-9])$
```
Regex options: None
Regex flavors: .NET, PCRE 7, Perl 5.10, Ruby 1.9

Week date, e.g., 2008-W35-6. The hyphens are optional:

```
^([0-9]{4})-?W(5[0-3]|[1-4][0-9]|0[1-9])-?([1-7])$
```
Regex options: None
Regex flavors: .NET, Java, JavaScript, PCRE, Perl, Python, Ruby

```
^(?<year>[0-9]{4})-?W(?<week>5[0-3]|[1-4][0-9]|0[1-9])-?(?<day>[1-7])$
```
Regex options: None
Regex flavors: .NET, PCRE 7, Perl 5.10, Ruby 1.9

Ordinal date, e.g., 2008-243. The hyphen is optional:

```
^([0-9]{4})-?(36[0-6]|3[0-5][0-9]|[12][0-9]{2}|0[1-9][0-9]|00[1-9])$
```
Regex options: None
Regex flavors: .NET, Java, JavaScript, PCRE, Perl, Python, Ruby

```
^(?<year>[0-9]{4})-?↵
(?<day>36[0-6]|3[0-5][0-9]|[12][0-9]{2}|0[1-9][0-9]|00[1-9])$
```
Regex options: None
Regex flavors: .NET, PCRE 7, Perl 5.10, Ruby 1.9

Hours and minutes, e.g., 17:21. The colon is optional:

```
^(2[0-3]|[01]?[0-9]):?([0-5]?[0-9])$
```
Regex options: None
Regex flavors: .NET, Java, JavaScript, PCRE, Perl, Python, Ruby

```
^(?<hour>2[0-3]|[01]?[0-9]):?(?<minute>[0-5]?[0-9])$
```
Regex options: None
Regex flavors: .NET, PCRE 7, Perl 5.10, Ruby 1.9

Hours, minutes, and seconds, e.g., 17:21:59. The colons are optional:

```
^(2[0-3]|[01]?[0-9]):?([0-5]?[0-9]):?([0-5]?[0-9])$
```
Regex options: None
Regex flavors: .NET, Java, JavaScript, PCRE, Perl, Python, Ruby

```
^(?<hour>2[0-3]|[01]?[0-9]):?(?<minute>[0-5]?[0-9]):?↵
(?<second>[0-5]?[0-9])$
```
Regex options: None

Regex flavors: .NET, PCRE 7, Perl 5.10, Ruby 1.9

Time zone designator, e.g., Z, +07 or +07:00. The colons and the minutes are optional:

```
^(Z|[+-](?:2[0-3]|[01]?[0-9])(?::?(?:[0-5]?[0-9]))?)$
```
Regex options: None

Regex flavors: .NET, Java, JavaScript, PCRE, Perl, Python, Ruby

Hours, minutes, and seconds with time zone designator, e.g., 17:21:59+07:00. All the colons are optional. The minutes in the time zone designator are also optional:

```
^(2[0-3]|[01]?[0-9]):?([0-5]?[0-9]):?([0-5]?[0-9])↵
(Z|[+-](?:2[0-3]|[01]?[0-9])(?::?(?:[0-5]?[0-9]))?)$
```
Regex options: None

Regex flavors: .NET, Java, JavaScript, PCRE, Perl, Python, Ruby

```
^(?<hour>2[0-3]|[01]?[0-9]):?(?<minute>[0-5]?[0-9]):?(?<sec>[0-5]?[0-9])↵
(?<timezone>Z|[+-](?:2[0-3]|[01]?[0-9])(?::?(?:[0-5]?[0-9]))?)$
```
Regex options: None

Regex flavors: .NET, PCRE 7, Perl 5.10, Ruby 1.9

Date, with optional time zone, e.g., 2008-08-30 or 2008-08-30+07:00. Hyphens are required. This is the XML Schema date type:

```
^(-?(?:[1-9][0-9]*)?[0-9]{4})-(1[0-2]|0[1-9])-(3[0-1]|0[1-9]|[1-2][0-9])↵
(Z|[+-](?:2[0-3]|[0-1][0-9]):[0-5][0-9])?$
```
Regex options: None

Regex flavors: .NET, Java, JavaScript, PCRE, Perl, Python, Ruby

```
^(?<year>-?(?:[1-9][0-9]*)?[0-9]{4})-(?<month>1[0-2]|0[1-9])-↵
(?<day>3[0-1]|0[1-9]|[1-2][0-9])↵
(?<timezone>Z|[+-](?:2[0-3]|[0-1][0-9]):[0-5][0-9])?$
```
Regex options: None

Regex flavors: .NET, PCRE 7, Perl 5.10, Ruby 1.9

Time, with optional microseconds and time zone, e.g., 01:45:36 or 01:45:36.123+07:00. This is the XML Schema dateTime type:

```
^(2[0-3]|[0-1][0-9]):([0-5][0-9]):([0-5][0-9])(\.[0-9]+)?↵
(Z|[+-](?:2[0-3]|[0-1][0-9]):[0-5][0-9])?$
```
Regex options: None

Regex flavors: .NET, Java, JavaScript, PCRE, Perl, Python, Ruby

```
^(?<hour>2[0-3]|[0-1][0-9]):(?<minute>[0-5][0-9]):(?<second>[0-5][0-9])↵
(?<ms>\.[0-9]+)?(?<timezone>Z|[+-](?:2[0-3]|[0-1][0-9]):[0-5][0-9])?$
```
Regex options: None

Regex flavors: .NET, PCRE 7, Perl 5.10, Ruby 1.9

Date and time, with optional microseconds and time zone, e.g., 2008-08-30T01:45:36 or 2008-08-30T01:45:36.123Z. This is the XML Schema dateTime type:

```
^(-?(?:[1-9][0-9]*)?[0-9]{4})-(1[0-2]|0[1-9])-(3[0-1]|0[1-9]|[1-2][0-9])↵
T(2[0-3]|[0-1][0-9]):([0-5][0-9]):([0-5][0-9])(\.[0-9]+)?↵
(Z|[+-](?:2[0-3]|[0-1][0-9]):[0-5][0-9])?$
```

Regex options: None
Regex flavors: .NET, Java, JavaScript, PCRE, Perl, Python, Ruby

```
^(?<year>-?(?:[1-9][0-9]*)?[0-9]{4})-(?<month>1[0-2]|0[1-9])-↵
(?<day>3[0-1]|0[1-9]|[1-2][0-9])T(?<hour>2[0-3]|[0-1][0-9]):↵
(?<minute>[0-5][0-9]):(?<second>[0-5][0-9])(?<ms>\.[0-9]+)?↵
(?<timezone>Z|[+-](?:2[0-3]|[0-1][0-9]):[0-5][0-9])?$
```

Regex options: None
Regex flavors: .NET, PCRE 7, Perl 5.10, Ruby 1.9

Discussion

ISO 8601 defines a wide range of date and time formats. The regular expressions presented here cover the most common formats, but most systems that use ISO 8601 use only a subset. For example, in XML Schema dates and times, the hyphens and colons are mandatory. To make hyphens and colons mandatory, simply remove the question marks after them. To disallow hyphens and colons, remove the hyphens and colons along with the question mark that follows them. Do watch out for the noncapturing groups, which use the ‹(?:group)› syntax. If a question mark and a colon follow an opening parenthesis, those three characters open a noncapturing group.

The regular expressions make the individual hyphens and colons optional, which does not follow ISO 8601 exactly. For example, 1733:26 is not a valid ISO 8601 time, but will be accepted by the time regexes. Requiring all hyphens and colons to be present or omitted at the same time makes your regex quite a bit more complex. We've done this as an example for the date regex, but in practice, as with the XML Schema types, the delimiters are usually required or disallowed rather than optional.

We put parentheses around all the number parts of the regex. That makes it easy to retrieve the numbers for the years, months, days, hours, minutes, seconds, and time zones. Recipe 2.9 explains how parentheses create capturing groups. Recipe 3.9 explains how you can retrieve the text matched by those capturing groups in procedural code.

For most regexes, we also show an alternative using named capture. Some of these date and time formats may be unfamiliar to you or your fellow developers. Named capture makes the regex easier to understand. .NET, PCRE 7, Perl 5.10, and Ruby 1.9 support the ‹(?<name>group)› syntax. All versions of PCRE and Python covered in this book support the alternative ‹(?P<name>group)› syntax, which adds a ‹P›. See Recipe 2.11 and Recipe 3.9 for details.

The number ranges in all the regexes are strict. For example, the calendar day is restricted between 01 and 31. You'll never end up with day 32 or month 13. None of the regexes here attempt to exclude invalid day and month combinations, such as February 31st; Recipe 4.5 explains how you can deal with that.

Though some of these regexes are quite long, they're all very straightforward and use the same techniques explained in Recipe 4.4 and Recipe 4.6.

See Also

Recipes 4.4, 4.5, 4.6

4.8 Limit Input to Alphanumeric Characters

Problem

Your application requires that users limit their responses to one or more alphanumeric characters from the English alphabet.

Solution

With regular expressions at your disposal, the solution is dead simple. A character class can set up the allowed range of characters. With an added quantifier that repeats the character class one or more times, and anchors that bind the match to the start and end of the string, you're good to go.

Regular expression

```
^[A-Z0-9]+$
```
Regex options: Case insensitive
Regex flavors: .NET, Java, JavaScript, PCRE, Perl, Python, Ruby

Ruby

```
if subject =~ /^[A-Z0-9]+$/i
    puts "Subject is alphanumeric"
else
    puts "Subject is not alphanumeric"
end
```

Other programming languages

See Recipes 3.4 and 3.5 for help implementing this regular expression with other programming languages.

Discussion

Let's look at the four pieces of this regular expression one at a time:

```
^           # Assert position at the beginning of the string.
[A-Z0-9]    # Match a character from "A" to "Z" or from "0" to "9"...
   +        #    between one and unlimited times.
$           # Assert position at the end of the string.
```

> **Regex options:** Case insensitive, free-spacing
> **Regex flavors:** .NET, Java, PCRE, Perl, Python, Ruby

The ‹^› and ‹$› assertions at the beginning and end of the regular expression ensure that the entire input string is tested. Without them, the regex could match any part of a longer string, letting invalid characters through. The plus quantifier ‹+› repeats the preceding element one or more times. If you wanted to allow the regex to match an entirely empty string, you could replace the ‹+› with ‹*›. The asterisk quantifier ‹*› allows zero or more repetitions, effectively making the preceding element optional.

Variations

Limit input to ASCII characters

The following regular expression limits input to the 128 characters in the seven-bit ASCII character table. This includes 33 nonvisible control characters:

```
^[\x00-\x7F]+$
```

> **Regex options:** None
> **Regex flavors:** .NET, Java, JavaScript, PCRE, Perl, Python, Ruby

Limit input to ASCII non-control characters and line breaks

Use the following regular expression to limit input to visible characters and whitespace in the ASCII character table, excluding control characters. The line feed and carriage return characters (at positions 0x0A and 0x0D, respectively) are the most commonly used control characters, so they're explicitly included using ‹\n› (line feed) and ‹\r› (carriage return):

```
^[\n\r\x20-\x7E]+$
```

> **Regex options:** None
> **Regex flavors:** .NET, Java, JavaScript, PCRE, Perl, Python, Ruby

Limit input to shared ISO-8859-1 and Windows-1252 characters

ISO-8859-1 and Windows-1252 (often referred to as ANSI) are two commonly used eight-bit character encodings that are both based on the Latin-1 standard (or more formally, ISO/IEC 8859-1). However, the characters they map to the positions between 0x80 and 0x9F are incompatible. ISO-8859-1 uses these positions for control codes, whereas Windows-1252 uses them for an extended range of letters and punctuation.

These differences sometimes lead to difficulty displaying characters, particularly with documents that do not declare their encoding or when the recipient is using a non-Windows system. The following regular expression can be used to limit input to characters that are shared by ISO-8859-1 and Windows-1252 (including shared control characters):

`^[\x00-\x7F\xA0-\xFF]+$`
Regex options: None
Regex flavors: .NET, Java, JavaScript, PCRE, Perl, Python, Ruby

The hexadecimal notation might make this regular expression hard to read, but it works the same way as the ‹[A-Z0-9]› character class shown earlier. It matches characters in two ranges: \x00-\x7F and \xA0-\xFF.

Limit input to alphanumeric characters in any language

This regular expression limits input to letters and numbers from any language or script. It uses a character class that includes properties for all code points in the Unicode letter and number categories:

`^[\p{L}\p{N}]+$`
Regex options: None
Regex flavors: .NET, Java, PCRE, Perl, Ruby 1.9

Unfortunately, Unicode properties are not supported by all of the regular expression flavors covered by this book. Specifically, this regex will not work with JavaScript, Python, or Ruby 1.8. Additionally, using this regex with PCRE requires PCRE to be compiled with UTF-8 support. Unicode properties can be used with PHP's `preg` functions (which rely on PCRE) if the `/u` option is appended to the regex.

The following regex shows a workaround for Python:

`^[^\W_]+$`
Regex options: Unicode
Regex flavors: Python

Here, we work around the lack of Unicode properties in Python by using the UNICODE or U flag when creating the regular expression. This changes the meaning of some regex tokens by making them use the Unicode character table. ‹\w› gets us most of the way to a solution since it matches alphanumeric characters and the underscore. By using its inverse (‹\W›) in a negated character class, we can remove the underscore from this set. Double negatives like this are occasionally quite useful in regular expressions, though perhaps a little difficult to wrap your head around.[*]

---

[*] For even more fun (if you have a twisted definition of fun), try creating triple, quadruple, or even greater levels of negatives by throwing in negative lookaround (see Recipe 2.16) and character class subtraction (see "Flavor-Specific Features" on page 33 in Recipe 2.3).

See Also

Recipe 4.9 shows how to limit text by length instead of character set.

4.9 Limit the Length of Text

Problem

You want to test whether a string is composed of between 1 and 10 letters from A to Z.

Solution

All the programming languages covered by this book provide a simple, efficient way to check the length of text. For example, JavaScript strings have a `length` property that holds an integer indicating the string's length. However, using regular expressions to check text length can be useful in some situations, particularly when length is only one of multiple rules that determine whether the subject text fits the desired pattern. The following regular expression ensures that text is between 1 and 10 characters long, and additionally limits the text to the uppercase letters A–Z. You can modify the regular expressions to allow any minimum or maximum text length, or allow characters other than A–Z.

Regular expression

```
^[A-Z]{1,10}$
```

Regex options: None
Regex flavors: .NET, Java, JavaScript, PCRE, Perl, Python, Ruby

Perl

```
if ($ARGV[0] =~ /^[A-Z]{1,10}$/) {
    print "Input is valid\n";
} else {
    print "Input is invalid\n";
}
```

Other programming languages

See Recipe 3.5 for help with implementing this regular expression with other programming languages.

Discussion

Here's the breakdown for this very straightforward regex:

```
^          # Assert position at the beginning of the string.
[A-Z]      # Match one letter from "A" to "Z"...
```

```
    {1,10}  #    between 1 and 10 times.
  $           # Assert position at the end of the string.
```
Regex options: Free-spacing
Regex flavors: .NET, Java, PCRE, Perl, Python, Ruby

The ‹^› and ‹$› anchors ensure that the regex matches the entire subject string; otherwise, it could match 10 characters within longer text. The ‹[A-Z]› character class matches any single uppercase character from A to Z, and the interval quantifier ‹{1,10}› repeats the character class from 1 to 10 times. By combining the interval quantifier with the surrounding start- and end-of-string anchors, the regex will fail to match if the subject text's length falls outside the desired range.

Note that the character class ‹[A-Z]› explicitly allows only uppercase letters. If you want to also allow the lowercase letters a to z, you can either change the character class to ‹[A-Za-z]› or apply the case insensitive option. Recipe 3.4 shows how to do this.

A mistake commonly made by new regular expression users is to try to save a few characters by using the character class range ‹[A-z]›. At first glance, this might seem like a clever trick to allow all uppercase and lowercase letters. However, the ASCII character table includes several punctuation characters in positions between the A to Z and a to z ranges. Hence, ‹[A-z]› is actually equivalent to ‹[A-Z[\]^_`a-z]›.

Variations

Limit the length of an arbitrary pattern

Because quantifiers such as ‹{1,10}› apply only to the immediately preceding element, limiting the number of characters that can be matched by patterns that include more than a single token requires a different approach.

As explained in Recipe 2.16, lookaheads (and their counterpart, lookbehinds) are a special kind of assertion that, like ‹^› and ‹$›, match a position within the subject string and do not consume any characters. Lookaheads can be either positive or negative, which means they can check if a pattern follows or does not follow the current position in the match. A positive lookahead, written as ‹(?=···)›, can be used at the beginning of the pattern to ensure that the string is within the target length range. The remainder of the regex can then validate the desired pattern without worrying about text length. Here's a simple example:

```
^(?=.{1,10}$).*
```
Regex options: Dot matches line breaks
Regex flavors: .NET, Java, PCRE, Perl, Python, Ruby

```
^(?=[\S\s]{1,10}$)[\S\s]*
```
Regex options: None
Regex flavor: JavaScript

It is important that the ‹$› anchor appears inside the lookahead because the maximum length test works only if we ensure that there are no more characters after we've reached the limit. Because the lookahead at the beginning of the regex enforces the length range, the following pattern can then apply any additional validation rules. In this case, the pattern ‹.*› (or ‹[\S\s]*› in the JavaScript version) is used to simply match the entire subject text with no added constraints.

This regex uses the "dot matches line breaks" option to allow the dots to match all characters, including line breaks. See Recipe 3.4 for details about how to apply this modifier with your programming language. The JavaScript regex is different, since JavaScript does not have a "dot matches line breaks" option. See "Any character including line breaks" on page 35 in Recipe 2.4 for more information.

Limit the number of nonwhitespace characters

The following regex matches any string that contains between 10 and 100 nonwhitespace characters:

```
^\s*(?:\S\s*){10,100}$
```
Regex options: None
Regex flavors: .NET, Java, JavaScript, PCRE, Perl, Python, Ruby

In Java, PCRE, Python, and Ruby, ‹\s› matches only ASCII whitespace characters, and ‹\S› matches everything else. In Python, you can make ‹\s› match all Unicode whitespace by passing the UNICODE or U flag when creating the regex. Developers using Java, PCRE, and Ruby 1.9 who want to avoid having any Unicode whitespace count against their character limit can switch to the following version that takes advantage of Unicode properties (described in Recipe 2.7):

```
^[\p{Z}\s]*(?:[^\p{Z}\s][\p{Z}\s]*){10,100}$
```
Regex options: None
Regex flavors: .NET, Java, PCRE, Perl, Ruby 1.9

PCRE must be compiled with UTF-8 support for this to work. In PHP, turn on UTF-8 support with the /u pattern modifier.

This latter regex combines the Unicode ‹\p{Z}› Separator property with the ‹\s› shorthand for whitespace. That's because the characters matched by ‹\p{Z}› and ‹\s› do not completely overlap. ‹\s› includes the characters at positions 0x09 through 0x0D (tab, line feed, vertical tab, form feed, and carriage return), which are not assigned the Separator property by the Unicode standard. By combining ‹\p{Z}› and ‹\s› in a character class, you ensure that all whitespace characters are matched.

In both regexes, the interval quantifier ‹{10,100}› is applied to the noncapturing group that precedes it, rather than a single token. The group matches any single nonwhitespace character followed by zero or more whitespace characters. The interval quantifier can reliably track how many nonwhitespace characters are matched because exactly one nonwhitespace character is matched during each iteration.

Limit the number of words

The following regex is very similar to the previous example of limiting the number of nonwhitespace characters, except that each repetition matches an entire word rather than a single, nonwhitespace character. It matches between 10 and 100 words, skipping past any nonword characters, including punctuation and whitespace:

```
^\W*(?:\w+\b\W*){10,100}$
```
Regex options: None
Regex flavors: .NET, Java, JavaScript, PCRE, Perl, Python, Ruby

In Java, JavaScript, PCRE, and Ruby, the word character token ‹\w› in this regex will only match the ASCII characters A–Z, a–z, 0–9, and _, and therefore this cannot correctly count words that contain non-ASCII letters and numbers. In .NET and Perl, ‹\w› is based on the Unicode table (as is its inverse, ‹\W›, and the word boundary ‹\b›) and will match letters and digits from all Unicode scripts. In Python, you can choose whether these tokens should be Unicode-based or not, based on whether you pass the UNICODE or U flag when creating the regex.

If you want to count words that contain non-ASCII letters and numbers, the following regexes provide this capability for additional regex flavors:

```
^[^\p{L}\p{N}_]*(?:[\p{L}\p{N}_]+\b[^\p{L}\p{N}_]*){10,100}$
```
Regex options: None
Regex flavors: .NET, Java, Perl

```
^[^\p{L}\p{N}_]*(?:[\p{L}\p{N}_]+(?:[^\p{L}\p{N}_]+|$)){10,100}$
```
Regex options: None
Regex flavors: .NET, Java, PCRE, Perl, Ruby 1.9

PCRE must be compiled with UTF-8 support for this to work. In PHP, turn on UTF-8 support with the /u pattern modifier.

As noted, the reason for these different (but equivalent) regexes is the varying handling of the word character and word boundary tokens explained in "Word Characters" on page 42 in Recipe 2.6.

The last two regexes use character classes that include the separate Unicode properties for letters and numbers (‹\p{L}› and ‹\p{N}›), and manually add the underscore character to each class to make them equivalent to the earlier regex that relied on ‹\w› and ‹\W›.

Each repetition of the noncapturing group in the first two of these three regexes matches an entire word followed by zero or more nonword characters. The ‹\w› (or ‹[^\p{L}\p{N}_]›) token inside the group is allowed to repeat zero times in case the string ends with a word character. However, since this effectively makes the nonword character sequence optional throughout the matching process, the word boundary assertion ‹\b› is needed between ‹\w› and ‹\W› (or ‹[\p{L}\p{N}_]› and ‹[^\p{L}\p{N}_]›), to ensure that each repetition of the group really matches an entire word. Without the word boundary, a single repetition would be allowed to match any part of a word, with subsequent repetitions matching additional pieces.

The third version of the regex (which adds support for PCRE and Ruby 1.9) works a bit differently. It uses a plus (one or more) instead of an asterisk (zero or more) quantifier, and explicitly allows matching zero characters only if the matching process has reached the end of the string. This allows us to avoid the word boundary token, which is necessary to ensure accuracy, since ‹\b› is not Unicode-enabled in PCRE or Ruby. ‹\b› *is* Unicode-enabled in Java, even though Java's ‹\w› is not.

Unfortunately, none of these options allow JavaScript or Ruby 1.8 to correctly handle words that use non-ASCII characters. A possible workaround is to reframe the regex to count whitespace rather than word character sequences, as shown here:

```
^\s*(?:\S+(?:\s+|$)){10,100}$
```
Regex options: None
Regex flavors: .NET, Java, JavaScript, Perl, PCRE, Python, Ruby

In many cases, this will work the same as the previous solutions, although it's not exactly equivalent. For example, one difference is that compounds joined by a hyphen (such as "far-reaching") will now be counted as one word instead of two.

See Also

Recipes 4.8 and 4.10

4.10 Limit the Number of Lines in Text

Problem

You need to check whether a string is comprised of five or fewer lines, without regard for how many total characters appear in the string.

Solution

The exact characters or character sequences used as line separators can vary depending on your operating system's convention, application or user preferences, and so on. Crafting an ideal solution therefore raises questions about what conventions should be supported to indicate the start of a new line. The following solutions support the standard MS-DOS/Windows (‹\r\n›), legacy Mac OS (‹\r›), and Unix/Linux/OS X (‹\n›) line break conventions.

Regular expression

The following three flavor-specific regexes contain two differences. The first regex uses atomic groups, written as ‹(?>⋯)›, instead of noncapturing groups, written as ‹(?:⋯)›, because they have the potential to provide a minor efficiency improvement here for the regex flavors that support them. Python and JavaScript do not support atomic groups, so they are not used with those flavors. The other difference is the tokens used to assert position at the beginning and end of the string (‹\A› or ‹^› for the beginning of the string, and ‹\z›, ‹\Z›, or ‹$› for the end). The reasons for this variation are discussed in depth later in this recipe. All three flavor-specific regexes match exactly the same strings:

```
\A(?>(?>\r\n?|\n)?[^\r\n]*){0,5}\z
```
Regex options: None
Regex flavors: .NET, Java, PCRE, Perl, Ruby

```
\A(?:(?:\r\n?|\n)?[^\r\n]*){0,5}\Z
```
Regex options: None
Regex flavor: Python

```
^(?:(?:\r\n?|\n)?[^\r\n]*){0,5}$
```
Regex options: None
Regex flavor: JavaScript

PHP (PCRE)

```
if (preg_match('/^(?>(?>\r\n?|\n)?[^\r\n]*){0,5}\z/', $_POST['subject'])) {
    print 'Subject contains five or fewer lines';
} else {
    print 'Subject contains more than five lines';
}
```

Other programming languages

See Recipe 3.5 for help implementing these regular expressions with other programming languages.

Discussion

All of the regular expressions shown so far in this recipe use a grouping that matches an MS-DOS/Windows, legacy Mac OS, or Unix/Linux/OS X line break sequence followed by any number of non-line-break characters. The grouping is repeated between zero and five times, since we're matching up to five lines.

In the following example, we've broken up the JavaScript version of the regex into its individual parts. We've used the JavaScript version here because its elements are probably familiar to the widest range of readers. We'll explain the variations for alternative regex flavors afterward:

```
^           # Assert position at the beginning of the string.
(?:         # Group but don't capture...
  (?:       #   Group but don't capture...
    \r      #     Match a carriage return (CR, ASCII position 0x0D).
    \n      #     Match a line feed (LF, ASCII position 0x0A)...
```

```
        ?       #         between zero and one time.
        |       #    or...
       \n       #      Match a line feed character.
       )        #    End the noncapturing group.
        ?       #       Repeat the preceding group between zero and one time.
    [^\r\n]     #    Match any single character except CR or LF...
        *       #         between zero and unlimited times.
   )            # End the noncapturing group.
     {0,5}      #    Repeat the preceding group between zero and five times.
   $            # Assert position at the end of the string.
```
Regex options: Free-spacing
Regex flavors: .NET, Java, PCRE, Perl, Python, Ruby

The leading ‹^› matches the position at the beginning of the string. This helps to ensure that the entire string contains no more than five lines, because unless the regex is forced to start at the beginning of the string, it can match any five lines within a longer string.

Next, a noncapturing group encloses the combination of a line break sequence and any number of non-line-break characters. The immediately following quantifier allows this group to repeat between zero and five times (zero repetitions would match a completely empty string). Within the outer group, an optional subgroup matches a line break sequence. Next is the character class that matches any number of non-line-break characters.

Take a close look at the order of the outer group's elements (first a line break, then a non-line-break sequence). If we reversed the order so that the group was instead written as ‹(?:[^\r\n]*(?:\r\n?|\n)?)›, a fifth repetition would allow a trailing line break. Effectively, such a change would allow an empty, sixth line.

The subgroup allows any of three line break sequences:

- A carriage return followed by a line feed (‹\r\n›, the conventional MS-DOS/ Windows line break sequence)
- A standalone carriage return (‹\r›, the legacy Mac OS line break character)
- A standalone line feed (‹\n›, the conventional Unix/Linux/OS X line break character)

Now let's move on to the cross-flavor differences.

The first version of the regex (used by all flavors except Python and JavaScript) uses atomic groups rather than simple noncapturing groups. Although in some cases the use of atomic groups can have a much more profound impact, in this case they simply let the regex engine avoid a bit of unnecessary backtracking that can occur if the match attempt fails (see Recipe 2.15 for more information about atomic groups).

The other cross-flavor differences are the tokens used to assert position at the beginning and end of the string. The breakdown shown earlier used ‹^› and ‹$› for these purposes. Although these anchors are supported by all of the regex flavors discussed here, the alternative regexes in this section used ‹\A›, ‹\Z›, and ‹\z› instead. The short explanation for this is that the meaning of these metacharacters differs slightly between regular expression flavors. The long explanation leads us to a bit of regex history....

When using Perl to read a line from a file, the resulting string ends with a line break. Hence, Perl introduced an "enhancement" to the traditional meaning of ‹$› that has since been copied by most regex flavors. In addition to matching the absolute end of a string, Perl's ‹$› matches just before a string-terminating line break. Perl also introduced two more assertions that match the end of a string: ‹\Z› and ‹\z›. Perl's ‹\Z› anchor has the same quirky meaning as ‹$›, except that it doesn't change when the option to let ‹^› and ‹$› match at line breaks is enabled. ‹\z› always matches only the absolute end of a string, no exceptions. Since this recipe explicitly deals with line breaks in order to count the lines in a string, it uses the ‹\z› assertion for the regex flavors that support it, to ensure that an empty, sixth line is not allowed.

Most of the other regex flavors copied Perl's end-of-line/string anchors. .NET, Java, PCRE, and Ruby all support both ‹\Z› and ‹\z› with the same meanings as Perl. Python includes only ‹\Z› (uppercase), but confusingly changes its meaning to match only the absolute end of the string, just like Perl's lowercase ‹\z›. JavaScript doesn't include any "z" anchors, but unlike all of the other flavors discussed here, its ‹$› anchor matches only at the absolute end of the string (when the option to let ‹^› and ‹$› match at line breaks is not enabled).

As for ‹\A›, the situation is slightly better. It always matches only at the start of a string, and it means exactly the same thing in all flavors discussed here, except JavaScript (which doesn't support it).

Although it's unfortunate that these kinds of confusing cross-flavor inconsistencies exist, one of the benefits of using the regular expressions in this book is that you generally won't need to worry about them. Gory details like the ones we've just described are included in case you care to dig deeper.

Variations

Working with esoteric line separators

The previously shown regexes limit support to the conventional MS-DOS/Windows, Unix/Linux/OS X, and legacy Mac OS line break character sequences. However, there are several rarer vertical whitespace characters that you might encounter occasionally. The following regexes take these additional characters into account while limiting matches to five lines of text or less.

```
\A(?>\R?\V*){0,5}\z
```
Regex options: None
Regex flavors: PCRE 7 (with the PCRE_BSR_UNICODE option), Perl 5.10

```
\A(?>(?>\r\n?|[\n-\f\x85\x{2028}\x{2029}])?↵
[^\n-\r\x85\x{2028}\x{2029}]*){0,5}\z
```
Regex options: None
Regex flavors: PCRE, Perl

```
\A(?>(?>\r\n?|[\n-\f\x85\u2028\u2029])?[^\n-\r\x85\u2028\u2029]*){0,5}\z
```
Regex options: None
Regex flavors: .NET, Java, Ruby

```
\A(?:(?:\r\n?|[\n-\f\x85\u2028\u2029])?[^\n-\r\x85\u2028\u2029]*){0,5}\Z
```
Regex options: None
Regex flavor: Python

```
^(?:(?:\r\n?|[\n-\f\x85\u2028\u2029])?[^\n-\r\x85\u2028\u2029]*){0,5}$
```
Regex options: None
Regex flavor: JavaScript

All of these regexes handle the line separators in Table 4-1, listed with their Unicode positions and names.

Table 4-1. Line separators

Unicode sequence	Regex equivalent	Name	When used
U+000D U+000A	‹\r\n›	Carriage return and line feed (CRLF)	Windows and MS-DOS text files
U+000A	‹\n›	Line feed (LF)	Unix, Linux, and OS X text files
U+000B	‹\v›	Line tabulation (aka vertical tab, or VT)	(Rare)
U+000C	‹\f›	Form feed (FF)	(Rare)
U+000D	‹\r›	Carriage return (CR)	Mac OS text files
U+0085	‹\x85›	Next line (NEL)	IBM mainframe text files (Rare)
U+2028	‹\u2028› or ‹\x{2028}›	Line separator	(Rare)
U+2029	‹\u2029› or ‹\x{2029}›	Paragraph separator	(Rare)

See Also

Recipe 4.9

4.11 Validate Affirmative Responses

Problem

You need to check a configuration option or command-line response for a positive value. You want to provide some flexibility in the accepted responses, so that true, t, yes, y, okay, ok, and 1 are all accepted in any combination of uppercase and lowercase.

Solution

Using a regex that combines all of the accepted forms allows you to perform the check with one simple test.

Regular expression

```
^(?:1|t(?:rue)?|y(?:es)?|ok(?:ay)?)$
```
Regex options: Case insensitive
Regex flavors: .NET, Java, JavaScript, PCRE, Perl, Python, Ruby

JavaScript

```javascript
var yes = /^(?:1|t(?:rue)?|y(?:es)?|ok(?:ay)?)$/i;

if (yes.test(subject)) {
    alert("Yes");
} else {
    alert("No");
}
```

Other programming languages

See Recipes 3.4 and 3.5 for help implementing this regular expression with other programming languages.

Discussion

The following breakdown shows the individual parts of the regex. Combinations of tokens that are easy to read together are shown on the same line:

```
^           # Assert position at the beginning of the string.
(?:         # Group but don't capture...
  1         #   Match a literal "1".
  |         #   or...
  t(?:rue)? #   Match "t", optionally followed by "rue".
  |         #   or...
  y(?:es)?  #   Match "y", optionally followed by "es".
  |         #   or...
  ok(?:ay)? #   Match "ok", optionally followed by "ay".
```

```
    )                    # End the noncapturing group.
    $                    # Assert position at the end of the string.
```
Regex options: Case insensitive, free-spacing
Regex flavors: .NET, Java, PCRE, Perl, Python, Ruby

This regex is essentially a simple test for one of seven literal, case-insensitive values. It could be written in a number of ways. For example, ‹^(?:[1ty]|true|yes|ok(?:ay)?)$› is an equally good approach. Simply alternating between all seven values as ‹^(?:1|t|true|y|yes|ok|okay)$› would also work fine, although for performance reasons it's generally better to reduce the amount of alternation via the pipe ‹|› operator in favor of character classes and optional suffixes (using the ‹?› quantifier). In this case, the performance difference is probably no more than a few microseconds, but it's a good idea to keep regex performance issues in the back of your mind. Sometimes the difference between these approaches can surprise you.

All of these examples surround the potential match values with a noncapturing group to limit the reach of the alternation operators. If we omit the grouping and instead use something like ‹^true|yes$›, the regex engine will search for "the start of the string followed by 'true'" or "'yes' followed by the end of the string." ‹^(?:true|yes)$› tells the regex engine to find the start of the string, then either "true" or "yes", and then the end of the string.

See Also

Recipes 5.2 and 5.3

4.12 Validate Social Security Numbers

Problem

You need to check whether someone entered text as a valid Social Security number.

Solution

If you simply need to ensure that a string follows the basic Social Security number format and that obvious, invalid numbers are eliminated, the following regex provides an easy solution. If you need a more rigorous solution that checks with the Social Security Administration to determine whether the number belongs to a living person, refer to the links in the "See Also" section of this recipe.

Regular expression

```
^(?!000|666)(?:[0-6][0-9]{2}|7(?:[0-6][0-9]|7[0-2]))-↵
(?!00)[0-9]{2}-(?!0000)[0-9]{4}$
```
Regex options: None
Regex flavors: .NET, Java, JavaScript, PCRE, Perl, Python, Ruby

Python

```
if re.match(r"^(?!000|666)(?:[0-6][0-9]{2}|7(?:[0-6][0-9]|7[0-2]))-↵
(?!00)[0-9]{2}-(?!0000)[0-9]{4}$", sys.argv[1]):
    print "SSN is valid"
else:
    print "SSN is invalid"
```

Other programming languages

See Recipe 3.5 for help with implementing this regular expression with other programming languages.

Discussion

United States Social Security numbers are nine-digit numbers in the format
AAA-GG-SSSS:

- The first three digits are assigned by geographical region and are called the *area
  number*. The area number cannot be 000 or 666, and as of this writing, no valid
  Social Security number contains an area number above 772.

- Digits four and five are called the *group number* and range from 01 to 99.

- The last four digits are *serial numbers* from 0001 to 9999.

This recipe follows all of the rules just listed. Here's the regular expression again, this
time explained piece by piece:

```
^              # Assert position at the beginning of the string.
(?!000|666)    # Assert that neither "000" nor "666" can be matched here.
(?:            # Group but don't capture...
  [0-6]        #   Match a character in the range between "0" and "6".
  [0-9]{2}     #   Match a digit, exactly two times.
  |            #   or...
  7            #   Match a literal "7".
  (?:          #   Group but don't capture...
    [0-6]      #     Match a character in the range between "0" and "6".
    [0-9]      #     Match a digit.
    |          #     or...
    7          #     Match a literal "7".
    [0-2]      #     Match a character in the range between "0" and "2".
  )            #   End the noncapturing group.
)              # End the noncapturing group.
-              # Match a literal "-".
(?!00)         # Assert that "00" cannot be matched here.
[0-9]{2}       # Match a digit, exactly two times.
-              # Match a literal "-".
(?!0000)       # Assert that "0000" cannot be matched here.
[0-9]{4}       # Match a digit, exactly four times.
$              # Assert position at the end of the string.
```

Regex options: Free-spacing
Regex flavors: .NET, Java, PCRE, Perl, Python, Ruby

Apart from the ‹^› and ‹$› tokens that assert position at the beginning and end of the string, this regex can be broken into three groups of digits separated by hyphens. The first group is the most complex. The second and third groups simply match any two or four-digit number, respectively, but use a preceding negative lookahead to rule out the possibility of matching all zeros.

The first group of digits is much more complex and harder to read than the others because it matches a numeric range. First, it uses the negative lookahead ‹(?!000| 666)› to rule out the specific values "000" and "666". Next comes the task of eliminating any number higher than 772.

Since regular expressions deal with text rather than numbers, we have to break down the numeric range character by character. First, we know that we can match any three-digit number starting with 0 through 6, because the preceding negative lookahead already ruled out the invalid numbers 000 and 666. This first part is easily accomplished using a couple of character classes and a quantifier: ‹[0-6][0-9]{2}›. Since we need to offer an alternative for numbers starting with 7, the pattern we just built is put into a grouping as ‹(?:[0-6][0-9]{2}|7)› in order to limit the reach of the alternation operator.

Numbers starting with 7 are allowed only if they fall between 700 and 772, so the next step is to further divide any number that starts with 7 based on the second digit. If it's between 0 and 6, any third digit is allowed. If the second digit is 7, the third digit must be between 0 and 2. Putting these rules for numbers starting with 7 together, we get ‹7(?:[0-6][0-9]|7[0-2])›, which matches the number 7 followed by one of two options for the second and third digit.

Finally, insert that into the outer grouping for the first set of digits, and you get ‹(?:[0-6][0-9]{2}|7(?:[0-6][0-9]|7[0-2]))›. That's it. You've successfully created a regex that matches a three-digit number between 000 and 772.

Variations

Find Social Security numbers in documents

If you're searching for Social Security numbers in a larger document or input string, replace the ‹^› and ‹$› anchors with word boundaries. Regular expression engines consider all alphanumeric characters and the underscore to be word characters.

```
\b(?!000|666)(?:[0-6][0-9]{2}|7(?:[0-6][0-9]|7[0-2]))-↵
(?!00)[0-9]{2}-(?!0000)[0-9]{4}\b
```
Regex options: None
Regex flavors: .NET, Java, JavaScript, PCRE, Perl, Python, Ruby

See Also

The Social Security Administration website at *http://www.socialsecurity.gov* provides answers to common questions as well as up-to-date lists of what area and group numbers have been assigned.

The Social Security Number Verification Service (SSNVS) at *http://www.socialsecurity .gov/employer/ssnv.htm* offers two ways to verify over the Internet that names and Social Security numbers match the Social Security Administration's records.

A more thorough discussion of matching numeric ranges, including examples of matching ranges with a variable number of digits, can be found in Recipe 6.5.

4.13 Validate ISBNs

Problem

You need to check the validity of an International Standard Book Number (ISBN), which can be in either the older ISBN-10 or the current ISBN-13 format. You want to allow a leading ISBN identifier, and ISBN parts can optionally be separated by hyphens or spaces. ISBN 978-0-596-52068-7, ISBN-13: 978-0-596-52068-7, 978 0 596 52068 7, 9780596520687, ISBN-10 0-596-52068-9, and 0-596-52068-9 are all examples of valid input.

Solution

You cannot validate an ISBN using a regex alone, because the last digit is computed using a checksum algorithm. The regular expressions in this section validate the format of an ISBN, whereas the subsequent code examples include a validity check for the final digit.

Regular expressions

ISBN-10:

```
^(?:ISBN(?:-10)?:?●)?(?=[-0-9X●]{13}$|[0-9X]{10}$)[0-9]{1,5}[-●]?↵
(?:[0-9]+[-●]?){2}[0-9X]$
```
    Regex options: None
    Regex flavors: .NET, Java, JavaScript, PCRE, Perl, Python, Ruby

ISBN-13:

```
^(?:ISBN(?:-13)?:?●)?(?=[-0-9●]{17}$|[0-9]{13}$)97[89][-●]?[0-9]{1,5}↵
[-●]?(?:[0-9]+[-●]?){2}[0-9]$
```
    Regex options: None
    Regex flavors: .NET, Java, JavaScript, PCRE, Perl, Python, Ruby

ISBN-10 or ISBN-13:

```
^(?:ISBN(?:-1[03])?:?●)?(?:=[-0-9●]{17}$|[-0-9X●]{13}$|[0-9X]{10}$)◄
(?:97[89][-●]?)?[0-9]{1,5}[-●]?(?:[0-9]+[-●]?){2}[0-9X]$
```
Regex options: None
Regex flavors: .NET, Java, JavaScript, PCRE, Perl, Python, Ruby

JavaScript

```javascript
// `regex` checks for ISBN-10 or ISBN-13 format
var regex = /^(?:ISBN(?:-1[03])?:? )?(?:=[-0-9 ]{17}$|[-0-9X ]{13}$|◄
[0-9X]{10}$)(?:97[89][- ]?)?[0-9]{1,5}[- ]?(?:[0-9]+[- ]?){2}[0-9X]$/;

if (regex.test(subject)) {
  // Remove non ISBN digits, then split into an array
  var chars = subject.replace(/[^0-9X]/g, "").split("");
  // Remove the final ISBN digit from `chars`, and assign it to `last`
  var last  = chars.pop();
  var sum   = 0;
  var digit = 10;
  var check;

  if (chars.length == 9) {
    // Compute the ISBN-10 check digit
    for (var i = 0; i < chars.length; i++) {
      sum += digit * parseInt(chars[i], 10);
      digit -= 1;
    }
    check = 11 - (sum % 11);
    if (check == 10) {
      check = "X";
    } else if (check == 11) {
      check = "0";
    }
  } else {
    // Compute the ISBN-13 check digit
    for (var i = 0; i < chars.length; i++) {
      sum += (i % 2 * 2 + 1) * parseInt(chars[i], 10);
    }
    check = 10 - (sum % 10);
    if (check == 10) {
      check = "0";
    }
  }

  if (check == last) {
    alert("Valid ISBN");
  } else {
    alert("Invalid ISBN check digit");
```

```
    }
  } else {
    alert("Invalid ISBN");
  }
```

Python

```python
import re
import sys

# `regex` checks for ISBN-10 or ISBN-13 format
regex = re.compile("^(?:ISBN(?:-1[03])?:? )?(?=[-0-9 ]{17}$|↵
[-0-9X ]{13}$|[0-9X]{10}$)(?:97[89][- ]?)?[0-9]{1,5}[- ]?↵
(?:[0-9]+[- ]?){2}[0-9X]$")

subject = sys.argv[1]

if regex.search(subject):
  # Remove non ISBN digits, then split into an array
  chars = re.sub("[^0-9X]", "", subject).split("")
  # Remove the final ISBN digit from `chars`, and assign it to `last`
  last  = chars.pop()

  if len(chars) == 9:
    # Compute the ISBN-10 check digit
    val = sum((x + 2) * int(y) for x,y in enumerate(reversed(chars)))
    check = 11 - (val % 11)
    if check == 10:
      check = "X"
    elif check == 11:
      check = "0"
  else:
    # Compute the ISBN-13 check digit
    val = sum((x % 2 * 2 + 1) * int(y) for x,y in enumerate(chars))
    check = 10 - (val % 10)
    if check == 10:
      check = "0"

  if (str(check) == last):
    print "Valid ISBN"
  else:
    print "Invalid ISBN check digit"
else:
  print "Invalid ISBN"
```

Other programming languages

See Recipe 3.5 for help with implementing these regular expressions in other programming languages.

Discussion

An ISBN is a unique identifier for commercial books and book-like products. The 10-digit ISBN format was published as an international standard, ISO 2108, in 1970. All ISBNs assigned since January 1, 2007 are 13 digits.

ISBN-10 and ISBN-13 numbers are divided into four or five elements, respectively. Three of the elements are of variable length; the remaining one or two elements are of fixed length. All five parts are usually separated with hyphens or spaces. A brief description of each element follows:

- 13-digit ISBNs start with the prefix 978 or 979.
- The *group identifier* identifies the language-sharing country group. It ranges from one to five digits long.
- The *publisher identifier* varies in length and is assigned by the national ISBN agency.
- The *title identifier* also varies in length and is selected by the publisher.
- The final character is called the *check digit*, and is computed using a checksum algorithm. An ISBN-10 check digit can be either a number from 0 to 9 or the letter X (Roman numeral for 10), while an ISBN-13 check digit ranges from 0 to 9. The allowed characters are different because the two ISBN types use different checksum algorithms.

The parts of the "ISBN-10 or ISBN-13" regex are shown in the following breakdown. Because this regex is written in free-spacing mode, the literal space characters in the regex have been escaped with backslashes. Java requires that even spaces within character classes be escaped in free-spacing mode:

```
^                      # Assert position at the beginning of the string.
(?:                    # Group but don't capture...
  ISBN                 #    Match the text "ISBN".
  (?:-1[03])?          #    Optionally match the text "-10" or "-13".
  :?                   #    Optionally match a literal ":".
  \                    #    Match a space character (escaped).
)?                     # Repeat the group between zero and one time.
(?=                    # Assert that the following can be matched here...
  [-0-9\ ]{17}$        #    Match 17 hyphens, digits, and spaces, then the end
  |                    #       of the string. Or...
  [-0-9X\ ]{13}$       #    Match 13 hyphens, digits, Xs, and spaces, then the
  |                    #       end of the string. Or...
  [0-9X]{10}$          #    Match 10 digits and Xs, then the end of the string.
)                      # End the positive lookahead.
(?:                    # Group but don't capture...
```

```
    97[89]          #   Match the text "978" or "979".
    [-\ ]?          #   Optionally match a hyphen or space.
  )?                # Repeat the group between zero and one time.
  [0-9]{1,5}        # Match a digit between one and five times.
  [-\ ]?            # Optionally match a hyphen or space.
  (?:               # Group but don't capture...
    [0-9]+          #   Match a digit between one and unlimited times.
    [-\ ]?          #   Optionally match a hyphen or space.
  ){2}              # Repeat the group exactly two times.
  [0-9X]            # Match a digit or "X".
  $                 # Assert position at the end of the string.
```
Regex options: Free-spacing
Regex flavors: .NET, Java, PCRE, Perl, Python, Ruby

The leading ‹(?:ISBN(?:-1[03])?:??•)?› has three optional elements, allowing it to match any one of the following seven strings (all except the empty-string option include a space character at the end):

- ISBN•
- ISBN-10•
- ISBN-13•
- ISBN:•
- ISBN-10:•
- ISBN-13:•
- *The empty string (no prefix)*

Next, the positive lookahead ‹(?=[-0-9•]{17}$|[-0-9X•]{13}$|[0-9X]{10}$)› enforces one of three options (separated by the ‹|› alternation operator) for the length and character set of the rest of the match. All three options (shown next) end with the ‹$› anchor, which ensures that there cannot be any trailing text that doesn't fit into one of the patterns:

‹[-0-9•]{17}$›
  Allows an ISBN-13 with four separators (17 total characters)

‹[-0-9X•]{13}$›
  Allows an ISBN-13 with no separators or an ISBN-10 with three separators (13 total characters)

‹[0-9X]{10}$›
  Allows an ISBN-10 with no separators (10 total characters)

After the positive lookahead validates the length and character set, we can match the individual elements of the ISBN without worrying about their combined length. ‹(?:97[89][-•]?)?› matches the "978" or "979" prefix required by an ISBN-13. The noncapturing group is optional because it will not match within an ISBN-10 subject string. ‹[0-9]{1,5}[-•]?› matches the one to five digit group identifier and an optional, following separator. ‹(?:[0-9]+[-•]?){2}› matches the variable-length publisher and title identifiers, along with their optional separators. Finally, ‹[0-9X]$› matches the check digit at the end of the string.

Although a regular expression can check that the final digit uses a valid character (a digit or X), it cannot determine whether it's correct for the ISBN's checksum. One of two checksum algorithms (determined by whether you're working with an ISBN-10 or ISBN-13 number) are used to provide some level of assurance that the ISBN digits haven't been accidentally transposed or otherwise entered incorrectly. The JavaScript and Python example code shown earlier implemented both algorithms. The following sections describe the checksum rules in order to help you implement these algorithms with other programming languages.

ISBN-10 checksum

The check digit for an ISBN-10 number ranges from 0 to 10 (with the Roman numeral X used instead of 10). It is computed as follows:

1. Multiply each of the first 9 digits by a number in the descending sequence from 10 to 2, and sum the results.
2. Divide the sum by 11.
3. Subtract the remainder (not the quotient) from 11.
4. If the result is 11, use the number 0; if 10, use the letter X.

Here's an example of how to derive the ISBN-10 check digit for 0-596-52068-?:

```
Step 1:
sum = 10×0 + 9×5 + 8×9 + 7×6 + 6×5 + 5×2 + 4×0 + 3×6 + 2×8
    =    0 +  45 +  72 +  42 +  30 +  10 +   0 +  18 +  16
    = 233
Step 2:
    233 ÷ 11 = 21, remainder 2
Step 3:
    11 - 2 = 9
Step 4:
    9 [no substitution required]
```

The check digit is 9, so the complete sequence is ISBN 0-596-52068-9.

ISBN-13 checksum

An ISBN-13 check digit ranges from 0 to 9, and is computed using similar steps.

1. Multiply each of the first 12 digits by 1 or 3, alternating as you move from left to right, and sum the results.
2. Divide the sum by 10.

3. Subtract the remainder (not the quotient) from 10.

4. If the result is 10, use the number 0.

For example, the ISBN-13 check digit for `978-0-596-52068-?` is calculated as follows:

```
Step 1:
sum = 1×9 + 3×7 + 1×8 + 3×0 + 1×5 + 3×9 + 1×6 + 3×5 + 1×2 + 3×0 + 1×6 + 3×8
    =   9 +  21 +   8 +   0 +   5 +  27 +   6 +  15 +   2 +   0 +   6 +  24
    = 123
Step 2:
    123 ÷ 10 = 12, remainder 3
Step 3:
    10 - 3 = 7
Step 4:
    7 [No substitution required]
```

The check digit is 7, and the complete sequence is ISBN `978-0-596-52068-7`.

Variations

Find ISBNs in documents

This version of the "ISBN-10 or ISBN-13" regex uses word boundaries instead of anchors to help you find ISBNs within longer text while ensuring that they stand on their own. The "ISBN" identifier has also been made a required string in this version, for two reasons. First, requiring it helps eliminate false positives (without it, the regex could potentially match any 10 or 13 digit number), and second, ISBNs are officially required to use this identifier when printed:

```
\bISBN(?:-1[03])?:?•(?=[-0-9•]{17}$|[-0-9X•]{13}$|[0-9X]{10}$)↵
(?:97[89][-•]?)?[0-9]{1,5}[-•]?(?:[0-9]+[-•]?){2}[0-9X]\b
```
Regex options: None
Regex flavors: .NET, Java, JavaScript, PCRE, Perl, Python, Ruby

Eliminate incorrect ISBN identifiers

A limitation of the previous regexes is that they allow matching an ISBN-10 number preceded by the "ISBN-13" identifier, and vice versa. The following regex uses regex conditionals (see Recipe 2.17) to ensure that an "ISBN-10" or "ISBN-13" identifier is followed by the appropriate ISBN type. It allows both ISBN-10 and ISBN-13 numbers when the type is not explicitly specified. This regex is overkill in most circumstances because the same result could be achieved more manageably using the ISBN-10 and ISBN-13 specific regexes that were shown earlier, one at a time. It's included here merely to demonstrate an interesting use of regular expressions:

```
^
(?:ISBN(-1(?:(0)|3))?:?\ )?
(?(1)
```

```
(?(2)
  (?=[-0-9X ]{13}$|[0-9X]{10}$)
  [0-9]{1,5}[- ]?(?:[0-9]+[- ]?){2}[0-9X]$
  |
  (?=[-0-9 ]{17}$|[0-9]{13}$)
  97[89][- ]?[0-9]{1,5}[- ]?(?:[0-9]+[- ]?){2}[0-9]$
)
|
  (?=[-0-9 ]{17}$|[-0-9X ]{13}$|[0-9X]{10}$)
  (?:97[89][- ]?)?[0-9]{1,5}[- ]?(?:[0-9]+[- ]?){2}[0-9X]$
)
$
```
Regex options: Free-spacing
Regex flavors: .NET, PCRE, Perl, Python

See Also

The most up-to-date version of the ISBN Users' Manual can be found on the International ISBN Agency's website at *http://www.isbn-international.org*.

The official Numerical List of Group Identifiers at *http://www.isbn-international.org/en/identifiers/allidentifiers.html* can help you identify a book's originating country or area based on the first 1 to 5 digits of its ISBN.

4.14 Validate ZIP Codes

Problem

You need to validate a ZIP code (U.S. postal code), allowing both the five-digit and nine-digit (*ZIP + 4*) formats. The regex should match **12345** and **12345-6789**, but not 1234, 123456, 123456789, or 1234-56789.

Solution

Regular expression

```
^[0-9]{5}(?:-[0-9]{4})?$
```
Regex options: None
Regex flavors: .NET, Java, JavaScript, PCRE, Perl, Python, Ruby

VB.NET

```
If Regex.IsMatch(subjectString, "^[0-9]{5}(?:-[0-9]{4})?$") Then
    Console.WriteLine("Valid ZIP code")
Else
    Console.WriteLine("Invalid ZIP code")
End If
```

Other programming languages

See Recipe 3.5 for help with implementing this regular expression with other programming languages.

Discussion

A breakdown of the ZIP code regular expression follows:

```
^            # Assert position at the beginning of the string.
[0-9]{5}     # Match a digit, exactly five times.
(?:          # Group but don't capture...
   -         #    Match a literal "-".
  [0-9]{4}   #    Match a digit, exactly four times.
)            # End the noncapturing group.
?            #    Repeat the preceding group between zero and one time.
$            # Assert position at the end of the string.
```
Regex options: Free-spacing
Regex flavors: .NET, Java, PCRE, Perl, Python, Ruby

This regex is pretty straightforward, so there isn't much to add. A simple change that allows you to find ZIP codes within a longer input string is to replace the ‹^› and ‹$› anchors with word boundaries, so you end up with ‹\b[0-9]{5}(?:-[0-9]{4})?\b›.

See Also

Recipes 4.15, 4.16, and 4.17

4.15 Validate Canadian Postal Codes

Problem

You want to check whether a string is a Canadian postal code.

Solution

```
^(?!.*[DFIOQU])[A-VXY][0-9][A-Z]●[0-9][A-Z][0-9]$
```
Regex options: None
Regex flavors: .NET, Java, JavaScript, PCRE, Perl, Python, Ruby

Discussion

The negative lookahead at the beginning of this regular expression prevents D, F, I, O, Q, or U anywhere in the subject string. The ‹[A-VXY]› character class further prevents W or Z as the first character. Aside from those two exceptions, Canadian postal codes simply use an alternating sequence of six alphanumeric characters with a space in the middle. For example, the regex will match K1A 0B1, which is the postal code for Canada Post's Ottawa headquarters.

See Also

Recipes 4.14, 4.16, and 4.17

4.16 Validate U.K. Postcodes

Problem

You need a regular expression that matches a U.K. postcode.

Solution

```
^[A-Z]{1,2}[0-9R][0-9A-Z]?•[0-9][ABD-HJLNP-UW-Z]{2}$
```
Regex options: None
Regex flavors: .NET, Java, JavaScript, PCRE, Perl, Python, Ruby

Discussion

Postal codes in the U.K. (or *postcodes*, as they're called) are composed of five to seven alphanumeric characters separated by a space. The rules covering which characters can appear at particular positions are rather complicated and fraught with exceptions. This regular expression sticks to the basic rules.

See Also

British Standard BS7666, available at *http://www.govtalk.gov.uk/gdsc/html/frames/Post Code.htm*, describes the U.K. postcode rules.

Recipes 4.14, 4.15, and 4.17.

4.17 Find Addresses with Post Office Boxes

Problem

You want to catch addresses that contain a P.O. box, and warn users that their shipping information must contain a street address.

Solution

Regular expression

```
^(?:Post•(?:Office•)?|P[.•]?O\.?•)?Box\b
```
Regex options: Case insensitive, ^ and $ match at line breaks
Regex flavors: .NET, Java, JavaScript, PCRE, Perl, Python, Ruby

C#

```
Regex regexObj = new Regex(
    @"^(?:Post (?:Office )?|P[. ]?O\.? )?Box\b",
    RegexOptions.IgnoreCase | RegexOptions.Multiline
);
if (regexObj.IsMatch(subjectString)) {
    Console.WriteLine("The value does not appear to be a street address");
} else {
    Console.WriteLine("Good to go");
}
```

Other programming languages

See Recipe 3.5 for help with implementing this regular expression with other programming languages.

Discussion

The following explanation is written in free-spacing mode, so each of the meaningful space characters in the regex has been escaped with a backslash:

```
^                  # Assert position at the beginning of a line.
(?:                # Group but don't capture...
   Post\           #   Match "Post ".
   (?:Office\ )?   #   Optionally match "Office ".
   |               # or...
   P[.\ ]?         #   Match "P" and an optional period or space character.
   O\.?\           #   Match "O", an optional period, and a space character.
)?                 # Repeat the group between zero and one time.
Box                # Match "Box".
\b                 # Assert position at a word boundary.
```
      Regex options: Case insensitive, ^ and $ match at line breaks
      Regex flavors: .NET, Java, PCRE, Perl, Python, Ruby

This regular expression matches all of the following example strings when they appear at the beginning of a line:

- Post Office Box
- post box
- P.O. box
- P O Box
- Po. box
- PO Box
- Box

Despite the precautions taken here, you might encounter a few false positives or false negatives because many people are used to shippers being quite flexible in deciphering addresses. To mitigate this risk, it's best to state up front that P.O. boxes are not allowed. If you get a match using this regular expression, consider warning the user that it appears she has entered a P.O. box, while still providing the option to keep the entry.

See Also

Recipes 4.14, 4.15, and 4.16

4.18 Reformat Names From "FirstName LastName" to "LastName, FirstName"

Problem

You want to convert people's names from the "FirstName LastName" format to "LastName, FirstName", for use in an alphabetical listing. You additionally want to account for other name parts, so that you can, e.g., convert "FirstName MiddleNames Particles LastName Suffix" to "LastName, FirstName MiddleNames Particles Suffix".

Solution

Unfortunately, it isn't possible to reliably parse names using a regular expression. Regular expressions are rigid, whereas names are so flexible that even humans get them wrong. Determining the structure of a name or how it should be listed alphabetically often requires taking traditional and national conventions, or even personal preferences, into account. Nevertheless, if you're willing to make certain assumptions about your data and can handle a moderate level of error, a regular expression can provide a quick solution.

The following regular expression has intentionally been kept simple, rather than trying to account for edge cases.

Regular expression

```
^(.+?)•([^\s,]+)(,?•(?:[JS]r\.?|III?|IV))?$
```
Regex options: Case insensitive
Regex flavors: .NET, Java, JavaScript, PCRE, Perl, Python, Ruby

Replacement

```
$2,•$1$3
```
Replacement text flavors: .NET, Java, JavaScript, Perl, PHP

```
\2,•\1\3
```
Replacement text flavors: Python, Ruby

JavaScript

```
function formatName (name) {
    return name.replace(/^(.+?) ([^\s,]+)(,? (?:[JS]r\.?|III?|IV))?$/i,
                        "$2, $1$3");
}
```

Other programming languages

See Recipe 3.15 for help implementing this regular expression with other programming languages.

Discussion

First, let's take a look at this regular expression piece by piece. Higher-level comments are provided afterward to help explain which parts of a name are being matched by various segments of the regex. Since the regex is written here in free-spacing mode, the literal space characters have been escaped with backslashes:

```
^              # Assert position at the beginning of the string.
(              # Capture the enclosed match to backreference 1...
  .+?          #   Match one or more characters, as few times as possible.
)              # End the capturing group.
\              # Match a literal space character.
(              # Capture the enclosed match to backreference 2...
  [^\s,]+      #   Match one or more characters that are not whitespace
               #   or commas.
)              # End the capturing group.
(              # Capture the enclosed match to backreference 3...
  ,?\          #   Match ", " or " ".
  (?:          #   Group but don't capture...
    [JS]r\.?   #     Match "Jr", "Jr.", "Sr", or "Sr.".
  |            #     or...
    III?       #     Match "II" or "III".
  |            #     or...
    IV         #     Match "IV".
  )            #   End the noncapturing group.
)?             # Repeat the group between zero and one time.
$              # Assert position at the end of the string.
```

Regex options: Case insensitive, free-spacing
Regex flavors: .NET, Java, PCRE, Perl, Python, Ruby

This regular expression makes the following assumptions about the subject data:

- It contains at least one first name and one last name (other name parts are optional).
- The first name is listed before the last name.
- If the name contains a suffix, it is one of the values "Jr", "Jr.", "Sr", "Sr.", "II", "III", or "IV", with an optional preceding comma.

A few more issues to consider:

- The regular expression cannot identify compound surnames that don't use hyphens. For example, `Sacha Baron Cohen` would be replaced with `Cohen, Sacha Baron`, rather than the correct listing, `Baron Cohen, Sacha`.

- It does not keep particles in front of the family name, although this is occasionally called for by convention or personal preference (for example, the correct alphabetical listing of "Charles de Gaulle" is "de Gaulle, Charles" according to the *Chicago Manual of Style*, 15th Edition, which contradicts *Merriam-Webster's Biographical Dictionary* on this particular name).

- Because of the ‹^› and ‹$› anchors that bind the match to the beginning and end of the string, no replacement can be made if the entire subject text does not fit the pattern. Hence, if no suitable match is found (for example, if the subject text contains only one name), the name is left unaltered.

As for how the regular expression works, it uses three capturing groups to split up the name. The pieces are then reassembled in the desired order via backreferences in the replacement string. Capturing group 1 uses the maximally flexible ‹.+?› pattern to grab the first name along with any number of middle names and surname particles, such as the German "von" or the French, Portuguese, and Spanish "de". These name parts are handled together because they are listed sequentially in the output. Lumping the first and middle names together also helps avoid errors, because the regular expression cannot distinguish between a compound first name, such as "Mary Lou" or "Norma Jeane," and a first name plus middle name. Even humans cannot accurately make the distinction just by visual examination.

Capturing group 2 matches the last name using ‹[^\s,]+›. Like the dot used in capturing group 1, the flexibility of this character class allows it to match accented characters and any other non-Latin characters. Capturing group 3 matches an optional suffix, such as "Jr." or "III," from a predefined list of possible values. The suffix is handled separately from the last name because it should continue to appear at the end of the reformatted name.

Let's go back for a minute to capturing group 1. Why was the dot within group 1 followed by the lazy ‹+?› quantifier, whereas the character class in group 2 was followed by the greedy ‹+› quantifier? If group 1 (which handles a variable number of elements and therefore needs to go as far as it can into the name) used a greedy quantifier, capturing group 3 (which attempts to match a suffix) wouldn't have a shot at participating in the match. The dot from group 1 would match until the end of the string, and since capturing group 3 is optional, the regex engine would only backtrack enough to find a match for group 2 before declaring success. Capturing group 2 can use a greedy quantifier because its more restrictive character class only allows it to match one name.

Table 4-2 shows some examples of how names are formatted using this regular expression and replacement string.

Table 4-2. Formatted names

Input	Output
Robert Downey, Jr.	Downey, Robert, Jr.
John F. Kennedy	Kennedy, John F.
Scarlett O'Hara	O'Hara, Scarlett
Pepé Le Pew	Pew, Pepé Le
J.R.R. Tolkien	Tolkien, J.R.R.
Catherine Zeta-Jones	Zeta-Jones, Catherine

Variations

List surname particles at the beginning of the name

An added segment in the following regular expression allows you to output surname particles from a predefined list in front of the last name. Specifically, this regular expression accounts for the values "De", "Du", "La", "Le", "St", "St.", "Ste", "Ste.", "Van", and "Von". Any number of these values are allowed in sequence (for example, "de la"):

```
^(.+?)•((?:(?:D[eu]|L[ae]|Ste?\.?|V[ao]n)•)*[^\s,]+)↵
(,?•(?:[JS]r\.?|III?|IV))?$
```
Regex options: Case insensitive
Regex flavors: .NET, Java, JavaScript, PCRE, Perl, Python, Ruby

```
$2,•$1$3
```
Replacement text flavors: .NET, Java, JavaScript, Perl, PHP

```
\2,•\1\3
```
Replacement text flavors: Python, Ruby

4.19 Validate Credit Card Numbers

Problem

You're given the job of implementing an order form for a company that accepts payment by credit card. Since the credit card processor charges for each transaction attempt, including failed attempts, you want to use a regular expression to weed out obviously invalid credit card numbers.

Doing this will also improve the customer's experience. A regular expression can instantly detect obvious typos as soon as the customer finishes filling in the field on the web form. A round trip to the credit card processor, by contrast, easily takes 10 to 30 seconds.

Solution

Strip spaces and hyphens

Retrieve the credit card number entered by the customer and store it into a variable. Before performing the check for a valid number, perform a search-and-replace to strip out spaces and hyphens. Replace this regular expression globally with blank replacement text:

```
[•-]
```
Regex options: None
Regex flavors: .NET, Java, JavaScript, PCRE, Perl, Python, Ruby

Recipe 3.14 shows you how to perform this initial replacement.

Validate the number

With spaces and hyphens stripped from the input, this regular expression checks if the credit card number uses the format of any of the six major credit card companies. It uses named capture to detect which brand of credit card the customer has:

```
^(?:
(?<visa>4[0-9]{12}(?:[0-9]{3})?) |
(?<mastercard>5[1-5][0-9]{14}) |
(?<discover>6(?:011|5[0-9][0-9])[0-9]{12}) |
(?<amex>3[47][0-9]{13}) |
(?<diners>3(?:0[0-5]|[68][0-9])[0-9]{11}) |
(?<jcb>(?:2131|1800|35\d{3})\d{11})
)$
```
Regex options: Free-spacing
Regex flavors: .NET, PCRE 7, Perl 5.10, Ruby 1.9

```
^(?:
(?P<visa>4[0-9]{12}(?:[0-9]{3})?) |
(?P<mastercard>5[1-5][0-9]{14}) |
(?P<discover>6(?:011|5[0-9][0-9])[0-9]{12}) |
(?P<amex>3[47][0-9]{13}) |
(?P<diners>3(?:0[0-5]|[68][0-9])[0-9]{11}) |
(?P<jcb>(?:2131|1800|35\d{3})\d{11})
)$
```
Regex options: Free-spacing
Regex flavors: PCRE, Python

Java, Perl 5.6, Perl 5.8, and Ruby 1.8 do not support named capture. You can use numbered capture instead. Group 1 will capture Visa cards, group 2 MasterCard, and so on up to group 6 for JCB:

```
^(?:
(4[0-9]{12}(?:[0-9]{3})?) |          # Visa
(5[1-5][0-9]{14}) |                  # MasterCard
```

```
(6(?:011|5[0-9][0-9])[0-9]{12}) |       # Discover
(3[47][0-9]{13}) |                       # AMEX
(3(?:0[0-5]|[68][0-9])[0-9]{11}) |       # Diners Club
((?:2131|1800|35\d{3})\d{11})            # JCB
)$
```
Regex options: Free-spacing
Regex flavors: .NET, Java, PCRE, Perl, Python, Ruby

JavaScript does not support free-spacing. Removing whitespace and comments, we get:

```
^(?:(4[0-9]{12}(?:[0-9]{3})?)|(5[1-5][0-9]{14})|↵
(6(?:011|5[0-9][0-9])[0-9]{12})|(3[47][0-9]{13})|↵
(3(?:0[0-5]|[68][0-9])[0-9]{11})|((?:2131|1800|35\d{3})\d{11}))$
```
Regex options: None
Regex flavors: .NET, Java, JavaScript, PCRE, Perl, Python, Ruby

If you don't need to determine which type the card is, you can remove the unnecessary capturing groups:

```
^(?:
4[0-9]{12}(?:[0-9]{3})? |       # Visa
5[1-5][0-9]{14} |               # MasterCard
6(?:011|5[0-9][0-9])[0-9]{12} | # Discover
3[47][0-9]{13} |                # AMEX
3(?:0[0-5]|[68][0-9])[0-9]{11} | # Diners Club
(?:2131|1800|35\d{3})\d{11}      # JCB
)$
```
Regex options: Free-spacing
Regex flavors: .NET, Java, PCRE, Perl, Python, Ruby

Or for JavaScript:

```
^(?:4[0-9]{12}(?:[0-9]{3})?|5[1-5][0-9]{14}|6(?:011|5[0-9][0-9])[0-9]{12}|↵
3[47][0-9]{13}|3(?:0[0-5]|[68][0-9])[0-9]{11}|(?:2131|1800|35\d{3})\d{11})$
```
Regex options: None
Regex flavors: .NET, Java, JavaScript, PCRE, Perl, Python, Ruby

Follow the recipe in Recipe 3.6 to add this regular expression to your order form to validate the card number. If you use different processors for different cards, or if you just want to keep some statistics, you can use Recipe 3.9 to check which named or numbered capturing group holds the match. That will tell you which brand of credit card the customer has.

Example web page with JavaScript

```
<html>
<head>
<title>Credit Card Test</title>
</head>
```

```
<body>
<h1>Credit Card Test</h1>

<form>
<p>Please enter your credit card number:</p>

<p><input type="text" size="20" name="cardnumber"
  onkeyup="validatecardnumber(this.value)"></p>

<p id="notice">(no card number entered)</p>
</form>

<script>
function validatecardnumber(cardnumber) {
  // Strip spaces and dashes
  cardnumber = cardnumber.replace(/[ -]/g, '');
  // See if the card is valid
  // The regex will capture the number in one of the capturing groups
  var match = /^(?:(4[0-9]{12}(?:[0-9]{3})?)|(5[1-5][0-9]{14})|↵
(6(?:011|5[0-9][0-9])[0-9]{12})|(3[47][0-9]{13})|(3(?:0[0-5]|[68][0-9])↵
[0-9]{11})|((?:2131|1800|35\d{3})\d{11}))$/.exec(cardnumber);
  if (match) {
    // List of card types, in the same order as the regex capturing groups
    var types = ['Visa', 'MasterCard', 'Discover', 'American Express',
                 'Diners Club', 'JCB'];
    // Find the capturing group that matched
    // Skip the zeroth element of the match array (the overall match)
    for (var i = 1; i < match.length; i++) {
      if (match[i]) {
        // Display the card type for that group
        document.getElementById('notice').innerHTML = types[i - 1];
        break;
      }
    }
  } else {
    document.getElementById('notice').innerHTML = '(invalid card number)';
  }
}
</script>
</body>
</html>
```

Discussion

Strip spaces and hyphens

On an actual credit card, the digits of the embossed card number are usually placed into groups of four. That makes the card number is easier for humans to read. Naturally, many people will try to enter the card number in the same way, including the spaces, on order forms.

Writing a regular expression that validates a card number, allowing for spaces, hyphens, and whatnot, is much more difficult that writing a regular expression that only allows digits. Thus, unless you want to annoy the customer with retyping the card number without spaces or hyphens, do a quick search-and-replace to strip them out before validating the card number and sending it to the card processor.

The regular expression ‹[•-]› matches a character that is a space or a hyphen. Replacing all matches of this regular expression with nothing effectively deletes all spaces and hyphens.

Credit card numbers can consist only of digits. Instead of using ‹[•-]› to remove only spaces and hyphens, you could use the shorthand character class ‹\D› to strip out all nondigits.

Validate the number

Each of the credit card companies uses a different number format. We'll exploit that difference to allow users to enter a number without specifying a company; the company can be determined from the number. The format for each company is:

Visa
> 13 or 16 digits, starting with 4.

MasterCard
> 16 digits, starting with 51 through 55.

Discover
> 16 digits, starting with 6011, or 15 digits starting with 5.

American Express
> 15 digits, starting with 34 or 37.

Diners Club
> 14 digits, starting with 300 through 305, 36, or 38.

JCB
> 15 digits, starting with 2131 or 1800, or 16 digits starting with 35.

If you accept only certain brands of credit cards, you can delete the cards that you don't accept from the regular expression. When deleting JCB, make sure to delete the last remaining ‹|› in the regular expression as well. If you end up with ‹||› or ‹|)› in your regular expression, it will accept the empty string as a valid card number.

For example, to accept only Visa, MasterCard, and AMEX, you can use:

```
^(?:
4[0-9]{12}(?:[0-9]{3})? |        # Visa
5[1-5][0-9]{14} |                # MasterCard
```

```
    3[47][0-9]{13}                         # AMEX
)$
```
   Regex options: Free-spacing
   Regex flavors: .NET, Java, PCRE, Perl, Python, Ruby

Alternatively:

```
^(?:4[0-9]{12}(?:[0-9]{3})?|5[1-5][0-9]{14}|3[47][0-9]{13})$
```
   Regex options: None
   Regex flavors: .NET, Java, JavaScript, PCRE, Perl, Python, Ruby

If you're searching for credit card numbers in a larger body of text, replace the anchors with ‹\b› word boundaries.

Incorporating the solution into a web page

The example in "Example web page with JavaScript" on page 273 shows how you could add these two regular expressions to your order form. The input box for the credit card number has an onkeyup event handler that calls the validatecardnumber() function. This function retrieves the card number from the input box, strips the spaces and hyphens, and then validates it using the regular expression with numbered capturing groups. The result of the validation is displayed by replacing the text in the last paragraph on the page.

If the regular expression fails to match, regexp.exec() returns null, and (invalid card number) is displayed. If the regex does match, regexp.exec() returns an array of strings. The zeroth element holds the overall match. Elements 1 through 6 hold the text matched by the six capturing groups.

Our regular expression has six capturing groups, divided by alternation. This means that exactly one capturing group will participate in the match and hold the card number. The other groups will be empty (either undefined or the empty string, depending on your browser). The function checks the six capturing groups, one by one. When it finds one that is not empty, the card number is recognized and displayed.

Extra Validation with the Luhn Algorithm

There is an extra validation check that you can do on the credit card number before processing the order. The last digit in the credit card number is a checksum calculated according to the *Luhn algoritm*. Since this algorithm requires basic arithmetic, you cannot implement it with a regular expression.

You can add the Luhn check to the web page example for this recipe by inserting the call luhn(cardnumber); before the "else" line in the validatecardnumber() function. This way, the Luhn check will be done only if the regular expression finds a valid match, and after determining the card brand. However, determining the brand of the credit card is not necessary for the Luhn check. All credit cards use the same method.

In JavaScript, you can code the Luhn function as follows:

```
function luhn(cardnumber) {
  // Build an array with the digits in the card number
  var getdigits = /\d/g;
  var digits = [];
  while (match = getdigits.exec(cardnumber)) {
    digits.push(parseInt(match[0], 10));
  }
  // Run the Luhn algorithm on the array
  var sum = 0;
  var alt = false;
  for (var i = digits.length - 1; i >= 0; i--) {
    if (alt) {
      digits[i] *= 2;
      if (digits[i] > 9) {
        digits[i] -= 9;
      }
    }
    sum += digits[i];
    alt = !alt;
  }
  // Card number turns out to be invalid anyway
  if (sum % 10 == 0) {
    document.getElementById("notice").innerHTML += '; Luhn check passed';
  } else {
    document.getElementById("notice").innerHTML += '; Luhn check failed';
  }
}
```

This function takes a string with the credit card number as a parameter. The card number should consist only of digits. In our example, validatecardnumber() has already stripped spaces and hyphens and determined the card number to have the right number of digits.

First, the function uses the regular expression ‹\d› to iterate over all the digits in the string. Notice the /g modifier. Inside the loop, match[0] retrieves the matched digit. Since regular expressions deal with text (strings) only, we call parseInt() to make sure the variable is stored as an integer instead of as a string. If we don't do this, the sum variable will end up as a string concatenation of the digits, rather than the integer addition of the numbers.

The actual algorithm runs on the array, calculating a checksum. If the sum modulus 10 is zero, then the card number is valid. If not, the number is invalid.

4.20 European VAT Numbers

Problem

You're given the job of implementing an online order form for a business in the European Union.

European tax laws stipulate that when a VAT-registered business (your customer) located in one EU country purchases from a vendor (your company) in another EU country, the vendor must not charge VAT (Value-Added Tax). If the buyer is not VAT-registered, the vendor must charge VAT and remit the VAT to the local tax office. The vendor must use the VAT registration number of the buyer as proof to the tax office that no VAT is due. This means that for the vendor, it is very important to validate the buyer's VAT number before proceeding with the tax-exempt sale.

The most common cause of invalid VAT numbers are simple typing mistakes by the customer. To make the ordering process faster and friendlier, you should use a regular expression to validate the VAT number immediately while the customer fills out your online order form. You can do this with some client-side JavaScript or in the CGI script on your web server that receives the order form. If the number does not match the regular expression, the customer can correct the typo right away.

Solution

Strip whitespace and punctuation

Retrieve the VAT number entered by the customer and store it into a variable. Before performing the check for a valid number, perform a search-and-replace to replace this regular expression globally with blank replacement text:

```
[-.•]
```
Regex options: None
Regex flavors: .NET, Java, JavaScript, PCRE, Perl, Python, Ruby

Recipe 3.14 shows you how to perform this initial replacement. We've assumed that the customer wouldn't enter any punctuation except hyphens, dots, and spaces. Any other extraneous characters will be caught by the upcoming check.

Validate the number

With whitespace and punctuation stripped, this regular expression checks whether the VAT number is valid for any of the 27 EU countries:

```
^(
(AT)?U[0-9]{8} |            # Austria
(BE)?0?[0-9]{9} |           # Belgium
(BG)?[0-9]{9,10} |          # Bulgaria
(CY)?[0-9]{8}L |            # Cyprus
```

```
(CZ)?[0-9]{8,10} |                                  # Czech Republic
(DE)?[0-9]{9} |                                     # Germany
(DK)?[0-9]{8} |                                     # Denmark
(EE)?[0-9]{9} |                                     # Estonia
(EL|GR)?[0-9]{9} |                                  # Greece
(ES)?[0-9A-Z][0-9]{7}[0-9A-Z] |                     # Spain
(FI)?[0-9]{8} |                                     # Finland
(FR)?[0-9A-Z]{2}[0-9]{9} |                          # France
(GB)?([0-9]{9}([0-9]{3})?|[A-Z]{2}[0-9]{3}) |       # United Kingdom
(HU)?[0-9]{8} |                                     # Hungary
(IE)?[0-9]S[0-9]{5}L |                              # Ireland
(IT)?[0-9]{11} |                                    # Italy
(LT)?([0-9]{9}|[0-9]{12}) |                         # Lithuania
(LU)?[0-9]{8} |                                     # Luxembourg
(LV)?[0-9]{11} |                                    # Latvia
(MT)?[0-9]{8} |                                     # Malta
(NL)?[0-9]{9}B[0-9]{2} |                            # Netherlands
(PL)?[0-9]{10} |                                    # Poland
(PT)?[0-9]{9} |                                     # Portugal
(RO)?[0-9]{2,10} |                                  # Romania
(SE)?[0-9]{12} |                                    # Sweden
(SI)?[0-9]{8} |                                     # Slovenia
(SK)?[0-9]{10}                                      # Slovakia
)$
```
Regex options: Free-spacing, case insensitive
Regex flavors: .NET, Java, PCRE, Perl, Python, Ruby

This regular expression uses free-spacing mode to make it easy to edit the regular expression later. Every now and then, new countries join the European Union, and member countries change their rules for VAT numbers. Unfortunately, JavaScript does not support free-spacing. In this case, you're stuck putting everything on one line:

```
^((AT)?U[0-9]{8}|(BE)?0?[0-9]{9}|(BG)?[0-9]{9,10}|(CY)?[0-9]{8}L| ↵
(CZ)?[0-9]{8,10}|(DE)?[0-9]{9}|(DK)?[0-9]{8}|(EE)?[0-9]{9}| ↵
(EL|GR)?[0-9]{9}|(ES)?[0-9A-Z][0-9]{7}[0-9A-Z]|(FI)?[0-9]{8}| ↵
(FR)?[0-9A-Z]{2}[0-9]{9}|(GB)?([0-9]{9}([0-9]{3})?|[A-Z]{2}[0-9]{3})| ↵
(HU)?[0-9]{8}|(IE)?[0-9]S[0-9]{5}L|(IT)?[0-9]{11}| ↵
(LT)?([0-9]{9}|[0-9]{12})|(LU)?[0-9]{8}|(LV)?[0-9]{11}|(MT)?[0-9]{8}| ↵
(NL)?[0-9]{9}B[0-9]{2}|(PL)?[0-9]{10}|(PT)?[0-9]{9}|(RO)?[0-9]{2,10}| ↵
(SE)?[0-9]{12}|(SI)?[0-9]{8}|(SK)?[0-9]{10})$
```
Regex options: Case insensitive
Regex flavors: .NET, Java, JavaScript, PCRE, Perl, Python, Ruby

Follow Recipe 3.6 to add this regular expression to your order form.

Discussion

Strip whitespace and punctuation

To make VAT numbers easier to read for humans, people often type them in with extra punctuation to split the digits into groups. For instance, a German customer might enter his VAT number DE123456789 as DE 123.456.789.

A single regular expression that matches VAT numbers from 27 countries in any possible notation is an impossible job. Since the punctuation is only for readability, it is much easier to first strip all the punctuation, then validate the resulting bare VAT number.

The regular expression ‹[-.●]› matches a character that is a hyphen, dot, or space. Replacing all matches of this regular expression with nothing effectively deletes the punctuation characters commonly used in VAT numbers.

VAT numbers consist only of letters and digits. Instead of using ‹[-.●]› to remove only common punctuation, you could use ‹[^A-Z0-9]› to strip out all invalid characters.

Validate the number

The two regular expressions for validating the number are identical. The only difference is that the first one uses the free-spacing syntax to make the regular expression more readable, and to indicate the countries. JavaScript does not support free-spacing, but the other flavors give you the choice.

The regex uses alternation to accommodate the VAT numbers of all 27 EU countries. The essential formats are:

Austria
    U99999999

Belgium
    999999999 or 0999999999

Bulgaria
    999999999 or 9999999999

Cyprus
    99999999L

Czech Republic
    99999999, 999999999, or 9999999999

Germany
    999999999

Denmark
    99999999

Estonia
999999999

Greece
999999999

Spain
X9999999X

Finland
99999999

France
XX999999999

United Kingdom
999999999, 999999999999, or XX999

Hungary
99999999

Ireland
9S99999L

Italy
99999999999

Lithuania
999999999 or 99999999999

Luxembourg
99999999

Latvia
99999999999

Malta
99999999

Netherlands
999999999B99

Poland
999999999

Portugal
999999999

Romania
99, 999, 9999, 99999, 999999, 9999999, 99999999, 999999999, or 9999999999

Sweden
99999999999

Slovenia
99999999

Slovakia
   999999999

Strictly speaking, the two-letter country code is part of the VAT number. However, people often omit it, since the billing address already indicates the country. The regular expression will accept VAT numbers with and without the country code. If you want the country code to be mandatory, remove all the question marks from the regular expression. If you do, mention that you require the country code in the error message that tells the user the VAT number is invalid.

If you accept orders only from certain countries, you can leave out the countries that don't appear in the country selection on your order form. When you delete an alternative, make sure to also delete the ‹|› operator that separates the alternative from the next or previous one. If you don't, you end up with ‹||› in your regular expression. ‹||› inserts an alternative that matches the empty string, which means your order form will accept the omission of a VAT number as a valid VAT number.

The 27 alternatives are grouped together. The group is placed between a caret and a dollar sign, which anchor the regular expression to the beginning and ending of the string you're validating. The whole input must validate as a VAT number.

If you're searching for VAT numbers in a larger body of text, replace the anchors with ‹\b› word boundaries.

Variations

The benefit of using one regular expression to check for all 27 countries is that you only need to add one regex validation to your order form. You could enhance your order form by using 27 separate regular expressions. First, check the country that the customer specified in the billing address. Then, look up the appropriate regular expression according to the country:

Austria
   ‹^(AT)?U[0-9]{8}$›
Belgium
   ‹^(BE)?0?[0-9]{9}$›
Bulgaria
   ‹^(BG)?[0-9]{9,10}$›
Cyprus
   ‹^(CY)?[0-9]{8}L$›
Czech Republic
   ‹^(CZ)?[0-9]{8,10}$›
Germany
   ‹^(DE)?[0-9]{9}$›

Denmark

`‹^(DK)?[0-9]{8}$›`

Estonia

`‹^(EE)?[0-9]{9}$›`

Greece

`‹^(EL|GR)?[0-9]{9}$›`

Spain

`‹^(ES)?[0-9A-Z][0-9]{7}[0-9A-Z]$›`

Finland

`‹^(FI)?[0-9]{8}$›`

France

`‹^(FR)?[0-9A-Z]{2}[0-9]{9}$›`

United Kingdom

`‹^(GB)?([0-9]{9}([0-9]{3})?|[A-Z]{2}[0-9]{3})$›`

Hungary

`‹^(HU)?[0-9]{8}$›`

Ireland

`‹^(IE)?[0-9]S[0-9]{5}L$›`

Italy

`‹^(IT)?[0-9]{11}$›`

Lithuania

`‹^(LT)?([0-9]{9}|[0-9]{12})$›`

Luxembourg

`‹^(LU)?[0-9]{8}$›`

Latvia

`‹^(LV)?[0-9]{11}$›`

Malta

`‹^(MT)?[0-9]{8}$›`

Netherlands

`‹^(NL)?[0-9]{9}B[0-9]{2}$›`

Poland

`‹^(PL)?[0-9]{10}$›`

Portugal

`‹^(PT)?[0-9]{9}$›`

Romania

`‹^(RO)?[0-9]{2,10}$›`

Sweden

`‹^(SE)?[0-9]{12}$›`

Slovenia
   ‹^(SI)?[0-9]{8}$›
Slovakia
   ‹^(SK)?[0-9]{10}$›

Implement Recipe 3.6 to validate the VAT number against the selected regular expression. That will tell you if the number is valid for the country the customer claims to reside in.

The main benefit of using the separate regular expressions is that you can force the VAT number to start with the correct country code, without asking the customer to type it in. When the regular expression matches the provided number, check the contents of the first capturing group. The recipe in Recipe 3.9 explains how to do this. If the first capturing group is empty, the customer did not type the country code at the start of the VAT number. You can then add the country code before storing the validated number in your order database.

Greek VAT numbers allow two country codes. EL is traditionally used for Greek VAT numbers, but GR is the ISO country code for Greece.

See Also

The regular expression merely checks if the number looks like a valid VAT number. This is enough to weed out honest mistakes. A regular expression obviously cannot check whether the VAT number is assigned to the business placing the order. The European Union provides a web page at *http://ec.europa.eu/taxation_customs/vies/vie shome.do* where you can check which business a particular VAT number belongs to, if any.

Techniques used in the regular expression are discussed in Recipes 2.3, 2.5 and 2.8.

## CHAPTER 5

Words, Lines, and Special Characters

This chapter contains recipes that deal with finding and manipulating text in a variety of contexts. Some of the recipes show how to do things you might expect from an advanced search engine, such as finding any one of several words or finding words that appear near each other. Other examples help you find entire lines that contain particular words, remove repeated words, or escape regular expression metacharacters.

The central theme of this chapter is showing a variety of regular expression constructs and techniques in action. Reading through it is like a workout for a large number of regular expression syntax features, and will help you apply regular expressions generally to the problems you encounter. In many cases, what we search for is simple, but the templates we provide in the solutions allow you to customize them for the specific problems you're facing.

5.1 Find a Specific Word

Problem

You're given the simple task of finding all occurrences of the word "cat", case insensitively. The catch is that it must appear as a complete word. You don't want to find pieces of longer words, such as `hellcat`, `application`, or `Catwoman`.

Solution

Word boundary tokens make this a very easy problem to solve:

```
\bcat\b
```
Regex options: Case insensitive
Regex flavors: .NET, Java, JavaScript, PCRE, Perl, Python, Ruby

Recipe 3.7 shows how you can use this regular expression to find all matches. Recipe 3.14 shows how you can replace matches with other text.

Discussion

The word boundaries at both ends of the regular expression ensure that cat is matched only when it appears as a complete word. More precisely, the word boundaries require that cat is set apart from other text by the beginning or end of the string, whitespace, punctuation, or other nonword characters.

Regular expression engines consider letters, numbers, and underscores to all be word characters. Word boundaries are discussed in greater depth in Recipe 2.6.

A problem can occur when working with international text in JavaScript, PCRE, and Ruby, since those regular expression flavors only consider letters in the ASCII table to create a word boundary. In other words, word boundaries are found only at the positions between a match of ‹^|[^A-Za-z0-9_]› and ‹[A-Za-z0-9_]›, or between ‹[A-Za-z0-9_]› and ‹[^A-Za-z0-9_]|$›. The same is true in Python when the UNICODE or U flag is not set. This prevents ‹\b› from being useful for a "whole word only" search on text that contains accented letters or words that use non-Latin scripts. For example, in JavaScript, PCRE, and Ruby, ‹\büber\b› will find a match within darüber, but not within dar über. In most cases, this is the exact opposite of what you would want. The problem occurs because ü is considered a nonword character, and a word boundary is therefore found between the two characters rü. No word boundary is found between a space character and ü, because they create a contiguous sequence of nonword characters.

You can deal with this problem by using lookahead and lookbehind (collectively, *lookaround*) instead of word boundaries. Like word boundaries, lookaround matches a zero-width position. In PCRE (when compiled with UTF-8 support) and Ruby 1.9, you can emulate Unicode-based word boundaries using, for example, ‹(?<=\P{L}|^)cat(?=\P{L}|$)›. This regular expression also uses negated Unicode Letter property tokens (‹\P{L}›), which are discussed in Recipe 2.7. Lookaround is discussed in Recipe 2.16. If you want the lookarounds to also treat numbers and underscore as word characters (like ‹\b› does), replace the two instances of ‹\P{L}› with the character class ‹[^\p{L}\p{N}_]›.

JavaScript and Ruby 1.8 support neither lookbehind nor Unicode properties. You can work around the lack of lookbehind support by matching the nonword character preceding each match, and then either removing it from each match or putting it back into the string when replacing matches (see the examples of using parts of a match in a replacement string in Recipe 3.15). The additional lack of support for matching Unicode properties (coupled with the fact that both programming languages' ‹\w› and ‹\W› tokens only match ASCII characters) means you might need to make do with a more restrictive solution. Code points in the letter category are scattered throughout Unicode's character set, so it would take thousands of characters to emulate ‹\p{L}› using Unicode escape sequences and character class ranges. A good compromise might be ‹[A-Za-z\xAA\xB5\xBA\xC0-\xD6\xD8-\xF6\xF8-\xFF]›, which matches all Unicode letter characters in eight-bit address space—i.e., the first 256 Unicode code points, from positions 0x0 to 0xFF (see Figure 5-1 for the list of matched characters). This character class lets you match (or in negated form, exclude) a variety of commonly used, accented characters that are outside the addressable space of seven-bit ASCII.

	0	1	2	3	4	5	6	7	8	9	A	B	C	D	E	F
⋮																
4		A	B	C	D	E	F	G	H	I	J	K	L	M	N	O
5	P	Q	R	S	T	U	V	W	X	Y	Z					
6		a	b	c	d	e	f	g	h	i	j	k	l	m	n	o
7	p	q	r	s	t	u	v	w	x	y	z					
⋮																
A											ª					
B						µ					º					
C	À	Á	Â	Ã	Ä	Å	Æ	Ç	È	É	Ê	Ë	Ì	Í	Î	Ï
D	Ð	Ñ	Ò	Ó	Ô	Õ	Ö		Ø	Ù	Ú	Û	Ü	Ý	Þ	ß
E	à	á	â	ã	ä	å	æ	ç	è	é	ê	ë	ì	í	î	ï
F	ð	ñ	ò	ó	ô	õ	ö		ø	ù	ú	û	ü	ý	þ	ÿ

Figure 5-1. Unicode letter characters in eight-bit address space

Following is an example of how to replace all instances of the word "cat" with "dog" in JavaScript. It correctly accounts for common, accented characters, so ëcat is not altered. To do this, you'll need to construct your own character class instead of relying on the built-in ‹\b› or ‹\w›:

```
// 8-bit-wide letter characters
var L = 'A-Za-z\xAA\xB5\xBA\xC0-\xD6\xD8-\xF6\xF8-\xFF';
var pattern = '([^{L}]|^)cat([^{L}]|$)'.replace(/{L}/g, L);
var regex = new RegExp(pattern, 'gi');

// replace cat with dog, and put back any
// additional matched characters
subject = subject.replace(regex, '$1dog$2');
```

Note that JavaScript string literals use \x*HH* (where *HH* is a two-digit hexadecimal number) to insert special characters. Hence, the L variable that is passed to the regular expression actually ends up containing the literal versions of the characters. If you wanted the \x*HH* metasequences to be passed through to the regex itself, you would have to escape the backslashes in the string literal (e.g., "\\x*HH*"). However, in this case it doesn't matter and will not change what the regular expression matches.

See Also

Recipes 5.2, 5.3, and 5.4

5.2 Find Any of Multiple Words

Problem

You want to find any one out of a list of words, without having to search through the subject string multiple times.

Solution

Using alternation

The simple solution is to alternate between the words you want to match:

```
\b(?:one|two|three)\b
```
Regex options: Case insensitive
Regex flavors: .NET, Java, JavaScript, PCRE, Perl, Python, Ruby

More complicated examples of matching similar words are shown in Recipe 5.3.

Example JavaScript solution

```javascript
var subject = 'One times two plus one equals three.';

var regex = /\b(?:one|two|three)\b/gi;

subject.match(regex);
// returns an array with four matches: ['One','two','one','three']

// This function does the same thing but accepts an array of words to
// match. Any regex metacharacters within the accepted words are escaped
// with a backslash before searching.

function match_words (subject, words) {
    var regex_metachars = /[(){}[\]*+?.\\^$|,\-]/g;

    for (var i = 0; i < words.length; i++) {
        words[i] = words[i].replace(regex_metachars, '\\$&');
    }

    var regex = new RegExp('\\b(?:' + words.join('|') + ')\\b', 'gi');

    return subject.match(regex) || [];
}

match_words(subject, ['one','two','three']);
// returns an array with four matches: ['One','two','one','three']
```

Discussion

Using alternation

There are three parts to this regular expression: the word boundaries on both ends, the noncapturing group, and the list of words (each separated by the ‹|› alternation operator). The word boundaries ensure that the regex does not match part of a longer word. The noncapturing group limits the reach of the alternation operators; otherwise, you'd need to write ‹\bone\b|\btwo\b|\bthree\b› to achieve the same effect. Each of the words simply matches itself.

Because the regex engine attempts to match each word in the list from left to right, you might see a very slight performance gain by placing the words that are most likely to be found in the subject text near the beginning of the list. Since the words are surrounded on both sides by word boundaries, they can appear in any order. Without the word boundaries, however, it might be important to put longer words first; otherwise, you'd never find "awesome" when searching for ‹awe|awesome›. The regex would always just match the "awe" at the beginning of the word.

Note that this regular expression is meant to generically demonstrate matching one out of a list of words. Because both the ‹two› and ‹three› in this example start with the same letter, you can more efficiently guide the regular expression engine by rewriting the regex as ‹\b(?:one|t(?:wo|hree))\b›. See Recipe 5.3 for more examples of how to efficiently match one out of a list of similar words.

Example JavaScript solution

The JavaScript example matches the same list of words in two different ways. The first approach is to simply create the regex and search the subject string using the `match` method that is available for JavaScript strings. When the `match` method is passed a regular expression that uses the `/g` ("global") flag, it returns an array of all matches found in the string, or `null` if no match is found.

The second approach uses a function (`match_words`) that accepts the subject string to search within and an array of words to search for. The function first escapes any regex metacharacters that might exist in the provided words, and then splices the word list into a new regular expression that is used to search the string. The function returns an array of any matches that are found, or an empty array if the generated regex doesn't match the string at all. The desired words can be matched in any combination of upper- and lowercase, thanks to the use of the case-insensitive (`/i`) flag.

See Also

Recipes 5.1, 5.3, and 5.4

5.3 Find Similar Words

Problem

You have several problems in this case:

- You want to find all occurrences of both color and colour in a string.
- You want to find any of three words that end with "at": bat, cat, or rat.
- You want to find any word ending with phobia.
- You want to find common variations on the name "Steven": Steve, Steven, and Stephen.
- You want to match any common form of the term "regular expression".

Solution

Regular expressions to solve each of the problems just listed are shown in turn. All of these solutions are listed with the case insensitive option.

Color or colour

```
\bcolou?r\b
```
Regex options: Case insensitive
Regex flavors: .NET, Java, JavaScript, PCRE, Perl, Python, Ruby

Bat, cat, or rat

```
\b[bcr]at\b
```
Regex options: Case insensitive
Regex flavors: .NET, Java, JavaScript, PCRE, Perl, Python, Ruby

Words ending with "phobia"

```
\b\w*phobia\b
```
Regex options: Case insensitive
Regex flavors: .NET, Java, JavaScript, PCRE, Perl, Python, Ruby

Steve, Steven, or Stephen

```
\bSte(?:ven?|phen)\b
```
Regex options: Case insensitive
Regex flavors: .NET, Java, JavaScript, PCRE, Perl, Python, Ruby

Variations of "regular expression"

```
\breg(?:ular•expressions?|ex(?:ps?|e[sn])?)\b
```
Regex options: Case insensitive
Regex flavors: .NET, Java, JavaScript, PCRE, Perl, Python, Ruby

---

Discussion

Use word boundaries to match complete words

All five of these regular expressions use word boundaries (‹\b›) to ensure that they match only complete words. The patterns use several different approaches to allow variation in the words that they match.

Let's take a closer look at each one.

Color or colour

This regular expression will match <u>color</u> or <u>colour</u>, but will not match within colorblind. It uses the ‹?› quantifier to make its preceding "u" optional. Quantifiers such as ‹?› do not work like the wildcards that many people are more familiar with. Instead, they bind to the immediately preceding element, which can be either a single token (in this case, the literal character "u") or a group of tokens wrapped in parentheses. The ‹?› quantifier repeats the preceding element zero or one time. The regex engine first tries to match the element that the quantifier is bound to, and if that doesn't work, the engine moves forward without matching it. Any quantifier that allows zero repetitions effectively makes the preceding element optional, which is exactly what we want here.

Bat, cat, or rat

This regular expression uses a character class to match "b", "c", or "r", followed by the literal characters "at". You could do the same thing using ‹\b(?:b|c|r)at\b›, ‹\b(?:bat| cat|rat)\b›, or ‹\bbat\b|\bcat\b|\brat\b›. However, any time the difference between allowed matches is a choice from one of a list of characters, you're better off using a character class. Not only do character classes provide a more compact and readable syntax (thanks to being able to drop all the vertical bars and use ranges such as A–Z), most regex engines also provide far superior optimization for character classes. Alternation using vertical bars requires the engine to use the computationally expensive backtracking algorithm, whereas character classes use a simpler search approach.

A few words of caution, though. Character classes are among the most frequently misused regular expression features. It's possible that they're not always documented well, or maybe some readers just skimmed over the details. Whatever the reasons, don't let yourself make the same newbie mistakes. Character classes are only capable of matching one character at a time from the characters specified within them—no exceptions.

Following are two of the most common ways that character classes are misused:

Putting words in character classes
> Sure, something like ‹[cat]{3}› will match <u>cat</u>, but it will also match <u>act</u>, <u>ttt</u>, and any other three-character combination of the listed characters. The same applies

to negated character classes such as ‹[^cat]›, which matches any single character that is not c, a, or t.

Trying to use the alternation operator within character classes

By definition, character classes allow a choice between the characters specified within them. ‹[a|b|c]› matches a single character from the set "abc|", which is probably not what you want. And even if it is, the class contains a redundant vertical bar.

See Recipe 2.3 for all the details you need to use character classes correctly and effectively.

Words ending with "phobia"

Like the previous regular expression, this one also uses a quantifier to provide the variation in the strings it matches. This regular expression matches, for example, <u>arachnophobia</u> and <u>hexakosioihexekontahexaphobia</u>, and because the ‹*› allows zero repetitions, it also matches <u>phobia</u> on its own. If you want to require at least one character before the "phobia" suffix, change the ‹*› to ‹+›.

Steve, Steven, or Stephen

This regex combines a couple of the features we've used in the previous examples. A noncapturing group, written as ‹(?:···)›, limits the reach of the ‹|› alternation operator. The ‹?› quantifier used inside the group's first alternation option makes the preceding ‹n› character optional. This improves efficiency (and brevity) versus the equivalent ‹\bSte(?:ve|ven|phen)\b›. The same principle explains why the literal string ‹Ste› appears at the front of the regular expression, rather than being repeated three times as with ‹\b(?:Steve|Steven|Stephen)\b› or ‹\bSteve\b|\bSteven\b|\bStephen\b›. Some backtracking regular expression engines are not smart enough to figure out that any text matched by these latter regexes must start with Ste. Instead, as the engine steps through the subject string looking for a match, it will first find a word boundary, then check the following character to see if it is an S. If not, the engine must try all alternative paths through the regular expression before it can move on and start over again at the next position in the string. Although it's easy for a human to see that this would be a waste of effort (since the alternative paths through the regex all start with "Ste"), the engine doesn't know this. If instead you write the regex as ‹\bSte(?:ven?|phen)\b›, the engine immediately realizes that it cannot match any string that does not start with those characters.

For an in-depth look under the hood of a backtracking regular expression engine, see Recipe 2.13.

Variations of "regular expression"

The final example for this recipe mixes alternation, character classes, and quantifiers to match any common variation of the term "regular expression". Since the regular expression can be a bit difficult to take in at a glance, let's break it down and examine each of its parts.

The regex is written here using the free-spacing option, which is not available in JavaScript. Since whitespace is ignored in free-spacing mode, the literal space character has been escaped with a backslash:

```
\b               # Assert position at a word boundary.
reg              # Match "reg".
(?:              # Group but don't capture...
  ular\          #   Match "ular ".
  expressions?   #   Match "expression" or "expressions".
  |              #   or...
  ex             #   Match "ex".
  (?:            #   Group but don't capture...
    ps?          #     Match "p" or "ps".
    |            #     or...
    e            #     Match "e".
    [sn]         #     Match one character from the set "sn".
  )              #   End the noncapturing group.
  ?              #     Repeat the preceding group zero or one time.
)                # End the noncapturing group.
\b               # Assert position at a word boundary.
```

Regex options: Free-spacing, case insensitive
Regex flavors: .NET, Java, PCRE, Perl, Python, Ruby

This pattern matches any of the following seven strings:

- regular expressions
- regular expression
- regexps
- regexp
- regexes
- regexen
- regex

See Also

Recipes 5.1, 5.2, and 5.4

5.4 Find All Except a Specific Word

Problem

You want to use a regular expression to match any complete word except cat. Catwoman and other words that merely contain the letters "cat" should be matched—just not cat.

Solution

A negative lookahead can help you rule out specific words, and is key to this next regex:

```
\b(?!cat\b)\w+
```

    Regex options: Case insensitive
    Regex flavors: .NET, Java, JavaScript, PCRE, Perl, Python, Ruby

Discussion

Although a negated character class (written as ‹[^…]›) makes it easy to match anything except a specific character, you can't just write ‹[^cat]› to match anything except the word cat. ‹[^cat]› is a valid regex, but it matches any character except c, a, or t. Hence, although ‹\b[^cat]+\b› would avoid matching the word cat, it wouldn't match the word cup either, because it contains the forbidden letter c. The regular expression ‹\b[^c][^a][^t]\w*› is no good either, because it would reject any word with c as its first letter, a as its second letter, or t as its third. Furthermore, that doesn't restrict the first three letters to word characters, and it only matches words with at least three characters since none of the negated character classes are optional.

With all that in mind, let's take another look at how the regular expression shown at the beginning of this recipe solved the problem:

```
\b      # Assert position at a word boundary.
(?!     # Assert that the regex below cannot be matched starting here...
  cat   #   Match "cat".
  \b    #   Assert position at a word boundary.
)       # End the negative lookahead.
\w+     # Match one or more word characters.
```

    Regex options: Free-spacing, case insensitive
    Regex flavors: .NET, Java, PCRE, Perl, Python, Ruby

The key to this pattern is a negative lookahead, which looks like ‹(?!…)›. The negative lookahead disallows the sequence cat followed by a word boundary, without preventing the use of those letters when they do not appear in that exact sequence, or when they appear as part of a longer or shorter word. There's no word boundary at the very end of the regular expression, because it wouldn't change what the regex matches. The ‹+› quantifier in ‹\w+› repeats the word character token as many times as possible, which means that it will always match until the next word boundary.

When applied to the subject string `categorically match any word except cat`, the regex will find five matches: <u>categorically</u>, <u>match</u>, <u>any</u>, <u>word</u>, and <u>except</u>.

Variations

Find words that don't contain another word

If, instead of trying to match any word that is not `cat`, you are trying to match any word that does not *contain* `cat`, a slightly different approach is needed:

> `\b(?:(?!cat)\w)+\b`
> **Regex options:** Case insensitive
> **Regex flavors:** .NET, Java, JavaScript, PCRE, Perl, Python, Ruby

In the earlier section of this recipe, the word boundary at the beginning of the regular expression provided a convenient anchor that allowed us to simply place the negative lookahead at the beginning of the word. The solution used here is not as efficient, but it's nevertheless a commonly used construct that allows you to match something other than a particular word or pattern. It does this by repeating a group containing a negative lookahead and a single word character. Before matching each character, the regex engine makes sure that the word `cat` cannot be matched starting at the current position.

Unlike the previous regular expression, this one requires a terminating word boundary. Otherwise, it could match just the first part of a word, up to where `cat` appears within it.

See Also

Recipe 2.16, which includes a more thorough discussion of lookaround (the collective term for positive and negative lookahead and lookbehind).

Recipes 5.1, 5.5, 5.6, and 5.11.

5.5 Find Any Word Not Followed by a Specific Word

Problem

You want to match any word that is not immediately followed by the word `cat`, ignoring any whitespace, punctuation, or other nonword characters that appear in between.

Solution

Negative lookahead is the secret ingredient for this regular expression:

> `\b\w+\b(?!\W+cat\b)`
> **Regex options:** Case insensitive
> **Regex flavors:** .NET, Java, JavaScript, PCRE, Perl, Python, Ruby

Recipes 3.7 and 3.14 show examples of how you might want to implement this regular expression in code.

Discussion

As with many other recipes in this chapter, word boundaries (‹\b›) and the word character token (‹\w›) work together to match a complete word. You can find in-depth descriptions of these features in Recipe 2.6.

The ‹(?!…)› surrounding the second part of this regex is a negative lookahead. Lookahead tells the regex engine to temporarily step forward in the string, to check whether the pattern inside the lookahead can be matched just ahead of the current position. It does not consume any of the characters matched inside the lookahead. Instead, it merely asserts whether a match is possible. Since we're using a negative lookahead, the result of the assertion is inverted. In other words, if the pattern inside the lookahead can be matched just ahead, the match attempt fails, and regex engine moves forward to try all over again starting from the next character in the subject string. You can find much more detail about lookahead (and its counterpart, lookbehind) in Recipe 2.16.

As for the pattern inside the lookahead, the ‹\W+› matches one or more nonword characters that appear before ‹cat›, and the word boundary at the end makes sure that we skip only words not followed by cat as a complete word, rather than just any word starting with cat.

Note that this regular expression even matches the word cat, as long as the subsequent word is not also cat. If you also want to avoid matching cat, you could combine this regex with the one in Recipe 5.4 to end up with ‹\b(?!cat\b)\w+\b(?!\W+cat\b)›.

Variations

If you want to only match words that *are* followed by cat (without including cat and its preceding nonword characters as part of the matched text), change the lookahead from negative to positive, then turn your frown upside-down:

```
\b\w+\b(?=\W+cat\b)
```
   Regex options: Case insensitive
   Regex flavors: .NET, Java, JavaScript, PCRE, Perl, Python, Ruby

See Also

Recipe 2.16, which includes a more thorough discussion of lookaround (the collective term for positive and negative lookahead and lookbehind).

Recipes 5.4 and 5.6.

5.6 Find Any Word Not Preceded by a Specific Word

Problem

You want to match any word that is not immediately preceded by the word cat, ignoring any whitespace, punctuation, or other nonword characters that come between.

Solution

Lookbehind you

Lookbehind lets you check if text appears before a given position. It works by instructing the regex engine to temporarily step backward in the string, checking whether something can be found ending at the position where you placed the lookbehind. See Recipe 2.16 if you need to brush up on the details of lookbehind.

The following three regexes use negative lookbehind, which looks like ‹(?<!⋯)›. Unfortunately, the regex flavors covered by this book differ in what kinds of patterns they allow you to place within lookbehind. As a result, the solutions end up working a bit differently in each case. Make sure to check out the "Discussion" on page 298 of this recipe for further details.

Words not preceded by "cat"

```
(?<!\bcat\W+)\b\w+
```
Regex options: Case insensitive
Regex flavor: .NET

```
(?<!\bcat\W{1,9})\b\w+
```
Regex options: Case insensitive
Regex flavors: .NET, Java, PCRE

```
(?<!\bcat)(?:\W+|^)(\w+)
```
Regex options: Case insensitive
Regex flavors: .NET, Java, PCRE, Perl, Python, Ruby 1.9

Simulate lookbehind

JavaScript and Ruby 1.8 do not support lookbehind at all, even though they do support lookahead. However, because the lookbehind for this problem appears at the very beginning of the regex, it is possible to perfectly simulate the lookbehind by splitting the regex into two parts, as demonstrated in the following JavaScript example:

```
var subject = 'My cat is furry.',
    main_regex = /\b\w+/g,
    lookbehind = /\bcat\W+$/i,
    lookbehind_type = false, // negative lookbehind
    matches = [],
```

```
    match,
    left_context;

while (match = main_regex.exec(subject)) {
    left_context = subject.substring(0, match.index);

    if (lookbehind_type == lookbehind.test(left_context)) {
        matches.push(match[0]);
    } else {
        main_regex.lastIndex = match.index + 1;
    }
}

// matches:  ['My','cat','furry']
```

Discussion

Fixed, finite, and infinite length lookbehind

The first regular expression uses the negative lookbehind ‹(?<!\bcat\W+)›. Because the ‹+› quantifier used inside the lookbehind has no upper limit on how many characters it can match, this version only works with the .NET regular expression flavor. All of the other regular expression flavors covered by this book require a fixed or maximum (finite) length for lookbehind patterns.

The second regular expression replaces the ‹+› within the lookbehind with ‹{1,9}›. As a result, it can be used with .NET, Java, and PCRE, all of which support variable-length lookbehind when there is a known upper limit to how many characters can be matched within them. I've arbitrarily chosen a maximum length of nine nonword characters to separate the words. That allows a bit of punctuation and a few blank lines to separate the words. Unless you're working with unusual subject text, this will probably end up working exactly like the previous .NET-only solution. Even in .NET, however, providing a reasonable repetition limit for any quantifiers inside lookbehind is likely to make your regular expression more efficient, if only because it reduces the amount of unanticipated backtracking that can potentially occur within the lookbehind.

The third regular expression was restructured in a way that lets the lookbehind test a fixed-length string, thereby adding support for even more regular expression flavors. In order to do so, the nonword character (‹\W›) shorthand class was moved outside of the lookbehind. This means that the nonword characters (such as punctuation and whitespace) preceding the words you're searching for will be part of the string that is actually matched (and returned) by the regular expression. To make it a little easier to ignore this portion of each match, a capturing group was added around the final word-character sequence. With a bit of additional code, you can read just the value of backreference 1 rather than the entire match, giving you the same result that you'd get from the prior regular expressions. Recipe 3.9 shows the code needed to work with backreferences.

Simulate lookbehind

JavaScript does not support lookbehind, but the JavaScript example code shows how you can simulate lookbehind that appears at the beginning of a regex by using two regular expressions. It doesn't impose any restrictions on the length of the text matched by the (simulated) lookbehind.

We start by splitting the ‹(?<!\bcat\W+)\b\w+› regular expression from the original solution into two pieces: the pattern inside the lookbehind (‹\bcat\W+›) and the pattern that comes after it (‹\b\w+›). Append a ‹$› to the end of the lookbehind regex. If you need to use the "caret and dollar sign match at line breaks" option (/m) with the lookbehind regex, use ‹$(?!\s)› instead of ‹$› to ensure that it can match only at the very end of its subject text. The lookbehind_type variable indicates whether we're emulating positive or negative lookbehind, using true for positive and false for negative.

After the variables are set up, we use main_regex and the exec method to iterate over the subject string (see Recipe 3.11 for a description of this process). When a match is found, the part of the subject text before the match is copied into a new string variable (left_context), and we test whether the lookbehind regex matches that string. Because of the anchor we appended to the end of the lookbehind regex, this effectively puts the second match immediately to the left of the first match. By comparing the result of the lookbehind test to lookbehind_type, we can determine whether the match meets the complete criteria for a successful match.

Finally, we take one of two steps. If we have a successful match, append the matched text to the matches array. If not, change the position at which to continue searching for a match (using main_regex.lastIndex) to the position one character after the starting position of the main_regex object's last match, rather than letting the next iteration of the exec method start at the end of the current match.

Whew! We're done.

This is an advanced trick that takes advantage of the lastIndex property that is dynamically updated with JavaScript regular expressions that use the /g ("global") flag. Usually, updating and resetting lastIndex is something that happens automagically. Here, we use it to take control of the regex's path through the subject string, moving forward and backward as necessary. This trick only lets you emulate lookbehind that appears at the beginning of a regex. With a few changes, this code could also be used to emulate lookbehind at the very end of a regex. However, it does not serve as a full substitute for lookbehind support. Due to the interplay of lookbehind and backtracking, this approach cannot help you accurately emulate the behavior of a lookbehind that appears in the middle of a regex.

Variations

If you only want to match words that *are* preceded by cat (without including cat and its following nonword characters as part of the matched text), change the negative lookbehind to a positive lookbehind:

```
(?<=\bcat\W+)\b\w+
```
Regex options: Case insensitive
Regex flavor: .NET

```
(?<=\bcat\W{1,9})\b\w+
```
Regex options: Case insensitive
Regex flavors: .NET, Java, PCRE

```
(?<=\bcat)(?:\W+|^)(\w+)
```
Regex options: Case insensitive
Regex flavors: .NET, Java, PCRE, Perl, Python, Ruby 1.9

See Also

Recipe 2.16, which includes a more thorough discussion of lookaround (the collective term for positive and negative lookahead and lookbehind).

Recipes 5.4 and 5.5.

5.7 Find Words Near Each Other

Problem

You want to emulate a NEAR search using a regular expression. For readers unfamiliar with the term, some search tools that use Boolean operators such as NOT and OR also have a special operator called NEAR. Searching for "word1 NEAR word2" finds word1 and word2 in any order, as long as they occur within a certain distance of each other.

Solution

If you're only searching for two different words, you can combine two regular expressions—one that matches word1 before word2, and another that flips the order of the words. The following regex allows up to five words to separate the two you're searching for:

```
\b(?:word1\W+(?:\w+\W+){0,5}?word2|word2\W+(?:\w+\W+){0,5}?word1)\b
```
Regex options: Case insensitive
Regex flavors: .NET, Java, JavaScript, PCRE, Perl, Python, Ruby

```
\b(?:
word1                 # first term
\W+ (?:\w+\W+){0,5}?  # up to five words
```

```
    word2                 # second term
|                         #   or, the same pattern in reverse...
    word2                 # second term
    \W+ (?:\w+\W+){0,5}?  # up to five words
    word1                 # first term
)\b
```
Regex options: Free-spacing, case insensitive
Regex flavors: .NET, Java, PCRE, Perl, Python, Ruby

The second regular expression here uses the free-spacing option and adds whitespace and comments for readability. Apart from that, the two regular expressions are identical. JavaScript doesn't support free-spacing mode, but the other listed regex flavors allow you to take your pick. Recipes 3.5 and 3.7 show examples of how you can add these regular expressions to your search form or other code.

Discussion

This regular expression puts two inverted copies of the same pattern back to back, and then surrounds them with word boundaries. The first subpattern matches word1, followed by between zero and five words, and then word2. The second subpattern matches the same thing, with the order of word1 and word2 reversed.

The lazy quantifier ‹{0,5}?› appears in both of the subpatterns. It causes the regular expression to match as few words as possible between the two terms you're searching for. If you run the regular expression over the subject text word1 word2 word2, it will match word1 word2 because that has fewer words (zero) between the start and end points. To configure the distance permitted between the target words, change the 0 and 5 within the two quantifiers to your preferred values. For example, if you changed them to ‹{1,15}?›, that would allow up to 15 words between the two you're looking for, and require that they be separated by at least one other word.

The shorthand character classes that are used to match word characters and nonword characters (‹\w› and ‹\W›, respectively) follow the quirky regular expression definition of which characters words are composed of (letters, numbers, and underscore).

Variations

Using a conditional

Often, there are many ways to write the same regular expression. In this book, we've tried hard to balance the trade-offs between portability, brevity, efficiency, and other considerations. However, sometimes solutions that are less than ideal can still be educational. The next two regular expressions illustrate alternative approaches to finding words near each other. We don't recommend actually using them, because although they match the same text, they will typically take a little longer to do so. They also work with fewer regular expression flavors.

This first regular expression uses a conditional to determine whether to match word1 or word2 at the end of the regex, rather than simply stringing reversed patterns together. The conditional checks if capturing group 1 participated in the match, which would mean that the match started with word2:

```
\b(?:word1|(word2))\W+(?:\w+\W+){0,5}?(?(1)word1|word2)\b
```
Regex options: None
Regex flavors: .NET, PCRE, Perl, Python

This next version once again uses a conditional to determine which word should be matched at the end, but it adds two more regular expression features into the mix:

```
\b(?:(?<w1>word1)|(?<w2>word2))\W+(?:\w+\W+){0,5}?(?(w2)(?&w1)|(?&w2))\b
```
Regex options: None
Regex flavors: PCRE 7, Perl 5.10

Here, named capturing groups, written as ‹(?<name>···)›, surround the first instances of ‹word1› and ‹word2›. This allows you to use the ‹(?&name)› *subroutine* syntax to reuse a subpattern that is called by name. This does not work the same as a backreference to a named group. A named backreference, such as ‹\k<name>› (.NET, PCRE 7, Perl 5.10) or ‹(?P=name)› (PCRE 4 and higher, Perl 5.10, Python) lets you re-match text that has already been matched by a named capturing group. A subroutine such as ‹(?&name)› allows you to reuse the actual pattern contained within the corresponding group. You can't use a backreference here, because that would only allow re-matching words that have already been matched. The subroutines within the conditional at the end of the regex match the word from the two provided options that *hasn't* already been matched, without having to spell out the words again. This means there is only one place in the regex to update if you need to reuse it to match different words.

Match three or more words near each other

Exponentially increasing permutations. Matching two words near each other is a fairly straightforward task. After all, there are only two possible ways to order them. But what if you want to match three words in any order? Now there are six possible orders (see Figure 5-2). The number of ways you can shift a given set of words around is $n!$, or the product of consecutive integers 1 through n ("n factorial"). With four words, there are 24 possible ways to order them. By the time you get to 10 words, the number of arrangements explodes into the millions. It is simply not viable to match more than a few words near each other using the regular expression techniques discussed so far.

The ugly solution. One way to solve this problem is by repeating a group that matches the required words or any other word (after a required word is first matched), and then using conditionals to prevent a match attempt from finishing successfully until all of the required words have been matched. Following is an example of matching three words in any order with up to five other words separating them:

```
\b(?:(?>(word1)|(word2)|(word3)|(?(1)|(?(2)|(?(3)|(?!)))))\w+)\b\W*?){3,8}↵
(?(1)(?(2)(?(3)|(?!))|(?!))|(?!))
```
Regex options: Case insensitive
Regex flavors: .NET, PCRE, Perl

```
Two values:
    [ 12, 21 ]
    = 2 possible arrangements

Three values:
    [ 123, 132,
      213, 231,
      312, 321 ]
    = 6 possible arrangements

Four values:
    [ 1234, 1243, 1324, 1342, 1423, 1432,
      2134, 2143, 2314, 2341, 2413, 2432,
      3124, 3142, 3214, 3241, 3412, 3421,
      4123, 4132, 4213, 4231, 4312, 4321 ]
    = 24 possible arrangements

Factorials:
    2! = 2 × 1                                    =        2
    3! = 3 × 2 × 1                                =        6
    4! = 4 × 3 × 2 × 1                            =       24
    5! = 5 × 4 × 3 × 2 × 1                        =      120
    ...
    10! = 10 × 9 × 8 × 7 × 6 × 5 × 4 × 3 × 2 × 1 = 3628800
```

Figure 5-2. Many ways to arrange a set

Here's the regex again with the atomic group (see Recipe 2.14) replaced with a standard, noncapturing group in order to add support for Python:

```
\b(?:(?:(word1)|(word2)|(word3)|(?(1)|(?(2)|(?(3)|(?!)))))\w+)\b\W*?){3,8}↵
(?(1)(?(2)(?(3)|(?!))|(?!))|(?!))
```
Regex options: Case insensitive
Regex flavors: .NET, PCRE, Perl, Python

The ‹{3,8}› quantifiers in the regular expressions just shown account for the three required words, and thus allows zero to five words in between them. The empty negative lookaheads, which look like ‹(?!)›, will never match and are therefore used to block certain paths through the regex until one or more of the required words have been matched. The logic that controls these paths is implemented using two sets of nested conditionals. The first set prevents matching any old word using ‹\w+› until at least one of the required words have been matched. The second set of conditionals at the end forces the regex engine to backtrack or fail unless all of the required words have been matched.

That's the brief overview of how this works, but rather than getting further into the weeds and describing how to add additional required words, let's take a look at an improved implementation that adds support for more regex flavors, and involves a bit of a trick.

Exploiting empty backreferences. The ugly solution works, but it could probably win a regex obfuscation contest for being so difficult to read and manage. It would only get worse if you added more required words into the mix.

Fortunately, there's a regular expression hack you can use that makes this a lot easier to follow, while also adding support for Java and Ruby (neither of which support conditionals).

 The behavior described in this section should be used with caution in production applications. We're pushing expectations for regex behavior into places that are undocumented for most regex libraries.

```
\b(?:(?>word1()|word2()|word3()|(?>\1|\2|\3)\w+)\b\W*?){3,8}\1\2\3
```
Regex options: Case insensitive
Regex flavors: .NET, Java, PCRE, Perl, Ruby

```
\b(?:(?:word1()|word2()|word3()|(?:\1|\2|\3)\w+)\b\W*?){3,8}\1\2\3
```
Regex options: Case insensitive
Regex flavors: .NET, Java, PCRE, Perl, Python, Ruby

Using this construct, it's easy to add more required words. Here's an example that allows four required words to appear in any order, with a total of up to five other words between them:

```
\b(?:(?>word1()|word2()|word3()|word4()| ↵
(?>\1|\2|\3|\4)\w+)\b\W*?){4,9}\1\2\3\4
```
Regex options: Case insensitive
Regex flavors: .NET, Java, PCRE, Perl, Ruby

```
\b(?:(?:word1()|word2()|word3()|word4()| ↵
(?:\1|\2|\3|\4)\w+)\b\W*?){4,9}\1\2\3\4
```
Regex options: Case insensitive
Regex flavors: .NET, Java, PCRE, Perl, Python, Ruby

These regular expressions intentionally use empty capturing groups after each of the required words. Since any attempt to match a backreference such as ‹\1› will fail if the corresponding capturing group has not yet participated in the match, backreferences to empty groups can be used to control the path a regex engine takes through a pattern, much like the more verbose conditionals we showed earlier. If the corresponding group has already participated in the match attempt when the engine reaches the backreference, it will simply match an empty string and move on.

Here, the ⟨(?>\1|\2|\3)⟩ grouping prevents matching a word using ⟨\w+⟩ until at least one of the required words has been matched. The backreferences are repeated at the end of the pattern to prevent any match from successfully completing until all of the required words have been found.

Python does not support atomic groups, so once again the examples that list Python among the regex flavors replace such groups with standard noncapturing groups. Although this makes the regexes less efficient, it doesn't change what they match. The outermost grouping cannot be atomic in any flavor, because in order for this to work, the regex engine must be able to backtrack into the outer group if the backreferences at the end of the pattern fail to match.

JavaScript backreferences by its own rules. Even though JavaScript supports all the syntax used in the Python versions of this pattern, it has two behavioral rules that prevent this trick from working like the other flavors. The first issue is what is matched by backreferences to capturing groups that have not yet participated in a match. The JavaScript specification dictates that such backreferences match the empty string, or in other words, they always match successfully. In just about every other regular expression flavor, the opposite is true: they never match, and as a result they force the regex engine to backtrack until either the entire match fails or the group they reference participates, thereby providing the possibility that the backreference too will match.

The second difference with the JavaScript flavor involves the value remembered by capturing groups nested within a repeated, outer group, e.g., ⟨((a)|(b))+⟩. With most regex flavors, the value remembered by a capturing group within a repeated grouping is whatever the group matched the last time it participated in the match. So, after ⟨(?: (a)|(b))+⟩ is used to match <u>ab</u>, the value of backreference 1 would be <u>a</u>. However, according to the JavaScript specification, the value of backreferences to nested groups is reset every time the outer group is repeated. Hence, ⟨(?:(a)|(b))+⟩ would still match <u>ab</u>, but backreference 1 after the match is complete would reference a nonparticipating capturing group, which in JavaScript would match an empty string within the regex itself and be returned as undefined in, for example, the array returned by the RegExp.prototype.exec method.

Either of these behavioral differences found in the JavaScript regex flavor are enough to prevent emulating conditionals using empty capturing groups, as described here.

Multiple words, any distance from each other

If you simply want to test whether a list of words can be found anywhere in a subject string without regard for their proximity, positive lookahead provides a way to do so using one search operation.

 In many cases it's simpler and more efficient to perform discrete searches for each term you're looking for, while keeping track of whether all tests come back positive.

```
\A(?=.*?\bword1\b)(?=.*?\bword2\b).*\Z
```
    Regex options: Case insensitive, dot matches line breaks
    Regex flavors: .NET, Java, PCRE, Perl, Python, Ruby

```
^(?=[\s\S]*?\bword1\b)(?=[\s\S]*?\bword2\b)[\s\S]*$
```
    Regex options: Case insensitive ("^ and $ match at line breaks" must not be set)
    Regex flavor: JavaScript

These regular expressions match the entire string they're run against if all of your target words are found within it; otherwise, they will not find any match. JavaScript programmers cannot use the first version, because JavaScript doesn't support the ‹\A› and ‹\Z› anchors or the "dot matches line breaks" option.

You can implement these regular expressions by following the code in Recipe 3.6. Simply change the ‹word1› and ‹word2› placeholders to the terms you're searching for. If you're checking for more than two words, you can add as many lookaheads to the front of the regex as you need. For example, ‹\A(?=.*?\bword1\b)(?=.*?\bword2\b)(?=.*? \bword3\b).*\Z› searches for three words.

See Also

Recipes 5.5 and 5.6

5.8 Find Repeated Words

Problem

You're editing a document and would like to check it for any incorrectly repeated words. You want to find these doubled words despite capitalization differences, such as with "The the". You also want to allow differing amounts of whitespace between words, even if this causes the words to extend across more than one line.

Solution

A backreference matches something that has been matched before, and therefore provides the key ingredient for this recipe:

```
\b([A-Z]+)\s+\1\b
```
    Regex options: Case insensitive
    Regex flavors: .NET, Java, JavaScript, PCRE, Perl, Python, Ruby

If you want to use this regular expression to keep the first word but remove subsequent duplicate words, replace all matches with backreference 1. Another approach is to highlight matches by surrounding them with other characters (such as an HTML tag), so you can more easily identify them during later inspection. Recipe 3.15 shows how you can use backreferences in your replacement text, which you'll need to do to implement either of these approaches.

If you just want to find repeated words so you can manually examine whether they need to be corrected, Recipe 3.7 shows the code you need. A text editor or grep-like tool, such as those mentioned in "Tools for Working with Regular Expressions" in Chapter 1, can help you find repeated words while providing the context needed to determine whether the words in question are in fact used correctly.

Discussion

There are two things needed to match something that was previously matched: a capturing group and a backreference. Place the thing you want to match more than once inside a capturing group, and then match it again using a backreference. This works differently from simply repeating a token or group using a quantifier. Consider the difference between the simplified regular expressions ‹(\w)\1› and ‹\w{2}›. The first regex uses a capturing group and backreference to match the same word character twice, whereas the latter uses a quantifier to match any two word characters. Recipe 2.10 discusses the magic of backreferences in greater depth.

Back to the problem at hand. This recipe only finds repeated words that are composed of letters from A to Z and a to z (since the case insensitive option is enabled). To also allow accented letters and letters from other scripts, you can use the Unicode Letter property (‹\p{L}›) if your regex flavor supports it (see "Unicode property or category" on page 45).

Between the capturing group and backreference, ‹\s+› matches any whitespace characters, such as spaces, tabs, or line breaks. If you want to restrict the characters that can separate repeated words to horizontal whitespace (i.e., no line breaks), replace the ‹\s› with ‹[^\S\r\n]›. This prevents matching repeated words that appear across multiple lines. PCRE 7 and Perl 5.10 include the shorthand character class ‹\h› that you might prefer to use here since it is specifically designed to match horizontal whitespace.

Finally, the word boundaries at the beginning and end of the regular expression ensure that it doesn't match within other words, e.g., with "this thistle".

Note that the use of repeated words is not always incorrect, so simply removing them without examination is potentially dangerous. For example, the constructions "that that" and "had had" are generally accepted in colloquial English. Homonyms, names, onomatopoeic words (such as "oink oink" or "ha ha"), and some other constructions also occasionally result in intentionally repeated words. Therefore, in most cases you will need to visually examine each match.

See Also

Recipe 2.10, which discusses backreferences in greater depth.

Recipe 5.9, which shows how to match repeated lines of text.

5.9 Remove Duplicate Lines

Problem

You have a logfile, database query output, or some other type of file or string with duplicate lines. You need to remove all but one of each duplicate line using a text editor or other similar tool.

Solution

There is a variety of software (including the Unix command-line utility `uniq` and Windows PowerShell cmdlet `Get-Unique`) that can help you remove duplicate lines in a file or string. The following sections contain three regex-based approaches that can be especially helpful when trying to accomplish this task in a nonscriptable text editor with regular expression search-and-replace support.

When programming, options two and three should be avoided since they are inefficient compared to other available approaches, such as using a hash object to keep track of unique lines. However, the first option (which requires that you sort the lines in advance, unless you only want to remove adjacent duplicates) may be an acceptable approach since it's quick and easy.

Option 1: Sort lines and remove adjacent duplicates

If you're able to sort lines in the file or string you're working with so that any duplicate lines appear next to each other, you should do so, unless the order of the lines must be preserved. This option will allow using a simpler and more efficient search-and-replace operation to remove the duplicates than would otherwise be possible.

After sorting the lines, use the following regex and replacement string to get rid of the duplicates:

```
^(.*)(?:(?:\r?\n|\r)\1)+$
```
Regex options: `^` and `$` match at line breaks ("dot matches line breaks" must not be set)
Regex flavors: .NET, Java, JavaScript, PCRE, Perl, Python, Ruby

Replace with:

```
$1
```
Replacement text flavors: .NET, Java, JavaScript, Perl, PHP

```
\1
```
Replacement text flavors: Python, Ruby

This regular expression uses a capturing group and a backreference (among other ingredients) to match two or more sequential, duplicate lines. A backreference is used in the replacement string to put back the first line. Recipe 3.15 shows example code that can be repurposed to implement this.

Option 2: Keep the last occurrence of each duplicate line in an unsorted file

If you are using a text editor that does not have the built-in ability to sort lines, or if it is important to preseve the original line order, the following solution lets you remove duplicates even when they are separated by other lines:

```
^([^\r\n]*)(?:\r?\n|\r)(?=.*^\1$)
```
Regex options: Dot matches line breaks, ^ and $ match at line breaks
Regex flavors: .NET, Java, PCRE, Perl, Python, Ruby

Here's the same thing as a JavaScript-compatible regex, without the requirement for the "dot matches line breaks" option:

```
^(.*)(?:\r?\n|\r)(?=[\s\S]*^\1$)
```
Regex options: ^ and $ match at line breaks
Regex flavor: JavaScript

Replace with:

(The empty string, i.e., nothing.)

Replacement text flavors: N/A

Option 3: Keep the first occurrence of each duplicate line in an unsorted file

If you want to preserve the first occurrence of each duplicate line, you'll need to use a somewhat different approach. First, here is the regular expression and replacement string we will use:

```
^([^\r\n]*)$(.*?)(?:(?:\r?\n|\r)\1$)+
```
Regex options: Dot matches line breaks, ^ and $ match at line breaks
Regex flavors: .NET, Java, PCRE, Perl, Python, Ruby

Once again, we need to make a couple changes to make this compatible with JavaScript-flavor regexes, since JavaScript doesn't have a "dot matches line breaks" option.

```
^(.*)$([\s\S]*?)(?:(?:\r?\n|\r)\1$)+
```
Regex options: ^ and $ match at line breaks
Regex flavors: JavaScript

Replace with:

```
$1$2
```
Replacement text flavors: .NET, Java, JavaScript, Perl, PHP

```
\1\2
```
Replacement text flavors: Python, Ruby

Unlike the option 1 and 2 regexes, this version cannot remove all duplicate lines with one search-and-replace operation. You'll need to continually apply "replace all" until the regex no longer matches your string, meaning that there are no more duplicates to remove. See the "Discussion" of this recipe for further details.

Discussion

Option 1: Sort lines and remove adjacent duplicates

This regex removes all but the first of duplicate lines that appear next to each other. It does not remove duplicates that are separated by other lines. Let's step through the process.

First, the caret (‹^›) at the front of the regular expression matches the start of a line. Normally it would only match at the beginning of the subject string, so you need to make sure that the option to let ^ and $ match at line breaks is enabled (Recipe 3.4 shows you how to set regex options). Next, the ‹.*› within the capturing parentheses matches the entire contents of a line (even if it's blank), and the value is stored as backreference 1. For this to work correctly, the "dot matches line breaks" option must not be set; otherwise, the dot-asterisk combination would match until the end of the string.

Within an outer, noncapturing group, we've used ‹(?:\r?\n|\r)› to match a line separator used in Windows (‹\r\n›), Unix/Linux/OS X (‹\n›), or legacy Mac OS (‹\r›) text files. The backreference ‹\1› then tries to match the line we just finished matching. If the same line isn't found at that position, the match attempt fails and the regex engine moves on. If it matches, we repeat the group (composed of a line break sequence and backreference 1) using the ‹+› quantifier to try to match additional duplicate lines.

Finally, we use the dollar sign at the end of the regex to assert position at the end of the line. This ensures that we only match identical lines, and not lines that merely start with the same characters as a previous line.

Because we're doing a search-and-replace, each entire match (including the original line and line separators) is removed from the string. We replace this with backreference 1 to put the original line back in.

Option 2: Keep the last occurrence of each duplicate line in an unsorted file

There are several changes here compared to the option 1 regex earlier in this recipe, which only finds duplicate lines when they appear next to each other. First, in the non-JavaScript version of the option 2 regex, the dot within the capturing group has been replaced with ‹[^\r\n]› (any character except a line break), and the "dot matches line breaks" option has been enabled. That's because a dot is used later in the regex to match any character, including line breaks. Second, a lookahead has been added to scan for duplicate lines at any position further along in the string. Since the lookahead does not consume any characters, the text matched by the regex is always a single line (along with its following line break) that is known to appear again later in the string. Replacing all matches with the empty string removes the duplicate lines, leaving behind only the last occurrence of each.

Option 3: Keep the first occurrence of each duplicate line in an unsorted file

Because lookbehind is not as widely supported as lookahead (and where it is supported, you still may not be able to look as far backwards as you need to), the Option 3 regex is significantly different from Option 2. Instead of matching lines that are known to be repeated earlier in the string (which would be comparable to option 2's tactic), this regex matches a line, the first duplicate of that line that occurs later in the string, and all the lines in between. The original line is stored as backreference 1, and the lines in between (if any) as backreference 2. By replacing each match with both backreference 1 and 2, you put back the parts you want to keep, leaving out the trailing, duplicate line and its preceding line break.

This alternative approach presents a couple of issues. First, because each match of a set of duplicate lines may include other lines in between, it's possible that there are duplicates of a different value within your matched text, and those will be skipped over during a "replace all" operation. Second, if a line is repeated more than twice, the regex will first match duplicates one and two, but after that, it will take another set of duplicates to get the regex to match again as it advances through the string. Thus, a single "replace all" action will at best remove only every other duplicate of any specific line. To solve both of these problems and make sure that all duplicates are removed, you'll need to continually apply the search-and-replace operation to your entire subject string until the regex no longer matches within it. Consider how this regex will work when applied to the following subject string:

```
value1
value2
value2
value3
value3
value1
value2
```

Removing all duplicate lines from this string will take three passes. Table 5-1 shows the result of each pass.

Table 5-1. Replacement passes

Pass one	Pass two	Pass three	Final string
value1	value1	value1	value1
value2	value2	value2	value2
value2	~~value2~~	value3	value3
value3	value3	~~value2~~	
value3	~~value3~~		
~~value1~~	value2		
value2			
One match/replacement	Two matches/replacements	One match/replacement	No duplicates remain

See Also

Recipe 2.10, which discusses backreferences in greater depth.

Recipe 5.8, which shows how to match repeated words.

5.10 Match Complete Lines That Contain a Word

Problem

You want to match all lines that contain the word `ninja` anywhere within them.

Solution

```
^.*\bninja\b.*$
```
Regex options: Case insensitive, ^ and $ match at line breaks ("dot matches line breaks" must not be set)
Regex flavors: .NET, Java, JavaScript, PCRE, Perl, Python, Ruby

Discussion

It's often useful to match complete lines in order to collect or remove them. To match any line that contains the word `ninja`, we start with the regular expression ‹\bninja \b›. The word boundary tokens on both ends make sure that we only match "ninja" when it appears as a complete word, as explained in Recipe 2.6.

To expand the regex to match a complete line, add ‹.*› at both ends. The dot-asterisk sequences match zero or more characters within the current line. The asterisk quantifiers are greedy, so they will match as much text as possible. The first dot-asterisk matches until the last occurrence of "ninja" on the line, and the second dot-asterisk matches any nonline-break characters that occur after it.

Finally, place caret and dollar sign anchors at the beginning and end of the regular expression, respectively, to ensure that matches contain a complete line. Strictly speaking, the dollar sign anchor at the end is redundant since the dot and greedy asterisk will always match until the end of the line. However, it doesn't hurt to add it, and makes the regular expression a little more self-explanatory. Adding line or string anchors to your regexes, when appropriate, can sometimes help you avoid unexpected issues, so it's not a bad habit to form. Note that unlike the dollar sign, the caret at the beginning of the regular expression is not necessarily redundant, since it ensures that the regex only matches complete lines, even if the search starts in the middle of a line for some reason.

Remember that the three key metacharacters used to restrict matches to a single line (the ‹^› and ‹$› anchors, and the dot) do not have fixed meanings. To make them all line-oriented, you have to enable the option to let ‹^› and ‹$› match at line breaks, and make sure that the option to let the dot match line breaks is not enabled. Recipe 3.4

shows you how to apply these options in your code. If you're using JavaScript or Ruby, there is one less option to worry about, because JavaScript does not have an option to let dot match line breaks, and Ruby's caret and dollar sign anchors always match at line breaks.

Variations

To search for lines that contain any one of multiple words, use alternation:

```
^.*\b(one|two|three)\b.*$
```
Regex options: Case insensitive, ^ and $ match at line breaks ("dot matches line breaks" must not be set)
Regex flavors: .NET, Java, JavaScript, PCRE, Perl, Python, Ruby

The regular expression just shown matches any line that contains at least one of the words "one", "two", or "three". The parentheses around the words serve two purposes. First, they limit the reach of the alternation, and second, they capture the word that actually appears on the line to backreference 1. If the line contains more than one of the words, the backreference will hold the one that occurs farthest to the right. This is because the asterisk quantifier that appears before the parentheses is greedy, and will expand the dot to match as much text as possible. If you make the asterisk lazy, as with ‹^.*?\b(one|two|three)\b.*$›, backreference 1 will contain the word from your list that appears farthest to the left.

To find lines that must contain multiple words, use lookahead:

```
^(?=.*?\bone\b)(?=.*?\btwo\b)(?=.*?\bthree\b).+$
```
Regex options: Case insensitive, ^ and $ match at line breaks ("dot matches line breaks" must not be set)
Regex flavors: .NET, Java, JavaScript, PCRE, Perl, Python, Ruby

This regular expression uses positive lookahead to match lines that contain three required words anywhere within them. The ‹.+› at the end is used to actually match the line, after the lookaheads have determined that the line meets the requirements.

See Also

Recipe 5.11 shows how to match complete lines that do *not* contain a particular word.

5.11 Match Complete Lines That Do Not Contain a Word

Problem

You want to match complete lines that do not contain the word `ninja`.

Solution

```
^(?:(?!\bninja\b).)*$
```

Regex options: Case insensitive, ^ and $ match at line breaks ("dot matches line breaks" must not be set)

Regex flavors: .NET, Java, JavaScript, PCRE, Perl, Python, Ruby

Discussion

In order to match a line that does *not* contain something, use negative lookahead (described in Recipe 2.16). Notice that in this regular expression, a negative lookahead and a dot are repeated together using a noncapturing group. This makes sure that the regex ‹\bninja\b› fails at every position in the line. The ‹^› and ‹$› anchors are placed at the edges of the regular expression to make sure you match a complete line.

The options you apply to this regular expression determine whether it tries to match the entire subject string or just one line at a time. With the option to let ‹^› and ‹$› match at line breaks enabled and the option to let dot match line breaks disabled, this regular expression works as described and matches line by line. If you invert the state of these two options, the regular expression will match any string that does not contain the word "ninja".

 Testing a negative lookahead against every position in a line or string is rather inefficient. This solution is only intended to be used in situations where one regular expression is all that can be used, such as when using an application that can't be programmed. When programming, Recipe 3.21 presents a far more efficient solution.

See Also

Recipe 5.10 shows how to match complete lines that *do* contain a particular word.

5.12 Trim Leading and Trailing Whitespace

Problem

You want to remove leading and trailing whitespace from a string.

Solution

To keep things simple and fast, the best all-around solution is to use two substitutions—one to remove leading whitespace, and another to remove trailing whitespace:

```
^\s+
```

Regex options: None ("^ and $ match at line breaks" must not be set)

Regex flavors: .NET, Java, JavaScript, PCRE, Perl, Python, Ruby

```
\s+$
```
Regex options: None ("^ and $ match at line breaks" must not be set)
Regex flavors: .NET, Java, JavaScript, PCRE, Perl, Python, Ruby

Simply replace matches found using both of these regular expressions with the empty string. Recipe 3.14 shows you how. With both regular expressions, you only need to replace the first match found since they match all leading or trailing whitespace in one go.

Discussion

Removing leading and trailing whitespace is a simple but common task. The two regular expressions just shown each contain three parts: an anchor to assert position at the beginning or end of the string (‹^› and ‹$›, respectively), the shorthand character class to match any whitespace character (‹\s›), and the quantifier to repeat the class one or more times (‹+›).

Many programming languages provide a function, usually called `trim` or `strip`, that can remove leading and trailing whitespace for you. Table 5-2 shows how to use this built-in function or method in a variety of programming languages.

Table 5-2. Standard functions to remove leading and trailing whitespace

Programming language(s)	Example usage
C#, VB.NET	`String.Trim([chars])`
Java	`string.trim()`
PHP	`trim($string)`
Python, Ruby	`string.strip()`

JavaScript and Perl do not have an equivalent function in their standard libraries, but you can easily create your own.

In Perl:

```
sub trim {
    my $string = shift;
    $string =~ s/^\s+//;
    $string =~ s/\s+$//;
    return $string;
}
```

In JavaScript:

```
function trim (string) {
    return string.replace(/^\s+/, '').replace(/\s+$/, '');
}
```

```
// Alternatively, use this to make trim a method of all strings:
String.prototype.trim = function () {
    return this.replace(/^\s+/, '').replace(/\s+$/, '');
};
```

 In both Perl and JavaScript, ‹\s› matches any character defined as white-space by the Unicode standard, in addition to the space, tab, line feed, and carriage return characters that are most commonly considered whitespace.

Variations

There are in fact a wide variety of ways you can write a regular expression to help you trim a string. However, they are invariably slower than using two simple substitutions when working with long strings (when performance matters most). Following are some of the more common alternative solutions that you might encounter. They are all written in JavaScript, and since JavaScript doesn't have a "dot matches line breaks" option, the regular expressions use ‹[\s\S]› to match any single character, including line breaks. In other programming languages, use a dot instead, and enable the "dot matches line breaks" option.

```
string.replace(/^\s+|\s+$/g, '');
```
> This is probably the most common solution. It combines the two simple regexes via alternation (see Recipe 2.8), and uses the /g (global) option to replace all matches, rather than just the first (it will match twice if there is both leading and trailing whitespace in the string). This isn't a terrible approach, but it's slower than using two simple substitutions when working with long strings.

```
string.replace(/^\s*([\s\S]*?)\s*$/, '$1')
```
> This regular expression works by matching the entire string and capturing the sequence from the first to the last nonwhitespace characters (if any) to backrefer-ence 1. By replacing the entire string with backreference 1, you're left with a trimmed version of the string.

> This approach is conceptually simple, but the lazy quantifier inside the capturing group makes the regex engine do a lot of extra work, and therefore tends to make this option slow with long subject strings. After the regex engine enters the capturing group during the matching process, the lazy quantifier requires that the ‹[\s\S]› character class be repeated as few times as possible. Thus, the regex engine matches one character at a time, stopping after each character to try to match the remaining pattern (‹\s*$›). If that fails because nonwhitespace characters remain somewhere after the current position in the string, the engine matches one more character and then tries the remainder of the pattern again.

```
string.replace(/^\s*([\s\S]*\S)?\s*$/, '$1')
```
> This is similar to the last regex, but it replaces the lazy quantifier with a greedy one for performance reasons. In order to make sure that the capturing group still only matches up to the last nonwhitespace character, we use a required trailing ‹\S›. However, since the regex must be able to match whitespace-only strings, the entire capturing group is made optional by adding a trailing question mark quantifier.
>
> Let's step back to look at how this actually works. Here, the greedy asterisk in ‹[\s\S]*› repeats the "any character" pattern until the end of the string. The regex engine then backtracks from the end of the string one character at a time until it's able to match the following ‹\S›, or until it's backtracked to the first character matched within the capturing group. Unless there's more trailing whitespace than there is text up until that point, this generally ends up being faster than the previous solution that used a lazy quantifier. Still, it can't compare to the performance of two simple substitutions.

```
string.replace(/^\s*(\S*(?:\s+\S+)*)\s*$/, '$1')
```
> This is a relatively common approach, so it's included here as a warning. There's no good reason to use this, because it's slower than all of the other solutions shown here. It's similar to the last two regexes in that it matches the entire string and replaces it with the part you want to keep, but because the inner, noncapturing group matches only one word at a time, there are a lot of discrete steps the regex engine must take. The performance hit will most likely be unnoticeable when trimming short strings, but with very long strings that contain lots of words, this regex can become a performance bottleneck.

Some regular expression implementations contain clever optimizations that alter the internal matching processes described here, and therefore make some of these options perform a bit better or worse than we've suggested. Nevertheless, the simplicity of using two substitutions provides consistently respectable performance with different string lengths and varying string contents, and it's therefore the best all-around solution.

See Also

Recipe 5.13

5.13 Replace Repeated Whitespace with a Single Space

Problem

As part of a cleanup routine for user input or other data, you want to replace repeated whitespace characters with a single space. Any tabs, line breaks, or other whitespace should also be replaced with a space.

Solution

To implement either of the following regular expressions, simply replace all matches with a single space character. Recipe 3.14 shows the code to do this.

Clean any whitespace characters

```
\s+
```
　　Regex options: None
　　Regex flavors: .NET, Java, JavaScript, PCRE, Perl, Python, Ruby

Clean horizontal whitespace characters

```
[●\t]+
```
　　Regex options: None
　　Regex flavors: .NET, Java, JavaScript, PCRE, Perl, Python, Ruby

Discussion

A common text cleanup routine is to replace repeated whitespace characters with a single space. In HTML, for example, repeated whitespace is simply ignored when rendering a page (with a few exceptions), so removing repeated whitespace can help to reduce the file size of pages without any negative effect.

Clean any whitespace characters

In this solution, any sequence of whitespace characters (line breaks, tabs, spaces, etc.) is replaced with a single space. Since the ‹+› quantifier repeats the whitespace class (‹\s›) one or more times, even a single tab character, for example, will be replaced with a space. If you replaced the ‹+› with ‹{2,}›, only sequences of two or more whitespace characters would be replaced. This could result in fewer replacements and thus improved performance, but it could also leave behind tab characters or line breaks that would otherwise be replaced with space characters. The better approach, therefore, depends on what you're trying to accomplish.

Clean horizontal whitespace characters

This works exactly like the previous solution, except that it leaves line breaks alone. Only tabs and spaces are replaced.

See Also

Recipe 5.12

5.14 Escape Regular Expression Metacharacters

Problem

You want to use a literal string provided by a user or from some other source as part of a regular expression. However, you want to escape all regular expression metacharacters within the string before embedding this string in your regex, to avoid any unintended consequences.

Solution

By adding a backslash before any characters that potentially have special meaning within a regular expression, you can safely use the resulting pattern to match a literal sequence of characters. Of the programming languages covered by this book, all except JavaScript have a built-in function or method to perform this task (listed in Table 5-3). However, for the sake of completeness, we'll show how to pull this off using your own regex, even in the languages that have a ready-made solution.

Built-in solutions

Table 5-3 lists the native functions designed to solve this problem.

Table 5-3. Native solutions for escaping regular expression metacharacters

Language	Function
C#, VB.NET	Regex.Escape(str)
Java	Pattern.quote(str)
Perl	quotemeta(str)
PHP	preg_quote(str, [delimiter])
Python	re.escape(str)
Ruby	Regexp.escape(str)

Notably absent from the list is JavaScript, which does not have a built-in function designed for this purpose.

Regular expression

Although it's best to use a built-in solution if available, you can pull this off on your own by using the following regular expression along with the appropriate replacement string (shown next). Just make sure to replace all matches, rather than only the first. Recipe 3.15 shows code for replacing matches with a string that contains a backreference. You'll need a backreference here to bring back the matched special character along with a preceding backslash:

```
[[\]{}()*+?.\\|^$\-,&#\s]
```

Regex options: None
Regex flavors: .NET, Java, JavaScript, PCRE, Perl, Python, Ruby

Replacement

 The following replacement strings contain a literal backslash character. The strings are shown without the extra backslashes that may be needed to escape backslashes when using string literals in some programming languages. See Recipe 2.19 for more details about replacement text flavors.

`\$&`
Replacement text flavors: .NET, JavaScript

`\\$&`
Replacement text flavor: Perl

`\\$0`
Replacement text flavors: Java, PHP

`\\\0`
Replacement text flavors: PHP, Ruby

`\\\&`
Replacement text flavor: Ruby

`\\\g<0>`
Replacement text flavor: Python

Example JavaScript function

Here's an example of how you can put the regular expression and replacement string to use to create a static method called `RegExp.escape` in JavaScript:

```
RegExp.escape = function (str) {
    return str.replace(/[[\]{}()*+?.\\|^$\-,&#\s]/g, "\\$&");
};

// Test it out...
var str = "Hello.World?";
var escaped_str = RegExp.escape(str);
alert(escaped_str == "Hello\\.World\\?"); // -> true
```

Discussion

This recipe's regular expression puts all the regex metacharacters inside a single character class. Let's take a look at each of those characters, and examine why they need to be escaped. Some are less obvious than others:

[] {} ()

‹[› and ‹]› create character classes. ‹{› and ‹}› create interval quantifiers and are also used with some other special constructs, such as Unicode properties. ‹(› and ‹)› are used for grouping, capturing, and other special constructs.

* + ?

These three characters are quantifiers that repeat their preceding element zero or more, one or more, or between zero and one time, respectively. The question mark is also used after an opening parenthesis to create special groupings and other constructs (the same is true for the asterisk in Perl 5.10 and PCRE 7).

. \ |

A dot matches any character within a line or string, a backslash escapes a special character or makes a literal character special, and a vertical bar alternates between multiple options.

^ $

The caret and dollar symbols are anchors that match the start or end of a line or string. The caret can also negate a character class.

The remaining characters matched by the regular expression are only special in special circumstances. They're included in the list to err on the side of caution.

-

A hyphen creates a range within a character class. It's escaped here to avoid inadvertently creating ranges when embedding text in the middle of a character class. Keep in mind that if you do embed text inside a character class, the resulting regex will not match the embedded string, but rather any one of the characters in the embedded string.

,

A comma is used inside an interval quantifier such as ‹{1,5}›. Since most regular expression flavors treat curly brackets as literal characters if they do not form a valid quantifier, it's possible (though a bit unlikely) to create a quantifier where there was none before when inserting literal text in a regex if you don't escape commas.

&

The ampersand is included in the list because two ampersands in a row are used for character class intersection in Java. In other programming languages, it's safe to remove the ampersand from the list of characters that need to be escaped, but it doesn't hurt to keep it.

and whitespace

The pound sign and whitespace (matched by ‹\s›) are metacharacters only if the free-spacing option is enabled. Again, it doesn't hurt to escape them anyway.

As for the replacement text, one of five tokens («$&», «\&», «$0», «\0», or «\g<0>») is used to restore the matched character along with a preceding backslash. In Perl, $& is actually a variable, and using it with any regular expression imposes a global performance penalty on all regular expressions. If $& is used elsewhere in your Perl program, it's OK to use it as much as you want because you've already paid the price. Otherwise, it's probably better to wrap the entire regex in a capturing group, and use $1 instead of $& in the replacement.

Variations

As explained in "Block escape" on page 27 in Recipe 2.1, you can create a block escape sequence within a regex using ‹\Q···\E›. However, block escapes are only supported by Java, PCRE, and Perl, and even in those languages block escapes are not foolproof. For complete safety, you'd still need to escape any occurrence of \E within the string you plan to embed in your regex. In most cases it's probably easier to just use the cross-language approach of escaping all regex metacharacters.

See Also

Recipe 2.1 discusses how to match literal characters; its list of characters that need to be escaped is shorter since it doesn't concern itself with characters that may need to be escaped in free-spacing mode or when dropped into an arbitrary, longer pattern.

## CHAPTER 6

Numbers

Regular expressions are designed to deal with text, and don't understand the numerical meanings that humans assign to strings of digits. To a regular expression, 56 is not the number fifty-six, but a string consisting of two characters displayed as the digits 5 and 6. The regex engine knows they're digits, because the shorthand character class ‹\d› matches them (see Recipe 2.3). But that's it. It doesn't know that 56 has a higher meaning, just as it doesn't know that :-) is anything but three punctuation characters matched by ‹\p{P}{3}›.

But numbers are some of the most important input you're likely to deal with, and sometimes you need to process them inside a regular expression instead of just passing them to a conventional programming language when you want to answer questions such as, "Is this number within the range 1 through 100?" So we've devoted a whole chapter to matching all kinds of numbers with regular expressions. We start off with a few recipes that may seem trivial, but actually explain important basic concepts. The later recipes that deal with more complicated regexes assume you grasp these basic concepts.

6.1 Integer Numbers

Problem

You want to find various kinds of integer decimal numbers in a larger body of text, or check whether a string variable holds an integer decimal number.

Solution

Find any positive integer decimal number in a larger body of text:

```
\b[0-9]+\b
```
Regex options: None
Regex flavors: .NET, Java, JavaScript, PCRE, Perl, Python, Ruby

Check if a text string holds just a positive integer decimal number:

`\A[0-9]+\Z`
Regex options: None
Regex flavors: .NET, Java, PCRE, Perl, Python, Ruby

`^[0-9]+$`
Regex options: None
Regex flavors: .NET, Java, JavaScript, PCRE, Perl, Python

Find any positive integer decimal number that stands alone in a larger body of text:

`(?<=^|\s)[0-9]+(?=$|\s)`
Regex options: None
Regex flavors: .NET, Java, PCRE, Perl, Python, Ruby 1.9

Find any positive integer decimal number that stands alone in a larger body of text, allowing leading whitespace to be included in the regex match:

`(^|\s)([0-9]+)(?=$|\s)`
Regex options: None
Regex flavors: .NET, Java, JavaScript, PCRE, Perl, Python, Ruby

Find any integer decimal number with an optional leading plus or minus sign:

`[+-]?\b[0-9]+\b`
Regex options: None
Regex flavors: .NET, Java, JavaScript, PCRE, Perl, Python, Ruby

Check whether a text string holds just an integer decimal number with optional sign:

`\A[+-]?[0-9]+\Z`
Regex options: None
Regex flavors: .NET, Java, PCRE, Perl, Python, Ruby

`^[+-]?[0-9]+$`
Regex options: None
Regex flavors: .NET, Java, JavaScript, PCRE, Perl, Python

Find any integer decimal number with optional sign, allowing whitespace between the number and the sign, but no leading whitespace without the sign:

`([+-]●*)?\b[0-9]+\b`
Regex options: None
Regex flavors: .NET, Java, JavaScript, PCRE, Perl, Python, Ruby

Discussion

An integer number is a contiguous series of one or more digits, each between zero and nine. We can easily represent this with a character class (Recipe 2.3) and a quantifier (Recipe 2.12): ‹[0-9]+›.

We prefer to use the explicit range ‹[0-9]› instead of the shorthand ‹\d›. In .NET and Perl, ‹\d› matches any digit in any script, but ‹[0-9]› always just matches the 10 digits in the ASCII table. If you know your subject text doesn't include any non-ASCII digits, you can save a few keystrokes and use ‹\d› instead of ‹[0-9]›.

If you don't know whether your subject will include digits outside the ASCII table, you need to think about what you want to do with the regex matches and what the user's expectations are in order to decide whether you should use ‹\d› or ‹[0-9]›. If you plan to convert the text matched by the regular expression into an integer, check whether the string-to-integer function in your programming language can interpret non-ASCII digits. Users writing documents in their native scripts will expect your software to recognize digits in their native scripts.

Beyond being a series of digits, the number must also stand alone. A4 is a paper size, not a number. There are several ways to make sure your regex only matches pure numbers.

If you want to check whether your string holds nothing but a number, simply put start-of-string and end-of-string anchors around your regex. ‹\A› and ‹\Z› are your best option, because their meaning doesn't change. Unfortunately, JavaScript doesn't support them. In JavaScript, use ‹^› and ‹$›, and make sure you don't specify the /m flag that makes the caret and dollar match at line breaks. In Ruby, the caret and dollar always match at line breaks, so you can't reliably use them to force your regex to match the whole string.

When searching for numbers within a larger body of text, word boundaries (Recipe 2.6) are an easy solution. When you place them before or after a regex token that matches a digit, the word boundary makes sure there is no word character before or after the matched digit. For example, ‹4› matches 4 in A4. ‹4\b› does too, because there's no word character after the 4. ‹\b4› and ‹\b4\b› don't match anything in A4, because ‹\b› fails between the two word characters A and 4. In regular expressions, word characters include letters, digits and underscores.

If you include nonword characters such as plus or minus signs or whitespace in your regex, you have to be careful with the placement of word boundaries. To match +4 while excluding +4B, use ‹\+4\b› instead of ‹\b\+4\b›. The latter does not match +4, because there's no word character before the plus in the subject string to satisfy the word boundary. ‹\b\+4\b› does match +4 in the text 3+4, because 3 is a word character and + is not.

‹\+4\b› only needs one word boundary. The first ‹\b› in ‹\+\b4\b› is superfluous. When this regex matches, the first ‹\b› is always between a + and a 4, and thus never excludes anything. The first ‹\b› becomes important when the plus sign is optional. ‹\+?\b4\b› does not match the 4 in A4, whereas ‹\+?4\b› does.

Word boundaries are not always the right solution. Consider the subject text `$123,456.78`. If you iterate over this string with the regex ‹\b[0-9]+\b›, it'll match 123, 456, and 78. The dollar sign, comma, and decimal point are not word characters, so the word boundary matches between a digit and any of these characters. Sometimes this is what you want, sometimes not.

If you only want to find integers surrounded by whitespace or the start or end of a string, you need to use lookaround instead of word boundaries. ‹(?=$|\s)› matches at the end of the string or before a character that is whitespace (whitespace includes line breaks). ‹(?<=^|\s)› matches either at the start of the string, or after a character that is whitespace. You can replace ‹\s› with a character class that matches any of the characters you want to allow before or after the number. See Recipe 2.16 to learn how lookaround works.

JavaScript and Ruby 1.8 don't support lookbehind. You can use a normal group instead of lookbehind to check if the number occurs at the start of the string, or if it is preceded by whitespace. The drawback is that the whitespace character will be included in the overall regex match if the number doesn't occur at the start of the string. An easy solution to that is to put the part of the regex that matches the number inside a capturing group. The fifth regex in the section "Solution" captures the whitespace character in the first capturing group and the matched integer in the second capturing group.

See Also

Recipes 2.3 and 2.12

6.2 Hexadecimal Numbers

Problem

You want to find hexadecimal numbers in a larger body of text, or check whether a string variable holds a hexadecimal number.

Solution

Find any hexadecimal number in a larger body of text:

    \b[0-9A-F]+\b
        Regex options: Case insensitive
        Regex flavors: .NET, Java, JavaScript, PCRE, Perl, Python, Ruby

    \b[0-9A-Fa-f]+\b
        Regex options: None
        Regex flavors: .NET, Java, JavaScript, PCRE, Perl, Python, Ruby

Check if a text string holds just a hexadecimal number:

> `\A[0-9A-F]+\Z`
>
> **Regex options:** Case insensitive
>
> **Regex flavors:** .NET, Java, PCRE, Perl, Python, Ruby

> `^[0-9A-F]+$`
>
> **Regex options:** Case insensitive
>
> **Regex flavors:** .NET, Java, JavaScript, PCRE, Perl, Python

Find a hexadecimal number with a `0x` prefix:

> `\b0x[0-9A-F]+\b`
>
> **Regex options:** Case insensitive
>
> **Regex flavors:** .NET, Java, JavaScript, PCRE, Perl, Python, Ruby

Find a hexadecimal number with an `&H` prefix:

> `&H[0-9A-F]+\b`
>
> **Regex options:** Case insensitive
>
> **Regex flavors:** .NET, Java, JavaScript, PCRE, Perl, Python, Ruby

Find a hexadecimal number with an `H` suffix:

> `\b[0-9A-F]+H\b`
>
> **Regex options:** Case insensitive
>
> **Regex flavors:** .NET, Java, JavaScript, PCRE, Perl, Python, Ruby

Find a hexadecimal byte value or 8-bit number:

> `\b[0-9A-F]{2}\b`
>
> **Regex options:** Case insensitive
>
> **Regex flavors:** .NET, Java, JavaScript, PCRE, Perl, Python, Ruby

Find a hexadecimal word value or 16-bit number:

> `\b[0-9A-F]{4}\b`
>
> **Regex options:** Case insensitive
>
> **Regex flavors:** .NET, Java, JavaScript, PCRE, Perl, Python, Ruby

Find a hexadecimal double word value or 32-bit number:

> `\b[0-9A-F]{8}\b`
>
> **Regex options:** Case insensitive
>
> **Regex flavors:** .NET, Java, JavaScript, PCRE, Perl, Python, Ruby

Find a hexadecimal quad word value or 64-bit number:

> `\b[0-9A-F]{16}\b`
>
> **Regex options:** Case insensitive
>
> **Regex flavors:** .NET, Java, JavaScript, PCRE, Perl, Python, Ruby

Find a string of hexadecimal bytes (i.e., an even number of hexadecimal digits):

```
\b(?:[0-9A-F]{2})+\b
```
Regex options: Case insensitive
Regex flavors: .NET, Java, JavaScript, PCRE, Perl, Python, Ruby

Discussion

The techniques for matching hexadecimal integers with a regular expression is the same as matching decimal integers. The only difference is that the character class that matches a single digit now has to include the letters A through F. You have to consider whether the letters must be either uppercase or lowercase, or if mixed case is permitted. The regular expressions shown here all allow mixed case.

By default, regular expressions are case-sensitive. ‹[0-9a-f]› allows only lowercase hexadecimal digits, and ‹[0-9A-F]› allows only uppercase hexadecimal digits. To allow mixed case, use ‹[0-9a-fA-F]› or turn on the option to make your regular expression case insensitive. Recipe 3.4 explains how to do that with the programming languages covered by this book. The first regex in the solution is shown twice, using the two different ways of making it case-insensitive. The others shown use only the second method.

If you only want to allow uppercase letters in hexadecimal numbers, use the regexes shown with case insensitivity turned off. To allow only lowercase letters, turn off case insensitivity and replace ‹A-F› with ‹a-f›.

‹(?:[0-9A-F]{2})+› matches an even number of hexadecimal digits. ‹[0-9A-F]{2}› matches exactly two hexadecimal digits. ‹(?:[0-9A-F]{2})+› does that one or more times. The noncapturing group (see Recipe 2.9) is required because the plus needs to repeat the character class and the quantifier ‹{2}› combined. ‹[0-9]{2}+› is not a syntax error in Java, PCRE, and Perl 5.10, but it doesn't do what you want. The extra ‹+› makes the ‹{2}› possessive. That has no effect, because ‹{2}› cannot repeat fewer than two times anyway.

Several of the solutions show how to require the hexadecimal number to have one of the prefixes or suffixes commonly used to identify hexadecimal numbers. These are used to differentiate between decimal numbers and hexadecimal numbers that happen to consist of only decimal digits. For example, 10 could be the decimal number between 9 and 11, or the hexadecimal number between F and 11.

Most solutions are shown with word boundaries (Recipe 2.6). Use word boundaries as shown to find numbers within a larger body of text. Notice that the regex using the &H prefix does not have a word boundary at the start. That's because the ampersand is not a word boundary. If we put a word boundary at the start of that regex, it would only find hexadecimal numbers immediately after a word character.

If you want to check whether your string holds nothing but a hexadecimal number, simply put start-of-string and end-of-string anchors around your regex. ‹\A› and ‹\Z› are your best options, because their meanings don't change. Unfortunately, JavaScript doesn't support them. In JavaScript, use ‹^› and ‹$›, and make sure you don't specify the /m flag that makes the caret and dollar match at line breaks. In Ruby, the caret and dollar always match at line breaks, so you can't reliably use them to force your regex to match the whole string.

See Also

Recipes 2.3 and 2.12

6.3 Binary Numbers

Problem

You want to find binary numbers in a larger body of text, or check whether a string variable holds a binary number.

Solution

Find a binary number in a larger body of text:

```
\b[01]+\b
```
Regex options: None
Regex flavors: .NET, Java, JavaScript, PCRE, Perl, Python, Ruby

Check whether a text string holds just a binary number:

```
\A[01]+\Z
```
Regex options: None
Regex flavors: .NET, Java, PCRE, Perl, Python, Ruby

```
^[01]+$
```
Regex options: None
Regex flavors: .NET, Java, JavaScript, PCRE, Perl, Python

Find a binary number with a B suffix:

```
\b[01]+B\b
```
Regex options: Case insensitive
Regex flavors: .NET, Java, JavaScript, PCRE, Perl, Python, Ruby

Find a binary byte value or 8-bit number:

```
\b[01]{8}\b
```
Regex options: None
Regex flavors: .NET, Java, JavaScript, PCRE, Perl, Python, Ruby

Find a binary word value or 16-bit number:

```
\b[01]{16}\b
```
Regex options: None
Regex flavors: .NET, Java, JavaScript, PCRE, Perl, Python, Ruby

Find a string of bytes (i.e., a multiple of eight bits):

```
\b(?:[01]{8})+\b
```
Regex options: None
Regex flavors: .NET, Java, JavaScript, PCRE, Perl, Python, Ruby

Discussion

All these regexes use techniques explained in the previous two recipes. The key difference is that each digit is now a 0 or a 1. We easily match that with a character class that includes just those two characters: ‹[01]›.

See Also

Recipes 2.3 and 2.12

6.4 Strip Leading Zeros

Problem

You want to match an integer number, and either return the number without any leading zeros or delete the leading zeros.

Solution

Regular expression

```
\b0*([1-9][0-9]*|0)\b
```
Regex options: None
Regex flavors: .NET, Java, JavaScript, PCRE, Perl, Python, Ruby

Replacement

```
$1
```
Replacement text flavors: .NET, Java, JavaScript, PHP, Perl

```
\1
```
Replacement text flavors: PHP, Python, Ruby

Getting the numbers in Perl

```perl
while ($subject =~ m/\b0*([1-9][0-9]*|0)\b/g) {
    push(@list, $1);
}
```

Stripping leading zeros in PHP

```php
$result = preg_replace('/\b0*([1-9][0-9]*|0)\b/', '$1', $subject);
```

Discussion

We use a capturing group to separate a number from its leading zeros. Before the group, ‹0*› matches the leading zeros, if any. Within the group, ‹[1-9][0-9]*› matches a number that consists of one or more digits, with the first digit being nonzero. The number can begin with a zero only if the number is zero itself. The word boundaries make sure we don't match partial numbers, as explained in Recipe 6.1.

To get a list of all numbers in the subject text without leading zeros, iterate over the regex matches as explained in Recipe 3.11. Inside the loop, retrieve the text matched by the first (and only) capturing group, as explained in Recipe 3.9. The solution for this shows how you could do this in Perl.

Stripping the leading zeros is easy with a search-and-replace. Our regex has a capturing group that separates the number from its leading zeros. If we replace the overall regex match (the number including the leading zeros) with the text matched by the first capturing group, we've effectively stripped out the leading zeros. The solution shows how to do this in PHP. Recipe 3.15 shows how to do it in other programming languages.

See Also

Recipes 3.15 and 6.1

6.5 Numbers Within a Certain Range

Problem

You want to match an integer number within a certain range of numbers. You want the regular expression to specify the range accurately, rather than just limiting the number of digits.

Solution

1 to 12 (hour or month):

```
^(1[0-2]|[1-9])$
```
Regex options: None
Regex flavors: .NET, Java, JavaScript, PCRE, Perl, Python, Ruby

1 to 24 (hour):

`^(2[0-4]|1[0-9]|[1-9])$`
Regex options: None
Regex flavors: .NET, Java, JavaScript, PCRE, Perl, Python, Ruby

1 to 31 (day of the month):

`^(3[01]|[12][0-9]|[1-9])$`
Regex options: None
Regex flavors: .NET, Java, JavaScript, PCRE, Perl, Python, Ruby

1 to 53 (week of the year):

`^(5[0-3]|[1-4][0-9]|[1-9])$`
Regex options: None
Regex flavors: .NET, Java, JavaScript, PCRE, Perl, Python, Ruby

0 to 59 (minute or second):

`^[1-5]?[0-9]$`
Regex options: None
Regex flavors: .NET, Java, JavaScript, PCRE, Perl, Python, Ruby

0 to 100 (percentage):

`^(100|[1-9]?[0-9])$`
Regex options: None
Regex flavors: .NET, Java, JavaScript, PCRE, Perl, Python, Ruby

1 to 100:

`^(100|[1-9][0-9]?)$`
Regex options: None
Regex flavors: .NET, Java, JavaScript, PCRE, Perl, Python, Ruby

32 to 126 (printable ASCII codes):

`^(12[0-6]|1[01][0-9]|[4-9][0-9]|3[2-9])$`
Regex options: None
Regex flavors: .NET, Java, JavaScript, PCRE, Perl, Python, Ruby

0 to 127 (nonnegative signed byte):

`^(12[0-7]|1[01][0-9]|[1-9]?[0-9])$`
Regex options: None
Regex flavors: .NET, Java, JavaScript, PCRE, Perl, Python, Ruby

−128 to 127 (signed byte):

`^(12[0-7]|1[01][0-9]|[1-9]?[0-9]|-(12[0-8]|1[01][0-9]|[1-9]?[0-9]))$`
Regex options: None
Regex flavors: .NET, Java, JavaScript, PCRE, Perl, Python, Ruby

0 to 255 (unsigned byte):

```
^(25[0-5]|2[0-4][0-9]|1[0-9]{2}|[1-9]?[0-9])$
```
Regex options: None
Regex flavors: .NET, Java, JavaScript, PCRE, Perl, Python, Ruby

1 to 366 (day of the year):

```
^(36[0-6]|3[0-5][0-9]|[12][0-9]{2}|[1-9][0-9]?)$
```
Regex options: None
Regex flavors: .NET, Java, JavaScript, PCRE, Perl, Python, Ruby

1900 to 2099 (year):

```
^(19|20)[0-9]{2}$
```
Regex options: None
Regex flavors: .NET, Java, JavaScript, PCRE, Perl, Python, Ruby

0 to 32767 (nonnegative signed word):

```
^(3276[0-7]|327[0-5][0-9]|32[0-6][0-9]{2}|3[01][0-9]{3}|[12][0-9]{4}|↵
[1-9][0-9]{1,3}|[0-9])$
```
Regex options: None
Regex flavors: .NET, Java, JavaScript, PCRE, Perl, Python, Ruby

−32768 to 32767 (signed word):

```
^(3276[0-7]|327[0-5][0-9]|32[0-6][0-9]{2}|3[01][0-9]{3}|[12][0-9]{4}|↵
[1-9][0-9]{1,3}|[0-9]|-(3276[0-8]|327[0-5][0-9]|32[0-6][0-9]{2}|↵
3[01][0-9]{3}|[12][0-9]{4}|[1-9][0-9]{1,3}|[0-9]))$
```
Regex options: None
Regex flavors: .NET, Java, JavaScript, PCRE, Perl, Python, Ruby

0 to 65535 (unsigned word):

```
^(6553[0-5]|655[0-2][0-9]|65[0-4][0-9]{2}|6[0-4][0-9]{3}|[1-5][0-9]{4}|↵
[1-9][0-9]{1,3}|[0-9])$
```
Regex options: None
Regex flavors: .NET, Java, JavaScript, PCRE, Perl, Python, Ruby

Discussion

The previous recipes matched integers with any number of digits, or with a certain number of digits. They allowed the full range of digits for all the digits in the number. Such regular expressions are very straightforward.

Matching a number in a specific range—e.g., a number between 0 and 255—is not a simple task with regular expressions. You can't write ‹[0-255]›. Well, you could, but it wouldn't match a number between 0 and 255. This character class, which is equivalent to ‹[0125]›, matches a single character that is one of the digits 0, 1, 2, or 5.

Because these regular expressions are quite a bit longer, the solutions all use anchors to make the regex suitable to check whether a string, such as user input, consists of a single acceptable number. Recipe 6.1 explains how you can use word boundaries or lookaround instead of the anchors for other purposes. In the discussion, we show the regexes without any anchors, keep the focus on dealing with numeric ranges. If you want to use any of these regexes, you'll have to add anchors or word boundaries to make sure your regex doesn't match digits that are part of a longer number.

Regular expressions work character by character. If we want to match a number that consists of more than one digit, we have to spell out all the possible combinations for the digits. The essential building blocks are character classes (Recipe 2.3) and alternation (Recipe 2.8).

In character classes, we can use ranges for single digits, such as ‹[0-5]›. That's because the characters for the digits 0 through 9 occupy consecutive positions in the ASCII and Unicode character tables. ‹[0-5]› matches one of six characters, just like ‹[j-o]› and ‹[\x09-\x0E]› match different ranges of six characters.

When a numeric range is represented as text, it consists of a number of positions. Each position allows a certain range of digits. Some ranges have a fixed number of positions, such as 12 to 24. Others have a variable number of positions, such as 1 to 12. The range of digits allowed by each position can be either interdependent or independent of the digits in the other positions. In the range 40 to 59, the positions are independent. In the range 44 to 55, the positions are interdependent.

The easiest ranges are those with a fixed number of independent positions, such as 40 to 59. To code these as a regular expression, all you need to do is to string together a bunch of character classes. Use one character class for each position, specifying the range of digits allowed at that position.

[45][0-9]
Regex options: None
Regex flavors: .NET, Java, JavaScript, PCRE, Perl, Python, Ruby

The range 40 to 59 requires a number with two digits. Thus we need two character classes. The first digit must be a 4 or 5. The character class ‹[45]› maches either digit. The second digit can be any of the 10 digits. ‹[0-9]› does the trick.

We could also have used the shorthand ‹\d› instead of ‹[0-9]›. We use the explicit range ‹[0-9]› for consistency with the other character classes, to help maintain readability. Reducing the number of backslashes in your regexes is also very helpful if you're working with a programming language such as Java that requires backslashes to be escaped in literal strings.

The numbers in the range 44 to 55 also need two positions, but they're not independent. The first digit must be 4 or 5. If the first digit is 4, the second digit must be between 4 and 9. That covers the numbers 44 to 49. If the first digit is 5, the second digit must be between 0 and 5. That covers the numbers 50 to 55. To create our regex, we simply use alternation to combine the two ranges:

4[4-9]|5[0-5]
Regex options: None
Regex flavors: .NET, Java, JavaScript, PCRE, Perl, Python, Ruby

By using alternation, we're telling the regex engine to match ‹4[4-9]› or ‹5[0-5]›. The alternation operator has the lowest precedence of all regex operators, and so we don't need to group the digits, as in ‹(4[4-9])|(5[0-5])›.

You can string together as many ranges using alternation as you want. The range 34 to 65 also has two interdependent positions. The first digit must be between 3 and 6. If the first digit is 3, the second must be 4 to 9. If the first is 4 or 5, the second can be any digit. If the first is 6, the second must be 0 to 5:

3[4-9]|[45][0-9]|6[0-5]
Regex options: None
Regex flavors: .NET, Java, JavaScript, PCRE, Perl, Python, Ruby

Just like we use alternation to split ranges with interdependent positions into multiple ranges with independent positions, we can use alternation to split ranges with a variable number of positions into multiple ranges with a fixed number of positions. The range 1 to 12 has numbers with one or two positions. We split this into the range 1 to 9 with one position, and the range 10 to 12 with two positions. The positions in each of these two ranges are independent, so we don't need to split them up further:

1[0-2]|[1-9]
Regex options: None
Regex flavors: .NET, Java, JavaScript, PCRE, Perl, Python, Ruby

We listed the range with two digits before the one with a single digit. This is intentional because the regular expression engine is *eager*. It scans the alternatives from left to right, and stops as soon as one matches. If your subject text is 12, then ‹1[0-2]|[1-9]› matches <u>12</u>, whereas ‹[1-9]|1[0-2]› matches just ‹1›. The first alternative, ‹[1-9]›, is tried first. Since that alternative is happy to match just <u>1</u>, the regex engine never tries to check whether ‹1[0-2]› might offer a "better" solution.

Some Regex Engines Are Not Eager

POSIX-compliant regex engines and DFA regex engines do not follow this rule. They try all alternatives, and return the one that finds the longest match. All the flavors discussed in this book, however, are NFA engines, which don't do the extra work required by POSIX. They will all tell you that ‹[1-9]|1[0-2]› matches <u>1</u> in 12.

In practice, you'll usually use anchors or word boundaries around your list of alternatives. Then the order of alternatives doesn't really matter. ‹^([1-9]|1[0-2])$› and ‹^(1[0-2]|[1-9])$› both match **12** in 12 with all regex flavors in this book, as well as POSIX "extended" regular expressions and DFA engines. The anchors require the regex to match either the whole string or nothing at all. DFA and NFA are defined in the sidebar "History of the Term 'Regular Expression'" on page 2 in Chapter 1.

The range 85 to 117 includes numbers of two different lengths. The range 85 to 99 has two positions, and the range 100 to 117 has three positions. The positions in these ranges are interdependent, and so we have to split them up further. For the two-digit range, if the first digit is 8, the second must be between 5 and 9. If the first digit is 9, the second digit can be any digit. For the three-digit range, the first position allows only the digit 1. If the second position has the digit 0, the third position allows any digit. But if the second digit is 1, then the third digit must be between 0 and 7. This gives us four ranges total: 85 to 89, 90 to 99, 100 to 109, and 110 to 117. Though things are getting long-winded, the regular expression remains as straightforward as the previous ones:

    8[5-9]|9[0-9]|10[0-9]|11[0-7]
    Regex options: None
    Regex flavors: .NET, Java, JavaScript, PCRE, Perl, Python, Ruby

That's all there really is to matching numeric ranges with regular expressions: simply split up the range until you have ranges with a fixed number of positions with independent digits. This way, you'll always get a correct regular expression that is easy to read and maintain, even if it may get a bit long-winded.

There are some extra techniques that allow for shorter regular expressions. For example, using the previous system, the range 0 to 65535 would require this regex:

    6553[0-5]|655[0-2][0-9]|65[0-4][0-9][0-9]|6[0-4][0-9][0-9][0-9]|↵
    [1-5][0-9][0-9][0-9][0-9]|[1-9][0-9][0-9][0-9]|[1-9][0-9][0-9]|↵
    [1-9][0-9]|[0-9]
    Regex options: None
    Regex flavors: .NET, Java, JavaScript, PCRE, Perl, Python, Ruby

This regular expression works perfectly, and you won't be able to come up with a regex that runs measurably faster. Any optimizations that could be made (e.g., there are various alternatives starting with a 6) are already made by the regular expression engine when it compiles your regular expression. There's no need to waste your time to make your regex more complicated in the hopes of getting it faster. But you can make your regex shorter, to reduce the amount of typing you need to do, while still keeping it readable.

Several of the alternatives have identical character classes next to each other. You can eliminate the duplication by using quantifiers. Recipe 2.12 tells you all about those.

```
6553[0-5]|655[0-2][0-9]|65[0-4][0-9]{2}|6[0-4][0-9]{3}|[1-5][0-9]{4}|↵
[1-9][0-9]{3}|[1-9][0-9]{2}|[1-9][0-9]|[0-9]
```
Regex options: None
Regex flavors: .NET, Java, JavaScript, PCRE, Perl, Python, Ruby

The ‹[1-9][0-9]{3}|[1-9][0-9]{2}|[1-9][0-9]› part of the regex has three very similar alternatives, and they all have the same pair of character classes. The only difference is the number of times the second class is repeated. We can easily combine that into ‹[1-9][0-9]{1,3}›.

```
6553[0-5]|655[0-2][0-9]|65[0-4][0-9]{2}|6[0-4][0-9]{3}|[1-5][0-9]{4}|↵
[1-9][0-9]{1,3}|[0-9]
```
Regex options: None
Regex flavors: .NET, Java, JavaScript, PCRE, Perl, Python, Ruby

Any further tricks will hurt readability. For example, you could isolate the leading 6 from the first four alternatives:

```
6(?:553[0-5]|55[0-2][0-9]|5[0-4][0-9]{2}|[0-4][0-9]{3})|[1-5][0-9]{4}|↵
[1-9][0-9]{1,3}|[0-9]
```
Regex options: None
Regex flavors: .NET, Java, JavaScript, PCRE, Perl, Python, Ruby

But this regex is actually one character longer because we had to add a noncapturing group to isolate the alternatives with the leading 6 from the other alternatives. You won't get a performance benefit with any of the regex flavors discussed in this book. They all make this optimization internally.

See Also

Recipes 2.8, 4.12, and 6.1

6.6 Hexadecimal Numbers Within a Certain Range

Problem

You want to match a hexadecimal number within a certain range of numbers. You want the regular expression to specify the range accurately, rather than just limiting the number of digits.

Solution

1 to C (1 to 12: hour or month):

```
^[1-9a-c]$
```
Regex options: Case insensitive
Regex flavors: .NET, Java, JavaScript, PCRE, Perl, Python, Ruby

1 to 18 (1 to 24: hour):

```
^(1[0-8]|[1-9a-f])$
```
Regex options: Case insensitive
Regex flavors: .NET, Java, JavaScript, PCRE, Perl, Python, Ruby

1 to 1F (1 to 31: day of the month):

```
^(1[0-9a-f]|[1-9a-f])$
```
Regex options: Case insensitive
Regex flavors: .NET, Java, JavaScript, PCRE, Perl, Python, Ruby

1 to 35 (1 to 53: week of the year):

```
^(3[0-5]|[12][0-9a-f]|[1-9a-f])$
```
Regex options: Case insensitive
Regex flavors: .NET, Java, JavaScript, PCRE, Perl, Python, Ruby

0 to 3B (0 to 59: minute or second):

```
^(3[0-9a-b]|[12]?[0-9a-f])$
```
Regex options: Case insensitive
Regex flavors: .NET, Java, JavaScript, PCRE, Perl, Python, Ruby

0 to 64 (0 to 100: percentage):

```
^(6[0-4]|[1-5]?[0-9a-f])$
```
Regex options: Case insensitive
Regex flavors: .NET, Java, JavaScript, PCRE, Perl, Python, Ruby

1 to 64 (1 to 100):

```
^(6[0-4]|[1-5][0-9a-f]|[1-9a-f])$
```
Regex options: Case insensitive
Regex flavors: .NET, Java, JavaScript, PCRE, Perl, Python, Ruby

20 to 7E (32 to 126: printable ASCII codes):

```
^(7[0-9a-e]|[2-6][0-9a-f])$
```
Regex options: Case insensitive
Regex flavors: .NET, Java, JavaScript, PCRE, Perl, Python, Ruby

0 to 7F (0 to 127: 7-bit number):

```
^[1-7]?[0-9a-f]$
```
Regex options: Case insensitive
Regex flavors: .NET, Java, JavaScript, PCRE, Perl, Python, Ruby

0 to FF (0 to 255: 8-bit number):

```
^[1-9a-f]?[0-9a-f]$
```
Regex options: Case insensitive
Regex flavors: .NET, Java, JavaScript, PCRE, Perl, Python, Ruby

1 to 16E (1 to 366: day of the year):

```
^(16[0-9a-e]|1[0-5][0-9a-f]|[1-9a-f][0-9a-f]?)$
```
Regex options: Case insensitive
Regex flavors: .NET, Java, JavaScript, PCRE, Perl, Python, Ruby

76C to 833 (1900 to 2099: year):

```
^(83[0-3]|8[0-2][0-9a-f]|7[7-9a-f][0-9a-f]|76[c-f])$
```
Regex options: Case insensitive
Regex flavors: .NET, Java, JavaScript, PCRE, Perl, Python, Ruby

0 to 7FFF: (0 to 32767: 15-bit number):

```
^([1-7][0-9a-f]{3}|[1-9a-f][0-9a-f]{1,2}|[0-9a-f])$
```
Regex options: Case insensitive
Regex flavors: .NET, Java, JavaScript, PCRE, Perl, Python, Ruby

0 to FFFF: (0 to 65535: 16-bit number):

```
^([1-9a-f][0-9a-f]{1,3}|[0-9a-f])$
```
Regex options: Case insensitive
Regex flavors: .NET, Java, JavaScript, PCRE, Perl, Python, Ruby

Discussion

There's no difference between matching decimal numeric ranges and hexadecimal numeric ranges with a regular expression. As the previous recipe explains, split the range into multiple ranges, until each range has a fixed number of positions with independent hexadecimal digits. Then it's just a matter of using a character class for each position, and combining the ranges with alternation.

Since letters and digits occupy separate areas in the ASCII and Unicode character tables, you cannot use the character class ‹[0-F]› to match any of the 16 hexadecimal decimal digits. Though this character class will actually do that, it will also match the punctuation symbols that sit between the digits and the letters in the ASCII table. Instead, place two character ranges in the character class: [0-9A-F].

Another issue that comes into play is case-sensitivity. By default, regular expressions are case-sensitive. ‹[0-9A-F]› matches only uppercase characters, and ‹[0-9a-f]› matches only lowercase characters. ‹[0-9A-Fa-f]› matches both.

Explicitly typing both the uppercase and lowercase ranges in each character class quickly gets tedious. Turning on the case insensitivity option is much easier. See Recipe 3.4 to learn how to do that in your favorite programming language.

See Also

Recipes 2.8 and 6.2

6.7 Floating Point Numbers

Problem

You want to match a floating-point number and specify whether the sign, integer, fraction and exponent parts of the number are required, optional, or disallowed. You don't want to use the regular expression to restrict the numbers to a specific range, and instead leave that to procedural code, as explained in Recipe 3.12.

Solution

Mandatory sign, integer, fraction, and exponent:

`^[-+][0-9]+\.[0-9]+[eE][-+]?[0-9]+$`
    Regex options: None
    Regex flavors: .NET, Java, JavaScript, PCRE, Perl, Python, Ruby

Mandatory sign, integer, and fraction, but no exponent:

`^[-+][0-9]+\.[0-9]+$`
    Regex options: None
    Regex flavors: .NET, Java, JavaScript, PCRE, Perl, Python, Ruby

Optional sign, mandatory integer and fraction, and no exponent:

`^[-+]?[0-9]+\.[0-9]+$`
    Regex options: None
    Regex flavors: .NET, Java, JavaScript, PCRE, Perl, Python, Ruby

Optional sign and integer, mandatory fraction, and no exponent:

`^[-+]?[0-9]*\.[0-9]+$`
    Regex options: None
    Regex flavors: .NET, Java, JavaScript, PCRE, Perl, Python, Ruby

Optional sign, integer, and fraction. If the integer part is omitted, the fraction is mandatory. If the fraction is omitted, the decimal dot must be omitted, too. No exponent.

`^[-+]?([0-9]+(\.[0-9]+)?|\.[0-9]+)$`
    Regex options: None
    Regex flavors: .NET, Java, JavaScript, PCRE, Perl, Python, Ruby

Optional sign, integer, and fraction. If the integer part is omitted, the fraction is mandatory. If the fraction is omitted, the decimal dot is optional. No exponent.

`^[-+]?([0-9]+(\.[0-9]*)?|\.[0-9]+)$`
    Regex options: None
    Regex flavors: .NET, Java, JavaScript, PCRE, Perl, Python, Ruby

Optional sign, integer, and fraction. If the integer part is omitted, the fraction is mandatory. If the fraction is omitted, the decimal dot must be omitted, too. Optional exponent.

`^[-+]?([0-9]+(\.[0-9]+)?|\.[0-9]+)([eE][-+]?[0-9]+)?$`
Regex options: None
Regex flavors: .NET, Java, JavaScript, PCRE, Perl, Python, Ruby

Optional sign, integer, and fraction. If the integer part is omitted, the fraction is mandatory. If the fraction is omitted, the decimal dot is optional. Optional exponent.

`^[-+]?([0-9]+(\.[0-9]*)?|\.[0-9]+)([eE][-+]?[0-9]+)?$`
Regex options: None
Regex flavors: .NET, Java, JavaScript, PCRE, Perl, Python, Ruby

The preceding regex, edited to find the number in a larger body of text:

`[-+]?(\b[0-9]+(\.[0-9]*)?|\.[0-9]+)([eE][-+]?[0-9]+\b)?`
Regex options: None
Regex flavors: .NET, Java, JavaScript, PCRE, Perl, Python, Ruby

Discussion

All regular expressions are wrapped between anchors (Recipe 2.5) to make sure we check whether the whole input is a floating-point number, as opposed to a floating-point number occurring in a larger string. You could use word boundaries or look-around as explained in Recipe 6.1 if you want to find floating-point numbers in a larger body of text.

The solutions without any optional parts are very straightforward: they simply spell things out from left to right. Character classes (Recipe 2.3) match the sign, digits, and the e. The plus and question mark quantifiers (Recipe 2.12) allow for any number of digits and an optional exponent sign.

Making just the sign and integer parts optional is easy. The question mark after the character class with the sign symbols makes it optional. Using an asterisk instead of a plus to repeat the integer digits allows for zero or more instead of one or more digits.

Complications arise when sign, integer, and fraction are all optional. Although they are optional on their own, they are not all optional at the same time, and the empty string is not a valid floating-point number. The naïve solution, ‹[-+]?[0-9]*\.?[0-9]*›, does match all valid floating-point numbers, but it also matches the empty string. And because we omitted the anchors, this regex will match the zero-length string between any two characters in your subject text. If you run a search-and-replace with this regex and the replacement «{$&}» on 123abc456, you'll get {123}{}a{}b{}c{456}{}. The regex does match 123 and 456 correctly, but it finds a zero-length match at every other match attempt, too.

When creating a regular expression in a situation where everything is optional, it's very important to consider whether everything else remains optional if one part is actually omitted. Floating-point numbers must have at least one digit.

The solutions for this recipe clearly spell out that when the integer and fractional parts are optional, either of them is still required. They also spell out whether 123. is a floating-point number with a decimal dot, or whether it's an integer number followed by a dot that's not part of the number. For example, in a programming language, that trailing dot might be a concatenation operator or the first dot in a range operator specified by two dots.

To implement the requirement that the integer and fractional can't be omitted at the same time, we use alternation (Recipe 2.8) inside a group (Recipe 2.9) to simply spell out the two situations. ‹[0-9]+(\.[0-9]+)?› matches a number with a required integer part and an optional fraction. ‹\.[0-9]+› matches just a fractional number.

Combined, ‹[0-9]+(\.[0-9]+)?|\.[0-9]+› covers all three situations. The first alternative covers numbers with both the integer and fractional parts, as well as numbers without a fraction. The second alternative matches just the fraction. Because the alternation operator has the lowest precedence of all, we have to place these two alternatives in a group before we can add them to a longer regular expression.

‹[0-9]+(\.[0-9]+)?|\.[0-9]+› requires the decimal dot to be omitted when the fraction is omitted. If the decimal dot can occur even without fractional digits, we use ‹[0-9]+(\.[0-9]*)?|\.[0-9]+› instead. In the first alternative in this regex, the fractional part is still grouped with the question mark quantifier, which makes it optional. The difference is that the fractional digits themselves are now optional. We changed the plus (one or more) into an asterisk (zero or more). The result is that the first alternative in this regex matches an integer with optional fractional part, where the fraction can either be a decimal dot with digits or just a decimal dot. The second alternative in the regex is unchanged.

This last example is interesting because we have a requirement change about one thing, but change the quantifier in the regex on something else. The requirement change is about the dot being optional on its own, rather than in combination with the fractional digits. We achieve this by changing the quantifier on the character class for the fractional digits. This works because the decimal dot and the character class were already inside a group that made both of them optional at the same time.

See Also

Recipes 2.3, 2.8, 2.9, and 2.12

6.8 Numbers with Thousand Separators

Problem

You want to match numbers that use the comma as the thousand separator and the dot as the decimal separator.

Solution

Mandatory integer and fraction:

```
^[0-9]{1,3}(,[0-9]{3})*\.[0-9]+$
```
Regex options: None
Regex flavors: .NET, Java, JavaScript, PCRE, Perl, Python, Ruby

Mandatory integer and optional fraction. Decimal dot must be omitted if the fraction is omitted.

```
^[0-9]{1,3}(,[0-9]{3})*(\.[0-9]+)?$
```
Regex options: None
Regex flavors: .NET, Java, JavaScript, PCRE, Perl, Python, Ruby

Optional integer and optional fraction. Decimal dot must be omitted if the fraction is omitted.

```
^([0-9]{1,3}(,[0-9]{3})*(\.[0-9]+)?|\.[0-9]+)$
```
Regex options: None
Regex flavors: .NET, Java, JavaScript, PCRE, Perl, Python, Ruby

The preceding regex, edited to find the number in a larger body of text:

```
\b[0-9]{1,3}(,[0-9]{3})*(\.[0-9]+)?\b|\.[0-9]+\b
```
Regex options: None
Regex flavors: .NET, Java, JavaScript, PCRE, Perl, Python, Ruby

Discussion

Since these are all regular expressions for matching floating-point numbers, they use the same techniques as the previous recipe. The only difference is that instead of simply matching the integer part with ‹[0-9]+›, we now use ‹[0-9]{1,3}(,[0-9]{3})*›. This regular expression matches between 1 and 3 digits, followed by zero or more groups that consist of a comma and 3 digits.

We cannot use ‹[0-9]{0,3}(,[0-9]{3})*› to make the integer part optional, because that would match numbers with a leading comma, e.g., ,123. It's the same trap of making everything optional, explained in the previous recipe. To make the integer part optional, we don't change the part of the regex for the integer, but instead make it optional in its entirety. The last two regexes in the solution do this using alternation. The regex for a mandatory integer and optional fraction is alternated with a regex that matches the fraction without the integer. That yields a regex where both integer and fraction are optional, but not at the same time.

See Also

Recipes 2.3, 2.9, and 2.12

6.9 Roman Numerals

Problem

You want to match Roman numerals such as IV, XIII, and MVIII.

Solution

Roman numerals without validation:

```
^[MDCLXVI]+$
```
Regex options: Case insensitive
Regex flavors: .NET, Java, JavaScript, PCRE, Perl, Python, Ruby

Modern Roman numerals, strict:

```
^(?=[MDCLXVI])M*(C[MD]|D?C{0,3})(X[CL]|L?X{0,3})(I[XV]|V?I{0,3})$
```
Regex options: Case insensitive
Regex flavors: .NET, Java, JavaScript, PCRE, Perl, Python, Ruby

Modern Roman numerals, flexible:

```
^(?=[MDCLXVI])M*(C[MD]|D?C*)(X[CL]|L?X*)(I[XV]|V?I*)$
```
Regex options: Case insensitive
Regex flavors: .NET, Java, JavaScript, PCRE, Perl, Python, Ruby

Simple Roman numerals:

```
^(?=[MDCLXVI])M*D?C{0,4}L?X{0,4}V?I{0,4}$
```
Regex options: Case insensitive
Regex flavors: .NET, Java, JavaScript, PCRE, Perl, Python, Ruby

Discussion

Roman numerals are written using the letters M, D, C, L, X, V, and I, representing the values 1000, 500, 100, 50, 10, 5, and 1, respectively. The first regex matches any string composed of these letters, without checking whether the letters appear in the order or quantity necessary to form a proper Roman numeral.

In modern times (meaning during the past few hundred years), Roman numerals have generally been written following a strict set of rules. These rules yield exactly one Roman numeral per number. For example, 4 is always written as IV, never as IIII.

The second regex in the solution matches only Roman numerals that follow these modern rules.

Each nonzero digit of the decimal number is written out separately in the Roman numeral. 1999 is written as MCMXCIX, where M is 1000, CM is 900, XC is 90, and IX is 9. We don't write MIM or IMM.

The thousands are easy: one M per thousand, easily matched with ‹M*›.

There are 10 variations for the hundreds, which we match using two alternatives. ‹C[MD]› matches CM and CD, which represent 900 and 400. ‹D?C{0,3}› matches DCCC, DCC, DC, D, CCC, CC, C, and the empty string, representing 800, 700, 600, 500, 300, 200, 100, and nothing. This gives us all of the 10 digits for the hundreds.

We match the tens with ‹X[CL]|L?X{0,3}› and the units with ‹I[XV]|V?I{0,3}›. These use the same syntax, but with different letters.

All four parts of the regex allow everything to be optional, because each of the digits could be zero. The Romans did not have a symbol, or even a word, to represent zero. Thus, zero is unwritten in Roman numerals. While each part of the regex should indeed be optional, they're not all optional at the same time. We have to make sure our regex does not allow zero-length matches. To do this, we put the lookahead ‹(?=[MDCLXVI])› at the start of the regex. This lookahead, as Recipe 2.16 explains, makes sure that there's at least one letter in the regex match. The lookahead does not consume the letter that it matches, so that letter can be matched again by the remainder of the regex.

The third regex is a bit more flexible. It also accepts numerals such as IIII, while still accepting IV.

The fourth regex only allows numerals written without using subtraction, and therefore all the letters must be in descending order. 4 must be written as IIII rather than IV. The Romans themselves usually wrote numbers this way.

 All regular expressions are wrapped between anchors (Recipe 2.5) to make sure we check whether the whole input is a Roman numeral, as opposed to a floating-point number occurring in a larger string. You can replace ‹^› and ‹$› with ‹\b› word boundaries if you want to find Roman numerals in a larger body of text.

Convert Roman Numerals to Decimal

This Perl function uses the "strict" regular expression from this recipe to check whether the input is a valid Roman numeral. If it is, it uses the regex ‹[MDLV]|C[MD]?|X[CL]?|I[XV]?› to iterate over all of the letters in the numeral, adding up their values:

```
sub roman2decimal {
    my $roman = shift;
```

```
        if ($roman =~
            m/^(?=[MDCLXVI])
                (M*)                    # 1000
                (C[MD]|D?C{0,3})        # 100
                (X[CL]|L?X{0,3})        # 10
                (I[XV]|V?I{0,3})        # 1
                $/ix)
        {
            # Roman numeral found
            my %r2d = ('I' =>      1, 'IV' =>   4, 'V' =>    5, 'IX' =>    9,
                       'X' =>     10, 'XL' =>  40, 'L' =>   50, 'XC' =>   90,
                       'C' =>    100, 'CD' => 400, 'D' =>  500, 'CM' =>  900,
                       'M' =>   1000);
            my $decimal = 0;
            while ($roman =~ m/[MDLV]|C[MD]?|X[CL]?|I[XV]?/ig) {
                $decimal += $r2d{uc($&)};
            }
            return $decimal;
        } else {
            # Not a Roman numeral
            return 0;
        }
    }
```

See Also

Recipes 2.3, 2.8, 2.9, 2.12, 2.16, 3.9, and 3.11

## CHAPTER 7

URLs, Paths, and Internet Addresses

Along with numbers, which were the subject of the previous chapter, another major subject that concerns a wide range of programs is the various paths and locators for finding data:

- URLs, URNs, and related strings
- Domain names
- IP addresses
- Microsoft Windows file and folder names

The URL format in particular has proven so flexible and useful that it has been adopted for a wide range of resources that have nothing to do with the World Wide Web. The toolbox of parsing regular expressions in this chapter will thus prove valuable in a surprising variety of situations.

7.1 Validating URLs

Problem

You want to check whether a given piece of text is a URL that is valid for your purposes.

Solution

Allow almost any URL:

```
^(https?|ftp|file)://.+$
```
Regex options: Case insensitive
Regex flavors: .NET, Java, JavaScript, PCRE, Perl, Python

```
\A(https?|ftp|file)://.+\Z
```
Regex options: Case insensitive
Regex flavors: .NET, Java, PCRE, Perl, Python, Ruby

Require a domain name, and don't allow a username or password:

```
\A                              # Anchor
(https?|ftp)://                 # Scheme
[a-z0-9-]+(\.[a-z0-9-]+)+       # Domain
([/?].*)?                       # Path and/or parameters
\Z                              # Anchor
```
Regex options: Free-spacing, case insensitive
Regex flavors: .NET, Java, PCRE, Perl, Python, Ruby

```
^(https?|ftp)://[a-z0-9-]+(\.[a-z0-9-]+)+↵
([/?].+)?$
```
Regex options: Case insensitive
Regex flavors: .NET, Java, JavaScript, PCRE, Perl, Python, Ruby

Require a domain name, and don't allow a username or password. Allow the scheme (http or ftp) to be omitted if it can be inferred from the subdomain (www or ftp):

```
\A                                  # Anchor
((https?|ftp)://|(www|ftp)\.)       # Scheme or subdomain
[a-z0-9-]+(\.[a-z0-9-]+)+           # Domain
([/?].*)?                           # Path and/or parameters
\Z                                  # Anchor
```
Regex options: Free-spacing, case insensitive
Regex flavors: .NET, Java, PCRE, Perl, Python, Ruby

```
^((https?|ftp)://|(www|ftp)\.)[a-z0-9-]+(\.[a-z0-9-]+)+([/?].*)?$
```
Regex options: Case insensitive
Regex flavors: .NET, Java, JavaScript, PCRE, Perl, Python

Require a domain name and a path that points to an image file. Don't allow a username, password, or parameters:

```
\A                              # Anchor
(https?|ftp)://                 # Scheme
[a-z0-9-]+(\.[a-z0-9-]+)+       # Domain
(/[\w-]+)*                      # Path
/[\w-]+\.(gif|png|jpg)          # File
\Z                              # Anchor
```
Regex options: Free-spacing, case insensitive
Regex flavors: .NET, Java, PCRE, Perl, Python, Ruby

```
^(https?|ftp)://[a-z0-9-]+(\.[a-z0-9-]+)+(/[\w-]+)*/[\w-]+\.(gif|png|jpg)$
```
Regex options: Case insensitive
Regex flavors: .NET, Java, JavaScript, PCRE, Perl, Python

Discussion

You cannot create a regular expression that matches every valid URL without matching any invalid URLs. The reason is that pretty much anything could be a valid URL in some as of yet uninvented scheme.

Validating URLs becomes useful only when we know the context in which those URLs have to be valid. We then can limit the URLs we accept to schemes supported by the software we're using. All the regular expressions for this recipe are for URLs used by web browsers. Such URLs use the form:

```
scheme://user:password@domain.name:80/path/file.ext?param=value&param2↵
=value2#fragment
```

All these parts are in fact optional. A `file:` URL has only a path. `http:` URLs only need a domain name.

The first regular expression in the solution checks whether the URL begins with one of the common schemes used by web browsers: `http`, `https`, `ftp`, and `file`. The caret anchors the regex to the start of the string (Recipe 2.5). Alternation (Recipe 2.8) is used to spell out the list of schemes. ‹https?› is a clever way of saying ‹http|https›.

Because the first regex allows for rather different schemes, such as `http` and `file`, it doesn't try to validate the text after the scheme. ‹.+$› simply grabs everything until the end of the string, as long as the string doesn't contain any line break characters.

By default, the dot (Recipe 2.4) matches all characters except line break characters, and the dollar (Recipe 2.5) does not match at embedded line breaks. Ruby is the exception here. In Ruby, caret and dollar always match at embedded line breaks, and so we have to use ‹\A› and ‹\Z› instead (Recipe 2.5). Strictly speaking, you'd have to make the same change for Ruby for all the other regular expressions shown in this recipe. You should… if your input could consist of multiple lines and you want to avoid matching a URL that takes up one line in several lines of text.

The next two regular expressions are the free-spacing (Recipe 2.18) and regular versions of the same regex. The free-spacing regex is easier to read, whereas the regular version is faster to type. JavaScript does not support free-spacing regular expressions.

These two regexes accept only web and FTP URLs, and require the HTTP or FTP scheme to be followed by something that looks like a valid domain name. The domain name must be in ASCII. Internationalized domains (IDNs) are not accepted. The domain can be followed by a path or a list of parameters, separated from the domain with a forward slash or a question mark. Since the question mark is inside a character class (Recipe 2.3), we don't need to escape it. The question mark is an ordinary character in character classes, and the forward slash is an ordinary character anywhere in a regular expression. (If you see it escaped in source code, that's because Perl and several other programming languages use forward slashes to delimit literal regular expressions.)

No attempt is made to validate the path or the parameters. ‹.*› simply matches anything that doesn't include line breaks. Since the path and parameters are both optional, ‹[/?].*› is placed inside a group that is made optional with a question mark (Recipe 2.12).

These regular expressions, and the ones that follow, don't allow a username or password to be specified as part of the URL. Putting user information in a URL is considered bad practice for security reasons.

Most web browsers accept URLs that don't specify the scheme, and correctly infer the scheme from the domain name. For example, `www.regexbuddy.com` is short for `http://www.regexbuddy.com`. To allow such URLs, we simply expand the list of schemes allowed by the regular expression to include the subdomains `www.` and `ftp.`.

‹`(https?|ftp)://|(www|ftp)\.`› does this nicely. This list has two alternatives, each of which starts with two alternatives. The first alternative allows ‹`https?`› and ‹`ftp`›, which must be followed by ‹`://`›. The second alternative allows ‹`www`› and ‹`ftp`›, which must be followed by a dot. You can easily edit both lists to change the schemes and subdomains the regex should accept.

The last two regular expressions require a scheme, an ASCII domain name, a path, and a filename to a GIF, PNG, or JPEG image file. The path and filename allow all letters and digits in any script, as well as underscores and hyphens. The shorthand character class ‹`\w`› includes all that, except the hyphens (Recipe 2.3).

Which of these regular expressions should you use? That really depends on what you're trying to do. In many situations, the answer may be to not use any regular expression at all. Simply try to resolve the URL. If it returns valid content, accept it. If you get a 404 or other error, reject it. Ultimately, that's the only real test to see whether a URL is valid.

See Also

Recipes 2.3, 2.8, 2.9, and 2.12

7.2 Finding URLs Within Full Text

Problem

You want to find URLs in a larger body of text. URLs may or may not be enclosed in punctuation, such as parentheses, that are not part of the URL.

Solution

URL without spaces:

> `\b(https?|ftp|file)://\S+`
> **Regex options:** Case insensitive
> **Regex flavors:** .NET, Java, JavaScript, PCRE, Perl, Python, Ruby

URL without spaces or final punctuation:

```
\b(https?|ftp|file)://[-A-Z0-9+&@#/%?=~_|$!:,.;]*↵
[A-Z0-9+&@#/%=~_|$]
```

   Regex options: Case insensitive
   Regex flavors: .NET, Java, JavaScript, PCRE, Perl, Python, Ruby

URL without spaces or final punctuation. URLs that start with the www or ftp subdomain can omit the scheme:

```
\b((https?|ftp|file)://|(www|ftp)\.)[-A-Z0-9+&@#/%?=~_|$!:,.;]*↵
[A-Z0-9+&@#/%=~_|$]
```

   Regex options: Case insensitive
   Regex flavors: .NET, Java, JavaScript, PCRE, Perl, Python, Ruby

Discussion

Given the text:

   Visit http://www.somesite.com/page, where you will find more information.

what is the URL?

Before you say http://www.somesite.com/page, think about this: punctuation and spaces are valid characters in URLs. Commas, dots, and even spaces do not have to be escaped as %20. Literal spaces are perfectly valid. Some WYSIWYG web authoring tools even make it easy for the user to put spaces in file and folder names, and include those spaces literally in links to those files.

That means that if we use a regular expression that allows all valid URLs, it will find this URL in the preceding text:

   http://www.somesite.com/page, where you will find more information.

The odds are small that the person who typed in this sentence intended the spaces to be part of the URL, since unescaped spaces in URLs are rare. The first regular expression in the solution excludes them using the shorthand character class ‹\S›, which includes all characters that are not whitespace. Though the regex specifies the "case insensitive" option, the S must be uppercase, because ‹\S› is not the same as ‹\s›. In fact, they're exactly the opposite. Recipe 2.3 has all the details.

The first regular expression is still quite crude. It will include the comma in the example text into the URL. Though it's not uncommon for URLs to include commas and other punctuation, punctuation rarely occurs at the end of the URL.

The next regular expression uses two character classes instead of the single shorthand ‹\S›. The first character class includes more punctuation than the second. The second class excludes those characters that are likely to appear as English language punctuation right after a URL when the URL is placed into an English sentence. The first character class has the asterisk quantifier (Recipe 2.12), to allow URLs of any length. The second character class has no quantifier, requiring the URL to end with one character from that class. The character classes don't include the lowercase letters; the "case insensitive" option takes care of those. See Recipe 3.4 to learn how to set such options in your programming language.

The second regex will work incorrectly with certain URLs that use odd punctuation, matching those URLs only partially. But this regex does solve the very common problem of a comma or full stop right after a URL, while still allowing commas and dots within the URL.

Most web browsers accept URLs that don't specify the scheme, and correctly infer the scheme from the domain name. For example, `www.regexbuddy.com` is short for `http://www.regexbuddy.com`. To allow such URLs, the final regex expands the list of allowed schemes to include the subdomains `www.` and `ftp.`.

‹`(https?|ftp)://|(www|ftp)\.`› does this nicely. This list has two alternatives, each of which starts with two alternatives. The first alternative allows ‹`https?`› and ‹`ftp`›, which must be followed by ‹`://`›. The second alternative allows ‹`www`› and ‹`ftp`›, which must be followed by a dot. You can easily edit both lists to change the schemes and subdomains the regex should accept.

See Also

Recipes 2.3 and 2.6

7.3 Finding Quoted URLs in Full Text

Problem

You want to find URLs in a larger body of text. URLs may or may not be enclosed in punctuation that is part of the larger body of text rather than part of the URL. You want to give users the option to place URLs between quotation marks, so they can explicitly indicate whether punctuation, or even spaces, should be part of the URL.

Solution

```
\b(?:(?:https?|ftp|file)://|(www|ftp)\.)[-A-Z0-9+&@#/%?=~_|$!:,.;]*
                                          [-A-Z0-9+&@#/%=~_|$]
|"(?:(?:https?|ftp|file)://|(www|ftp)\.)[^"\r\n]+"
|'(?:(?:https?|ftp|file)://|(www|ftp)\.)[^'\r\n]+'
```

Regex options: Free-spacing, case insensitive, dot matches line breaks, anchors match at line breaks
Regex flavors: .NET, Java, JavaScript, PCRE, Perl, Python, Ruby

Discussion

The previous recipe explains the issue of mixing URLs with English text, and how to differentiate between English punctuation and URL characters. Though the solution to the previous recipe is a very useful one that gets it right most of the time, no regex will get it right all of the time.

If your regex will be used on text to be written in the future, you can provide a way for your users to quote their URLs. The solution we present allows a pair of single quotes or a pair of double quotes to be placed around the URL. When a URL is quoted, it must start with one of several schemes: ‹https?|ftp|file› or one of two subdomains ‹www| ftp›. After the scheme or subdomain, the regex allows the URL to include any character, except for line breaks, and the delimiting quote.

The regular expression as a whole is split into three alternatives. The first alternative is the regex from the previous recipe, which matches an unquoted URL, trying to differentiate between English punctuation and URL characters. The second alternative matches a double-quoted URL. The third alternative matches a single-quoted URL. We use two alternatives rather than a single alternative with a capturing group around the opening quote and a backreference for the closing quote, because we cannot use a backreference inside the negated character class that excludes the quote character from the URL.

We chose to use single and double quotes because that's how URLs commonly appear in HTML and XHTML files. Quoting URLs this way is natural to people who work on the Web, but you can easily edit the regex to allow different pairs of characters to delimit URLs.

See Also

Recipes 2.8 and 2.9

7.4 Finding URLs with Parentheses in Full Text

Problem

You want to find URLs in a larger body of text. URLs may or may not be enclosed in punctuation that is part of the larger body of text rather than part of the URL. You want to correctly match URLs that include pairs of parentheses as part of the URL, without matching parentheses placed around the entire URL.

Solution

```
\b(?:(?:https?|ftp|file)://|www\.|ftp\.)
(?:\([-A-Z0-9+&@#/%=~_|$?!:,.]*\)|[-A-Z0-9+&@#/%=~_|$?!:,.])*
(?:\([-A-Z0-9+&@#/%=~_|$?!:,.]*\)|[A-Z0-9+&@#/%=~_|$])
```
Regex options: Free-spacing, case insensitive
Regex flavors: .NET, Java, PCRE, Perl, Python, Ruby

```
\b(?:(?:https?|ftp|file)://|www\.|ftp\.)(?:\([-A-Z0-9+&@#/%=~_|$?!:,.]*\)↵
|[-A-Z0-9+&@#/%=~_|$?!:,.])*(?:\([-A-Z0-9+&@#/%=~_|$?!:,.]*\)|↵
[A-Z0-9+&@#/%=~_|$])
```
Regex options: Case insensitive
Regex flavors: .NET, Java, JavaScript, PCRE, Perl, Python, Ruby

Discussion

Pretty much any character is valid in URLs, including parentheses. Parentheses are very rare in URLs, however, and that's why we don't include them in any of the regular expressions in the previous recipes. But certain important websites have started using them:

```
http://en.wikipedia.org/wiki/PC_Tools_(Central_Point_Software)
http://msdn.microsoft.com/en-us/library/aa752574(VS.85).aspx
```

One solution is to require your users to quote such URLs. The other is to enhance your regex to accept such URLs. The hard part is how to determine whether a closing parenthesis is part of the URL or is used as punctuation around the URL, as in this example:

```
RegexBuddy's web site (at http://www.regexbuddy.com) is really cool.
```

Since it's possible for one of the parentheses to be adjacent to the URL while the other one isn't, we can't use the technique for quoting regexes from the previous recipe. The most straightforward solution is to allow parentheses in URLs only when they occur in unnested pairs of opening and closing parentheses. The Wikipedia and Microsoft URLs meet that requirement.

The two regular expressions in the solution are the same. The first uses free-spacing mode to make it a bit more readable.

These regular expressions are essentially the same as the last regex in the solution to Recipe 7.2. There are three parts to all these regexes: the list of schemes, followed by the body of the URL that uses the asterisk quantifier to allow URLs of any length, and the end of the URL, which has no quantifier (i.e., it must occur once). In the original regex in Recipe 7.2, both the body of the URL and the end of the URL consisted of just one character class.

The solutions to this recipe replace the two character classes with more elaborate things. The middle character class:

```
[-A-Z0-9+&@#/%=~_|$?!:,.]
```

has become:

```
\([-A-Z0-9+&@#/%=~_|$?!:,.]*\)|[-A-Z0-9+&@#/%=~_|$?!:,.]
```

The final character class:

```
[A-Z0-9+&@#/%=~_|$]
```

has become:

`\([-A-Z0-9+&@#/%=~_|$?!:,.]*\)|[A-Z0-9+&@#/%=~_|$]`

Both character classes were replaced with something involving alternation (Recipe 2.8). Because alternation has the lowest precedence of all regex operators, we use noncapturing groups (Recipe 2.9) to keep the two alternatives together.

For both character classes, we've added the alternative ‹`\([-A-Z0-9+&@#/%=~_|$?!:,.]*\)`› while leaving the original character class as the other alternative. The new alternative matches a pair of parentheses, with any number of any of the characters we allow in the URL in between.

The final character class was given the same alternative, allowing the URL to end with text between parentheses or with a single character that is not likely to be English language punctuation.

Combined, this results in a regex that matches URLs with any number of parentheses, including URLs without parentheses and even URLs that consist of nothing but parentheses, and as long as those parentheses occur in pairs.

For the body of the URL, we put the asterisk quantifier around the whole noncapturing group. This allows any number of pairs of parentheses to occur in the URL. Because we have the asterisk around the noncapturing group, we no longer need an asterisk directly on the original character class. In fact, we must make sure not to include the asterisk.

The regex in the solution has the form ‹(ab*c|d)*› in the middle, where ‹a› and ‹c› are the literal parentheses, and ‹b› and ‹d› are character classes. Writing this as ‹(ab*c|d*)*› would be a mistake. It might seem logical at first, because we allow any number of the characters from ‹d›, but the outer ‹*› already repeats ‹d› just fine. If we add an inner asterisk directly on ‹d›, the complexity of the regular expression becomes exponential. ‹(d*)*› can match dddd in many ways. For example, the outer asterisk could repeat four times, repeating the inner asterisk once each time. The outer asterisk could repeat three times, with the inner asterisk doing 2-1-1, 1-2-1, or 1-1-2. The outer asterisk could repeat twice, with the inner asterisk doing 2-2, 1-3, or 3-1. You can imagine that as the length of the string grows, the number of combinations quickly explodes. We call this catastrophic backtracking, a term introduced in Recipe 2.15. This problem will arise when the regular expression cannot find a valid match, e.g., because you've appended something to the regex to find URLs that end with or contain something specific to your requirements.

See Also

Recipes 2.8 and 2.9

7.5 Turn URLs into Links

Problem

You have a body of text that may contain one or more URLs. You want to convert the URLs that it contains into links by placing HTML anchor tags around the URLs. The URL itself will be both the destination for the link and the text being linked.

Solution

To find the URLs in the text, use one of the regular expressions from Recipes 7.2 or 7.4. As the replacement text, use:

`<a•href="$&">$&</a>`
Replacement text flavors: .NET, JavaScript, Perl

`<a•href="$0">$0</a>`
Replacement text flavors: .NET, Java, PHP

`<a•href="\0">\0</a>`
Replacement text flavors: PHP, Ruby

`<a•href="\&">\&</a>`
Replacement text flavor: Ruby

`<a•href="\g<0>">\g<0></a>`
Replacement text flavor: Python

When programming, you can implement this search-and-replace as explained in Recipe 3.15.

Discussion

The solution to this problem is very straightforward. We use a regular expression to match a URL, and then replace it with «`<a•href="URL">URL</a>`», where *URL* represents the URL that we matched. Different programming languages use different syntax for the replacement text, hence the long list of solutions to this problem. But they all do exactly the same thing. Recipe 2.20 explains the replacement text syntax.

See Also

Recipes 2.21, 3.15, 7.2, and 7.4

7.6 Validating URNs

Problem

You want to check whether a string represents a valid Uniform Resource Name (URN), as specified in RFC 2141, or find URNs in a larger body of text.

Solution

Check whether a string consists entirely of a valid URN:

```
\Aurn:
# Namespace Identifier
[a-z0-9][a-z0-9-]{0,31}:
# Namespace Specific String
[a-z0-9()+,\-.:=@;$_!*'%/?#]+
\Z
```
Regex options: Free-spacing, case insensitive
Regex flavors: .NET, Java, PCRE, Perl, Python, Ruby

```
^urn:[a-z0-9][a-z0-9-]{0,31}:[a-z0-9()+,\-.:=@;$_!*'%/?#]+$
```
Regex options: Case insensitive
Regex flavors: .NET, Java, JavaScript, PCRE, Perl, Python

Find a URN in a larger body of text:

```
\burn:
# Namespace Identifier
[a-z0-9][a-z0-9-]{0,31}:
# Namespace Specific String
[a-z0-9()+,\-.:=@;$_!*'%/?#]+
```
Regex options: Free-spacing, case insensitive
Regex flavors: .NET, Java, PCRE, Perl, Python, Ruby

```
\burn:[a-z0-9][a-z0-9-]{0,31}:[a-z0-9()+,\-.:=@;$_!*'%/?#]+
```
Regex options: Case insensitive
Regex flavors: .NET, Java, JavaScript, PCRE, Perl, Python, Ruby

Find a URN in a larger body of text, assuming that punctuation at the end of the URN is part of the (English) text in which the URN is quoted rather than part of the URN itself:

```
\burn:
# Namespace Identifier
[a-z0-9][a-z0-9-]{0,31}:
# Namespace Specific String
[a-z0-9()+,\-.:=@;$_!*'%/?#]*[a-z0-9+=@$/]
```
Regex options: Free-spacing, case insensitive
Regex flavors: .NET, Java, PCRE, Perl, Python, Ruby

```
\burn:[a-z0-9][a-z0-9-]{0,31}:[a-z0-9()+,\-.:=@;$_!*'%/?#]*[a-z0-9+=@$/]
```
Regex options: Case insensitive
Regex flavors: .NET, Java, JavaScript, PCRE, Perl, Python, Ruby

Discussion

A URN consists of three parts. The first part is the four characters urn:, which we can add literally to the regular expression.

The second part is the Namespace Identifier (NID). It is between 1 and 32 characters long. The first character must be a letter or a digit. The remaining characters can be letters, digits, and hyphens. We match this using two character classes (Recipe 2.3): the first one matches a letter or a digit, and the second one matches between 0 and 31 letters, digits, and hyphens. The NID must be delimited with a colon, which we again add literally to the regex.

The third part of the URN is the Namespace Specific String (NSS). It can be of any length, and can include a bunch of punctuation characters in addition to letters and digits. We easily match this with another character class. The plus after the character class repeats it one or more times (Recipe 2.12).

If you want to check whether a string represents a valid URN, all that remains is to add anchors to the start and the end of the regex that match at the start and the end of the string. We can do this with ‹^› and ‹$› in all flavors except Ruby, and with ‹\A› and ‹\Z› in all flavors except JavaScript. Recipe 2.5 has all the details on these anchors.

Things are a little trickier if you want to find URNs in a larger body of text. The punctuation issue with URLs discussed in Recipe 7.2 also exists for URNs. Suppose you have the text:

    The URN is urn:nid:nss, isn't it?

The issue is whether the comma is part of the URN. URNs that end with commas are syntactically valid, but any human reading this English-language sentence would see the comma as English punctuation, not as part of the URN. The last regular expression in the "Solution" section solves this issue by being a little more strict than RFC 2141. It restricts the last character of the URN to be a character that is valid for the NSS part, and is not likely to appear as English punctuation in a sentence mentioning a URN.

This is easily done by replacing the plus quantifier (one or more) with an asterisk (zero or more), and adding a second character class for the final character. If we added the character class without changing the quantifier, we'd require the NSS to be at least two characters long, which isn't what we want.

See Also

Recipes 2.3 and 2.12

7.7 Validating Generic URLs

Problem

You want to check whether a given piece of text is a valid URL according to RFC 3986.

Solution

```
\A
(# Scheme
 [a-z][a-z0-9+\-.]*:
 (# Authority & path
  //
  ([a-z0-9\-._~%!$&'()*+,;=]+@)?              # User
  ([a-z0-9\-._~%]+                            # Named host
  |\[[a-f0-9:.]+\]                            # IPv6 host
  |\[v[a-f0-9][a-z0-9\-._~%!$&'()*+,;=:]+\])  # IPvFuture host
  (:[0-9]+)?                                  # Port
  (/[a-z0-9\-._~%!$&'()*+,;=:@]+)*/?          # Path
 |# Path without authority
  (/?[a-z0-9\-._~%!$&'()*+,;=:@]+(/[a-z0-9\-._~%!$&'()*+,;=:@]+)*/?)?
 )
|# Relative URL (no scheme or authority)
 (# Relative path
  [a-z0-9\-._~%!$&'()*+,;=@]+(/[a-z0-9\-._~%!$&'()*+,;=:@]+)*/?
 |# Absolute path
  (/[a-z0-9\-._~%!$&'()*+,;=:@]+)+/?
 )
)
# Query
(\?[a-z0-9\-._~%!$&'()*+,;=:@/?]*)?
# Fragment
(\#[a-z0-9\-._~%!$&'()*+,;=:@/?]*)?
\Z
```

Regex options: Free-spacing, case insensitive
Regex flavors: .NET, Java, PCRE, Perl, Python, Ruby

```
\A
(# Scheme
 (?<scheme>[a-z][a-z0-9+\-.]*):
 (# Authority & path
  //
  (?<user>[a-z0-9\-._~%!$&'()*+,;=]+@)?        # User
  (?<host>[a-z0-9\-._~%]+                      # Named host
  |       \[[a-f0-9:.]+\]                      # IPv6 host
  |       \[v[a-f0-9][a-z0-9\-._~%!$&'()*+,;=:]+\]) # IPvFuture host
  (?<port>:[0-9]+)?                            # Port
  (?<path>(/[a-z0-9\-._~%!$&'()*+,;=:@]+)*/?)  # Path
 |# Path without authority
  (?<path>/?[a-z0-9\-._~%!$&'()*+,;=:@]+
          (/[a-z0-9\-._~%!$&'()*+,;=:@]+)*/?)?
 )
|# Relative URL (no scheme or authority)
 (?<path>
  # Relative path
```

```
   [a-z0-9\-._~%!$&'()*+,;=@]+(/[a-z0-9\-._~%!$&'()*+,;=:@]+)*/?
 |# Absolute path
   (/[a-z0-9\-._~%!$&'()*+,;=:@]+)+/?
 )
)
# Query
(?<query>\?[a-z0-9\-._~%!$&'()*+,;=:@/?]*)?
# Fragment
(?<fragment>\#[a-z0-9\-._~%!$&'()*+,;=:@/?]*)?
\Z
```

Regex options: Free-spacing, case insensitive
Regex flavor: .NET

```
\A
(# Scheme
 (?<scheme>[a-z][a-z0-9+\-.]*):
 (# Authority & path
  //
  (?<user>[a-z0-9\-._~%!$&'()*+,;=]+@)?               # User
  (?<host>[a-z0-9\-._~%]+                             # Named host
  |      \[[a-f0-9:.]+\]                              # IPv6 host
  |      \[v[a-f0-9][a-z0-9\-._~%!$&'()*+,;=:]+\])    # IPvFuture host
  (?<port>:[0-9]+)?                                   # Port
  (?<hostpath>(/[a-z0-9\-._~%!$&'()*+,;=:@]+)*/?)     # Path
 |# Path without authority
  (?<schemepath>/?[a-z0-9\-._~%!$&'()*+,;=:@]+
              (/[a-z0-9\-._~%!$&'()*+,;=:@]+)*/?)?
 )
|# Relative URL (no scheme or authority)
 (?<relpath>
  # Relative path
  [a-z0-9\-._~%!$&'()*+,;=@]+(/[a-z0-9\-._~%!$&'()*+,;=:@]+)*/?
 |# Absolute path
  (/[a-z0-9\-._~%!$&'()*+,;=:@]+)+/?
 )
)
# Query
(?<query>\?[a-z0-9\-._~%!$&'()*+,;=:@/?]*)?
# Fragment
(?<fragment>\#[a-z0-9\-._~%!$&'()*+,;=:@/?]*)?
\Z
```

Regex options: Free-spacing, case insensitive
Regex flavors: .NET, PCRE 7, Perl 5.10, Ruby 1.9

```
\A
(# Scheme
 (?P<scheme>[a-z][a-z0-9+\-.]*):
 (# Authority & path
  //
```

```
(?P<user>[a-z0-9\-._~%!$&'()*+,;=]+@)?        # User
(?P<host>[a-z0-9\-._~%]+                       # Named host
|          \[[a-f0-9:.]+\]                     # IPv6 host
|          \[v[a-f0-9][a-z0-9\-._~%!$&'()*+,;=:]+\])   # IPvFuture host
(?P<port>:[0-9]+)?                             # Port
(?P<hostpath>(/[a-z0-9\-._~%!$&'()*+,;=:@]+)*/?)       # Path
|# Path without authority
(?P<schemepath>/?[a-z0-9\-._~%!$&'()*+,;=:@]+
                (/[a-z0-9\-._~%!$&'()*+,;=:@]+)*/?)?
)
|# Relative URL (no scheme or authority)
(?P<relpath>
 # Relative path
 [a-z0-9\-._~%!$&'()*+,;=@]+(/[a-z0-9\-._~%!$&'()*+,;=:@]+)*/?
|# Absolute path
 (/[a-z0-9\-._~%!$&'()*+,;=:@]+)+/?
)
)
# Query
(?P<query>\?[a-z0-9\-._~%!$&'()*+,;=:@/?]*)?
# Fragment
(?P<fragment>\#[a-z0-9\-._~%!$&'()*+,;=:@/?]*)?
\Z
```

Regex options: Free-spacing, case insensitive
Regex flavors: PCRE 4 and later, Perl 5.10, Python

```
^([a-z][a-z0-9+\-.]*):(\/\/([a-z0-9\-._~%!$&'()*+,;=]+@)?([a-z0-9\-._~%]+|↵
\[[a-f0-9:.]+\]|\[v[a-f0-9][a-z0-9\-._~%!$&'()*+,;=:]+\])(:[0-9]+)?↵
(\/[a-z0-9\-._~%!$&'()*+,;=:@]+)*\/?|(\/?[a-z0-9\-._~%!$&'()*+,;=:@]+↵
(\/[a-z0-9\-._~%!$&'()*+,;=:@]+)*\/?)?)|([a-z0-9\-._~%!$&'()*+,;=@]+↵
(\/[a-z0-9\-._~%!$&'()*+,;=:@]+)*\/?|(\/[a-z0-9\-._~%!$&'()*+,;=:@]+)↵
+\/?))
(\?[a-z0-9\-._~%!$&'()*+,;=:@\/?]*)?(#[a-z0-9\-._~%!$&'()*+,;=:@\/?]*)?$
```

Regex options: Case insensitive
Regex flavors: .NET, Java, JavaScript, PCRE, Perl, Python

Discussion

Most of the preceding recipes in this chapter deal with URLs, and the regular expressions in those recipes deal with specific kinds of URLs. Some of the regexes are adapted to specific purposes, such as determining whether punctuation is part of the URL or the text that quotes the URL.

The regular expressions in this recipe deal with generic URLs. They're not intended for searching for URLs in larger text, but for validating strings that are supposed to hold URLs, and for splitting URLs into their various parts. They accomplish these tasks for any kind of URL, but in practice, you'll likely want to make the regexes more specific. The recipes after this one show examples of more specific regexes.

RFC 3986 describes what a valid URL should look like. It covers every possible URL, including relative URLs and URLs for schemes that haven't even been invented yet. As a result, RFC 3986 is very broad, and a regular expression that implements it is quite long. The regular expressions in this recipe only implement the basics. They're enough to reliably split the URL into its various parts, but not to validate each of those parts. Validating all the parts would require specific knowledge of each URL scheme anyway.

RFC 3986 does not cover all URLs that you may encounter in the wild. For example, many browsers and web servers accept URLs with literal spaces in them, but RFC 3986 requires spaces to be escaped as %20.

An absolute URL must begin with a scheme, such as http: or ftp:. The first character of the scheme must be a letter. The following characters may be letters, digits, and a few specific punctuation characters. We can easily match that with two character classes: ‹[a-z][a-z0-9+\-.]*›.

Many URL schemes require what RFC 3986 calls an "authority." The authority is the domain name or IP address of the server, optionally preceded by a username, and optionally followed by a port number.

The username can consist of letters, digits, and a bunch of punctuation. It must be delimited from the domain name or IP address with an @ sign. ‹[a-z0-9\-._~%!$&'()*+,;=]+@› matches the username and delimiter.

RFC 3986 is quite liberal in what it allows for the domain name. Recipe 7.15 explains what is commonly allowed for domains: letters, digits, hyphens, and dots. RFC 3986 also allows tildes, and any other character via the percentage notation. The domain name must be converted to UTF-8, and any byte that is not a letter, digit, hyphen, or tilde must be encoded as %FF, where FF is the hexadecimal representation of the byte.

To keep our regular expression simple, we don't check if each percentage sign is followed by exactly two hexadecimal digits. It is better to do such validation after the various parts of the URL have been separated. So we match the hostname with just ‹[a-z0-9\-._~%]+›, which also matches IPv4 addresses (allowed under RFC 3986).

Instead of a domain name or IPv4 address, the host also can be specified as an IPv6 address between square brackets, or even a future version of IP addresses. We match the IPv6 addresses with ‹\[[a-f0-9:.]+\]› and the future addresses with ‹\[v[a-f0-9][a-z0-9\-._~%!$&'()*+,;=:]+\]›. Although we can't validate IP addresses using a version of IP that hasn't been defined yet, we could be more strict about the IPv6 addresses. But this is again better left for a second regex, after extracting the address from the URL. Recipe 7.17 shows that validating IPv6 addresses is far from trivial.

The port number, if specified, is simply a decimal number separated from the hostname with a colon. ‹:[0-9]+› is all we need.

If an authority is specified, it must be followed by either an absolute path or no path at all. An absolute path starts with a forward slash, followed by one or more segments delimited by forward slashes. A segment consists of one or more letters, digits, or punctuation characters. There can be no consecutive forward slashes. The path may end with a forward slash. ‹(/[a-z0-9\-._~%!$&'()*+,;=:@]+)*/?› matches such paths.

If the URL does not specify an authority, the path can be absolute, relative, or omitted. Absolute paths start with a forward slash, whereas relative paths don't. Because the leading forward slash is now optional, we need a slightly longer regex to match both absolute and relative paths: ‹/?[a-z0-9\-._~%!$&'()*+,;=:@]+(/[a-z0-9\-._~%!$&'()*+,;=:@]+)*/?›.

Relative URLs do not specify a scheme, and therefore no authority. The path becomes mandatory, and it can be absolute or relative. Since the URL does not specify a scheme, the first segment of a relative path cannot contain any colons. Otherwise, that colon would be seen as the delimiter of the scheme. So we need two regular expressions to match the path of a relative URL. We match relative paths with ‹[a-z0-9\-._~%!$&'()*+,;=@]+(/[a-z0-9\-._~%!$&'()*+,;=:@]+)*/?›. This is very similar to the regex for paths with a scheme but no authority. The only differences are the optional forward slash at the start, which is missing, and the first character class, which does not include the colon. We match absolute paths with ‹(/[a-z0-9\-._~%!$&'()*+,;=:@]+)+/?›. This is the same regex as the one for paths in URLs that specify a scheme and an authority, except that the asterisk that repeats the segments of the path has become a plus. Relative URLs require at least one path segment.

The query part of the URL is optional. If present, it must start with a question mark. The query runs until the first hash sign in the URL or until the end of the URL. Since the hash sign is not among valid punctuation characters for the query part of the URL, we can easily match this with ‹\?[a-z0-9\-._~%!$&'()*+,;=:@/?]*›. Both of the question marks in this regex are literal characters. The first one is outside a character class, and must be escaped. The second one is inside a character class, where it is always a literal character.

The final part of a URL is the fragment, which is also optional. It begins with a hash sign and runs until the end of the URL. ‹\#[a-z0-9\-._~%!$&'()*+,;=:@/?]*› matches this.

To make it easier to work with the various parts of the URL, we use named capturing groups. Recipe 2.11 explains how named capture works in the different regex flavors discussed in this book. .NET is the only flavor that treats multiple groups with the same name as if they were one group. This is very handy in this situation, because our regex has multiple ways of matching the URL's path, depending on whether the scheme and/or the authority are specified. If we give these three groups the same name, we can simply query the "path" group to get the path, regardless of whether the URL has a scheme and/or an authority.

The other flavors don't support this behavior for named capture in .NET, even though most support the same syntax for named capture. For the other flavors, the three capturing groups for the path all have different names. Only one of them will actually hold the URL's path when a match is found. The other two won't have participated in the match.

See Also

Recipes 2.3, 2.8, 2.9, and 2.12

7.8 Extracting the Scheme from a URL

Problem

You want to extract the URL scheme from a string that holds a URL. For example, you want to extract http from http://www.regexcookbook.com.

Solution

Extract the scheme from a URL known to be valid

```
^([a-z][a-z0-9+\-.]*):
```
Regex options: Case insensitive
Regex flavors: .NET, Java, JavaScript, PCRE, Perl, Python, Ruby

Extract the scheme while validating the URL

```
\A
([a-z][a-z0-9+\-.]*):
(# Authority & path
 //
 ([a-z0-9\-._~%!$&'()*+,;=]+@)?              # User
 ([a-z0-9\-._~%]+                            # Named host
 |\[[a-f0-9:.]+\]                            # IPv6 host
 |\[v[a-f0-9][a-z0-9\-._~%!$&'()*+,;=:]+\])  # IPvFuture host
 (:[0-9]+)?                                  # Port
 (/[a-z0-9\-._~%!$&'()*+,;=:@]+)*/?          # Path
|# Path without authority
 (/?[a-z0-9\-._~%!$&'()*+,;=:@]+(/[a-z0-9\-._~%!$&'()*+,;=:@]+)*/?)?
)
# Query
(\?[a-z0-9\-._~%!$&'()*+,;=:@/?]*)?
# Fragment
(\#[a-z0-9\-._~%!$&'()*+,;=:@/?]*)?
\Z
```
Regex options: Case insensitive
Regex flavors: .NET, Java, PCRE, Perl, Python, Ruby

```
^([a-z][a-z0-9+\-.]*):(//([a-z0-9\-._~%!$&'()*+,;=]+@)?([a-z0-9\-._~%]+|↵
\[[a-f0-9:.]+\]|\[v[a-f0-9][a-z0-9\-._~%!$&'()*+,;=:]+\])(:[0-9]+)?↵
(/[a-z0-9\-._~%!$&'()*+,;=:@]+)*/?|(/?[a-z0-9\-._~%!$&'()*+,;=:@]+↵
(/[a-z0-9\-._~%!$&'()*+,;=:@]+)*/?)?)(\?[a-z0-9\-._~%!$&'()*+,;=:@/?]*)?↵
(#[a-z0-9\-._~%!$&'()*+,;=:@/?]*)?$
```
Regex options: Case insensitive
Regex flavors: .NET, Java, JavaScript, PCRE, Perl, Python

Discussion

Extracting the scheme from a URL is easy if you already know that your subject text is a valid URL. A URL's scheme always occurs at the very start of the URL. The caret (Recipe 2.5) specifies that requirement in the regex. The scheme begins with a letter, which can be followed by additional letters, digits, plus signs, hyphens, and dots. We match this with the two character classes ‹[a-z][a-z0-9+\-.]*› (Recipe 2.3).

The scheme is delimited from the rest of the URL with a colon. We add this colon to the regex to make sure we match the scheme only if the URL actually starts with a scheme. Relative URLs do not start with a scheme. The URL syntax specified in RFC 3986 makes sure that relative URLs don't contain any colons, unless those colons are preceded by characters that aren't allowed in schemes. That's why we had to exclude the colon from one of the character classes for matching the path in Recipe 7.7. If you use the regexes in this recipe on a valid but relative URL, they won't find a match at all.

Since the regex matches more than just the scheme itself (it includes the colon), we've added a capturing group to the regular expression. When the regex finds a match, you can retrieve the text matched by the first (and only) capturing group to get the scheme without the colon. Recipe 2.9 tells you all about capturing groups. See Recipe 3.9 to learn how to retrieve text matched by capturing groups in your favorite programming language.

If you don't already know that your subject text is a valid URL, you can use a simplified version of the regex from Recipe 7.7. Since we want to extract the scheme, we can exclude relative URLs, which don't specify a scheme. That makes the regular expression slightly simpler.

Since this regex matches the whole URL, we added an extra capturing group around the part of the regex that matches the scheme. Retrieve the text matched by capturing group number 1 to get the URL's scheme.

See Also

Recipes 2.9, 3.9, and 7.7

7.9 Extracting the User from a URL

Problem

You want to extract the user from a string that holds a URL. For example, you want to extract jan from `http://jan@www.regexcookbook.com`.

Solution

Extract the user from a URL known to be valid

```
^[a-z0-9+\-.]+://([a-z0-9\-._~%!$&'()*+,;=]+)@
```
Regex options: Case insensitive
Regex flavors: .NET, Java, JavaScript, PCRE, Perl, Python, Ruby

Extract the user while validating the URL

```
\A
[a-z][a-z0-9+\-.]*://              # Scheme
([a-z0-9\-._~%!$&'()*+,;=]+)@       # User
([a-z0-9\-._~%]+                    # Named host
|\[[a-f0-9:.]+\]                    # IPv6 host
|\[v[a-f0-9][a-z0-9\-._~%!$&'()*+,;=:]+\])  # IPvFuture host
(:[0-9]+)?                          # Port
(/[a-z0-9\-._~%!$&'()*+,;=:@]+)*/?  # Path
(\?[a-z0-9\-._~%!$&'()*+,;=:@/?]*)? # Query
(\#[a-z0-9\-._~%!$&'()*+,;=:@/?]*)? # Fragment
\Z
```
Regex options: Case insensitive
Regex flavors: .NET, Java, PCRE, Perl, Python, Ruby

```
^[a-z][a-z0-9+\-.]*://([a-z0-9\-._~%!$&'()*+,;=]+)@([a-z0-9\-._~%]+|↵
\[[a-f0-9:.]+\]|\[v[a-f0-9][a-z0-9\-._~%!$&'()*+,;=:]+\])(:[0-9]+)?↵
(/[a-z0-9\-._~%!$&'()*+,;=:@]+)*/?(\?[a-z0-9\-._~%!$&'()*+,;=:@/?]*)?↵
(#[a-z0-9\-._~%!$&'()*+,;=:@/?]*)?$
```
Regex options: Case insensitive
Regex flavors: .NET, Java, JavaScript, PCRE, Perl, Python

Discussion

Extracting the user from a URL is easy if you already know that your subject text is a valid URL. The username, if present in the URL, occurs right after the scheme and the two forward slashes that begin the "authority" part of the URL. The username is separated from the hostname that follows it with an @ sign. Since @ signs are not valid in hostnames, we can be sure that we're extracting the username portion of a URL if we find an @ sign after the two forward slashes and before the next forward slash in the URL. Forward slashes are not valid in usernames, so we don't need to do any special checking for them.

All these rules mean we can very easily extract the username if we know the URL to be valid. We just skip over the scheme with ‹[a-z0-9+\-.]+› and the ://. Then, we grab the username that follows. If we can match the @ sign, we know that the characters before it are the username. The character class ‹[a-z0-9\-._~%!$&'()*+,;=]› lists all the characters that are valid in usernames.

This regex will find a match only if the URL actually specifies a user. When it does, the regex will match both the scheme and the user parts of the URL. Therefore, we've added a capturing group to the regular expression. When the regex finds a match, you can retrieve the text matched by the first (and only) capturing group to get the username without any delimiters or other URL parts. Recipe 2.9 tells you all about capturing groups. See Recipe 3.9 to learn how to retrieve text matched by capturing groups in your favorite programming language.

If you don't already know that your subject text is a valid URL, you can use a simplified version of the regex from Recipe 7.7. Since we want to extract the user, we can exclude URLs that don't specify an authority. The regex in the solution actually matches only URLs that specify an authority that includes a username. Requiring the authority part of the URL makes the regular expression quite a bit simpler. It's even simpler than the one we used in Recipe 7.8.

Since this regex matches the whole URL, we added an extra capturing group around the part of the regex that matches the user. Retrieve the text matched by capturing group number 1 to get the URL's user.

If you want a regex that matches any valid URL, including those that don't specify the user, you can use one of the regexes from Recipe 7.7. The first regex in that recipe captures the user, if present, in the third capturing group. The capturing group will include the @ symbol. You can add an extra capturing group to the regex if you want to capture the username without the @ symbol.

See Also

Recipes 2.9, 3.9, and 7.7

7.10 Extracting the Host from a URL

Problem

You want to extract the host from a string that holds a URL. For example, you want to extract www.regexcookbook.com from http://www.regexcookbook.com/.

Solution

Extract the host from a URL known to be valid

```
\A
[a-z][a-z0-9+\-.]*://              # Scheme
([a-z0-9\-._~%!$&'()*+,;=]+@)?     # User
([a-z0-9\-._~%]+                   # Named or IPv4 host
|\[[a-z0-9\-._~%!$&'()*+,;=:]+\])  # IPv6+ host
```
Regex options: Free-spacing, case insensitive
Regex flavors: .NET, Java, JavaScript, PCRE, Perl, Python, Ruby

```
^[a-z][a-z0-9+\-.]*://([a-z0-9\-._~%!$&'()*+,;=]+@)?([a-z0-9\-._~%]+| ↵
\[[a-z0-9\-._~%!$&'()*+,;=:]+\])
```
Regex options: Case insensitive
Regex flavors: .NET, Java, JavaScript, PCRE, Perl, Python, Ruby

Extract the host while validating the URL

```
\A
[a-z][a-z0-9+\-.]*://                    # Scheme
([a-z0-9\-._~%!$&'()*+,;=]+@)?           # User
([a-z0-9\-._~%]+                         # Named host
|\[[a-f0-9:.]+\]                         # IPv6 host
|\[v[a-f0-9][a-z0-9\-._~%!$&'()*+,;=:]+\])  # IPvFuture host
(:[0-9]+)?                               # Port
(/[a-z0-9\-._~%!$&'()*+,;=:@]+)*/?       # Path
(\?[a-z0-9\-._~%!$&'()*+,;=:@/?]*)?      # Query
(\#[a-z0-9\-._~%!$&'()*+,;=:@/?]*)?      # Fragment
\Z
```
Regex options: Case insensitive
Regex flavors: .NET, Java, PCRE, Perl, Python, Ruby

```
^[a-z][a-z0-9+\-.]*://([a-z0-9\-._~%!$&'()*+,;=]+@)?([a-z0-9\-._~%]+| ↵
\[[a-f0-9:.]+\]|\[v[a-f0-9][a-z0-9\-._~%!$&'()*+,;=:]+\])(:[0-9]+)? ↵
(/[a-z0-9\-._~%!$&'()*+,;=:@]+)*/?(\?[a-z0-9\-._~%!$&'()*+,;=:@/?]*)? ↵
(#[a-z0-9\-._~%!$&'()*+,;=:@/?]*)?$
```
Regex options: Case insensitive
Regex flavors: .NET, Java, JavaScript, PCRE, Perl, Python

Discussion

Extracting the host from a URL is easy if you already know that your subject text is a valid URL. We use ‹\A› or ‹^› to anchor the match to the start of the string. ‹[a-z][a-z0-9+\-.]*://› skips over the scheme, and ‹([a-z0-9\-._~%!$&'()*+,;=]+@)?› skips over the optional user. The hostname follows right after that.

RFC 3986 allows two different notations for the host. Domain names and IPv4 addresses are specified without square brackets, whereas IPv6 and future IP addresses are specified with square brackets. We need to handle those separately because the notation with square brackets allows more punctuation than the notation without. In particular, the colon is allowed between square brackets, but not in domain names or IPv4 addresses. The colon is also used to delimit the hostname (with or without square brackets) from the port number.

‹[a-z0-9\-._~%]+› matches domain names and IPv4 addresses. ‹\[[a-z0-9\-._~%! $&'()*+,;=:]+\]› handles IP version 6 and later. We combine these two using alternation (Recipe 2.8) in a group. The capturing group also allows us to extract the hostname.

This regex will find a match only if the URL actually specifies a host. When it does, the regex will match the scheme, user, and host parts of the URL. When the regex finds a match, you can retrieve the text matched by the second capturing group to get the hostname without any delimiters or other URL parts. The capturing group will include the square brackets for IPv6 addresses. Recipe 2.9 tells you all about capturing groups. See Recipe 3.9 to learn how to retrieve text matched by capturing groups in your favorite programming language.

If you don't already know that your subject text is a valid URL, you can use a simplified version of the regex from Recipe 7.7. Since we want to extract the host, we can exclude URLs that don't specify an authority. This makes the regular expression quite a bit simpler. It's very similar to the one we used in Recipe 7.9. The only difference is that now the user part of the authority is optional again, as it was in Recipe 7.7.

This regex also uses alternation for the various notations for the host, which is kept together by a capturing group. Retrieve the text matched by capturing group number 2 to get the URL's host.

If you want a regex that matches any valid URL, including those that don't specify the user, you can use one of the regexes from Recipe 7.7. The first regex in that recipe captures the host, if present, in the fourth capturing group.

See Also

Recipes 2.9, 3.9, and 7.7

7.11 Extracting the Port from a URL

Problem

You want to extract the port number from a string that holds a URL. For example, you want to extract 80 from http://www.regexcookbook.com:80/.

Solution

Extract the port from a URL known to be valid

```
\A
[a-z][a-z0-9+\-.]*://                      # Scheme
([a-z0-9\-._~%!$&'()*+,;=]+@)?             # User
([a-z0-9\-._~%]+                           # Named or IPv4 host
|\[[a-z0-9\-._~%!$&'()*+,;=:]+\])          # IPv6+ host
:(?<port>[0-9]+)                           # Port number
```
Regex options: Free-spacing, case insensitive
Regex flavors: .NET, Java, JavaScript, PCRE, Perl, Python, Ruby

```
^[a-z][a-z0-9+\-.]*://([a-z0-9\-._~%!$&'()*+,;=]+@)?↵
([a-z0-9\-._~%]+|\[[a-z0-9\-._~%!$&'()*+,;=:]+\]):([0-9]+)
```
Regex options: Case insensitive
Regex flavors: .NET, Java, JavaScript, PCRE, Perl, Python, Ruby

Extract the host while validating the URL

```
\A
[a-z][a-z0-9+\-.]*://                            # Scheme
([a-z0-9\-._~%!$&'()*+,;=]+@)?                   # User
([a-z0-9\-._~%]+                                 # Named host
|\[[a-f0-9:.]+\]                                 # IPv6 host
|\[v[a-f0-9][a-z0-9\-._~%!$&'()*+,;=:]+\])       # IPvFuture host
:([0-9]+)                                        # Port
(/[a-z0-9\-._~%!$&'()*+,;=:@]+)*/?               # Path
(\?[a-z0-9\-._~%!$&'()*+,;=:@/?]*)?              # Query
(\#[a-z0-9\-._~%!$&'()*+,;=:@/?]*)?              # Fragment
\Z
```
Regex options: Case insensitive
Regex flavors: .NET, Java, PCRE, Perl, Python, Ruby

```
^[a-z][a-z0-9+\-.]*:\/\/([a-z0-9\-._~%!$&'()*+,;=]+@)?↵
([a-z0-9\-._~%]+|\[[a-f0-9:.]+\]|\[v[a-f0-9][a-z0-9\-._~%!$&'()*+,;=:]↵
+\]):([0-9]+)(\/[a-z0-9\-._~%!$&'()*+,;=:@]+)*\/?↵
(\?[a-z0-9\-._~%!$&'()*+,;=:@\/?]*)?(#[a-z0-9\-._~%!$&'()*+,;=:@\/?]*)?$
```
Regex options: Case insensitive
Regex flavors: .NET, Java, JavaScript, PCRE, Perl, Python

Discussion

Extracting the port number from a URL is easy if you already know that your subject text is a valid URL. We use ‹\A› or ‹^› to anchor the match to the start of the string. ‹[a-z][a-z0-9+\-.]*://› skips over the scheme, and ‹([a-z0-9\-._~%!$&'()*+,;=]+@)?› skips over the optional user. ‹([a-z0-9\-._~%]+|\[[a-z0-9\-._~%!$&'()*+,;=:]+\])› skips over the hostname.

The port number is separated from the hostname with a colon, which we add as a literal character to the regular expression. The port number itself is simply a string of digits, easily matched with ‹[0-9]+›.

This regex will find a match only if the URL actually specifies a port number. When it does, the regex will match the scheme, user, host, and port number parts of the URL. When the regex finds a match, you can retrieve the text matched by the third capturing group to get the port number without any delimiters or other URL parts.

The other two groups are used to make the username optional, and to keep the two alternatives for the hostname together. Recipe 2.9 tells you all about capturing groups. See Recipe 3.9 to learn how to retrieve text matched by capturing groups in your favorite programming language.

If you don't already know that your subject text is a valid URL, you can use a simplified version of the regex from Recipe 7.7. Since we want to extract the host, we can exclude URLs that don't specify an authority. This makes the regular expression quite a bit simpler. It's very similar to the one we used in Recipe 7.10.

The only difference is that this time the port number isn't optional, and we moved the port number's capturing group to exclude the colon that separates the port number from the hostname. The capturing group's number is 3.

If you want a regex that matches any valid URL, including those that don't specify the port, you can use one of the regexes from Recipe 7.7. The first regex in that recipe captures the port, if present, in the fifth capturing group.

See Also

Recipes 2.9, 3.9, and 7.7

7.12 Extracting the Path from a URL

Problem

You want to extract the path from a string that holds a URL. For example, you want to extract /index.html from http://www.regexcookbook.com/index.html or from /index.html#fragment.

Solution

Extract the path from a string known to hold a valid URL. The following finds a match for all URLs, even for URLs that have no path:

```
\A
# Skip over scheme and authority, if any
([a-z][a-z0-9+\-.]*:(//[^/?#]+)?)?
```

```
# Path
([a-z0-9\-._~%!$&'()*+,;=:@/]*)
```
    Regex options: Free-spacing, case insensitive
    Regex flavors: .NET, Java, PCRE, Perl, Python, Ruby

```
^([a-z][a-z0-9+\-.]*:(//[^/?#]+)?)?([a-z0-9\-._~%!$&'()*+,;=:@/]*)
```
    Regex options: Case insensitive
    Regex flavors: .NET, Java, JavaScript, PCRE, Perl, Python, Ruby

Extract the path from a string known to hold a valid URL. Only match URLs that actually have a path:

```
\A
# Skip over scheme and authority, if any
([a-z][a-z0-9+\-.]*:(//[^/?#]+)?)?
# Path
(/?[a-z0-9\-._~%!$&'()*+,;=@]+(/[a-z0-9\-._~%!$&'()*+,;=:@]+)*/?|/)
# Query, fragment, or end of URL
([#?]|\Z)
```
    Regex options: Free-spacing, case insensitive
    Regex flavors: .NET, Java, PCRE, Perl, Python, Ruby

```
^([a-z][a-z0-9+\-.]*:(//[^/?#]+)?)?(/?[a-z0-9\-._~%!$&'()*+,;=@]+↵
(/[a-z0-9\-._~%!$&'()*+,;=:@]+)*/?|/)([#?]|$)
```
    Regex options: Case insensitive
    Regex flavors: .NET, Java, JavaScript, PCRE, Perl, Python, Ruby

Extract the path from a string known to hold a valid URL. Use atomic grouping to match only those URLs that actually have a path:

```
\A
# Skip over scheme and authority, if any
(?>([a-z][a-z0-9+\-.]*:(//[^/?#]+)?)?)
# Path
([a-z0-9\-._~%!$&'()*+,;=:@/]+)
```
    Regex options: Free-spacing, case insensitive
    Regex flavors: .NET, Java, PCRE, Perl, Ruby

Discussion

You can use a much simpler regular expression to extract the path if you already know that your subject text is a valid URL. While the generic regex in Recipe 7.7 has three different ways to match the path, depending on whether the URL specifies a scheme and/or authority, the specific regex for extracting the path from a URL known to be valid needs to match the path only once.

We start with ‹\A› or ‹^› to anchor the match to the start of the string. ‹[a-z][a-z0-9+\-.]*:› skips over the scheme, and ‹//[^/?#]+› skips over the authority. We can use this very simple regex for the authority because we already know it to be valid, and we're not interested in extracting the user, host, or port from the authority.

The authority starts with two forward slashes, and runs until the start of the path (forward slash), query (question mark), or fragment (hash). The negated character class matches everything up to the first forward slash, question mark, or hash (Recipe 2.3).

Because the authority is optional, we put it into a group followed by the question mark quantifier: ‹(//[^/?#]+)?›. The scheme is also optional. If the scheme is omitted, the authority must be omitted, too. To match this, we place the parts of the regex for the scheme and the optional authority in another group, also made optional with a question mark.

Since we know the URL to be valid, we can easily match the path with a single character class ‹[a-z0-9\-._~%!$&'()*+,;=:@/]*› that includes the forward slash. We don't need to check for consecutive forward slashes, which aren't allowed in paths in URLs.

We indeed use an asterisk rather than a plus as the quantifier on the character class for the path. It may seem strange to make the path optional in a regex that only exists to extract the path from a URL. Actually, making the path optional is essential because of the shortcuts we took in skipping over the scheme and the authority.

In the generic regex for URLs in Recipe 7.7, we have three different ways of matching the path, depending on whether the scheme and/or authority are present in the URL. This makes sure the scheme isn't accidentally matched as the path.

Now we're trying to keep things simple by using only one character class for the path. Consider the URL http://www.regexcookbook.com, which has a scheme and an authority but no path. The first part of our regex will happily match the scheme and the authority. The regex engine then tries to match the character class for the path, but there are no characters left. If the path is optional (using the asterisk quantifier), the regex engine is perfectly happy not to match any characters for the path. It reaches the end of the regex and declares that an overall match has been found.

But if the character class for the path is not optional, the regex engine backtracks. (See Recipe 2.13 if you're not familiar with backtracking.) It remembered that the authority and scheme parts of our regex are optional, so the engine says: let's try this again, without allowing ‹(//[^/?#]+)?› to match anything. ‹[a-z0-9\-._~%!$&'()*+,;=:@/]+› would then match //www.regexcookbook.com for the path, clearly not what we want. If we used a more accurate regex for the path to disallow the double forward slashes, the regex engine would simply backtrack again, and pretend the URL has no scheme. With an accurate regex for the path, it would match http as the path. To prevent that as well, we would have to add an extra check to make sure the path is followed by the query, fragment, or nothing at all. If we do all that, we end up with the regular expressions indicated as "only match URLs that actually have a path" in this Recipe's "Solution". These are quite a bit more complicated than the first two, all just to make the regex not match URLs without a path.

If your regex flavor supports atomic grouping, there's an easier way. All flavors discussed in this book, except JavaScript and Python, support atomic grouping (see Recipe 2.15). Essentially, an atomic group tells the regex engine not to backtrack. If we place the scheme and authority parts of our regex inside an atomic group, the regex engine will be forced to keep the matches of the scheme and authority parts once they've been matched, even if that allows no room for the character class for the path to match. This solution is just as efficient as making the path optional.

Regardless of which regular expression you choose from this recipe, the third capturing group will hold the path. The third capturing group may return the empty string, or null in JavaScript, if you use one of the first two regexes that allow the path to be optional.

If you don't already know that your subject text is a valid URL, you can use the regex from Recipe 7.7. If you're using .NET, you can use the .NET-specific regex that includes three groups named "path" to capture the three parts of the regex that could match the URL's path. If you use another flavor that supports named capture, one of three groups will have captured it: "hostpath", "schemepath", or "relpath". Since only one of the three groups will actually capture anything, a simple trick to get the path is to concatenate the strings returned by the three groups. Two of them will return the empty string, so no actual concatenation is done.

If your flavor does not support named capture, you can use the first regex in Recipe 7.7. It captures the path in group 6, 7, or 8. You can use the same trick to concatenate the text captured by these three groups, as two of them will return the empty string. In JavaScript, however, this won't work. JavaScript returns undefined for groups that don't participate.

Recipe 3.9 has more information on retrieving the text matched by named and numbered capturing groups in your favorite programming language.

See Also

Recipes 2.9, 3.9, and 7.7

7.13 Extracting the Query from a URL

Problem

You want to extract the query from a string that holds a URL. For example, you want to extract param=value from http://www.regexcookbook.com?param=value or from /index.html?param=value.

Solution

```
^[^?#]+\?([^#]+)
```

Regex options: Case insensitive
Regex flavors: .NET, Java, JavaScript, PCRE, Perl, Python, Ruby

Discussion

Extracting the query from a URL is trivial if you know that your subject text is a valid URL. The query is delimited from the part of the URL before it with a question mark. That is the first question mark allowed anywhere in URLs. Thus, we can easily skip ahead to the first question mark with ‹^[^?#]+\?›. The question mark is a metacharacter only outside character classes, but not inside, so we escape the literal question mark outside the character class. The first ‹^› is an anchor (Recipe 2.5), whereas the second ‹^› negates the character class (Recipe 2.3).

Question marks can appear in URLs as part of the (optional) fragment after the query. So we do need to use ‹^[^?#]+\?›, rather than just ‹\?›, to make sure we have the first question mark in the URL, and make sure that it isn't part of the fragment in a URL without a query.

The query runs until the start of the fragment, or the end of the URL if there is no fragment. The fragment is delimited from the rest of the URL with a hash sign. Since hash signs are not permitted anywhere except in the fragment, ‹[^#]+› is all we need to match the query. The negated character class matches everything up to the first hash sign, or everything until the end of the subject if it doesn't contain any hash signs.

This regular expression will find a match only for URLs that actually contain a query. When it matches a URL, the match includes everything from the start of the URL, so we put the ‹[^#]+› part of the regex that matches the query inside a capturing group. When the regex finds a match, you can retrieve the text matched by the first (and only) capturing group to get the query without any delimiters or other URL parts. Recipe 2.9 tells you all about capturing groups. See Recipe 3.9 to learn how to retrieve text matched by capturing groups in your favorite programming language.

If you don't already know that your subject text is a valid URL, you can use one of the regexes from Recipe 7.7. The first regex in that recipe captures the query, if one is present in the URL, into capturing group number 12.

See Also

Recipes 2.9, 3.9, and 7.7

7.14 Extracting the Fragment from a URL

Problem

You want to extract the fragment from a string that holds a URL. For example, you want to extract <u>top</u> from `http://www.regexcookbook.com#top` or from `/index.html#top`.

Solution

    #(.+)

Regex options: Case insensitive
Regex flavors: .NET, Java, JavaScript, PCRE, Perl, Python, Ruby

Discussion

Extracting the fragment from a URL is trivial if you know that your subject text is a valid URL. The query is delimited from the part of the URL before it with a hash sign. The fragment is the only part of URLs in which hash signs are allowed, and the fragment is always the last part of the URL. Thus, we can easily extract the fragment by finding the first hash sign and grabbing everything until the end of the string. ‹#.+› does that nicely. Make sure to turn off free-spacing mode; otherwise, you need to escape the literal hash sign with a backslash.

This regular expression will find a match only for URLs that actually contain a fragment. The match consists of just the fragment, but includes the hash sign that delimits the fragment from the rest of the URL. The solution has an extra capturing group to retrieve just the fragment, without the delimiting #.

If you don't already know that your subject text is a valid URL, you can use one of the regexes from Recipe 7.7. The first regex in that recipe captures the fragment, if one is present in the URL, into capturing group number 13.

See Also

Recipes 2.9, 3.9, and 7.7

7.15 Validating Domain Names

Problem

You want to check whether a string looks like it may be a valid, fully qualified domain name, or find such domain names in longer text.

Solution

Check whether a string looks like a valid domain name:

```
^([a-z0-9]+(-[a-z0-9]+)*\.)+[a-z]{2,}$
```
Regex options: Case insensitive
Regex flavors: .NET, Java, JavaScript, PCRE, Perl, Python

```
\A([a-z0-9]+(-[a-z0-9]+)*\.)+[a-z]{2,}\Z
```
Regex options: Case insensitive
Regex flavors: .NET, Java, PCRE, Perl, Python, Ruby

Find valid domain names in longer text:

```
\b([a-z0-9]+(-[a-z0-9]+)*\.)+[a-z]{2,}\b
```
Regex options: Case insensitive
Regex flavors: .NET, Java, JavaScript, PCRE, Perl, Python, Ruby

Check whether each part of the domain is not longer than 63 characters:

```
\b((?=[a-z0-9-]{1,63}\.)[a-z0-9]+(-[a-z0-9]+)*\.)+[a-z]{2,63}\b
```
Regex options: Case insensitive
Regex flavors: .NET, Java, JavaScript, PCRE, Perl, Python, Ruby

Allow internationalized domain names using the punycode notation:

```
\b((xn--)?[a-z0-9]+(-[a-z0-9]+)*\.)+[a-z]{2,}\b
```
Regex options: Case insensitive
Regex flavors: .NET, Java, JavaScript, PCRE, Perl, Python, Ruby

Check whether each part of the domain is not longer than 63 characters, and allow internationalized domain names using the punycode notation:

```
\b((?=[a-z0-9-]{1,63}\.)(xn--)?[a-z0-9]+(-[a-z0-9]+)*\.)+[a-z]{2,63}\b
```
Regex options: Case insensitive
Regex flavors: .NET, Java, JavaScript, PCRE, Perl, Python, Ruby

Discussion

A domain name has the form of `domain.tld`, or `subdomain.domain.tld`, or any number of additional subdomains. The top-level domain (`tld`) consists of two or more letters. That's the easiest part of the regex: ‹[a-z]{2,}›.

The domain, and any subdomains, consist of letters, digits, and hyphens. Hyphens cannot appear in pairs, and cannot appear as the first or last character in the domain. We handle this with the regular expression ‹[a-z0-9]+(-[a-z0-9]+)*›. This regex allows any number of letters and digits, optionally followed by any number of groups that consist of a hyphen followed by another sequence of letters and digits. Remember that the hyphen is a metacharacter inside character classes (Recipe 2.3) but an ordinary character outside of character classes, so we don't need to escape any hyphens in this regex.

The domain and the subdomains are delimited with a literal dot, which we match with ‹\.› in a regular expression. Since we can have any number of subdomains in addition to the domain, we place the domain name part of the regex and the literal dot in a group that we repeat: ‹([a-z0-9]+(-[a-z0-9]+)*\.)+›. Since the subdomains follow the same syntax as the domain, this one group handles both.

If you want to check whether a string represents a valid domain name, all that remains is to add anchors to the start and the end of the regex that match at the start and the end of the string. We can do this with ‹^› and ‹$› in all flavors except Ruby, and with ‹\A› and ‹\Z› in all flavors except JavaScript. Recipe 2.5 has all the details.

If you want to find domain names in a larger body of text, you can add word boundaries (‹\b›; see Recipe 2.6).

Our first set of regular expressions doesn't check whether each part of the domain is no longer than 63 characters. We can't easily do this, because our regex for each domain part, ‹[a-z0-9]+(-[a-z0-9]+)*›, has three quantifiers in it. There's no way to tell the regex engine to make these add up to 63.

We could use ‹[-a-z0-9]{1,63}› to match a domain part that is 1 to 63 characters long, or ‹\b([-a-z0-9]{1,63}\.)+[a-z]{2,63}› for the whole domain name. But then we're no longer excluding domains with hyphens in the wrong places.

What we can do is to use lookahead to match the same text twice. Review Recipe 2.16 first if you're not familiar with lookahead. We use the same regex ‹[a-z0-9]+(-[a-z0-9]+)*\.› to match a domain name with valid hyphens, and add ‹[-a-z0-9]{1,63}\.› inside a lookahead to check that its length is also 63 characters or less. The result is ‹(?=[-a-z0-9]{1,63}\.)[a-z0-9]+(-[a-z0-9]+)*\.›.

The lookahead ‹(?=[-a-z0-9]{1,63}\.)› first checks that there are 1 to 63 letters, digits, and hyphens until the next dot. It's important to include the dot in the lookahead. Without it, domains longer than 63 characters would still satisfy the lookahead's requirement for 63 characters. Only by putting the literal dot inside the lookahead do we enforce the requirement that we want at most 63 characters.

The lookahead does not consume the text that it matched. Thus, if the lookahead succeeds, ‹[a-z0-9]+(-[a-z0-9]+)*\.› is applied to the same text already matched by the lookahead. We've confirmed there are no more than 63 characters, and now we test that they're the right combination of hyphens and nonhyphens.

Internationalized domain names (IDNs) theoretically can contain pretty much any character. The actual list of characters depends on the registry that manages the top-level domain. For example, .es allows domain names with Spanish characters.

In practice, internationalized domain names are often encoded using a scheme called *punycode*. Although the punycode algorithm is quite complicated, what matters here is that it results in domain names that are a combination of letters, digits, and hyphens, following the rules we're already handling with our regular expression for domain names. The only difference is that the domain name produced by punycode is prefixed with xn--. To add support for such domains to our regular expression, we only need to add ‹(xn--)?› to the group in our regular expression that matches the domain name parts.

See Also

Recipes 2.3, 2.12, and 2.16

7.16 Matching IPv4 Addresses

Problem

You want to check whether a certain string represents a valid IPv4 address in 255.255.255.255 notation. Optionally, you want to convert this address into a 32-bit integer.

Solution

Regular expression

Simple regex to check for an IP address:

```
^(?:[0-9]{1,3}\.){3}[0-9]{1,3}$
```
Regex options: None
Regex flavors: .NET, Java, JavaScript, PCRE, Perl, Python, Ruby

Accurate regex to check for an IP address:

```
^(?:(?:25[0-5]|2[0-4][0-9]|[01]?[0-9][0-9]?)\.){3}
(?:25[0-5]|2[0-4][0-9]|[01]?[0-9][0-9]?)$
```
Regex options: None
Regex flavors: .NET, Java, JavaScript, PCRE, Perl, Python, Ruby

Simple regex to extract IP addresses from longer text:

```
\b(?:[0-9]{1,3}\.){3}[0-9]{1,3}\b
```
Regex options: None
Regex flavors: .NET, Java, JavaScript, PCRE, Perl, Python, Ruby

Accurate regex to extract IP addresses from longer text:

```
\b(?:(?:25[0-5]|2[0-4][0-9]|[01]?[0-9][0-9]?)\.){3}
(?:25[0-5]|2[0-4][0-9]|[01]?[0-9][0-9]?)\b
```
Regex options: None
Regex flavors: .NET, Java, JavaScript, PCRE, Perl, Python, Ruby

Simple regex that captures the four parts of the IP address:

```
^([0-9]{1,3})\.([0-9]{1,3})\.([0-9]{1,3})\.([0-9]{1,3})$
```
Regex options: None
Regex flavors: .NET, Java, JavaScript, PCRE, Perl, Python, Ruby

Accurate regex that captures the four parts of the IP address:

```
^(25[0-5]|2[0-4][0-9]|[01]?[0-9][0-9]?)\. ↵
(25[0-5]|2[0-4][0-9]|[01]?[0-9][0-9]?)\. ↵
(25[0-5]|2[0-4][0-9]|[01]?[0-9][0-9]?)\. ↵
(25[0-5]|2[0-4][0-9]|[01]?[0-9][0-9]?)$
```

Regex options: None
Regex flavors: .NET, Java, JavaScript, PCRE, Perl, Python, Ruby

Perl

```perl
if ($subject =~ m/^([0-9]{1,3})\.([0-9]{1,3})\.([0-9]{1,3})\.([0-9]{1,3})/)
{
    $ip = $1 << 24 | $2 << 16 | $3 << 8 | $4;
}
```

Discussion

A version 4 IP address is usually written in the form 255.255.255.255, where each of the four numbers must be between 0 and 255. Matching such IP addresses with a regular expression is very straightforward.

In the solution we present four regular expressions. Two of them are billed as "simple," while the other two are marked "accurate."

The simple regexes use ‹[0-9]{1,3}› to match each of the four blocks of digits in the IP address. These actually allow numbers from 0 to 999 rather than 0 to 255. The simple regexes are more efficient when you already know your input will contain only valid IP addresses, and you only need to separate the IP addresses from the other stuff.

The accurate regexes use ‹25[0-5]|2[0-4][0-9]|[01]?[0-9][0-9]?› to match each of the four numbers in the IP address. This regex accurately matches a number in the range 0 to 255, with one optional leading zero for numbers between 10 and 99, and two optional leading zeros for numbers between 0 and 9. ‹25[0-5]› matches 250 through 255, ‹2[0-4][0-9]› matches 200 to 249, and ‹[01]?[0-9][0-9]?› takes care of 0 to 199, including the optional leading zeros. Recipe 6.5 explains in detail how to match numeric ranges with a regular expression.

If you want to check whether a string is a valid IP address in its entirety, use one of the regexes that begin with a caret and end with a dollar. These are the start-of-string and end-of-string anchors, explained in Recipe 2.5. If you want to find IP addresses within longer text, use one of the regexes that begin and end with the word boundaries ‹\b› (Recipe 2.6).

The first four regular expressions use the form ‹(?:number\.){3}number›. The first three numbers in the IP address are matched by a noncapturing group (Recipe 2.9) that is repeated three times (Recipe 2.12). The group matches a number and a literal dot, of which there are three in an IP address. The last part of the regex matches the final number in the IP address. Using the noncapturing group and repeating it three times makes our regular expression shorter and more efficient.

To convert the textual representation of the IP address into an integer, we need to capture the four numbers separately. The last two regexes in the solution do this. Instead of using the trick of repeating a group three times, they have four capturing groups, one for each number. Spelling things out this way is the only way we can separately capture all four numbers in the IP address.

Once we've captured the number, combining them into a 32-bit number is easy. In Perl, the special variables $1, $2, $3, and $4 hold the text matched by the four capturing groups in the regular expression. Recipe 3.9 explains how to retrieve capturing groups in other programming languages. In Perl, the string variables for the capturing groups are automatically coerced into numbers when we apply the bitwise left shift operator (<<) to them. In other languages, you may have to call `String.toInteger()` or something similar before you can shift the numbers and combine them with a bitwise **or**.

See Also

Recipes 2.3, 2.8, 2.9, and 2.12

7.17 Matching IPv6 Addresses

Problem

You want to check whether a string represents a valid IPv6 address using the standard, compact, and/or mixed notations.

Solution

Standard notation

Match an IPv6 address in standard notation, which consists of eight 16-bit words using hexadecimal notation, delimited by colons (e.g.: `1762:0:0:0:0:B03:1:AF18`). Leading zeros are optional.

Check whether the whole subject text is an IPv6 address using standard notation:

```
^(?:[A-F0-9]{1,4}:){7}[A-F0-9]{1,4}$
```
Regex options: Case insensitive
Regex flavors: .NET, Java, JavaScript, PCRE, Perl, Python

```
\A(?:[A-F0-9]{1,4}:){7}[A-F0-9]{1,4}\Z
```
Regex options: Case insensitive
Regex flavors: .NET, Java, PCRE, Perl, Python, Ruby

Find an IPv6 address using standard notation within a larger collection of text:

```
(?<![:.\w])(?:[A-F0-9]{1,4}:){7}[A-F0-9]{1,4}(?![:.\w])
```
Regex options: Case insensitive
Regex flavors: .NET, Java, PCRE, Perl, Python, Ruby 1.9

JavaScript and Ruby 1.8 don't support lookbehind. We have to remove the check at the start of the regex that keeps it from finding IPv6 addresses within longer sequences of hexadecimal digits and colons. A word boundary performs part of the test:

```
\b(?:[A-F0-9]{1,4}:){7}[A-F0-9]{1,4}\b
```
Regex options: Case insensitive
Regex flavors: .NET, Java, JavaScript, PCRE, Perl, Python, Ruby

Mixed notation

Match an IPv6 address in mixed notation, which consists of six 16-bit words using hexadecimal notation, followed by four bytes using decimal notation. The words are delimited with colons, and the bytes with dots. A colon separates the words from the bytes. Leading zeros are optional for both the hexadecimal words and the decimal bytes. This notation is used in situations where IPv4 and IPv6 are mixed, and the IPv6 addresses are extensions of the IPv4 addresses. `1762:0:0:0:0:B03:127.32.67.15` is an example of an IPv6 address in mixed notation.

Check whether the whole subject text is an IPv6 address using mixed notation:

```
^(?:[A-F0-9]{1,4}:){6}(?:(?:25[0-5]|2[0-4][0-9]|[01]?[0-9][0-9]?)\.){3}↵
(?:25[0-5]|2[0-4][0-9]|[01]?[0-9][0-9]?)$
```
Regex options: Case insensitive
Regex flavors: .NET, Java, JavaScript, PCRE, Perl, Python, Ruby

Find IPv6 address using mixed notation within a larger collection of text:

```
(?<![:.\w])(?:[A-F0-9]{1,4}:){6}↵
(?:(?:25[0-5]|2[0-4][0-9]|[01]?[0-9][0-9]?)\.){3}↵
(?:25[0-5]|2[0-4][0-9]|[01]?[0-9][0-9]?)(?![:.\w])
```
Regex options: Case insensitive
Regex flavors: .NET, Java, JavaScript, PCRE, Perl, Python, Ruby

JavaScript and Ruby 1.8 don't support lookbehind. We have to remove the check at the start of the regex that keeps it from finding IPv6 addresses within longer sequences of hexadecimal digits and colons. A word boundary performs part of the test:

```
\b(?:[A-F0-9]{1,4}:){6}(?:(?:25[0-5]|2[0-4][0-9]|[01]?[0-9][0-9]?)\.){3}↵
(?:25[0-5]|2[0-4][0-9]|[01]?[0-9][0-9]?)\b
```
Regex options: Case insensitive
Regex flavors: .NET, Java, JavaScript, PCRE, Perl, Python, Ruby

Standard or mixed notation

Match an IPv6 address using standard or mixed notation.

Check whether the whole subject text is an IPv6 address using standard or mixed notation:

```
\A                                            # Start of string
(?:[A-F0-9]{1,4}:){6}                          # 6 words
(?:[A-F0-9]{1,4}:[A-F0-9]{1,4}                 # 2 words
|  (?:(?:25[0-5]|2[0-4][0-9]|[01]?[0-9][0-9]?)\.){3} # or 4 bytes
   (?:25[0-5]|2[0-4][0-9]|[01]?[0-9][0-9]?)
)\Z                                            # End of string
```
> **Regex options:** Free-spacing, case insensitive
> **Regex flavors:** .NET, Java, PCRE, Perl, Python, Ruby

```
^(?:[A-F0-9]{1,4}:){6}(?:[A-F0-9]{1,4}:[A-F0-9]{1,4}| ↵
(?:(?:25[0-5]|2[0-4][0-9]|[01]?[0-9][0-9]?)\.){3}↵
(?:25[0-5]|2[0-4][0-9]|[01]?[0-9][0-9]?))$
```
> **Regex options:** Case insensitive
> **Regex flavors:** .NET, Java, JavaScript, PCRE, Perl, Python

Find IPv6 address using standard or mixed notation within a larger collection of text:

```
(?<![:.\w])                                    # Anchor address
(?:[A-F0-9]{1,4}:){6}                          # 6 words
(?:[A-F0-9]{1,4}:[A-F0-9]{1,4}                 # 2 words
|  (?:(?:25[0-5]|2[0-4][0-9]|[01]?[0-9][0-9]?)\.){3} # or 4 bytes
   (?:25[0-5]|2[0-4][0-9]|[01]?[0-9][0-9]?)
)(?![:.\w])                                    # Anchor address
```
> **Regex options:** Free-spacing, case insensitive
> **Regex flavors:** .NET, Java, PCRE, Perl, Python, Ruby 1.9

JavaScript and Ruby 1.8 don't support lookbehind. We have to remove the check at the start of the regex that keeps it from finding IPv6 addresses within longer sequences of hexadecimal digits and colons. A word boundary performs part of the test:

```
\b                                            # Word boundary
(?:[A-F0-9]{1,4}:){6}                          # 6 words
(?:[A-F0-9]{1,4}:[A-F0-9]{1,4}                 # 2 words
|  (?:(?:25[0-5]|2[0-4][0-9]|[01]?[0-9][0-9]?)\.){3} # or 4 bytes
   (?:25[0-5]|2[0-4][0-9]|[01]?[0-9][0-9]?)
)\b                                            # Word boundary
```
> **Regex options:** Free-spacing, case insensitive
> **Regex flavors:** .NET, Java, PCRE, Perl, Python, Ruby

```
\b(?:[A-F0-9]{1,4}:){6}(?:[A-F0-9]{1,4}:[A-F0-9]{1,4}| ↵
(?:(?:25[0-5]|2[0-4][0-9]|[01]?[0-9][0-9]?)\.){3}↵
(?:25[0-5]|2[0-4][0-9]|[01]?[0-9][0-9]?))\b
```
> **Regex options:** Case insensitive
> **Regex flavors:** .NET, Java, JavaScript, PCRE, Perl, Python, Ruby

Compressed notation

Match an IPv6 address using compressed notation. Compressed notation is the same as standard notation, except that one sequence of one or more words that are zero may be omitted, leaving only the colons before and after the omitted zeros. Addresses using compressed notation can be recognized by the occurrence of two adjacent colons in the address. Only one sequence of zeros may be omitted; otherwise, it would be impossible to determine how many words have been omitted in each sequence. If the omitted sequence of zeros is at the start or the end of the IP address, it will begin or end with two colons. If all numbers are zero, the compressed IPv6 address consists of just two colons, without any digits.

For example, `1762::B03:1:AF18` is the compressed form of `1762:0:0:0:0:B03:1:AF18`. The regular expressions in this section will match both the compressed and the standard form of the IPv6 address. Check whether the whole subject text is an IPv6 address using standard or compressed notation:

```
\A(?:
 # Standard
 (?:[A-F0-9]{1,4}:){7}[A-F0-9]{1,4}
 # Compressed with at most 7 colons
|(?=(?:[A-F0-9]{0,4}:){0,7}[A-F0-9]{0,4}
    \Z) # and anchored
 # and at most 1 double colon
 (([0-9A-F]{1,4}:){1,7}|:)((:[0-9A-F]{1,4}){1,7}|:)
)\Z
```
Regex options: Free-spacing, case insensitive
Regex flavors: .NET, Java, PCRE, Perl, Python, Ruby

```
^(?:(?:[A-F0-9]{1,4}:){7}[A-F0-9]{1,4}|↵
(?=(?:[A-F0-9]{0,4}:){0,7}[A-F0-9]{0,4}$)(([0-9A-F]{1,4}:){1,7}|:)↵
((:[0-9A-F]{1,4}){1,7}|:))$
```
Regex options: Case insensitive
Regex flavors: .NET, Java, JavaScript, PCRE, Perl, Python

Find IPv6 address using standard or compressed notation within a larger collection of text:

```
(?<![:.\w])(?:
 # Standard
 (?:[A-F0-9]{1,4}:){7}[A-F0-9]{1,4}
 # Compressed with at most 7 colons
|(?=(?:[A-F0-9]{0,4}:){0,7}[A-F0-9]{0,4}
    (?![:.\w])) # and anchored
 # and at most 1 double colon
 (([0-9A-F]{1,4}:){1,7}|:)((:[0-9A-F]{1,4}){1,7}|:)
)(?![:.\w])
```
Regex options: Free-spacing, case insensitive
Regex flavors: .NET, Java, PCRE, Perl, Python, Ruby 1.9

JavaScript and Ruby 1.8 don't support lookbehind, so we have to remove the check at the start of the regex that keeps it from finding IPv6 addresses within longer sequences of hexadecimal digits and colons. We cannot use a word boundary, because the address may start with a colon, which is not a word character:

```
(?:
 # Standard
 (?:[A-F0-9]{1,4}:){7}[A-F0-9]{1,4}
 # Compressed with at most 7 colons
|(?=(?:[A-F0-9]{0,4}:){0,7}[A-F0-9]{0,4}
    (?![:.\w])) # and anchored
 # and at most 1 double colon
 (([0-9A-F]{1,4}:){1,7}|:)((:[0-9A-F]{1,4}){1,7}|:)
)(?![:.\w])
```
> **Regex options:** Free-spacing, case insensitive
> **Regex flavors:** .NET, Java, PCRE, Perl, Python, Ruby

```
(?:(?:[A-F0-9]{1,4}:){7}[A-F0-9]{1,4}|(?=(?:[A-F0-9]{0,4}:){0,7}↵
[A-F0-9]{0,4}(?![:.\w]))(([0-9A-F]{1,4}:){1,7}|:)((:[0-9A-F]{1,4})↵
{1,7}|:))(?![:.\w])
```
> **Regex options:** Case insensitive
> **Regex flavors:** .NET, Java, JavaScript, PCRE, Perl, Python, Ruby

Compressed mixed notation

Match an IPv6 address using compressed mixed notation. Compressed mixed notation is the same as mixed notation, except that one sequence of one or more words that are zero may be omitted, leaving only the colons before and after the omitted zeros. The 4 decimal bytes must all be specified, even if they are zero. Addresses using compressed mixed notation can be recognized by the occurrence of two adjacent colons in the first part of the address and the three dots in the second part. Only one sequence of zeros may be omitted; otherwise, it would be impossible to determine how many words have been omitted in each sequence. If the omitted sequence of zeros is at the start of the IP address, it will begin with two colons rather than with a digit.

For example, the IPv6 address `1762::B03:127.32.67.15` is the compressed form of `1762:0:0:0:0:B03:127.32.67.15`. The regular expressions in this section will match both compressed and noncompressed IPv6 address using mixed notation.

Check whether the whole subject text is an IPv6 address using compressed or non-compressed mixed notation:

```
\A
(?:
 # Non-compressed
 (?:[A-F0-9]{1,4}:){6}
 # Compressed with at most 6 colons
|(?=(?:[A-F0-9]{0,4}:){0,6}
    (?:[0-9]{1,3}\.){3}[0-9]{1,3}  # and 4 bytes
```

```
    \Z)                                          # and anchored
   # and at most 1 double colon
   (([0-9A-F]{1,4}:){0,5}|:)((:[0-9A-F]{1,4}){1,5}:|:)
   )
   # 255.255.255.
   (?:(?:25[0-5]|2[0-4][0-9]|[01]?[0-9][0-9]?)\.){3}
   # 255
   (?:25[0-5]|2[0-4][0-9]|[01]?[0-9][0-9]?)
   \Z
```

Regex options: Free-spacing, case insensitive
Regex flavors: .NET, Java, PCRE, Perl, Python, Ruby

```
^(?:(?:[A-F0-9]{1,4}:){6}|(?=(?:[A-F0-9]{0,4}:){0,6}(?:[0-9]{1,3}\.)↵
{3}[0-9]{1,3}$)(([0-9A-F]{1,4}:){0,5}|:)((:[0-9A-F]{1,4}){1,5}:|:))↵
(?:(?:25[0-5]|2[0-4][0-9]|[01]?[0-9][0-9]?)\.){3}(?:25[0-5]|2[0-4]↵
[0-9]|[01]?[0-9][0-9]?)$
```

Regex options: Case insensitive
Regex flavors: .NET, Java, JavaScript, PCRE, Perl, Python

Find IPv6 address using compressed or noncompressed mixed notation within a larger collection of text:

```
(?<![:.\w])
(?:
 # Non-compressed
 (?:[A-F0-9]{1,4}:){6}
 # Compressed with at most 6 colons
|(?=(?:[A-F0-9]{0,4}:){0,6}
    (?:[0-9]{1,3}\.){3}[0-9]{1,3}   # and 4 bytes
    (?![:.\w]))                     # and anchored
 # and at most 1 double colon
  (([0-9A-F]{1,4}:){0,5}|:)((:[0-9A-F]{1,4}){1,5}:|:)
 )
 # 255.255.255.
 (?:(?:25[0-5]|2[0-4][0-9]|[01]?[0-9][0-9]?)\.){3}
 # 255
 (?:25[0-5]|2[0-4][0-9]|[01]?[0-9][0-9]?)
 (?![:.\w])
```

Regex options: Free-spacing, case insensitive
Regex flavors: .NET, Java, PCRE, Perl, Python, Ruby 1.9

JavaScript and Ruby 1.8 don't support lookbehind, so we have to remove the check at the start of the regex that keeps it from finding IPv6 addresses within longer sequences of hexadecimal digits and colons. We cannot use a word boundary, because the address may start with a colon, which is not a word character.

```
(?:
 # Non-compressed
 (?:[A-F0-9]{1,4}:){6}
 # Compressed with at most 6 colons
```

```
|(?=(?:[A-F0-9]{0,4}:){0,6}
    (?:[0-9]{1,3}\.){3}[0-9]{1,3}    # and 4 bytes
    (?![:.\w]))                       # and anchored
 # and at most 1 double colon
 (([0-9A-F]{1,4}:){0,5}|:)((:[0-9A-F]{1,4}){1,5}:|:)
)
# 255.255.255.
(?:(?:25[0-5]|2[0-4][0-9]|[01]?[0-9][0-9]?)\.){3}
# 255
(?:25[0-5]|2[0-4][0-9]|[01]?[0-9][0-9]?)
(?![:.\w])
```
Regex options: Free-spacing, case insensitive
Regex flavors: .NET, Java, PCRE, Perl, Python, Ruby

```
(?:(?:[A-F0-9]{1,4}:){6}|(?=(?:[A-F0-9]{0,4}:){0,6}(?:[0-9]{1,3}\.){3}↵
[0-9]{1,3}(?![:.\w]))(([0-9A-F]{1,4}:){0,5}|:)((:[0-9A-F]{1,4}){1,5}:|:))↵
(?:(?:25[0-5]|2[0-4][0-9]|[01]?[0-9][0-9]?)\.){3}↵
(?:25[0-5]|2[0-4][0-9]|[01]?[0-9][0-9]?)(?![:.\w])
```
Regex options: Case insensitive
Regex flavors: .NET, Java, JavaScript, PCRE, Perl, Python, Ruby

Standard, mixed, or compressed notation

Match an IPv6 address using any of the notations explained earlier: standard, mixed, compressed, and compressed mixed.

Check whether the whole subject text is an IPv6 address:

```
\A(?:
# Mixed
 (?:
  # Non-compressed
  (?:[A-F0-9]{1,4}:){6}
  # Compressed with at most 6 colons
 |(?=(?:[A-F0-9]{0,4}:){0,6}
     (?:[0-9]{1,3}\.){3}[0-9]{1,3}    # and 4 bytes
     \Z)                               # and anchored
  # and at most 1 double colon
  (([0-9A-F]{1,4}:){0,5}|:)((:[0-9A-F]{1,4}){1,5}:|:)
 )
 # 255.255.255.
 (?:(?:25[0-5]|2[0-4][0-9]|[01]?[0-9][0-9]?)\.){3}
 # 255
 (?:25[0-5]|2[0-4][0-9]|[01]?[0-9][0-9]?)
|# Standard
 (?:[A-F0-9]{1,4}:){7}[A-F0-9]{1,4}
|# Compressed with at most 7 colons
 (?=(?:[A-F0-9]{0,4}:){0,7}[A-F0-9]{0,4}
     \Z)  # and anchored
```

```
      # and at most 1 double colon
      ((([0-9A-F]{1,4}:){1,7}|:)((:[0-9A-F]{1,4}){1,7}|:)
      )\Z
```
Regex options: Free-spacing, case insensitive
Regex flavors: .NET, Java, PCRE, Perl, Python, Ruby

```
^(?:(?:(?:[A-F0-9]{1,4}:){6}|(?=(?:[A-F0-9]{0,4}:){0,6}(?:[0-9]{1,3}\.){3}↵
[0-9]{1,3}$)(([0-9A-F]{1,4}:){0,5}|:)((:[0-9A-F]{1,4}){1,5}:|:))↵
(?:(?:25[0-5]|2[0-4][0-9]|[01]?[0-9][0-9]?)\.){3}↵
(?:25[0-5]|2[0-4][0-9]|[01]?[0-9][0-9]?)|(?:[A-F0-9]{1,4}:){7}↵
[A-F0-9]{1,4}|(?=(?:[A-F0-9]{0,4}:){0,7}[A-F0-9]{0,4}$)↵
(([0-9A-F]{1,4}:){1,7}|:)((:[0-9A-F]{1,4}){1,7}|:))$
```
Regex options: Case insensitive
Regex flavors: .NET, Java, JavaScript, PCRE, Perl, Python

Find an IPv6 address using standard or mixed notation within a larger collection of text:

```
(?<![:.\w])(?:
# Mixed
 (?:
  # Non-compressed
  (?:[A-F0-9]{1,4}:){6}
  # Compressed with at most 6 colons
 |(?=(?:[A-F0-9]{0,4}:){0,6}
     (?:[0-9]{1,3}\.){3}[0-9]{1,3}  # and 4 bytes
     (?![:.\w]))                    # and anchored
  # and at most 1 double colon
  ((([0-9A-F]{1,4}:){0,5}|:)((:[0-9A-F]{1,4}){1,5}:|:)
  )
 # 255.255.255.
 (?:(?:25[0-5]|2[0-4][0-9]|[01]?[0-9][0-9]?)\.){3}
 # 255
 (?:25[0-5]|2[0-4][0-9]|[01]?[0-9][0-9]?)
|# Standard
 (?:[A-F0-9]{1,4}:){7}[A-F0-9]{1,4}
|# Compressed with at most 7 colons
 (?=(?:[A-F0-9]{0,4}:){0,7}[A-F0-9]{0,4}
     (?![:.\w]))  # and anchored
  # and at most 1 double colon
  (([0-9A-F]{1,4}:){1,7}|:)((:[0-9A-F]{1,4}){1,7}|:)
)(?![:.\w])
```
Regex options: Free-spacing, case insensitive
Regex flavors: .NET, Java, PCRE, Perl, Python, Ruby 1.9

JavaScript and Ruby 1.8 don't support lookbehind, so we have to remove the check at the start of the regex that keeps it from finding IPv6 addresses within longer sequences of hexadecimal digits and colons. We cannot use a word boundary, because the address may start with a colon, which is not a word character.

```
(?:
 # Mixed
 (?:
  # Non-compressed
  (?:[A-F0-9]{1,4}:){6}
  # Compressed with at most 6 colons
  |(?=(?:[A-F0-9]{0,4}:){0,6}
      (?:[0-9]{1,3}\.){3}[0-9]{1,3}   # and 4 bytes
      (?![:.\w]))                       # and anchored
   # and at most 1 double colon
   (([0-9A-F]{1,4}:){0,5}|:)((:[0-9A-F]{1,4}){1,5}:|:)
 )
 # 255.255.255.
 (?:(?:25[0-5]|2[0-4][0-9]|[01]?[0-9][0-9]?)\.){3}
 # 255
 (?:25[0-5]|2[0-4][0-9]|[01]?[0-9][0-9]?)
|# Standard
 (?:[A-F0-9]{1,4}:){7}[A-F0-9]{1,4}
|# Compressed with at most 7 colons
 (?=(?:[A-F0-9]{0,4}:){0,7}[A-F0-9]{0,4}
     (?![:.\w]))   # and anchored
  # and at most 1 double colon
  (([0-9A-F]{1,4}:){1,7}|:)((:[0-9A-F]{1,4}){1,7}|:)
)(?![:.\w])
```
Regex options: Free-spacing, case insensitive

Regex flavors: .NET, Java, PCRE, Perl, Python, Ruby

```
(?:(?:(?:[A-F0-9]{1,4}:){6}|(?=(?:[A-F0-9]{0,4}:){0,6}(?:[0-9]{1,3}\.){3}↵
[0-9]{1,3}(?![:.\w]))(([0-9A-F]{1,4}:){0,5}|:)((:[0-9A-F]{1,4}){1,5}:|:))↵
(?:(?:25[0-5]|2[0-4][0-9]|[01]?[0-9][0-9]?)\.){3}(?:25[0-5]|2[0-4][0-9]|↵
[01]?[0-9][0-9]?)|(?:[A-F0-9]{1,4}:){7}[A-F0-9]{1,4}|↵
(?=(?:[A-F0-9]{0,4}:){0,7}[A-F0-9]{0,4}(?![:.\w]))↵
(([0-9A-F]{1,4}:){1,7}|:)((:[0-9A-F]{1,4}){1,7}|:))(?![:.\w])
```
Regex options: Case insensitive

Regex flavors: .NET, Java, JavaScript, PCRE, Perl, Python, Ruby

Discussion

Because of the different notations, matching an IPv6 address isn't nearly as simple as matching an IPv4 address. Which notations you want to accept will greatly impact the complexity of your regular expression. Basically, there are two notations: standard and mixed. You can decide to allow only one of the two notations, or both. That gives us three sets of regular expressions.

Both the standard and mixed notations have a compressed form that omits zeros. Allowing compressed notation gives us another three sets of regular expressions.

You'll need slightly different regexes depending on whether you want to check if a given string is a valid IPv6 address, or whether you want to find IP addresses in a larger body of text. To validate the IP address, we use anchors, as Recipe 2.5 explains. JavaScript uses the ‹^› and ‹$› anchors, whereas Ruby uses ‹\A› and ‹\Z›. All other flavors support both. Ruby also supports ‹^› and ‹$›, but allows them to match at embedded line breaks in the string as well. You should use the caret and dollar in Ruby only if you know your string doesn't have any embedded line breaks.

To find IPv6 addresses within larger text, we use negative lookbehind ‹(?<![:.\w])› and negative lookahead ‹(?![:.\w])› to make sure the address isn't preceded or followed by a word character (letter, digit, or underscore) or by a dot or colon. This makes sure we don't match parts of longer sequences of digits and colons. Recipe 2.16 explains how lookbehind and lookahead work. If lookaround isn't available, word boundaries can check that the address isn't preceded or followed by a word character, but only if the first and last character in the address are sure to be (hexadecimal) digits. Compressed notation allows addresses that start and end with a colon. If we were to put a word boundary before or after a colon, it would require an adjacent letter or digit, which isn't what we want. Recipe 2.6 explains everything about word boundaries.

Standard notation

Standard IPv6 notation is very straightforward to handle with a regular expression. We need to match eight words in hexadecimal notation, delimited by seven colons. ‹[A-F0-9]{1,4}› matches 1 to 4 hexadecimal characters, which is what we need for a 16-bit word with optional leading zeros. The character class (Recipe 2.3) lists only the uppercase letters. The case-insensitive matching mode takes care of the lowercase letters. See Recipe 3.4 to learn how to set matching modes in your programming language.

The noncapturing group ‹(?:[A-F0-9]{1,4}:){7}› matches a hexadecimal word followed by a literal colon. The quantifier repeats the group seven times. The first colon in this regex is part of the regex syntax for noncapturing groups, as Recipe 2.9 explains, and the second is a literal colon. The colon is not a metacharacter in regular expressions, except in a few very specific situations as part of a larger regex token. Therefore, we don't need to use backslashes to escape literal colons in our regular expressions. We could escape them, but it would only make the regex harder to read.

Mixed notation

The regex for the mixed IPv6 notation consists of two parts. ‹(?:[A-F0-9]{1,4}:){6}› matches six hexadecimal words, each followed by a literal colon, just like we have a sequence of seven such words in the regex for the standard IPv6 notation.

Instead of having one more hexadecimal word at the end, we now have a full IPv4 address at the end. We match this using the "accurate" regex shown in Recipe 7.16.

Standard or mixed notation

Allowing both standard and mixed notation requires a slightly longer regular expression. The two notations differ only in their representation of the last 32 bits of the IPv6 address. Standard notation uses two 16-bit words, whereas mixed notation uses 4 decimal bytes, as with IPv4.

The first part of the regex matches six hexadecimal words, as in the regex that supports mixed notation only. The second part of the regex is now a noncapturing group with the two alternatives for the last 32 bits. As Recipe 2.8 explains, the alternation operator (vertical bar) has the lowest precedence of all regex operators. Thus, we need the noncapturing group to exclude the six words from the alternation.

The first alternative, located to the left of the vertical bar, matches two hexadecimal words with a literal colon in between. The second alternative matches an IPv4 address.

Compressed notation

Things get quite a bit more complicated when we allow compressed notation. The reason is that compressed notation allows a variable number of zeros to be omitted. 1:0:0:0:0:6:0:0, 1::6:0:0, and 1:0:0:0:0:6:: are three ways of writing the same IPv6 address. The address may have at most eight words, but it needn't have any. If it has less than eight, it must have one double-colon sequence that represents the omitted zeros.

Variable repetition is easy with regular expressions. If an IPv6 address has a double colon, there can be at most seven words before and after the double colon. We could easily write this as:

```
(
  ([0-9A-F]{1,4}:){1,7}   # 1 to 7 words to the left
| :                       # or a double colon at the start
)
(
  (:[0-9A-F]{1,4}){1,7}   # 1 to 7 words to the right
| :                       # or a double colon at the end
)
```
Regex options: Free-spacing, case insensitive
Regex flavors: .NET, Java, PCRE, Perl, Python, Ruby

 This regular expression and the ones that follow in this discussion also work with JavaScript if you eliminate the comments and extra whitespace. JavaScript supports all the features used in these regexes, except free-spacing, which we use here to make these regexes easier to understand.

This regular expression matches all compressed IPv6 addresses, but it doesn't match any addresses that use noncompressed standard notation.

This regex is quite simple. The first part matches 1 to 7 words followed by a colon, or just the colon for addresses that don't have any words to the left of the double colon.

The second part matches 1 to 7 words preceded by a colon, or just the colon for addresses that don't have any words to the right of the double colon. Put together, valid matches are a double colon by itself, a double colon with 1 to 7 words at the left only, a double colon with 1 to 7 words at the right only, and a double colon with 1 to 7 words at both the left and the right.

It's the last part that is troublesome. The regex allows 1 to 7 words at both the left and the right, as it should, but it doesn't specify that the total number of words at the left and right must be 7 or less. An IPv6 address has 8 words. The double colon indicates we're omitting at least one word, so at most 7 remain.

Regular expressions don't do math. They can count if something occurs between 1 and 7 times. But they cannot count if two things occur for a total of 7 times, splitting those 7 times between the two things in any combination.

To understand this problem better, let's examine a simple analog. Say we want to match something in the form of aaaaxbbb. The string must be between 1 and 8 characters long and consist of 0 to 7 times a, exactly one x, and 0 to 7 times b.

There are two ways to solve this problem with a regular expression. One way is to spell out all the alternatives. The next section discussing compressed mixed notation uses this. It can result in a long-winded regex, but it will be easy to understand.

```
\A(?:a{7}x
 |   a{6}xb?
 |   a{5}xb{0,2}
 |   a{4}xb{0,3}
 |   a{3}xb{0,4}
 |   a{2}xb{0,5}
 |   axb{0,6}
 |   xb{0,7}
)\Z
```
Regex options: Free-spacing
Regex flavors: .NET, Java, PCRE, Perl, Python, Ruby

This regular expression has one alternative for each of the possible number of letters a. Each alternative spells out how many letters b are allowed after the given number of letters a and the x have been matched. The other solution is to use lookahead. This is the method used for the regex within the "Solution" section that matches an IPv6 address using compressed notation. If you're not familiar with lookahead, see Recipe 2.16 first. Using lookahead, we can essentially match the same text twice, checking it for two conditions.

```
\A
  (?=[abx]{1,8}\Z)
  a{0,7}xb{0,7}
\Z
```
Regex options: Free-spacing
Regex flavors: .NET, Java, PCRE, Perl, Python, Ruby

The ⟨\A⟩ at the start of the regex anchors it to the start of the subject text. Then the positive lookahead kicks in. It checks whether a series of 1 to 8 letters ⟨a⟩, ⟨b⟩, and/or ⟨x⟩ can be matched, and that the end of the string is reached when those 1 to 8 letters have been matched. The ⟨\Z⟩ inside the lookahead is crucial. In order to limit the regex to strings of eight characters or less, the lookahead must test that there aren't any further characters after those that it matched.

In a different scenario, you might use another kind of delimiter instead of ⟨\A⟩ and ⟨\Z⟩. If you wanted to do a "whole words only" search for aaaaxbbb and friends, you would use word boundaries. But to restrict the regex match to the right length, you have to use some kind of delimiter, and you have to put the delimiter that matches the end of the string both inside the lookahead and at the end of the regular expression. If you don't, the regular expression will partly match a string that has too many characters.

When the lookahead has satisfied its requirement, it gives up the characters that it has matched. Thus, when the regex engine attempts ⟨a{0,7}⟩, it is back at the start of the string. The fact that the lookahead doesn't consume the text that it matched is the key difference between a lookahead and a noncapturing group, and is what allows us to apply two patterns to a single piece of text.

Although ⟨a{0,7}xb{0,7}⟩ on its own could match up to 15 letters, in this case it can match only 8, because the lookahead already made sure there are only 8 letters. All ⟨a{0,7}xb{0,7}⟩ has to do is to check that they appear in the right order. In fact, ⟨a*xb*⟩ would have the exact same effect as ⟨a{0,7}xb{0,7}⟩ in this regular expression.

The second ⟨\Z⟩ at the end of the regex is also essential. Just like the lookahead needs to make sure there aren't too many letters, the second test after the lookahead needs to make sure that all the letters are in the right order. This makes sure we don't match something like axba, even though it satisfies the lookahead by being between 1 and 8 characters long.

Compressed mixed notation

Mixed notation can be compressed just like standard notation. Although the four bytes at the end must always be specified, even when they are zero, the number of hexadecimal words before them again becomes variable. If all the hexadecimal words are zero, the IPv6 address could end up looking like an IPv4 address with two colons before it.

Creating a regex for compressed mixed notation involves solving the same issues as for compressed standard notation. The previous section explains all this.

The main difference between the regex for compressed mixed notation and the regex for compressed (standard) notation is that the one for compressed mixed notation needs to check for the IPv4 address after the six hexadecimal words. We do this check at the end of the regex, using the same regex for accurate IPv4 addresses from Recipe 7.16 that we used in this recipe for noncompressed mixed notation.

We have to match the IPv4 part of the address at the end of the regex, but we also have to check for it inside the lookahead that makes sure we have no more than six colons or six hexadecimal words in the IPv6 address. Since we're already doing an accurate test at the end of the regex, the lookahead can suffice with a simple IPv4 check. The lookahead doesn't need to validate the IPv4 part, as the main regex already does that. But it does have to match the IPv4 part, so that the end-of-string anchor at the end of the lookahead can do its job.

Standard, mixed, or compressed notation

The final set of regular expressions puts it all together. These match an IPv6 address in any notation: standard or mixed, compressed or not.

These regular expressions are formed by alternating the ones for compressed mixed notation and compressed (standard) notation. These regexes already use alternation to match both the compressed and noncompressed variety of the IPv6 notation they support.

The result is a regular expression with three top-level alternatives, with the first alternative consisting of two alternatives of its own. The first alternative matches an IPv6 address using mixed notation, either noncompressed or compressed. The second alternative matches an IPv6 address using standard notation. The third alternative covers the compressed (standard) notation.

We have three top-level alternatives instead of two alternatives that each contain their own two alternatives because there's no particular reason to group the alternatives for standard and compressed notation. For mixed notation, we do keep the compressed and noncompressed alternatives together, because it saves us having to spell out the IPv4 part twice.

Essentially, we combined this regex:

    ^(6words|compressed6words)ip4$

and this regex:

    ^(8words|compressed8words)$

into:

    ^((6words|compressed6words)ip4|8words|compressed8words)$

rather than:

    ^((6words|compressed6words)ip4|(8words|compressed8words))$

See Also

Recipes 2.16 and 7.16

7.18 Validate Windows Paths

Problem

You want to check whether a string looks like a valid path to a folder or file on the Microsoft Windows operating system.

Solution

Drive letter paths

```
\A
[a-z]:\\                     # Drive
(?:[^\\/:*?"<>|\r\n]+\\)*    # Folder
[^\\/:*?"<>|\r\n]*           # File
\Z
```
Regex options: Free-spacing, case insensitive
Regex flavors: .NET, Java, PCRE, Perl, Python, Ruby

```
^[a-z]:\\(?:[^\\/:*?"<>|\r\n]+\\)*[^\\/:*?"<>|\r\n]*$
```
Regex options: Case insensitive
Regex flavors: .NET, Java, JavaScript, PCRE, Perl, Python

Drive letter and UNC paths

```
\A
(?:[a-z]:|\\\\[a-z0-9_.$]+\\[a-z0-9_.$]+)\\  # Drive
(?:[^\\/:*?"<>|\r\n]+\\)*                     # Folder
[^\\/:*?"<>|\r\n]*                            # File
\Z
```
Regex options: Free-spacing, case insensitive
Regex flavors: .NET, Java, PCRE, Perl, Python, Ruby

```
^(?:[a-z]:|\\\\[a-z0-9_.$]+\\[a-z0-9_.$]+)\\(?:[^\\/:*?"<>|\r\n]+\\)*↵
[^\\/:*?"<>|\r\n]*$
```
Regex options: Case insensitive
Regex flavors: .NET, Java, JavaScript, PCRE, Perl, Python

Drive letter, UNC, and relative paths

```
\A
(?:(?:[a-z]:|\\\\[a-z0-9_.$]+\\[a-z0-9_.$]+)\\|  # Drive
    \\?[^\\/:*?"<>|\r\n]+\\?)                    # Relative path
(?:[^\\/:*?"<>|\r\n]+\\)*                         # Folder
[^\\/:*?"<>|\r\n]*                                # File
\Z
```
Regex options: Free-spacing, case insensitive
Regex flavors: .NET, Java, PCRE, Perl, Python, Ruby

```
^(?:(?:[a-z]:|\\\\[a-z0-9_.$]+\\[a-z0-9_.$]+)\\|\\?[^\\/:*?"<>|\r\n]+\\?)↵
(?:[^\\/:*?"<>|\r\n]+\\)*[^\\/:*?"<>|\r\n]*$
```
Regex options: Case insensitive
Regex flavors: .NET, Java, JavaScript, PCRE, Perl, Python

Discussion

Drive letter paths

Matching a full path to a file or folder on a drive that has a drive letter is very straight-forward. The drive is indicated with a single letter, followed by a colon and a backslash. We easily match this with ‹[a-z]:\\›. The backslash is a metacharacter in regular expressions, and so we need to escape it with another backslash to match it literally.

Folder and filenames on Windows can contain all characters, except these: \/:*?"<>|. Line breaks aren't allowed either. We can easily match a sequence of all characters except these with the negated character class ‹[^\\/:*?"<>|\r\n]+›. The backslash is a metacharacter in character classes too, so we escape it. ‹\r› and ‹\n› are the two line break characters. See Recipe 2.3 to learn more about (negated) character classes. The plus quantifier (Recipe 2.12) specifies we want one or more such characters.

Folders are delimited with backslashes. We can match a sequence of zero or more folders with ‹(?:[^\\/:*?"<>|\r\n]+\\)*›, which puts the regex for the folder name and a literal backslash inside a noncapturing group (Recipe 2.9) that is repeated zero or more times with the asterisk (Recipe 2.12).

To match the filename, we use ‹[^\\/:*?"<>|\r\n]*›. The asterisk makes the filename optional, to allow paths that end with a backslash. If you don't want to allow paths that end with a backslash, change the last ‹*› in the regex into a ‹+›.

Drive letter and UNC paths

Paths to files on network drives that aren't mapped to drive letters can be accessed using Universal Naming Convention (UNC) paths. UNC paths have the form *server* *share\folder\file*.

We can easily adapt the regex for drive letter paths to support UNC paths as well. All we have to do is to replace the ‹[a-z]:› part that matches the drive letter with something that matches a drive letter or server name.

‹(?:[a-z]:|\\\\[a-z0-9_.$]+\\[a-z0-9_.$]+)› does that. The vertical bar is the alternation operator (Recipe 2.8). It gives the choice between a drive letter matched with ‹[a-z]:› or a server and share name matched with ‹\\\\[a-z0-9_.$]+\\[a-z0-9_.$]+›. The alternation operator has the lowest precedence of all regex operators. To group the two alternatives together, we use a noncapturing group. As Recipe 2.9 explains, the characters ‹(?:› form the somewhat complicated opening bracket of a noncapturing group. The question mark does not have its usual meaning after a parenthesis.

The rest of the regular expression can remain the same. The name of the share in UNC paths will be matched by the part of the regex that matches folder names.

Drive letter, UNC, and relative paths

A relative path is one that begins with a folder name (perhaps the special folder `..` to select the parent folder) or consists of just a filename. To support relative paths, we add a third alternative to the "drive" portion of our regex. This alternative matches the start of a relative path rather than a drive letter or server name.

‹\\?[^\\/:*?"<>|\r\n]+\\?› matches the start of the relative path. The path can begin with a backslash, but it doesn't have to. ‹\\?› matches the backslash if present, or nothing otherwise. ‹[^\\/:*?"<>|\r\n]+› matches a folder or filename. If the relative path consists of just a filename, the final ‹\\?› won't match anything, and neither will the "folder" and "file" parts of the regex, which are both optional. If the relative path specifies a folder, the final ‹\\?› will match the backslash that delimits the first folder in the relative path from the rest of the path. The "folder" part then matches the remaining folders in the path, if any, and the "file" part matches the filename.

The regular expression for matching relative paths no longer neatly uses distinct parts of the regex to match distinct parts of the subject text. The regex part labeled "relative path" will actually match a folder or filename if the path is relative. If the relative path specifies one or more folders, the "relative path" part matches the first folder, and the "folder" and "file" paths match what's left. If the relative path is just a filename, it will be matched by the "relative path" part, leaving nothing for the "folder" and "file" parts. Since we're only interested in validating the path, this doesn't matter. The comments in the regex are just labels to help us understand it.

If we wanted to extract parts of the path into capturing groups, we'd have to be more careful to match the drive, folder, and filename separately. The next recipe handles that problem.

See Also

Recipes 2.3, 2.8, 2.9, and 2.12

7.19 Split Windows Paths into Their Parts

Problem

You want to check whether a string looks like a valid path to a folder or file on the Microsoft Windows operating system. If the string turns out to hold a valid Windows path, then you also want to extract the drive, folder, and filename parts of the path separately.

Solution

Drive letter paths

```
\A
(?<drive>[a-z]:)\\
(?<folder>(?:[^\\/:*?"<>|\r\n]+\\)*)
(?<file>[^\\/:*?"<>|\r\n]*)
\Z
```

Regex options: Free-spacing, case insensitive
Regex flavors: .NET, PCRE 7, Perl 5.10, Ruby 1.9

```
\A
(?P<drive>[a-z]:)\\
(?P<folder>(?:[^\\/:*?"<>|\r\n]+\\)*)
(?P<file>[^\\/:*?"<>|\r\n]*)
\Z
```

Regex options: Free-spacing, case insensitive
Regex flavors: PCRE 4 and later, Perl 5.10, Python

```
\A
([a-z]:)\\
((?:[^\\/:*?"<>|\r\n]+\\)*)
([^\\/:*?"<>|\r\n]*)
\Z
```

Regex options: Free-spacing, case insensitive
Regex flavors: .NET, Java, PCRE, Perl, Python, Ruby

```
^([a-z]:)\\((?:[^\\/:*?"<>|\r\n]+\\)*)([^\\/:*?"<>|\r\n]*)$
```

Regex options: Case insensitive
Regex flavors: .NET, Java, JavaScript, PCRE, Perl, Python

Drive letter and UNC paths

```
\A
(?<drive>[a-z]:|\\\\[a-z0-9_.$]+\\[a-z0-9_.$]+)\\
(?<folder>(?:[^\\/:*?"<>|\r\n]+\\)*)
(?<file>[^\\/:*?"<>|\r\n]*)
\Z
```

Regex options: Free-spacing, case insensitive
Regex flavors: .NET, PCRE 7, Perl 5.10, Ruby 1.9

```
\A
(?P<drive>[a-z]:|\\\\[a-z0-9_.$]+\\[a-z0-9_.$]+)\\
(?P<folder>(?:[^\\/:*?"<>|\r\n]+\\)*)
(?P<file>[^\\/:*?"<>|\r\n]*)
\Z
```

Regex options: Free-spacing, case insensitive
Regex flavors: PCRE 4 and later, Perl 5.10, Python

```
\A
([a-z]:|\\\\[a-z0-9_.$]+\\[a-z0-9_.$]+)\\
((?:[^\\/:*?"<>|\r\n]+\\)*)
([^\\/:*?"<>|\r\n]*)
\Z
```
Regex options: Free-spacing, case insensitive
Regex flavors: .NET, Java, PCRE, Perl, Python, Ruby

```
^([a-z]:|\\\\[a-z0-9_.$]+\\[a-z0-9_.$]+)\\((?:[^\\/:*?"<>|\r\n]+\\)*)↵
([^\\/:*?"<>|\r\n]*)$
```
Regex options: Case insensitive
Regex flavors: .NET, Java, JavaScript, PCRE, Perl, Python

Drive letter, UNC, and relative paths

 These regular expressions can match the empty string. See the Discussion for more details and an alternative solution.

```
\A
(?<drive>[a-z]:\\|\\\\[a-z0-9_.$]+\\[a-z0-9_.$]+\\|\\?)
(?<folder>(?:[^\\/:*?"<>|\r\n]+\\)*)
(?<file>[^\\/:*?"<>|\r\n]*)
\Z
```
Regex options: Free-spacing, case insensitive
Regex flavors: .NET, PCRE 7, Perl 5.10, Ruby 1.9

```
\A
(?P<drive>[a-z]:\\|\\\\[a-z0-9_.$]+\\[a-z0-9_.$]+\\|\\?)
(?P<folder>(?:[^\\/:*?"<>|\r\n]+\\)*)
(?P<file>[^\\/:*?"<>|\r\n]*)
\Z
```
Regex options: Free-spacing, case insensitive
Regex flavors: PCRE 4 and later, Perl 5.10, Python

```
\A
([a-z]:\\|\\\\[a-z0-9_.$]+\\[a-z0-9_.$]+\\|\\?)
((?:[^\\/:*?"<>|\r\n]+\\)*)
([^\\/:*?"<>|\r\n]*)
\Z
```
Regex options: Free-spacing, case insensitive
Regex flavors: .NET, Java, PCRE, Perl, Python, Ruby

```
^([a-z]:\\|\\\\[a-z0-9_.$]+\\[a-z0-9_.$]+\\|\\?)↵
((?:[^\\/:*?"<>|\r\n]+\\)*)([^\\/:*?"<>|\r\n]*)$
```
Regex options: Case insensitive
Regex flavors: .NET, Java, JavaScript, PCRE, Perl, Python

Discussion

The regular expressions in this recipe are very similar to the ones in the previous recipe. This discussion assumes you've already read and understood the discussion of the previous recipe.

Drive letter paths

We've made only one change to the regular expressions for drive letter paths, compared to the ones in the previous recipe. We've added three capturing groups that you can use to retrieve the various parts of the path: ‹drive›, ‹folder›, and ‹file›. You can use these names if your regex flavor supports named capture (Recipe 2.11). If not, you'll have to reference the capturing groups by their numbers: 1, 2, and 3. See Recipe 3.9 to learn how to get the text matched by named and/or numbered groups in your favorite programming language.

Drive letter and UNC paths

We've added the same three capturing groups to the regexes for UNC paths.

Drive letter, UNC, and relative paths

Things get a bit more complicated if we also want to allow relative paths. In the previous recipe, we could just add a third alternative to the drive part of the regex to match the start of the relative path. We can't do that here. In case of a relative path, the capturing group for the drive should remain empty.

Instead, the literal backslash that was after the capturing group for the drives in the regex in the "drive letter and UNC paths" section is now moved into that capturing group. We add it to the end of the alternatives for the drive letter and the network share. We add a third alternative with an optional backslash for relative paths that may or may not begin with a backslash. Because the third alternative is optional, the whole group for the drive is essentially optional.

The resulting regular expression correctly matches all Windows paths. The problem is that by making the drive part optional, we now have a regex in which everything is optional. The folder and file parts were already optional in the regexes that support absolute paths only. In other words: our regular expression will match the empty string.

If we want to make sure the regex doesn't match empty strings, we'd have to add additional alternatives to deal with relative paths that specify a folder (in which case the filename is optional), and relative paths that don't specify a folder (in which case the filename is mandatory):

```
\A
(?:
    (?<drive>[a-z]:|\\\\[a-z0-9_.$]+\\[a-z0-9_.$]+)\\
    (?<folder>(?:[^\\/:*?"<>|\r\n]+\\)*)
```

```
    (?<file>[^\\/:*?"<>|\r\n]*)
|   (?<relativefolder>\\?(?:[^\\/:*?"<>|\r\n]+\\)+)
    (?<file2>[^\\/:*?"<>|\r\n]*)
|   (?<relativefile>[^\\/:*?"<>|\r\n]+)
)
\Z
```
Regex options: Free-spacing, case insensitive
Regex flavors: .NET, PCRE 7, Perl 5.10, Ruby 1.9

```
\A
(?:
    (?P<drive>[a-z]:|\\\\[a-z0-9_.$]+\\[a-z0-9_.$]+)\\
    (?P<folder>(?:[^\\/:*?"<>|\r\n]+\\)*)
    (?P<file>[^\\/:*?"<>|\r\n]*)
|   (?P<relativefolder>\\?(?:[^\\/:*?"<>|\r\n]+\\)+)
    (?P<file2>[^\\/:*?"<>|\r\n]*)
|   (?P<relativefile>[^\\/:*?"<>|\r\n]+)
)
\Z
```
Regex options: Free-spacing, case insensitive
Regex flavors: PCRE 4 and later, Perl 5.10, Python

```
\A
(?:
    ([a-z]:|\\\\[a-z0-9_.$]+\\[a-z0-9_.$]+)\\
    ((?:[^\\/:*?"<>|\r\n]+\\)*)
    ([^\\/:*?"<>|\r\n]*)
|   (\\?(?:[^\\/:*?"<>|\r\n]+\\)+)
    ([^\\/:*?"<>|\r\n]*)
|   ([^\\/:*?"<>|\r\n]+)
)
\Z
```
Regex options: Free-spacing, case insensitive
Regex flavors: .NET, Java, PCRE, Perl, Python, Ruby

```
^(?:([a-z]:|\\\\[a-z0-9_.$]+\\[a-z0-9_.$]+)\\((?:[^\\/:*?"<>|\r\n]+\\)*)↵
([^\\/:*?"<>|\r\n]*)|(\\?(?:[^\\/:*?"<>|\r\n]+\\)+)([^\\/:*?"<>|\r\n]*)|↵
([^\\/:*?"<>|\r\n]+))$
```
Regex options: Case insensitive
Regex flavors: .NET, Java, JavaScript, PCRE, Perl, Python

The price we pay for excluding zero-length strings is that we now have six capturing groups to capture the three different parts of the path. You'll have to look at the scenario in which you want to use these regular expressions to determine whether it's easier to do an extra check for empty strings before using the regex or to spend more effort in dealing with multiple capturing groups after a match has been found.

If you're using the .NET regex flavor, you can give multiple named groups the same name. The .NET flavor is the only one that treats groups with the same name as if they were a single capturing group. With this regex in .NET, you can simply get the match of the folder or file group, without worrying about which of the two folder groups or three file groups actually participated in the regex match:

```
\A
(?:
    (?<drive>[a-z]:|\\\\[a-z0-9_.$]+\\[a-z0-9_.$]+)\\
    (?<folder>(?:[^\\/:*?"<>|\r\n]+\\)*)
    (?<file>[^\\/:*?"<>|\r\n]*)
 |  (?<folder>\\?(?:[^\\/:*?"<>|\r\n]+\\)+)
    (?<file>[^\\/:*?"<>|\r\n]*)
 |  (?<file>[^\\/:*?"<>|\r\n]+)
)
\Z
```

Regex options: Free-spacing, case insensitive
Regex flavor: .NET

See Also

Recipes 2.9, 2.11, 3.9, and 7.18

7.20 Extract the Drive Letter from a Windows Path

Problem

You have a string that holds a (syntactically) valid path to a file or folder on a Windows PC or network. You want to extract the drive letter, if any, from the path. For example, you want to extract c from c:\folder\file.ext.

Solution

```
^([a-z]):
```

Regex options: Case insensitive
Regex flavors: .NET, Java, JavaScript, PCRE, Perl, Python, Ruby

Discussion

Extracting the drive letter from a string known to hold a valid path is trivial, even if you don't know whether the path actually starts with a drive letter. The path could be a relative path or a UNC path.

Colons are invalid characters in Windows paths, except to delimit the drive letter. Thus, if we have a letter followed by a colon at the start of the string, we know the letter is the drive letter.

The anchor ‹^› matches at the start of the string (Recipe 2.5). The fact that the caret also matches at embedded line breaks in Ruby doesn't matter, because valid Windows paths don't include line breaks. The character class ‹[a-z]› matches a single letter (Recipe 2.3). We place the character class between a pair of parentheses (which form a capturing group) so you can get the drive letter without the literal colon that is also matched by the regular expression. We add the colon to the regular expression to make sure we're extracting the drive letter, rather than the first letter in a relative path.

See Also

Recipe 2.9 tells you all about capturing groups.

See Recipe 3.9 to learn how to retrieve text matched by capturing groups in your favorite programming language.

Follow Recipe 7.19 if you don't know in advance that your string holds a valid Windows path.

7.21 Extract the Server and Share from a UNC Path

Problem

You have a string that holds a (syntactically) valid path to a file or folder on a Windows PC or network. If the path is a UNC path, then you want to extract the name of the network server and the share on the server that the path points to. For example, you want to extract <u>server</u> and <u>share</u> from \\server\share\folder\file.ext.

Solution

```
^\\\\([a-z0-9_.$]+)\\([a-z0-9_.$]+)
```
Regex options: Case insensitive
Regex flavors: .NET, Java, JavaScript, PCRE, Perl, Python, Ruby

Discussion

Extracting the network server and share from a string known to hold a valid path is easy, even if you don't know whether the path is a UNC path. The path could be a relative path or use a drive letter.

UNC paths begin with two backslashes. Two consecutive backslashes are not allowed in Windows paths, except to begin a UNC path. Thus, if a known valid path begins with two backslashes, we know that the server and share name must follow.

The anchor ‹^› matches at the start of the string (Recipe 2.5). The fact that the caret also matches at embedded line breaks in Ruby doesn't matter, because valid Windows paths don't include line breaks. ‹\\\\› matches two literal backslashes. Since the backslash is a metacharacter in regular expressions, we have to escape a backslashsh with another backslash if we want to match it as a literal character. The first character class, ‹[a-z0-9_.$]+›, matches the name of the network server. The second one, after another literal backslash, matches the name of the share. We place both character classes between a pair of parentheses, which form a capturing group. That way you can get the server name alone from the first capturing group, and the share name alone from the second capturing group. The overall regex match will be \\server\share.

See Also

Recipe 2.9 tells you all about capturing groups.

See Recipe 3.9 to learn how to retrieve text matched by capturing groups in your favorite programming language.

Follow Recipe 7.19 if you don't know in advance that your string holds a valid Windows path.

7.22 Extract the Folder from a Windows Path

Problem

You have a string that holds a (syntactically) valid path to a file or folder on a Windows PC or network, and you want to extract the folder from the path. For example, you want to extract \folder\subfolder\ from c:\folder\subfolder\file.ext or \\server \share\folder\subfolder\file.ext.

Solution

```
^([a-z]:|\\\\[a-z0-9_.$]+\\[a-z0-9_.$]+)?((?:\\|^)↵
(?:[^\\/:*?"<>|\r\n]+\\)+)
```
Regex options: Case insensitive
Regex flavors: .NET, Java, JavaScript, PCRE, Perl, Python, Ruby

Discussion

Extracting the folder from a Windows path is a bit tricky if we want to support UNC paths, because we can't just grab the part of the path between backslashes. If we did, we'd be grabbing the server and share from UNC paths too.

The first part of the regex, ‹^([a-z]:|\\\\[a-z0-9_.$]+\\[a-z0-9_.$]+)?›, skips over the drive letter or the network server and network share names at the start of the path. This piece of the regex consists of a capturing group with two alternatives. The first alternative matches the drive letter, as in Recipe 7.20, and the second alternative matches the server and share in UNC paths, as in Recipe 7.21. Recipe 2.8 explains the alternation operator.

The question mark after the group makes it optional. This allows us to support relative paths, which don't have a drive letter or network share.

The folders are easily matched with ‹(?:[^\\/:*?"<>|\r\n]+\\)+›. The character class matches a folder name. The noncapturing group matches a folder name followed by a literal backslash that delimits the folders from each other and from the filename. We repeat this group one or more times. This means our regular expression will match only those paths that actually specify a folder. Paths that specify only a filename, drive, or network share won't be matched.

If the path begins with a drive letter or network share, that must be followed by a backslash. A relative path may or may not begin with a backslash. Thus, we need to add an optional backslash to the start of the group that matches the folder part of the path. Since we will only use our regex on paths known to be valid, we don't have to be strict about requiring the backslash in case of a drive letter or network share. We only have to allow for it.

Because we require the regex to match at least one folder, we have to make sure that our regex doesn't match e\ as the folder in \\server\share\. That's why we use ‹(\\|^)› rather than ‹\\?› to add the optional backslash at the start of the capturing group for the folder.

If you're wondering why \\server\shar might be matched as the drive and e\ as the folder, review Recipe 2.13. Regular expression engines backtrack. Imagine this regex:

```
^([a-z]:|\\\\[a-z0-9_.$]+\\[a-z0-9_.$]+)?↵
((?:\\?(?:[^\\/:*?"<>|\r\n]+\\)+)
```

This regex, just like the regex in the solution, requires at least one nonbackslash character and one backslash for the path. If the regex has matched \\server\share for the drive in \\server\share and then fails to match the folder group, it doesn't just give up; it tries different permutations of the regex.

In this case, the engine has remembered that the character class ‹[a-z0-9_.$]+›, which matches the network share, doesn't have to match all available characters. One character is enough to satisfy the ‹+›. The engine backtracks by forcing the character class to give up one character, and then it tries to continue.

When the engine continues, it has two remaining characters in the subject string to match the folder: e\. These two characters are enough to satisfy ‹(?:[^\\/:*?"<>|\r\n]+\\)+›, and we have an overall match for the regex. But it's not the match we wanted.

Using ‹(\\|^)› instead of ‹\\?› solves this. It still allows for an optional backslash, but when the backslash is missing, it requires the folder to begin at the start of the string. This means that if a drive has been matched, and thus the regex engine has proceeded beyond the start of the string, the backslash is required. The regex engine will still try to backtrack if it can't match any folders, but it will do so in vain because ‹(\\|^)› will fail to match. The regex engine will backtrack until it is back at the start of the string. The capturing group for the drive letter and network share is optional, so the regex engine is welcome to try to match the folder at the start of the string. Although ‹(\\|^)› will match there, the rest of the regex will not, because ‹(?:[^\\/:*?"<>|\r\n]+\\)+› does not allow the colon that follows the drive letter or the double backslash of the network share.

If you're wondering why we don't use this technique in Recipes 7.18 and 7.19, that's because those regular expressions don't require a folder. Since everything after the part that matches the drive in those regexes is optional, the regex engine never does any backtracking. Of course, making things optional can lead to different problems, as discussed in Recipe 7.19.

When this regular expression finds a match, the first capturing group will hold the drive letter or network share, and the second capturing group will hold the folder. The first capturing group will be empty in case of a relative path. The second capturing group will always contain at least one folder. If you use this regex on a path that doesn't specify a folder, the regex won't find a match at all.

See Also

Recipe 2.9 tells you all about capturing groups.

See Recipe 3.9 to learn how to retrieve text matched by capturing groups in your favorite programming language.

Follow Recipe 7.19 if you don't know in advance that your string holds a valid Windows path.

7.23 Extract the Filename from a Windows Path

Problem

You have a string that holds a (syntactically) valid path to a file or folder on a Windows PC or network, and you want to extract the filename, if any, from the path. For example, you want to extract <u>file.ext</u> from c:\folder\file.ext.

Solution

```
[^\\/:*?"<>|\r\n]+$
```
Regex options: Case insensitive
Regex flavors: .NET, Java, JavaScript, PCRE, Perl, Python, Ruby

Discussion

Extracting the filename from a string known to hold a valid path is trivial, even if you don't know whether the path actually ends with a filename.

The filename always occurs at the end of the string. It can't contain any colons or backslashes, so it cannot be confused with folders, drive letters, or network shares, which all use backslashes and/or colons.

The anchor ‹$› matches at the end of the string (Recipe 2.5). The fact that the dollar also matches at embedded line breaks in Ruby doesn't matter, because valid Windows paths don't include line breaks. The negated character class ‹[^\\/:*?"<>| \r\n]+› (Recipe 2.3) matches the characters that can occur in filenames. Though the regex engine scans the string from left to right, the anchor at the end of the regex makes sure that only the last run of filename characters in the string will be matched, giving us our filename.

If the string ends with a backslash, as it will for paths that don't specify a filename, the regex won't match at all. When it does match, it will match only the filename, so we don't need to use any capturing groups to separate the filename from the rest of the path.

See Also

See Recipe 3.7 to learn how to retrieve text matched by the regular expression in your favorite programming language.

Follow Recipe 7.19 if you don't know in advance that your string holds a valid Windows path.

7.24 Extract the File Extension from a Windows Path

Problem

You have a string that holds a (syntactically) valid path to a file or folder on a Windows PC or network, and you want to extract the file extension, if any, from the path. For example, you want to extract **.ext** from c:\folder\file.ext.

Solution

```
\.[^.\\/:*?"<>|\r\n]+$
```
Regex options: Case insensitive
Regex flavors: .NET, Java, JavaScript, PCRE, Perl, Python, Ruby

Discussion

We can use the same technique for extracting the file extension as we used for extracting the whole filename in Recipe 7.23.

The only difference is in how we handle dots. The regex in Recipe 7.23 does not include any dots. The negated character class in that regex will simply match any dots that happen to be in the filename.

A file extension must begin with a dot. Thus, we add ⟨\.⟩ to match a literal dot at the start of the regex.

Filenames such as `Version 2.0.txt` may contain multiple dots. The last dot is the one that delimits the extension from the filename. The extension itself should not contain any dots. We specify this in the regex by putting a dot inside the character class. The dot is simply a literal character inside character classes, so we don't need to escape it. The ⟨$⟩ anchor at the end of the regex makes sure we match **.txt** instead of **.0**.

If the string ends with a backslash, or with a filename that doesn't include any dots, the regex won't match at all. When it does match, it will match the extension, including the dot that delimits the extension and the filename.

See Also

Follow Recipe 7.19 if you don't know in advance that your string holds a valid Windows path.

7.25 Strip Invalid Characters from Filenames

Problem

You want to strip a string of characters that aren't valid in Windows filenames. For example, you have a string with the title of a document that you want to use as the default filename when the user clicks the Save button the first time.

Solution

Regular expression

```
[\\/:"*?<>|]+
```

> **Regex options:** None
> **Regex flavors:** .NET, Java, JavaScript, PCRE, Perl, Python, Ruby

Replacement

Leave the replacement text blank.

> **Replacement text flavors:** .NET, Java, JavaScript, PHP, Perl, Python, Ruby

Discussion

The characters \/:"*?<>| are not valid in Windows filenames. These characters are used to delimit drives and folders, to quote paths, or to specify wildcards and redirection on the command line.

We can easily match those characters with the character class ‹[\\/:"*?<>|]›. The backslash is a metacharacter inside character classes, so we need to escape it with another backslash. All the other characters are always literal characters inside character classes.

We repeat the character class with a ‹+› for efficiency. This way, if the string contains a sequence of invalid characters, the whole sequence will be deleted at once, rather than character by character. You won't notice the performance difference when dealing with very short strings, such as filenames, but it is a good technique to keep in mind when you're dealing with larger sets of data that are more likely to have longer runs of characters that you want to delete.

Since we just want to delete the offending characters, we run a search-and-replace with the empty string as the replacement text.

See Also

Recipe 3.14 explains how to run a search-and-replace with a fixed replacement text in your favorite programming language.

## CHAPTER 8

Markup and Data Interchange

This final chapter focuses on common tasks that come up when working with an assortment of common markup languages and formats: HTML, XHTML, XML, CSV, and INI. Although we'll assume at least basic familiarity with these technologies, a brief description of each is included at the start of the chapter to make sure we're on the same page before digging in. The descriptions here concentrate on the basic syntax rules needed to correctly search through the data structures of each format. Other details will be introduced as we encounter relevant issues.

Although it's not always apparent on the surface, some of these formats can be surprisingly complex to process and manipulate accurately, at least using regular expressions. It's usually best to use dedicated parsers and APIs instead of regular expressions when performing many of the tasks in this chapter, especially if accuracy is critical (e.g., if your processing might have security implications). Nevertheless, these recipes show useful techniques that can be used with many quick processing tasks.

So let's look at what we're up against. Many of the difficulties we'll encounter throughout this chapter involve how we should handle cases that deviate from the following rules in expected or unexpected ways.

Hypertext Markup Language (HTML)

HTML is used to describe the structure, semantics, and appearance of billions of web pages and other documents. It's common to want to process HTML using regular expressions, but you should know up front that the language is poorly suited to the rigidity and precision of regular expressions. This is especially true of the bastardized HTML that is common on many web pages, thanks in part to the extreme tolerance for poorly constructed HTML that web browsers are known for. In this chapter we'll concentrate on the rules needed to process the key components of well-formed HTML: elements (and the attributes they contain), character references, comments, and document type declarations. This book covers HTML 4.01, which was finalized in 1999 and remains the latest finalized version of the standard as of this writing.

The basic HTML building blocks are called *elements*. Elements are written using *tags*, which are surrounded by angle brackets. Elements are classified as either block-level (e.g., paragraphs, headings, lists, tables, and forms) or inline (e.g., hyperlinks, citations, italics, and form input controls). Elements usually have both a start tag (e.g., `<html>`) and end tag (`</html>`). An element's start tag may contain *attributes*, which are described later. Between the tags is the element's *content*, which can be composed of text and other elements or left empty. Elements may be nested, but cannot overlap (e.g., `<div><div></div></div>` is OK, but not `<div><span></div></span>`). For some elements (such as `<p>`, which marks a paragraph), the end tag is optional. Elements with an optional end tag are automatically closed by the start of new block-level elements. A few elements (including `<br>`, which terminates a line) cannot contain content, and never use an end tag. However, an empty element may still contain attributes. HTML element names start with a letter from A–Z. All valid elements use only letters and numbers in their names. Element names are not case-sensitive.

`<script>` and `<style>` elements warrant special consideration because they let you embed scripting language code and stylesheets in your document. These elements end after the first occurrence of `</style>` or `</script>`, even if it appears within a comment or string inside the style or scripting language.

Attributes appear within an element's start tag after the element name, and are separated by one or more whitespace characters. Most attributes are written as name-value pairs. Thus, the following example shows an `<a>` (anchor) element with two attributes and the content "Click me!":

```
<a href="http://www.regexcookbook.com"
    title = 'Regex Cookbook'>Click me!</a>
```

As shown here, an attribute's name and value are separated by an equals sign and optional whitespace. The value is enclosed with single or double quotes. To use the enclosing quote type within the value, you must use a character reference (described next). The enclosing quote characters are not required if the value contains only the characters A–Z, a–z, 0–9, underscore, period, colon, and hyphen (written in regex, that's ‹^[-.0-9:A-Z_a-z]+$›). A few attributes (such as the `selected` and `checked` attributes used with some form elements) affect the element that contains them simply by their presence, and do not require a value. In these cases, the equals sign that separates an attribute's name and value is also omitted. Alternatively, these "minimized" attributes may reuse their name as their value (e.g., `selected="selected"`). Attribute names start with a letter from A–Z. All valid attributes use only letters and hyphens in their names. Attributes may appear in any order, and their names are not case-sensitive.

HTML version 4 defines 252 *character entity references* and more than a million *numeric character references* (collectively, we'll call these *character references*). Numeric character references refer to a character by its Unicode code point, and use the format &#*nnnn*; or &#x*hhhh*;, where *nnnn* is one or more decimal digits from 0–9 and *hhhh* is one or more hexadecimal digits from 0–9 and A–F (case-insensitive). Character entity references are written as &*entityname*; (case-sensitive, unlike most other aspects of HTML), and are especially helpful when entering literal characters that are sensitive in some contexts, such as angle brackets (< and >), double quotes ("), and ampersand (&).

Also common is the   entity (no-break space, position 0xA0), which is particularly useful since all occurrences of this character are rendered, even when they appear in sequence. Spaces, tabs, and line breaks are all normally rendered as a single space character, even if many of them are entered in a row. The ampersand character (&) cannot be used outside of character references.

HTML comments have the following syntax:

```
<!-- this is a comment -->
<!-- so is this, but this comment
     spans more than one line -->
```

Content within comments has no special meaning, and is hidden from view by most user agents. Whitespace is allowed between the closing -- and >. For compatibility with ancient (pre-1995) browsers, some people surround the content of <script> and <style> elements with an HTML comment. Modern browsers ignore these comments and process the script or style content normally.

Finally, HTML documents often start with a *document type declaration* (informally, a "DOCTYPE"), which identifies a machine-readable specification of the permitted and prohibited content for the document. The DOCTYPE looks a bit similar to an HTML element, as shown in the following line used with documents wishing to conform to the HTML 4.01 Strict definition:

```
<!DOCTYPE html PUBLIC "-//W3C//DTD HTML 4.01//EN"
     "http://www.w3.org/TR/html4/strict.dtd">
```

So, that's the physical structure of an HTML document in a nutshell. Be aware that real-world HTML is often rife with deviations from these rules that most browsers are happy to accommodate. Beyond these basics, each element has restrictions on the content and attributes that may appear within it in order for an HTML document to be considered valid. Such content rules are beyond the scope of this book, but O'Reilly's *HTML & XHTML: The Definitive Guide* by Chuck Musciano and Bill Kennedy is a good source if you need more information.

 Because the structure of HTML is very similar to XHTML and XML (both described next), many regular expressions in this chapter are written to support all three markup languages.

Extensible Hypertext Markup Language (XHTML)

XHTML was designed as the successor to HTML 4.01, and migrates HTML from its SGML heritage to an XML foundation. However, development of HTML is now continuing separately, and thus XHTML is more accurately considered an alternative to HTML. This book covers XHTML 1.0 and 1.1. Although these versions of the standard are mostly backward-compatible with HTML, there are a few key differences from the HTML structure we've just described:

- XHTML documents may start with an *XML declaration* such as `<?xml version="1.0" encoding="UTF-8"?>`.

- Nonempty elements must have a closing tag. Empty elements must either use a closing tag or end with `/>`.

- Element and attribute names are case-sensitive and use lowercase.

- Due to the use of XML namespace prefixes, element and attribute names may include a colon, in addition to the characters found in HTML names.

- Unquoted attribute values are not allowed. Attribute values must be enclosed in single or double quotes.

- Attributes must have an accompanying value.

There are a number of other differences between HTML and XHTML that mostly affect edge cases and error handling, but generally they do not affect the regexes in this chapter. For more on the differences between HTML and XHTML, see *http://www.w3.org/TR/xhtml1/#diffs* and *http://wiki.whatwg.org/wiki/HTML_vs._XHTML*.

 Because the syntax of XHTML is very similar to HTML and is formed from XML, many regular expressions in this chapter are written to support all three of these markup languages. Recipes that refer to "(X)HTML" handle HTML and XHTML equally. You usually cannot depend on a document using only HTML or XHTML conventions, since mix-ups are common and web browsers generally don't mind.

Extensible Markup Language (XML)

XML is a general-purpose language designed primarily for sharing structured data. It is used as the foundation to create a wide array of markup languages, including XHTML, which we've just discussed. This book covers XML versions 1.0 and 1.1. A full description of XML features and grammar is beyond the scope of this book, but for our purposes, there are only a few key differences from the HTML structure we've already described:

- XML documents may start with an XML declaration such as `<?xml version="1.0" encoding="UTF-8"?>`, and may contain other, similarly formatted processing *instructions*. For example, `<?xml-stylesheet type="text/xsl"`

`href="transform.xslt"?>` specifies that the XSL transformation file *transform.xslt* should be applied to the document.

- The DOCTYPE may include internal markup declarations within square brackets. For example:

```
<!DOCTYPE example [
  <!ENTITY copy "&#169;">
  <!ENTITY copyright-notice "Copyright &copy; 2008, O'Reilly Media">
]>
```

- *CDATA sections* are used to escape blocks of text. They begin with the string `<![CDATA[` and end with the first occurrence of `]]>`.

- Nonempty elements must have a closing tag. Empty elements must either use a closing tag or end with `/>`.

- XML *names* (which govern the rules for element, attribute, and entity reference names) are case-sensitive, and may use a large group of Unicode characters. The allowed characters include A–Z, a–z, colon (:), and underscore (_), as well as 0–9, hyphen (-), and period (.) after the first character. See Recipe 8.4 for more precise details.

- Unquoted attribute values are not allowed. Attribute values must be enclosed in single or double quotes.

- Attributes must have an accompanying value.

There are many other rules that must be adhered to when authoring well-formed XML documents, or if you want to write your own conforming XML parser. However, the rules we've just described (appended to the structure we've already outlined for HTML documents) are generally enough for simple regex searches.

> Because the structure of XML is very similar to HTML and forms the basis of XHTML, many regular expressions in this chapter are written to support all three markup languages. Recipes that refer to "XML-style" markup handle XML, XHTML, and HTML equally.

Comma-Separated Values (CSV)

CSV is an old but still very common file format used for spreadsheet-like data. The CSV format is supported by most spreadsheets and database management systems, and is especially popular for exchanging data between applications. Although there is no official CSV specification, an attempt at a common definition was published in October 2005 as RFC 4180 and registered with IANA as MIME type "text/csv". Before this RFC was published, the CSV conventions used by Microsoft Excel had been established as more or less a de facto standard. Since the RFC specifies rules that are very similar to those used by Excel, this doesn't present much of a problem.

This chapter covers the CSV formats specified by RFC 4180 and used by Microsoft Excel 2003 and later.

As the name suggests, CSV files contain a list of values, or *fields*, separated by commas. Each row, or *record*, appears on its own line. The last field in a record is not followed by a comma. The last record in a file may or may not be followed by a line break. Throughout the entire file, each record should have the same number of fields.

The value of each CSV field may be unadorned or enclosed with double quotes. Fields also may be entirely empty. Any field that contains commas, double quotes, or line breaks must be enclosed in double quotes. A double quote appearing inside a field is escaped by preceding it with another double quote.

The first record in a CSV file is sometimes used as a header with the names of each column. This cannot be programmatically determined from the content of a CSV file alone, so some applications prompt the user to decide how the first row should be handled.

RFC 4180 specifies that leading and trailing spaces in a field are part of the value. Some older versions of Excel ignored these spaces, but Excel 2003 and later follow the RFC on this point. The RFC does not specify error handling for unescaped double quotes or pretty much anything else. Excel's handling can be a bit unpredictable in edge cases, so it's important to ensure that double quotes are escaped, fields containing double quotes are themselves enclosed with double quotes, and quoted fields do not contain leading or trailing spaces outside of the quotes.

The following CSV example demonstrates many of the rules we've just discussed. It contains two records with three fields each:

```
aaa,b b,"""c"" cc"
1,,"333, three,
still more threes"
```

Table 8-1 shows how the CSV content just shown would be displayed in a table.

Table 8-1. Example CSV output

aaa	b b	"c" cc
1	*(empty)*	333, three, still more threes

Although we've described the CSV rules observed by the chapters in this recipe, there is a fair amount of variation in how different programs read and write CSV files. Many applications even allow files with the "csv" extension to use any delimiter, not just commas. Other common variations include how commas (or other field delimiters), double quotes, and line breaks are embedded within fields, and whether leading and trailing whitespace in unquoted fields is ignored or treated as literal text.

Initialization files (INI)

The lightweight INI file format is commonly used for configuration files. It is poorly defined, and as a result, there is plenty of variation in how the format is interpreted by different programs and systems. The regexes in this chapter adhere to the most common INI file conventions, which we'll describe here.

INI file *parameters* are name-value pairs, separated by an equals sign and optional spaces or tabs. Values may be enclosed in single or double quotes, which allows them to contain leading and trailing whitespace and other special characters.

Parameters may be grouped into *sections*, which start with the section's name enclosed in square brackets on its own line. Sections continue until either the next section declaration or the end of the file. Sections cannot be nested.

A semicolon marks the start of a *comment*, which continues until the end of the line. A comment may appear on the same line as a parameter or section declaration. Content within comments has no special meaning.

Following is an example INI file with an introductory comment (noting when the file was last modified), two sections ("user" and "post"), and a total of three parameters ("name", "title", and "content"):

```
; last modified 2008-12-25

[user]
name=J. Random Hacker

[post]
title = Regular Expressions Rock!
content = "Let me count the ways..."
```

8.1 Find XML-Style Tags

Problem

You want to match any HTML, XHTML, or XML tags in a string, in order to remove, modify, count, or otherwise deal with them.

Solution

The most appropriate solution depends on several factors, including the level of accuracy, efficiency, and tolerance for erroneous markup that is acceptable to you. Once you've determined the approach that works for your needs, there are any number of things you might want to do with the results. But whether you want to remove the tags, search within them, add or remove attributes, or replace them with alternative markup, the first step is to find them.

Be forewarned that this will be a long recipe, fraught with subtleties, exceptions, and variations. If you're looking for a quick fix and are not willing to put in the effort to determine the best solution for your needs, you might want to jump to the section "(X)HTML tags (loose)" of this recipe, which offers a decent mix of tolerance versus precaution.

Quick and dirty

This first solution is simple and more commonly used than you might expect, but it's included here mostly for comparison and examination of its flaws. It may be good enough when you know exactly what type of content you're dealing with and are not overly concerned about the consequences of incorrect handling. This regex starts by matching <, then simply continues until the first >:

```
<[^>]*>
```
Regex options: None
Regex flavors: .NET, Java, JavaScript, PCRE, Perl, Python, Ruby

Allow > in attribute values

This next regex is again rather simplistic and does not handle all cases correctly. However, it might work well for your needs if it will be used to process only snippets of valid (X)HTML. It's advantage over the previous regex is that it correctly passes over > characters that appear within attribute values:

```
<(?:[^>"']|"[^"]*"|'[^']*')*>
```
Regex options: None
Regex flavors: .NET, Java, JavaScript, PCRE, Perl, Python, Ruby

Here is the same regex, with added whitespace and comments for readability:

```
<
(?: [^>"']    # Non-quoted character, or...
  | "[^"]*"   # Double-quoted attribute value, or...
  | '[^']*'   # Single-quoted attribute value
)*
>
```
Regex options: Free-spacing
Regex flavors: .NET, Java, PCRE, Perl, Python, Ruby

The two regexes just shown work identically, so you can use whichever you prefer. JavaScripters are stuck with the first option since JavaScript lacks a free-spacing option.

(X)HTML tags (loose)

In addition to supporting > characters embedded in attribute values, this next regex emulates the lenient rules for (X)HTML tag names that browsers generally implement. This lets the regex avoid content that does not look like a tag, including comments, DOCTYPEs, and unencoded < characters in text. It uses the same handling for attributes and other stray characters that may appear inside a tag as the previous regex, but it adds special handling for the tag name. Specifically, it requires that the name begin with an English letter. The tag name is captured to backreference 1 in case you need to refer back to it:

```
</?([A-Za-z][^\s>/]*)(?:[^>"']|"[^"]*"|'[^']*')*>
```
Regex options: None
Regex flavors: .NET, Java, JavaScript, PCRE, Perl, Python, Ruby

And in free-spacing mode:

```
<
/?                      # Permit closing tags
([A-Za-z][^\s>/]*)      # Capture the tag name to backreference 1
(?: [^>"']              # Non-quoted character, or...
  | "[^"]*"             # Double-quoted attribute value, or...
  | '[^']*'             # Single-quoted attribute value
)*
>
```
Regex options: Free-spacing
Regex flavors: .NET, Java, PCRE, Perl, Python, Ruby

The last two regexes work identically, although the latter cannot be used in JavaScript, since it lacks a free-spacing option.

(X)HTML tags (strict)

This regex is more complicated than those we've already seen in this recipe, because it actually follows the rules for (X)HTML tags explained in the introductory section of this chapter. This is not always desirable, since browsers don't strictly adhere to these rules. In other words, this regex will avoid matching content that does not look like valid (X)HTML tags, at the cost of possibly not matching some content that browsers would in fact interpret as a tag (e.g., if your markup uses an attribute name that includes characters not accounted for here, or if attributes are included in a closing tag). Both HTML and XHTML tag rules are handled together since it is common for their conventions to be mixed. The tag name is captured to backreference 1 or 2 (depending on whether it is an opening or closing tag), in case you need to refer back to it:

```
<(?:([A-Z][-:A-Z0-9]*)(?:\s+[A-Z][-:A-Z0-9]*(?:\s*=\s*(?:"[^"]*"|↵
'[^']*'|[-.:\w]+))?)*\s*/?|/([A-Z][-:A-Z0-9]*)\s*)>
```
Regex options: Case insensitive
Regex flavors: .NET, Java, JavaScript, PCRE, Perl, Python, Ruby

To make it a little less cryptic, here is the same regex in free-spacing mode with comments:

```
<                       #
(?:                     # Branch for opening tags...
  ([A-Z][-:A-Z0-9]*)    #   Capture the opening tag name to backreference 1
```

```
(?:                       #   Permit zero or more attributes...
  \s+                     #   ...separated by whitespace
  [A-Z][-:A-Z0-9]*        #     Attribute name
  (?:                     #
    \s*=\s*               #       Attribute name-value delimiter
    (?: "[^"]*"           #         Double-quoted attribute value
      | '[^']*'           #         Single-quoted attribute value
      | [-.:\w]+          #         Unquoted attribute value (HTML)
    )                     #
  )?                      #       Permit attributes without a value (HTML)
)*                        #
\s*                       #   Permit trailing whitespace
/?                        #   Permit self-closed tags (XHTML)
|                         # Branch for closing tags...
/                         #
([A-Z][-:A-Z0-9]*)        #   Capture the closing tag name to backreference 2
\s*                       #   Permit trailing whitespace
)                         #
>                         #
```
Regex options: Case insensitive, free-spacing
Regex flavors: .NET, Java, PCRE, Perl, Python, Ruby

XML tags (strict)

XML is a very precisely specified language, and requires that user agents strictly adhere to and enforce its rules. This is a stark change from HTML and the commonly used, long-suffering browsers that process it:

```
<(?:([_:A-Z][-.:\w]*)(?:\s+[_:A-Z][-.:\w]*\s*=\s*(?:"[^"]*"|'[^']*'))*\s*↵
/?|/([_:A-Z][-.:\w]*)\s*)>
```
Regex options: Case insensitive
Regex flavors: .NET, Java, JavaScript, PCRE, Perl, Python, Ruby

Once again, here is the same regex in free-spacing mode with added comments:

```
<                         #
(?:                       # Branch for opening tags...
  ([_:A-Z][-.:\w]*)       #   Capture the opening tag name to backreference 1
  (?:                     #   Permit zero or more attributes...
    \s+                   #   ...separated by whitespace
    [_:A-Z][-.:\w]*       #     Attribute name
    \s*=\s*               #     Attribute name-value delimiter
    (?: "[^"]*"           #       Double-quoted attribute value
      | '[^']*'           #       Single-quoted attribute value
    )                     #
  )*                      #
  \s*                     #   Permit trailing whitespace
  /?                      #   Permit self-closed tags
|                         # Branch for closing tags...
```

```
/                            #
([_:A-Z][-.:\w]*)            #   Capture the closing tag name to backreference 2
\s*                          #   Permit trailing whitespace
)                            #
>                            #
```
Regex options: Case insensitive, free-spacing
Regex flavors: .NET, Java, PCRE, Perl, Python, Ruby

Like the previous two solutions shown for (X)HTML tags, these regexes capture the tag name to backreference 1 or 2, depending on whether an opening or closing tag is matched. The XML tag regex is a little shorter than the (X)HTML versions since it doesn't have to deal with HTML-only syntax (minimized attributes and unquoted values). It also allows a wider range of characters to be used for element and attribute names.

Discussion

A few words of caution

Although it's common to want to match XML-style tags using regular expressions, doing it safely requires balancing trade-offs and thinking carefully about the data you're working with. Because of these difficulties, some people choose to forgo the use of regular expressions for any sort of XML or (X)HTML processing in favor of specialized parsers and APIs. That's an approach you should strongly consider, since such tools are typically optimized to perform their designated tasks quickly, and they include robust detection or handling for incorrect markup. In browser-land, for example, it's usually best to take advantage of the tree-based Document Object Model (DOM) for your HTML search and manipulation needs. Elsewhere, you might be well-served by a SAX parser or XPath. However, you may occasionally find places where regex-based solutions make a lot of sense and work perfectly fine.

With that disclaimer out of the way, let's examine the regexes we've already seen in this recipe. The first two solutions are overly simplistic for most cases, but handle XML-style markup languages equally. The latter three follow stricter rules and are tailored to their respective markup languages. Even in the latter solutions, however, HTML and XHTML tag conventions are handled together since it's common for them to be mixed, often inadvertently. For example, an author may use an XHTML-style, self-closing `<br />` tag in an HTML document, or incorrectly use an uppercase element name in a document with an XHTML DOCTYPE.

Quick and dirty

The advantage of this solution is its simplicity, which makes it easy to remember and type, and also fast to run. The trade-off is that it incorrectly handles certain valid and invalid XML and (X)HTML constructs. If you're working with markup you wrote yourself and know that such cases will never appear in your subject text, or if you are not concerned about the consequences if they do, this trade-off might be OK. Another example of where this solution might be good enough is when you're working with a text editor that lets you preview regex matches.

The regex starts off by finding a literal ‹<› character (the start of a tag). It then uses a negated character class and greedy asterisk quantifier ‹[^>]*› to match zero or more following characters that are not >. This takes care of matching the name of the tag, attributes, and a leading or trailing /. We could use a lazy quantifier (‹[^>]*?›) instead, but that wouldn't change anything other than making the regex a tiny bit slower since it would cause more backtracking (Recipe 2.13 explains why). To end the tag, the regex then matches a literal ‹>›.

If you prefer to use a dot instead of the negated character class ‹[^>]›, go for it. A dot will work fine as long as you also use a lazy asterisk along with it (‹.*?›) and make sure to enable the "dot matches line breaks" option (in JavaScript, you could use ‹[\s \S]*?› instead). A dot with a greedy asterisk (making the full pattern ‹<.*>›) would change the regex's meaning, causing it to incorrectly match from the first < until the very last > in the subject string, even if the regex has to swallow multiple tags along the way in order to do so.

It's time for a few examples. This regex matches each of the following lines in full:

```
<div>
</div>
<div class="box">
<div id="pandoras-box" class="box" />
<!-- comment -->
<!DOCTYPE html>
<< < w00t! >
<>
```

Notice that the pattern matches more than just tags. Worse, it will not correctly match the entire tags in the subject strings `<input type="button" value=">>">` or `<input type="button" onclick="alert(2 > 1)">`. Instead, it will only match until the first > that appears within the attribute values. It will have similar problems with comments, XML CDATA sections, DOCTYPEs, code within `<script>` elements, and anything else that contains embedded > symbols.

If you're processing anything more than the most basic markup, especially if the subject text is coming from mixed or unknown sources, you will be better served by one of the more robust solutions further along in this recipe.

Allow > in attribute values

Like the quick and dirty regex we've just described, this next one is included primarily to contrast it with the later, more robust solutions. Nevertheless, it covers the basics needed to match XML-style tags, and thus it might work well for your needs if it will be used to process snippets of valid markup that include only elements and text. The difference from the last regex is that it passes over > characters that appear within attribute values. For example, it will correctly match the entire <input> tags in the example subject strings we've previously shown: `<input type="button" value=">>">` and `<input type="button" onclick="alert(2 > 1)">`.

As before, the regex uses literal angle bracket characters at the edges of the regex to match the start and end of a tag. In between, it repeats a noncapturing group containing three alternatives, each separated by the ‹|› alternation metacharacter.

The first alternative is the negated character class ‹[^>"']›, which matches any single character other than a right angle bracket (which closes the tag), double quote, or single quote (both quote marks indicate the start of an attribute value). This first alternative is responsible for matching the tag and attribute names as well as any other characters outside of quoted values. The order of the alternatives is intentional, and written with performance in mind. Regular expression engines attempt alternative paths through a regex from left to right, and attempts at matching this first option will most likely succeed more often than the alternatives for quoted values (especially since it matches only one character at a time).

Next come the alternatives for matching double and single quoted attribute values (‹"[^"]*"› and ‹'[^']*'›). Their use of negated character classes allows them to continue matching past any included > characters, line breaks, and anything else that isn't a closing quote mark.

Note that this solution has no special handling that allows it to exclude or properly match comments and other special nodes in your documents. Make sure you're familiar with the kind of content you're working with before putting this regex to use.

A (Safe) Efficiency Optimization

After reading this section, you might think you could make the regex a bit faster by adding a ‹*› or ‹+› quantifier after the leading negated character class (‹[^>"']›). At positions within the subject string where the regex finds matches, you'd be right. By matching more than one character at a time, you'd let the regex engine skip a lot of unnecessary steps on the way to a successful match.

What might not be as readily apparent is the negative consequence such a change could lead to in places where the regex engine finds only a partial match. When the regex matches an opening < character but there is no following > that would allow the match attempt to complete successfully, you'll run into the "catastrophic backtracking" problem described in Recipe 2.15. This is because of the huge number of ways the new, inner quantifier could be combined with the outer quantifier (following the noncapturing group) to match the text that follows <, all of which the engine must try before giving up on the match attempt. Watch out!

With regex flavors that support possessive quantifiers or atomic groups (JavaScript and Python have neither), it's possible to avoid this problem while still gaining the performance advantage of matching more than one nonquoted character at a time. In fact, we can go further and reduce potential backtracking elsewhere in the regex as well. If the regex flavor you're using supports both features, possessive quantifiers (shown here in the second regex) are the better option since they keep the regex shorter and more readable.

With atomic groups:

```
<(?>(?:(?>[^>"']+)|"[^"]*"|'[^']*')*)>
```
Regex options: None
Regex flavors: .NET, Java, PCRE, Perl, Ruby

With possessive quantifiers:

```
<(?:[^>"']++|"[^"]*"|'[^']*')*+>
```
Regex options: None
Regex flavors: Java, PCRE, Perl 5.10, Ruby 1.9

(X)HTML tags (loose)

Via a simple addition, this regex gets a lot closer to emulating the easygoing rules that web browsers use to identify (X)HTML tags in source code. That makes it a good solution in cases where you're trying to copy browser behavior and don't care whether the tags you match actually follow all the rules for valid markup. Keep in mind that it's still possible to create horrifically invalid HTML that this regex will not handle in the same way as one or more browsers, since browsers parse edge cases of erroneous markup in their own, unique ways.

This regex's most significant difference from the previous solution is that it requires the character following the opening left angle bracket (‹<›) to be a letter from A–Z or a–z, optionally preceded by / (for closing tags). This constraint rules out matching stray, unencoded < characters in text, as well as comments, DOCTYPEs, XML declarations and processing instructions, CDATA sections, etc. That doesn't protect it from matching something that looks like a tag *within* comments, scripting language code, the content of ‹textarea› elements, and so on. The upcoming section, "Skip tricky (X)HTML and XML sections" on page 428, shows a workaround for this issue. But first, let's look at how this regex works.

‹<› starts off the match with a literal left angle bracket. The ‹/?› that follows allows an optional forward slash, for closing tags. Next comes the capturing group ‹([A-Za-z][^\s>/]*)›, which matches the tag's name and remembers it as backreference 1. If you don't need to refer back to the tag name (e.g., if you're simply removing all tags), you can remove the capturing parentheses (just don't get rid of the pattern within them). Within the group are two character classes. The first, ‹[A-Za-z]›, sets the tag name's initial-character rule. The next class, ‹[^\s>/]›, allows nearly any characters to follow as part of the name. The only exceptions are whitespace (‹\s›, which separates the tag name from any following attributes), > (which ends the tag), and / (used before the closing > for XHTML-style singleton tags). Any other characters (even including quote marks) are treated as part of the tag's name. That might seem a bit overly permissive, but it's how most browsers operate. Bogus tags might not have any effect on the way a page is rendered, but they neverthess become accessible via the DOM tree and are not rendered as text, although any content within them will show up.

After the tag name comes the attribute handling, which is taken directly out of the previous regex: ‹(?:[^>"']|"[^"]*"|'[^']*')*›. Add a right angle bracket to finish the tag, and we're done.

The following regexes show how this pattern can be tweaked to match only opening, closing, or singleton (self-closing) tags:

Opening tags

```
<([A-Za-z][^\s>/]*)(?:[^>"'/]|"[^"]*"|'[^']*')*>
```
Regex options: None
Regex flavors: .NET, Java, JavaScript, PCRE, Perl, Python, Ruby

This version adds a forward slash (/) within the first negated character class in the noncapturing group, to prevent forward slashes from occuring anywhere other than within quoted attribute values.

Singleton tags

```
<([A-Za-z][^\s>/]*)(?:[^>"']|"[^"]*"|'[^']*')*/>
```
Regex options: None
Regex flavors: .NET, Java, JavaScript, PCRE, Perl, Python, Ruby

Here, we've added a required forward slash just before the closing right angle bracket.

Opening and singleton tags

```
<([A-Za-z][^\s>/]*)(?:[^>"']|"[^"]*"|'[^']*')*>
```
Regex options: None
Regex flavors: .NET, Java, JavaScript, PCRE, Perl, Python, Ruby

There is no addition here. Instead, the ‹/?› that appeared after the the opening ‹<› in the original regex has been removed.

Closing tags

```
</([A-Za-z][^\s>/]*)(?:[^>"']|"[^"]*"|'[^']*')*>
```
Regex options: None
Regex flavors: .NET, Java, JavaScript, PCRE, Perl, Python, Ruby

The forward slash after the opening left angle bracket has been made a required part of the match here. Note that we are intentionally allowing attributes inside closing tags, since this is based on the "loose" solution. Although browsers don't use attributes that occur in closing tags, they don't mind if such attributes exist.

The sidebar "A (Safe) Efficiency Optimization" on page 423 showed how to improve performance when matching tags through the use of atomic groups or possessive quantifiers. This time around, the potential performance improvement is even greater since the characters that can be matched by the ‹[^\s>/]› character class overlaps with the latter part of the regex, thereby providing lots of pattern combinations to try before the regex engine can give up on a partial match.

If atomic groups or possessive quantifiers are available in the regex flavor you're using, you may get significantly better performance by taking advantage of them here. The following changes can also be transferred to the opening/closing/singleton-specific regexes just shown:

```
</?([A-Za-z](?>[^\s>/]*))(?>(?:(?>[^>"']+)|"[^"]*"|'[^']*')*)>
```
Regex options: None
Regex flavors: .NET, Java, PCRE, Perl, Ruby

```
</?([A-Za-z][^\s>/]*+)(?:[^>"']++|"[^"]*"|'[^']*')*+>
```
Regex options: None
Regex flavors: Java, PCRE, Perl 5.10, Ruby 1.9

(X)HTML tags (strict)

By saying that this solution is strict, we mean that it attempts to follow the HTML and XHTML syntax rules explained in the introductory section of this chapter, rather than emulating the rules browsers actually use when parsing the source code of a document. This strictness adds the following rules compared to the previous regexes:

- Both tag and attribute names must start with a letter from A–Z or a–z, and their names may only use the characters A–Z, a–z, 0–9, hyphen, and colon (in regex, that's ‹^[-:A-Za-z0-9]+$›).

- Inappropriate, stray characters are not allowed after the tag name. Only white-space, attributes (with or without an accompanying value), and optionally a trailing forward slash (/) may appear after the tag name.

- Unquoted attribute values may only use the characters A–Z, a–z, 0–9, underscore, hyphen, period, and colon (in regex, ‹^[-.:A-Za-z0-9_]+$›).

- Closing tags cannot include attributes.

Since the pattern is split into two branches (the first for opening and singleton tags, and the second for closing tags), the tag name is captured to either backreference 1 or 2, depending on what type of tag is matched. Both sets of capturing parentheses may be removed if you have no need to refer back to the tag names.

In the following examples, the two branches of the pattern are separated into their own regexes. Both capture the tag name to backreference 1:

Opening and singleton tags

```
<([A-Z][-:A-Z0-9]*)(?:\s+[A-Z][-:A-Z0-9]*(?:\s*=\s*↵
(?:"[^"]*"|'[^']*'|[-.:\w]+))?)*\s*/?>
```
Regex options: Case insensitive
Regex flavors: .NET, Java, JavaScript, PCRE, Perl, Python, Ruby

The ‹/?› that appears just before the closing ‹>› is what allows this regex to match both opening and singleton tags. Remove it to match only opening tags. Remove just the question mark quantifier (making the ‹/› required), and it will only match singleton tags.

Closing tags

```
</([A-Z][-:A-Z0-9]*)\s*>
```
Regex options: Case insensitive
Regex flavors: .NET, Java, JavaScript, PCRE, Perl, Python, Ruby

In the last couple of sections, we've shown how to get a potential performance boost by adding atomic groups or possessive quantifiers. The strictly defined paths through this regex means that there is no potential to match the same strings more than one way, and therefore less potential backtracking to worry about. This regex doesn't *rely* on backtracking, so if you wanted to, you could make every last ‹*›, ‹+›, and ‹?› quantifier possessive (or achieve the same effect using atomic groups). Although that could only help, we're going to skip such variations for this (and the next) regex, to try to keep the crazy amount of options in this recipe under control.

See "Skip tricky (X)HTML and XML sections" on page 428 for a way to avoid matching tags within comments, ‹script› tags, and so on.

XML tags (strict)

XML precludes the need for a "loose" solution through its precise specification and requirement that conforming parsers do not process markup that is not well-formed. Although you could use one of the preceding regexes when processing XML documents, their simplicity won't give you the advantage of actually providing a more reliable search, since there is no loose XML user agent behavior to emulate.

This regex is basically a simpler version of the "(X)HTML tags (strict)" regex, since we're able to remove support for two HTML features that are not allowed in XML: unquoted attribute values and minimized attributes (attributes without an accompanying value). The only other difference is the characters that are allowed as part of the tag and attribute names. In fact, the rules for XML names (which govern the requirements for both tag and attribute names) are more permissive than shown here, allowing hundreds of thousands of additional Unicode characters. If you need to allow these characters in your search, you can replace the three occurrences of ‹[_:A-Z][-.:\w]*› with one of the patterns found in Recipe 8.4. Note that the list of characters allowed differs depending on the version of XML in use.

As with the (X)HTML regexes, the tag name is captured to backreference 1 or 2, depending on whether an opening/singleton or closing tag is matched. And once again, you can remove the capturing parentheses if you don't need to refer back to the tag names.

In the following examples, the two branches of the pattern are separated into their own regexes. As a result, both regexes capture the tag name to backreference 1:

Opening and singleton tags

```
<([_:A-Z][-.:\w]*)(?:\s+[_:A-Z][-.:\w]*\s*=\s*↲
(?:"[^"]*"|'[^']*'))*\s*/?>
```
Regex options: Case insensitive
Regex flavors: .NET, Java, JavaScript, PCRE, Perl, Python, Ruby

The ‹/?› that appears just before the closing ‹>› is what allows this regex to match both opening and singleton tags. Remove it to match only opening tags. Remove just the question mark quantifier, and it will match only singleton tags.

Closing tags

```
</([_:A-Z][-.:\w]*)\s*>
```
Regex options: Case insensitive
Regex flavors: .NET, Java, JavaScript, PCRE, Perl, Python, Ruby

See the section "Skip tricky (X)HTML and XML sections" for a way to avoid matching tags within comments, CDATA sections, and DOCTYPEs.

Skip tricky (X)HTML and XML sections

When trying to match XML-style tags within a source file or string, much of the battle is avoiding content that looks like a tag, even though its placement or other context precludes it from being interpreted as a tag. The (X)HTML- and XML-specific regexes we've shown in this recipe avoid some problematic content by restricting the initial character of an element's name. Some went even further, requiring tags to fulfill the (X)HTML or XML syntax rules. Still, a robust solution requires that we also avoid any content that appears within comments, scripting language code (which may use greater-than and less-than symbols for mathematical operations), XML CDATA sections, and various other constructs. We can solve this issue by first searching for these problematic sections, and then searching for tags only in the content outside of those matches.

Recipe 3.18 shows how to write code that searches between matches of another regex. It takes two patterns: an inner regex and outer regex. The solutions we've already shown will serve as our inner regex. The outer regex is shown next, with separate patterns for (X)HTML and XML. This approach hides the problematic sections from the inner regex's view, and thereby lets us keep things relatively simple.

Outer regex for (X)HTML. The following regex matches comments as well as `<script>`, `<style>`, `<textarea>`, and `<xmp>`[*] elements (including their content):

```
<!--.*?--\s*>|<(script|style|textarea|xmp)\b(?:[^>"']|"[^"]*"|↵
'[^']*')*?(?:/>|>.*?</\1\s*>)
```
Regex options: Case insensitive, dot matches line breaks
Regex flavors: .NET, Java, PCRE, Perl, Python, Ruby

In case that's not the most readable line of code you've ever read, here is the regex again in free-spacing mode, with a few comments added:

```
# Comment
<!-- .*? --\s*>

|

# Special element and its content
<( script | style | textarea | xmp )\b
   (?: [^>"']   # Non-quoted character
     | "[^"]*"  # Double-quoted value
     | '[^']*'  # Single-quoted value
   )*?
(?: # Singleton tag
    />
  | # Otherwise, include the element's content and matching closing tag
    > .*? </\1\s*>
)
```
Regex options: Case insensitive, dot matches line breaks, free-spacing
Regex flavors: .NET, Java, PCRE, Perl, Python, Ruby

Neither of the above regexes work correctly in JavaScript, since JavaScript lacks both the "dot matches line breaks" and "free-spacing" options. The following regex reverts back to being unreadable and replaces the dots with ‹[\s\S]›, so it can be used in JavaScript:

```
<!--[\s\S]*?--\s*>|<(script|style|textarea|xmp)\b(?:[^>"']|"[^"]*"|↵
'[^']*')*?(?:/>|>[\s\S]*?</\1\s*>)
```
Regex options: Case insensitive
Regex flavors: JavaScript

These regexes present a bit of a dilemma: because they match `<script>`, `<style>`, `<textarea>`, and `<xmp>` tags, those tags are never matched by the second (inner) regex, even though we're supposedly searching for all tags. However, it should just be a matter of adding a bit of extra code to handle those tags specially. These (outer) regexes already

---

[*] `<xmp>` is a little-known but widely supported element similar to `<pre>`. Like `<pre>`, it preserves all whitespace and uses a fixed-width font by default, but it goes one step further and displays all of its contents (including HTML tags) as plain text. `<xmp>` was deprecated in HTML 3.2, and removed entirely from HTML 4.

capture the tag names to backreference 1, which can serve as a good check of whether they matched a comment or tag (and if it was a tag, you'll know which one).

Outer regex for XML. This regex matches comments, CDATA sections, and DOCTYPEs. Each of these cases are matched using a discrete pattern, all of which are combined into one regex using the ‹|› alternation metacharacter:

```
<!--.*?--\s*>|<!\[CDATA\[.*?]]>|<!DOCTYPE\s(?:[^<>"']|"[^"]*"|↵
'[^']*'|<!(?:[^>"']|"[^"]*"|'[^']*')*>)*>
```
    Regex options: Case insensitive, dot matches line breaks
    Regex flavors: .NET, Java, PCRE, Perl, Python, Ruby

Here it is again in free-spacing mode:

```
# Comment
<!-- .*? --\s*>

|

# CDATA section
<!\[CDATA\[ .*? ]]>

|

# Document type declaration
<!DOCTYPE\s
    (?: [^<>"']   # Non-special character
      | "[^"]*"   # Double-quoted value
      | '[^']*'   # Single-quoted value
      | <!(?:[^>"']|"[^"]*"|'[^']*')*>  # Markup declaration
    )*
>
```
    Regex options: Case insensitive, dot matches line breaks, free-spacing
    Regex flavors: .NET, Java, PCRE, Perl, Python, Ruby

And here is a version that works in JavaScript (which lacks the "dot matches line breaks" and "free-spacing" options):

```
<!--[\s\S]*?--\s*>|<!\[CDATA\[[\s\S]*?]]>|<!DOCTYPE\s(?:[^<>"']|"[^"]*"|↵
'[^']*'|<!(?:[^>"']|"[^"]*"|'[^']*')*>)*>
```
    Regex options: Case insensitive
    Regex flavors: JavaScript

Variations

Match valid HTML 4 tags

Occasionally, you may want to limit your search to only valid HTML elements, especially when searching for tags in non-HTML documents where extra precaution against false positives may be in order. The following regex matches only the 91 valid HTML

4 elements. This list does not include nonstandard HTML, such as the proprietary tags `<blink>`, `<bgsound>`, `<embed>`, and `<nobr>`. It also doesn't include XHTML 1.1-only elements (XHTML 1.0 adds no new tags) or fancy new elements planned for HTML 5:

```
</?(a|abbr|acronym|address|applet|area|b|base|basefont|bdo|big|blockquote|↵
body|br|button|caption|center|cite|code|col|colgroup|dd|del|dfn|dir|div|↵
dl|dt|em|fieldset|font|form|frame|frameset|h1|h2|h3|h4|h5|h6|head|hr|html|↵
i|iframe|img|input|ins|isindex|kbd|label|legend|li|link|map|menu|meta|↵
noframes|noscript|object|ol|optgroup|option|p|param|pre|q|s|samp|script|↵
select|small|span|strike|strong|style|sub|sup|table|tbody|td|textarea|↵
tfoot|th|thead|title|tr|tt|u|ul|var)\b(?:[^>"']|"[^"]*"|'[^']*')*>
```
Regex options: None
Regex flavors: .NET, Java, JavaScript, PCRE, Perl, Python, Ruby

We can make this regex faster by reducing the number of alternatives separated by the ‹|› metacharacter. Instead, we'll use character classes and optional suffixes wherever possible. These changes can dramatically reduce the amount of backtracking required by the regex engine. Consider what happens when the engine encounters `<0` in the subject text. This cannot possibly be the start of a tag, since no tag name starts with the number 0, but before the regex engine can rule this out as a match, it must check whether any of the 91 alternatives start with a literal 0. By reducing the number of alternatives to the minimum (one for each letter that can start a tag), we bring the number of steps that must be tried after a left angle bracket is found from 91 down to just 19. Here's how such a regex looks:

```
</?(a(?:bbr|cronym|ddress|pplet|rea)?|b(?:ase(?:font)?|do|ig|lockquote|↵
ody|r|utton)?|c(?:aption|enter|ite|o(?:de|l(?:group)?))|d(?:[dlt]|el|fn|↵
i[rv])|em|f(?:ieldset|o(?:nt|rm)|rame(?:set)?)|h(?:[1-6r]|ead|tml)|↵
i(?:frame|mg|n(?:put|s)|sindex)?|kbd|l(?:abel|egend|i(?:nk)?)|m(?:ap|↵
e(?:nu|ta))|no(?:frames|script)|o(?:bject|l|p(?:tgroup|tion))|p(?:aram|↵
re)?|q|s(?:amp|cript|elect|mall|pan|t(?:rike|rong|yle)|u[bp])?|t(?:able|↵
body|[dhrt]|extarea|foot|head|itle)|ul?|var)\b(?:[^>"']|"[^"]*"|'[^']*')*>
```
Regex options: Case insensitive
Regex flavors: .NET, Java, JavaScript, PCRE, Perl, Python, Ruby

That's certainly harder to read, but free-spacing mode can help a little:

```
<
/?  # Permit closing tags
(   # Capture the tag name to backreference 1

    a(?:bbr|cronym|ddress|pplet|rea)?|
    b(?:ase(?:font)?|do|ig|lockquote|ody|r|utton)?|
    c(?:aption|enter|ite|o(?:de|l(?:group)?))|
    d(?:[dlt]|el|fn|i[rv])|
    em|
    f(?:ieldset|o(?:nt|rm)|rame(?:set)?)|
    h(?:[1-6r]|ead|tml)|
    i(?:frame|mg|n(?:put|s)|sindex)?|
```

```
    kbd|
    l(?:abel|egend|i(?:nk)?)|
    m(?:ap|e(?:nu|ta))|
    no(?:frames|script)|
    o(?:bject|l|p(?:tgroup|tion))|
    p(?:aram|re)?|
    q|
    s(?:amp|cript|elect|mall|pan|t(?:rike|rong|yle)|u[bp])?|
    t(?:able|body|[dhrt]|extarea|foot|head|itle)|
    ul?|
    var

  ) \b         # Don't permit partial name matches
  (?: [^>"']   # Any character except >, ", or '
    | "[^"]*"  # Double-quoted attribute value
    | '[^']*'  # Single-quoted attribute value
  )*
>
```

Regex options: Case insensitive

Regex flavors: .NET, Java, PCRE, Perl, Python, Ruby

If you want to go crazy with whitespace, here's yet another way to write the same regex in free-spacing mode that might make it even easier to read:

```
<
/?  # Permit closing tags
(   # Capture the tag name to backreference 1

    a (?: bbr              #
        | cronym           #
        | ddress           #
        | pplet            #
        | rea              #
      )?|                  # Optional group (allow <a>)
    b (?: ase (?:font)?    # <base>, <basefont>
        | do               #
        | ig               #
        | lockquote        #
        | ody              #
        | r                #
        | utton            #
      )?|                  # Optional group (allow <b>)
    c (?: aption           #
        | enter            #
        | ite              #
        | o (?:de|l(?:group)?) # <code>, <col>, <colgroup>
      ) |                  #
    d (?: [dlt]            # <dd>, <dl>, <dt>
        | el               #
```

```
        |  fn                    #
        |  i[rv]                 #  <dir>, <div>
      ) |                        #
  em    |                        #
  f (?: ieldset                  #
        |  o (?:nt|rm)           #  <font>, <form>
        |  rame (?:set)?         #  <frame>, <frameset>
      ) |                        #
  h (?: [1-6r]                   #  <h1>, <h2>, <h3>, <h4>, <h5>, <h6>, <hr>
        |  ead                   #
        |  tml                   #
      ) |                        #
  i (?: frame                    #
        |  mg                    #
        |  n (?:put|s)           #  <input>, <ins>
        |  sindex                #
      )?|                        #  Optional group (allow <i>)
  kbd   |                        #
  l (?: abel                     #
        |  egend                 #
        |  i (?:nk)?             #  <li>, <link>
      ) |                        #
  m (?: ap                       #
        |  e (?:nu|ta)           #  <menu>, <meta>
      ) |                        #
  no (?: frames                  #
        |  script                #
      ) |                        #
  o (?: bject                    #
        |  l                     #
        |  p (?:tgroup|tion)     #  <optgroup>, <option>
      ) |                        #
  p (?: aram                     #
        |  re                    #
      )?|                        #  Optional group (allow <p>)
  q     |                        #
  s (?: amp                      #
        |  cript                 #
        |  elect                 #
        |  mall                  #
        |  pan                   #
        |  t (?:rike|rong|yle)   #  <strike>, <strong>, <style>
        |  u[bp]                 #  <sub>, <sup>
      )?|                        #  Optional group (allow <s>)
  t (?: able                     #
        |  body                  #
        |  [dhrt]                #  <td>, <th>, <tr>, <tt>
        |  extarea               #
```

```
              | foot                #
              | head                #
              | itle                #
            ) |                     #
        ul? |                       # <u>, <ul>
        var                         #

    ) \b           # Don't permit partial name matches
    (?: [^>"']     # Any character except >, ", or '
      | "[^"]*"    # Double-quoted attribute value
      | '[^']*'    # Single-quoted attribute value
    )*
    >
```
Regex options: Case insensitive
Regex flavors: .NET, Java, PCRE, Perl, Python, Ruby

If you're working with XHTML, note that although XHTML 1.0 adds no new tags, it removes the following 14: <applet>, <basefont>, <center>, <dir>, <font>, <frame>, <frameset>, <iframe>, <isindex>, <menu>, <noframes>, <s>, <strike>, and <u>.

XHTML 1.1 keeps all the elements from XHTML 1.0, and adds six new ones (all related to ruby text for Asian languages): <rb>, <rbc>, <rp>, <rt>, <rtc>, and <ruby>. Creating regexes dedicated to matching only the valid XHTML 1.0 or 1.1 elements is something we'll leave to you.

See Also

Matching any and all tags can be useful, but it's also common to want to match a specific one or a few out of the bunch; Recipe 8.2 shows how to pull off both of these tasks.

Recipe 8.4 describes the characters that can be used in valid XML element and attribute names.

8.2 Replace <b> Tags with <strong>

Problem

You want to replace all opening and closing <b> tags in a string with corresponding <strong> tags, while preserving any existing attributes.

Solution

This regex matches opening and closing <b> tags, with or without attributes:

```
<(/?)b\b((?:[^>"']|"[^"]*"|'[^']*')*)>
```
Regex options: Case insensitive
Regex flavors: .NET, Java, JavaScript, PCRE, Perl, Python, Ruby

---

In free-spacing mode:

```
<                    #
(/?)                 # Capture the optional leading slash to backreference 1
b \b                 # Complete tag name, with word boundary
(                    # Capture any attributes, etc. to backreference 2
    (?: [^>"']       #     Any character except >, ", or '
      | "[^"]*"      #     Double-quoted attribute value
      | '[^']*'      #     Single-quoted attribute value
    )*               #
)                    #
>                    #
```

Regex options: Case insensitive, free-spacing
Regex flavors: .NET, Java, PCRE, Perl, Python, Ruby

To preserve all attributes while changing the tag name, use the following replacement text:

```
<$1strong$2>
```
Replacement text flavors: .NET, Java, JavaScript, Perl, PHP

```
<\1strong\2>
```
Replacement text flavors: Python, Ruby

If you want to discard any attributes in the same process, omit backreference 2 in the replacement string:

```
<$1strong>
```
Replacement text flavors: .NET, Java, JavaScript, Perl, PHP

```
<\1strong>
```
Replacement text flavors: Python, Ruby

Recipe 3.15 shows the code needed to implement this.

Discussion

The previous recipe included a detailed discussion of many ways to match *any* XML-style tag. That frees this recipe to focus on a straightforward approach to search for a specific type of tag. ‹b› and its replacement ‹strong› are offered as examples, but you can substitute those tag names with any two others.

The regex starts by matching a literal ‹<›—the first character of any tag. It then optionally matches the forward slash found in closing tags using ‹/?›, within capturing parentheses. Capturing the result of this pattern (which will be either an empty string or a forward slash) allows you to easily restore the forward slash in the replacement string, without any conditional logic.

Next, we match the tag name itself, ‹b›. You could use any other tag name instead if you wanted to. We're using the case-insensitive option to make sure that we also match an uppercase B.

The word boundary (‹\b›) that follows the tag name is easy to forget, but it's one of the most important pieces of this regex. The word boundary lets us match only <b> tags, and not <br>, <body>, <blockquote>, or any other tags that merely start with the letter "b". We could alternatively match a whitespace token (‹\s›) after the name as a safe-guard against this same problem, but that wouldn't work for tags that have no attributes and thus might not have any whitespace following their tag name. The word boundary solves this problem simply and elegantly.

 When working with XML and XHTML, be aware that the colon used for namespaces, as well as hyphens and some other characters allowed as part of XML names, create a word boundary. For example, the regex could end up matching something like <b-sharp>. If you're worried about this, you might want to use the lookahead ‹(?=[\s/>])› instead of a word boundary. It achieves the same result of ensuring that we do not match partial tag names, and does so more reliably.

After the tag name, the pattern ‹((?:[^>"']|"[^"]*"|'[^']*')*)› is used to match any-thing remaining within the tag up until the closing right angle bracket. Wrapping this pattern in a capturing group as we've done here lets us easily bring back any attributes and other characters (such as the trailing slash for singleton tags) in our replacement string. Within the capturing parentheses, the pattern repeats a noncapturing group with three alternatives. The first, ‹[^>"']›, matches any single character except >, ", or '. The remaining two alternatives match an entire double- or single-quoted string, which lets you match attribute values that contain right angle brackets without having the regex think it has found the end of the tag.

Variations

Replace a list of tags

If you want to match any from a list of tag names, a simple change is needed. Place all of the desired tag names within a group, and alternate between them. Placing the names in a group limits the reach of the alternation metacharacter (‹|›).

The following regex matches opening and closing <b>, <i>, <em>, and <big> tags. The replacement text shown later replaces all of them with a corresponding <strong> or </strong> tag, while preserving any attributes:

```
<(/?)([bi]|em|big)\b((?:[^>"']|"[^"]*"|'[^']*')*)>
    Regex options: Case insensitive
    Regex flavors: .NET, Java, JavaScript, PCRE, Perl, Python, Ruby
```

Here's the same regex in free-spacing mode:

```
<                       #
(/?)                    # Capture the optional leading slash to backreference 1
```

```
([bi]|em|big) \b   # Capture the tag name to backreference 2
(                  # Capture any attributes, etc. to backreference 3
    (?: [^>"']     #       Any character except >, ", or '
      | "[^"]*"    #       Double-quoted attribute value
      | '[^']*'    #       Single-quoted attribute value
    )*             #
)                  #
>                  #
```

Regex options: Case insensitive, free-spacing
Regex flavors: .NET, Java, PCRE, Perl, Python, Ruby

We've used the character class ‹[bi]› to match both <b> and <i> tags, rather than separating them with the alternation metacharacter (|) as we've done for <em> and <big>. Character classes perform faster than alternation, since they don't use backtracking to get their job done. When the difference between two options is a single character, use a character class.

We've also added a capturing group for the tag name, which shifted the group that matches attributes, etc. to store its match as backreference 3. Although there's no need to refer back to the tag name if you're just going to replace all matches with <strong> tags, storing the tag name in its own backreference can help you check what type of tag was matched, when needed.

To preserve all attributes while replacing the tag name, use the following replacement text:

```
<$1strong$3>
```
Replacement text flavors: .NET, Java, JavaScript, Perl, PHP

```
<\1strong\3>
```
Replacement text flavors: Python, Ruby

Omit backreference 3 in the replacement string if you want to discard attributes for matched tags as part of the same process:

```
<$1strong>
```
Replacement text flavors: .NET, Java, JavaScript, Perl, PHP

```
<\1strong>
```
Replacement text flavors: Python, Ruby

See Also

Recipe 8.1 shows how to match all XML-style tags while balancing trade-offs, including tolerance for invalid markup.

Recipe 8.3 is the opposite of this recipe, and shows how to match all except a select list of tags.

8.3 Remove All XML-Style Tags Except \<em> and \<strong>

Problem

You want to remove all tags in a string except \<em> and \<strong>.

In a separate case, you not only want to remove all tags other than \<em> and \<strong>, you also want to remove \<em> and \<strong> tags that contain attributes.

Solution

This is a perfect setting to put negative lookahead (explained in Recipe 2.16) to use. Applied to this problem, negative lookahead lets you match what looks like a tag, *except* when certain words come immediately after the opening < or </. If you then replace all matches with an empty string (Recipe 3.14 shows you how), only the approved tags are left behind.

Solution 1: Match tags except \<em> and \<strong>

```
</?(?!(?:em|strong)\b)[a-z](?:[^>"']|"[^"]*"|'[^']*')*>
```
Regex options: Case insensitive
Regex flavors: .NET, Java, JavaScript, PCRE, Perl, Python, Ruby

In free-spacing mode:

```
< /?                      # Permit closing tags
(?!                       # Negative lookahead
    (?: em | strong )     #     List of tags to avoid matching
    \b                    #     Word boundary avoids partial word matches
)                         #
[a-z]                     # Tag name initial character must be a-z
(?: [^>"']                #     Any character except >, ", or '
  | "[^"]*"               #     Double-quoted attribute value
  | '[^']*'               #     Single-quoted attribute value
)*                        #
>                         #
```
Regex options: Case insensitive, free-spacing
Regex flavors: .NET, Java, PCRE, Perl, Python, Ruby

Solution 2: Match tags except \<em> and \<strong>, and any tags that contain attributes

With one change (replacing the ‹\b› with ‹\s*›), you can make the regex also match any \<em> and \<strong> tags that contain attributes:

```
</?(?!(?:em|strong)\s*>)[a-z](?:[^>"']|"[^"]*"|'[^']*')*>
```
Regex options: Case insensitive
Regex flavors: .NET, Java, JavaScript, PCRE, Perl, Python, Ruby

---

Once again, the same regex in free-spacing mode:

```
< /?                        # Permit closing tags
(?!                         # Negative lookahead
    (?: em | strong )       #    List of tags to avoid matching
    \s* >                   #    Only avoid tags if they contain no attributes
)                           #
[a-z]                       # Tag name initial character must be a-z
(?: [^>"']                  #    Any character except >, ", or '
  | "[^"]*"                 #    Double-quoted attribute value
  | '[^']*'                 #    Single-quoted attribute value
)*                          #
>                           #
```

Regex options: Case insensitive, free-spacing
Regex flavors: .NET, Java, PCRE, Perl, Python, Ruby

Discussion

This recipe's regular expressions have a lot in common with those we've included earlier in this chapter for matching XML-style tags. Apart from the negative lookahead added to prevent some tags from being matched, these regexes are nearly equivalent to the "(X)HTML tags (loose)" regex from Recipe 8.1. The other main difference here is that we're not capturing the tag name to backreference 1.

So let's look more closely at what's new in this recipe. Solution 1 never matches <em> or <strong> tags, regardless of whether they have any attributes, but matches all other tags. Solution 2 matches all the same tags as Solution 1, and additionally matches <em> and <strong> tags that contain one or more attributes. Table 8-2 shows a few example subject strings that illustrate this.

Table 8-2. A few example subject strings

Subject string	Solution 1	Solution 2
<i>	Match	Match
</i>	Match	Match
<i style="font-size:500%; color:red;">	Match	Match
<em>	No match	No match
</em>	No match	No match
<em style="font-size:500%; color:red;">	No match	Match

Since the point of these regexes is to replace matches with empty strings (i.e., remove the tags), Solution 2 is less prone to abuse of the allowed <em> and <strong> tags to provide unexpected formatting or other shenanigans.

This recipe has (until now) intentionally avoided the word "whitelist" when describing how only a few tags are left in place, since that word has security connotations. There are a variety of ways to work around this pattern's constraints using specially crafted, malicious HTML strings. If you're worried about malicious HTML and cross-site scripting (XSS) attacks, your safest bet is to convert all <, >, and & characters to their corresponding character entity references (<, >, and &), then bring back tags that are known to be safe (as long as they contain no attributes or only use those within a select list of approved attributes). style is an example of an attribute that is not safe, since some browsers let you embed scripting language code in your CSS. For example, to bring back tags after replacing <, >, and & with entity references, you might search using the regex ‹<(/?)em>› and replace matches with «<$1em>» (or in Python and Ruby, «<\1em>»).

Variations

Whitelist specific attributes

Consider these new requirements: you need to match all tags except <a>, <em>, and <strong>, with two exceptions. Any <a> tags that have attributes other than href or title should be matched, and if <em> or <strong> tags have any attributes at all, match them too. All matched strings will be removed.

In other words, you want to remove all tags, except those on your whitelist (<a>, <em>, and <strong>). The only whitelisted attributes are href and title, and they are allowed only within <a> tags. If a nonwhitelisted attribute appears in any tag, the entire tag should be removed.

Here's a regex that can get the job done, shown with and without free-spacing mode:

```
<(?!(?:em|strong|a(?:\s+(?:href|title)\s*=\s*(?:"[^"]*"|'[^']*'))*)\s*>)↵
[a-z](?:[^>"']|"[^"]*"|'[^']*')*>
```
Regex options: Case insensitive
Regex flavors: .NET, Java, JavaScript, PCRE, Perl, Python, Ruby

```
< /?             # Permit closing tags
(?!              # Negative lookahead
   (?: em        #     Dont match <em>...
    | strong     #     or <strong>...
    | a          #     or <a>...
      (?:        #         Only avoid matching <a> tags that stick to...
        \s+  #                 href and/or title attributes
        (?:href|title)
        \s*=\s*
        (?:"[^"]*"|'[^']*')  # Double- or single-quoted attribute value
      )*
   )
```

```
        \s* >          # Only avoid matching these tags when they stick to the...
    )                  #     attributes listed above
    [a-z]              # Tag name initial character must be a-z
    (?: [^>"']         #     Any character except >, ", or '
      | "[^"]*"        #     Double-quoted attribute value
      | '[^']*'        #     Single-quoted attribute value
    )*
    >
```

Regex options: Case insensitive, free-spacing
Regex flavors: .NET, Java, PCRE, Perl, Python, Ruby

This pushes the boundary of where it makes sense to use such a complicated regex. If your rules get any more complex than this, it would probably be better to write some code based on Recipes 3.11 or 3.16 that checks the value of each matched tag to determine how to process it (based on the tag name, included attributes, or whatever else is needed).

See Also

Recipe 8.1 shows how to match all XML-style tags, while balancing trade-offs, including tolerance for invalid markup.

Recipe 8.2 is the opposite of this recipe, and shows how to match a select list of tags.

8.4 Match XML Names

Problem

You want to check whether a string is a legitimate XML *name* (a common syntactic construct). XML provides precise rules for the characters that can occur in a name, and reuses those rules for element, attribute, and entity names, processing instruction targets, and more. Names must be composed of a letter, underscore, or colon as the first character, followed by any combination of letters, digits, underscores, colons, hyphens, and periods. That's actually an approximate description, but it's pretty close. The exact list of permitted characters depends on the version of XML in use.

Alternatively, you might want to splice a pattern for matching valid names into other XML-handling regexes, when the extra precision warrants the added complexity.

Following are some examples of valid names:

- `thing`
- `_thing_2_`
- `:Российские-Вещь`
- `fantastic4:the.thing`
- `日本の物`

Note that letters from non-Latin scripts are allowed, even including the ideographic characters in the last example. Likewise, any Unicode digit is allowed after the first character, not just the Arabic numerals 0–9.

For comparison, here are several examples of invalid names that should not be matched by the regex:

- `thing!`
- `thing with spaces`
- `.thing.with.a.dot.in.front`
- `-thingamajig`
- `2nd_thing`

Solution

Like identifiers in many programming languages, there is a set of characters that can occur in an XML name, and a subset that can be used as the first character. Those character lists are dramatically different for XML 1.0 Fourth Edition (and earlier) and XML 1.1 and 1.0 Fifth Edition. Essentially, XML 1.1 names can use all the characters permitted by 1.0 Fourth Edition, plus almost a million more. However, the majority of the additional characters are nothing more than positions in the Unicode table. Most don't have a character assigned to them yet, but are allowed for future compatibility as the Unicode character database expands.

For brevity's sake, references to XML 1.0 in this recipe describe the first through fourth editions of XML 1.0. When we talk about XML 1.1 names, we're also describing the XML 1.0 Fifth Edition rules. The fifth edition only became an official W3C Recommendation at the end of November 2008, nearly five years after XML 1.1.

 Regexes in this recipe are shown with start and end of string anchors (using either ‹^…$› or ‹\A…\Z›) that cause your subject string to be matched in its entirety or not at all. If you want to embed these patterns in a longer regular expression that deals with matching, say, XML elements, make sure to remove the anchors at the beginning and end of the patterns displayed here. Anchors are explained in Recipe 2.5.

XML 1.0 names (approximate)

```
\A[:_\p{Ll}\p{Lu}\p{Lt}\p{Lo}\p{Nl}][:_\-.\p{L}\p{M}\p{Nd}\p{Nl}]*\Z
```
Regex options: None
Regex flavors: .NET, Java, PCRE, Perl, Ruby 1.9

PCRE must be compiled with UTF-8 support for the Unicode properties (‹\p{…}›) to work. In PHP, turn on UTF-8 support with the /u pattern modifier.

Unicode properties are not supported by JavaScript, Python, or Ruby 1.8. The XML 1.1 names regex that comes next doesn't rely on Unicode properties and therefore might be a good alternative if you're using one of these programming languages. See the "Discussion" on page 444 of this recipe for details on why you might be better off using the XML 1.1-based solution anyway, even if your regex flavor supports Unicode properties.

XML 1.1 names (exact)

Following are three versions of the same regular expression, due to flavor differences. The only difference between the first two is the anchors used at the start and end of the patterns. The third version uses ⟨\x{⋯}⟩ instead of ⟨\u⟩ to specify Unicode code points greater than FF hexadecimal (255 decimal).

```
\A[:_A-Za-z\xC0-\xD6\xD8-\xF6\xF8-\u02FF\u0370-\u037D\u037F-\u1FFF\u200C↵
\u200D\u2070-\u218F\u2C00-\u2FEF\u3001-\uD7FF\uF900-\uFDCF\uFDF0-\uFFFD]↵
[:_\-.A-Za-z0-9\xB7\xC0-\xD6\xD8-\xF6\xF8-\u036F\u0370-\u037D\u037F-\u1FFF↵
\u200C\u200D\u203F\u2040\u2070-\u218F\u2C00-\u2FEF\u3001-\uD7FF\uF900-↵
\uFDCF\uFDF0-\uFFFD]*\Z
```
Regex options: None
Regex flavors: .NET, Java, Python, Ruby 1.9

```
^[:_A-Za-z\xC0-\xD6\xD8-\xF6\xF8-\u02FF\u0370-\u037D\u037F-\u1FFF\u200C↵
\u200D\u2070-\u218F\u2C00-\u2FEF\u3001-\uD7FF\uF900-\uFDCF\uFDF0-\uFFFD]↵
[:_\-.A-Za-z0-9\xB7\xC0-\xD6\xD8-\xF6\xF8-\u036F\u0370-\u037D\u037F-\u1FFF↵
\u200C\u200D\u203F\u2040\u2070-\u218F\u2C00-\u2FEF\u3001-\uD7FF\uF900-↵
\uFDCF\uFDF0-\uFFFD]*$
```
Regex options: None ("^ and $ match at line breaks" must not be set)
Regex flavors: .NET, Java, JavaScript, Python

```
\A[:_A-Za-z\xC0-\xD6\xD8-\xF6\xF8-\x{2FF}\x{370}-\x{37D}\x{37F}-\x{1FFF}↵
\x{200C}\x{200D}\x{2070}-\x{218F}\x{2C00}-\x{2FEF}\x{3001}-\x{D7FF}↵
\x{F900}-\x{FDCF}\x{FDF0}-\x{FFFD}][:_\-.A-Za-z0-9\xB7\xC0-\xD6\xD8-\xF6↵
\xF8-\x{36F}\x{370}-\x{37D}\x{37F}-\x{1FFF}\x{200C}\x{200D}\x{203F}↵
\x{2040}\x{2070}-\x{218F}\x{2C00}-\x{2FEF}\x{3001}-\x{D7FF}\x{F900}-↵
\x{FDCF}\x{FDF0}-\x{FFFD}]*\Z
```
Regex options: None
Regex flavors: PCRE, Perl

PCRE must be compiled with UTF-8 support for the ⟨\x{⋯}⟩ metasequences to work with values greater than FF hexadecimal. In PHP, turn on UTF-8 support with the /u pattern modifier.

Ruby 1.8 does not support Unicode regular expressions at all, but see the section "Variations" on page 446 of this recipe for a possible alternative solution that is less precise.

Although we've claimed these regular expressions follow the XML 1.1 name rules exactly, that's actually only true for characters up to 16-bits wide (positions 0x0 through 0xFFFF). XML 1.1 additionally allows the 917,503 code points between positions 0x10000 and 0xEFFFF to occur after the name start character. However, only PCRE, Perl, and Python are even capable of referencing code points beyond 0xFFFF, and you are unlikely to encounter any in the wild (for one thing, most of the positions in this range have not been assigned an actual character). If you need to add support for these extra code points, in PCRE and Perl you could add ‹\x{10000}-\x{EFFFF}› at the end of the second character class, and in Python you could add ‹\U00010000-\U000EFFFF› (note the uppercase U, which must be followed by eight hexadecimal digits). But even without adding this massive range, the XML 1.1 name character list we've just shown is much more permissive than XML 1.0.

Discussion

Since many of the regular expressions in this chapter deal with matching XML elements, this recipe largely serves to provide a fuller discussion of the patterns that can be used when you want to get very specific about how tag and attribute names are matched. Elsewhere, we mostly stick to simpler patterns that are less precise, in the interest of readability and efficiency.

So let's dig a little deeper into the rules behind these patterns.

XML 1.0 names

The XML 1.0 specification uses a whitelist approach for its name rules, and explicitly lists all the characters that are allowed. The name start character can be a colon (:), underscore (_), or approximately any character in the following Unicode categories:

- Lowercase letter (Ll)
- Uppercase letter (Lu)
- Titlecase letter (Lt)
- Letter without case (Lo)
- Letter number (Nl)

After the initial character, hyphen (-), period (.), and any character in the following categories are allowed in addition to the characters already mentioned:

- Mark (M), which combines the subcategories non-spacing mark (Mn), spacing combining mark (Mc), and enclosing mark (Me)
- Modifier letter (Lm)
- Decimal digit (Nd)

These rules lead us to the regular expression shown in the "Solution" of this recipe. Here it is again in free-spacing mode:

```
\A                                    # Start of string
[:_\p{Ll}\p{Lu}\p{Lt}\p{Lo}\p{Nl}]    # Name start character
[:_\-.\p{L}\p{M}\p{Nd}\p{Nl}]*        # Name characters (zero or more)
\Z                                    # End of string
```
Regex options: Free-spacing
Regex flavors: .NET, Java, PCRE, Perl, Ruby 1.9

Again, PCRE must be compiled with UTF-8 support. In PHP, turn on UTF-8 support with the /u pattern modifier.

Notice that in the second character class, all of the letter subcategories (Ll, Lu, Lt, Lo, and Lm) have been combined into their base category using ‹\p{L}›.

Earlier, we noted that the rules described here are approximate. There are a couple of reasons for that. First, the XML 1.0 specification (remember that we're not talking about the fifth edition and later here) lists a number of exceptions to these rules. Second, the XML 1.0 character lists were derived from Unicode 2.0, which was released back in 1996. Later versions of the Unicode standard have added support for an assortment of new scripts whose characters are not permitted by the XML 1.0 rules. However, decoupling the regex from whatever Unicode version your regex engine uses so you can restrict matches to Unicode 2.0 characters would turn this pattern into a page-long monstrosity filled with hundreds of ranges and code points. If you really want to create this monster, refer to *XML 1.0*, Fourth Edition (*http://www.w3.org/TR/2006/REC-xml-20060816*) section 2.3, "Common Syntactic Constructs," and Appendix B, "Character Classes."

Following are several flavor-specific ways to shorten the regex we've already seen.

Perl and PCRE let you combine the lowercase letter (Ll), uppercase letter (Lu), and titlecase letter (Lt) subcategories into the special "letter with case" (L&) category. These regex flavors also let you omit the curly brackets in the ‹\p{···}› escape sequence if only one letter is used within. We've taken advantage of this in the following regex by using ‹\pL\pM› instead of ‹\p{L}\p{M}›:

```
\A[:_\p{L&}\p{Lo}\p{Nl}][:_\-.\pL\pM\p{Nd}\p{Nl}]*\Z
```
Regex options: None
Regex flavors: PCRE, Perl

.NET supports character class subtraction, which is used in the first character class here to subtract the Lm subcategory from L, rather than explicitly listing all the other letter subcategories:

```
\A[:_\p{L}\p{Nl}-[\p{Lm}]][:_\-.\p{L}\p{M}\p{Nd}\p{Nl}]*\Z
```
Regex options: None
Regex flavor: .NET

Java, like PCRE and Perl, lets you omit the curly brackets around one-letter Unicode categories. The following regex also takes advantage of Java's more complicated version of character class subtraction (implemented via intersection with a negated class) to subtract the Lm subcategory from L:

```
\A[:_\pL\p{Nl}&&[^\p{Lm}]][:_\-.\pL\pM\p{Nd}\p{Nl}]*\Z
```
Regex options: None
Regex flavor: Java

JavaScript, Python, and Ruby 1.8 don't support Unicode categories at all. Ruby 1.9 doesn't have the fancy features just described, but it does support the more portable version of these regexes shown in the "Solution" of this recipe.

XML 1.1 names

XML 1.0 made the mistake of explicitly tying itself to Unicode 2.0. Later versions of the Unicode standard have added support for many more characters, some of which are from scripts that weren't previously accounted for at all (e.g., Cherokee, Ethiopic, and Mongolian). Since XML wants to be regarded as a universal format, it has tried to fix this problem with XML 1.1 and 1.0 Fifth Edition. These later versions switch from a whitelist to a blacklist approach for name characters in order to support not only the characters added since Unicode 2.0, but also those that may be added in the future.

This new strategy of allowing anything that isn't explicitly forbidden improves future compatibility, and it also makes it easier and less verbose to precisely follow the rules. That's why the XML 1.1 name regexes are labeled as being exact, whereas the XML 1.0 regex is approximate.

Variations

In some of this chapter's recipes (e.g., Recipe 8.1), the pattern segments that deal with XML names employ next to no restrictions or disallow foreign scripts and other characters that are in fact perfectly valid. This is done to keep things simple. However, if you want to allow foreign scripts while still providing a base level of restrictions (and you don't need the more precise name validation of earlier regexes in this recipe), these next regexes might do the trick.

 We've left the start- and end-of-string anchors off of these regexes since they're not meant to be used on their own, but rather as parts of longer patterns.

This first regex simply avoids matching the characters used as separators and delimiters within XML tags, and additionally prevents matching a digit as the first character:

```
[^\d\s"'/<=>][^\s"'/<=>]*
```
Regex options: None
Regex flavors: .NET, Java, JavaScript, PCRE, Perl, Python, Ruby

---

Following is another, even shorter way to accomplish the same thing. Instead of using two separate character classes, it uses negative lookahead to forbid a digit as the initial character. This ban applies to the first matched character only, even though the ‹+› quantifier after the character class lets the regex match an unlimited number of characters:

```
(?!\d)[^\s"'/<=>]+
```
Regex options: None
Regex flavors: .NET, Java, JavaScript, PCRE, Perl, Python, Ruby

See Also

John Cowan, one of the editors of the XML 1.1 specification, explains which characters are forbidden in XML 1.1 names and why in a blog post at *http://recycledknowledge .blogspot.com/2008/02/which-characters-are-excluded-in-xml.html*.

The document "Background to Changes in XML 1.0, 5th Edition" at *http://www.w3 .org/XML/2008/02/xml10_5th_edition_background.html* discusses the rationale for backporting XML 1.1's name rules to XML 1.0, Fifth Edition.

8.5 Convert Plain Text to HTML by Adding <p> and
 Tags

Problem

Given a plain text string, such as a multiline value submitted via a form, you want to convert it to an HTML fragment to display within a web page. Paragraphs, separated by two line breaks in a row, should be surrounded with <p>···</p>. Additional line breaks should be replaced with <br> tags.

Solution

This problem can be solved in four simple steps. In most programming languages, only the middle two steps benefit from regular expressions.

Step 1: Replace HTML special characters with character entity references

As we're converting plain text to HTML, the first step is to convert the three special HTML characters &, <, and > to character entity references (see Table 8-3). Otherwise, the resulting markup could lead to unintended results when displayed in a web browser.

Table 8-3. HTML special character substitutions

Search for	Replace with
‹&›	«&»
‹<›	«<»
‹>›	«>»

Ampersands (&) must be replaced first, since you'll be adding additional ampersands to the subject string as part of the character entity references.

Step 2: Replace all line breaks with

Search for:

```
\r\n?|\n
```

> **Regex options:** None
> **Regex flavors:** .NET, Java, JavaScript, PCRE, Perl, Python, Ruby

```
\R
```

> **Regex options:** None
> **Regex flavors:** PCRE 7, Perl 5.10

Replace with:

```
<br>
```

> **Replacement text flavors:** .NET, Java, JavaScript, Perl, PHP, Python, Ruby

Step 3: Replace double <br> tags with </p><p>

Search for:

```
<br>\s*<br>
```

> **Regex options:** None
> **Regex flavors:** .NET, Java, JavaScript, PCRE, Perl, Python, Ruby

Replace with:

```
</p><p>
```

> **Replacement text flavors:** .NET, Java, JavaScript, Perl, PHP, Python, Ruby

Step 4: Wrap the entire string with <p>···</p>

This step is a simple string concatenation, and doesn't require regular expressions.

JavaScript example

As we tie all four steps together, we'll create a JavaScript function called `html_from_plaintext`. This function accepts a string, processes it using the steps we've just described, then returns the new HTML string:

```javascript
function html_from_plaintext (subject) {
    // step 1 (plain text searches)
    subject = subject.replace(/&/g, "&amp;").
                      replace(/</g, "&lt;").
                      replace(/>/g, "&gt;");

    // step 2
    subject = subject.replace(/\r\n?|\n/g, "<br>");
```

```
        // step 3
        subject = subject.replace(/<br>\s*<br>/g, "</p><p>");

        // step 4
        subject = "<p>" + subject + "</p>";

        return subject;
}

/*
html_from_plaintext("Test.")           -> "<p>Test.</p>"
html_from_plaintext("Test.\n")         -> "<p>Test.<br></p>"
html_from_plaintext("Test.\n\n")       -> "<p>Test.</p><p></p>"
html_from_plaintext("Test1.\nTest2.")  -> "<p>Test1.<br>Test2.</p>"
html_from_plaintext("Test1.\n\nTest2.") -> "<p>Test1.</p><p>Test2.</p>"
html_from_plaintext("< AT&T >")        -> "<p>&lt; AT&amp;T &gt;</p>"
*/
```

Several examples are included at the end of the code snippet that show the output when this function is applied to various subject strings. If JavaScript is foreign to you, note that the /g modifier appended to each of the regex literals causes the replace method to replace all occurrences of the pattern, rather than just the first. The \n metasequence in the example subject strings inserts a line feed character (ASCII position 0x0A) in a JavaScript string literal.

Discussion

Step 1: Replace HTML special characters with character entity references

The easiest way to complete this step is to use three discrete search-and-replace operations (see Table 8-3, shown earlier, for the list of replacements). JavaScript always uses regular expressions for global search-and-replace operations, but in other programming languages you will typically get better performance from simple plain-text substitutions.

Step 2: Replace all line breaks with

In this step, we use the regular expression ‹\r\n?|\n› to find line breaks that follow the Windows/MS-DOS (CRLF), Unix/Linux/OS X (LF), and legacy Mac OS (CR) conventions. Perl 5.10 and PCRE 7 users can use the dedicated ‹\R› token (note the uppercase R) instead for matching those and other line break sequences.

Replacing all line breaks with <br> before adding paragraph tags in the next step keeps things simpler overall, since it gives you the option to add whitespace between your </p><p> tags in later substitutions. Doing so can help keep your HTML code readable by not smashing it all together.

If you prefer to use XHTML-style singleton tags, use «<br•/>» instead of «
» as your replacement string. You'll also need to alter the regular expression in Step 3 to match this change.

Step 3: Replace double <br> tags with </p><p>

Two line breaks in a row indicate the end of one paragraph and the start of another, so our replacement text for this step is a closing </p> tag followed by an opening <p>. If the subject text contains only one paragraph (i.e., two line breaks never appear in a row), no substitutions will be made. Step 2 already replaced several line break conventions (leaving behind only <br> tags), so this step could be handled with a plain text substitution. However, using a regex here makes it easy to take things one step further and ignore whitespace that appears between line breaks. Any extra space characters won't be rendered in an HTML document anyway.

If you're generating XHTML and therefore replaced line breaks with «<br•/>» instead of «
», you'll need to adjust the regex for this step to ‹<br•/>\s*<br•/>›.

Step 4: Wrap the entire string with <p>···</p>

Step 3 merely added markup between paragraphs. Now you need to add a <p> tag at the very beginning of the subject string, and a closing </p> at the very end. That completes the process, whether there were 1 or 100 paragraphs in the text.

See Also

Recipe 4.10 includes more information about Perl and PCRE's ‹\R› token, and shows how to manually match the additional, esoteric line separators that are supported by ‹\R›.

8.6 Find a Specific Attribute in XML-Style Tags

Problem

You want to find tags within an (X)HTML or XML file that contain a specific attribute, such as id.

This recipe covers several variations on the same problem. Suppose that you want to match each of the following types of strings using separate regular expressions:

- Tags that contain an id attribute.
- <div> tags that contain an id attribute.
- Tags that contain an id attribute with the value my-id.
- Tags that contain my-class within their class attribute value (classes are separated by whitespace).

Solution

Tags that contain an id attribute (quick and dirty)

If you want to do a quick search in a text editor that lets you preview your results, the following (overly simplistic) regex might do the trick:

```
<[^>]+\sid\b[^>]*>
```
Regex options: Case insensitive
Regex flavors: .NET, Java, JavaScript, PCRE, Perl, Python, Ruby

Here's a breakdown of the regex in free-spacing mode:

```
<           # Start of the tag
[^>]+       # Tag name, attributes, etc.
\s id \b    # The target attribute name, as a whole word
[^>]*       # The remainder of the tag, including the id attribute's value
>           # End of the tag
```
Regex options: Case insensitive, free-spacing
Regex flavors: .NET, Java, PCRE, Perl, Python, Ruby

Tags that contain an id attribute (more reliable)

Unlike the regex just shown, this next take on the same problem supports quoted attribute values that contain literal > characters, and it doesn't match tags that merely contain the word id within one of their attributes' values:

```
<(?:[^>"']|"[^"]*"|'[^']*')+?\sid\s*=\s*("[^"]*"|'[^']*')↵
(?:[^>"']|"[^"]*"|'[^']*')*>
```
Regex options: Case insensitive
Regex flavors: .NET, Java, JavaScript, PCRE, Perl, Python, Ruby

In free-spacing mode:

```
<                       #
(?: [^>"']              # Tag and attribute names, etc.
  | "[^"]*"             #     ...and quoted attribute values
  | '[^']*'             #
)+?                     #
\s id                   # The target attribute name, as a whole word
\s* = \s*               # Attribute name-value delimiter
( "[^"]*" | '[^']*' )   # Capture the attribute value to backreference 1
(?: [^>"']              # Any remaining characters
  | "[^"]*"             #     ...and quoted attribute values
  | '[^']*'             #
)*                      #
>                       #
```
Regex options: Case insensitive, free-spacing
Regex flavors: .NET, Java, PCRE, Perl, Python, Ruby

This regex captures the `id` attribute's value and surrounding quote marks to backreference 1. This allows you to use the value in code outside of the regex or in a replacement string. If you don't need to reuse the value, you can switch to a noncapturing group or replace the entire ‹\s*=\s*("[^"]*"|'[^']*')› sequence with ‹\b›. The remainder of the regex will pick up the slack and match the `id` attribute's value.

<div> tags that contain an id attribute

To search for a specific tag type, you need to add its name to the beginning of the regex and make a couple of other minor changes to the previous regex. In the following example, we've added ‹div\s› after the opening ‹<›. The ‹\s› (whitespace) token ensures that we don't match tags whose names merely start with the three letters "div". We know there will be a whitespace character following the tag name because the tags we're searching for have at least one attribute (`id`). Additionally, the ‹+?\s› sequence has been changed to ‹*?\b›, so that the regex works when `id` is the first attribute within the tag and there are no additional separating characters (beyond the initial space) after the tag name:

```
<div\s(?:[^>"']|"[^"]*"|'[^']*')*?\bid\s*=\s*("[^"]*"|'[^']*')↵
(?:[^>"']|"[^"]*"|'[^']*')*>
```

Regex options: Case insensitive
Regex flavors: .NET, Java, JavaScript, PCRE, Perl, Python, Ruby

Here is the same thing in free-spacing mode:

```
<div \s                    # Tag name and following whitespace character
(?: [^>"']                 # Tag and attribute names, etc.
  | "[^"]*"                #    ...and quoted attribute values
  | '[^']*'                #
)*?                        #
\b id                      # The target attribute name, as a whole word
\s* = \s*                  # Attribute name-value delimiter
( "[^"]*" | '[^']*' )      # Capture the attribute value to backreference 1
(?: [^>"']                 # Any remaining characters
  | "[^"]*"                #    ...and quoted attribute values
  | '[^']*'                #
)*                         #
>                          #
```

Regex options: Case insensitive, free-spacing
Regex flavors: .NET, Java, PCRE, Perl, Python, Ruby

Tags that contain an id attribute with the value "my-id"

Compared to the regex titled "Tags that contain an id attribute (more reliable)" on page 451, this time we'll remove the capturing group around the `id` attribute's value since you already know the value in advance. Specifically, the subpattern ‹("[^"]*"|'[^']*')› has been replaced with ‹(?:"my-id"|'my-id')›:

```
<(?:[^>"']|"[^"]*"|'[^']*')+?\sid\s*=\s*(?:"my-id"|'my-id')↵
(?:[^>"']|"[^"]*"|'[^']*')*>
```
Regex options: Case insensitive

Regex flavors: .NET, Java, JavaScript, PCRE, Perl, Python, Ruby

And the free-spacing version:

```
<                      #
(?: [^>"']             # Tag and attribute names, etc.
  | "[^"]*"            #     ...and quoted attribute values
  | '[^']*'            #
)+?                    #
\s id                  # The target attribute name, as a whole word
\s* = \s*              # Attribute name-value delimiter
(?: "my-id"            # The target attribute value
  | 'my-id' )          #     ...surrounded by single or double quotes
(?: [^>"']             # Any remaining characters
  | "[^"]*"            #     ...and quoted attribute values
  | '[^']*'            #
)*                     #
>                      #
```
Regex options: Case insensitive, free-spacing

Regex flavors: .NET, Java, PCRE, Perl, Python, Ruby

Going back to the ‹(?:"my-id"|'my-id')› subpattern for a second, you could alternatively avoid repeating "my-id" (at the cost of some efficiency) by using ‹(["'])my-id \1›. That uses a capturing group and backreference to ensure that the value starts and ends with the same type of quote mark.

Tags that contain "my-class" within their class attribute value

If the previous regular expressions haven't already passed this threshold, this is where it becomes obvious that we're pushing the boundary of what can sensibly be accomplished using a single regex. Splitting the process into multiple regexes helps a little, so we'll split this search into three parts. The first regex will match tags, the next will find the class attribute within it (and store its value within a backreference), and finally we'll search within the value for my-class.

Find tags:

```
<(?:[^>"']|"[^"]*"|'[^']*')+>
```
Regex options: None

Regex flavors: .NET, Java, JavaScript, PCRE, Perl, Python, Ruby

 Recipe 8.1 is dedicated to matching XML-style tags. It explains how the regex just shown works, and provides a number of alternatives with varying degrees of complexity and accuracy.

Next, follow the code in Recipe 3.13 to search within each match for a `class` attribute using the following regex:

```
^(?:[^>"']|"[^"]*"|'[^']*')+?\sclass\s*=\s*("[^"]*"|'[^']*')
```
Regex options: Case insensitive
Regex flavors: .NET, Java, JavaScript, PCRE, Perl, Python, Ruby

This captures the entire `class` value and its surrounding quote marks to backreference 1. Everything before the `class` attribute is matched using ‹`^(?:[^>"']|"[^"]*"|'[^']*')+?`›, which matches quoted values in single steps to avoid finding the word "class" inside another attribute's value. On the right side of the pattern, the match ends as soon as we reach the end of the `class` attribute's value. Nothing after that is relevant to our search, so there's no reason to match all the way to the end of the tag within which you're searching.

The caret at the beginning of the regex anchors it to the start of the subject string. This doesn't change what is matched, but it's there so that if the regex engine can't find a match starting at the beginning of the string, it doesn't try again (and inevitably fail) at each subsequent character position.

Finally, if both of the previous regexes matched successfully, you'll want to search within backreference 1 of the second regex's matches using the following pattern:

```
(?:^|\s)my-class(?:\s|$)
```
Regex options: None
Regex flavors: .NET, Java, JavaScript, PCRE, Perl, Python, Ruby

Since classes are separated by whitespace, `my-class` must be bordered on both ends by either whitespace or nothing at all. If it weren't for the fact that class names can include hyphens, you could use word boundary tokens instead of the two noncapturing groups here. However, hyphens create word boundaries, and thus ‹`\bmy-class\b`› would match within `not-my-class`.

Discussion

The "Solution" of this recipe already covers the details of how these regular expressions work, so we'll avoid rehashing it all here. Remember that regular expressions are often not the ideal solution for markup searches, especially those that reach the complexity described in this recipe. Before using these regular expressions, consider whether you'd be better served by an alternative solution, such as XPath, a SAX parser, or a DOM. We've included these regexes since it's not uncommon for people to try to pull off this kind of thing, but don't say you weren't warned. Hopefully this has at least helped to show some of the issues involved in markup searches, and helped you avoid even more naïve solutions.

See Also

Recipe 8.7 is the conceptual inverse of this recipe, and finds tags that do not contain a specific attribute.

8.7 Add a cellspacing Attribute to <table> Tags That Do Not Already Include It

Problem

You want to search through an (X)HTML file and add `cellspacing="0"` to all tables that do not already include a `cellspacing` attribute.

This recipe serves as an example of adding an attribute to XML-style tags that do not already include it. You can swap in whatever tag and attribute names and values you prefer.

Solution

Regex 1: Simplistic solution

You can use negative lookahead to match `<table>` tags that do not contain the word `cellspacing`, as follows:

```
<table\b(?![^>]*?\scellspacing\b)([^>]*)>
```
Regex options: Case insensitive
Regex flavors: .NET, Java, JavaScript, PCRE, Perl, Python, Ruby

Here's the regex again in free-spacing mode:

```
<table \b            # Match "<table", followed by a word boundary
(?!                  # Assert that the regex below cannot be matched here
  [^>]               #   Match any character except ">"...
    *?               #     zero or more times, as few as possible (lazy)
  \s cellspacing \b  #   Match "cellspacing" as a complete word
)                    #
(                    # Capture the regex below to backreference 1
  [^>]               #   Match any character except ">"...
    *                #     zero or more times, as many as possible (greedy)
)                    #
>                    # Match a literal ">" to end the tag
```
Regex options: Case insensitive
Regex flavors: .NET, Java, PCRE, Perl, Python, Ruby

Regex 2: More reliable solution

The following regex replaces both instances of the negated character class ‹[^>]› from the simplistic solution with ‹(?:[^>"']|"[^"]*"|'[^']*')›. This improves the regular expression's reliability in two ways. First, it adds support for quoted attribute values that contain literal ">" characters. Second, it ensures that we don't preclude matching tags that merely contain the word "cellspacing" within an attribute's value.

Here's how the regex looks with the change we've just described:

```
<table\b(?!(?:[^>"']|"[^"]*"|'[^']*')*?\scellspacing\b)↵
((?:[^>"']|"[^"]*"|'[^']*')*)>
```
Regex options: Case insensitive
Regex flavors: .NET, Java, JavaScript, PCRE, Perl, Python, Ruby

And here it is in free-spacing mode:

```
<table \b            # Match "<table", followed by a word boundary
(?!                  # Assert that the regex below cannot be matched here
  (?: [^>"']         #   Match any character except >, ", or '
   | "[^"]*"         #     Or, a double-quoted value
   | '[^']*'         #     Or, a single-quoted value
  )*?                #   Zero or more times, as few as possible (lazy)
  \s cellspacing \b  #   Match "cellspacing" as a complete word
)                    #
(                    # Capture the regex below to backreference 1
  (?: [^>"']         #   Match any character except >, ", or '
   | "[^"]*"         #     Or, a double-quoted value
   | '[^']*'         #     Or, a single-quoted value
  )*                 #   Zero or more times, as many as possible (greedy)
)                    #
>                    #
```
Regex options: Case insensitive
Regex flavors: .NET, Java, PCRE, Perl, Python, Ruby

Insert the new attribute

All of the regexes shown in this recipe can use the same replacement strings, since the regexes all capture attributes within the matched `<table>` tags (if any) to backreference 1. This lets you bring back those attributes as part of your replacement value, while adding the new `cellspacing` attribute. Here are the necessary replacement strings:

```
<table•cellspacing="0"$1>
```
Replacement text flavors: .NET, Java, JavaScript, Perl, PHP

```
<table•cellspacing="0"\1>
```
Replacement text flavors: Python, Ruby

Recipe 3.15 shows how to perform substitutions that use a backreference in the replacement string.

Discussion

In order to examine how these regexes work, we'll first break down the simplistic solution. As you'll see, it has four logical parts.

The first part, ‹<table\b›, matches the literal characters <table, followed by a word boundary (‹\b›). The word boundary prevents matching tag names that merely start with "table". Although that might seem unnecessary here when working with (X)HTML (since there are no valid elements named "tablet", "tableau", or "tablespoon", for example), it's good practice nonetheless, and can help you avoid bugs when adapting this regex to search for other tags.

The second part of the regex, ‹(?![^>]*?\scellspacing\b)›, is a negative lookahead. It doesn't consume any text as part of the match, but it asserts that the match attempt should fail if the word cellspacing occurs anywhere within the opening tag. Since we're going to add the cellspacing attribute to all matches, we don't want to match tags that already contain it.

Since the lookahead peeks forward from the current position in the match attempt, it uses the leading ‹[^>]*?› to let it search as far forward as it needs to, up until what is assumed to be the end of the tag (the first occurrence of >). The remainder of the lookahead subpattern (‹\scellspacing\b›) simply matches the literal characters "cellspacing" as a complete word. We match a leading whitespace character (‹\s›) since whitespace must always separate an attribute name from the tag name or preceding attributes. We match a trailing word boundary instead of another whitespace character since a word boundary fulfills the need to match cellspacing as a complete word, yet works even if the attribute has no value or if the attribute name is immediately followed by an equals sign.

Moving along, we get to the third piece of the regex: ‹([^>]*)›. This is a negated character class and a following "zero or more" quantifier, wrapped in a capturing group. Capturing this part of the match allows you to easily bring back the attributes that each matched tag contained as part of the replacement string. And unlike the negative lookahead, this part actually adds the attributes within the tag to the string matched by the regex.

Finally, the regex matches the literal character ‹>› to end the tag.

Regex 2, the so-called more reliable version, works exactly the same as the regex we've just described, except that both instances of the negated character class ‹[^>]› are replaced with ‹(?:[^>"']|"[^"]*"|'[^']*')›. This longer pattern passes over double- and single-quoted attribute values in one step.

As for the replacement strings, they work with both regexes, replacing each matched <table> tag with a new tag that includes cellspacing as the first attribute, followed by whatever attributes occurred within the original tag (backreference 1).

See Also

Recipe 8.6 is the conceptual inverse of this recipe, and finds tags that contain a specific attribute.

8.8 Remove XML-Style Comments

Problem

You want to remove comments from an (X)HTML or XML document. For example, you want to remove comments from a web page before it is served to web browsers in order to reduce the file size of the page and thereby reduce load time for people with slow Internet connections.

Solution

Finding comments is not a difficult task, thanks to the availability of lazy quantifiers. Here is the regular expression for the job:

```
<!--.*?-->
```

Regex options: Dot matches line breaks
Regex flavors: .NET, Java, PCRE, Perl, Python, Ruby

That's pretty straightforward. As usual, though, JavaScript's lack of a "dot matches line breaks" option means that you'll need to replace the dot with an all-inclusive character class in order for the regular expression to match comments that span more than one line. Following is a version that works with JavaScript:

```
<!--[\s\S]*?-->
```

Regex options: None
Regex flavor: JavaScript

To remove the comments, replace all matches with the empty string (i.e., nothing). Recipe 3.14 lists code to replace all matches of a regex.

Discussion

How it works

At the beginning and end of this regular expression are the literal character sequences ‹<!--› and ‹-->›. Since none of those characters are special in regex syntax (except within character classes, where hyphens create ranges), they don't need to be escaped. That just leaves the ‹.*?› or ‹[\s\S]*?› in the middle of the regex to examine further.

Thanks to the "dot matches line breaks" option, the dot in the regex shown first matches any single character. In the JavaScript version, the character class ‹[\s\S]› takes its place. However, the two regexes are exactly equivalent. ‹\s› matches any whitespace character, and ‹\S› matches everything else. Combined, they match any character.

The lazy ‹*?› quantifier repeats its preceding "any character" element zero or more times, as few times as possible. Thus, the preceding token is repeated only until the first occurrence of --›, rather than matching all the way to the end of the subject string, and then backtracking until the last --›. (See Recipe 2.13 for more on how backtracking works with lazy and greedy quantifiers.) This simple strategy works well since XML-style comments cannot be nested within each other. In other words, they always end at the first (leftmost) occurrence of --›.

When comments can't be removed

Most web developers are familiar with using HTML comments within `<script>` and `<style>` elements for backward compatibility with ancient browsers. These days, it's mostly just a meaningless incantation, but its use lives on thanks in part to copy-and-paste coding. We're going to assume that when you remove comments from an (X)HTML document, you don't want to strip out embedded JavaScript and CSS. You probably also want to leave the contents of `<textarea>` elements, CDATA sections, and the values of attributes within tags alone.

Earlier, we said removing comments wasn't a difficult task. As it turns out, that was only true if you ignore some of the tricky areas of (X)HTML or XML where the syntax rules change. In other words, if you ignore the hard parts of the problem, it's easy.

Of course, in some cases you might evaluate the markup you're dealing with and decide it's OK to ignore these problem cases, maybe because you wrote the markup yourself and know what to expect. It might also be OK if you're doing a search-and-replace in a text editor and are able to manually inspect each match before removing it.

But getting back to how to work around these issues, in "Skip tricky (X)HTML and XML sections" on page 428 we discussed some of these same problems in the context of matching XML-style tags. We can use a similar line of attack when searching for comments. Use the code in Recipe 3.18 to first search for tricky sections using the regular expression shown next, and then replace comments found between matches with the empty string (i.e., remove the comments):

```
<(script|style|textarea|xmp)\b(?:[^>"']|"[^"]*"|'[^']*')*?↵
(?:/>|>.*?</\1\s*>)|<[a-z](?:[^>"']|"[^"]*"|'[^']*')*>|<!\[CDATA\[.*?]]>
```
Regex options: Case insensitive, dot matches line breaks
Regex flavors: .NET, Java, PCRE, Perl, Python, Ruby

Adding some whitespace and a few comments to the regex in free-spacing mode makes this a lot easier to follow:

```
# Special element: tag and content
<( script | style | textarea | xmp )\b
    (?: [^>"']    # Match any attribute names
      | "[^"]*"   #     ...and values
```

```
      | '[^']*'  #
    )*?
  (?: # Singleton tag
      />
    | # Otherwise, include the element's content and matching closing tag
      > .*? </\1\s*>
  )

  |

  # Standard element: tag only
  <[a-z]           # Tag name initial character
     (?: [^>"']    # Match the rest of the tag name
       | "[^"]*"   #     ...along with attribute
       | '[^']*'   #     ...names and values
     )*
  >

  |

  # CDATA section
  <!\[CDATA\[ .*? ]]>
```

> **Regex options:** Case insensitive, dot matches line breaks, free-spacing
> **Regex flavors:** .NET, Java, PCRE, Perl, Python, Ruby

Here's an equivalent version for JavaScript, which lacks both "dot matches line breaks" and "free-spacing" options:

```
<(script|style|textarea|xmp)\b(?:[^>"']|"[^"]*"|'[^']*')*?↵
(?:/>|>[\s\S]*?</\1\s*>)|<[a-z](?:[^>"']|"[^"]*"|'[^']*')*>|<!\[CDATA\[↵
[\s\S]*?]]>
```

> **Regex options:** Case insensitive
> **Regex flavor:** JavaScript

Variations

Find valid XML-style comments

There are in fact a few syntax rules for (X)HTML and XML comments that go beyond simply starting with `<!--` and ending with `-->`. Specifically:

- Two hyphens cannot appear in a row within a comment. For example, `<!-- com--ment -->` is invalid because of the two hyphens in the middle.

- The closing delimiter cannot be preceded by a hyphen that is part of the comment. For example, `<!-- comment --->` is invalid, but the completely empty comment `<!---->` is allowed.

- Whitespace may occur between the closing `--` and `>`. For example, `<!-- comment -- >` is a valid, complete comment.

It's not hard to work these rules into a regex:

```
<!--[^-]*(?:-[^-]+)*--\s*>
```
Regex options: None
Regex flavors: .NET, Java, JavaScript, PCRE, Perl, Python, Ruby

Notice that everything between the opening and closing comment delimiters is still optional, so it matches the completely empty comment `<!---->`. However, if a hyphen occurs between the delimiters, it must be followed by at least one nonhyphen character. And since the inner portion of the regex can no longer match two hyphens in a row, the lazy quantifier from the regexes at the beginning of this recipe has been replaced with greedy quantifiers. Lazy quantifiers would still work fine, but sticking with them here would result in unnecessary backtracking (see Recipe 2.13).

Some readers might look at this new regex and wonder why the ‹[^-]› negated character class is used twice, rather than just making the hyphen inside the noncapturing group optional (i.e., ‹<!--(?:-?[^-]+)*--\s*>›). There's a good reason, which brings us back to the discussion of "catastrophic backtracking" from Recipe 2.15.

So-called *nested quantifiers* always warrant extra attention and care in order to ensure that you're not creating the potential for catastrophic backtracking. A quantifier is nested when it occurs within a grouping that is itself repeated by a quantifier. For example, the pattern ‹(?:-?[^-]+)*› contains two nested quantifiers: the question mark following the hyphen and the plus sign following the negated character class.

However, nesting quantifiers is not really what makes this dangerous, performance-wise. Rather, it's that there are a potentially massive number of ways that the outer ‹*› quantifier can be combined with the inner quantifiers while attempting to match a string. If the regex engine fails to find `-->` at the end of a partial match (as is required when you plug this pattern segment into the comment-matching regex), the engine must try all possible repetition combinations before failing the match attempt and moving on. This number of options expands extremely rapidly with each additional character that the engine must try to match. However, there is nothing dangerous about the nested quantifiers if this situation is avoided. For example, the pattern ‹(?:-[^-]+)*› does not pose a risk, even though it contains a nested ‹+› quantifier, because now that exactly one hyphen must be matched per repetition of the group, the potential number of backtracking points increases linearly with the length of the subject string.

Another way to avoid the potential backtracking problem we've just described is to use an atomic group. The following is equivalent to the first regex shown in this section, but it's a few characters shorter and isn't supported by JavaScript or Python:

```
<!--(?>-?[^-]+)*--\s*>
```
Regex options: None
Regex flavors: .NET, Java, PCRE, Perl, Ruby

See Recipe 2.14 for the details about how atomic groups (and their counterpart, possessive quantifiers) work.

Find C-style comments

The same type of pattern as shown for XML-style comments works well with other nonnested, multiline comments. C-style comments either start with /* and end with the first occurrence of */, or start with // and continue until the end of the line. The following regex matches both of these comment types by combining a pattern for each type using a vertical bar:

```
/\*[\s\S]*?\*/|//.*
```

Regex options: None ("dot matches line breaks" must not be set)
Regex flavors: .NET, Java, JavaScript, PCRE, Perl, Python, Ruby

See Also

Recipe 8.9 shows how to find specific words when they occur within XML-style comments.

8.9 Find Words Within XML-Style Comments

Problem

You want to find all occurrences of the word TODO within (X)HTML or XML comments. For example, you want to match only the underlined text within the following string:

```
This "TODO" is not within a comment, but the next one is. <!-- TODO: ↵
Come up with a cooler comment for this example. -->
```

Solution

There are at least two approaches to this problem, and both have their advantages. The first tactic, described as the "Two-step approach" on page 463, is to find comments with an outer regex, and then search within each match using a separate regex or even a plain text search. That works best if you're writing code to do the job, since separating the task into two steps keeps things simple and fast. However, if you're searching through files using a text editor or grep tool, splitting the task in two won't work unless your tool of choice offers a special option to search within matches found by another regex.[†]

When you need to find words within comments using a single regex, you can accomplish this with the help of lookaround. This second method is shown in the upcoming section "Single-step approach".

[†] PowerGREP—described in "Tools for Working with Regular Expressions" in Chapter 1—is one tool that's able to search within matches.

Two-step approach

When it's a workable option, the better solution is to split the task in two: search for comments, and then search within those comments for TODO.

Here's how you can find comments:

```
<!--.*?-->
```
Regex options: Dot matches line breaks
Regex flavors: .NET, Java, PCRE, Perl, Python, Ruby

JavaScript doesn't have a "dot matches line breaks" option, but you can use an all-inclusive character class in place of the dot, as follows:

```
<!--[\s\S]*?-->
```
Regex options: None
Regex flavor: JavaScript

For each comment you find using one of the regexes just shown, you can then search within the matched text for the literal characters ‹TODO›. If you prefer, you can make it a case-insensitive regex with word boundaries on each end to make sure that only the complete word TODO is matched, like so:

```
\bTODO\b
```
Regex options: Case insensitive
Regex flavors: .NET, Java, JavaScript, PCRE, Perl, Python, Ruby

Recipe 3.13 shows how to search within matches of an outer regex.

Single-step approach

Lookahead (described in Recipe 2.16) lets you solve this problem with a single regex, albeit less efficiently. In the following regex, positive lookahead is used to make sure that the word TODO is followed by the closing comment delimiter -->. On its own, that doesn't tell whether the word appears within a comment or is simply followed by a comment, so a nested negative lookahead is used to ensure that the opening comment delimiter <!-- does not appear before the -->:

```
\bTODO\b(?=(?:(?!<!--).)*?-->)
```
Regex options: Case insensitive, dot matches line breaks
Regex flavors: .NET, Java, PCRE, Perl, Python, Ruby

Since JavaScript doesn't have a "dot matches line breaks" option, use ‹[\s\S]› in place of the dot:

```
\bTODO\b(?=(?:(?!<!--)[\s\S])*?-->)
```
Regex options: Case insensitive
Regex flavor: JavaScript

Discussion

Two-step approach

Recipe 3.13 shows the code you need to search within matches of another regex. It takes an inner and outer regex. The comment regex serves as the outer regex, and ‹\bTODO\b› as the inner regex. The main thing to note here is the lazy ‹*?› quantifier that follows the dot or character class in the comment regex. As explained in Recipe 2.13, that lets you match up to the first --> (the one that ends the comment), rather than the very last occurrence of --> in your subject string.

Single-step approach

This solution is more complex, and slower. On the plus side, it combines the two steps of the previous approach into one regex. Thus, it can be used when working with a text editor, IDE, or other tool that doesn't allow searching within matches of another regex.

Let's break this regex down in free-spacing mode, and take a closer look at each part:

```
\b TODO \b      # Match the characters "TODO", as a complete word
(?=             # Assert that the regex below can match here
  (?:           #   Group but don't capture...
    (?! <!-- )  #     Assert that "<!--" cannot match here
    .           #     Match any single character
  )*?           #   Repeat zero or more times, as few as possible (lazy)
  -->           #   Match the characters "-->"
)               #
```

Regex options: Dot matches line breaks, free-spacing
Regex flavors: .NET, Java, PCRE, Perl, Python, Ruby

This commented version of the regex doesn't work in JavaScript, since JavaScript lacks both "free-spacing" and "dot matches line breaks" modes.

Notice that the regex contains a negative lookahead nested within an outer, positive lookahead. That lets you require that any match of TODO is followed by --> and that <!-- does not occur in between.

If it's clear to you how all of this works together, great: you can skip the rest of this section. But in case it's still a little hazy, let's take another step back and build the outer, positive lookahead in this regex step by step.

Let's say for a moment that we simply want to match occurrences of the word TODO that are followed at some point in the string by -->. That gives us the regex ‹\bTODO \b(?=.*?-->)› (with "dot matches line breaks" enabled), which matches the underlined text in <!--TODO--> just fine. We need the ‹.*?› at the beginning of the lookahead, because otherwise the regex would match only when TODO is *immediately* followed by -->, with no characters in between. The ‹*?› quantifier repeats the dot zero or more times, as few times as possible, which is great since we only want to match until the first following `-->`.

As an aside, the regex so far could be rewritten as ‹\bTODO(?=.*?-->)\b›—with the second ‹\b› moved after the lookahead—without any affect on the text that is matched. That's because both the word boundary and the lookahead are zero-length assertions (see "Lookaround" on page 75). However, it's better to place the word boundary first for readability and efficiency. In the middle of a partial match, the regex engine can more quickly test a word boundary, fail, and move forward to try again at the next character in the string without having to spend time testing the lookahead when it isn't necessary because TODO is not a complete word.

OK, so the regex ‹\bTODO\b(?=.*?-->)› seems to work fine so far, but what about when it's applied to the subject string TODO <!-- separate comment -->? The regex still matches TODO since it's followed by `-->`, even though TODO is not within a comment. Thus, we need to change the dot within the lookahead from matching any character to any character that is not part of the string `<!--`, since that would indicate the start of a new comment. We can't use a negated character class such as ‹[^<!-]›, because we want to allow `<`, `!`, and `-` characters that are not grouped into the exact sequence `<!--`.

That's where the nested negative lookahead comes in. ‹(?!<!--).› matches any single character that is not part of an opening comment delimiter. Placing that pattern within a noncapturing group as ‹(?:(?!<!--).)› allows us to repeat the whole sequence with the lazy ‹*?› quantifier we'd previously applied to just the dot.

Putting it all together, we get the final regex that was listed as the solution for this problem: ‹\bTODO\b(?=(?:(?!<!--).)*?-->)›. In JavaScript, which lacks the necessary "dot matches line breaks" option, ‹\bTODO\b(?=(?:(?!<!--)[\s\S])*?-->)› is equivalent.

Variations

Although the "single-step approach" regex ensures that any match of TODO is followed by `-->` without `<!--` occurring in between, it doesn't check the reverse: that the target word is also preceded by `<!--` without `-->` in between. There are several reasons we left that rule out:

- You can usually get away with not doing this double-check, especially since the single-step regex is meant to be used with text editors and the like, where you can visually verify your results.

- Having less to verify means less time spent performing the verification (i.e., it's faster to leave the extra check out).

- Most importantly, since you don't know how far back the comment may have started, looking backward like this requires infinite-length lookbehind, which is supported by the .NET regex flavor only.

If you're working with .NET and want to include this added check, use the following regex:

```
(?<=<!--(?:(?!-->).)*?)\bTODO\b(?=(?:(?!<!--).)*?-->)
```
Regex options: Case insensitive, dot matches line breaks
Regex flavor: .NET

This stricter, .NET-only regex adds a positive lookbehind at the front, which works just like the lookahead at the end but in reverse. Because the lookbehind works forward from the position where it finds <!--, the lookbehind contains a nested negative look-ahead that lets it match any characters that are not part of the sequence -->.

Since the leading lookahead and trailing lookbehind are both zero-length assertions, the final match is just the word TODO. The strings matched within the lookarounds do not become a part of the final matched text.

See Also

Recipe 8.8 includes a detailed discussion of how to match XML-style comments.

8.10 Change the Delimiter Used in CSV Files

Problem

You want to change all field-delimiting commas in a CSV file to tabs. Commas that occur within double-quoted values should be left alone.

Solution

The following regular expression matches an individual CSV field along with its preceding delimiter, if any. The preceding delimiter is usually a comma, but can also be an empty string (i.e., nothing) when matching the first field of the first record, or a line break when matching the first field of any subsequent record. Every time a match is found, the field itself, including the double quotes that may surround it, is captured to backreference 2, and its preceding delimiter is captured to backreference 1.

 The regular expressions in this recipe are designed to work correctly only with valid CSV files, according to the format rules under the term "Comma-Separated Values (CSV)" that was discussed earlier in this book.

```
(,|\r?\n|^)([^",\r\n]+|"(?:[^"]|"")*")?
```
Regex options: None ("^ and $ match at line breaks" must not be set)
Regex flavors: .NET, Java, JavaScript, PCRE, Perl, Python, Ruby

Here is the same regular expression again in free-spacing mode:

```
( , | \r?\n | ^ )     # Capturing group 1 matches field delimiters
                      #    or the beginning of the string
(                     # Capturing group 2 matches a single field:
  [^",\r\n]+          #    a non-quoted field
|                     #    or...
  " (?:[^"]|"")* "    #    a quoted field (may contain escaped double-quotes)
)?                    # The group is optional because fields may be empty
```
Regex options: Free-spacing ("^ and $ match at line breaks" must not be set)
Regex flavors: .NET, Java, PCRE, Perl, Python, Ruby

Using this regex and the code in Recipe 3.11, you can iterate over your CSV file and check the value of backreference 1 after each match. The necessary replacement string for each match depends on the value of this backreference. If it's a comma, replace it with a tab character. If the backreference is empty or contains a line break, leave the value in place (i.e., do nothing, or put it back as part of a replacement string). Since CSV fields are captured to backreference 2 as part of each match, you'll also have to put that back as part of each replacement string. The only things you're actually replacing are the commas that are captured to backreference 1.

JavaScript example

The following code is a complete web page that includes two multiline text input fields, with a button labeled *Replace* between them. Clicking the button takes whatever string you put into the first text box (labeled *Input*), converts any comma delimiters to tabs with the help of the regular expression just shown, then puts the new string into the second text box (labeled *Output*). If you use valid CSV content as your input, it should show up in the second text box with all comma delimiters replaced with tabs. To test it, save this code into a file with the ".html" extension and open it in your favorite web browser:

```
<html>
<head>
<title>Change CSV delimiters from commas to tabs</title>
</head>

<body>
<p>Input:</p>
<textarea id="input" rows="5" cols="75"></textarea>

<p><input type="button" value="Replace" onclick="commas_to_tabs()"></p>

<p>Output:</p>
<textarea id="output" rows="5" cols="75"></textarea>

<script>
function commas_to_tabs () {
```

```
var input  = document.getElementById('input'),
    output = document.getElementById('output'),
    regex  = /(,|\r?\n|^)([^",\r\n]+|"(?:[^"]|"")*")?/g,
    result = '',
    match;

while (match = regex.exec(input.value)) {
    // Check the value of backreference 1
    if (match[1] == ',') {
        // Add a tab (in place of the matched comma)
        // and backreference 2 to the result.
        // If backreference 2 is undefined (because the
        // optional, second capturing group did not participate
        // in the match), use an empty string instead.
        result += '\t' + (match[2] || '');
    } else {
        // Add the entire match to the result
        result += match[0];
    }

    // Prevent some browsers from getting stuck in an infinite loop
    if (match.index == regex.lastIndex) regex.lastIndex++;
}

output.value = result;
}
</script>
</body>
</html>
```

Discussion

The approach prescribed by this recipe allows you to pass over each complete CSV field (including any embedded line breaks, escaped double quotes, and commas) one at a time. Each match then starts just before the next field delimiter.

The first capturing group in the regex, ‹(,|\r?\n|^)›, matches a comma, line break, or the position at the beginning of the subject string. Since the regex engine will attempt alternatives from left to right, these options are listed in the order in which they will most frequently occur in the average CSV file. This capturing group is the only part of the regex that is required to match. Therefore, it's possible for the complete regex to match an empty string since the ‹^› anchor can always match once. The value matched by this first capturing group must be checked in code outside of the regex that replaces commas with your substitute delimiter (e.g., a tab).

We haven't yet gotten through the entire regex, but the approach described so far is already somewhat convoluted. You might be wondering why the regex is not written to match *only* the commas that should be replaced with tabs. If you could do that, a

---

simple substitution of all matched text would avoid the need for code outside of the regex to check whether capturing group 1 matched a comma or some other string. After all, it should be possible to use lookahead and lookbehind to determine whether a comma is inside or outside a quoted CSV field, right?

Unfortunately, in order for such an approach to accurately determine which commas are outside of double-quoted fields, you'd need infinite-length lookbehind, which is available only in the .NET regex flavor (see "Different levels of lookbehind" on page 77 for a discussion of the varying lookbehind limitations). Even .NET developers should avoid a lookaround-based approach since it would add significant complexity and also make the regex slower.

Getting back to how the regex works, most of the pattern appears within the next set of parentheses: capturing group 2. This second group matches a single CSV field, including any surrounding double quotes. Unlike the previous capturing group, this one is optional in order to allow matching empty fields.

Note that group 2 within the regex contains two alternative patterns separated by the ‹|› metacharacter. The first alternative, ‹[^",\r\n]+›, is a negated character class followed by a one-or-more (‹+›) quantifier that, together, match an entire nonquoted field. For this to match, the field cannot contain any double quotes, commas, or line breaks.

The second alternative within group 2, ‹"(?:[^"]|"")*"›, matches a field surrounded by double quotes. More precisely, it matches a double-quote character, followed by zero or more nondouble-quote characters and repeated (escaped) double quotes, followed by a closing double quote.

The ‹*› quantifier at the end of the inner, noncapturing group repeats the two inner options as many times as possible, until you get to a double quote that is not repeated and therefore ends the field.

Assuming you're working with a valid CSV file, the first match found by this regex should occur at the beginning of the subject string, and each subsequent match should occur immediately after the end of the last match.

See Also

Recipe 8.11 describes how to reuse the regex in this recipe to extract CSV fields from a specific column.

8.11 Extract CSV Fields from a Specific Column

Problem

You want to extract every field from the third column of a CSV file.

Solution

The regular expressions from Recipe 8.10 can be reused here to iterate over each field in a CSV subject string. With a bit of extra code, you can count the number of fields from left to right in each row, or *record*, and extract the fields at the position you're interested in.

The following regular expression (shown with and without the free-spacing option) matches a single CSV field and its preceding delimiter in two separate capturing groups. Since line breaks can appear within double-quoted fields, it would not be accurate to simply search from the beginning of each line in your CSV string. By matching and stepping past fields one by one, you can easily determine which line breaks appear outside of double-quoted fields and therefore start a new record.

 The regular expressions in this recipe are designed to work correctly only with valid CSV files, according to the format rules discussed in "Comma-Separated Values (CSV) on page 415."

```
(,|\r?\n|^)([^",\r\n]+|"(?:[^"]|"")*")?
```
Regex options: None ("^ and $ match at line breaks" must not be set)
Regex flavors: .NET, Java, JavaScript, PCRE, Perl, Python, Ruby

```
( , | \r?\n | ^ )    # Capturing group 1 matches field delimiters
                     #   or the beginning of the string
(                    # Capturing group 2 matches a single field:
  [^",\r\n]+         #   a non-quoted field
|                    #   or...
  " (?:[^"]|"")* "   #   a quoted field (may contain escaped double-quotes)
)?                   # The group is optional because fields may be empty
```
Regex options: Free-spacing ("^ and $ match at line breaks" must not be set)
Regex flavors: .NET, Java, PCRE, Perl, Python, Ruby

These regular expressions are exactly the same as those in Recipe 8.10, and they can be repurposed for plenty of other CSV processing tasks as well. The following example code demonstrates how you can use the version without the free-spacing option to help you extract a CSV column.

JavaScript example

The following code is a complete web page that includes two multiline text input fields and a button between them labeled *Extract Column 3*. Clicking the button takes whatever string you put into the *Input* text box, extracts the value of the third field in each record with the help of the regular expression shown earlier in this recipe, then puts the entire column (with each value separated by a line break) into the *Output* field. To test it, save this code into a file with the ".html" extension and open it in your favorite web browser:

```
<html>
<head>
<title>Extract the third column from a CSV string</title>
</head>

<body>
<p>Input:</p>
<textarea id="input" rows="5" cols="75"></textarea>

<p><input type="button" value="Extract Column 3"
    onclick="display_csv_column(2)"></p>

<p>Output:</p>
<textarea id="output" rows="5" cols="75"></textarea>

<script>
function display_csv_column (index) {
    var input  = document.getElementById('input'),
        output = document.getElementById('output'),
        column_fields = get_csv_column(input.value, index);

    if (column_fields.length > 0) {
        // Show each record on its own line, separated by a line feed (\n)
        output.value = column_fields.join('\n');
    } else {
        output.value = '[No data found to extract]';
    }
}

// Return an array of CSV fields at the provided, zero-based index
function get_csv_column (csv, index) {
    var regex   = /(,|\r?\n|^)([^",\r\n]+|"(?:[^"]|"")*")?/g,
        result = [],
        column_index = 0,
        match;

    while (match = regex.exec(csv)) {
        // Check the value of backreference 1. If it's a comma,
        // increment column_index. Otherwise, reset it to zero.
        if (match[1] == ',') {
            column_index++;
        } else {
            column_index = 0;
        }
        if (column_index == index) {
            // Add the field (backref 2) at the end of the result array
            result.push(match[2]);
        }
```

```
            // Prevent some browsers from getting stuck in an infinite loop
            if (match.index == regex.lastIndex) regex.lastIndex++;
        }

        return result;
    }
</script>
</body>
</html>
```

Discussion

Since the regular expressions here are repurposed from Recipe 8.10, we won't repeat the detailed explanation of how they work. However, this recipe includes new JavaScript example code that uses the regex to extract fields at a specific index from each record in the CSV subject string.

In the provided code, the `get_csv_column` function works by iterating over the subject string one match at a time. After each match, backreference 1 is examined to check whether it contains a comma. If so, you've matched something other than the first field in a row, so the `column_index` variable is incremented to keep track of which column you're at. If backreference 1 is anything other than a comma (i.e., an empty string or a line break), you've matched the first field in a new row and `column_index` is reset to zero.

The next step in the code is to check whether the `column_index` counter has reached the index you're looking to extract. Every time it does, the value of backreference 2 (everything after the leading delimiter) is pushed to the `result` array. After you've iterated over the entire subject string, the `get_csv_column` function returns an array containing values for the entire specified column (in this example, the third column). The list of matches is then dumped into the second text box on the page, with each value separated by a line feed character (\n).

A simple improvement would be to let the user specify which column index should be extracted, via a prompt or additional text field. The `get_csv_column` function we've been discussing is already written with this feature in mind, and lets you specify the desired column as a zero-based integer via the second parameter (`index`).

Variations

Although using code to iterate over a string one CSV field at a time allows for extra flexibility, if you're using a text editor to get the job done, you may be limited to just search-and-replace. In this situation, you can achieve a similar result by matching each complete record and replacing it with the value of the field at the column index you're searching for (using a backreference). The following regexes illustrate this technique for particular column indexes, replacing each record with the field in a specific column.

With all of these regexes, if any record does not contain at least as many fields as the column index you're searching for, that record will not be matched and will be left in place.

Match a CSV record and capture the field in column 1 to backreference 1

```
^([^",\r\n]+|"(?:[^"]|"")*")?(?:,(?:[^",\r\n]+|"(?:[^"]|"")*")?)*
```
Regex options: ^ and $ match at line breaks
Regex flavors: .NET, Java, JavaScript, PCRE, Perl, Python, Ruby

Match a CSV record and capture the field in column 2 to backreference 1

```
^(?:[^",\r\n]+|"(?:[^"]|"")*")?,([^",\r\n]+|"(?:[^"]|"")*")?↵
(?:,(?:[^",\r\n]+|"(?:[^"]|"")*")?)*
```
Regex options: ^ and $ match at line breaks
Regex flavors: .NET, Java, JavaScript, PCRE, Perl, Python, Ruby

Match a CSV record and capture the field in column 3 or higher to backreference 1

```
^(?:[^",\r\n]+|"(?:[^"]|"")*")?(?:,(?:[^",\r\n]+|"(?:[^"]|"")*")?){1},↵
([^",\r\n]+|"(?:[^"]|"")*")?(?:,(?:[^",\r\n]+|"(?:[^"]|"")*")?)*
```
Regex options: ^ and $ match at line breaks
Regex flavors: .NET, Java, JavaScript, PCRE, Perl, Python, Ruby

Increment the number within the ‹{1}› quantifier to make this last regex work for anything higher than column 3. For example, change it to ‹{2}› to capture fields from column 4, ‹{3}› for column 5, and so on. If you're working with column 3, you can simply remove the ‹{1}› if you prefer, since it has no effect here.

Replacement string

The same replacement string (backreference 1) is used with all of these regexes. Replacing each match with backreference 1 should leave you with just the fields you're searching for.

```
$1
```
Replacement text flavors: .NET, Java, JavaScript, Perl, PHP

```
\1
```
Replacement text flavors: Python, Ruby

8.12 Match INI Section Headers

Problem

You want to match all section headers in an INI file.

Solution

This one is easy. INI section headers appear at the beginning of a line, and are designated by placing a name within square brackets (e.g., [Section1]). Those rules are simple to translate into a regex:

```
^\[[^\]\r\n]+]
```
Regex options: ^ and $ match at line breaks
Regex flavors: .NET, Java, JavaScript, PCRE, Perl, Python, Ruby

Discussion

There aren't many parts to this regex, so it's easy to break down:

- The leading ‹^› matches the position at the beginning of a line, since the "^ and $ match at line breaks" option is enabled.

- ‹\[› matches a literal [character. It's escaped with a backslash to prevent [from starting a character class.

- ‹[^\]\r\n]› is a negated character class that matches any character except], a carriage return (\r), or a line feed (\n). The immediately following ‹+› quantifier lets the class match one or more characters, which brings us to....

- The trailing ‹]› matches a literal] character to end the section header. There's no need to escape this character with a backslash because it does not occur within a character class.

If you only want to find a specific section header, that's even easier. The following regex matches the header for a section called Section1:

```
^\[Section1]
```
Regex options: ^ and $ match at line breaks
Regex flavors: .NET, Java, JavaScript, PCRE, Perl, Python, Ruby

In this case, the only difference from a plain-text search for "[Section1]" is that the match must occur at the beginning of a line. This prevents matching commented-out section headers (preceded by a semicolon) or what looks like a header but is actually part of a parameter's value (e.g., Item1=[Value1]).

See Also

Recipe 8.13 describes how to match INI section blocks.

Recipe 8.14 does the same for INI name-value pairs.

8.13 Match INI Section Blocks

Problem

You need to match each complete INI section block (i.e., a section header and all of the section's parameter-value pairs), in order to split up an INI file or process each block separately.

Solution

Recipe 8.12 showed how to match an INI section header. To match an entire section, we'll start with the same pattern from that recipe, but continue matching until we reach the end of the string or a [character that occurs at the beginning of a line (since that indicates the start of a new section):

```
^\[[^\]\r\n]+](?:\r?\n(?:[^[\r\n].*)?)*
```

Regex options: ^ and $ match at line breaks ("dot matches line breaks" must not be set)

Regex flavors: .NET, Java, JavaScript, PCRE, Perl, Python, Ruby

Or in free-spacing mode:

```
^ \[ [^\]\r\n]+ ]   # Match a section header
(?:                 # Followed by the rest of the section...
  \r?\n             #   Match a line break character sequence
  (?:               #   After each line starts, match...
    [^[\r\n]        #     Any character except "[" or a line break character
    .*              #     Match the rest of the line
  )?                #   The group is optional to allow matching empty lines
)*                  # Continue until the end of the section
```

Regex options: ^ and $ match at line breaks, free-spacing ("dot matches line breaks" must not be set)

Regex flavors: .NET, Java, PCRE, Perl, Python, Ruby

Discussion

This regular expression starts by matching an INI section header with the pattern ‹^\ [[^\]\r\n]+]›, and continues matching one line at a time as long as the lines do not start with [. Consider the following subject text:

```
[Section1]
Item1=Value1
Item2=[Value2]

; [SectionA]
; The SectionA header has been commented out

ItemA=ValueA ; ItemA is not commented out, and is part of Section1
```

```
[Section2]
Item3=Value3
Item4 = Value4
```

Given the string just shown, this regex finds two matches. The first match extends from the beginning of the string up to and including the empty line before "[Section2]". The second match extends from the start of the Section2 header until the end of the string.

See Also

Recipe 8.12 shows how to match INI section headers.

Recipe 8.14 does the same for INI name-value pairs.

8.14 Match INI Name-Value Pairs

Problem

You want to match INI parameter name-value pairs (e.g., Item1=Value1), separating each match into two parts using capturing groups. Backreference 1 should contain the parameter name (Item1), and backreference 2 should contain the value (Value1).

Solution

Here's the regular expression to get the job done (the second is shown with free-spacing mode):

```
^([^=;\r\n]+)=([^;\r\n]*)
```
   Regex options: ^ and $ match at line breaks
   Regex flavors: .NET, Java, JavaScript, PCRE, Perl, Python, Ruby

```
^                   # Start of a line
( [^=;\r\n]+ )      # Capture the name to backreference 1
=                   # Name-value delimiter
( [^;\r\n]* )       # Capture the value to backreference 2
```
   Regex options: ^ and $ match at line breaks, free-spacing
   Regex flavors: .NET, Java, PCRE, Perl, Python, Ruby

Discussion

Like the other INI recipes in this chapter, we're working with pretty straightforward ingredients here. The regex starts with ‹^›, to match the position at the start of a line (make sure the "^ and $ match at line breaks" option is enabled). This is important because without the assurance that matches start at the beginning of a line, you could match part of a commented-out line.

Next, the regex uses a capturing group that contains a negated character class (‹[^=;\r \n]›) followed by the one-or-more quantifier (‹+›) to match the name of the parameter and remember it as backreference 1. The negated class matches any character except the following four: equals sign, semicolon, carriage return (‹\r›), and line feed (‹\n›). The carriage return and line feed characters are both used to end an INI parameter, a semicolon marks the start of a comment, and an equals sign separates a parameter's name and value.

After matching the parameter name, the regex matches a literal equals sign (the name-value delimiter), and then the parameter value. The value is matched using a second capturing group that is similar to the pattern used to match the parameter name but has two less restrictions. First, this second subpattern allows matching equals signs as part of the value (i.e., there is one less negated character in the character class). Second, it uses a ‹*› quantifier to remove the need to match at least one character (since, unlike names, values may be empty).

And we're done.

See Also

Recipe 8.12 explains how to match INI section headers.

Recipe 8.13 gives the details on INI section blocks.

Index

We'd like to hear your suggestions for improving our indexes. Send email to *index@oreilly.com*.

for matching previously matched text,
60–62
reproducing lookbehind, 79
escaping, 321
as metacharacters, 26, 220
+ (plus sign)
escaping, 321
as metacharacter, 26
for possessive quantifiers, 70, 217
? (question mark)
escaping, 321
for lazy quantifiers, 69
as metacharacter, 26
for zero-or-once matching, 66
| (vertical bar)
as alternation operator, 56, 235, 288
escaping, 321

A

\a (bell character), 28
\A anchor, 37, 38, 218
accented letters, 52
ActionScript language, 98
addresses with post office boxes, finding, 266–
268
affirmative responses, validating, 253–254
alphanumeric characters, limiting input to,
241–244
alternation, 56
finding numbers within a range, 335
finding words from a list, 288
verifying time formats, 235
ampersand (&), escaping, 321
anchors, 37
ANSI characters, limiting to, 242
appendReplacement() method, 185
appendTail() method, 185
ASCII control characters (see control
characters)
assertions, 220
asterisk (*)
as anchor (assertion), 220
escaping, 321
as greedy, 68
as metacharacter, 26
for possessive quantifiers, 217
at sign (@)
encoding in Perl, 104
matching, 216

atomic groups, 71–72, 74, 248
atomic lookaround and lookbehind, 78
attributes (markup languages), 412
finding specific, 450–455
whitelisting, 440

B

<b> tags, replacing with <strong>, 434–437
\b word boundary, 32, 41, 218, 222, 236, 286
(see also words)
\B nonboundary, 42
backreferences
empty, using, 304
finding repeated words, 306–307
named, 64
named capture for (see named capture)
to nonexistent groups, 90
reinserting parts of match, 176–181
with splitting strings, 203–208
backreferencing, 60–62
backslash (\)
escaping, 321
in replacement text, 85–87
for escaping characters, 26, 319–322
within character classes, 31
as metacharacters, 26
in source code, 102
backtracking, 68
catastrophic, 73
unnecessary, eliminating, 70–72
balanced matching, 168
!~ operator, 126
begin() method, Ruby (MatchData class), 143
bell character (\a), 28
binary numbers, finding, 329–330
block escapes, 27, 322
blocks, Unicode, 48–51
listing all characters in, 53
braces { }
escaping, 321
as metacharacters, 26
for repetition, 65
brackets [ ]
for character classes, 216
for defining character classes, 31
escaping, 321
as metacharacter, 26

I

(?i) mode modifier, 27
(?-i) mode modifier, 27
IGNORECASE constant (Regexp), 118
IgnoreCase option (RegexOptions), 115
IgnorePatternWhitespace option
        (RegexOptions), 115
importing regular expression library, 106–107
Index property (.NET), 141
index property (JavaScript), 141
infinite repetition, 66
infinite-length lookaround, 298
INI files, 417
    matching name-value pairs in, 476–477
    matching section blocks in, 475–476
    matching section headers in, 473–474
initialization files (see INI files)
input validation, 254
    (see also validating)
    affirmative responses, 253–254
    allowing only alphanumeric characters,
        241–244
    credit card numbers, 271–277
    line count, 248–252
    string length, 244–248
integers
    containing comma (thousands separator),
        343–344
    finding or identifying, 323–326
    stripping leading zeros, 330–331
    within a certain range, finding, 331–337
international phone numbers, validating, 224–
        226
intersections of character classes, 33
interval quantifier, 246
IPv4 addresses, matching, 379–381
IPv6 addresses, matching, 381–394
ISBNs, validating, 257–264
IsMatch() method (.NET), 125, 152
ISO 8601 formats, 237–241
ISO-8859-1 characters, limiting to, 242
iterating over all matches, 155–161

J

Java language, xiv
    (see also Matcher class (Java); Pattern class
    (Java); String class (Java))
    creating regular expression objects, 110
    importing regular expression library, 107
    literal regular expressions in, 103
    regular expression options, 116, 118
    regular expressions support, 4, 96
    regular replacement text, 6
java.util.regex package, 4, 6, 96
    to use regular expression library, 107
JavaScript language, xiv
    (see also RegExp class (JavaScript); String
    class (JavaScript))
    creating regular expression objects, 111
    literal regular expressions in, 103
    regular expression library, 107
    regular expression options, 116, 119
    regular expressions support, 4, 96
    replacement text, 7

K

ksort() method (PHP), 175

L

languages, Unicode scripts for, 51
last names, reformatting, 268–271
last occurrences of lines, storing, 309, 310
lastIndex property (JavaScript), 141, 159
lastIndex property, JavaScript (RegExp class),
        299
lazy quantifiers, 69
    eliminating backtracking with, 70–72
leading whitespace, trimming, 314–317
leading zeros, stripping, 330–331
left context, 92
length of match, determining, 138–143
length of strings, validating, 244–248
Length property (.NET), 141
length() method, Ruby (MatchData class), 143
letters, Unicode category for, 45
line breaks, 42, 251
    in HTML documents, 449
line count, validating, 248–252
line feed (see newline)
line start or end, matching characters at, 36–
        41
    (see also word boundaries)
line-by-line searching, 208–211
lines, 308
    (see also words)
    defined, 37

S

About the Authors

Regular Expressions Cookbook is written by **Jan Goyvaerts** and **Steven Levithan**, two of the world's experts on regular expressions.

Jan Goyvaerts runs Just Great Software, where he designs and develops some of the most popular regular expression software. His products include RegexBuddy, the world's only regular expression editor that emulates the peculiarities of 15 regular expression flavors, and PowerGREP, the most feature-rich grep tool for Microsoft Windows.

Steven Levithan is a leading JavaScript regular expression expert and runs a popular regular expression centric blog at *http://blog.stevenlevithan.com*. Expanding his knowledge of the regular expression flavor and library landscape has been one of his hobbies for the last several years.

Colophon

The image on the cover of *Regular Expressions Cookbook* is a musk shrew (genus *Crocidura*, family *Soricidae*). Several types of musk shrews exist, including white- and red-toothed shrews, gray musk shrews, and red musk shrews. The shrew is native to South Africa and India.

While several physical characteristics distinguish one type of shrew from another, all shrews share certain commonalities. For instance, shrews are thought to be the smallest insectivores in the world, and all have stubby legs, five claws on each foot, and an elongated snout with tactile hairs. Differences include color variations among their teeth (most noticeably in the aptly named white- and red-toothed shrews) and in the color of their fur, which ranges from red to brown to gray.

Though the shrew usually forages for insects, it will also help farmers keep vermin in check by eating mice or other small rodents in their fields.

Many musk shrews give off a strong, musky odor (hence their common name), which they use to mark their territory. At one time it was rumored that the musk shrew's scent was so strong that it would permeate any wine or beer bottles that the shrew happened to pass by, thus giving the liquor a musky taint, but the rumor has since proved to be false.

The cover image is from Lydekker's *Royal Natural History*. The cover font is Adobe ITC Garamond. The text font is Linotype Birka; the heading font is Adobe Myriad Condensed; and the code font is LucasFont's TheSansMonoCondensed.

The O'Reilly Advantage

Stay Current and Save Money